The JOKER

His Greatest Jokes

WHITNEY ELLSWORTH, JULIUS SCHWARTZ, JACK SCHIFF, LEN WEIN, DAN RASPLER, PETER J. TOMASI, MIKE MARTS, CHRIS CONROY Editors – Original Series
MURRAY BOLTINOFF, GEORGE KASHDAN, JEANINE SCHAEFER Associate Editors – Original Series
E. NELSON BRIDWELL, CARL GAFFORD, NICOLA CUTI, ELISABETH V. GEHRLEIN, DAVE WIELGOSZ Assistant Editors – Original Series
JEB WOODARD Group Editor – Collected Editions ALEX GALER Editor – Collected Edition
STEVE COOK Design Director – Books DAMIAN RYLAND Publication Design TOM VALENTE Publication Production

BOB HARRAS Senior VP – Editor-in-Chief, DC Comics
PAT McCALLUM Executive Editor, DC Comics

DAN DIDIO Publisher JIM LEE Publisher & Chief Creative Officer BOBBIE CHASE VP – New Publishing Initiatives & Talent Development
DON FALLETTI VP – Manufacturing Operations & Workflow Management LAWRENCE GANEM VP – Talent Services ALISON GILL Senior VP – Manufacturing & Operations
HANK KANALZ Senior VP – Publishing Strategy & Support Services DAN MIRON VP – Publishing Operations NICK J. NAPOLITANO VP – Manufacturing Administration & Design
NANCY SPEARS VP – Sales MICHELE R. WELLS VP & Executive Editor, Young Reader

THE JOKER: HIS GREATEST JOKES

DC Comics, 2900 West Alameda Ave., Burbank, CA 91505

Printed by LSC Communications, Kendallville, IN, USA. 8/2/19. First Printing. ISBN: 978-1-4012-9441-0.

Library of Congress Cataloging-in-Publication Data is available.

PEFC Certified
This product is from sustainably managed forests and controlled sources
PEFC/29-31-337
www.pefc.org

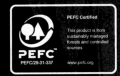

Table of Contents

JIM LEE, SCOTT WILLIAMS and ALEX SINCLAIR collection cover artists
BATMAN created by BOB KANE with BILL FINGER
HARLEY QUINN created by PAUL DINI and BRUCE TIMM
THE SPECTRE created by JERRY SIEGEL and BERNARD BAILY

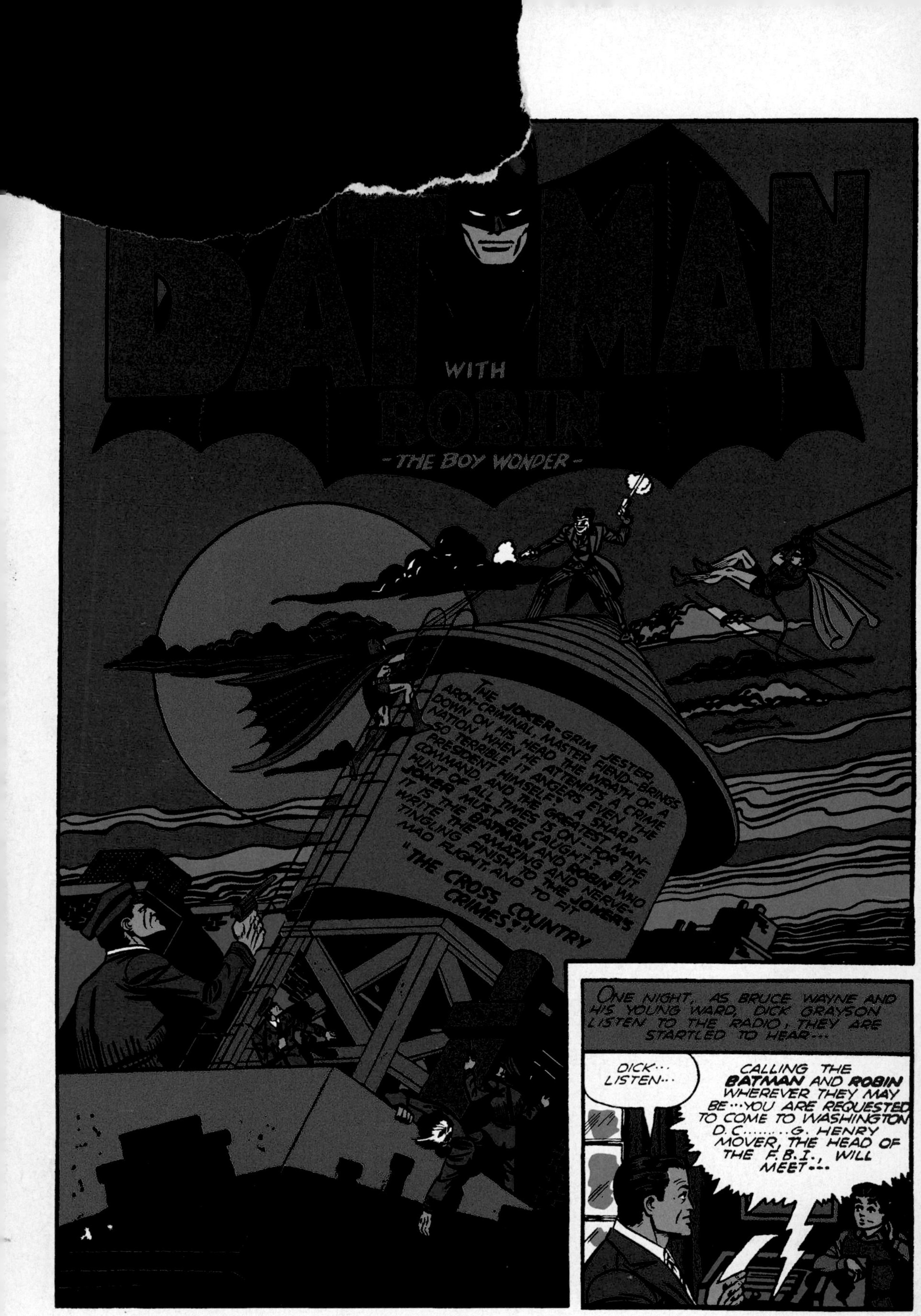
BATMAN
WITH ROBIN
-THE BOY WONDER-
THE JOKER-GRIM JESTER, ARCH-CRIMINAL, MASTER FIEND--BRINGS DOWN ON HIS HEAD THE WRATH OF A NATION WHEN HE ATTEMPTS A CRIME SO TERRIBLE IT ANGERS EVEN THE PRESIDENT HIMSELF! A SHARP COMMAND, AND THE GREATEST MAN-HUNT OF ALL TIMES IS ON--FOR THE JOKER MUST BE CAUGHT? BUT IT IS THE BATMAN AND ROBIN WHO WRITE THE AMAZING AND NERVE-TINGLING FINISH TO THE JOKER'S MAD FLIGHT, AND TO "THE CROSS COUNTRY CRIMES!"
ONE NIGHT, AS BRUCE WAYNE AND HIS YOUNG WARD, DICK GRAYSON LISTEN TO THE RADIO, THEY ARE STARTLED TO HEAR...
DICK... LISTEN...
CALLING THE BATMAN AND ROBIN WHEREVER THEY MAY BE...YOU ARE REQUESTED TO COME TO WASHINGTON D.C.........G. HENRY MOVER, THE HEAD OF THE F.B.I., WILL MEET...

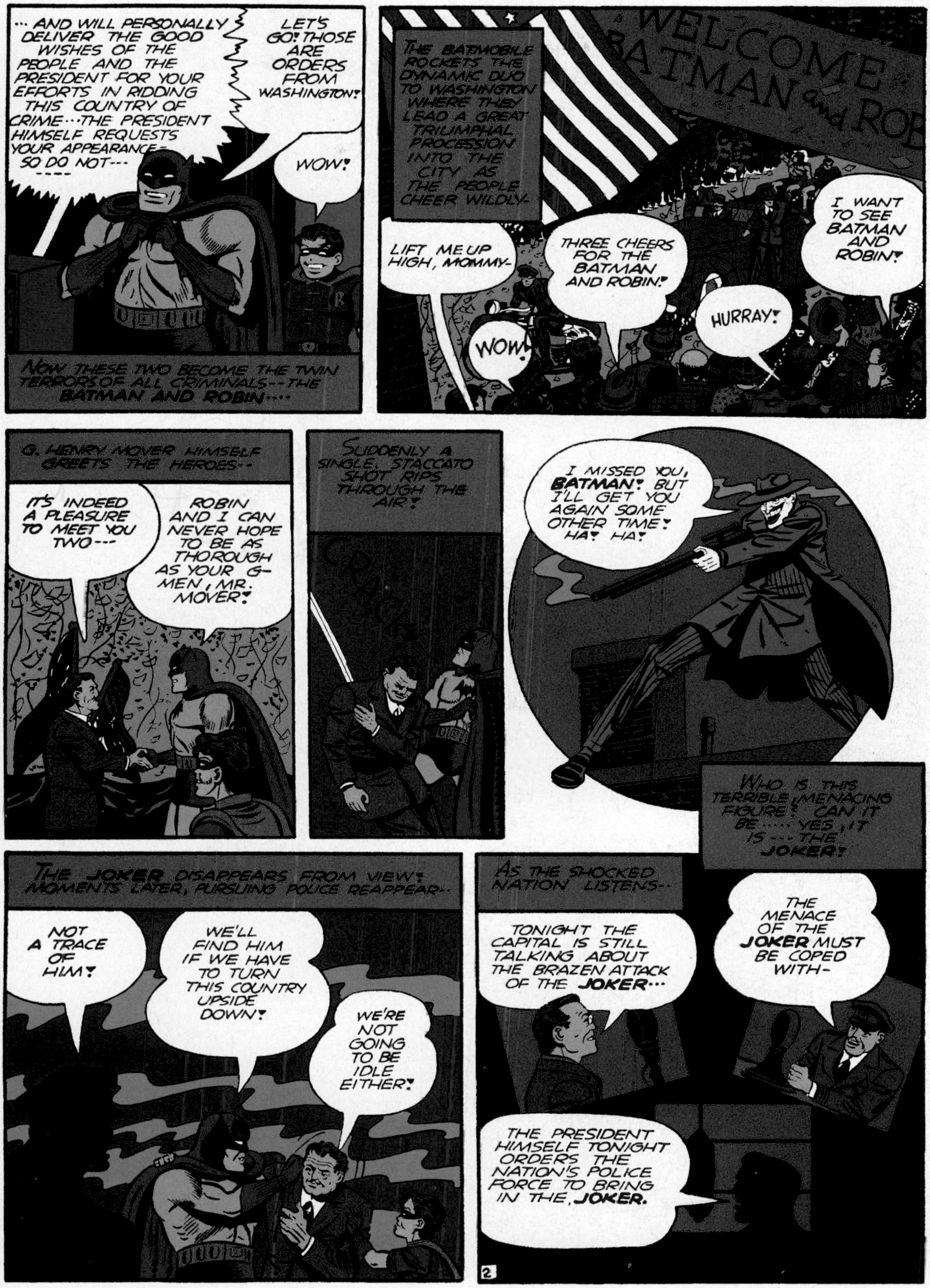
... AND WILL PERSONALLY DELIVER THE GOOD WISHES OF THE PEOPLE AND THE PRESIDENT FOR YOUR EFFORTS IN RIDDING THIS COUNTRY OF CRIME...THE PRESIDENT HIMSELF REQUESTS YOUR APPEARANCE-- SO DO NOT--- ----
LET'S GO! THOSE ARE ORDERS FROM WASHINGTON!
WOW!
NOW THESE TWO BECOME THE TWIN TERRORS OF ALL CRIMINALS--THE BATMAN AND ROBIN....
THE BATMOBILE ROCKETS THE DYNAMIC DUO TO WASHINGTON WHERE THEY LEAD A GREAT TRIUMPHAL PROCESSION INTO THE CITY AS THE PEOPLE CHEER WILDLY-
WELCOME BATMAN and ROB
LIFT ME UP HIGH, MOMMY-
THREE CHEERS FOR THE BATMAN AND ROBIN!
I WANT TO SEE BATMAN AND ROBIN!
HURRAY!
WOW!
G. HENRY MOVER HIMSELF GREETS THE HEROES--
IT'S INDEED A PLEASURE TO MEET YOU TWO---
ROBIN AND I CAN NEVER HOPE TO BE AS THOROUGH AS YOUR G-MEN, MR. MOVER!
SUDDENLY A SINGLE, STACCATO SHOT RIPS THROUGH THE AIR!
CRACK
I MISSED YOU, BATMAN! BUT I'LL GET YOU AGAIN SOME OTHER TIME! HA! HA!
WHO IS THIS TERRIBLE, MENACING FIGURE? CAN IT BE..... YES, IT IS --- THE JOKER!
THE JOKER DISAPPEARS FROM VIEW! MOMENTS LATER, PURSUING POLICE REAPPEAR--
NOT A TRACE OF HIM!
WE'LL FIND HIM IF WE HAVE TO TURN THIS COUNTRY UPSIDE DOWN!
WE'RE NOT GOING TO BE IDLE EITHER!
AS THE SHOCKED NATION LISTENS--
TONIGHT THE CAPITAL IS STILL TALKING ABOUT THE BRAZEN ATTACK OF THE JOKER...
THE MENACE OF THE JOKER MUST BE COPED WITH-
THE PRESIDENT HIMSELF TONIGHT ORDERS THE NATION'S POLICE FORCE TO BRING IN THE JOKER.
2

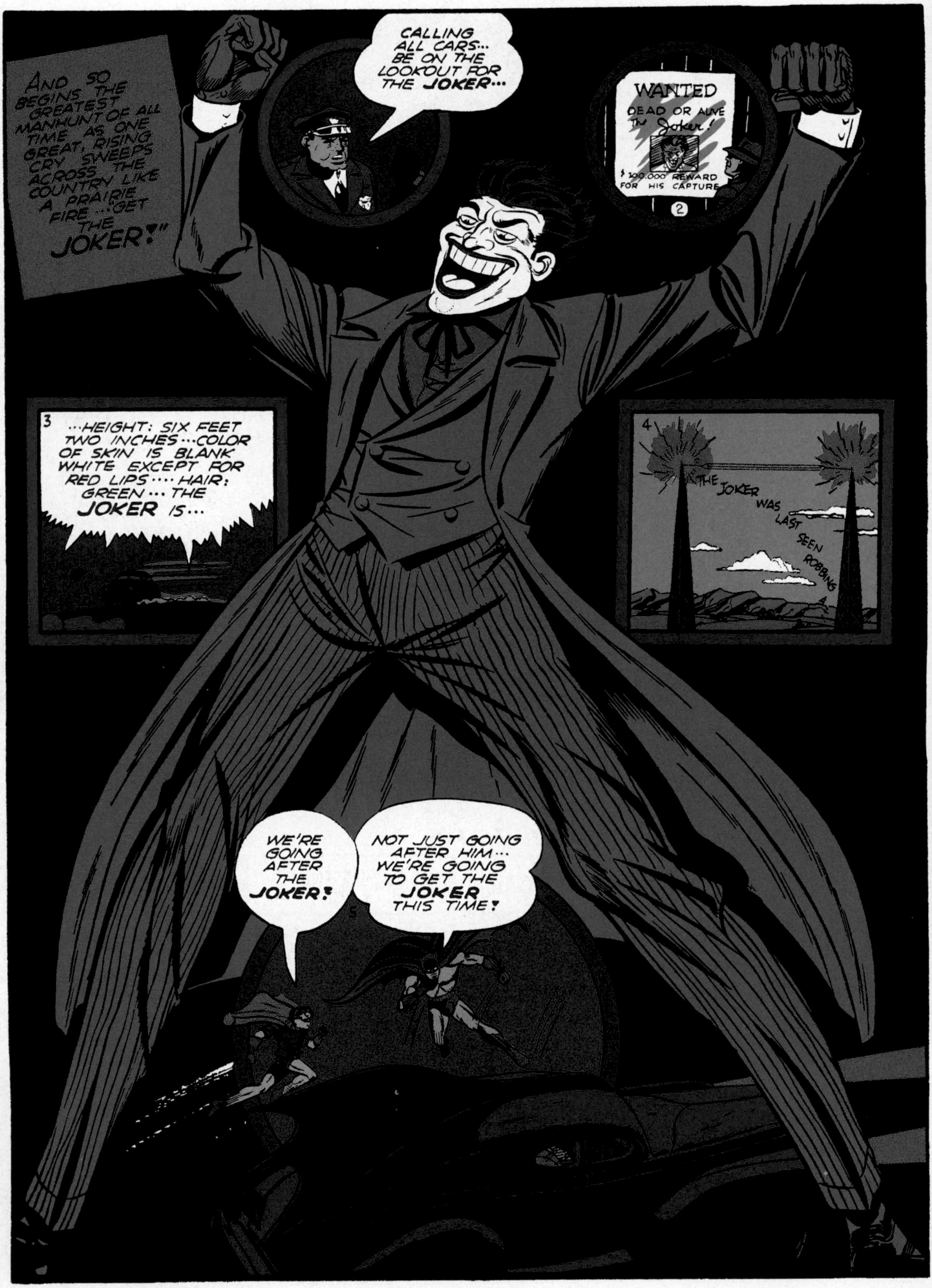
AND SO BEGINS THE GREATEST MANHUNT OF ALL TIME AS ONE GREAT, RISING CRY SWEEPS ACROSS THE COUNTRY LIKE A PRAIRIE FIRE ... "GET THE JOKER!"
CALLING ALL CARS... BE ON THE LOOKOUT FOR THE JOKER...
WANTED
DEAD OR ALIVE
The Joker!
$100,000 REWARD FOR HIS CAPTURE
...HEIGHT: SIX FEET TWO INCHES...COLOR OF SKIN IS BLANK WHITE EXCEPT FOR RED LIPS.... HAIR: GREEN... THE JOKER IS...
THE JOKER WAS LAST SEEN ROBBING
WE'RE GOING AFTER THE JOKER!
NOT JUST GOING AFTER HIM... WE'RE GOING TO GET THE JOKER THIS TIME!

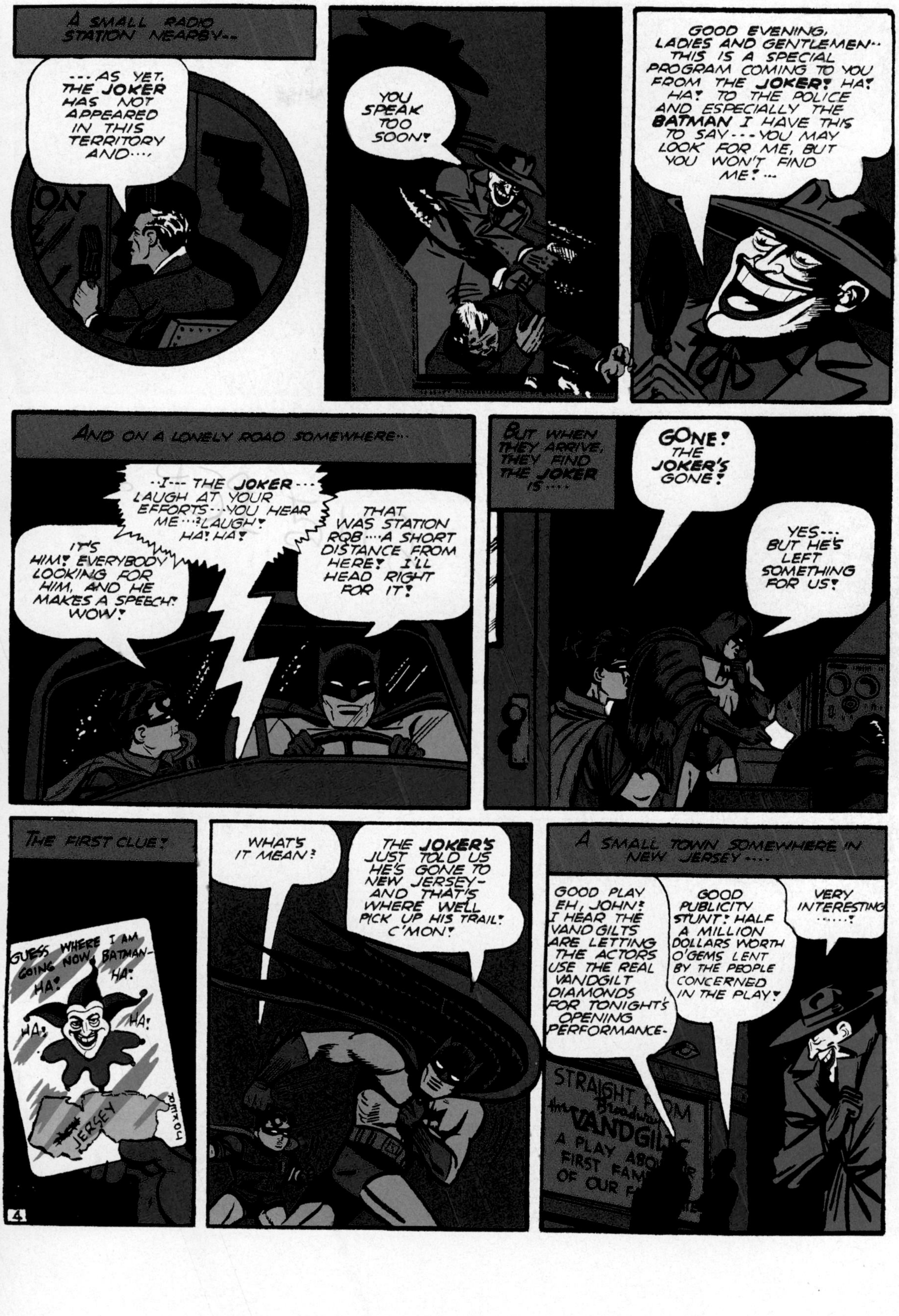
A SMALL RADIO STATION NEARBY--
--- AS YET, THE JOKER HAS NOT APPEARED IN THIS TERRITORY AND...,
YOU SPEAK TOO SOON!
GOOD EVENING, LADIES AND GENTLEMEN-- THIS IS A SPECIAL PROGRAM COMING TO YOU FROM THE JOKER! HA! HA! TO THE POLICE AND ESPECIALLY THE BATMAN I HAVE THIS TO SAY---YOU MAY LOOK FOR ME, BUT YOU WON'T FIND ME!...
AND ON A LONELY ROAD SOMEWHERE...
--I--- THE JOKER--- LAUGH AT YOUR EFFORTS---YOU HEAR ME---?LAUGH! HA! HA!
IT'S HIM! EVERYBODY LOOKING FOR HIM, AND HE MAKES A SPEECH! WOW!
THAT WAS STATION RQB----A SHORT DISTANCE FROM HERE! I'LL HEAD RIGHT FOR IT!
BUT WHEN THEY ARRIVE, THEY FIND THE JOKER IS....
GONE! THE JOKER'S GONE!
YES--- BUT HE'S LEFT SOMETHING FOR US!
THE FIRST CLUE!
GUESS WHERE I AM GOING NOW, BATMAN-- HA! HA! HA! HA!
JERSEY
WHAT'S IT MEAN?
THE JOKER'S JUST TOLD US HE'S GONE TO NEW JERSEY- AND THAT'S WHERE WE'LL PICK UP HIS TRAIL! C'MON!
A SMALL TOWN SOMEWHERE IN NEW JERSEY....
GOOD PLAY EH, JOHN? I HEAR THE VANDGILTS ARE LETTING THE ACTORS USE THE REAL VANDGILT DIAMONDS FOR TONIGHT'S OPENING PERFORMANCE-
GOOD PUBLICITY STUNT! HALF A MILLION DOLLARS WORTH O'GEMS LENT BY THE PEOPLE CONCERNED IN THE PLAY!
VERY INTERESTING.....!
STRAIGHT FROM Broadway VANDGILTS A PLAY ABOUT FIRST FAM OF OUR

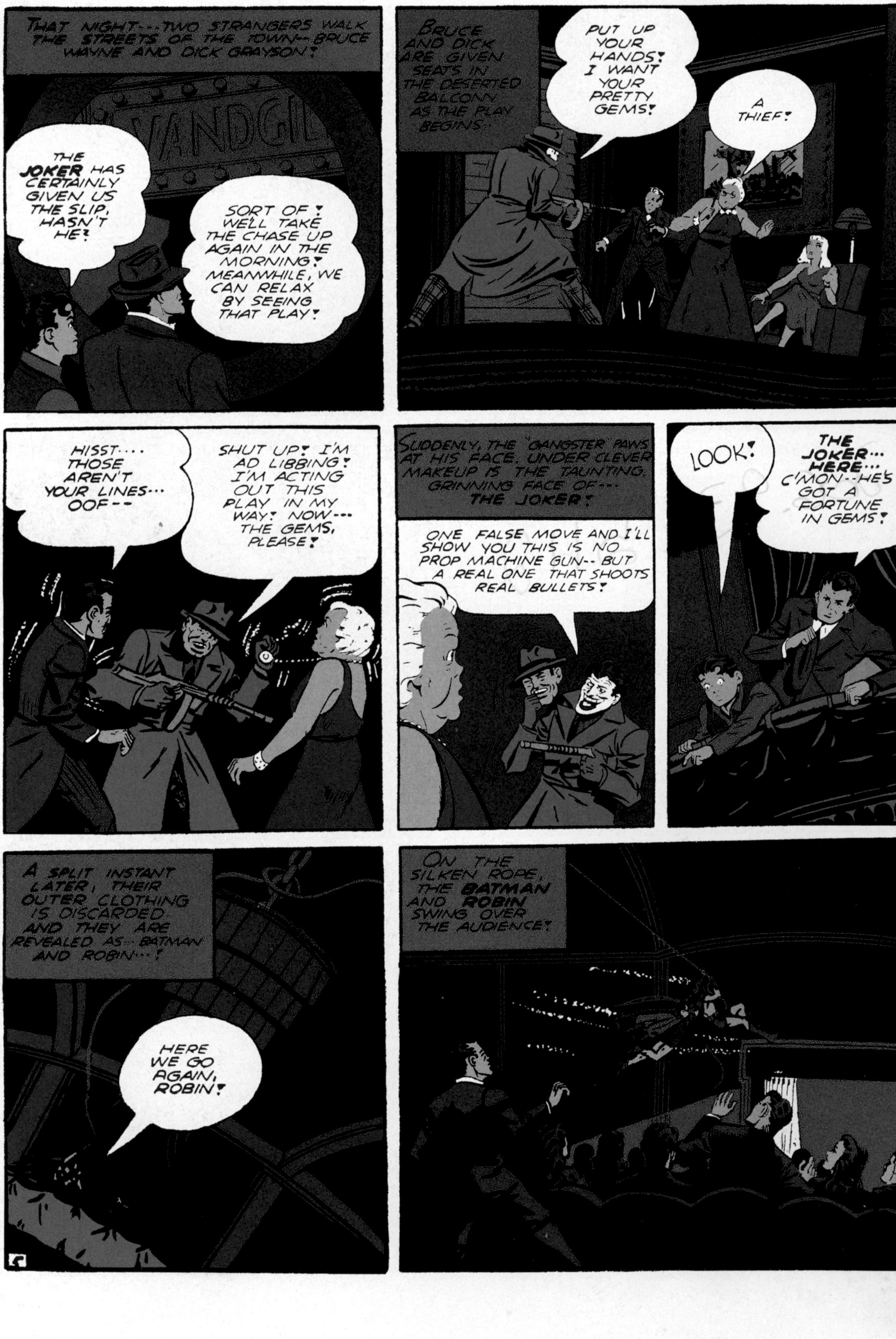
THAT NIGHT---TWO STRANGERS WALK THE STREETS OF THE TOWN--BRUCE WAYNE AND DICK GRAYSON!
THE JOKER HAS CERTAINLY GIVEN US THE SLIP, HASN'T HE?
SORT OF! WE'LL TAKE THE CHASE UP AGAIN IN THE MORNING! MEANWHILE, WE CAN RELAX BY SEEING THAT PLAY!
BRUCE AND DICK ARE GIVEN SEATS IN THE DESERTED BALCONY AS THE PLAY BEGINS..
PUT UP YOUR HANDS! I WANT YOUR PRETTY GEMS!
A THIEF!
HISST.... THOSE AREN'T YOUR LINES... OOF--
SHUT UP! I'M AD LIBBING! I'M ACTING OUT THIS PLAY IN MY WAY! NOW--- THE GEMS, PLEASE!
SUDDENLY, THE "GANGSTER" PAWS AT HIS FACE. UNDER CLEVER MAKEUP IS THE TAUNTING GRINNING FACE OF--- THE JOKER!
ONE FALSE MOVE AND I'LL SHOW YOU THIS IS NO PROP MACHINE GUN-- BUT A REAL ONE THAT SHOOTS REAL BULLETS!
LOOK!
THE JOKER... HERE... C'MON--HE'S GOT A FORTUNE IN GEMS!
A SPLIT INSTANT LATER, THEIR OUTER CLOTHING IS DISCARDED. AND THEY ARE REVEALED AS-- BATMAN AND ROBIN---!
HERE WE GO AGAIN, ROBIN!
ON THE SILKEN ROPE, THE BATMAN AND ROBIN SWING OVER THE AUDIENCE!

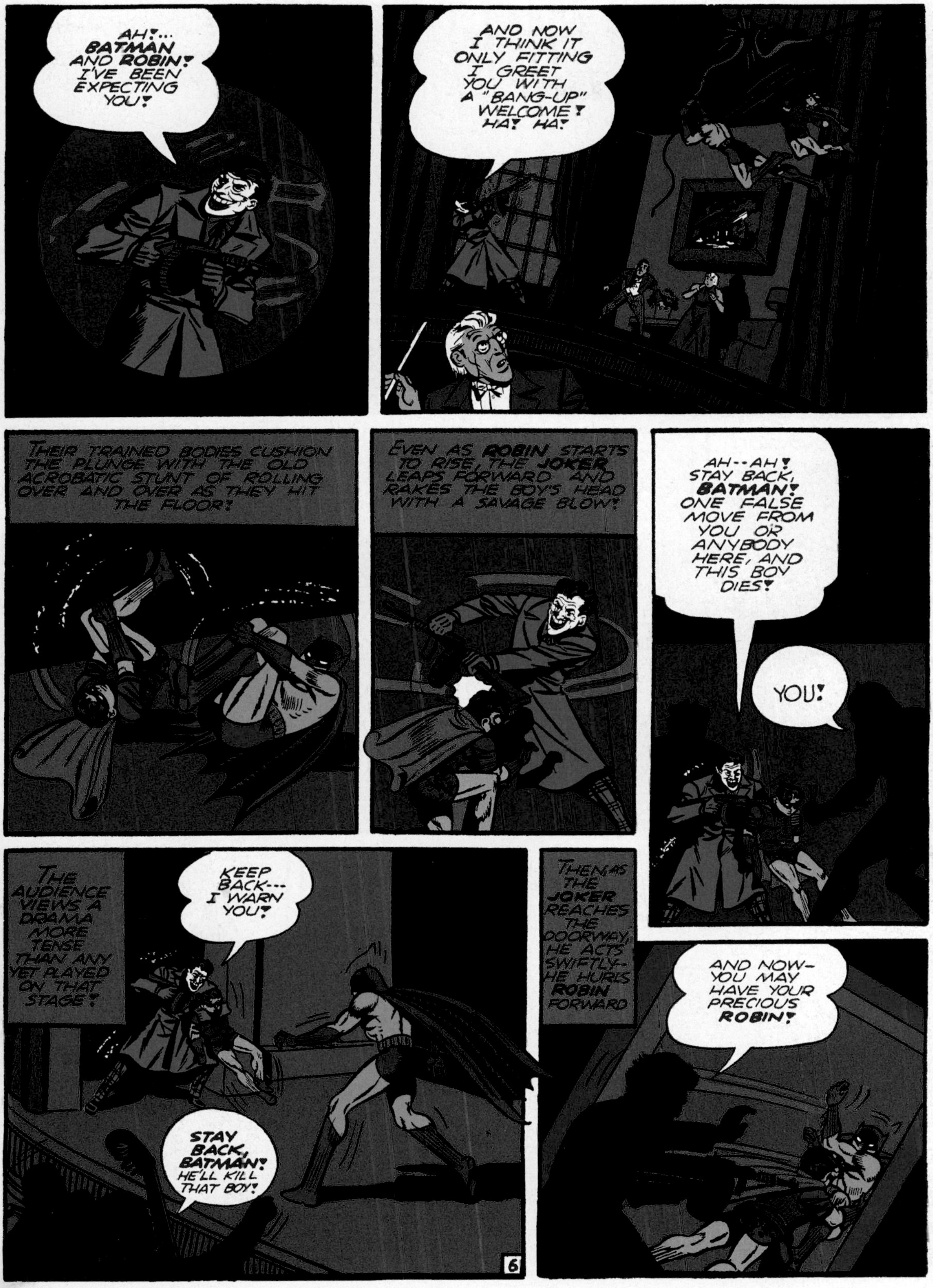
AH!... BATMAN AND ROBIN! I'VE BEEN EXPECTING YOU!
AND NOW I THINK IT ONLY FITTING I GREET YOU WITH A "BANG-UP" WELCOME! HA! HA!
THEIR TRAINED BODIES CUSHION THE PLUNGE WITH THE OLD ACROBATIC STUNT OF ROLLING OVER AND OVER AS THEY HIT THE FLOOR!
EVEN AS ROBIN STARTS TO RISE, THE JOKER LEAPS FORWARD AND RAKES THE BOY'S HEAD WITH A SAVAGE BLOW!
AH--AH! STAY BACK, BATMAN! ONE FALSE MOVE FROM YOU OR ANYBODY HERE, AND THIS BOY DIES!
YOU!
THE AUDIENCE VIEWS A DRAMA MORE TENSE THAN ANY YET PLAYED ON THAT STAGE!
KEEP BACK--- I WARN YOU!
STAY BACK, BATMAN! HE'LL KILL THAT BOY!
6
THEN, AS THE JOKER REACHES THE DOORWAY, HE ACTS SWIFTLY-- HE HURLS ROBIN FORWARD
AND NOW- YOU MAY HAVE YOUR PRECIOUS ROBIN!

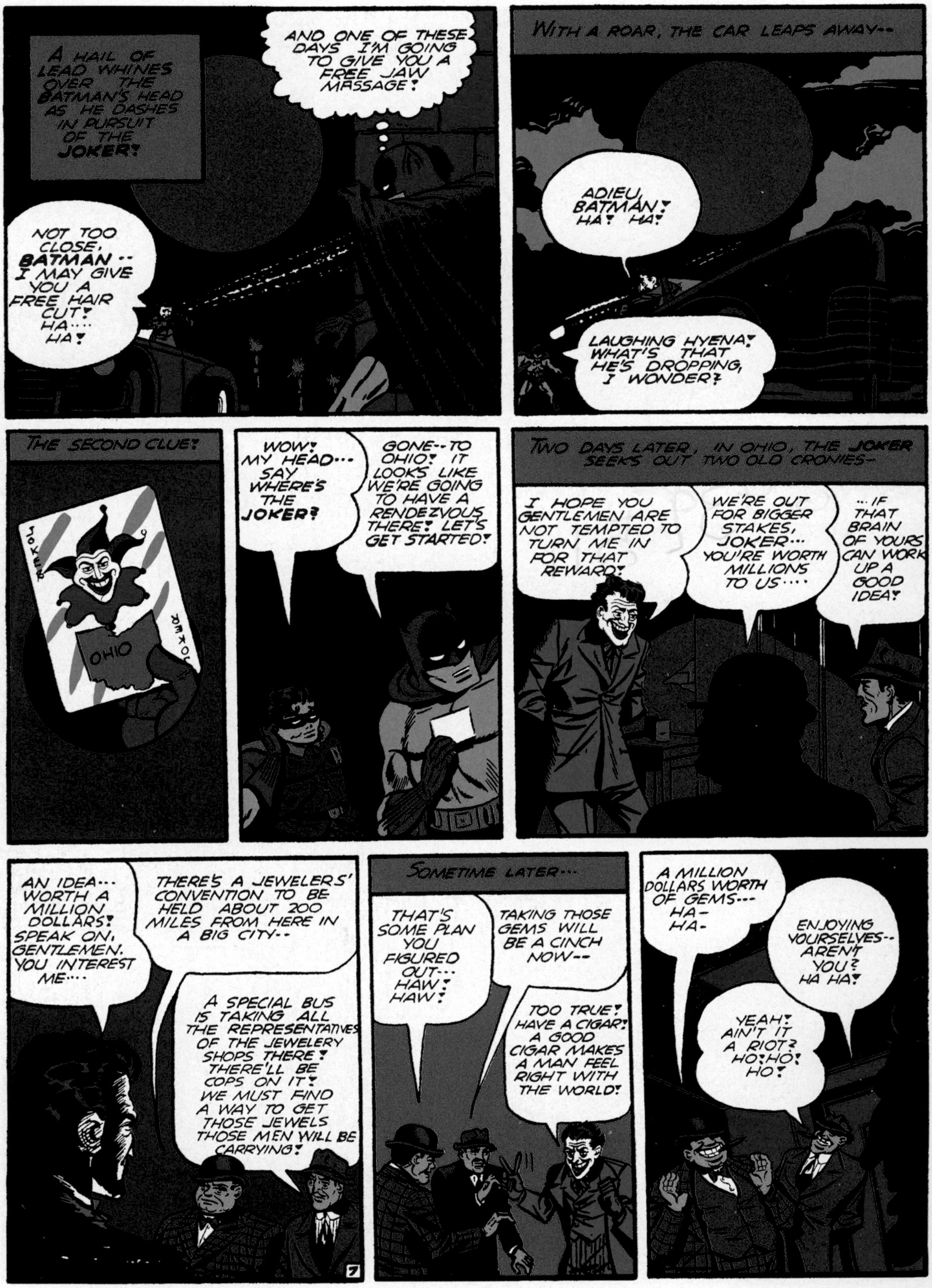
A HAIL OF LEAD WHINES OVER THE BATMAN'S HEAD AS HE DASHES IN PURSUIT OF THE JOKER!
AND ONE OF THESE DAYS I'M GOING TO GIVE YOU A FREE JAW MASSAGE!
NOT TOO CLOSE, BATMAN -- I MAY GIVE YOU A FREE HAIR CUT! HA.... HA!
WITH A ROAR, THE CAR LEAPS AWAY--
ADIEU, BATMAN! HA! HA!
LAUGHING HYENA! WHAT'S THAT HE'S DROPPING, I WONDER?
THE SECOND CLUE!
JOKER
OHIO
JOKER
WOW! MY HEAD... SAY WHERE'S THE JOKER?
GONE--TO OHIO! IT LOOKS LIKE WE'RE GOING TO HAVE A RENDEZVOUS THERE! LET'S GET STARTED!
TWO DAYS LATER, IN OHIO, THE JOKER SEEKS OUT TWO OLD CRONIES--
I HOPE YOU GENTLEMEN ARE NOT TEMPTED TO TURN ME IN FOR THAT REWARD!
WE'RE OUT FOR BIGGER STAKES, JOKER... YOU'RE WORTH MILLIONS TO US....
...IF THAT BRAIN OF YOURS CAN WORK UP A GOOD IDEA!
AN IDEA... WORTH A MILLION DOLLARS! SPEAK ON, GENTLEMEN. YOU INTEREST ME....
THERE'S A JEWELERS' CONVENTION TO BE HELD ABOUT 200 MILES FROM HERE IN A BIG CITY--
A SPECIAL BUS IS TAKING ALL THE REPRESENTATIVES OF THE JEWELERY SHOPS THERE! THERE'LL BE COPS ON IT! WE MUST FIND A WAY TO GET THOSE JEWELS THOSE MEN WILL BE CARRYING!
7
SOMETIME LATER...
THAT'S SOME PLAN YOU FIGURED OUT... HAW! HAW!
TAKING THOSE GEMS WILL BE A CINCH NOW--
TOO TRUE! HAVE A CIGAR! A GOOD CIGAR MAKES A MAN FEEL RIGHT WITH THE WORLD!
A MILLION DOLLARS WORTH OF GEMS--- HA- HA-
ENJOYING YOURSELVES-- AREN'T YOU? HA HA!
YEAH! AIN'T IT A RIOT? HO! HO! HO!

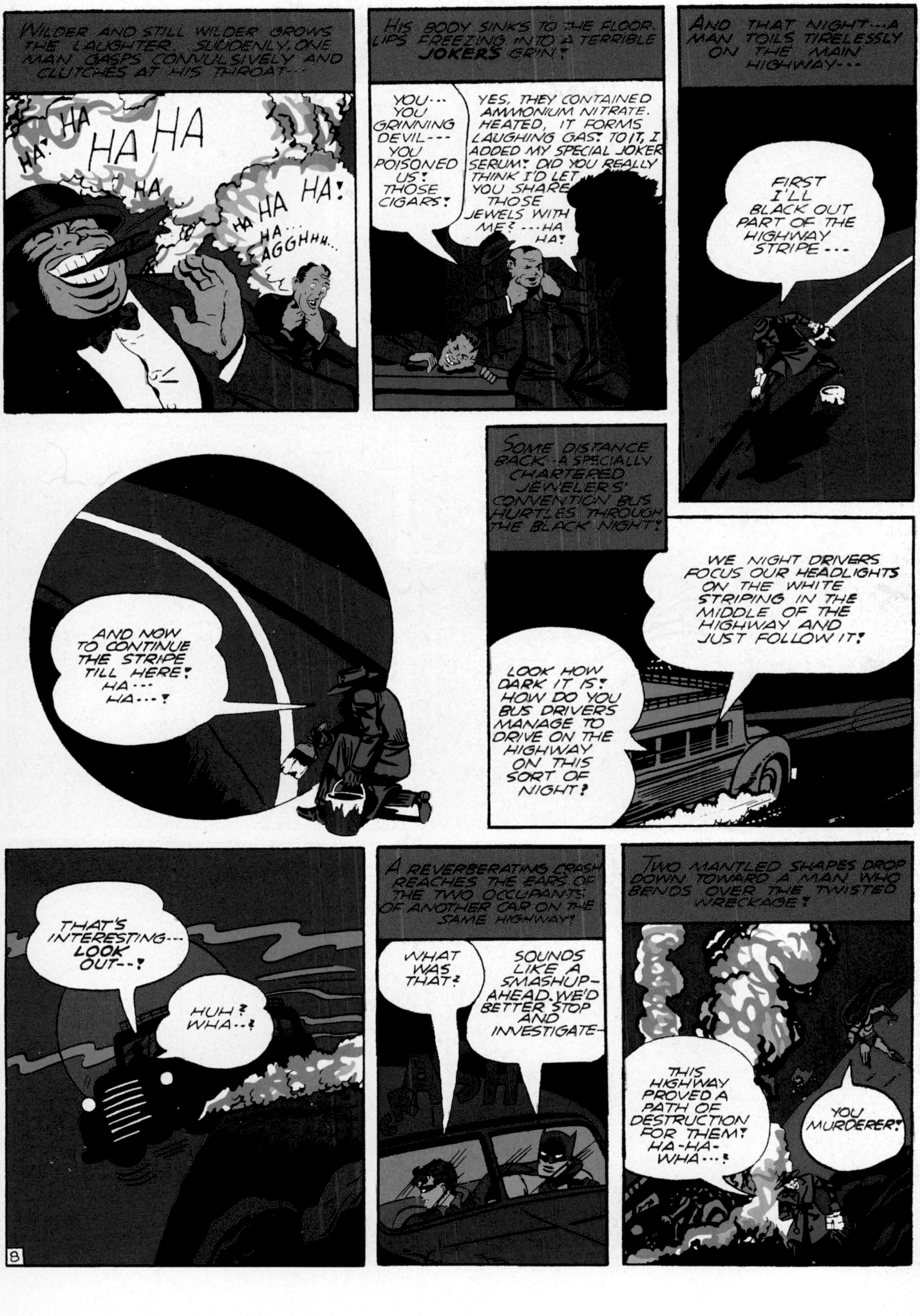
WILDER AND STILL WILDER GROWS THE LAUGHTER. SUDDENLY, ONE MAN GASPS CONVULSIVELY AND CLUTCHES AT HIS THROAT---
HA! HA HA HA HA
HA HA
HA HA HA!
HA... AGGHHH...
HIS BODY SINKS TO THE FLOOR, LIPS FREEZING INTO A TERRIBLE JOKERS GRIN!
YOU--- YOU GRINNING DEVIL--- YOU POISONED US! THOSE CIGARS!
YES, THEY CONTAINED AMMONIUM NITRATE. HEATED, IT FORMS LAUGHING GAS! TO IT, I ADDED MY SPECIAL JOKER SERUM! DID YOU REALLY THINK I'D LET YOU SHARE THOSE JEWELS WITH ME? ---HA HA!
AND THAT NIGHT--A MAN TOILS TIRELESSLY ON THE MAIN HIGHWAY---
FIRST I'LL BLACK OUT PART OF THE HIGHWAY STRIPE---
AND NOW TO CONTINUE THE STRIPE TILL HERE! HA--- HA---!
SOME DISTANCE BACK--A SPECIALLY CHARTERED JEWELERS' CONVENTION BUS HURTLES THROUGH THE BLACK NIGHT!
LOOK HOW DARK IT IS! HOW DO YOU BUS DRIVERS MANAGE TO DRIVE ON THE HIGHWAY ON THIS SORT OF NIGHT?
WE NIGHT DRIVERS FOCUS OUR HEADLIGHTS ON THE WHITE STRIPING IN THE MIDDLE OF THE HIGHWAY AND JUST FOLLOW IT!
THAT'S INTERESTING--- LOOK OUT--!
HUH? WHA--?
8
A REVERBERATING CRASH REACHES THE EARS OF THE TWO OCCUPANTS OF ANOTHER CAR ON THE SAME HIGHWAY!
WHAT WAS THAT?
SOUNDS LIKE A SMASHUP-AHEAD. WE'D BETTER STOP AND INVESTIGATE-
TWO MANTLED SHAPES DROP DOWN TOWARD A MAN WHO BENDS OVER THE TWISTED WRECKAGE!
THIS HIGHWAY PROVED A PATH OF DESTRUCTION FOR THEM! HA-HA-WHA---?
YOU MURDERER!

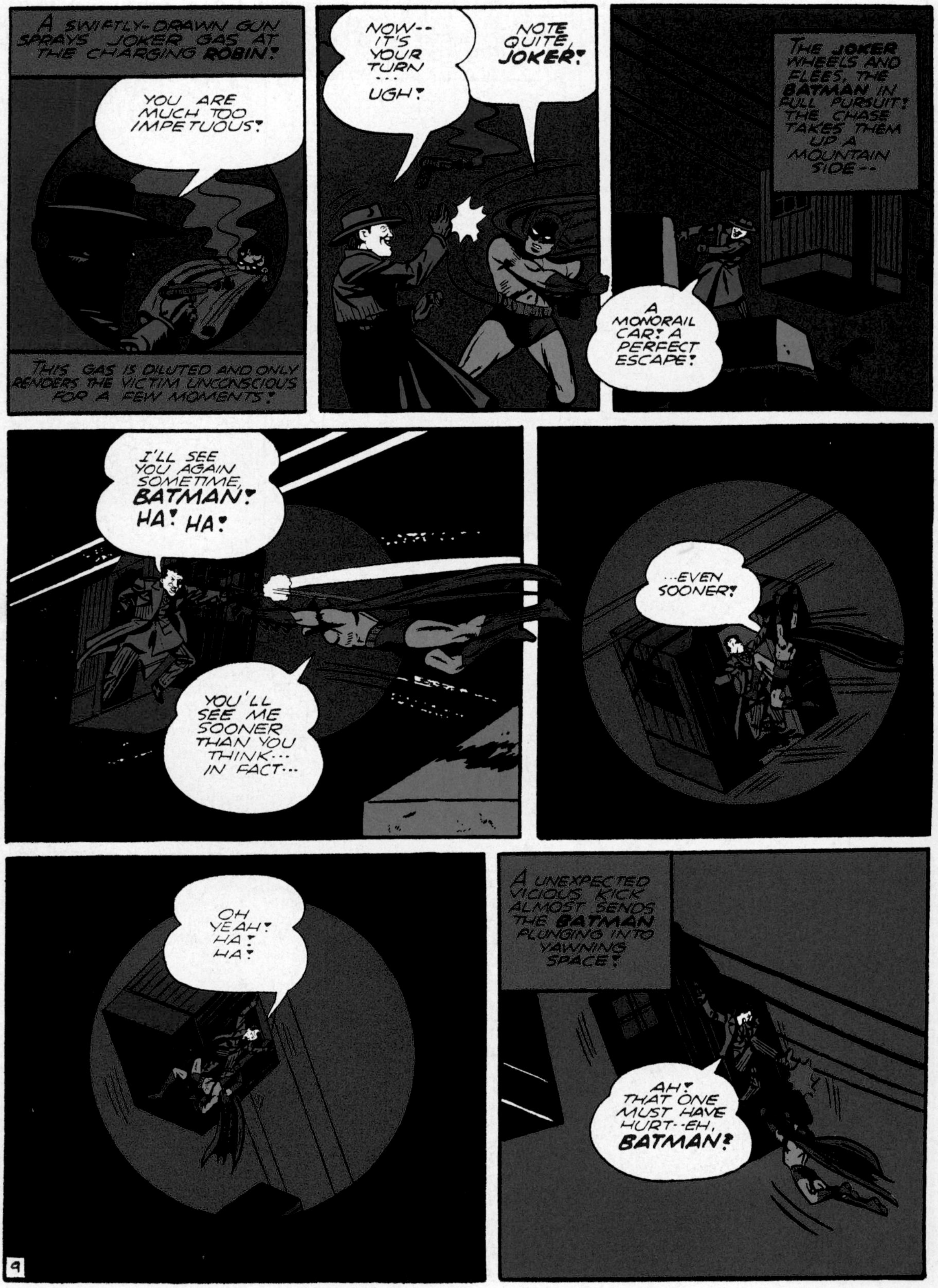
A SWIFTLY-DRAWN GUN SPRAYS JOKER GAS AT THE CHARGING ROBIN!
YOU ARE MUCH TOO IMPETUOUS!
THIS GAS IS DILUTED AND ONLY RENDERS THE VICTIM UNCONSCIOUS FOR A FEW MOMENTS!
NOW-- IT'S YOUR TURN ... UGH!
NOTE QUITE, JOKER!
THE JOKER WHEELS AND FLEES, THE BATMAN IN FULL PURSUIT! THE CHASE TAKES THEM UP A MOUNTAIN SIDE--
A MONORAIL CAR! A PERFECT ESCAPE!
I'LL SEE YOU AGAIN SOMETIME, BATMAN! HA! HA!
YOU'LL SEE ME SOONER THAN YOU THINK... IN FACT...
...EVEN SOONER!
OH YEAH! HA! HA!
9
A UNEXPECTED VICIOUS KICK ALMOST SENDS THE BATMAN PLUNGING INTO YAWNING SPACE!
AH! THAT ONE MUST HAVE HURT--EH, BATMAN?

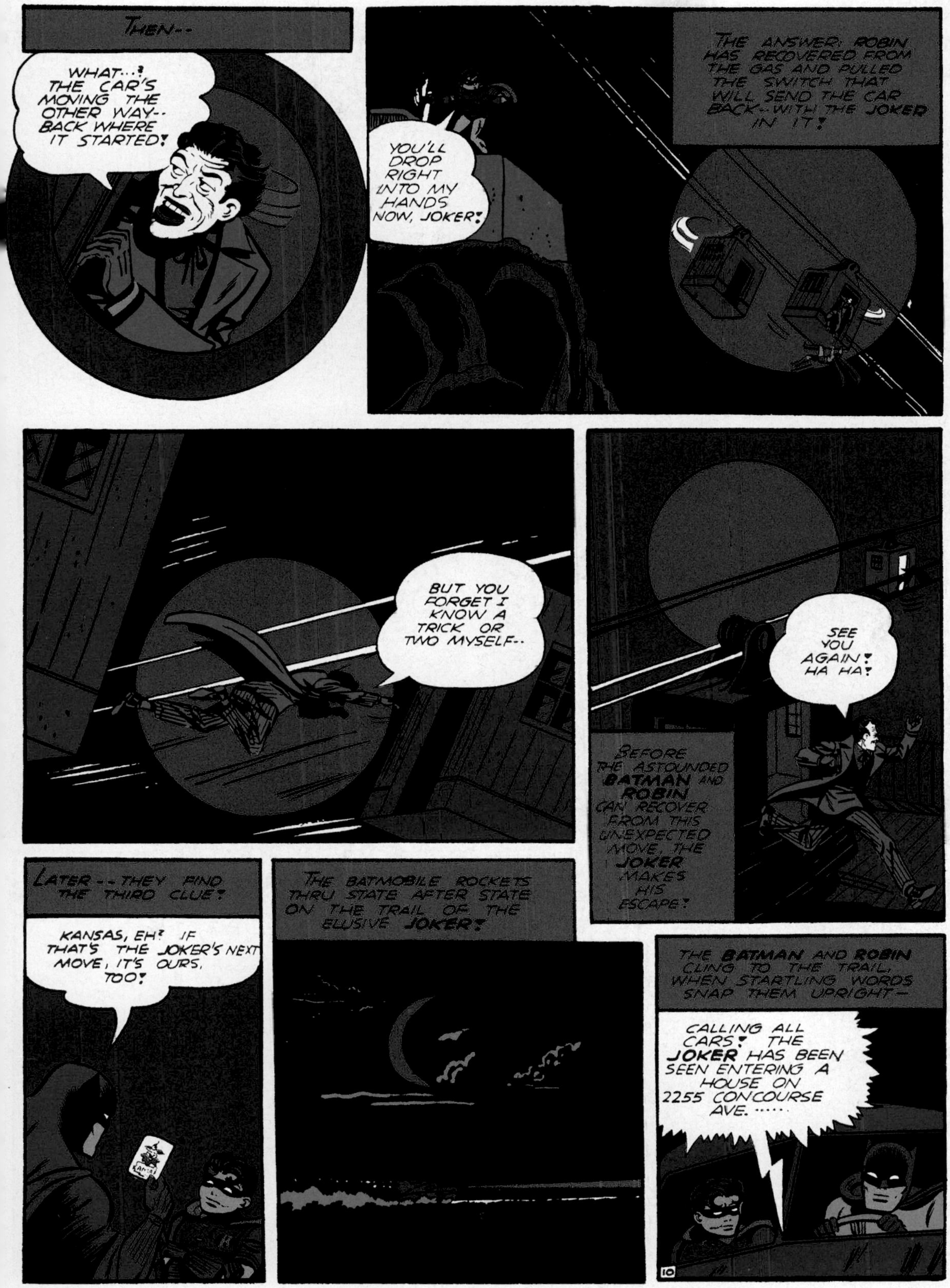

THEN--
WHAT...? THE CAR'S MOVING THE OTHER WAY--BACK WHERE IT STARTED!
THE ANSWER: ROBIN HAS RECOVERED FROM THE GAS AND PULLED THE SWITCH THAT WILL SEND THE CAR BACK--WITH THE JOKER IN IT!
YOU'LL DROP RIGHT INTO MY HANDS NOW, JOKER!
BUT YOU FORGET I KNOW A TRICK OR TWO MYSELF--
SEE YOU AGAIN! HA HA!
BEFORE THE ASTOUNDED BATMAN AND ROBIN CAN RECOVER FROM THIS UNEXPECTED MOVE, THE JOKER MAKES HIS ESCAPE!
LATER--THEY FIND THE THIRD CLUE!
KANSAS, EH? IF THAT'S THE JOKER'S NEXT MOVE, IT'S OURS, TOO!
THE BATMOBILE ROCKETS THRU STATE AFTER STATE ON THE TRAIL OF THE ELUSIVE JOKER!
THE BATMAN AND ROBIN CLING TO THE TRAIL, WHEN STARTLING WORDS SNAP THEM UPRIGHT—
CALLING ALL CARS! THE JOKER HAS BEEN SEEN ENTERING A HOUSE ON 2255 CONCOURSE AVE......
10

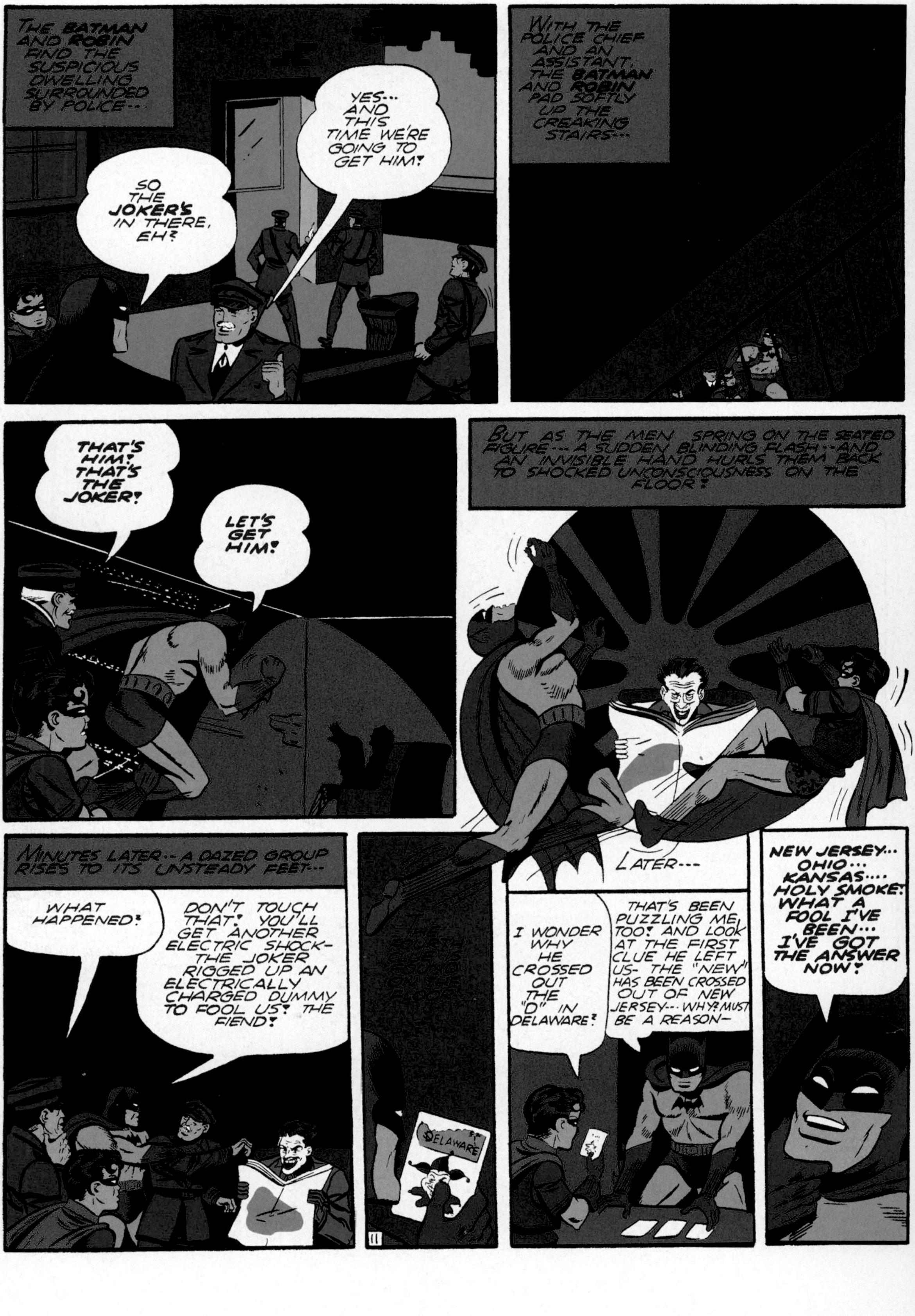
THE BATMAN AND ROBIN FIND THE SUSPICIOUS DWELLING SURROUNDED BY POLICE--
SO THE JOKER'S IN THERE, EH?
YES--- AND THIS TIME WE'RE GOING TO GET HIM!
WITH THE POLICE CHIEF AND AN ASSISTANT, THE BATMAN AND ROBIN PAD SOFTLY UP THE CREAKING STAIRS---
THAT'S HIM! THAT'S THE JOKER!
LET'S GET HIM!
BUT AS THE MEN SPRING ON THE SEATED FIGURE--- A SUDDEN BLINDING FLASH--AND AN INVISIBLE HAND HURLS THEM BACK TO SHOCKED UNCONSCIOUSNESS ON THE FLOOR!
MINUTES LATER-- A DAZED GROUP RISES TO ITS UNSTEADY FEET---
WHAT HAPPENED?
DON'T TOUCH THAT! YOU'LL GET ANOTHER ELECTRIC SHOCK- THE JOKER RIGGED UP AN ELECTRICALLY CHARGED DUMMY TO FOOL US! THE FIEND!
DELAWARE
LATER---
I WONDER WHY HE CROSSED OUT THE "D" IN DELAWARE?
THAT'S BEEN PUZZLING ME, TOO! AND LOOK AT THE FIRST CLUE HE LEFT US- THE "NEW" HAS BEEN CROSSED OUT OF NEW JERSEY--- WHY? MUST BE A REASON-
NEW JERSEY... OHIO... KANSAS.... HOLY SMOKE! WHAT A FOOL I'VE BEEN... I'VE GOT THE ANSWER NOW!

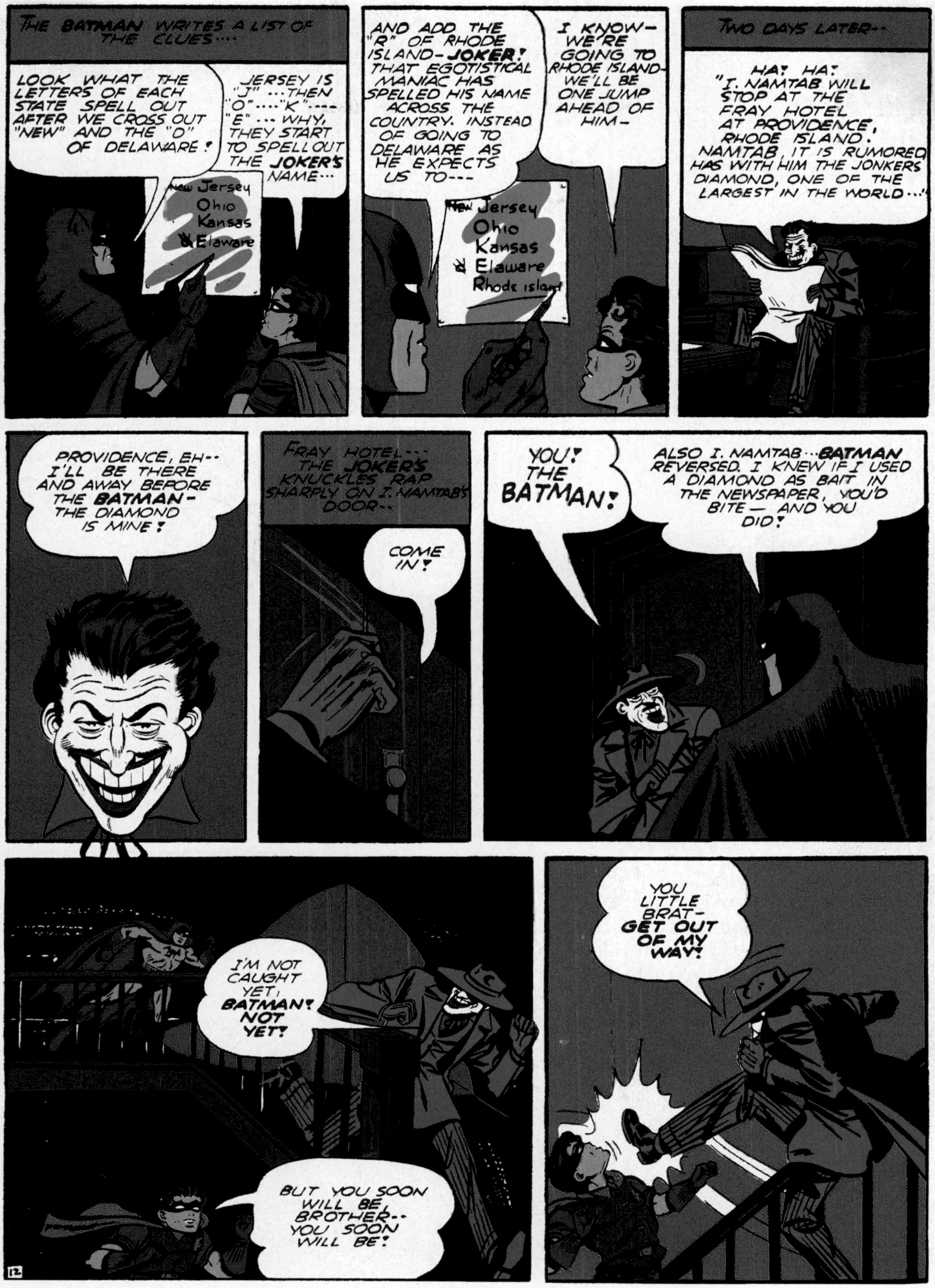
THE BATMAN WRITES A LIST OF THE CLUES....
LOOK WHAT THE LETTERS OF EACH STATE SPELL OUT AFTER WE CROSS OUT "NEW" AND THE "D" OF DELAWARE!
JERSEY IS "J" ... THEN "O" ... "K" ... "E" ... WHY, THEY START TO SPELL OUT THE JOKER'S NAME...
New Jersey
Ohio
Kansas
Elaware
AND ADD THE "R" OF RHODE ISLAND- JOKER! THAT EGOTISTICAL MANIAC HAS SPELLED HIS NAME ACROSS THE COUNTRY. INSTEAD OF GOING TO DELAWARE AS HE EXPECTS US TO---
I KNOW- WE'RE GOING TO RHODE ISLAND- WE'LL BE ONE JUMP AHEAD OF HIM-
Rhode island
TWO DAYS LATER--
HA! HA! "I. NAMTAB WILL STOP AT THE FRAY HOTEL AT PROVIDENCE, RHODE ISLAND. NAMTAB, IT IS RUMORED, HAS WITH HIM THE JONKERS DIAMOND, ONE OF THE LARGEST IN THE WORLD..."
PROVIDENCE, EH-- I'LL BE THERE AND AWAY BEFORE THE BATMAN- THE DIAMOND IS MINE!
FRAY HOTEL--- THE JOKER'S KNUCKLES RAP SHARPLY ON I. NAMTAB'S DOOR--
COME IN!
YOU! THE BATMAN!
ALSO I. NAMTAB...BATMAN REVERSED. I KNEW IF I USED A DIAMOND AS BAIT IN THE NEWSPAPER, YOU'D BITE— AND YOU DID!
I'M NOT CAUGHT YET, BATMAN! NOT YET!
BUT YOU SOON WILL BE, BROTHER-- YOU SOON WILL BE!
12
YOU LITTLE BRAT- GET OUT OF MY WAY!

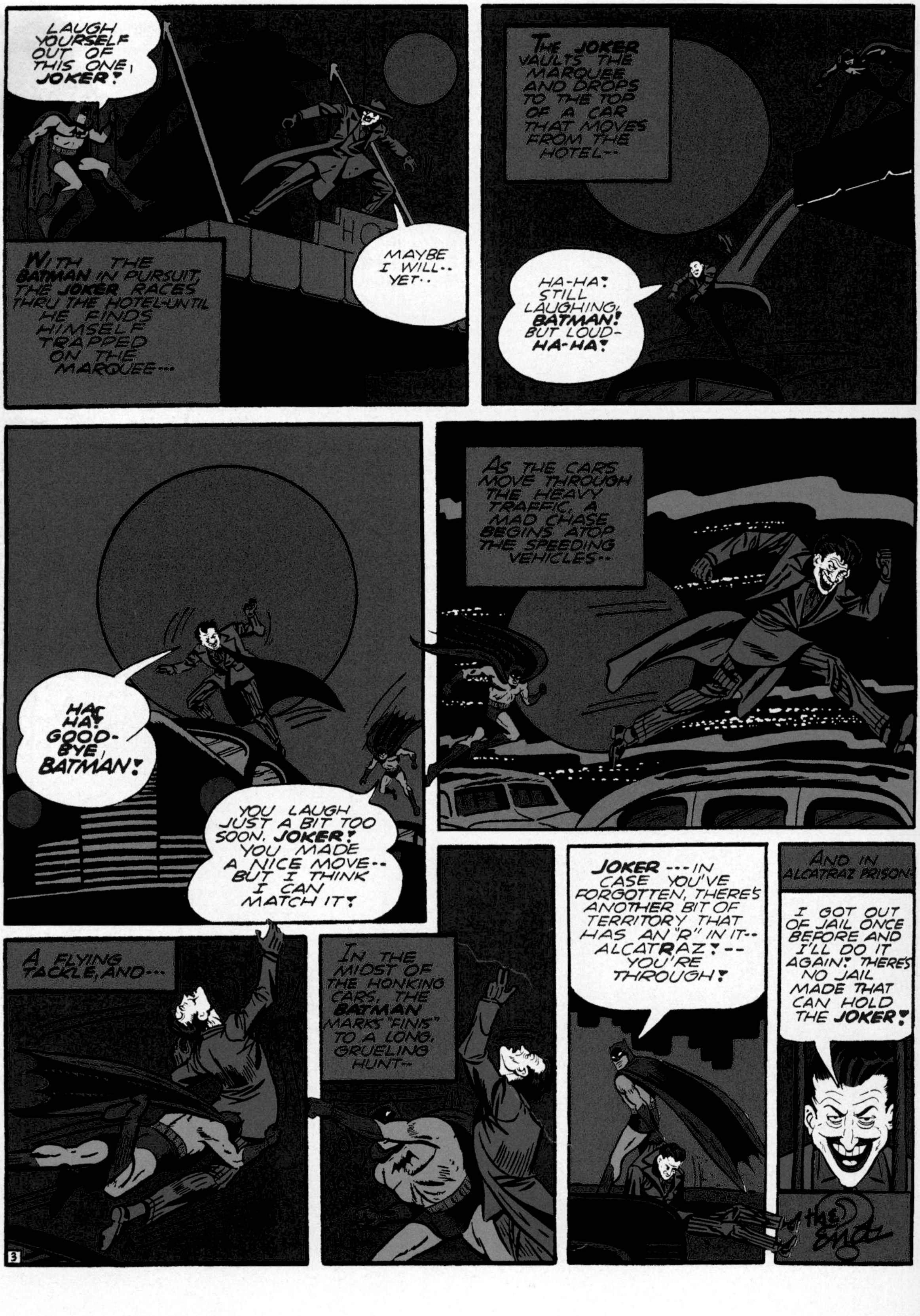
LAUGH YOURSELF OUT OF THIS ONE, JOKER!
WITH THE BATMAN IN PURSUIT, THE JOKER RACES THRU THE HOTEL-UNTIL HE FINDS HIMSELF TRAPPED ON THE MARQUEE---
MAYBE I WILL-- YET--
THE JOKER VAULTS THE MARQUEE AND DROPS TO THE TOP OF A CAR THAT MOVES FROM THE HOTEL--
HA-HA! STILL LAUGHING, BATMAN! BUT LOUD-HA-HA!
HA! HA! GOOD-BYE, BATMAN!
YOU LAUGH JUST A BIT TOO SOON, JOKER! YOU MADE A NICE MOVE-- BUT I THINK I CAN MATCH IT!
AS THE CARS MOVE THROUGH THE HEAVY TRAFFIC, A MAD CHASE BEGINS ATOP THE SPEEDING VEHICLES--
A FLYING TACKLE, AND---
IN THE MIDST OF THE HONKING CARS, THE BATMAN MARKS "FINIS" TO A LONG, GRUELING HUNT--
JOKER --- IN CASE YOU'VE FORGOTTEN, THERE'S ANOTHER BIT OF TERRITORY THAT HAS AN "R" IN IT-- ALCATRAZ! -- YOU'RE THROUGH!
AND IN ALCATRAZ PRISON--
I GOT OUT OF JAIL ONCE BEFORE AND I'LL DO IT AGAIN! THERE'S NO JAIL MADE THAT CAN HOLD THE JOKER!
THE END

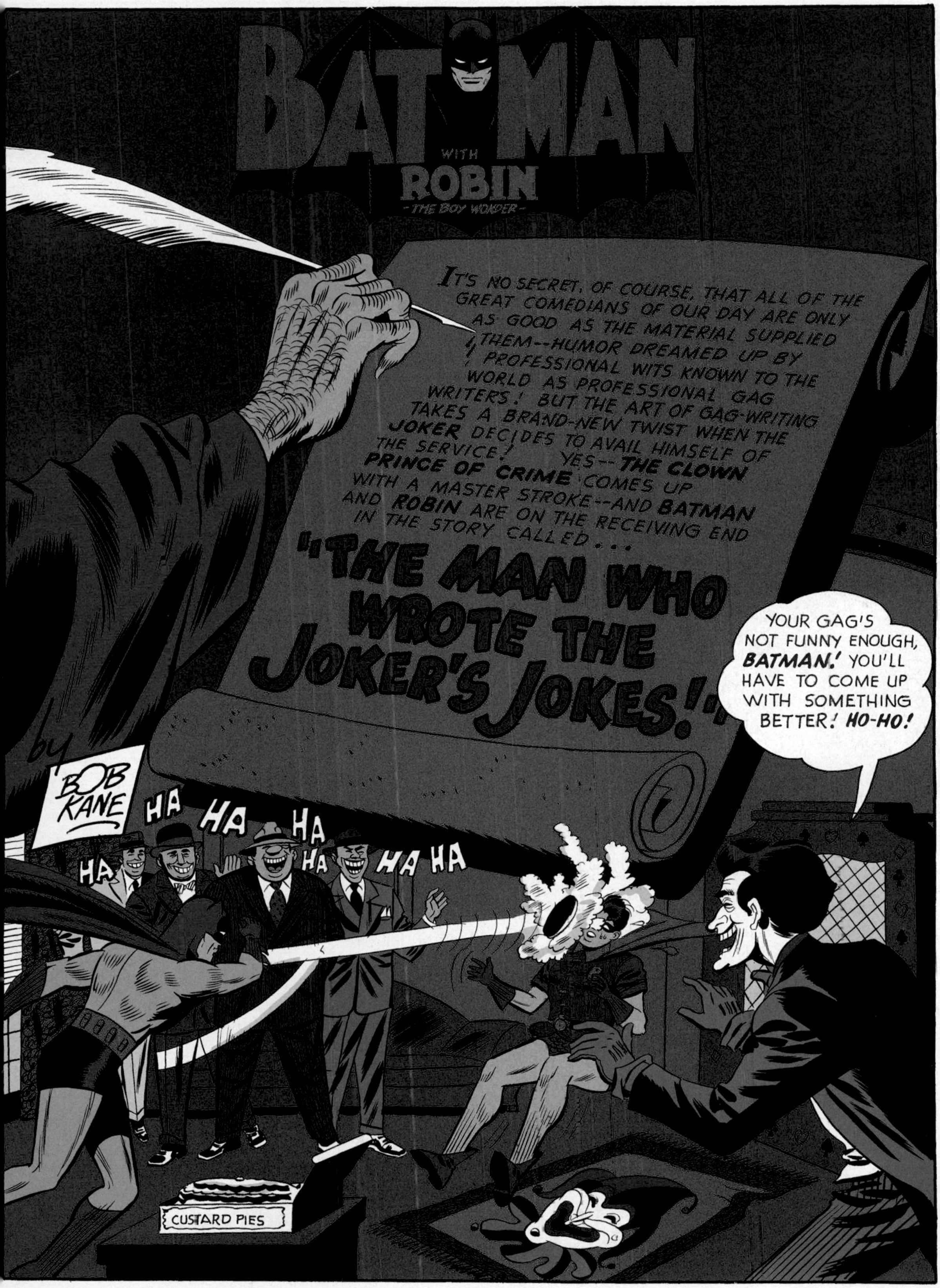
BATMAN
WITH
ROBIN
-THE BOY WONDER-
IT'S NO SECRET, OF COURSE, THAT ALL OF THE GREAT COMEDIANS OF OUR DAY ARE ONLY AS GOOD AS THE MATERIAL SUPPLIED THEM--HUMOR DREAMED UP BY PROFESSIONAL WITS KNOWN TO THE WORLD AS PROFESSIONAL GAG WRITERS! BUT THE ART OF GAG-WRITING TAKES A BRAND-NEW TWIST WHEN THE JOKER DECIDES TO AVAIL HIMSELF OF THE SERVICE! YES--THE CLOWN PRINCE OF CRIME COMES UP WITH A MASTER STROKE--AND BATMAN AND ROBIN ARE ON THE RECEIVING END IN THE STORY CALLED...
"THE MAN WHO WROTE THE JOKER'S JOKES!"
YOUR GAG'S NOT FUNNY ENOUGH, BATMAN! YOU'LL HAVE TO COME UP WITH SOMETHING BETTER! HO-HO!
by BOB KANE
HA HA HA HA HA HA HA HA
CUSTARD PIES

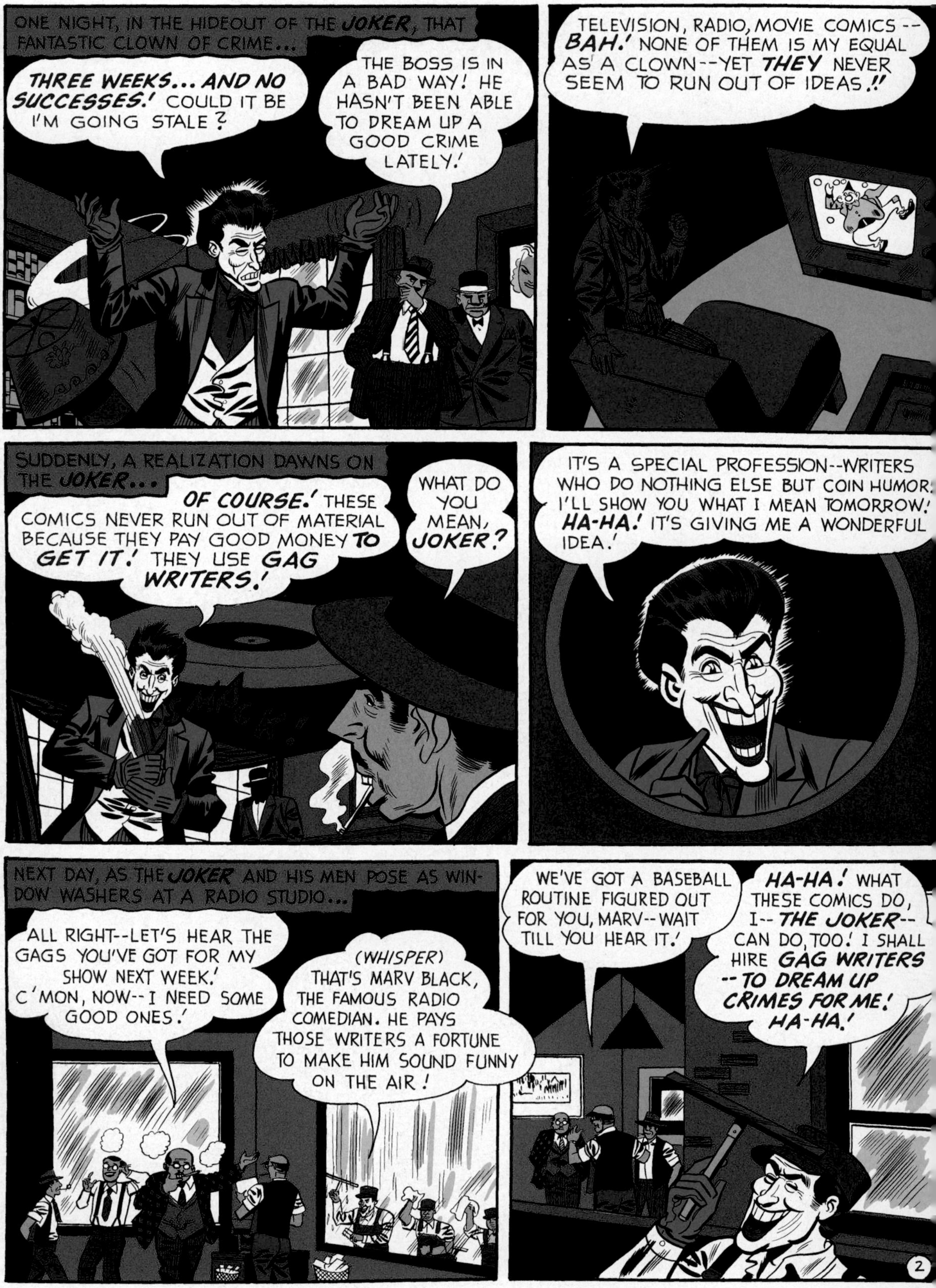
ONE NIGHT, IN THE HIDEOUT OF THE JOKER, THAT FANTASTIC CLOWN OF CRIME...
THREE WEEKS... AND NO SUCCESSES! COULD IT BE I'M GOING STALE?
THE BOSS IS IN A BAD WAY! HE HASN'T BEEN ABLE TO DREAM UP A GOOD CRIME LATELY!
TELEVISION, RADIO, MOVIE COMICS -- BAH! NONE OF THEM IS MY EQUAL AS A CLOWN--YET THEY NEVER SEEM TO RUN OUT OF IDEAS!!
SUDDENLY, A REALIZATION DAWNS ON THE JOKER...
OF COURSE! THESE COMICS NEVER RUN OUT OF MATERIAL BECAUSE THEY PAY GOOD MONEY TO GET IT! THEY USE GAG WRITERS!
WHAT DO YOU MEAN, JOKER?
IT'S A SPECIAL PROFESSION--WRITERS WHO DO NOTHING ELSE BUT COIN HUMOR! I'LL SHOW YOU WHAT I MEAN TOMORROW! HA-HA! IT'S GIVING ME A WONDERFUL IDEA!
NEXT DAY, AS THE JOKER AND HIS MEN POSE AS WINDOW WASHERS AT A RADIO STUDIO...
ALL RIGHT--LET'S HEAR THE GAGS YOU'VE GOT FOR MY SHOW NEXT WEEK! C'MON, NOW--I NEED SOME GOOD ONES!
(WHISPER) THAT'S MARV BLACK, THE FAMOUS RADIO COMEDIAN. HE PAYS THOSE WRITERS A FORTUNE TO MAKE HIM SOUND FUNNY ON THE AIR!
WE'VE GOT A BASEBALL ROUTINE FIGURED OUT FOR YOU, MARV--WAIT TILL YOU HEAR IT!
HA-HA! WHAT THESE COMICS DO, I-- THE JOKER-- CAN DO, TOO! I SHALL HIRE GAG WRITERS --TO DREAM UP CRIMES FOR ME! HA-HA!
2

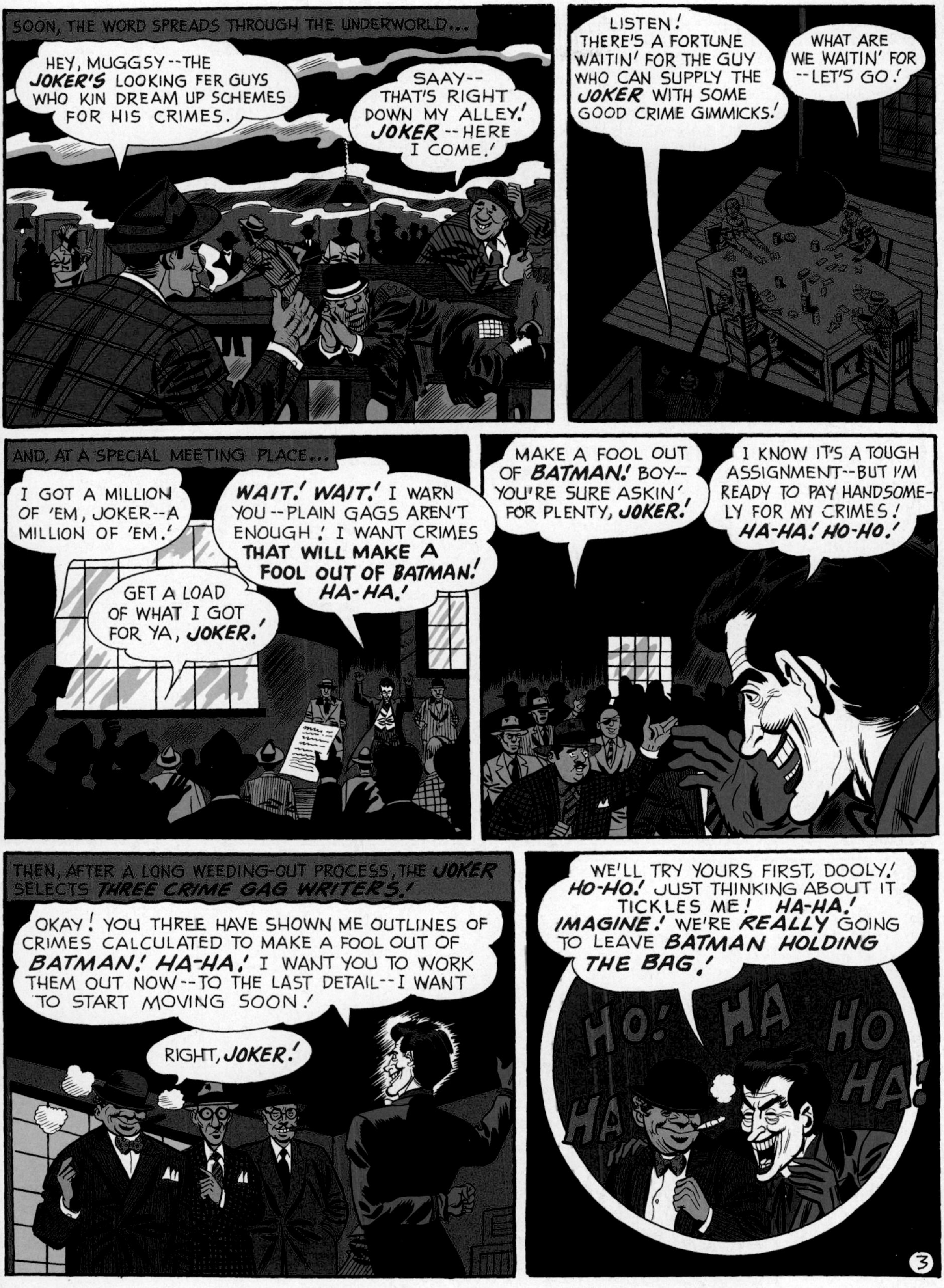

SOON, THE WORD SPREADS THROUGH THE UNDERWORLD...
HEY, MUGGSY--THE JOKER'S LOOKING FER GUYS WHO KIN DREAM UP SCHEMES FOR HIS CRIMES.
SAAY--THAT'S RIGHT DOWN MY ALLEY! JOKER--HERE I COME!
LISTEN! THERE'S A FORTUNE WAITIN' FOR THE GUY WHO CAN SUPPLY THE JOKER WITH SOME GOOD CRIME GIMMICKS!
WHAT ARE WE WAITIN' FOR--LET'S GO!
AND, AT A SPECIAL MEETING PLACE...
I GOT A MILLION OF 'EM, JOKER--A MILLION OF 'EM!
GET A LOAD OF WHAT I GOT FOR YA, JOKER!
WAIT! WAIT! I WARN YOU--PLAIN GAGS AREN'T ENOUGH! I WANT CRIMES THAT WILL MAKE A FOOL OUT OF BATMAN! HA-HA!
MAKE A FOOL OUT OF BATMAN! BOY--YOU'RE SURE ASKIN' FOR PLENTY, JOKER!
I KNOW IT'S A TOUGH ASSIGNMENT--BUT I'M READY TO PAY HANDSOME-LY FOR MY CRIMES! HA-HA! HO-HO!
THEN, AFTER A LONG WEEDING-OUT PROCESS, THE JOKER SELECTS THREE CRIME GAG WRITERS!
OKAY! YOU THREE HAVE SHOWN ME OUTLINES OF CRIMES CALCULATED TO MAKE A FOOL OUT OF BATMAN! HA-HA! I WANT YOU TO WORK THEM OUT NOW--TO THE LAST DETAIL--I WANT TO START MOVING SOON!
RIGHT, JOKER!
WE'LL TRY YOURS FIRST, DOOLY! HO-HO! JUST THINKING ABOUT IT TICKLES ME! HA-HA! IMAGINE! WE'RE REALLY GOING TO LEAVE BATMAN HOLDING THE BAG!
HO! HA HO HA HA!
3

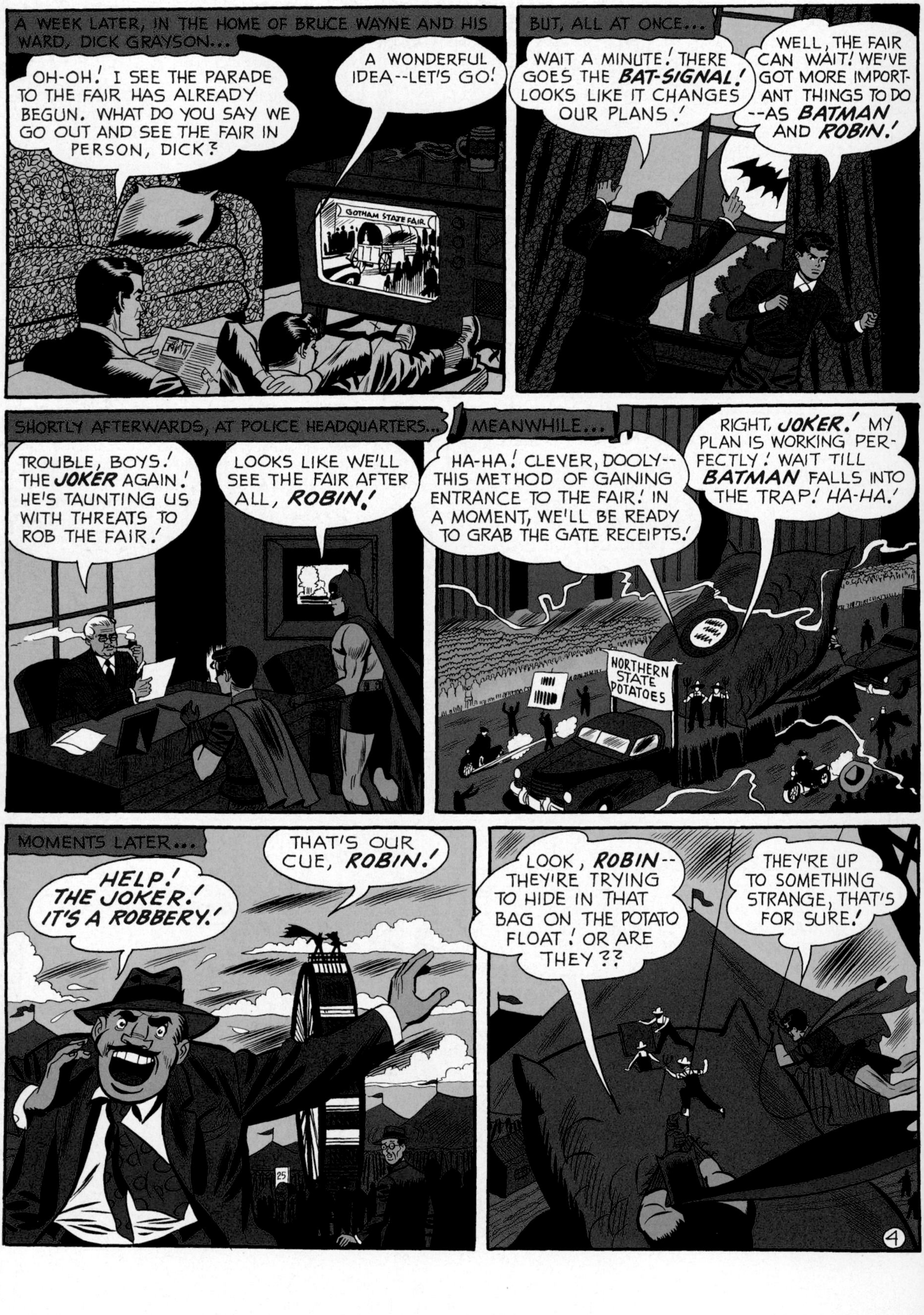
A WEEK LATER, IN THE HOME OF BRUCE WAYNE AND HIS WARD, DICK GRAYSON...
OH-OH! I SEE THE PARADE TO THE FAIR HAS ALREADY BEGUN. WHAT DO YOU SAY WE GO OUT AND SEE THE FAIR IN PERSON, DICK?
A WONDERFUL IDEA--LET'S GO!
GOTHAM STATE FAIR
BUT, ALL AT ONCE...
WAIT A MINUTE! THERE GOES THE BAT-SIGNAL! LOOKS LIKE IT CHANGES OUR PLANS!
WELL, THE FAIR CAN WAIT! WE'VE GOT MORE IMPORTANT THINGS TO DO --AS BATMAN AND ROBIN!
SHORTLY AFTERWARDS, AT POLICE HEADQUARTERS...
TROUBLE, BOYS! THE JOKER AGAIN! HE'S TAUNTING US WITH THREATS TO ROB THE FAIR!
LOOKS LIKE WE'LL SEE THE FAIR AFTER ALL, ROBIN!
MEANWHILE...
HA-HA! CLEVER, DOOLY-- THIS METHOD OF GAINING ENTRANCE TO THE FAIR! IN A MOMENT, WE'LL BE READY TO GRAB THE GATE RECEIPTS!
RIGHT, JOKER! MY PLAN IS WORKING PERFECTLY! WAIT TILL BATMAN FALLS INTO THE TRAP! HA-HA!
NORTHERN STATE POTATOES
MOMENTS LATER...
HELP! THE JOKER! IT'S A ROBBERY!
THAT'S OUR CUE, ROBIN!
25
LOOK, ROBIN-- THEY'RE TRYING TO HIDE IN THAT BAG ON THE POTATO FLOAT! OR ARE THEY??
THEY'RE UP TO SOMETHING STRANGE, THAT'S FOR SURE!
4

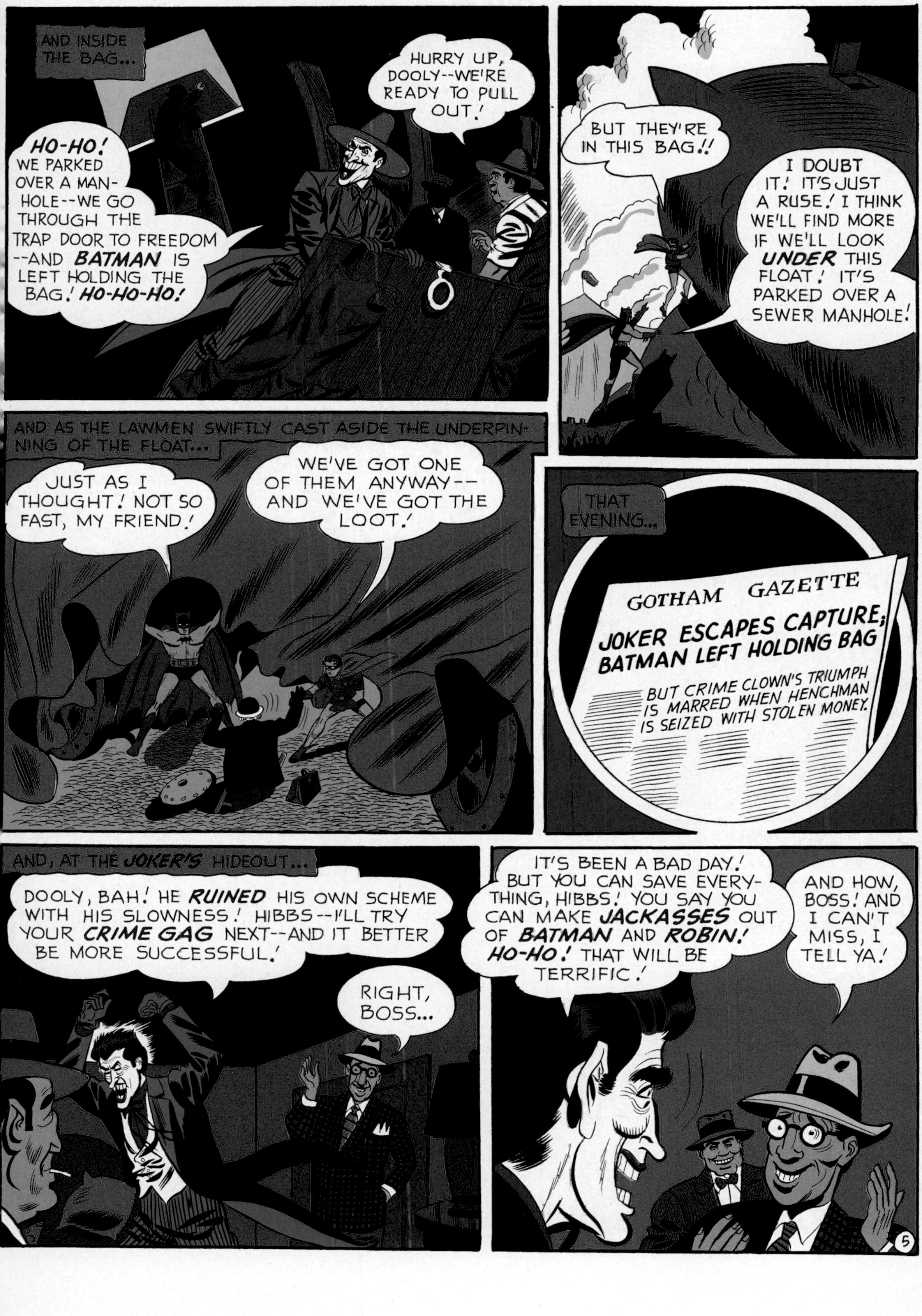

AND INSIDE THE BAG...
HURRY UP, DOOLY--WE'RE READY TO PULL OUT!
HO-HO! WE PARKED OVER A MAN-HOLE--WE GO THROUGH THE TRAP DOOR TO FREEDOM --AND BATMAN IS LEFT HOLDING THE BAG! HO-HO-HO!
BUT THEY'RE IN THIS BAG!!
I DOUBT IT! IT'S JUST A RUSE! I THINK WE'LL FIND MORE IF WE'LL LOOK UNDER THIS FLOAT! IT'S PARKED OVER A SEWER MANHOLE!
AND AS THE LAWMEN SWIFTLY CAST ASIDE THE UNDERPIN-NING OF THE FLOAT...
JUST AS I THOUGHT! NOT SO FAST, MY FRIEND!
WE'VE GOT ONE OF THEM ANYWAY-- AND WE'VE GOT THE LOOT!
THAT EVENING...
GOTHAM GAZETTE
JOKER ESCAPES CAPTURE; BATMAN LEFT HOLDING BAG
BUT CRIME CLOWN'S TRIUMPH IS MARRED WHEN HENCHMAN IS SEIZED WITH STOLEN MONEY.
AND, AT THE JOKER'S HIDEOUT...
DOOLY, BAH! HE RUINED HIS OWN SCHEME WITH HIS SLOWNESS! HIBBS--I'LL TRY YOUR CRIME GAG NEXT--AND IT BETTER BE MORE SUCCESSFUL!
RIGHT, BOSS...
IT'S BEEN A BAD DAY! BUT YOU CAN SAVE EVERY-THING, HIBBS! YOU SAY YOU CAN MAKE JACKASSES OUT OF BATMAN AND ROBIN! HO-HO! THAT WILL BE TERRIFIC!
AND HOW, BOSS! AND I CAN'T MISS, I TELL YA!
5

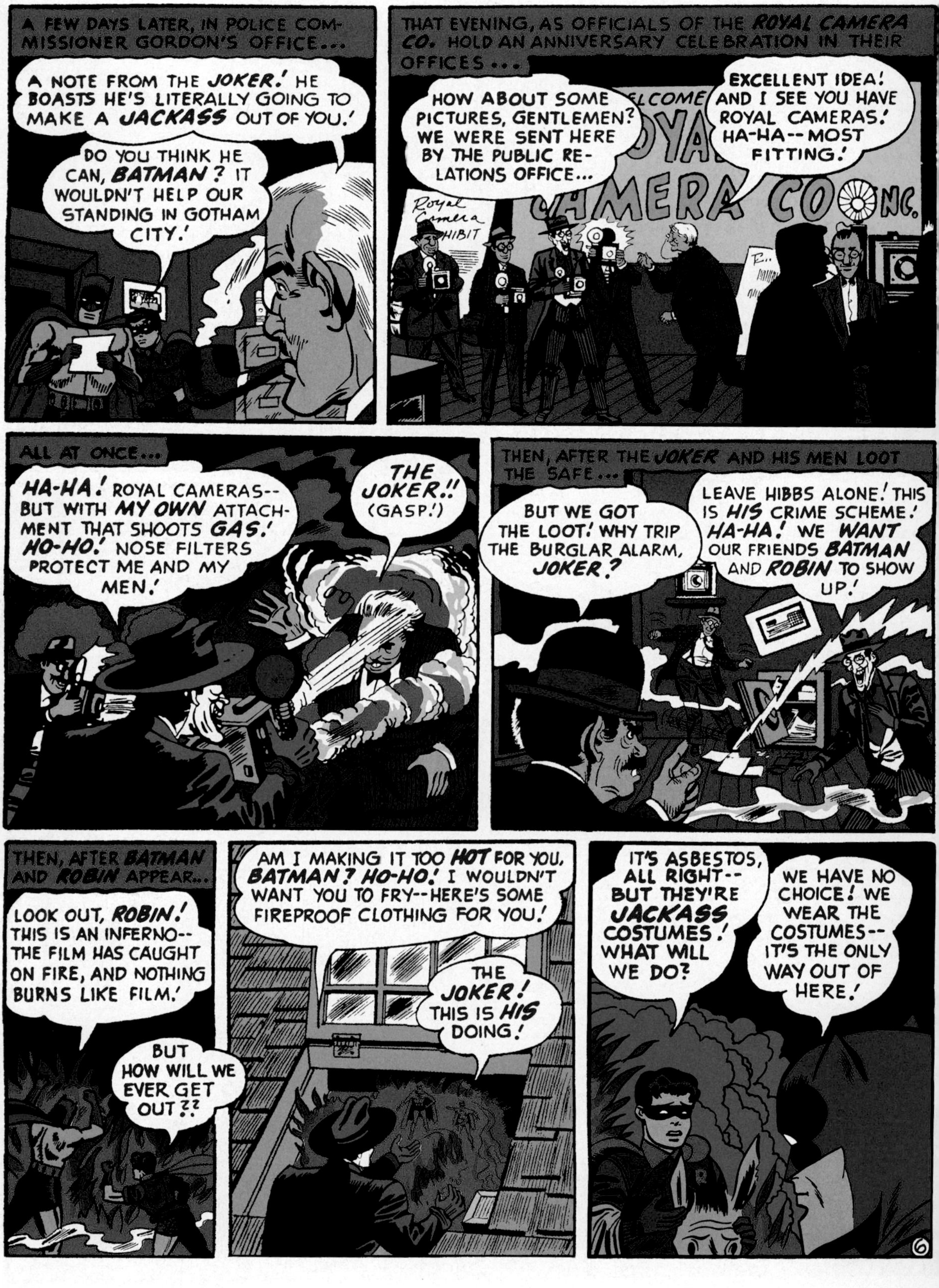
A FEW DAYS LATER, IN POLICE COMMISSIONER GORDON'S OFFICE...
A NOTE FROM THE JOKER! HE BOASTS HE'S LITERALLY GOING TO MAKE A JACKASS OUT OF YOU!
DO YOU THINK HE CAN, BATMAN? IT WOULDN'T HELP OUR STANDING IN GOTHAM CITY!
THAT EVENING, AS OFFICIALS OF THE ROYAL CAMERA CO. HOLD AN ANNIVERSARY CELEBRATION IN THEIR OFFICES...
HOW ABOUT SOME PICTURES, GENTLEMEN? WE WERE SENT HERE BY THE PUBLIC RELATIONS OFFICE...
EXCELLENT IDEA! AND I SEE YOU HAVE ROYAL CAMERAS! HA-HA--MOST FITTING!
CAMERA CO INC.
ALL AT ONCE...
HA-HA! ROYAL CAMERAS--BUT WITH MY OWN ATTACHMENT THAT SHOOTS GAS! HO-HO! NOSE FILTERS PROTECT ME AND MY MEN!
THE JOKER!! (GASP!)
THEN, AFTER THE JOKER AND HIS MEN LOOT THE SAFE...
BUT WE GOT THE LOOT! WHY TRIP THE BURGLAR ALARM, JOKER?
LEAVE HIBBS ALONE! THIS IS HIS CRIME SCHEME! HA-HA! WE WANT OUR FRIENDS BATMAN AND ROBIN TO SHOW UP!
THEN, AFTER BATMAN AND ROBIN APPEAR...
LOOK OUT, ROBIN! THIS IS AN INFERNO--THE FILM HAS CAUGHT ON FIRE, AND NOTHING BURNS LIKE FILM!
BUT HOW WILL WE EVER GET OUT??
AM I MAKING IT TOO HOT FOR YOU, BATMAN? HO-HO! I WOULDN'T WANT YOU TO FRY--HERE'S SOME FIREPROOF CLOTHING FOR YOU!
THE JOKER! THIS IS HIS DOING!
IT'S ASBESTOS, ALL RIGHT--BUT THEY'RE JACKASS COSTUMES! WHAT WILL WE DO?
WE HAVE NO CHOICE! WE WEAR THE COSTUMES--IT'S THE ONLY WAY OUT OF HERE!
6

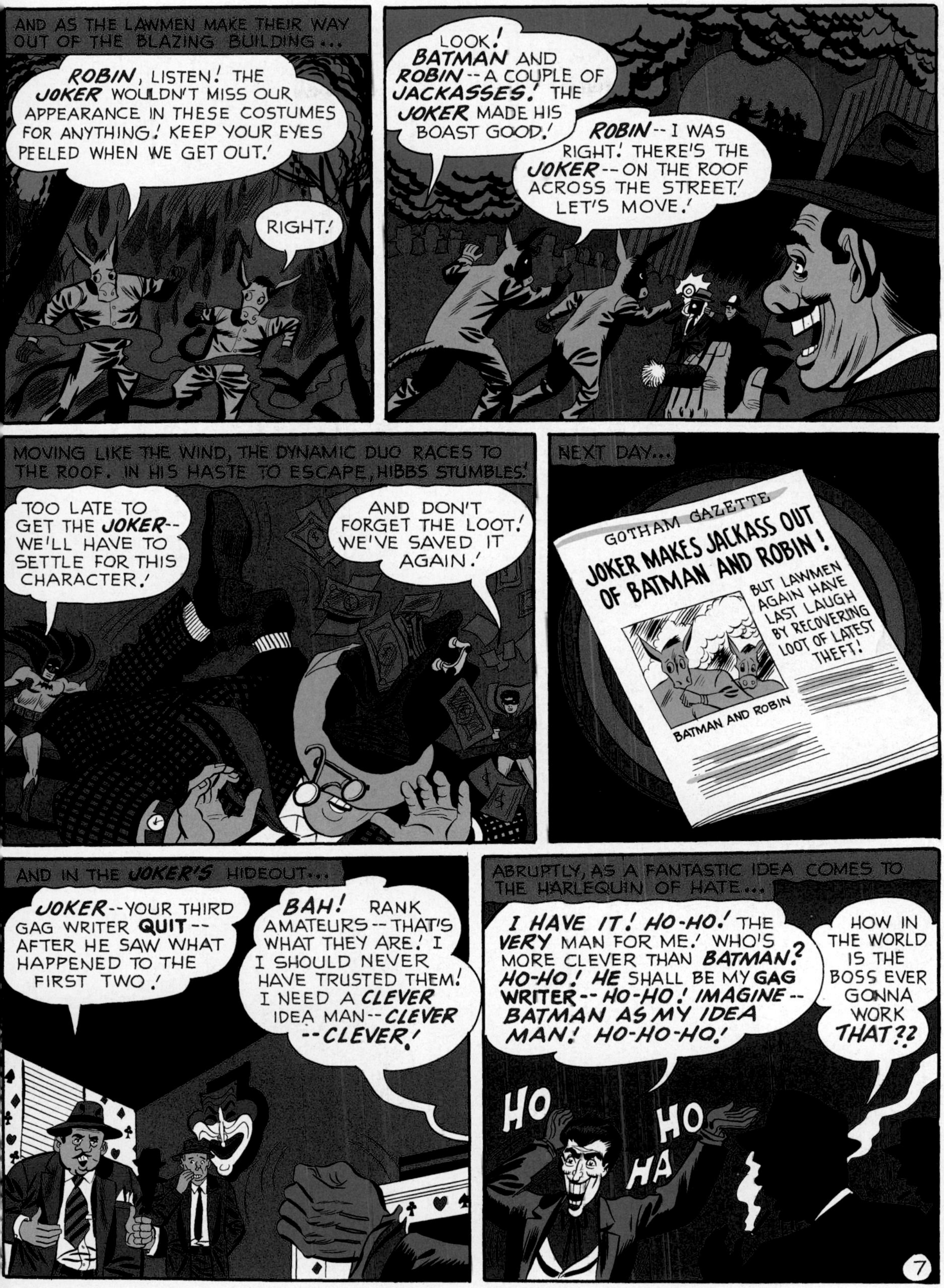
AND AS THE LAWMEN MAKE THEIR WAY OUT OF THE BLAZING BUILDING...
ROBIN, LISTEN! THE JOKER WOULDN'T MISS OUR APPEARANCE IN THESE COSTUMES FOR ANYTHING! KEEP YOUR EYES PEELED WHEN WE GET OUT!
RIGHT!
LOOK! BATMAN AND ROBIN -- A COUPLE OF JACKASSES! THE JOKER MADE HIS BOAST GOOD!
ROBIN -- I WAS RIGHT! THERE'S THE JOKER -- ON THE ROOF ACROSS THE STREET! LET'S MOVE!
MOVING LIKE THE WIND, THE DYNAMIC DUO RACES TO THE ROOF. IN HIS HASTE TO ESCAPE, HIBBS STUMBLES!
TOO LATE TO GET THE JOKER -- WE'LL HAVE TO SETTLE FOR THIS CHARACTER!
AND DON'T FORGET THE LOOT! WE'VE SAVED IT AGAIN!
NEXT DAY...
GOTHAM GAZETTE
JOKER MAKES JACKASS OUT OF BATMAN AND ROBIN!
BUT LAWMEN AGAIN HAVE LAST LAUGH BY RECOVERING LOOT OF LATEST THEFT!
BATMAN AND ROBIN
AND IN THE JOKER'S HIDEOUT...
JOKER -- YOUR THIRD GAG WRITER QUIT -- AFTER HE SAW WHAT HAPPENED TO THE FIRST TWO!
BAH! RANK AMATEURS -- THAT'S WHAT THEY ARE! I SHOULD NEVER HAVE TRUSTED THEM! I NEED A CLEVER IDEA MAN -- CLEVER -- CLEVER!
ABRUPTLY, AS A FANTASTIC IDEA COMES TO THE HARLEQUIN OF HATE...
I HAVE IT! HO-HO! THE VERY MAN FOR ME! WHO'S MORE CLEVER THAN BATMAN? HO-HO! HE SHALL BE MY GAG WRITER -- HO-HO! IMAGINE -- BATMAN AS MY IDEA MAN! HO-HO-HO!
HOW IN THE WORLD IS THE BOSS EVER GONNA WORK THAT??
HO
HO
HA
7

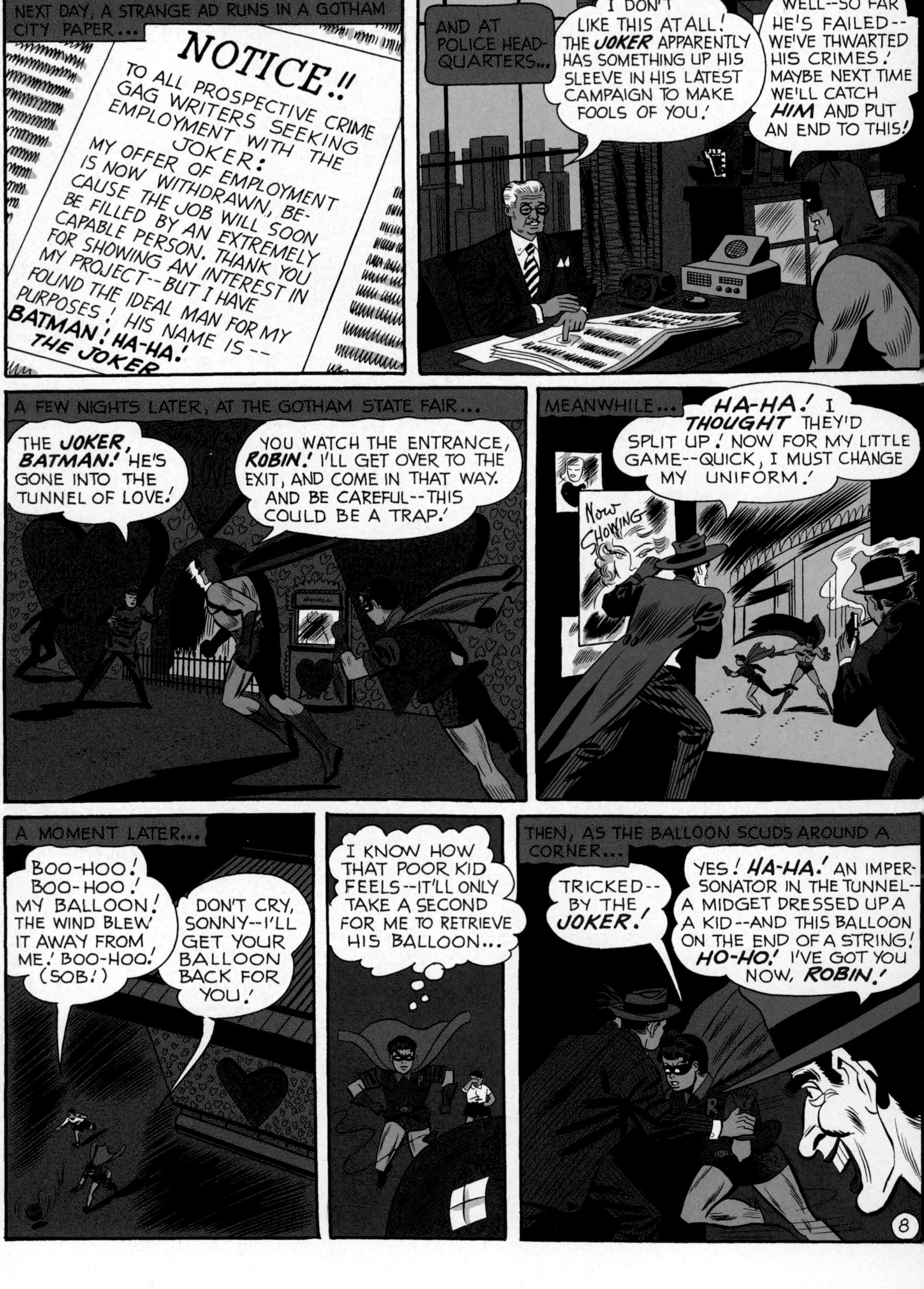
NEXT DAY, A STRANGE AD RUNS IN A GOTHAM CITY PAPER...
NOTICE!!
TO ALL PROSPECTIVE CRIME GAG WRITERS SEEKING EMPLOYMENT WITH THE JOKER:
MY OFFER OF EMPLOYMENT IS NOW WITHDRAWN, BECAUSE THE JOB WILL SOON BE FILLED BY AN EXTREMELY CAPABLE PERSON. THANK YOU FOR SHOWING AN INTEREST IN MY PROJECT--BUT I HAVE FOUND THE IDEAL MAN FOR MY PURPOSES! HIS NAME IS -- BATMAN! HA-HA!
THE JOKER
AND AT POLICE HEADQUARTERS...
I DON'T LIKE THIS AT ALL! THE JOKER APPARENTLY HAS SOMETHING UP HIS SLEEVE IN HIS LATEST CAMPAIGN TO MAKE FOOLS OF YOU!
WELL--SO FAR HE'S FAILED--WE'VE THWARTED HIS CRIMES! MAYBE NEXT TIME WE'LL CATCH HIM AND PUT AN END TO THIS!
A FEW NIGHTS LATER, AT THE GOTHAM STATE FAIR...
THE JOKER, BATMAN! HE'S GONE INTO THE TUNNEL OF LOVE!
YOU WATCH THE ENTRANCE, ROBIN! I'LL GET OVER TO THE EXIT, AND COME IN THAT WAY. AND BE CAREFUL--THIS COULD BE A TRAP!
MEANWHILE...
HA-HA! I THOUGHT THEY'D SPLIT UP! NOW FOR MY LITTLE GAME--QUICK, I MUST CHANGE MY UNIFORM!
Now Showing
A MOMENT LATER...
BOO-HOO! BOO-HOO! MY BALLOON! THE WIND BLEW IT AWAY FROM ME! BOO-HOO! (SOB!)
DON'T CRY, SONNY--I'LL GET YOUR BALLOON BACK FOR YOU!
I KNOW HOW THAT POOR KID FEELS--IT'LL ONLY TAKE A SECOND FOR ME TO RETRIEVE HIS BALLOON...
THEN, AS THE BALLOON SCUDS AROUND A CORNER...
TRICKED--BY THE JOKER!
YES! HA-HA! AN IMPERSONATOR IN THE TUNNEL--A MIDGET DRESSED UP A A KID--AND THIS BALLOON ON THE END OF A STRING! HO-HO! I'VE GOT YOU NOW, ROBIN!
8

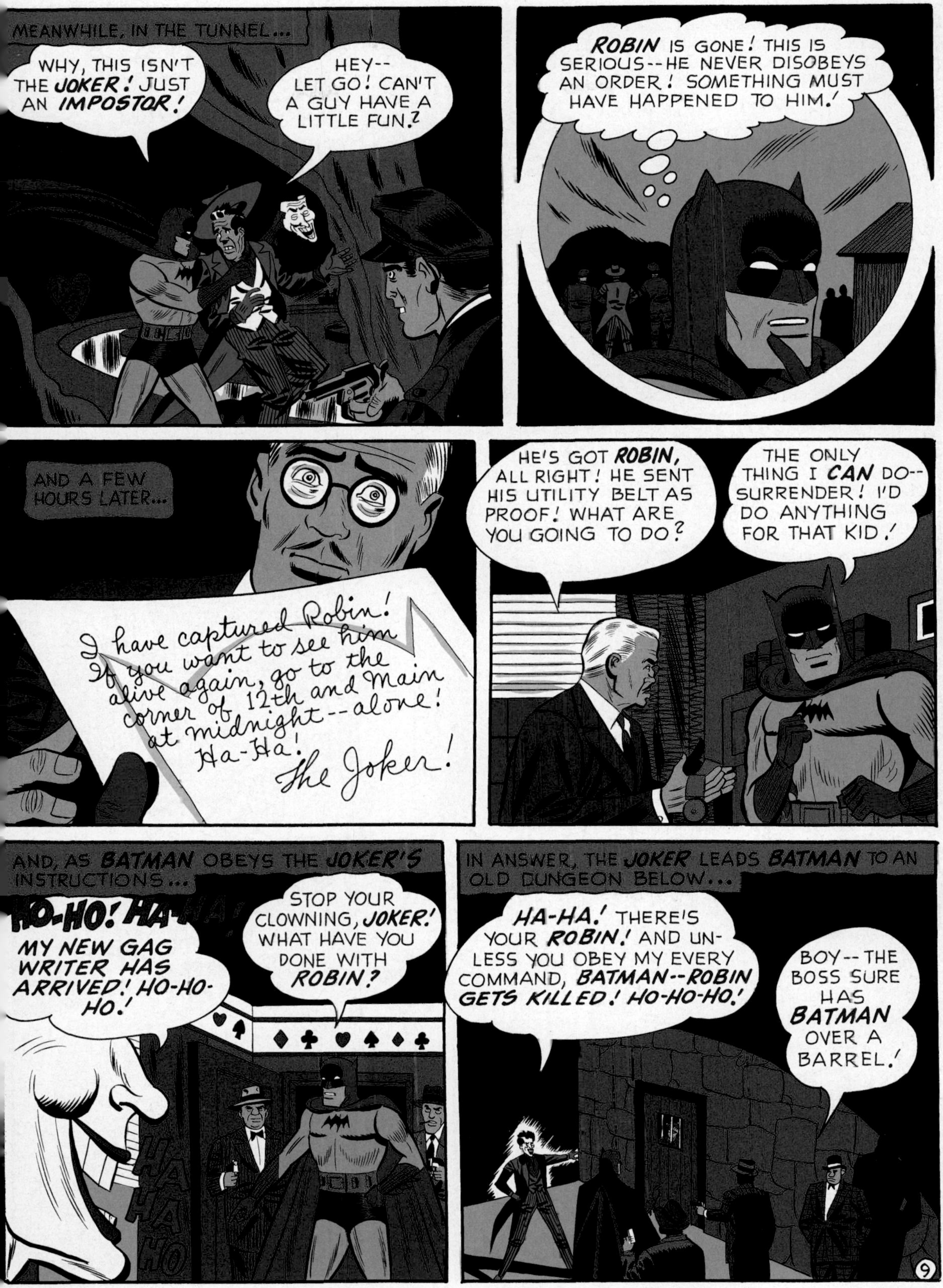
MEANWHILE, IN THE TUNNEL...
WHY, THIS ISN'T THE JOKER! JUST AN IMPOSTOR!
HEY-- LET GO! CAN'T A GUY HAVE A LITTLE FUN?
ROBIN IS GONE! THIS IS SERIOUS--HE NEVER DISOBEYS AN ORDER! SOMETHING MUST HAVE HAPPENED TO HIM!
AND A FEW HOURS LATER...
I have captured Robin! If you want to see him alive again, go to the corner of 12th and Main at midnight--alone! Ha-Ha! The Joker!
HE'S GOT ROBIN, ALL RIGHT! HE SENT HIS UTILITY BELT AS PROOF! WHAT ARE YOU GOING TO DO?
THE ONLY THING I CAN DO-- SURRENDER! I'D DO ANYTHING FOR THAT KID!
AND, AS BATMAN OBEYS THE JOKER'S INSTRUCTIONS...
HO-HO! HA-HA! MY NEW GAG WRITER HAS ARRIVED! HO-HO-HO!
STOP YOUR CLOWNING, JOKER! WHAT HAVE YOU DONE WITH ROBIN?
HA HA HA HO
IN ANSWER, THE JOKER LEADS BATMAN TO AN OLD DUNGEON BELOW...
HA-HA! THERE'S YOUR ROBIN! AND UNLESS YOU OBEY MY EVERY COMMAND, BATMAN--ROBIN GETS KILLED! HO-HO-HO!
BOY--THE BOSS SURE HAS BATMAN OVER A BARREL!
9

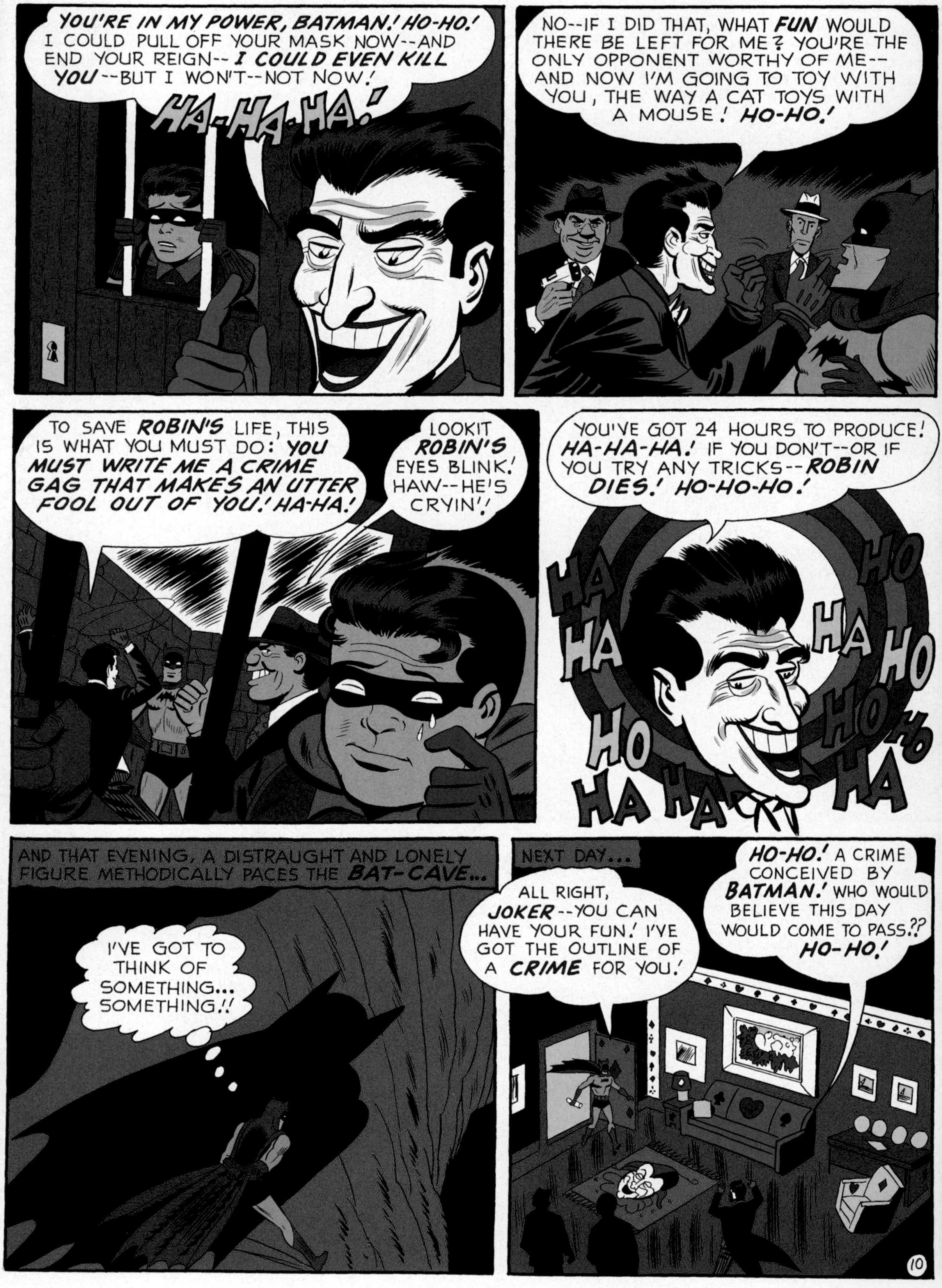
YOU'RE IN MY POWER, BATMAN! HO-HO! I COULD PULL OFF YOUR MASK NOW--AND END YOUR REIGN-- I COULD EVEN KILL YOU--BUT I WON'T--NOT NOW!
HA-HA-HA!
NO--IF I DID THAT, WHAT FUN WOULD THERE BE LEFT FOR ME? YOU'RE THE ONLY OPPONENT WORTHY OF ME-- AND NOW I'M GOING TO TOY WITH YOU, THE WAY A CAT TOYS WITH A MOUSE! HO-HO!
TO SAVE ROBIN'S LIFE, THIS IS WHAT YOU MUST DO: YOU MUST WRITE ME A CRIME GAG THAT MAKES AN UTTER FOOL OUT OF YOU! HA-HA!
LOOKIT ROBIN'S EYES BLINK! HAW--HE'S CRYIN'!
YOU'VE GOT 24 HOURS TO PRODUCE! HA-HA-HA! IF YOU DON'T--OR IF YOU TRY ANY TRICKS--ROBIN DIES! HO-HO-HO!
HA HA HO HA HO HO HO HO HA HA HA HA
AND THAT EVENING, A DISTRAUGHT AND LONELY FIGURE METHODICALLY PACES THE BAT-CAVE...
I'VE GOT TO THINK OF SOMETHING... SOMETHING!!
NEXT DAY...
ALL RIGHT, JOKER--YOU CAN HAVE YOUR FUN! I'VE GOT THE OUTLINE OF A CRIME FOR YOU!
HO-HO! A CRIME CONCEIVED BY BATMAN! WHO WOULD BELIEVE THIS DAY WOULD COME TO PASS?? HO-HO!
10

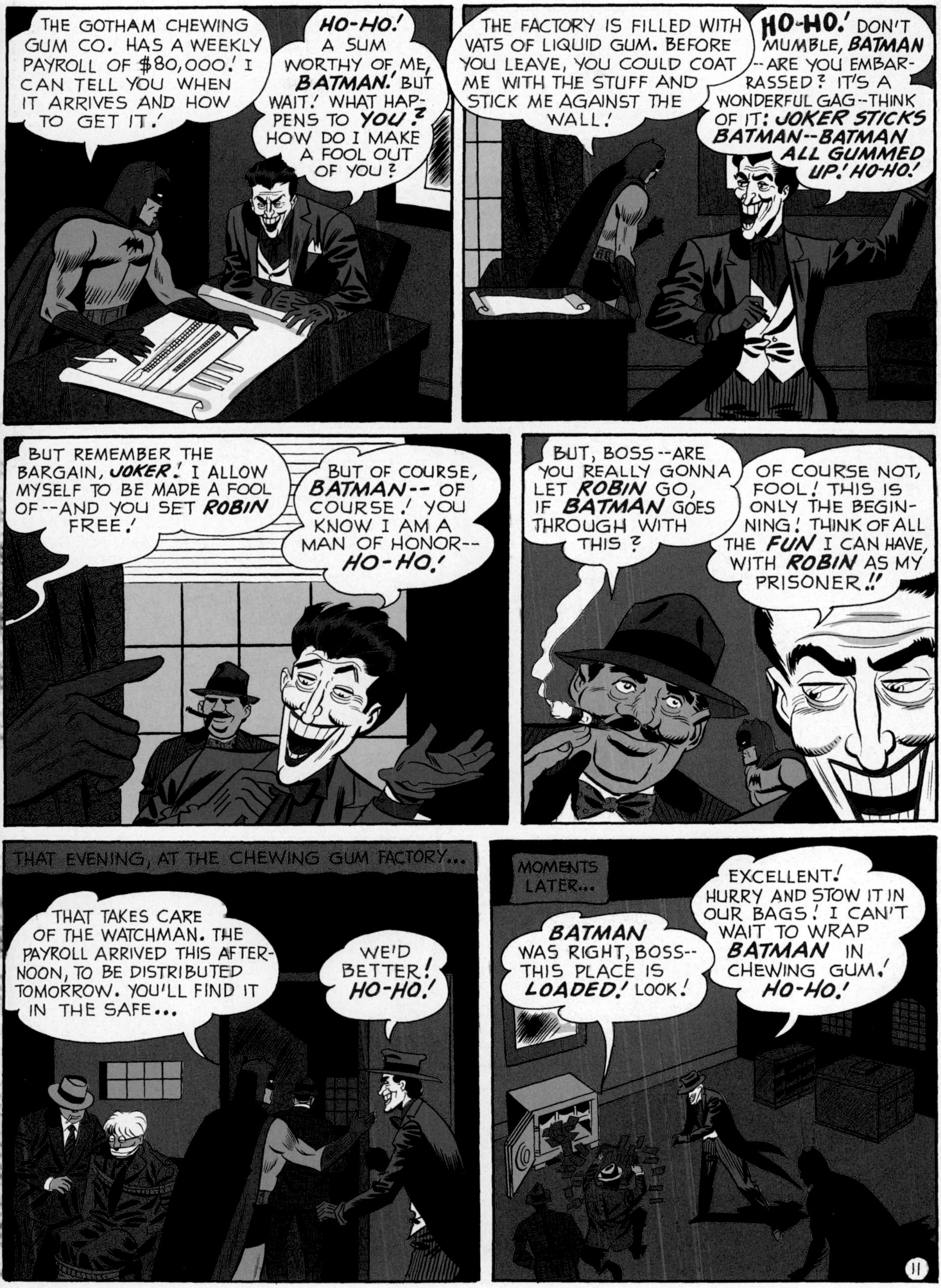
THE GOTHAM CHEWING GUM CO. HAS A WEEKLY PAYROLL OF $80,000! I CAN TELL YOU WHEN IT ARRIVES AND HOW TO GET IT!
HO-HO! A SUM WORTHY OF ME, BATMAN! BUT WAIT! WHAT HAPPENS TO YOU? HOW DO I MAKE A FOOL OUT OF YOU?
THE FACTORY IS FILLED WITH VATS OF LIQUID GUM. BEFORE YOU LEAVE, YOU COULD COAT ME WITH THE STUFF AND STICK ME AGAINST THE WALL!
HO-HO! DON'T MUMBLE, BATMAN -- ARE YOU EMBARRASSED? IT'S A WONDERFUL GAG--THINK OF IT: JOKER STICKS BATMAN--BATMAN ALL GUMMED UP! HO-HO!
BUT REMEMBER THE BARGAIN, JOKER! I ALLOW MYSELF TO BE MADE A FOOL OF--AND YOU SET ROBIN FREE!
BUT OF COURSE, BATMAN-- OF COURSE! YOU KNOW I AM A MAN OF HONOR-- HO-HO!
BUT, BOSS--ARE YOU REALLY GONNA LET ROBIN GO, IF BATMAN GOES THROUGH WITH THIS?
OF COURSE NOT, FOOL! THIS IS ONLY THE BEGINNING! THINK OF ALL THE FUN I CAN HAVE, WITH ROBIN AS MY PRISONER!!
THAT EVENING, AT THE CHEWING GUM FACTORY...
THAT TAKES CARE OF THE WATCHMAN. THE PAYROLL ARRIVED THIS AFTERNOON, TO BE DISTRIBUTED TOMORROW. YOU'LL FIND IT IN THE SAFE...
WE'D BETTER! HO-HO!
MOMENTS LATER...
BATMAN WAS RIGHT, BOSS-- THIS PLACE IS LOADED! LOOK!
EXCELLENT! HURRY AND STOW IT IN OUR BAGS! I CAN'T WAIT TO WRAP BATMAN IN CHEWING GUM! HO-HO!
11

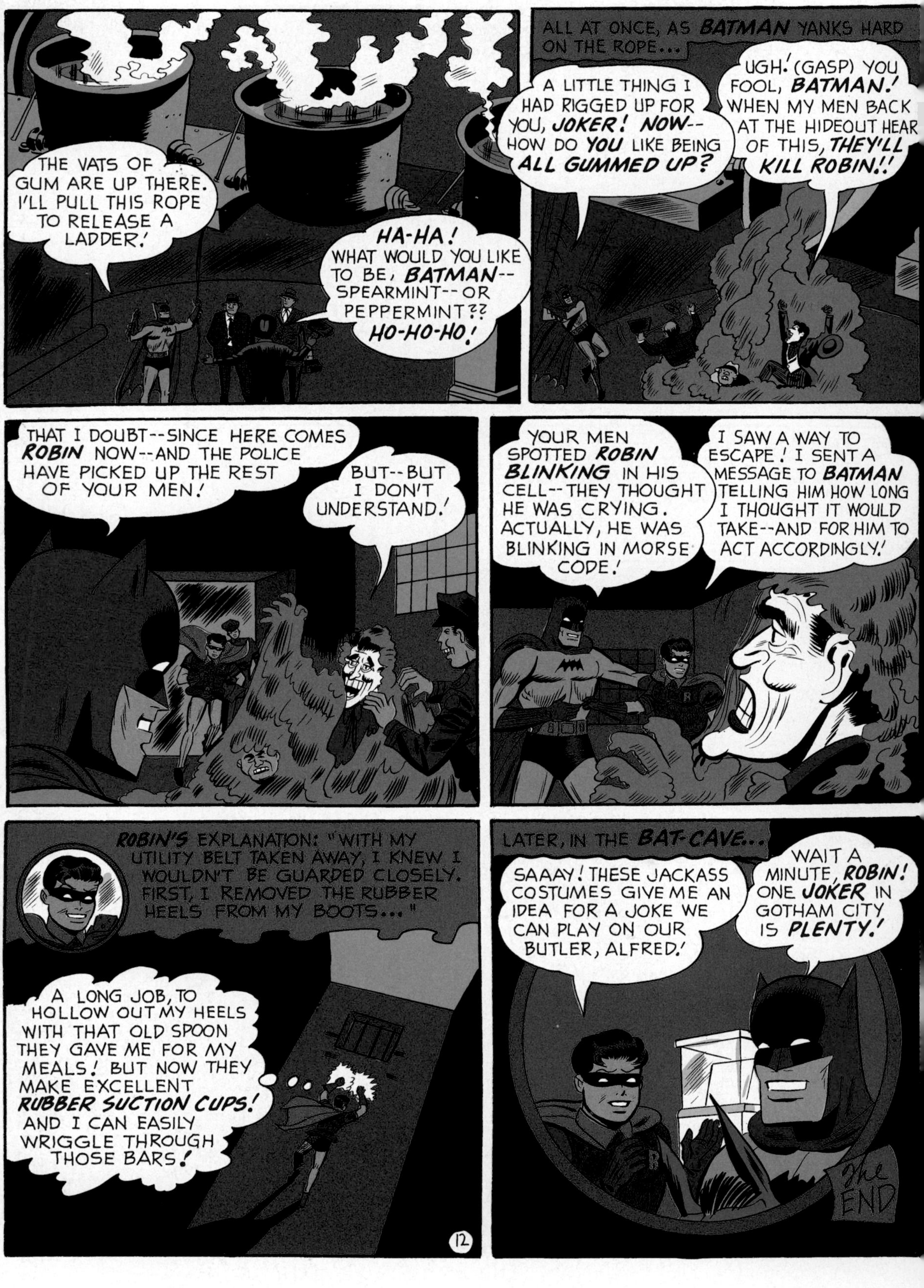
THE VATS OF GUM ARE UP THERE. I'LL PULL THIS ROPE TO RELEASE A LADDER!
HA-HA! WHAT WOULD YOU LIKE TO BE, BATMAN-- SPEARMINT--OR PEPPERMINT?? HO-HO-HO!
ALL AT ONCE, AS BATMAN YANKS HARD ON THE ROPE...
A LITTLE THING I HAD RIGGED UP FOR YOU, JOKER! NOW-- HOW DO YOU LIKE BEING ALL GUMMED UP?
UGH! (GASP) YOU FOOL, BATMAN! WHEN MY MEN BACK AT THE HIDEOUT HEAR OF THIS, THEY'LL KILL ROBIN!!
THAT I DOUBT--SINCE HERE COMES ROBIN NOW--AND THE POLICE HAVE PICKED UP THE REST OF YOUR MEN!
BUT--BUT I DON'T UNDERSTAND!
YOUR MEN SPOTTED ROBIN BLINKING IN HIS CELL--THEY THOUGHT HE WAS CRYING. ACTUALLY, HE WAS BLINKING IN MORSE CODE!
I SAW A WAY TO ESCAPE! I SENT A MESSAGE TO BATMAN TELLING HIM HOW LONG I THOUGHT IT WOULD TAKE--AND FOR HIM TO ACT ACCORDINGLY!
ROBIN'S EXPLANATION: "WITH MY UTILITY BELT TAKEN AWAY, I KNEW I WOULDN'T BE GUARDED CLOSELY. FIRST, I REMOVED THE RUBBER HEELS FROM MY BOOTS..."
A LONG JOB, TO HOLLOW OUT MY HEELS WITH THAT OLD SPOON THEY GAVE ME FOR MY MEALS! BUT NOW THEY MAKE EXCELLENT RUBBER SUCTION CUPS! AND I CAN EASILY WRIGGLE THROUGH THOSE BARS!
12
LATER, IN THE BAT-CAVE...
SAAAY! THESE JACKASS COSTUMES GIVE ME AN IDEA FOR A JOKE WE CAN PLAY ON OUR BUTLER, ALFRED!
WAIT A MINUTE, ROBIN! ONE JOKER IN GOTHAM CITY IS PLENTY!
The END

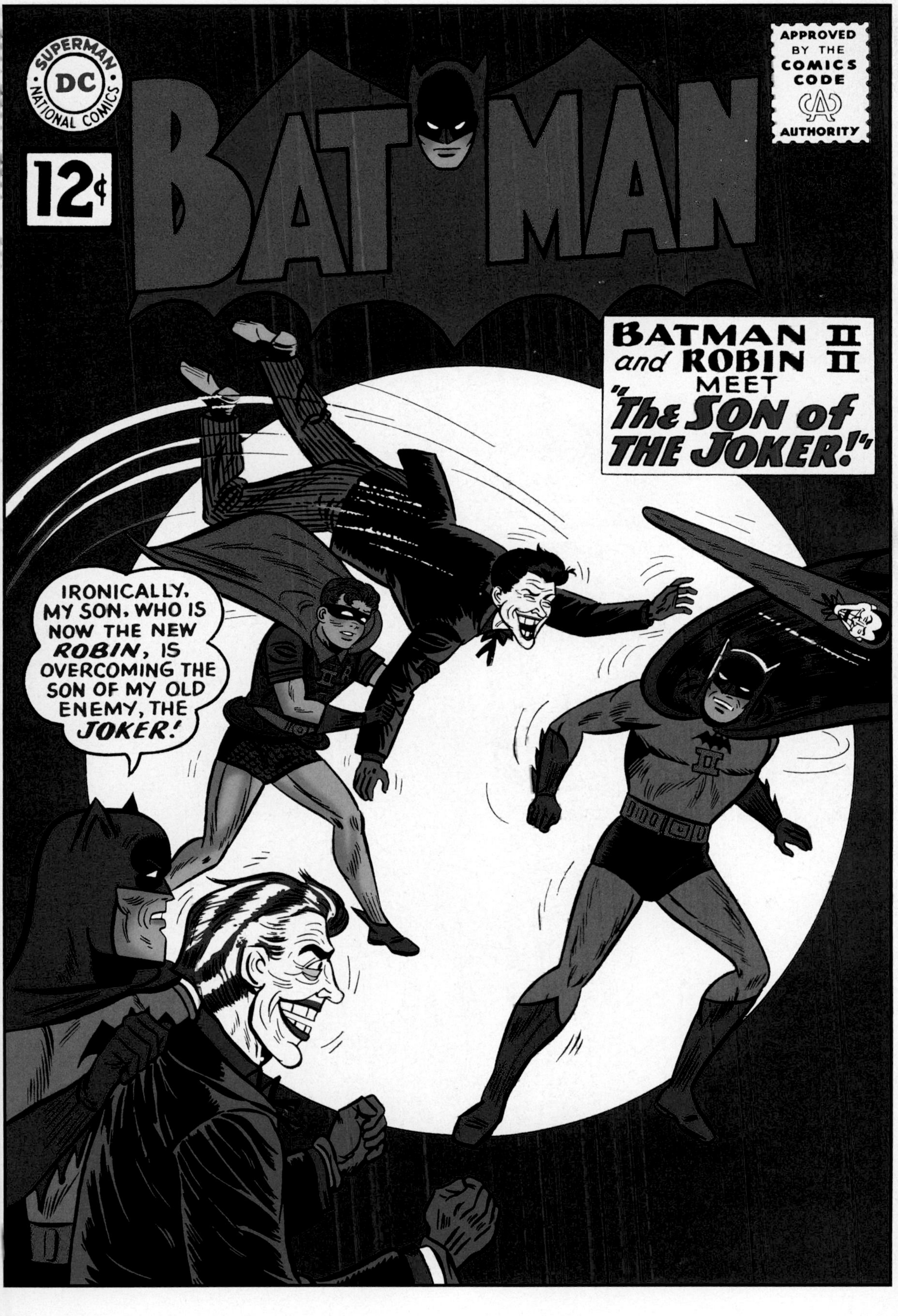
SUPERMAN DC NATIONAL COMICS
12¢
BATMAN
APPROVED BY THE COMICS CODE AUTHORITY
BATMAN II and ROBIN II MEET "The SON of THE JOKER!"
IRONICALLY, MY SON, WHO IS NOW THE NEW ROBIN, IS OVERCOMING THE SON OF MY OLD ENEMY, THE JOKER!

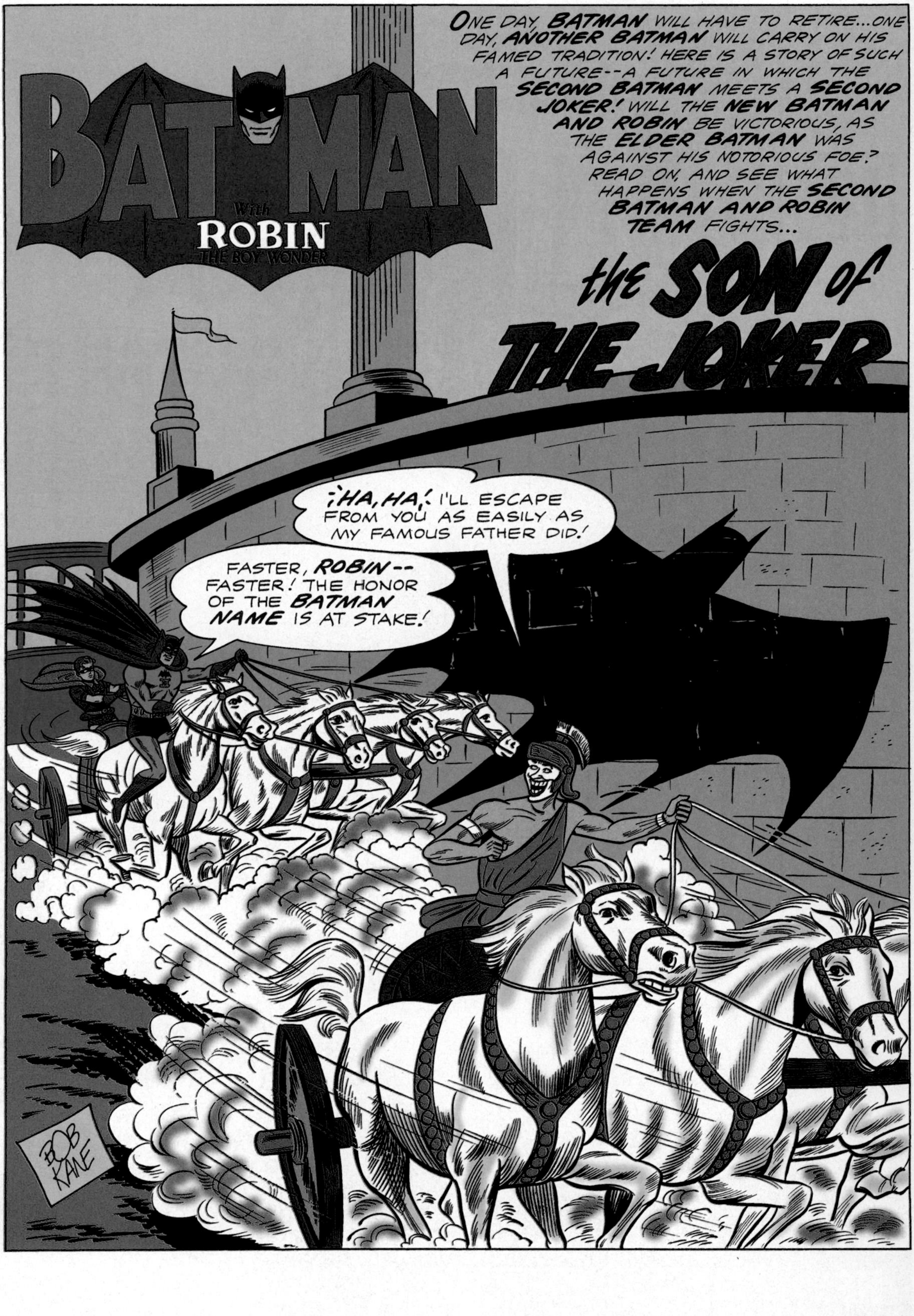
BATMAN
With ROBIN THE BOY WONDER
ONE DAY BATMAN WILL HAVE TO RETIRE...ONE DAY, ANOTHER BATMAN WILL CARRY ON HIS FAMED TRADITION! HERE IS A STORY OF SUCH A FUTURE--A FUTURE IN WHICH THE SECOND BATMAN MEETS A SECOND JOKER! WILL THE NEW BATMAN AND ROBIN BE VICTORIOUS, AS THE ELDER BATMAN WAS AGAINST HIS NOTORIOUS FOE? READ ON, AND SEE WHAT HAPPENS WHEN THE SECOND BATMAN AND ROBIN TEAM FIGHTS...
the SON of THE JOKER
¡HA, HA,¡ I'LL ESCAPE FROM YOU AS EASILY AS MY FAMOUS FATHER DID!
FASTER, ROBIN-- FASTER! THE HONOR OF THE BATMAN NAME IS AT STAKE!
BOB KANE

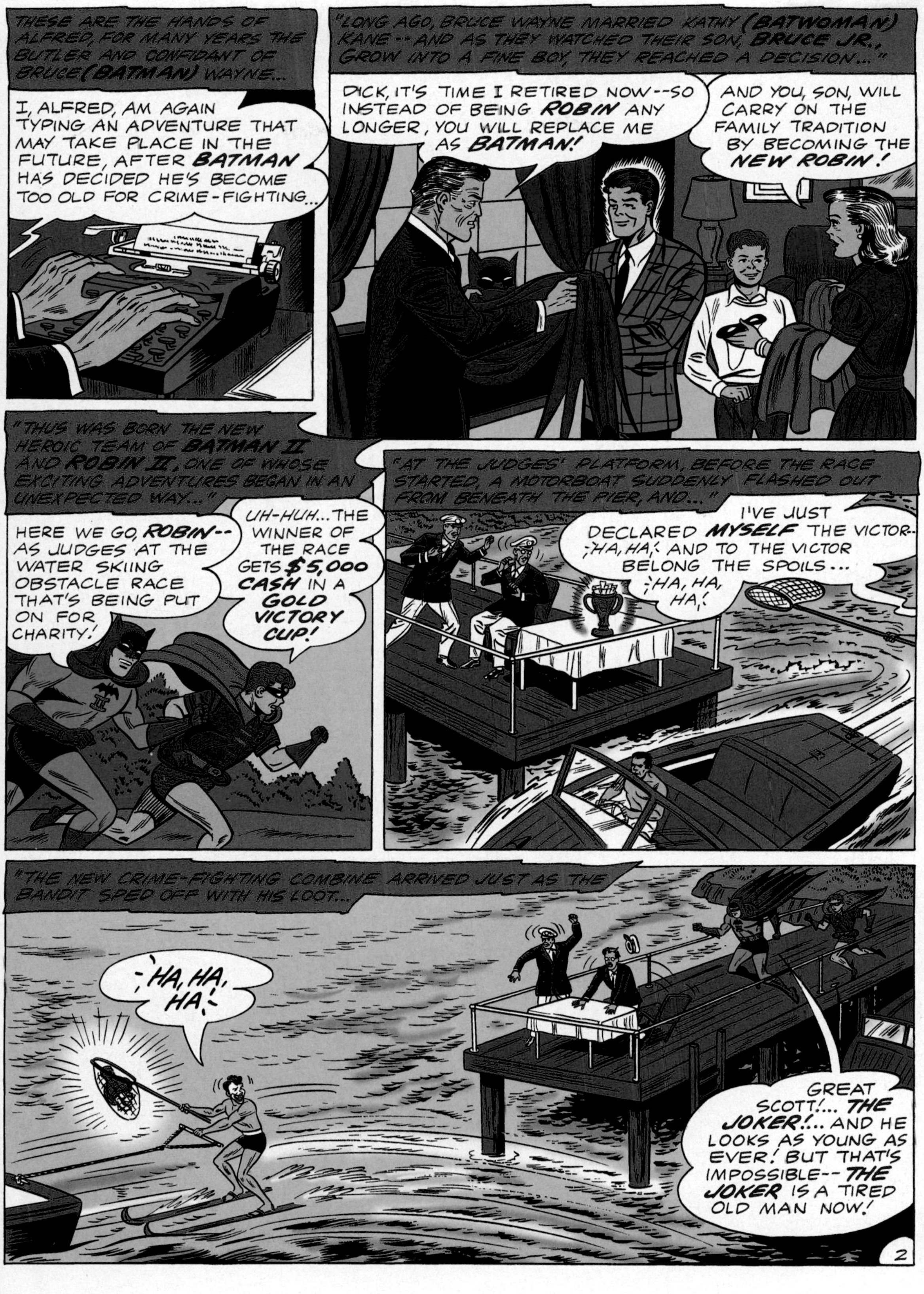
THESE ARE THE HANDS OF ALFRED, FOR MANY YEARS THE BUTLER AND CONFIDANT OF BRUCE (BATMAN) WAYNE...
I, ALFRED, AM AGAIN TYPING AN ADVENTURE THAT MAY TAKE PLACE IN THE FUTURE, AFTER BATMAN HAS DECIDED HE'S BECOME TOO OLD FOR CRIME-FIGHTING...
"LONG AGO, BRUCE WAYNE MARRIED KATHY (BATWOMAN) KANE -- AND AS THEY WATCHED THEIR SON, BRUCE JR., GROW INTO A FINE BOY, THEY REACHED A DECISION..."
DICK, IT'S TIME I RETIRED NOW--SO INSTEAD OF BEING ROBIN ANY LONGER, YOU WILL REPLACE ME AS BATMAN!
AND YOU, SON, WILL CARRY ON THE FAMILY TRADITION BY BECOMING THE NEW ROBIN!
"THUS WAS BORN THE NEW HEROIC TEAM OF BATMAN II AND ROBIN II, ONE OF WHOSE EXCITING ADVENTURES BEGAN IN AN UNEXPECTED WAY..."
HERE WE GO, ROBIN-- AS JUDGES AT THE WATER SKIING OBSTACLE RACE THAT'S BEING PUT ON FOR CHARITY!
UH-HUH...THE WINNER OF THE RACE GETS $5,000 CASH IN A GOLD VICTORY CUP!
"AT THE JUDGES' PLATFORM, BEFORE THE RACE STARTED, A MOTORBOAT SUDDENLY FLASHED OUT FROM BENEATH THE PIER, AND..."
I'VE JUST DECLARED MYSELF THE VICTOR-- HA, HA! AND TO THE VICTOR BELONG THE SPOILS... HA, HA, HA!
"THE NEW CRIME-FIGHTING COMBINE ARRIVED JUST AS THE BANDIT SPED OFF WITH HIS LOOT..."
HA, HA, HA!
GREAT SCOTT!... THE JOKER!... AND HE LOOKS AS YOUNG AS EVER! BUT THAT'S IMPOSSIBLE-- THE JOKER IS A TIRED OLD MAN NOW!
2

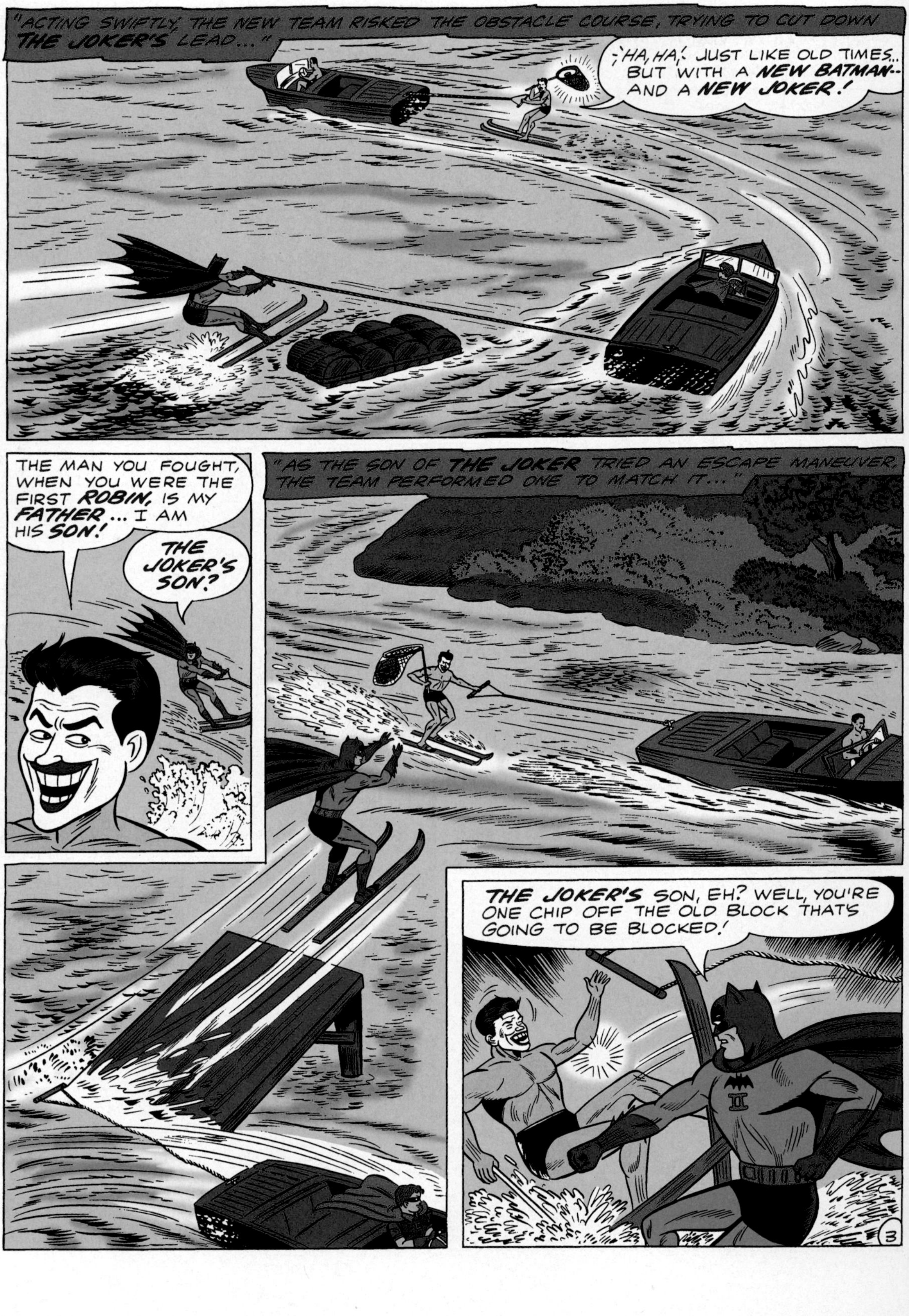
"ACTING SWIFTLY, THE NEW TEAM RISKED THE OBSTACLE COURSE, TRYING TO CUT DOWN THE JOKER'S LEAD..."
HA, HA! JUST LIKE OLD TIMES... BUT WITH A NEW BATMAN-- AND A NEW JOKER!
THE MAN YOU FOUGHT, WHEN YOU WERE THE FIRST ROBIN, IS MY FATHER... I AM HIS SON!
THE JOKER'S SON?
"AS THE SON OF THE JOKER TRIED AN ESCAPE MANEUVER, THE TEAM PERFORMED ONE TO MATCH IT..."
THE JOKER'S SON, EH? WELL, YOU'RE ONE CHIP OFF THE OLD BLOCK THAT'S GOING TO BE BLOCKED!
3

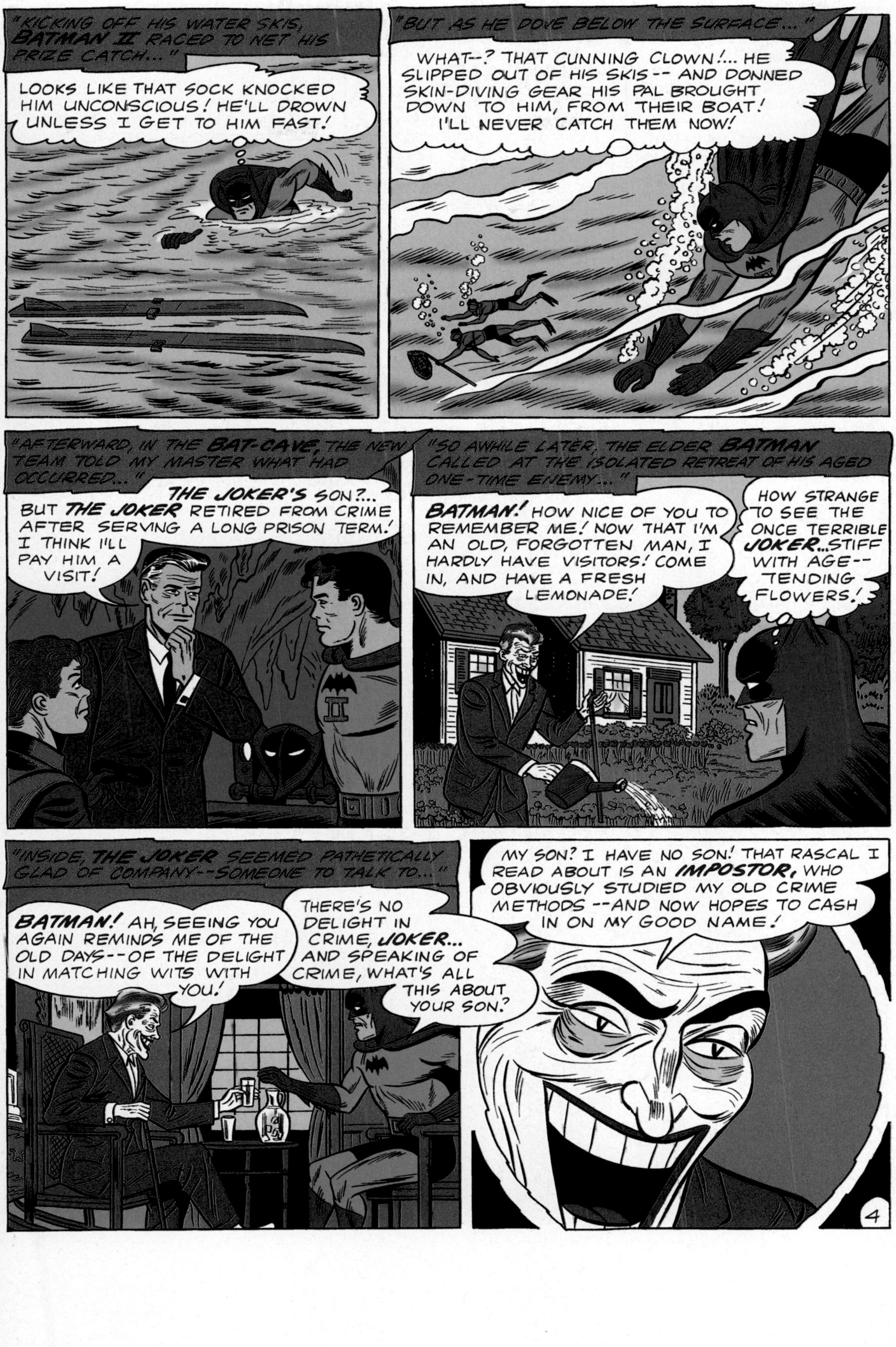
"KICKING OFF HIS WATER SKIS, BATMAN II RACED TO NET HIS PRIZE CATCH..."
LOOKS LIKE THAT SOCK KNOCKED HIM UNCONSCIOUS! HE'LL DROWN UNLESS I GET TO HIM FAST!
"BUT AS HE DOVE BELOW THE SURFACE..."
WHAT--? THAT CUNNING CLOWN!... HE SLIPPED OUT OF HIS SKIS -- AND DONNED SKIN-DIVING GEAR HIS PAL BROUGHT DOWN TO HIM, FROM THEIR BOAT! I'LL NEVER CATCH THEM NOW!
"AFTERWARD, IN THE BAT-CAVE, THE NEW TEAM TOLD MY MASTER WHAT HAD OCCURRED..."
THE JOKER'S SON?... BUT THE JOKER RETIRED FROM CRIME AFTER SERVING A LONG PRISON TERM! I THINK I'LL PAY HIM A VISIT!
"SO AWHILE LATER, THE ELDER BATMAN CALLED AT THE ISOLATED RETREAT OF HIS AGED ONE-TIME ENEMY..."
BATMAN! HOW NICE OF YOU TO REMEMBER ME! NOW THAT I'M AN OLD, FORGOTTEN MAN, I HARDLY HAVE VISITORS! COME IN, AND HAVE A FRESH LEMONADE!
HOW STRANGE TO SEE THE ONCE TERRIBLE JOKER...STIFF WITH AGE-- TENDING FLOWERS!
"INSIDE, THE JOKER SEEMED PATHETICALLY GLAD OF COMPANY--SOMEONE TO TALK TO..."
BATMAN! AH, SEEING YOU AGAIN REMINDS ME OF THE OLD DAYS--OF THE DELIGHT IN MATCHING WITS WITH YOU!
THERE'S NO DELIGHT IN CRIME, JOKER... AND SPEAKING OF CRIME, WHAT'S ALL THIS ABOUT YOUR SON?
MY SON? I HAVE NO SON! THAT RASCAL I READ ABOUT IS AN IMPOSTOR, WHO OBVIOUSLY STUDIED MY OLD CRIME METHODS --AND NOW HOPES TO CASH IN ON MY GOOD NAME!
4

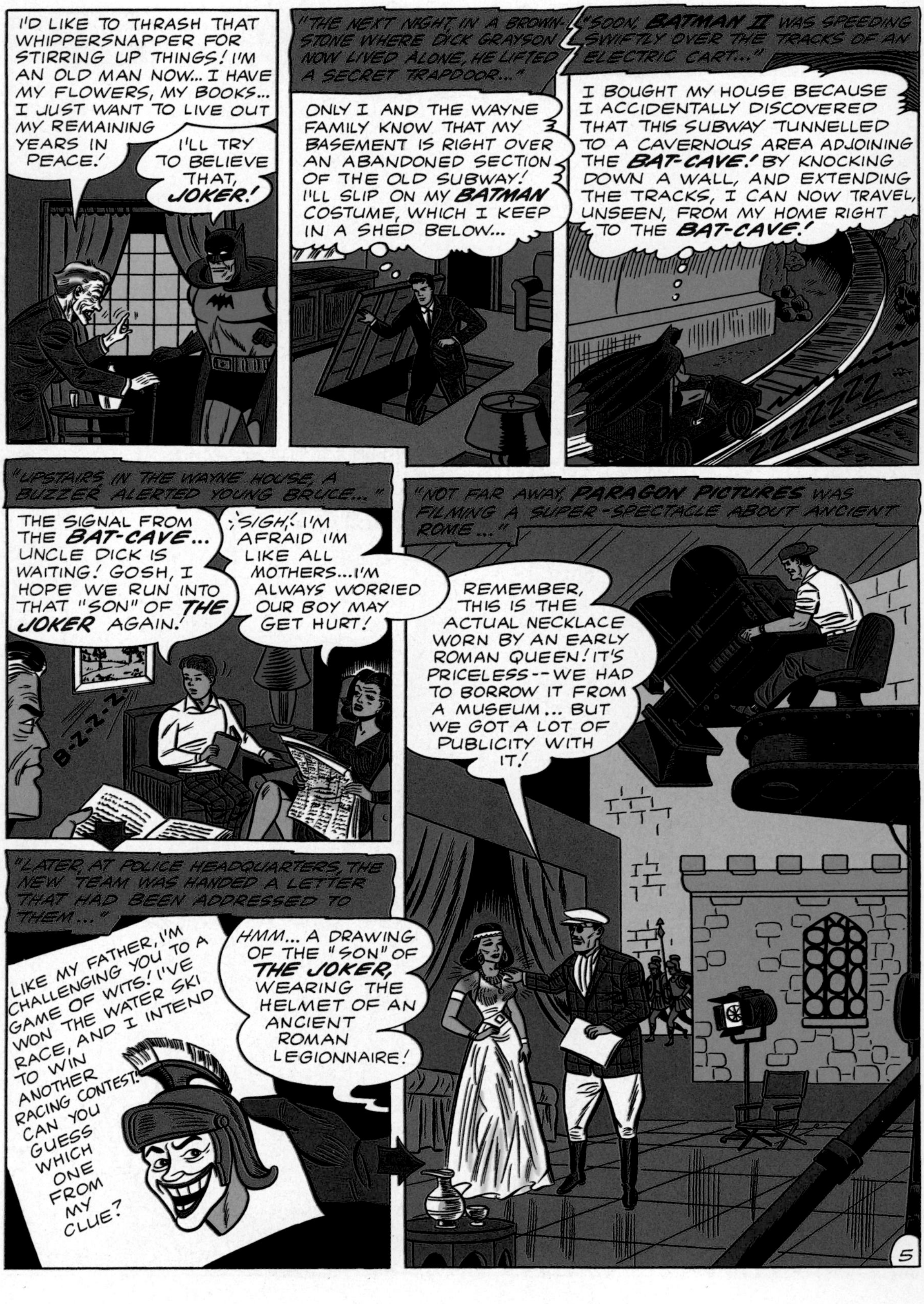
I'D LIKE TO THRASH THAT WHIPPERSNAPPER FOR STIRRING UP THINGS! I'M AN OLD MAN NOW... I HAVE MY FLOWERS, MY BOOKS... I JUST WANT TO LIVE OUT MY REMAINING YEARS IN PEACE!
I'LL TRY TO BELIEVE THAT, JOKER!
"THE NEXT NIGHT, IN A BROWN-STONE WHERE DICK GRAYSON NOW LIVED ALONE, HE LIFTED A SECRET TRAPDOOR..."
ONLY I AND THE WAYNE FAMILY KNOW THAT MY BASEMENT IS RIGHT OVER AN ABANDONED SECTION OF THE OLD SUBWAY! I'LL SLIP ON MY BATMAN COSTUME, WHICH I KEEP IN A SHED BELOW...
"SOON, BATMAN II WAS SPEEDING SWIFTLY OVER THE TRACKS OF AN ELECTRIC CART..."
I BOUGHT MY HOUSE BECAUSE I ACCIDENTALLY DISCOVERED THAT THIS SUBWAY TUNNELLED TO A CAVERNOUS AREA ADJOINING THE BAT-CAVE! BY KNOCKING DOWN A WALL, AND EXTENDING THE TRACKS, I CAN NOW TRAVEL, UNSEEN, FROM MY HOME RIGHT TO THE BAT-CAVE!
ZZZZZZZZ
"UPSTAIRS IN THE WAYNE HOUSE, A BUZZER ALERTED YOUNG BRUCE..."
THE SIGNAL FROM THE BAT-CAVE... UNCLE DICK IS WAITING! GOSH, I HOPE WE RUN INTO THAT "SON" OF THE JOKER AGAIN!
SIGH! I'M AFRAID I'M LIKE ALL MOTHERS...I'M ALWAYS WORRIED OUR BOY MAY GET HURT!
B-Z-Z-Z-Z
"LATER, AT POLICE HEADQUARTERS, THE NEW TEAM WAS HANDED A LETTER THAT HAD BEEN ADDRESSED TO THEM..."
LIKE MY FATHER, I'M CHALLENGING YOU TO A GAME OF WITS! I'VE WON THE WATER SKI RACE, AND I INTEND TO WIN ANOTHER RACING CONTEST! CAN YOU GUESS WHICH ONE FROM MY CLUE?
HMM... A DRAWING OF THE "SON" OF THE JOKER, WEARING THE HELMET OF AN ANCIENT ROMAN LEGIONNAIRE!
"NOT FAR AWAY, PARAGON PICTURES WAS FILMING A SUPER-SPECTACLE ABOUT ANCIENT ROME..."
REMEMBER, THIS IS THE ACTUAL NECKLACE WORN BY AN EARLY ROMAN QUEEN! IT'S PRICELESS--WE HAD TO BORROW IT FROM A MUSEUM... BUT WE GOT A LOT OF PUBLICITY WITH IT!
5

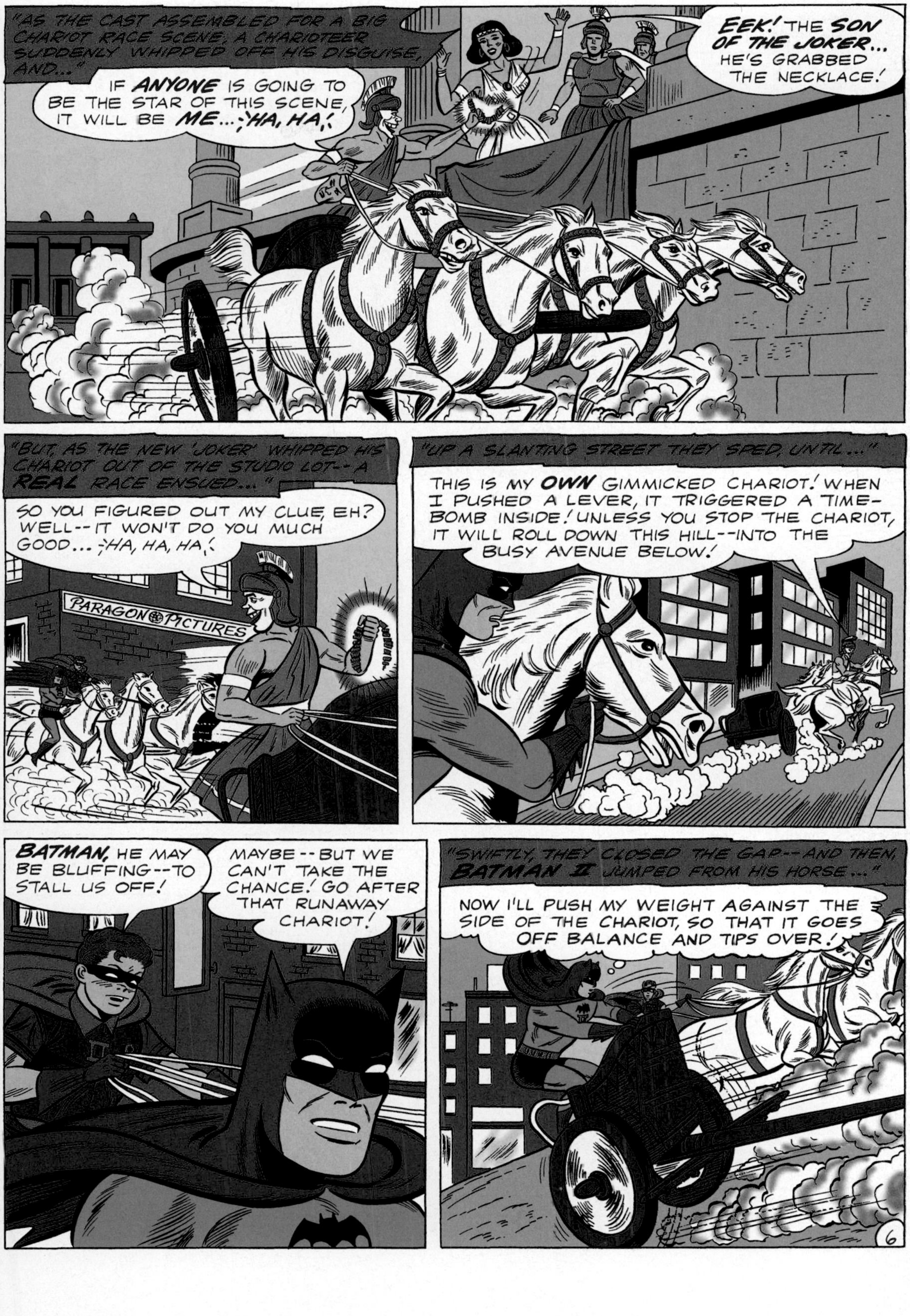
"AS THE CAST ASSEMBLED FOR A BIG CHARIOT RACE SCENE, A CHARIOTEER SUDDENLY WHIPPED OFF HIS DISGUISE, AND..."
IF ANYONE IS GOING TO BE THE STAR OF THIS SCENE, IT WILL BE ME...;HA, HA;
EEK! THE SON OF THE JOKER... HE'S GRABBED THE NECKLACE!
"BUT, AS THE NEW 'JOKER' WHIPPED HIS CHARIOT OUT OF THE STUDIO LOT--A REAL RACE ENSUED..."
SO YOU FIGURED OUT MY CLUE, EH? WELL--IT WON'T DO YOU MUCH GOOD...;HA, HA, HA;
PARAGON PICTURES
"UP A SLANTING STREET THEY SPED, UNTIL..."
THIS IS MY OWN GIMMICKED CHARIOT! WHEN I PUSHED A LEVER, IT TRIGGERED A TIME-BOMB INSIDE! UNLESS YOU STOP THE CHARIOT, IT WILL ROLL DOWN THIS HILL--INTO THE BUSY AVENUE BELOW!
BATMAN, HE MAY BE BLUFFING--TO STALL US OFF!
MAYBE--BUT WE CAN'T TAKE THE CHANCE! GO AFTER THAT RUNAWAY CHARIOT!
"SWIFTLY, THEY CLOSED THE GAP--AND THEN, BATMAN II JUMPED FROM HIS HORSE..."
NOW I'LL PUSH MY WEIGHT AGAINST THE SIDE OF THE CHARIOT, SO THAT IT GOES OFF BALANCE AND TIPS OVER!
6

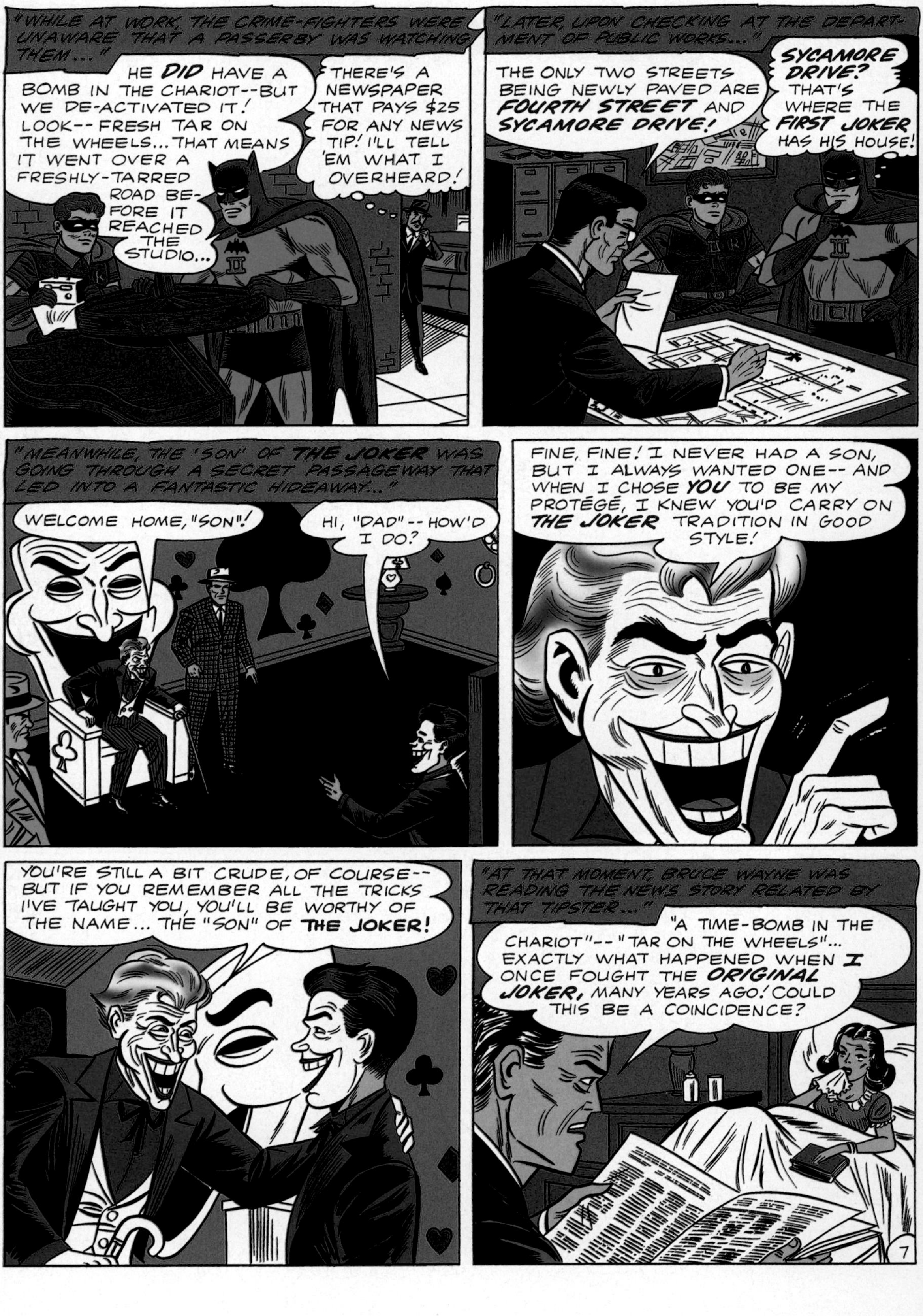
"WHILE AT WORK, THE CRIME-FIGHTERS WERE UNAWARE THAT A PASSERBY WAS WATCHING THEM..."
HE DID HAVE A BOMB IN THE CHARIOT--BUT WE DE-ACTIVATED IT! LOOK--FRESH TAR ON THE WHEELS...THAT MEANS IT WENT OVER A FRESHLY-TARRED ROAD BEFORE IT REACHED THE STUDIO...
THERE'S A NEWSPAPER THAT PAYS $25 FOR ANY NEWS TIP! I'LL TELL 'EM WHAT I OVERHEARD!
"LATER, UPON CHECKING AT THE DEPARTMENT OF PUBLIC WORKS..."
THE ONLY TWO STREETS BEING NEWLY PAVED ARE FOURTH STREET AND SYCAMORE DRIVE!
SYCAMORE DRIVE? THAT'S WHERE THE FIRST JOKER HAS HIS HOUSE!
"MEANWHILE, THE 'SON' OF THE JOKER WAS GOING THROUGH A SECRET PASSAGEWAY THAT LED INTO A FANTASTIC HIDEAWAY..."
WELCOME HOME, "SON"!
HI, "DAD"--HOW'D I DO?
FINE, FINE! I NEVER HAD A SON, BUT I ALWAYS WANTED ONE--AND WHEN I CHOSE YOU TO BE MY PROTÉGÉ, I KNEW YOU'D CARRY ON THE JOKER TRADITION IN GOOD STYLE!
YOU'RE STILL A BIT CRUDE, OF COURSE--BUT IF YOU REMEMBER ALL THE TRICKS I'VE TAUGHT YOU, YOU'LL BE WORTHY OF THE NAME... THE "SON" OF THE JOKER!
"AT THAT MOMENT, BRUCE WAYNE WAS READING THE NEWS STORY RELATED BY THAT TIPSTER..."
"A TIME-BOMB IN THE CHARIOT"--"TAR ON THE WHEELS"... EXACTLY WHAT HAPPENED WHEN I ONCE FOUGHT THE ORIGINAL JOKER, MANY YEARS AGO! COULD THIS BE A COINCIDENCE?
7

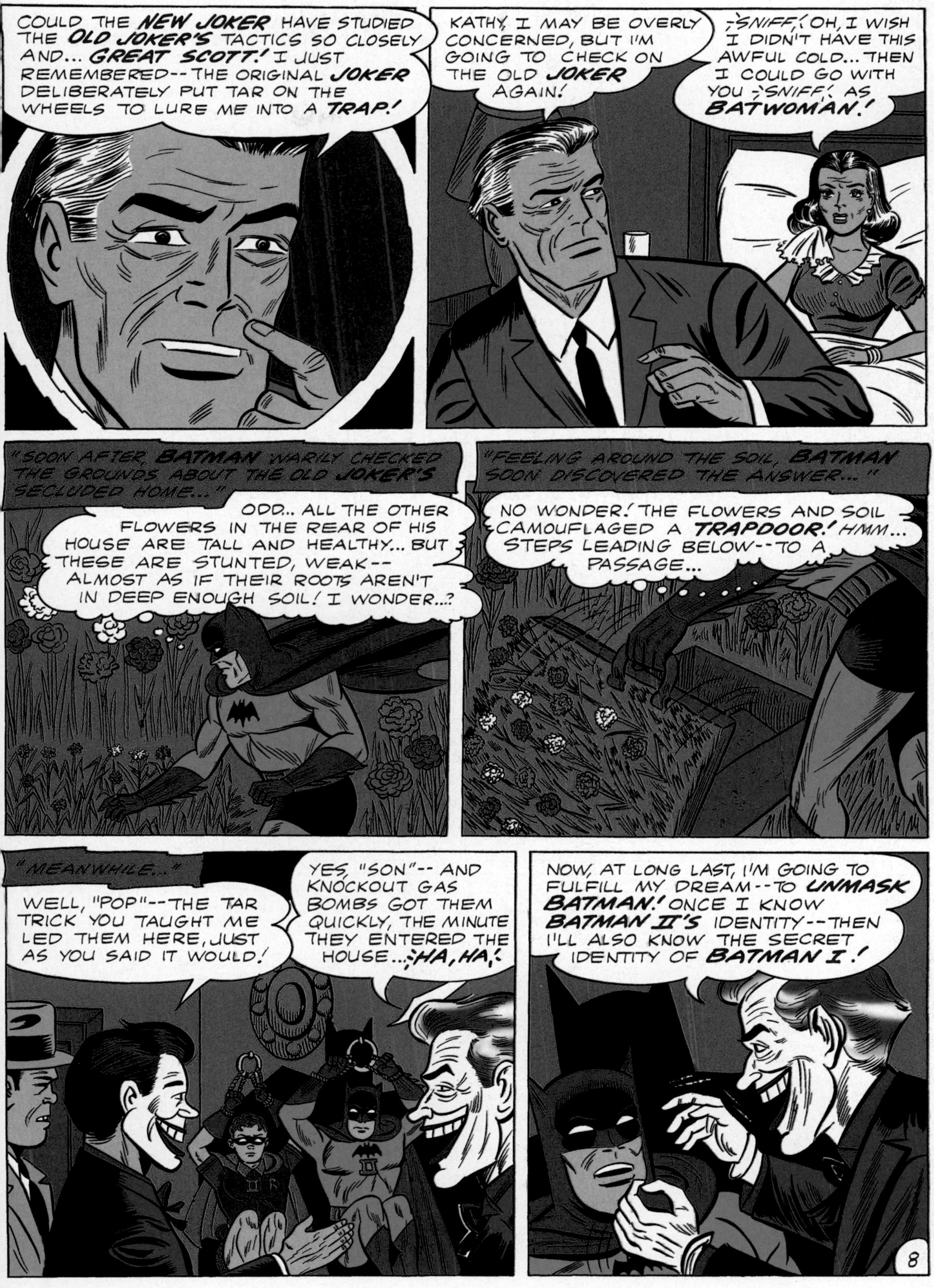

COULD THE NEW JOKER HAVE STUDIED THE OLD JOKER'S TACTICS SO CLOSELY AND... GREAT SCOTT! I JUST REMEMBERED--THE ORIGINAL JOKER DELIBERATELY PUT TAR ON THE WHEELS TO LURE ME INTO A TRAP!
KATHY, I MAY BE OVERLY CONCERNED, BUT I'M GOING TO CHECK ON THE OLD JOKER AGAIN!
-SNIFF!- OH, I WISH I DIDN'T HAVE THIS AWFUL COLD... THEN I COULD GO WITH YOU -SNIFF!- AS BATWOMAN!
"SOON AFTER, BATMAN WARILY CHECKED THE GROUNDS ABOUT THE OLD JOKER'S SECLUDED HOME..."
ODD.. ALL THE OTHER FLOWERS IN THE REAR OF HIS HOUSE ARE TALL AND HEALTHY... BUT THESE ARE STUNTED, WEAK-- ALMOST AS IF THEIR ROOTS AREN'T IN DEEP ENOUGH SOIL! I WONDER...?
"FEELING AROUND THE SOIL, BATMAN SOON DISCOVERED THE ANSWER..."
NO WONDER! THE FLOWERS AND SOIL CAMOUFLAGED A TRAPDOOR! HMM... STEPS LEADING BELOW--TO A PASSAGE...
"MEANWHILE..."
WELL, "POP"--THE TAR TRICK YOU TAUGHT ME LED THEM HERE, JUST AS YOU SAID IT WOULD!
YES, "SON"-- AND KNOCKOUT GAS BOMBS GOT THEM QUICKLY, THE MINUTE THEY ENTERED THE HOUSE... -HA, HA!-
NOW, AT LONG LAST, I'M GOING TO FULFILL MY DREAM--TO UNMASK BATMAN! ONCE I KNOW BATMAN II'S IDENTITY--THEN I'LL ALSO KNOW THE SECRET IDENTITY OF BATMAN I!
8

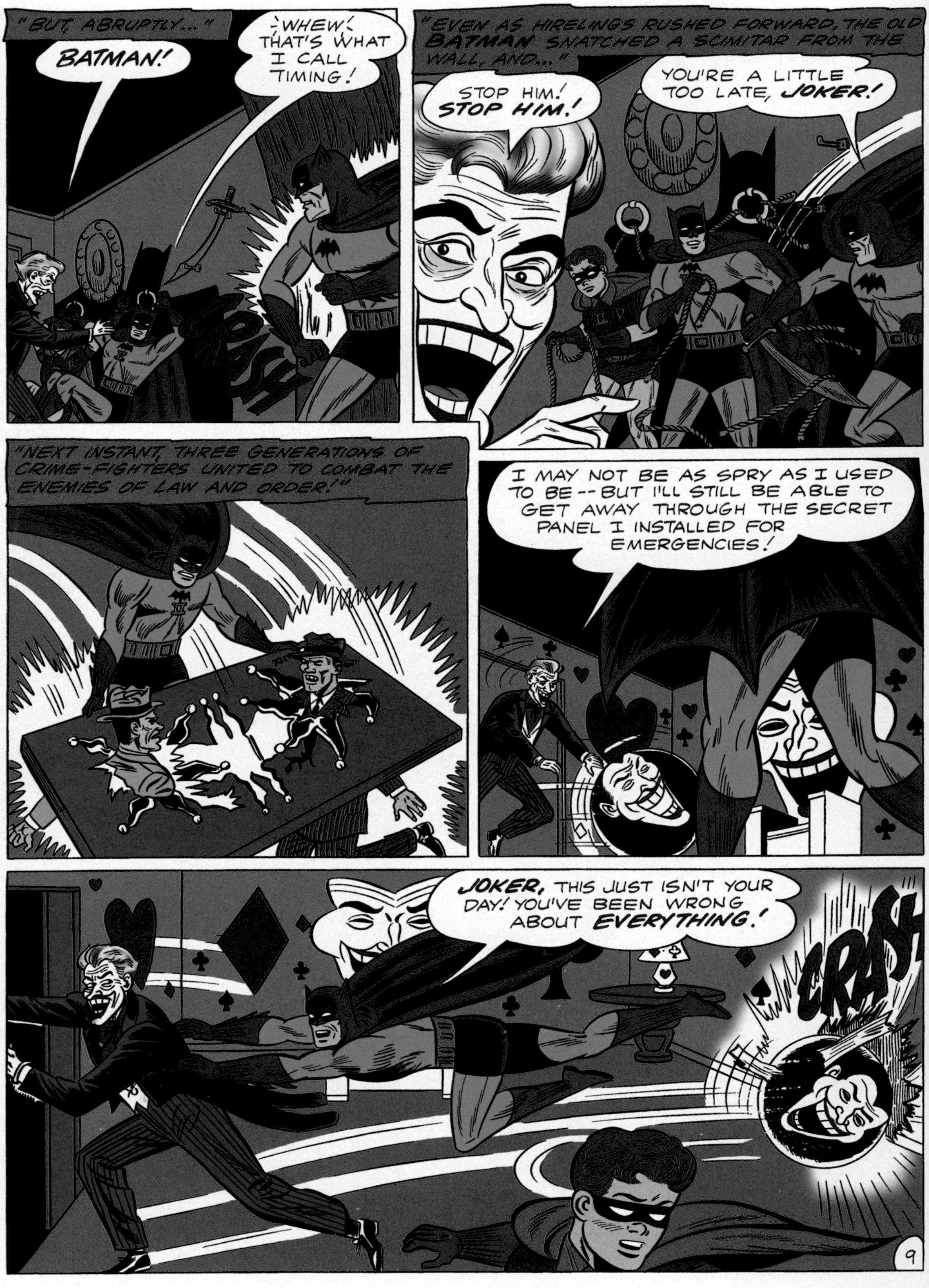
"BUT, ABRUPTLY..."
BATMAN!
WHEW! THAT'S WHAT I CALL TIMING!
CRASH
"EVEN AS HIRELINGS RUSHED FORWARD, THE OLD BATMAN SNATCHED A SCIMITAR FROM THE WALL, AND..."
STOP HIM! STOP HIM!
YOU'RE A LITTLE TOO LATE, JOKER!
"NEXT INSTANT, THREE GENERATIONS OF CRIME-FIGHTERS UNITED TO COMBAT THE ENEMIES OF LAW AND ORDER!"
I MAY NOT BE AS SPRY AS I USED TO BE -- BUT I'LL STILL BE ABLE TO GET AWAY THROUGH THE SECRET PANEL I INSTALLED FOR EMERGENCIES!
JOKER, THIS JUST ISN'T YOUR DAY! YOU'VE BEEN WRONG ABOUT EVERYTHING!
CRASH
9

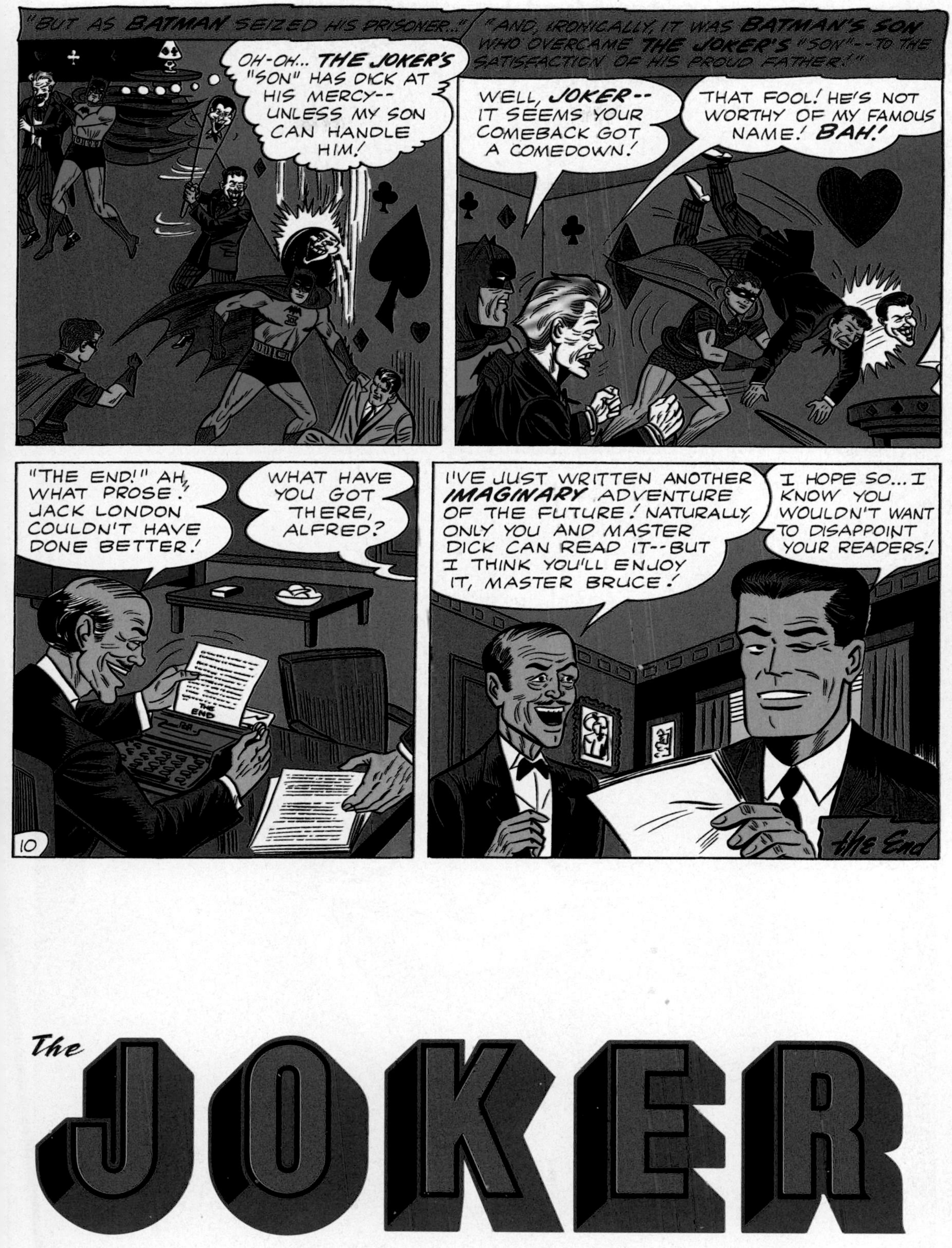
"BUT AS BATMAN SEIZED HIS PRISONER..."
OH-OH... THE JOKER'S "SON" HAS DICK AT HIS MERCY-- UNLESS MY SON CAN HANDLE HIM!
"AND, IRONICALLY, IT WAS BATMAN'S SON WHO OVERCAME THE JOKER'S "SON"--TO THE SATISFACTION OF HIS PROUD FATHER!"
WELL, JOKER-- IT SEEMS YOUR COMEBACK GOT A COMEDOWN!
THAT FOOL! HE'S NOT WORTHY OF MY FAMOUS NAME! BAH!
"THE END!" AH, WHAT PROSE. JACK LONDON COULDN'T HAVE DONE BETTER!
WHAT HAVE YOU GOT THERE, ALFRED?
10
I'VE JUST WRITTEN ANOTHER IMAGINARY ADVENTURE OF THE FUTURE! NATURALLY, ONLY YOU AND MASTER DICK CAN READ IT--BUT I THINK YOU'LL ENJOY IT, MASTER BRUCE!
I HOPE SO... I KNOW YOU WOULDN'T WANT TO DISAPPOINT YOUR READERS!
THE END

The JOKER

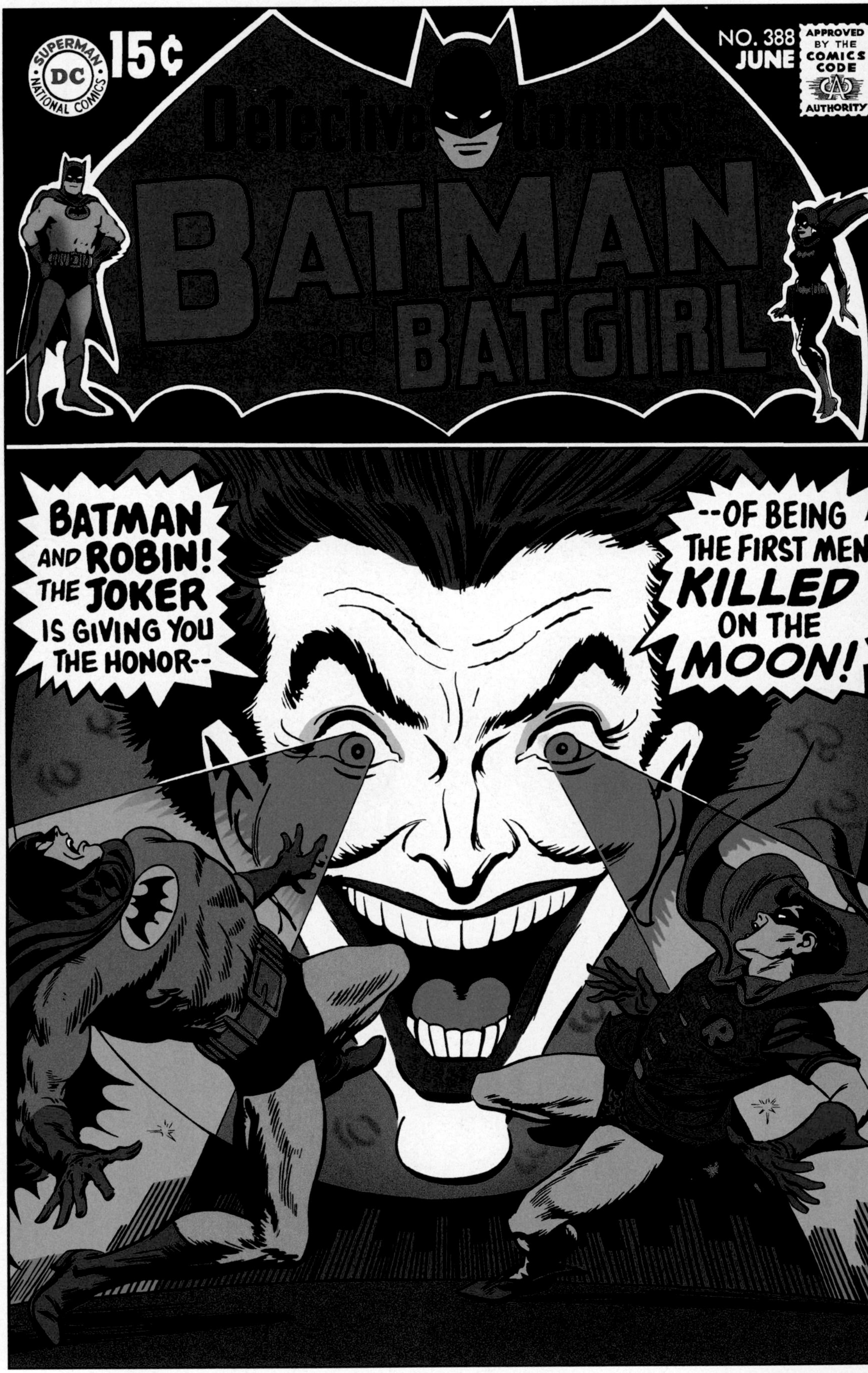
SUPERMAN DC NATIONAL COMICS
15¢
NO. 388 JUNE
APPROVED BY THE COMICS CODE AUTHORITY
Detective Comics
BATMAN and BATGIRL
BATMAN AND ROBIN! THE JOKER IS GIVING YOU THE HONOR--
--OF BEING THE FIRST MEN KILLED ON THE MOON!

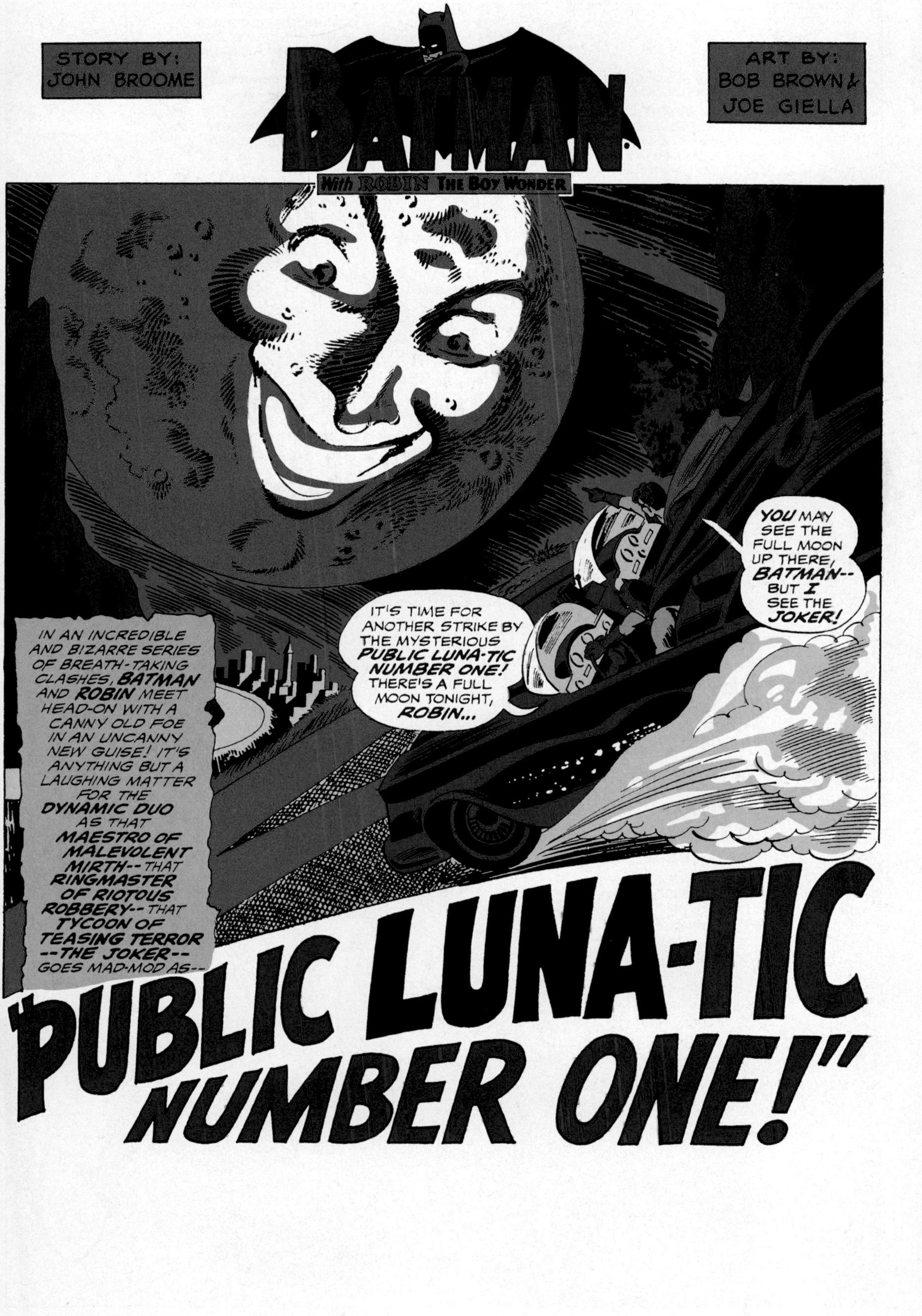
STORY BY: JOHN BROOME
BATMAN
With ROBIN THE BOY WONDER
ART BY: BOB BROWN & JOE GIELLA
IN AN INCREDIBLE AND BIZARRE SERIES OF BREATH-TAKING CLASHES, BATMAN AND ROBIN MEET HEAD-ON WITH A CANNY OLD FOE IN AN UNCANNY NEW GUISE! IT'S ANYTHING BUT A LAUGHING MATTER FOR THE DYNAMIC DUO AS THAT MAESTRO OF MALEVOLENT MIRTH--THAT RINGMASTER OF RIOTOUS ROBBERY--THAT TYCOON OF TEASING TERROR --THE JOKER-- GOES MAD-MOD AS--
IT'S TIME FOR ANOTHER STRIKE BY THE MYSTERIOUS PUBLIC LUNA-TIC NUMBER ONE! THERE'S A FULL MOON TONIGHT, ROBIN...
YOU MAY SEE THE FULL MOON UP THERE, BATMAN-- BUT I SEE THE JOKER!
"PUBLIC LUNA-TIC NUMBER ONE!"

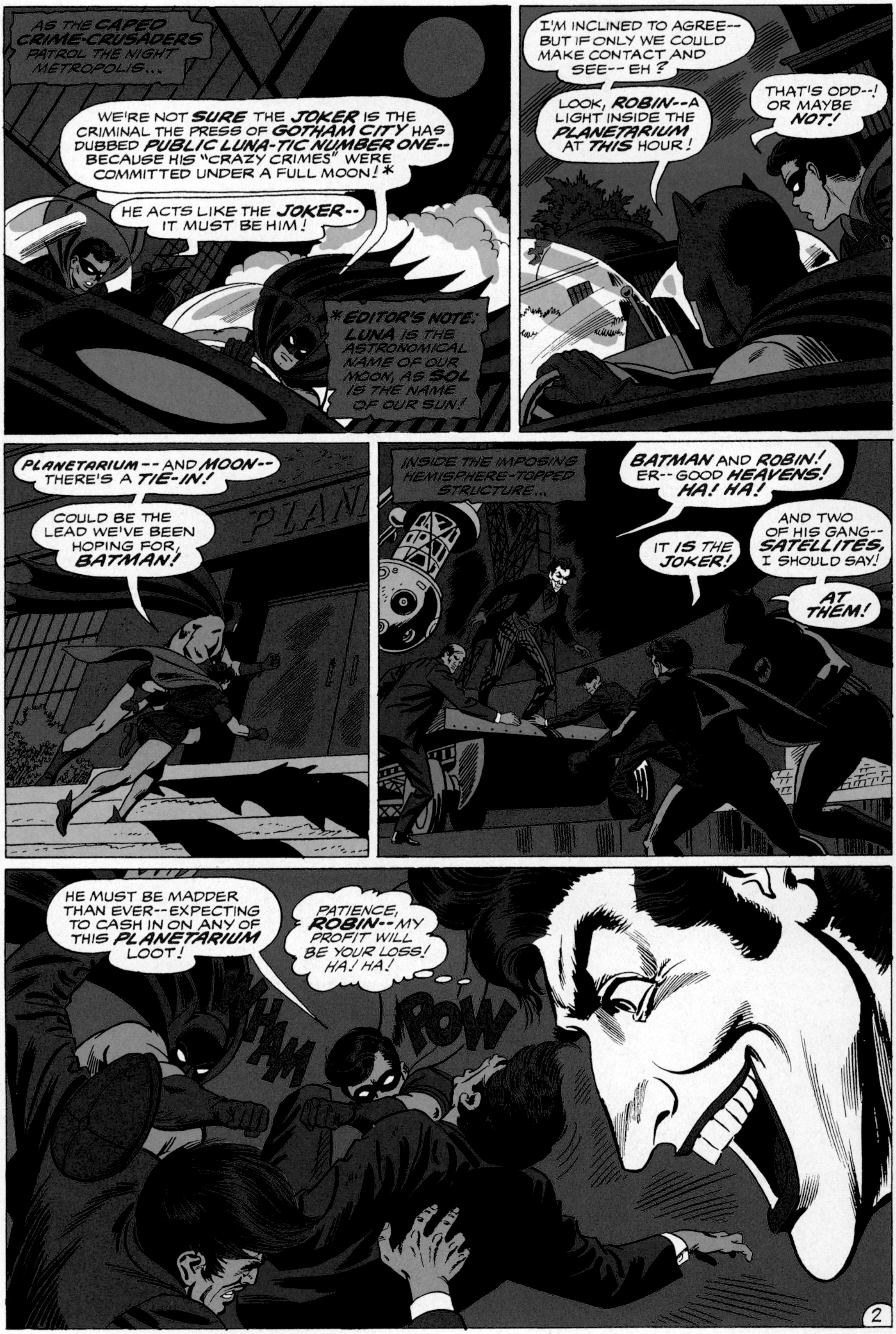
AS THE CAPED CRIME-CRUSADERS PATROL THE NIGHT METROPOLIS...
WE'RE NOT SURE THE JOKER IS THE CRIMINAL THE PRESS OF GOTHAM CITY HAS DUBBED PUBLIC LUNA-TIC NUMBER ONE-- BECAUSE HIS "CRAZY CRIMES" WERE COMMITTED UNDER A FULL MOON! *
HE ACTS LIKE THE JOKER-- IT MUST BE HIM!
* EDITOR'S NOTE: LUNA IS THE ASTRONOMICAL NAME OF OUR MOON, AS SOL IS THE NAME OF OUR SUN!
I'M INCLINED TO AGREE-- BUT IF ONLY WE COULD MAKE CONTACT AND SEE-- EH?
LOOK, ROBIN--A LIGHT INSIDE THE PLANETARIUM AT THIS HOUR!
THAT'S ODD--! OR MAYBE NOT!
PLANETARIUM-- AND MOON-- THERE'S A TIE-IN!
COULD BE THE LEAD WE'VE BEEN HOPING FOR, BATMAN!
PLAN
INSIDE THE IMPOSING HEMISPHERE-TOPPED STRUCTURE...
BATMAN AND ROBIN! ER-- GOOD HEAVENS! HA! HA!
IT IS THE JOKER!
AND TWO OF HIS GANG-- SATELLITES, I SHOULD SAY!
AT THEM!
HE MUST BE MADDER THAN EVER--EXPECTING TO CASH IN ON ANY OF THIS PLANETARIUM LOOT!
PATIENCE, ROBIN--MY PROFIT WILL BE YOUR LOSS! HA! HA!
WHAM
POW
2

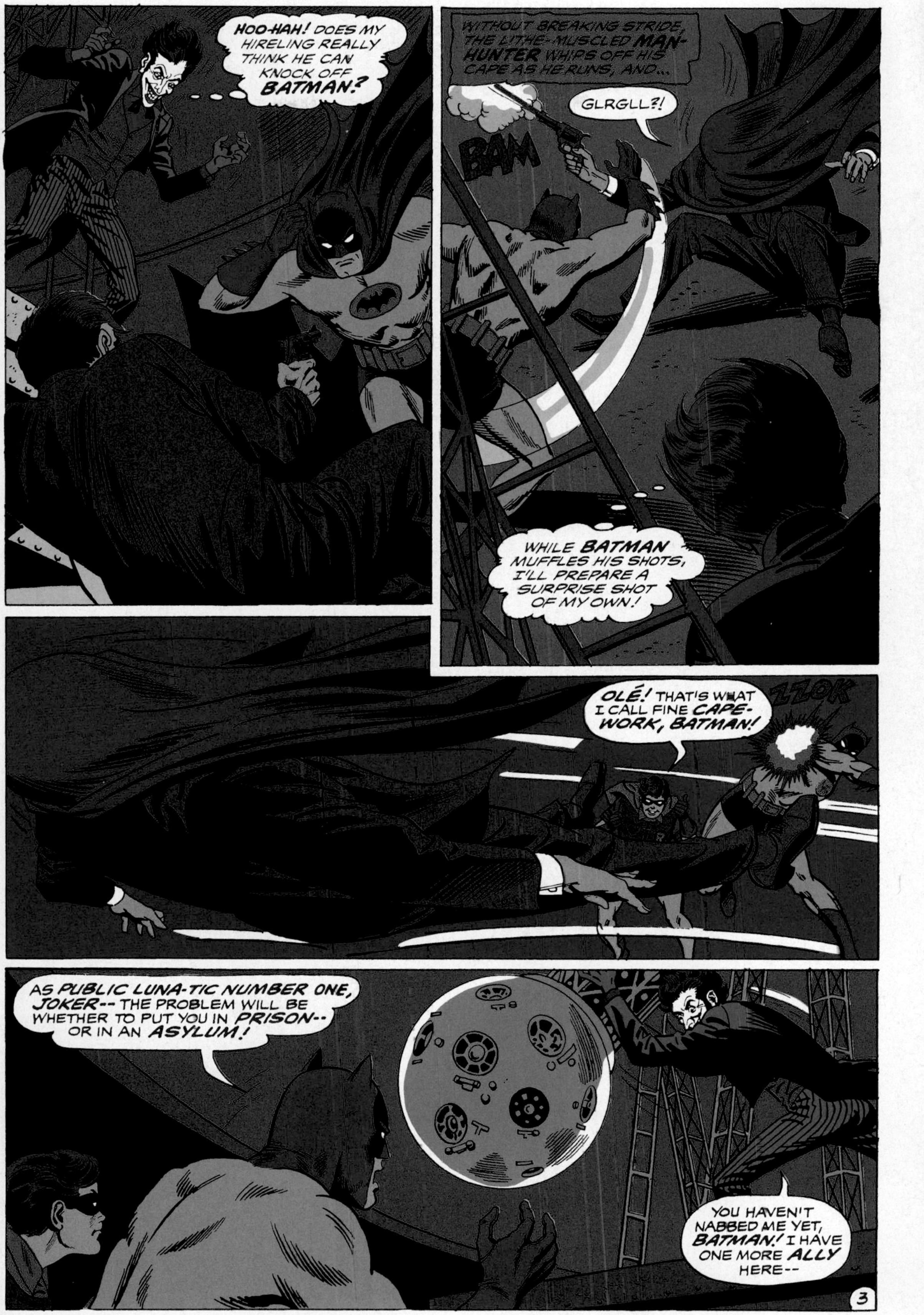
HOO-HAH! DOES MY HIRELING REALLY THINK HE CAN KNOCK OFF BATMAN?
WITHOUT BREAKING STRIDE, THE LITHE-MUSCLED MAN-HUNTER WHIPS OFF HIS CAPE AS HE RUNS, AND...
GLRGLL?!
BAM
WHILE BATMAN MUFFLES HIS SHOTS, I'LL PREPARE A SURPRISE SHOT OF MY OWN!
OLÉ! THAT'S WHAT I CALL FINE CAPE-WORK, BATMAN!
ZZOK
AS PUBLIC LUNA-TIC NUMBER ONE, JOKER-- THE PROBLEM WILL BE WHETHER TO PUT YOU IN PRISON-- OR IN AN ASYLUM!
YOU HAVEN'T NABBED ME YET, BATMAN! I HAVE ONE MORE ALLY HERE--
3

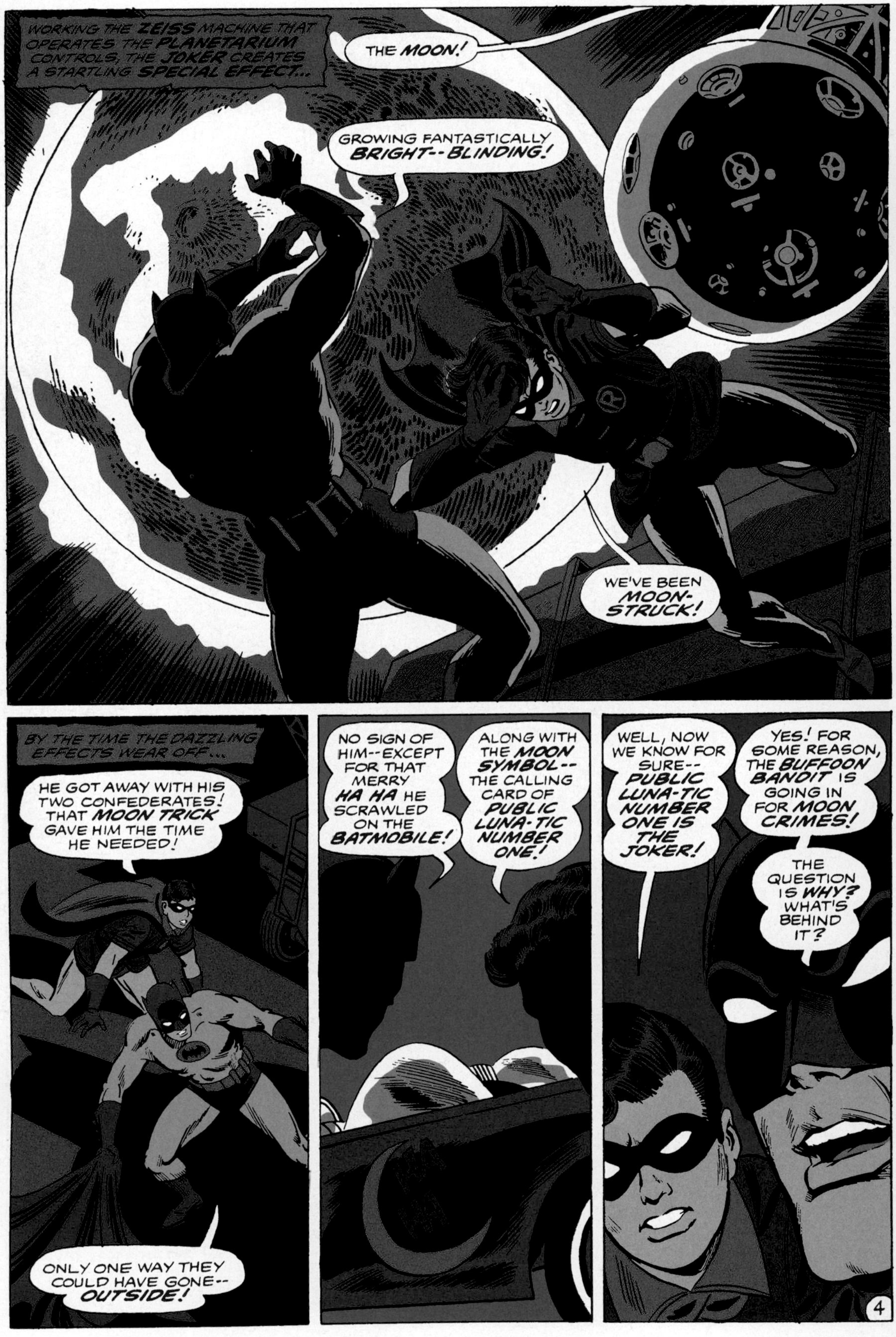
WORKING THE ZEISS MACHINE THAT OPERATES THE PLANETARIUM CONTROLS, THE JOKER CREATES A STARTLING SPECIAL EFFECT...
THE MOON!
GROWING FANTASTICALLY BRIGHT--BLINDING!
WE'VE BEEN MOON-STRUCK!
BY THE TIME THE DAZZLING EFFECTS WEAR OFF...
HE GOT AWAY WITH HIS TWO CONFEDERATES! THAT MOON TRICK GAVE HIM THE TIME HE NEEDED!
ONLY ONE WAY THEY COULD HAVE GONE--OUTSIDE!
NO SIGN OF HIM--EXCEPT FOR THAT MERRY HA HA HE SCRAWLED ON THE BATMOBILE!
ALONG WITH THE MOON SYMBOL--THE CALLING CARD OF PUBLIC LUNA-TIC NUMBER ONE!
WELL, NOW WE KNOW FOR SURE--PUBLIC LUNA-TIC NUMBER ONE IS THE JOKER!
YES! FOR SOME REASON, THE BUFFOON BANDIT IS GOING IN FOR MOON CRIMES!
THE QUESTION IS WHY? WHAT'S BEHIND IT?
4

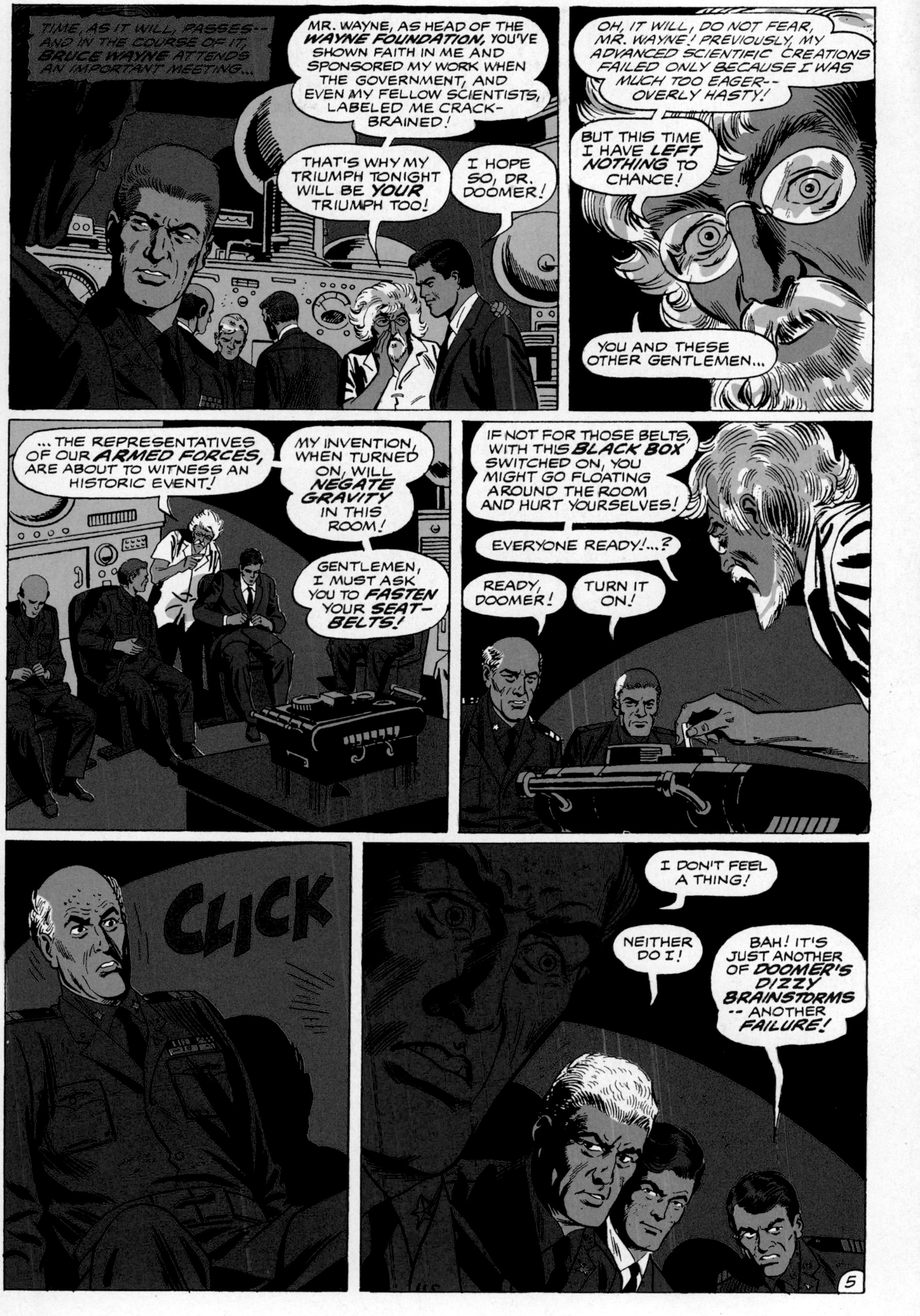
TIME, AS IT WILL, PASSES-- AND IN THE COURSE OF IT, BRUCE WAYNE ATTENDS AN IMPORTANT MEETING...
MR. WAYNE, AS HEAD OF THE WAYNE FOUNDATION, YOU'VE SHOWN FAITH IN ME AND SPONSORED MY WORK WHEN THE GOVERNMENT, AND EVEN MY FELLOW SCIENTISTS, LABELED ME CRACK-BRAINED!
THAT'S WHY MY TRIUMPH TONIGHT WILL BE YOUR TRIUMPH TOO!
I HOPE SO, DR. DOOMER!
OH, IT WILL, DO NOT FEAR, MR. WAYNE! PREVIOUSLY, MY ADVANCED SCIENTIFIC CREATIONS FAILED ONLY BECAUSE I WAS MUCH TOO EAGER-- OVERLY HASTY!
BUT THIS TIME I HAVE LEFT NOTHING TO CHANCE!
YOU AND THESE OTHER GENTLEMEN...
...THE REPRESENTATIVES OF OUR ARMED FORCES, ARE ABOUT TO WITNESS AN HISTORIC EVENT!
MY INVENTION, WHEN TURNED ON, WILL NEGATE GRAVITY IN THIS ROOM!
GENTLEMEN, I MUST ASK YOU TO FASTEN YOUR SEAT-BELTS!
IF NOT FOR THOSE BELTS, WITH THIS BLACK BOX SWITCHED ON, YOU MIGHT GO FLOATING AROUND THE ROOM AND HURT YOURSELVES!
EVERYONE READY!...?
READY, DOOMER!
TURN IT ON!
CLICK
I DON'T FEEL A THING!
NEITHER DO I!
BAH! IT'S JUST ANOTHER OF DOOMER'S DIZZY BRAINSTORMS -- ANOTHER FAILURE!
5

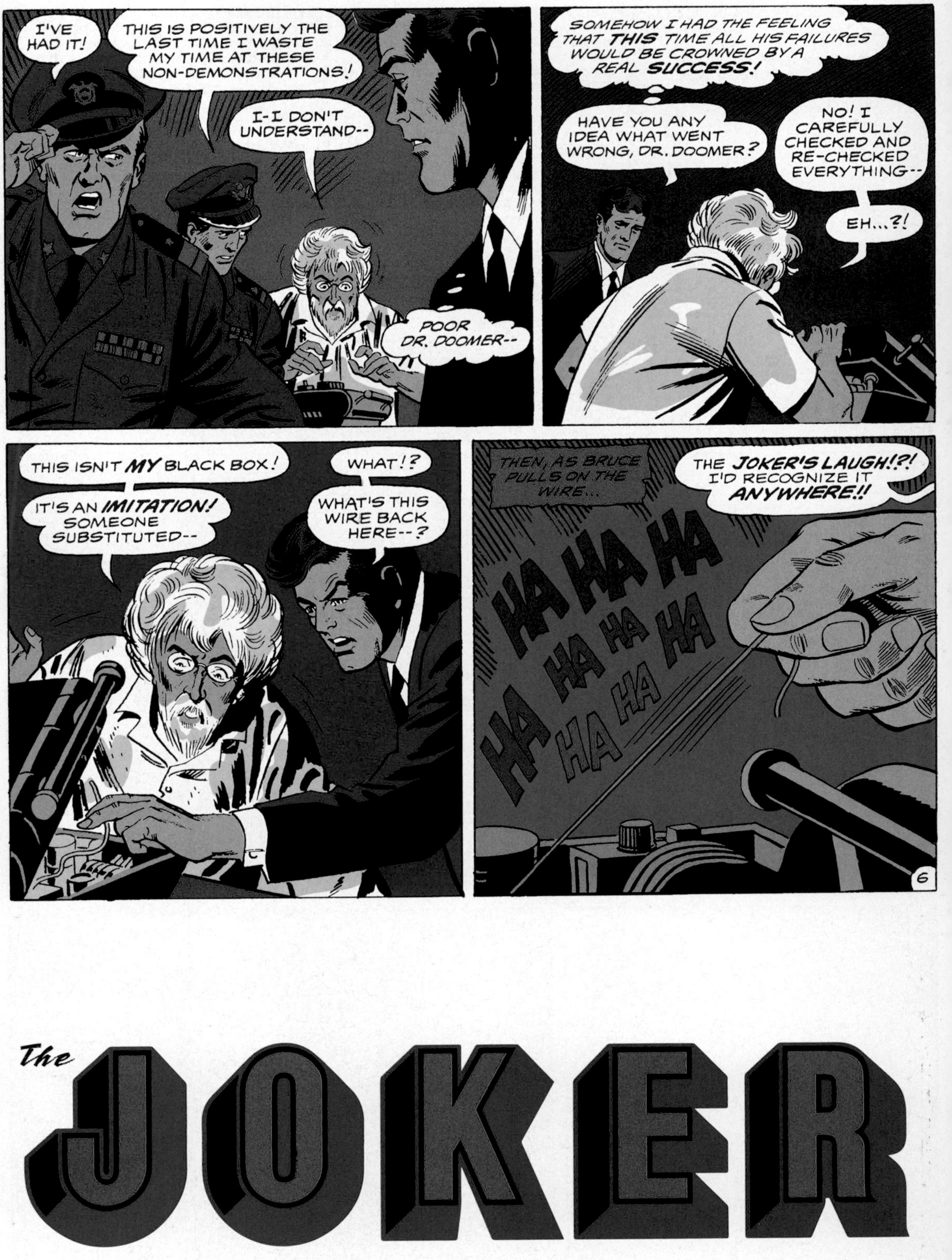
I'VE HAD IT!
THIS IS POSITIVELY THE LAST TIME I WASTE MY TIME AT THESE NON-DEMONSTRATIONS!
I-I DON'T UNDERSTAND--
POOR DR. DOOMER--
SOMEHOW I HAD THE FEELING THAT THIS TIME ALL HIS FAILURES WOULD BE CROWNED BY A REAL SUCCESS!
HAVE YOU ANY IDEA WHAT WENT WRONG, DR. DOOMER?
NO! I CAREFULLY CHECKED AND RE-CHECKED EVERYTHING--
EH...?!
THIS ISN'T MY BLACK BOX!
IT'S AN IMITATION! SOMEONE SUBSTITUTED--
WHAT!?
WHAT'S THIS WIRE BACK HERE--?
THEN, AS BRUCE PULLS ON THE WIRE...
THE JOKER'S LAUGH!?! I'D RECOGNIZE IT ANYWHERE!!
HA HA HA HA
HA HA HA HA
HA HA HA
6

The JOKER

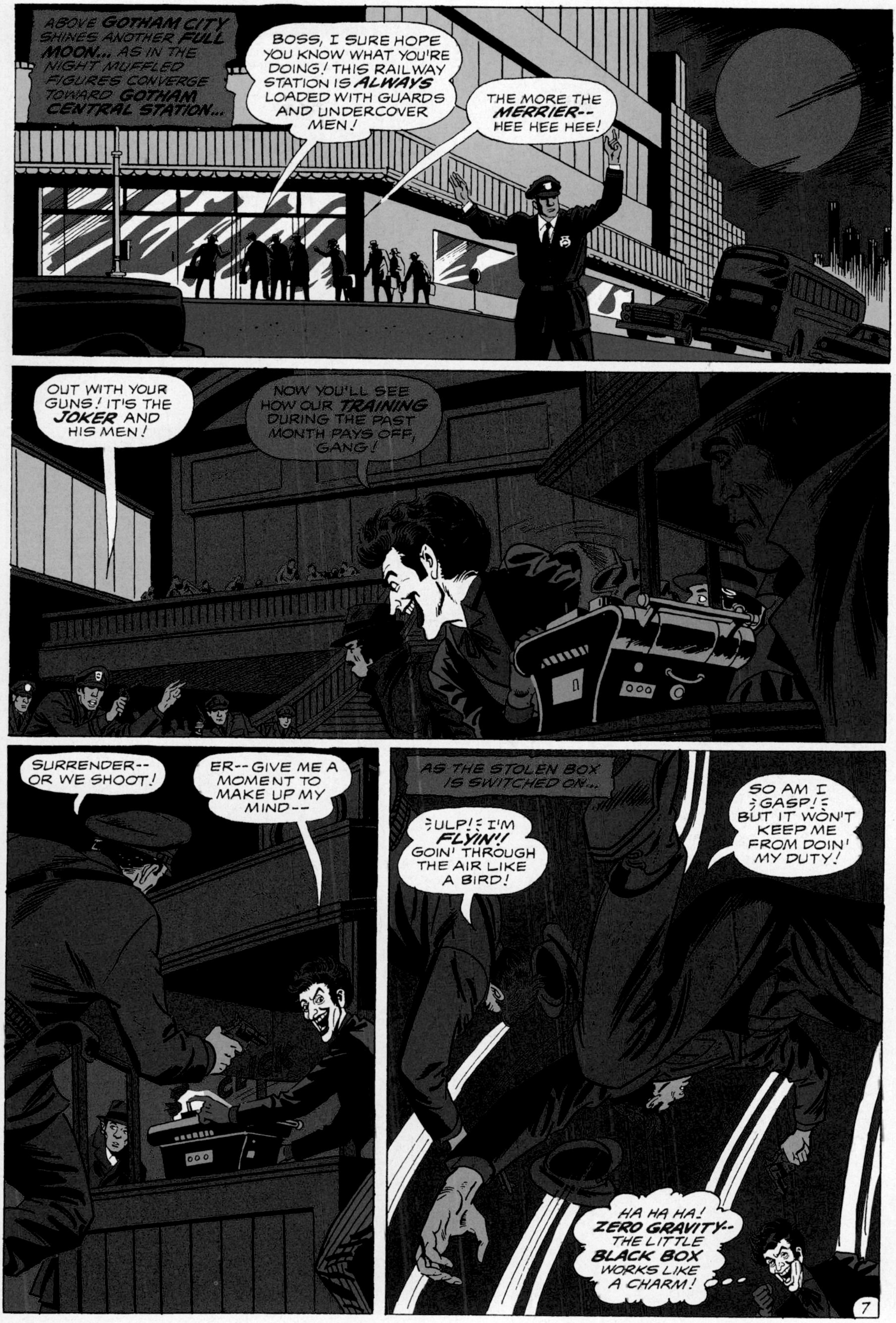

ABOVE GOTHAM CITY SHINES ANOTHER FULL MOON... AS IN THE NIGHT MUFFLED FIGURES CONVERGE TOWARD GOTHAM CENTRAL STATION...
BOSS, I SURE HOPE YOU KNOW WHAT YOU'RE DOING! THIS RAILWAY STATION IS ALWAYS LOADED WITH GUARDS AND UNDERCOVER MEN!
THE MORE THE MERRIER-- HEE HEE HEE!
OUT WITH YOUR GUNS! IT'S THE JOKER AND HIS MEN!
NOW YOU'LL SEE HOW OUR TRAINING DURING THE PAST MONTH PAYS OFF, GANG!
SURRENDER-- OR WE SHOOT!
ER-- GIVE ME A MOMENT TO MAKE UP MY MIND--
AS THE STOLEN BOX IS SWITCHED ON...
ULP! I'M FLYIN'! GOIN' THROUGH THE AIR LIKE A BIRD!
SO AM I -GASP!- BUT IT WON'T KEEP ME FROM DOIN' MY DUTY!
HA HA HA! ZERO GRAVITY-- THE LITTLE BLACK BOX WORKS LIKE A CHARM!
7

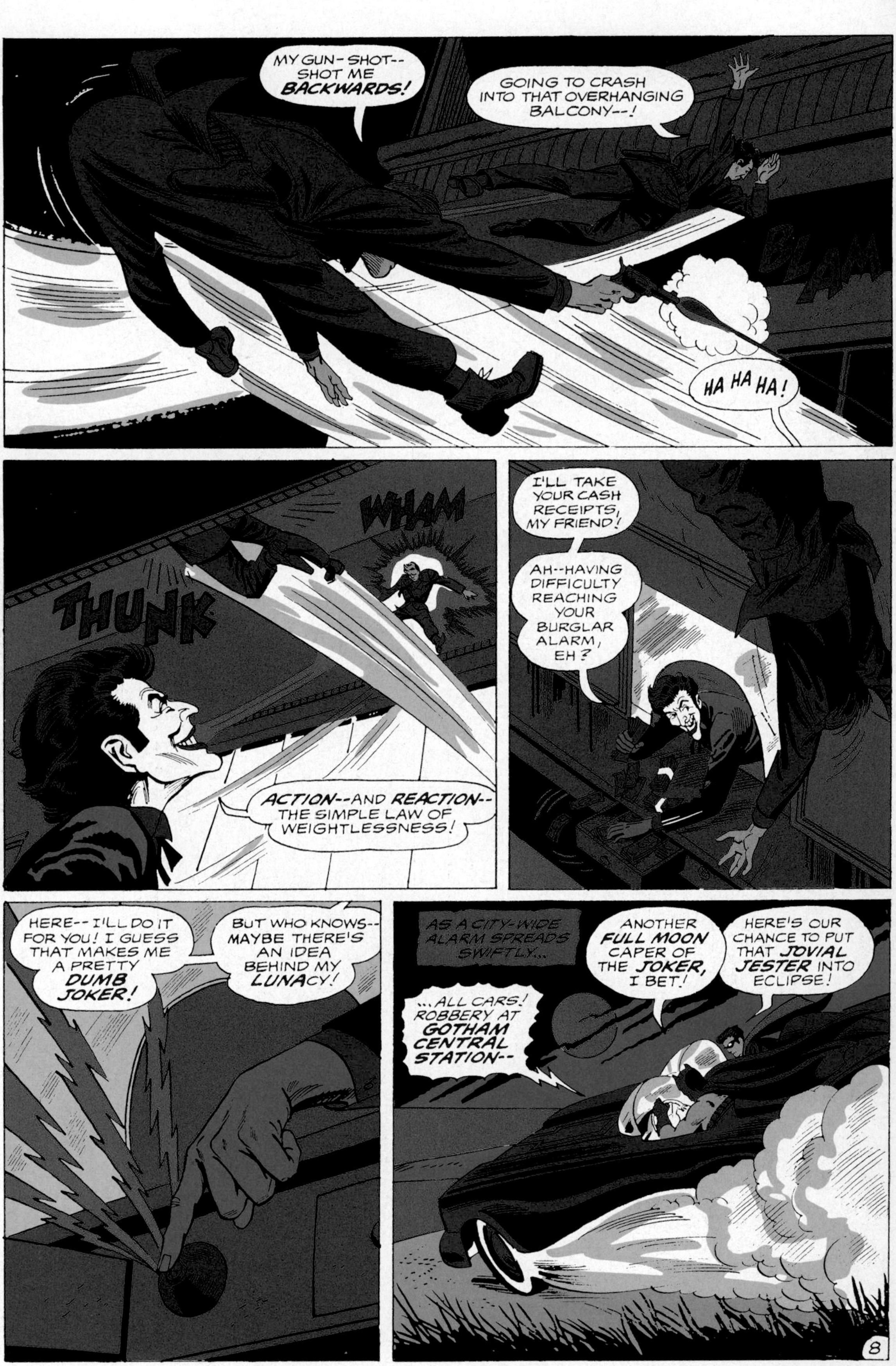
MY GUN-SHOT--SHOT ME BACKWARDS!
GOING TO CRASH INTO THAT OVERHANGING BALCONY--!
BLAM
HA HA HA!
WHAM
THUNK
ACTION--AND REACTION--THE SIMPLE LAW OF WEIGHTLESSNESS!
I'LL TAKE YOUR CASH RECEIPTS, MY FRIEND!
AH--HAVING DIFFICULTY REACHING YOUR BURGLAR ALARM, EH?
HERE--I'LL DO IT FOR YOU! I GUESS THAT MAKES ME A PRETTY DUMB JOKER!
BUT WHO KNOWS--MAYBE THERE'S AN IDEA BEHIND MY LUNACY!
AS A CITY-WIDE ALARM SPREADS SWIFTLY...
...ALL CARS! ROBBERY AT GOTHAM CENTRAL STATION--
ANOTHER FULL MOON CAPER OF THE JOKER, I BET!
HERE'S OUR CHANCE TO PUT THAT JOVIAL JESTER INTO ECLIPSE!
8

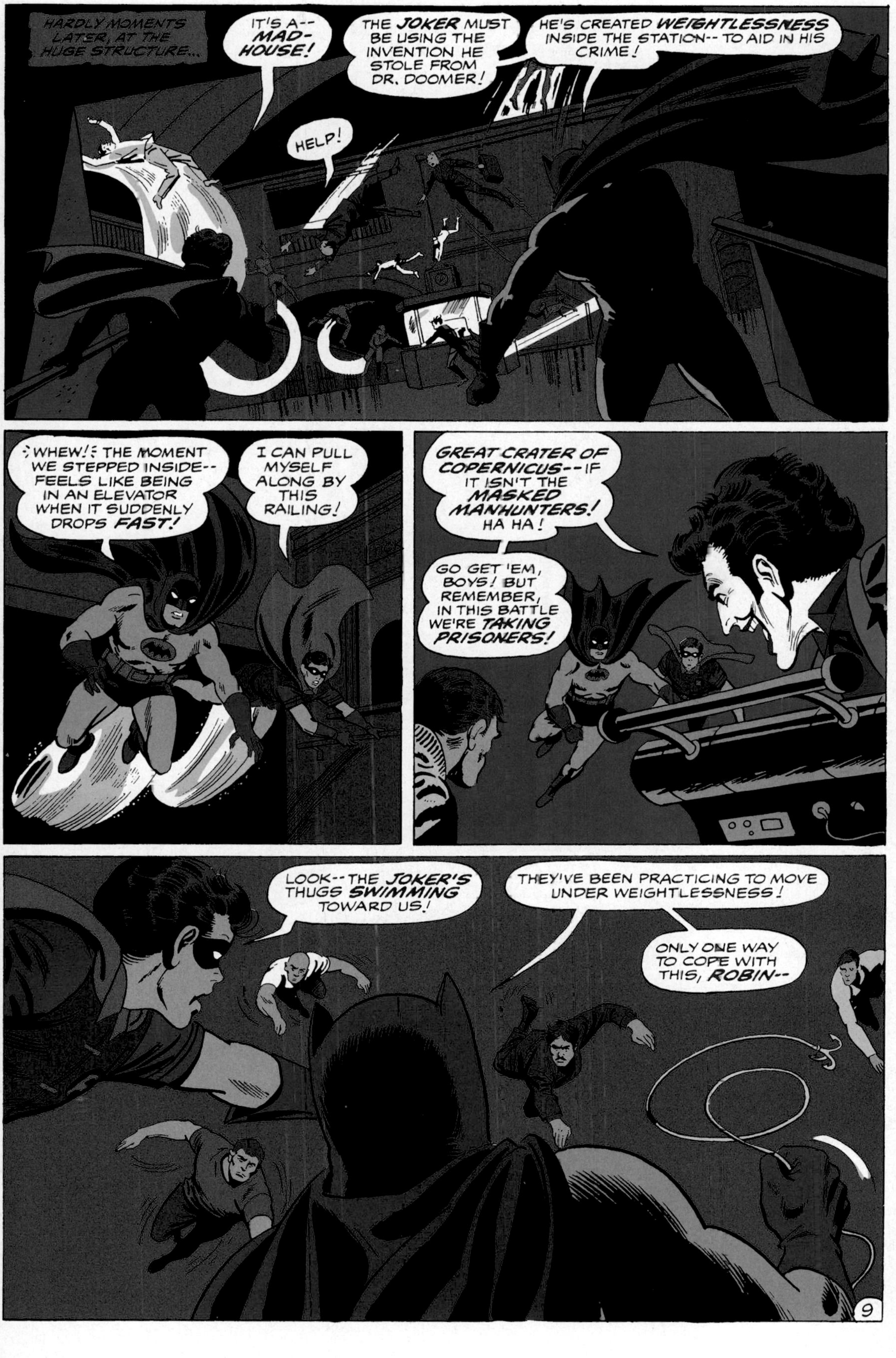
HARDLY MOMENTS LATER, AT THE HUGE STRUCTURE...
IT'S A-- MAD-HOUSE!
THE JOKER MUST BE USING THE INVENTION HE STOLE FROM DR. DOOMER!
HE'S CREATED WEIGHTLESSNESS INSIDE THE STATION-- TO AID IN HIS CRIME!
HELP!
WHEW! THE MOMENT WE STEPPED INSIDE-- FEELS LIKE BEING IN AN ELEVATOR WHEN IT SUDDENLY DROPS FAST!
I CAN PULL MYSELF ALONG BY THIS RAILING!
GREAT CRATER OF COPERNICUS-- IF IT ISN'T THE MASKED MANHUNTERS! HA HA!
GO GET 'EM, BOYS! BUT REMEMBER, IN THIS BATTLE WE'RE TAKING PRISONERS!
LOOK-- THE JOKER'S THUGS SWIMMING TOWARD US!
THEY'VE BEEN PRACTICING TO MOVE UNDER WEIGHTLESSNESS!
ONLY ONE WAY TO COPE WITH THIS, ROBIN--
9

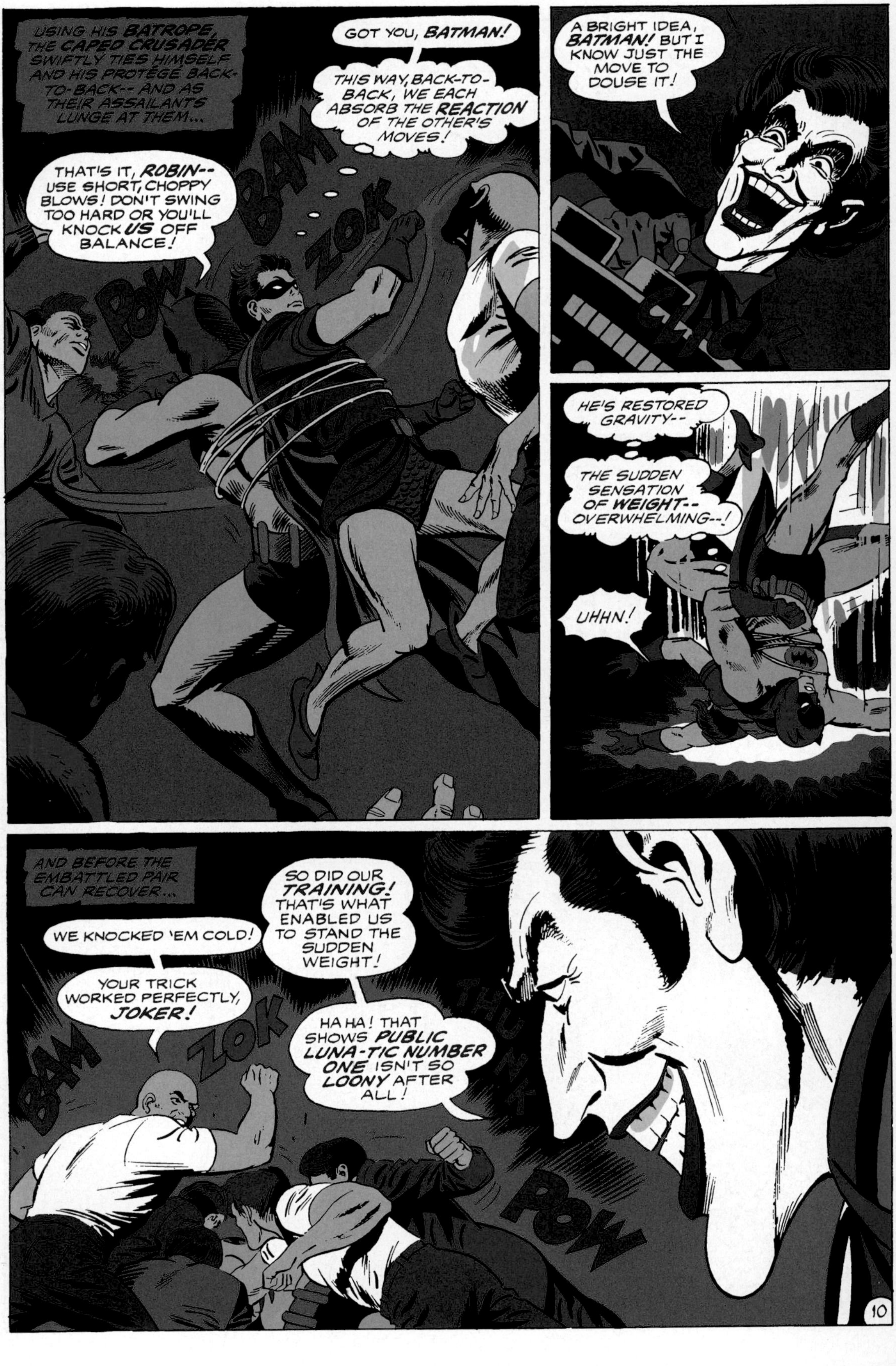

USING HIS BATROPE, THE CAPED CRUSADER SWIFTLY TIES HIMSELF AND HIS PROTÉGÉ BACK-TO-BACK-- AND AS THEIR ASSAILANTS LUNGE AT THEM...
GOT YOU, BATMAN!
THIS WAY, BACK-TO-BACK, WE EACH ABSORB THE REACTION OF THE OTHER'S MOVES!
THAT'S IT, ROBIN-- USE SHORT, CHOPPY BLOWS! DON'T SWING TOO HARD OR YOU'LL KNOCK US OFF BALANCE!
BAM
ZOK
POW
A BRIGHT IDEA, BATMAN! BUT I KNOW JUST THE MOVE TO DOUSE IT!
CLICK
HE'S RESTORED GRAVITY--
THE SUDDEN SENSATION OF WEIGHT-- OVERWHELMING--!
UHHN!
AND BEFORE THE EMBATTLED PAIR CAN RECOVER...
WE KNOCKED 'EM COLD!
YOUR TRICK WORKED PERFECTLY, JOKER!
SO DID OUR TRAINING! THAT'S WHAT ENABLED US TO STAND THE SUDDEN WEIGHT!
HA HA! THAT SHOWS PUBLIC LUNA-TIC NUMBER ONE ISN'T SO LOONY AFTER ALL!
BAM
ZOK
THUNK
POW
10

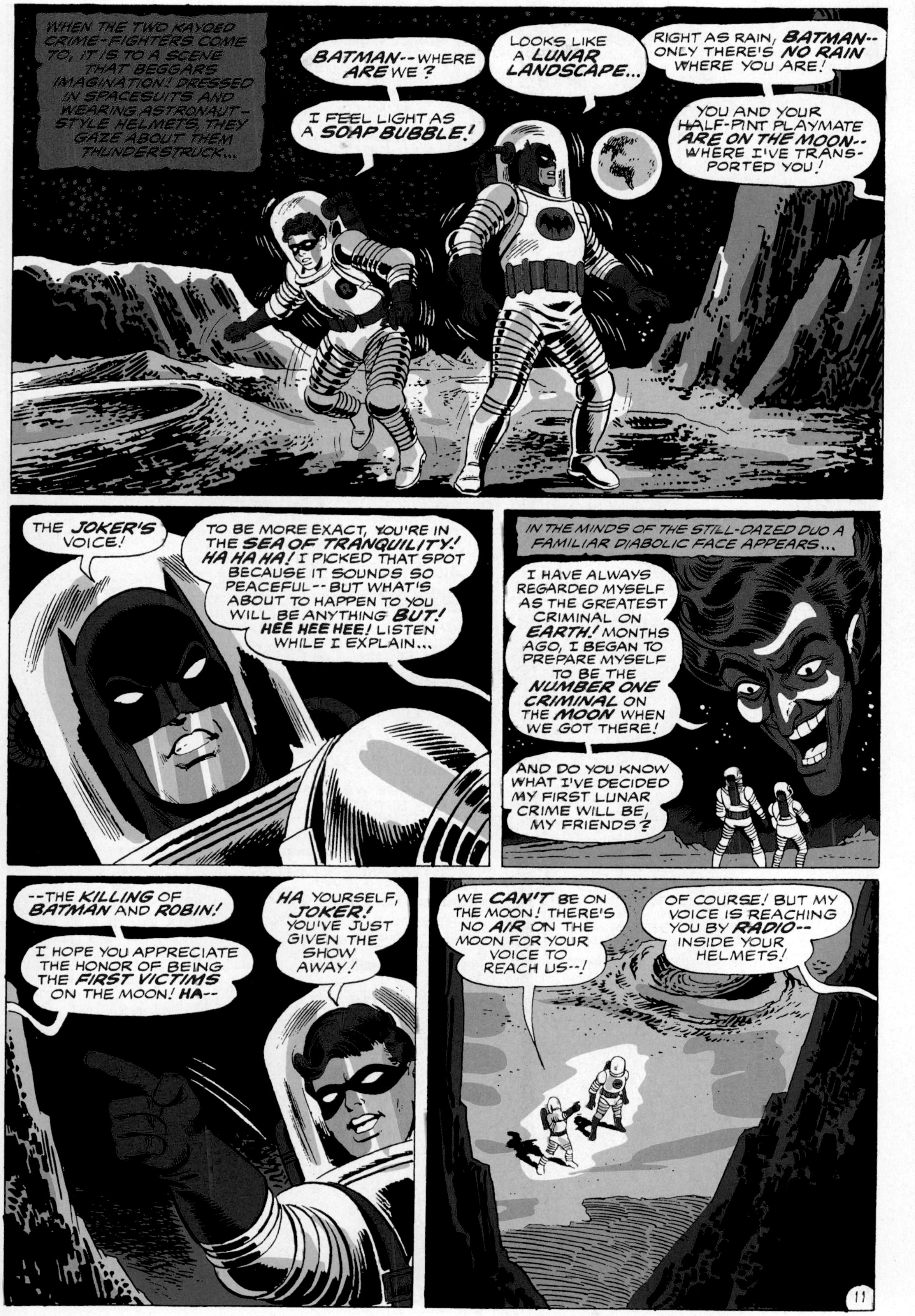

WHEN THE TWO KAYOED CRIME-FIGHTERS COME TO, IT IS TO A SCENE THAT BEGGARS IMAGINATION! DRESSED IN SPACESUITS AND WEARING ASTRONAUT-STYLE HELMETS, THEY GAZE ABOUT THEM THUNDERSTRUCK...
BATMAN--WHERE ARE WE?
I FEEL LIGHT AS A SOAP BUBBLE!
LOOKS LIKE A LUNAR LANDSCAPE...
RIGHT AS RAIN, BATMAN--ONLY THERE'S NO RAIN WHERE YOU ARE!
YOU AND YOUR HALF-PINT PLAYMATE ARE ON THE MOON--WHERE I'VE TRANSPORTED YOU!
THE JOKER'S VOICE!
TO BE MORE EXACT, YOU'RE IN THE SEA OF TRANQUILITY! HA HA HA! I PICKED THAT SPOT BECAUSE IT SOUNDS SO PEACEFUL--BUT WHAT'S ABOUT TO HAPPEN TO YOU WILL BE ANYTHING BUT! HEE HEE HEE! LISTEN WHILE I EXPLAIN...
IN THE MINDS OF THE STILL-DAZED DUO A FAMILIAR DIABOLIC FACE APPEARS...
I HAVE ALWAYS REGARDED MYSELF AS THE GREATEST CRIMINAL ON EARTH! MONTHS AGO, I BEGAN TO PREPARE MYSELF TO BE THE NUMBER ONE CRIMINAL ON THE MOON WHEN WE GOT THERE!
AND DO YOU KNOW WHAT I'VE DECIDED MY FIRST LUNAR CRIME WILL BE, MY FRIENDS?
--THE KILLING OF BATMAN AND ROBIN!
I HOPE YOU APPRECIATE THE HONOR OF BEING THE FIRST VICTIMS ON THE MOON! HA--
HA YOURSELF, JOKER! YOU'VE JUST GIVEN THE SHOW AWAY!
WE CAN'T BE ON THE MOON! THERE'S NO AIR ON THE MOON FOR YOUR VOICE TO REACH US--!
OF COURSE! BUT MY VOICE IS REACHING YOU BY RADIO--INSIDE YOUR HELMETS!
11

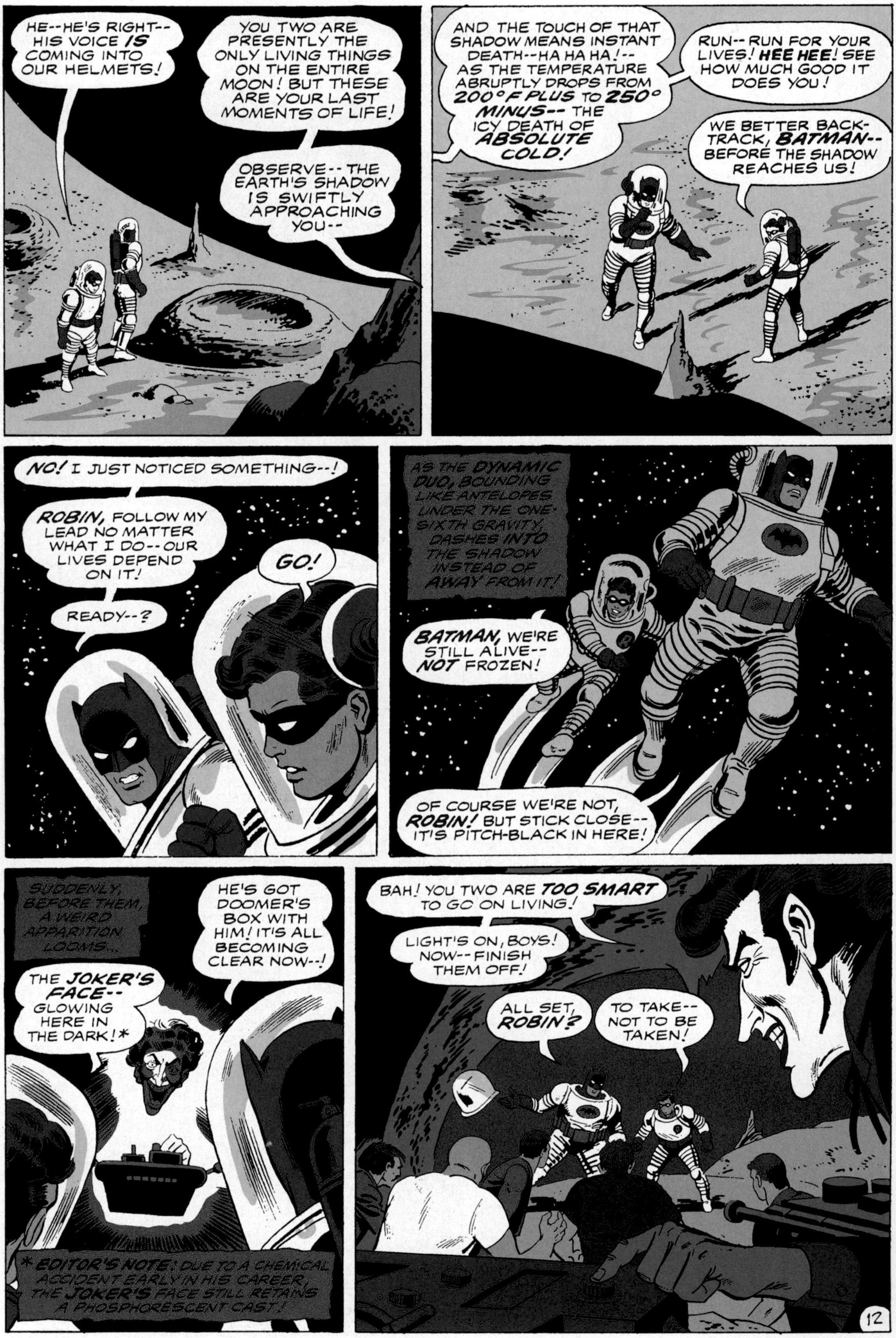
HE--HE'S RIGHT--HIS VOICE IS COMING INTO OUR HELMETS!
YOU TWO ARE PRESENTLY THE ONLY LIVING THINGS ON THE ENTIRE MOON! BUT THESE ARE YOUR LAST MOMENTS OF LIFE!
OBSERVE--THE EARTH'S SHADOW IS SWIFTLY APPROACHING YOU--
AND THE TOUCH OF THAT SHADOW MEANS INSTANT DEATH--HA HA HA!--AS THE TEMPERATURE ABRUPTLY DROPS FROM 200°F PLUS TO 250° MINUS--THE ICY DEATH OF ABSOLUTE COLD!
RUN--RUN FOR YOUR LIVES! HEE HEE! SEE HOW MUCH GOOD IT DOES YOU!
WE BETTER BACK-TRACK, BATMAN--BEFORE THE SHADOW REACHES US!
NO! I JUST NOTICED SOMETHING--!
ROBIN, FOLLOW MY LEAD NO MATTER WHAT I DO--OUR LIVES DEPEND ON IT!
READY--?
GO!
AS THE DYNAMIC DUO, BOUNDING LIKE ANTELOPES UNDER THE ONE-SIXTH GRAVITY, DASHES INTO THE SHADOW INSTEAD OF AWAY FROM IT!
BATMAN, WE'RE STILL ALIVE--NOT FROZEN!
OF COURSE WE'RE NOT, ROBIN! BUT STICK CLOSE--IT'S PITCH-BLACK IN HERE!
SUDDENLY, BEFORE THEM, A WEIRD APPARITION LOOMS...
HE'S GOT DOOMER'S BOX WITH HIM! IT'S ALL BECOMING CLEAR NOW--!
THE JOKER'S FACE--GLOWING HERE IN THE DARK!*
*EDITOR'S NOTE: DUE TO A CHEMICAL ACCIDENT EARLY IN HIS CAREER, THE JOKER'S FACE STILL RETAINS A PHOSPHORESCENT CAST!
BAH! YOU TWO ARE TOO SMART TO GO ON LIVING!
LIGHT'S ON, BOYS! NOW--FINISH THEM OFF!
ALL SET, ROBIN?
TO TAKE--NOT TO BE TAKEN!
12

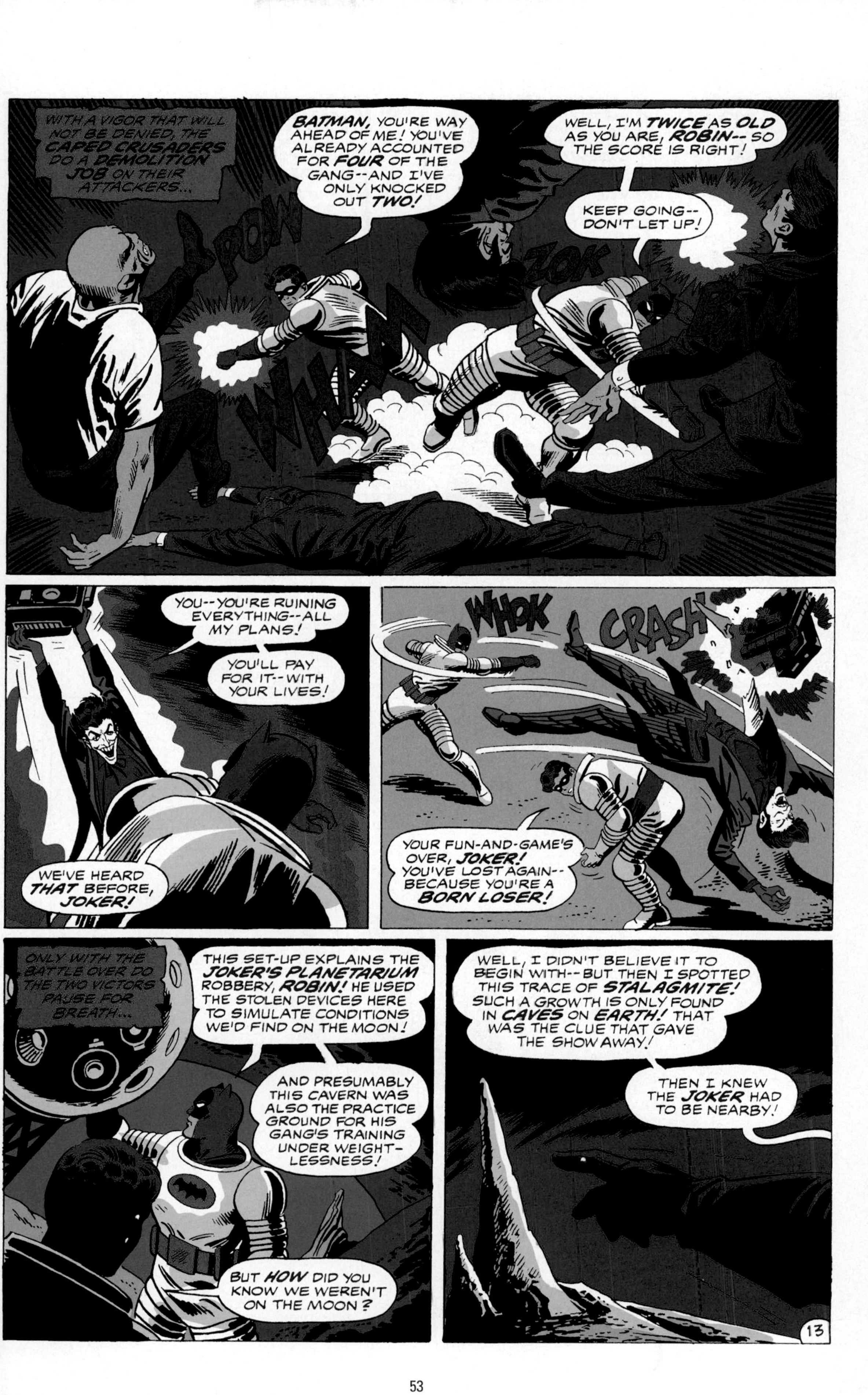
WITH A VIGOR THAT WILL NOT BE DENIED, THE CAPED CRUSADERS DO A DEMOLITION JOB ON THEIR ATTACKERS...
BATMAN, YOU'RE WAY AHEAD OF ME! YOU'VE ALREADY ACCOUNTED FOR FOUR OF THE GANG--AND I'VE ONLY KNOCKED OUT TWO!
WELL, I'M TWICE AS OLD AS YOU ARE, ROBIN-- SO THE SCORE IS RIGHT!
KEEP GOING-- DON'T LET UP!
POW
WHAM
ZOK
YOU--YOU'RE RUINING EVERYTHING--ALL MY PLANS!
YOU'LL PAY FOR IT--WITH YOUR LIVES!
WE'VE HEARD THAT BEFORE, JOKER!
WHOK
CRASH
YOUR FUN-AND-GAME'S OVER, JOKER! YOU'VE LOST AGAIN-- BECAUSE YOU'RE A BORN LOSER!
ONLY WITH THE BATTLE OVER DO THE TWO VICTORS PAUSE FOR BREATH...
THIS SET-UP EXPLAINS THE JOKER'S PLANETARIUM ROBBERY, ROBIN! HE USED THE STOLEN DEVICES HERE TO SIMULATE CONDITIONS WE'D FIND ON THE MOON!
AND PRESUMABLY THIS CAVERN WAS ALSO THE PRACTICE GROUND FOR HIS GANG'S TRAINING UNDER WEIGHT-LESSNESS!
BUT HOW DID YOU KNOW WE WEREN'T ON THE MOON?
WELL, I DIDN'T BELIEVE IT TO BEGIN WITH--BUT THEN I SPOTTED THIS TRACE OF STALAGMITE! SUCH A GROWTH IS ONLY FOUND IN CAVES ON EARTH! THAT WAS THE CLUE THAT GAVE THE SHOW AWAY!
THEN I KNEW THE JOKER HAD TO BE NEARBY!
13

LATER, WITH PUBLIC LUNA-TIC NUMBER ONE AND HIS HENCHMEN BEHIND BARS...
IN TRYING TO MAKE US BELIEVE WE WERE ACTUALLY ON THE MOON, THE JOKER TRIED TO FRIGHTEN US TO DEATH!
THAT WAS TO BE HIS GREATEST-- AND GHASTLIEST JEST!
THE ONLY TROUBLE WAS HE WASN'T THOROUGH ENOUGH!
YOU MEAN OVERLOOKING THE STALAGMITE?
YES-- BUT IF IT WASN'T THAT IT WOULD HAVE BEEN SOMETHING ELSE!
THE JOKER WAS TOO EAGER TO ENJOY HIS VICTORY OVER US-- OVERLY HASTY! THAT'S WHAT LED TO HIS DOWNFALL!
STILL-- I'M GOING TO FLINCH WHENEVER I SEE A FULL MOON!
LATER, IN DR. DOOMER'S LABORATORY...
MY ANTI-GRAVITY DEVICE-- COMPLETELY SMASHED! IT WILL TAKE ME YEARS TO REBUILD ANOTHER ONE!
THE WORLD WILL BE PATIENTLY WAITING, DR. DOOMER--
--AND WHEN IT'S COMPLETED, YOU'LL BE HONORED AS-- PUBLIC SCIENTIST NUMBER ONE!
14
THE End

The JOKER

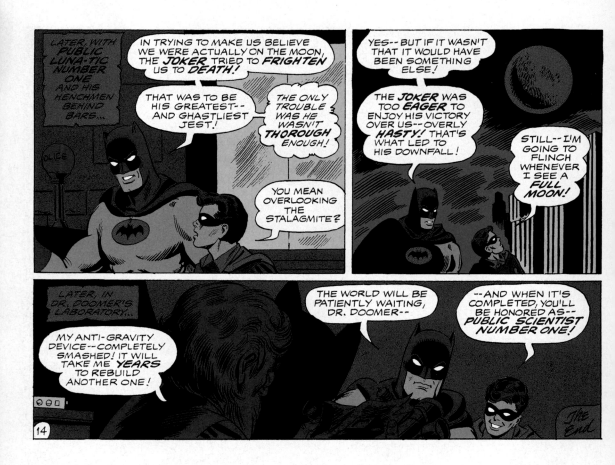

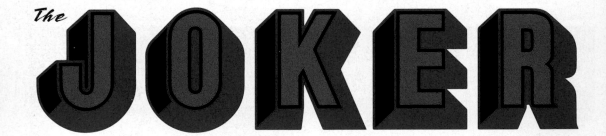

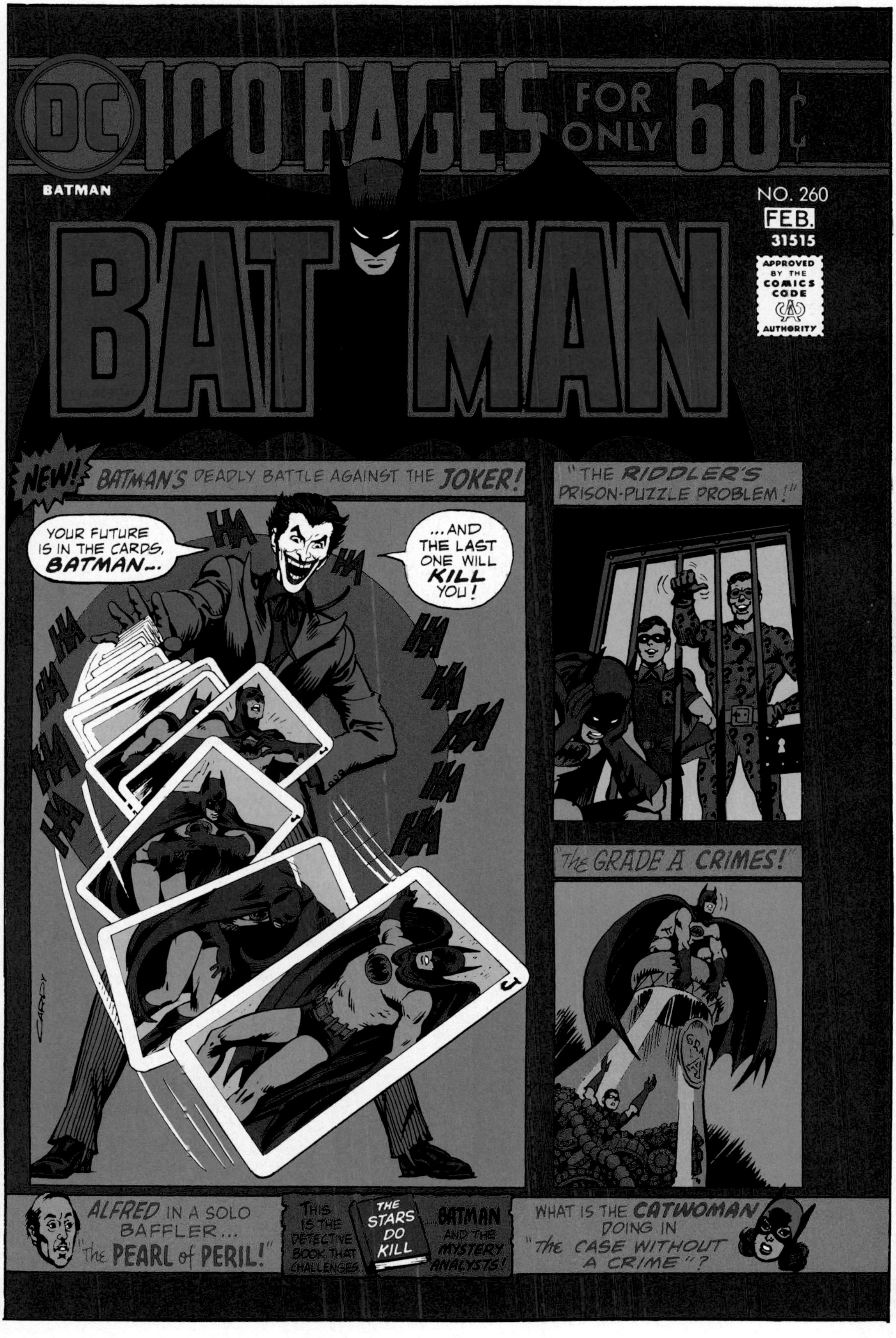
DC
100 PAGES FOR ONLY 60¢
BATMAN
NO. 260
FEB.
31515
APPROVED BY THE COMICS CODE AUTHORITY
BATMAN
NEW!
BATMAN'S DEADLY BATTLE AGAINST THE JOKER!
YOUR FUTURE IS IN THE CARDS, BATMAN...
...AND THE LAST ONE WILL KILL YOU!
"THE RIDDLER'S PRISON-PUZZLE PROBLEM!"
"The GRADE A CRIMES!"
CARDY
ALFRED IN A SOLO BAFFLER... "The PEARL of PERIL!"
THIS IS THE DETECTIVE BOOK THAT CHALLENGES...
THE STARS DO KILL
...BATMAN AND THE MYSTERY ANALYSTS!
WHAT IS THE CATWOMAN DOING IN "The CASE WITHOUT A CRIME"?

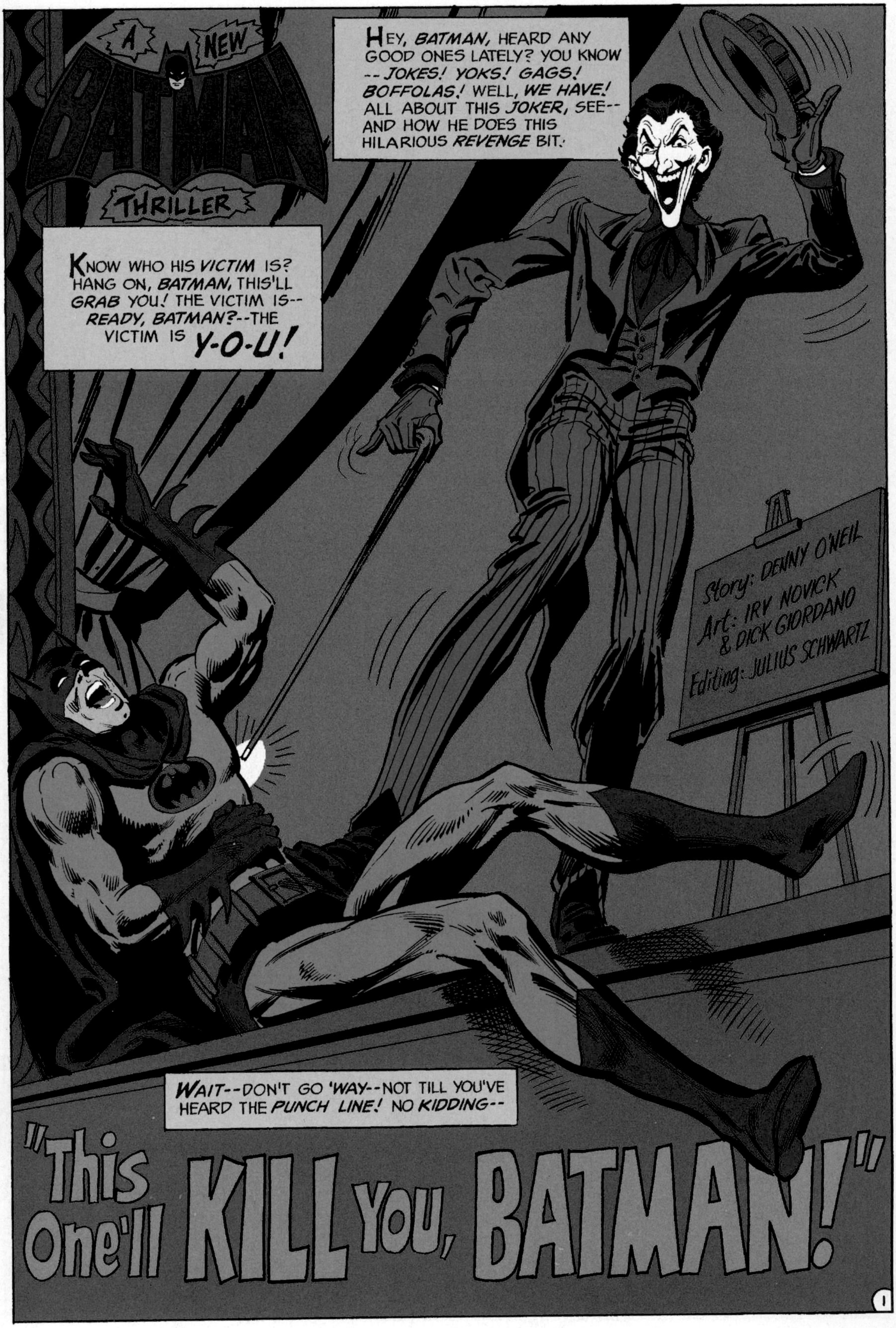
A NEW BATMAN THRILLER
HEY, BATMAN, HEARD ANY GOOD ONES LATELY? YOU KNOW --JOKES! YOKS! GAGS! BOFFOLAS! WELL, WE HAVE! ALL ABOUT THIS JOKER, SEE-- AND HOW HE DOES THIS HILARIOUS REVENGE BIT.
KNOW WHO HIS VICTIM IS? HANG ON, BATMAN, THIS'LL GRAB YOU! THE VICTIM IS-- READY, BATMAN?--THE VICTIM IS Y-O-U!
Story: DENNY O'NEIL
Art: IRV NOVICK & DICK GIORDANO
Editing: JULIUS SCHWARTZ
WAIT--DON'T GO 'WAY--NOT TILL YOU'VE HEARD THE PUNCH LINE! NO KIDDING--
"This One'll KILL You, BATMAN!"
1

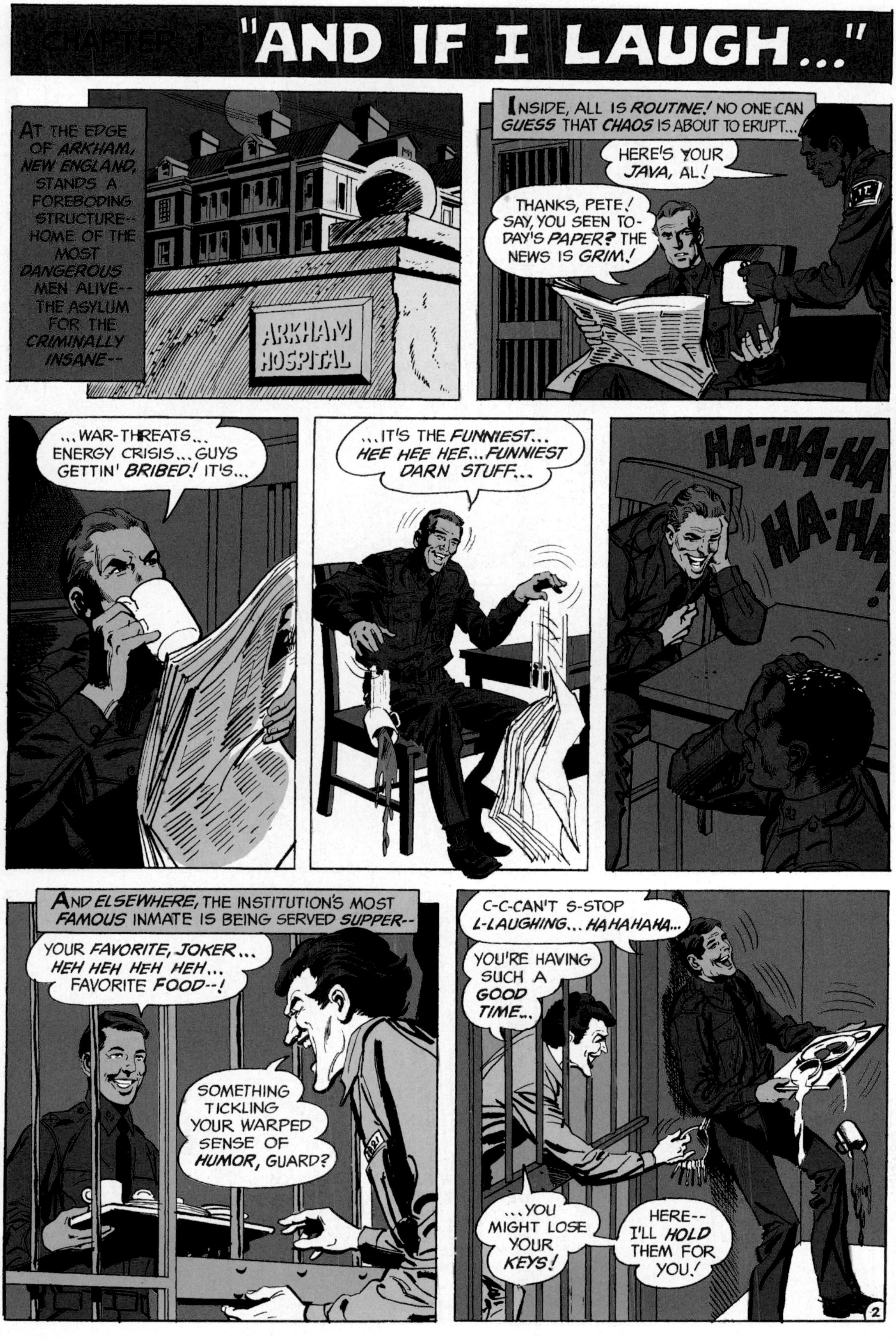
"AND IF I LAUGH..."
AT THE EDGE OF ARKHAM, NEW ENGLAND, STANDS A FOREBODING STRUCTURE-- HOME OF THE MOST DANGEROUS MEN ALIVE-- THE ASYLUM FOR THE CRIMINALLY INSANE--
ARKHAM HOSPITAL
INSIDE, ALL IS ROUTINE! NO ONE CAN GUESS THAT CHAOS IS ABOUT TO ERUPT...
HERE'S YOUR JAVA, AL!
THANKS, PETE! SAY, YOU SEEN TO-DAY'S PAPER? THE NEWS IS GRIM!
...WAR-THREATS... ENERGY CRISIS... GUYS GETTIN' BRIBED! IT'S...
...IT'S THE FUNNIEST... HEE HEE HEE... FUNNIEST DARN STUFF...
HA-HA-HA HA-HA!
AND ELSEWHERE, THE INSTITUTION'S MOST FAMOUS INMATE IS BEING SERVED SUPPER--
YOUR FAVORITE, JOKER... HEH HEH HEH HEH... FAVORITE FOOD--!
SOMETHING TICKLING YOUR WARPED SENSE OF HUMOR, GUARD?
C-C-CAN'T S-STOP L-LAUGHING... HAHAHAHA...
YOU'RE HAVING SUCH A GOOD TIME...
...YOU MIGHT LOSE YOUR KEYS!
HERE-- I'LL HOLD THEM FOR YOU!
2

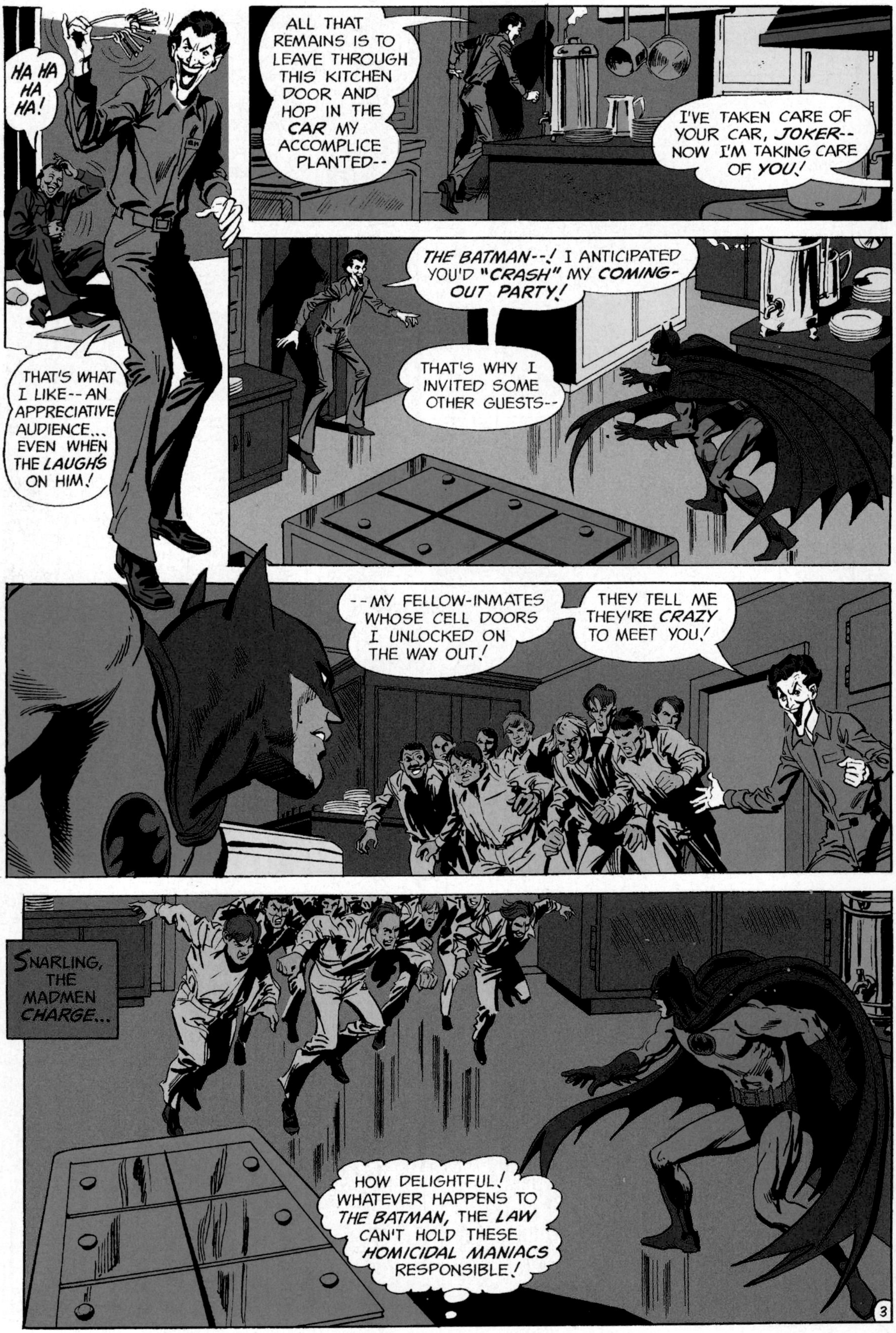
HA HA HA HA!
ALL THAT REMAINS IS TO LEAVE THROUGH THIS KITCHEN DOOR AND HOP IN THE CAR MY ACCOMPLICE PLANTED--
I'VE TAKEN CARE OF YOUR CAR, JOKER-- NOW I'M TAKING CARE OF YOU!
THAT'S WHAT I LIKE--AN APPRECIATIVE AUDIENCE... EVEN WHEN THE LAUGH'S ON HIM!
THE BATMAN--! I ANTICIPATED YOU'D "CRASH" MY COMING-OUT PARTY!
THAT'S WHY I INVITED SOME OTHER GUESTS--
--MY FELLOW-INMATES WHOSE CELL DOORS I UNLOCKED ON THE WAY OUT!
THEY TELL ME THEY'RE CRAZY TO MEET YOU!
SNARLING, THE MADMEN CHARGE...
HOW DELIGHTFUL! WHATEVER HAPPENS TO THE BATMAN, THE LAW CAN'T HOLD THESE HOMICIDAL MANIACS RESPONSIBLE!
3

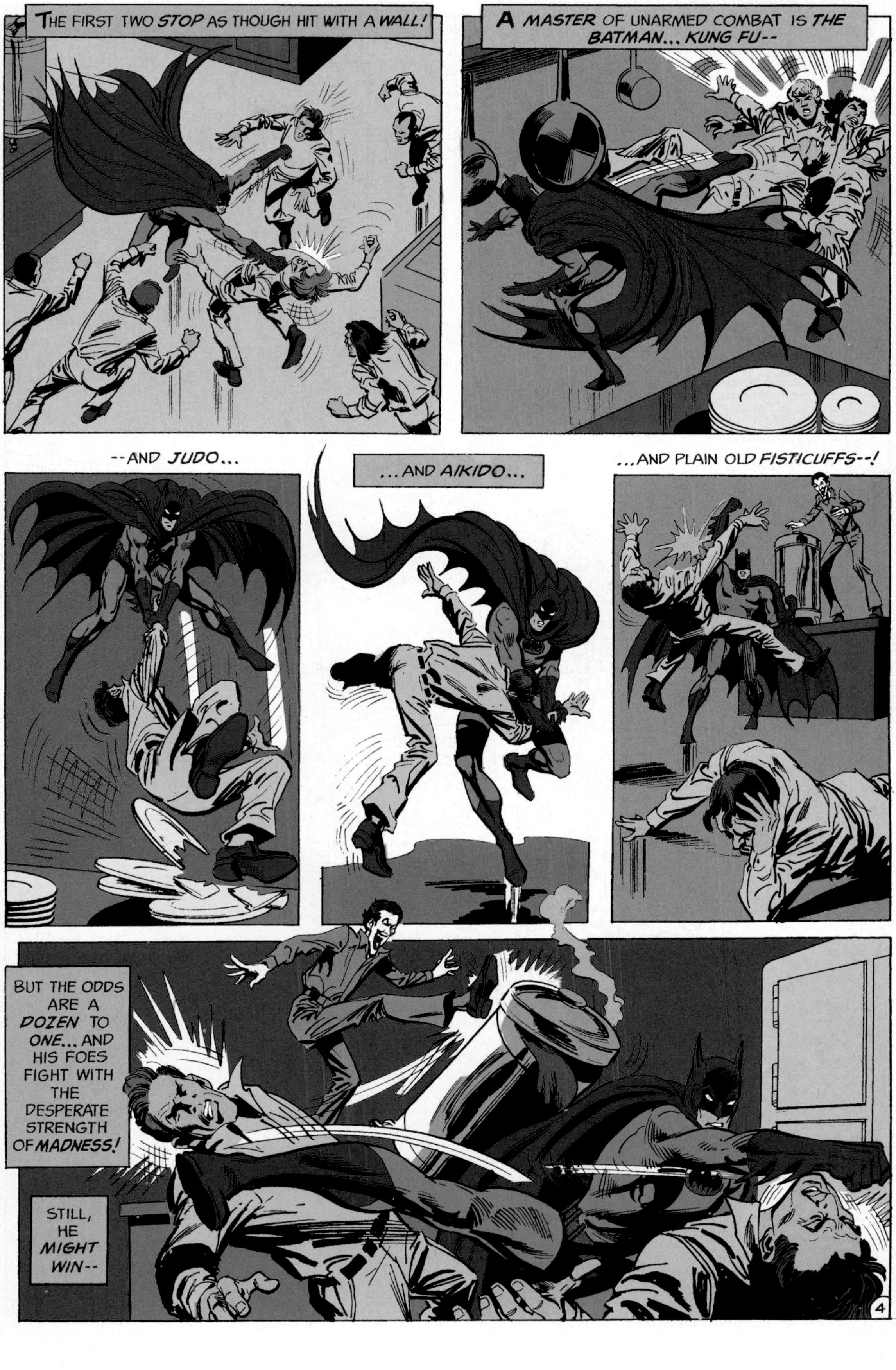
THE FIRST TWO STOP AS THOUGH HIT WITH A WALL!
A MASTER OF UNARMED COMBAT IS THE BATMAN... KUNG FU--
--AND JUDO...
...AND AIKIDO...
...AND PLAIN OLD FISTICUFFS--!
BUT THE ODDS ARE A DOZEN TO ONE... AND HIS FOES FIGHT WITH THE DESPERATE STRENGTH OF MADNESS!
STILL, HE MIGHT WIN--
4

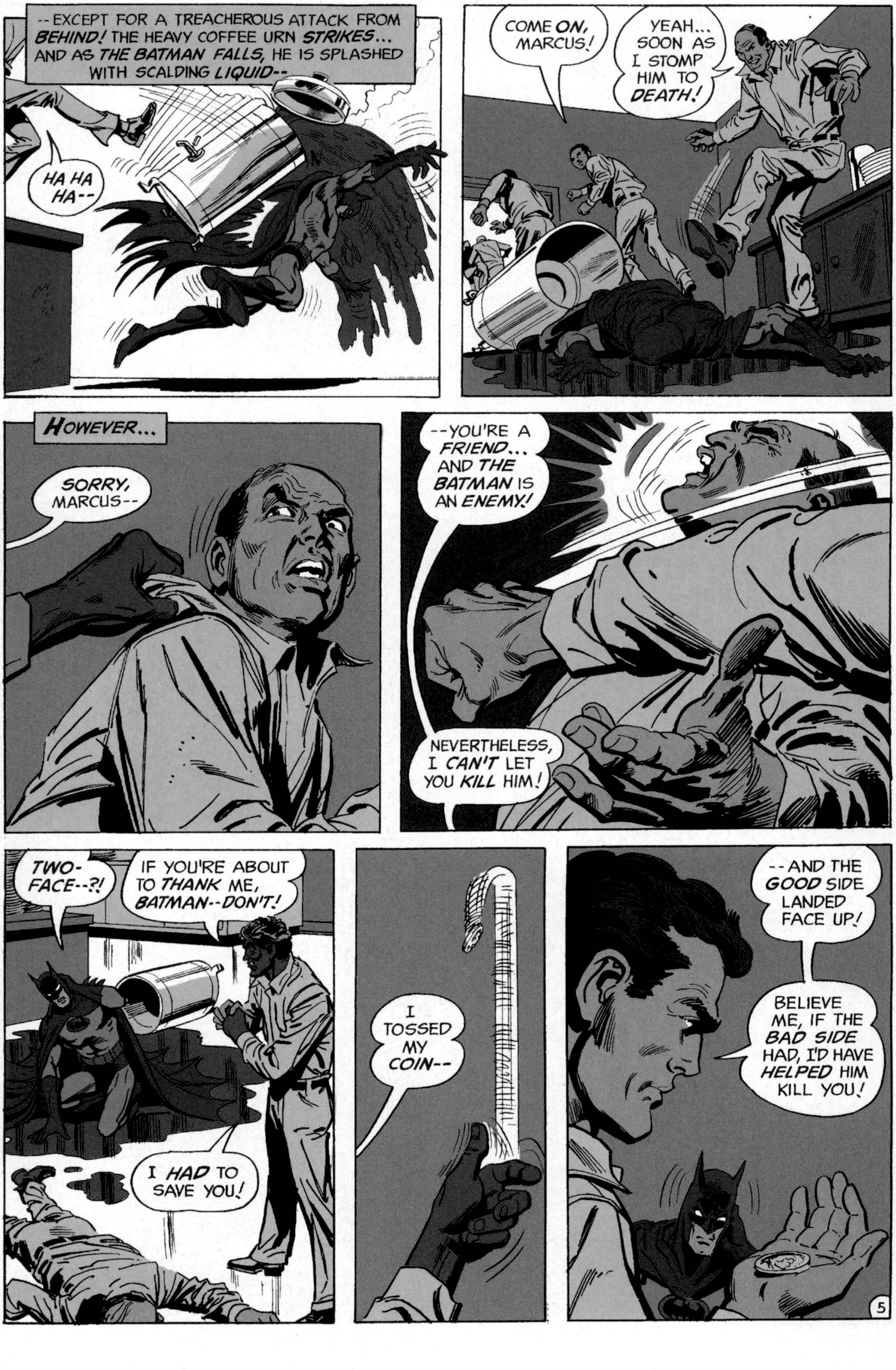
--EXCEPT FOR A TREACHEROUS ATTACK FROM BEHIND! THE HEAVY COFFEE URN STRIKES... AND AS THE BATMAN FALLS, HE IS SPLASHED WITH SCALDING LIQUID--
HA HA HA--
COME ON, MARCUS!
YEAH... SOON AS I STOMP HIM TO DEATH!
HOWEVER...
SORRY, MARCUS--
--YOU'RE A FRIEND... AND THE BATMAN IS AN ENEMY!
NEVERTHELESS, I CAN'T LET YOU KILL HIM!
TWO-FACE--?!
IF YOU'RE ABOUT TO THANK ME, BATMAN--DON'T!
I HAD TO SAVE YOU!
I TOSSED MY COIN--
--AND THE GOOD SIDE LANDED FACE UP!
BELIEVE ME, IF THE BAD SIDE HAD, I'D HAVE HELPED HIM KILL YOU!
5

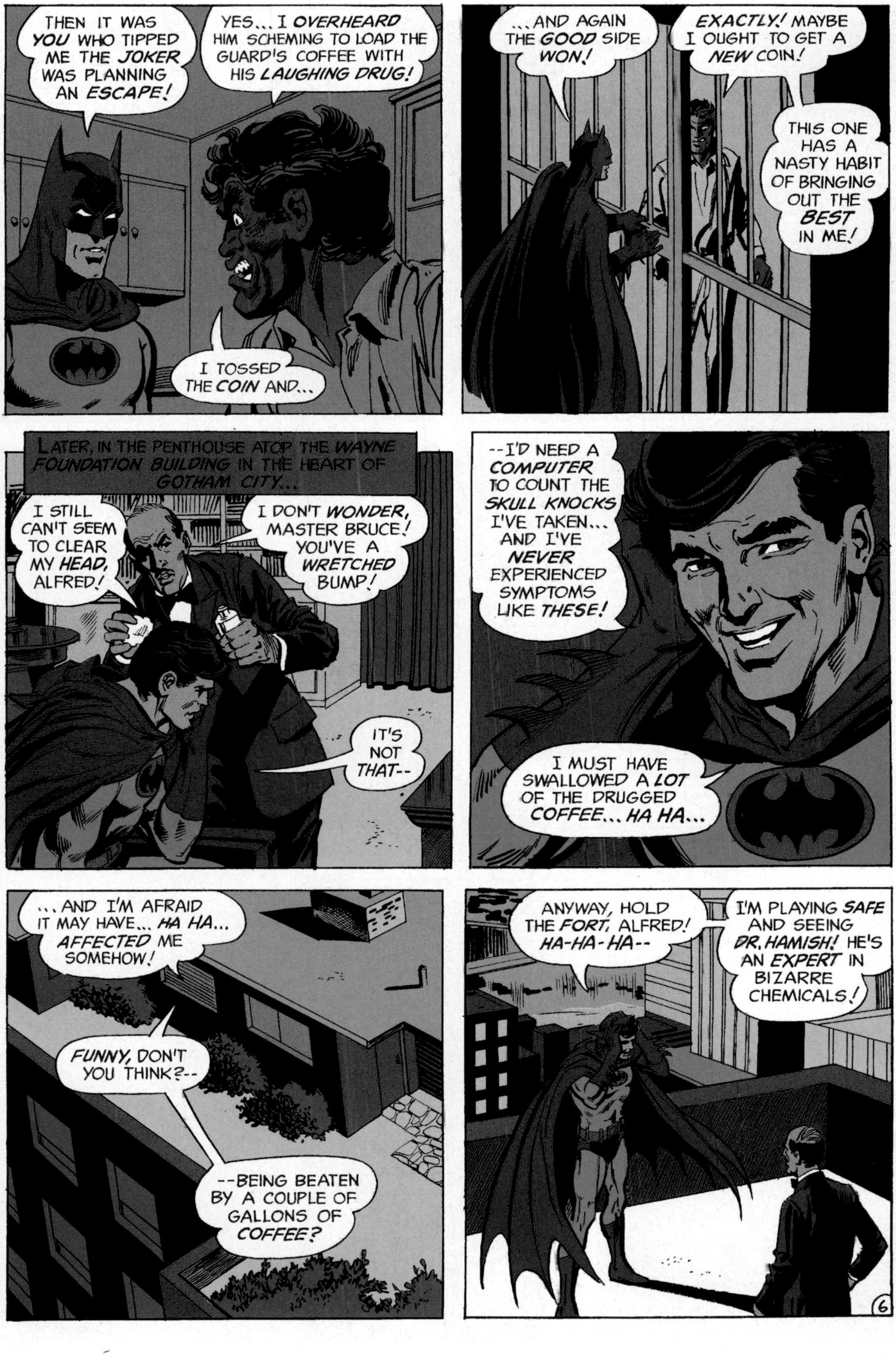
THEN IT WAS YOU WHO TIPPED ME THE JOKER WAS PLANNING AN ESCAPE!
YES... I OVERHEARD HIM SCHEMING TO LOAD THE GUARD'S COFFEE WITH HIS LAUGHING DRUG!
I TOSSED THE COIN AND...
...AND AGAIN THE GOOD SIDE WON!
EXACTLY! MAYBE I OUGHT TO GET A NEW COIN!
THIS ONE HAS A NASTY HABIT OF BRINGING OUT THE BEST IN ME!
LATER, IN THE PENTHOUSE ATOP THE WAYNE FOUNDATION BUILDING IN THE HEART OF GOTHAM CITY...
I STILL CAN'T SEEM TO CLEAR MY HEAD, ALFRED!
I DON'T WONDER, MASTER BRUCE! YOU'VE A WRETCHED BUMP!
IT'S NOT THAT--
--I'D NEED A COMPUTER TO COUNT THE SKULL KNOCKS I'VE TAKEN... AND I'VE NEVER EXPERIENCED SYMPTOMS LIKE THESE!
I MUST HAVE SWALLOWED A LOT OF THE DRUGGED COFFEE... HA HA...
...AND I'M AFRAID IT MAY HAVE... HA HA... AFFECTED ME SOMEHOW!
FUNNY, DON'T YOU THINK?--
--BEING BEATEN BY A COUPLE OF GALLONS OF COFFEE?
ANYWAY, HOLD THE FORT, ALFRED! HA-HA-HA--
I'M PLAYING SAFE AND SEEING DR. HAMISH! HE'S AN EXPERT IN BIZARRE CHEMICALS!
6

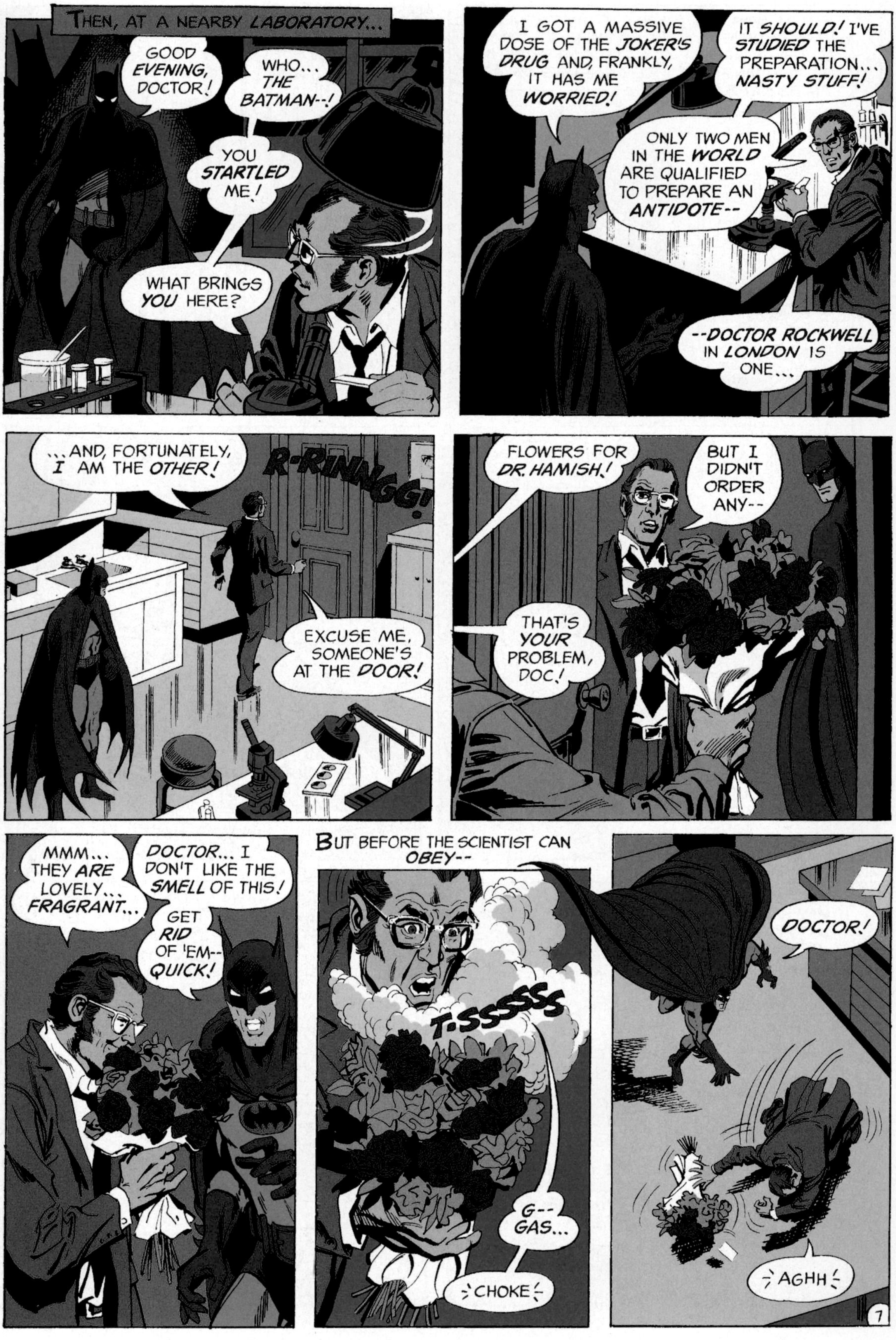
THEN, AT A NEARBY LABORATORY...
GOOD EVENING, DOCTOR!
WHO... THE BATMAN--!
YOU STARTLED ME!
WHAT BRINGS YOU HERE?
I GOT A MASSIVE DOSE OF THE JOKER'S DRUG AND, FRANKLY, IT HAS ME WORRIED!
IT SHOULD! I'VE STUDIED THE PREPARATION... NASTY STUFF!
ONLY TWO MEN IN THE WORLD ARE QUALIFIED TO PREPARE AN ANTIDOTE--
--DOCTOR ROCKWELL IN LONDON IS ONE...
...AND, FORTUNATELY, I AM THE OTHER!
R-RINNGG!
EXCUSE ME, SOMEONE'S AT THE DOOR!
FLOWERS FOR DR. HAMISH!
BUT I DIDN'T ORDER ANY--
THAT'S YOUR PROBLEM, DOC!
MMM... THEY ARE LOVELY... FRAGRANT...
DOCTOR... I DON'T LIKE THE SMELL OF THIS!
GET RID OF 'EM-- QUICK!
BUT BEFORE THE SCIENTIST CAN OBEY--
T-SSSSSS
G-- GAS...
CHOKE
DOCTOR!
AGHH
7

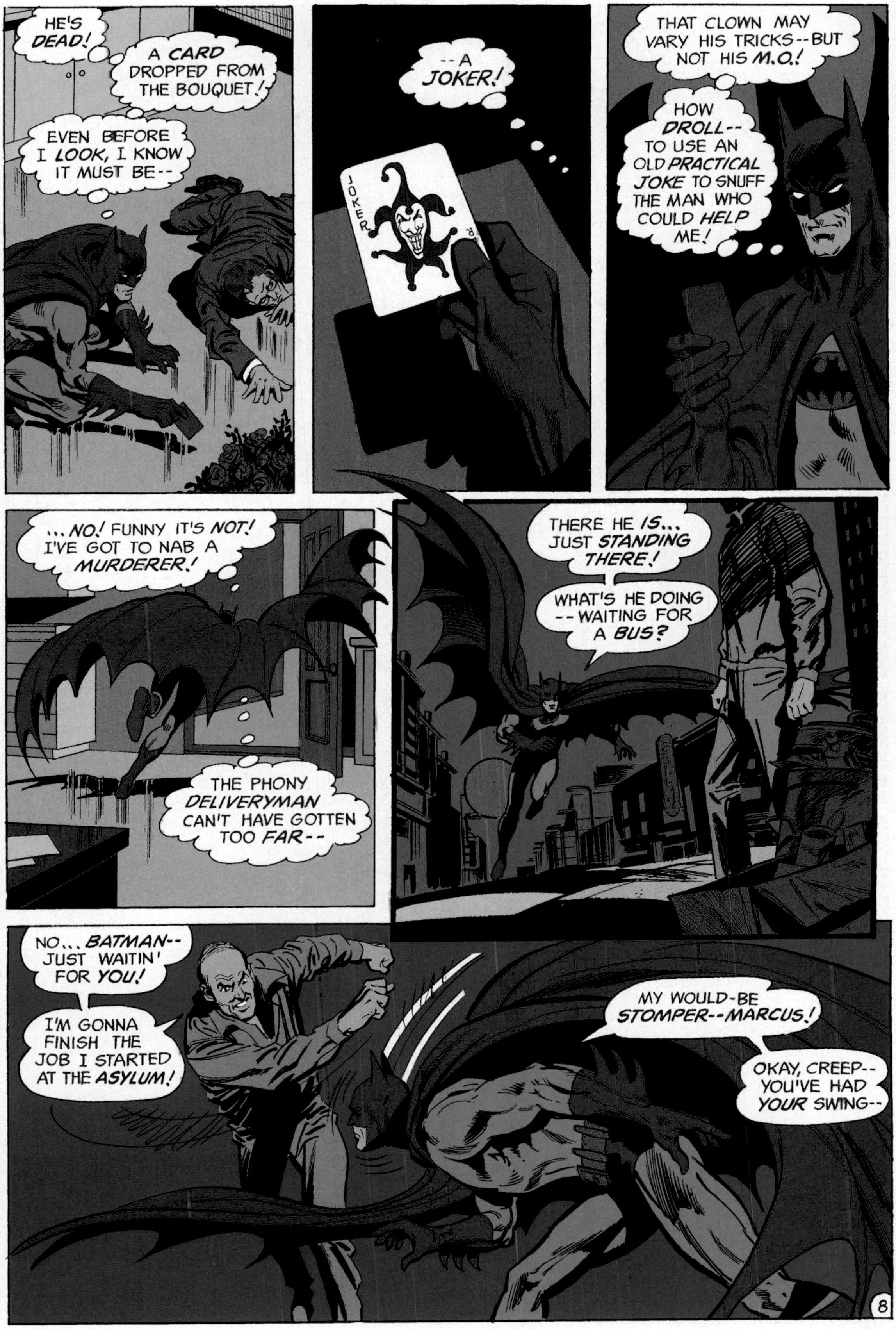
HE'S DEAD!
A CARD DROPPED FROM THE BOUQUET!
EVEN BEFORE I LOOK, I KNOW IT MUST BE--
--A JOKER!
JOKER
THAT CLOWN MAY VARY HIS TRICKS--BUT NOT HIS M.O.!
HOW DROLL-- TO USE AN OLD PRACTICAL JOKE TO SNUFF THE MAN WHO COULD HELP ME!
...NO! FUNNY IT'S NOT! I'VE GOT TO NAB A MURDERER!
THE PHONY DELIVERYMAN CAN'T HAVE GOTTEN TOO FAR--
THERE HE IS... JUST STANDING THERE!
WHAT'S HE DOING --WAITING FOR A BUS?
NO... BATMAN-- JUST WAITIN' FOR YOU!
I'M GONNA FINISH THE JOB I STARTED AT THE ASYLUM!
MY WOULD-BE STOMPER--MARCUS!
OKAY, CREEP-- YOU'VE HAD YOUR SWING--
8

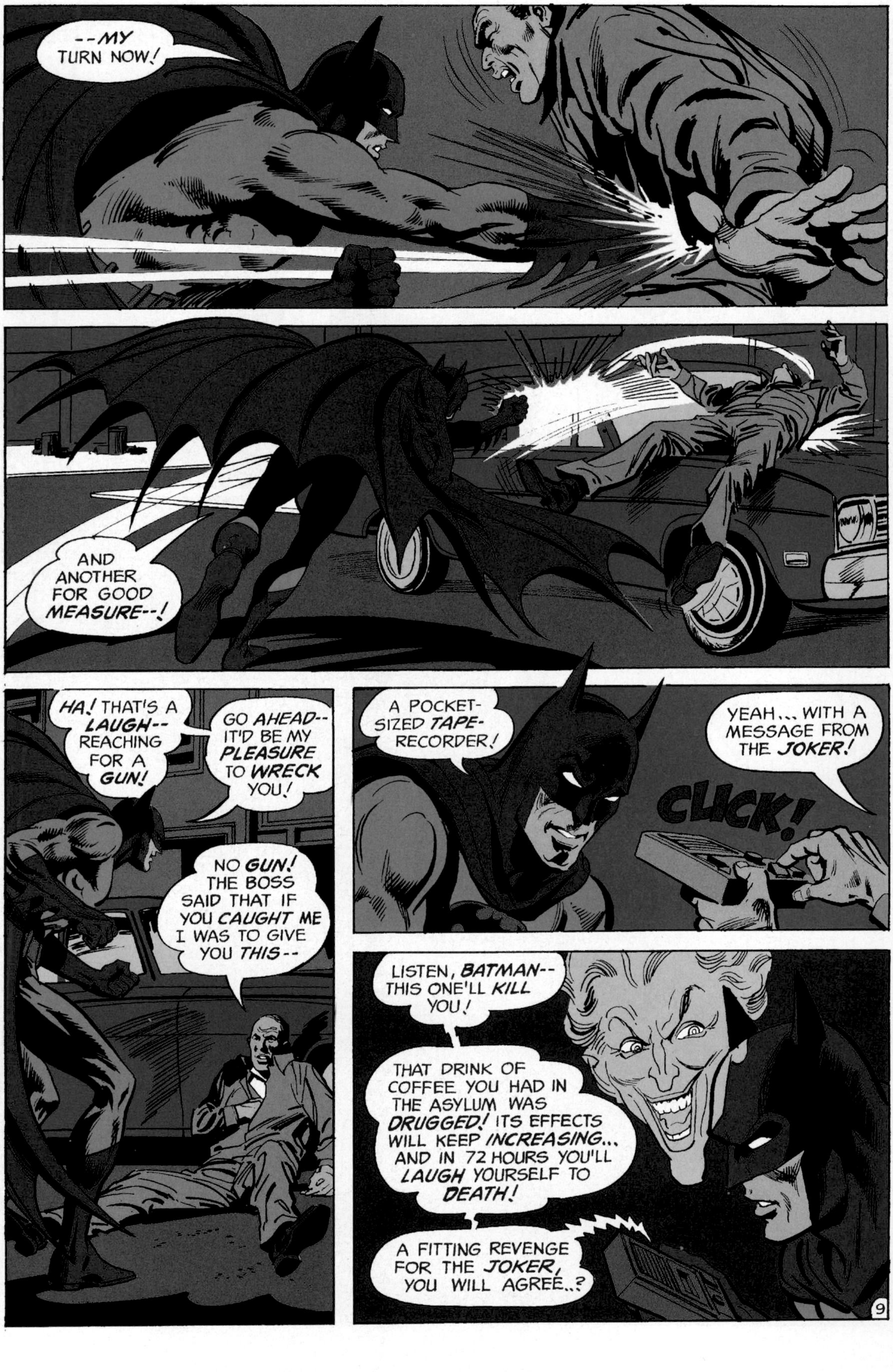
--MY TURN NOW!
AND ANOTHER FOR GOOD MEASURE--!
HA! THAT'S A LAUGH--REACHING FOR A GUN!
GO AHEAD--IT'D BE MY PLEASURE TO WRECK YOU!
NO GUN! THE BOSS SAID THAT IF YOU CAUGHT ME I WAS TO GIVE YOU THIS--
A POCKET-SIZED TAPE-RECORDER!
YEAH... WITH A MESSAGE FROM THE JOKER!
CLICK!
LISTEN, BATMAN--THIS ONE'LL KILL YOU!
THAT DRINK OF COFFEE YOU HAD IN THE ASYLUM WAS DRUGGED! ITS EFFECTS WILL KEEP INCREASING... AND IN 72 HOURS YOU'LL LAUGH YOURSELF TO DEATH!
A FITTING REVENGE FOR THE JOKER, YOU WILL AGREE..?
9

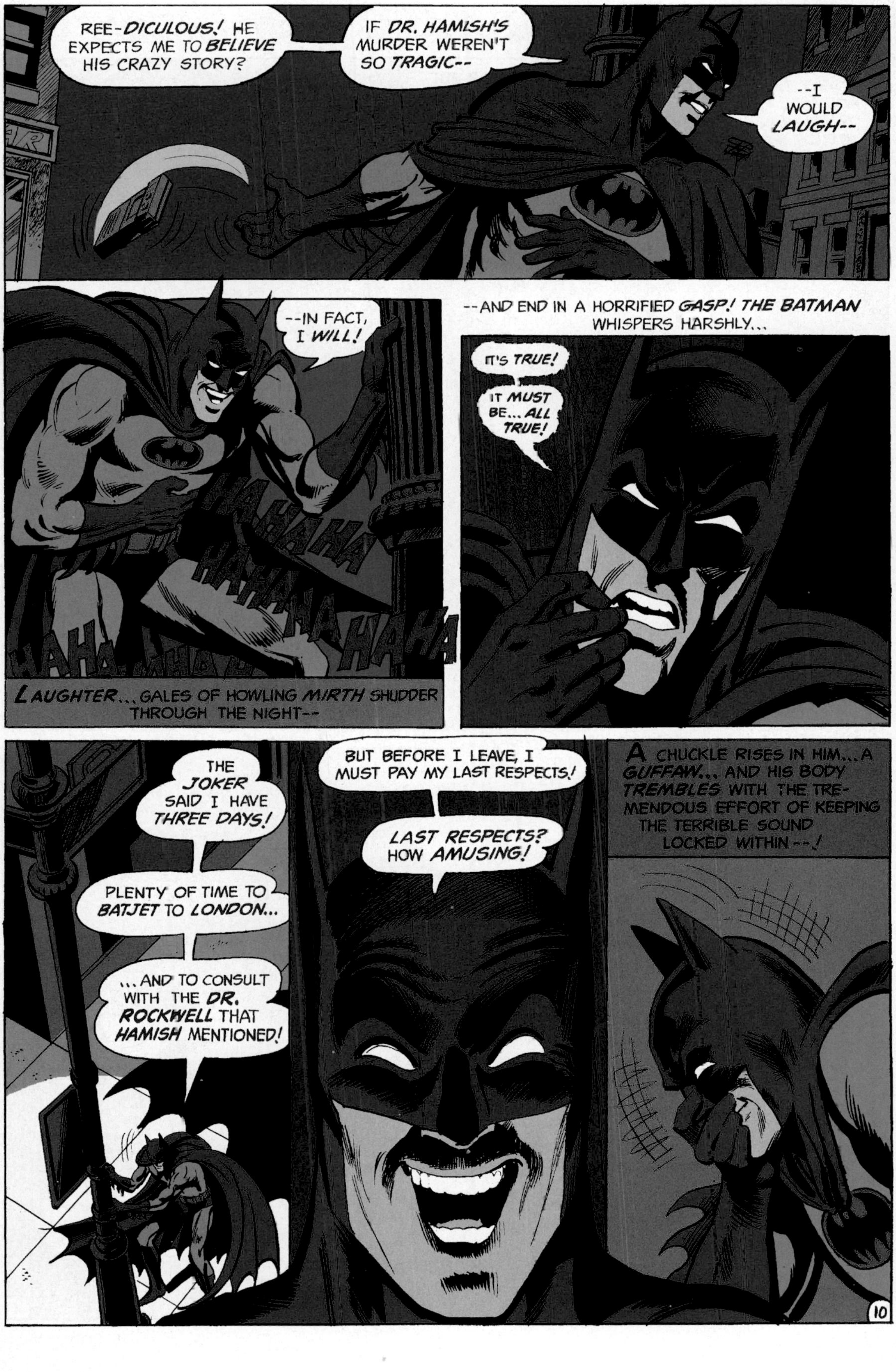

REE-DICULOUS! HE EXPECTS ME TO BELIEVE HIS CRAZY STORY?
IF DR. HAMISH'S MURDER WEREN'T SO TRAGIC--
--I WOULD LAUGH--
--IN FACT, I WILL!
HA HA HA HA HA HA HA HA HA HA HA HA
LAUGHTER... GALES OF HOWLING MIRTH SHUDDER THROUGH THE NIGHT--
--AND END IN A HORRIFIED GASP! THE BATMAN WHISPERS HARSHLY...
IT'S TRUE!
IT MUST BE... ALL TRUE!
THE JOKER SAID I HAVE THREE DAYS!
PLENTY OF TIME TO BATJET TO LONDON...
...AND TO CONSULT WITH THE DR. ROCKWELL THAT HAMISH MENTIONED!
BUT BEFORE I LEAVE, I MUST PAY MY LAST RESPECTS!
LAST RESPECTS? HOW AMUSING!
A CHUCKLE RISES IN HIM... A GUFFAW... AND HIS BODY TREMBLES WITH THE TREMENDOUS EFFORT OF KEEPING THE TERRIBLE SOUND LOCKED WITHIN--!
10

CHAPTER 2: "...'TIS THAT I MAY NOT WEEP!"

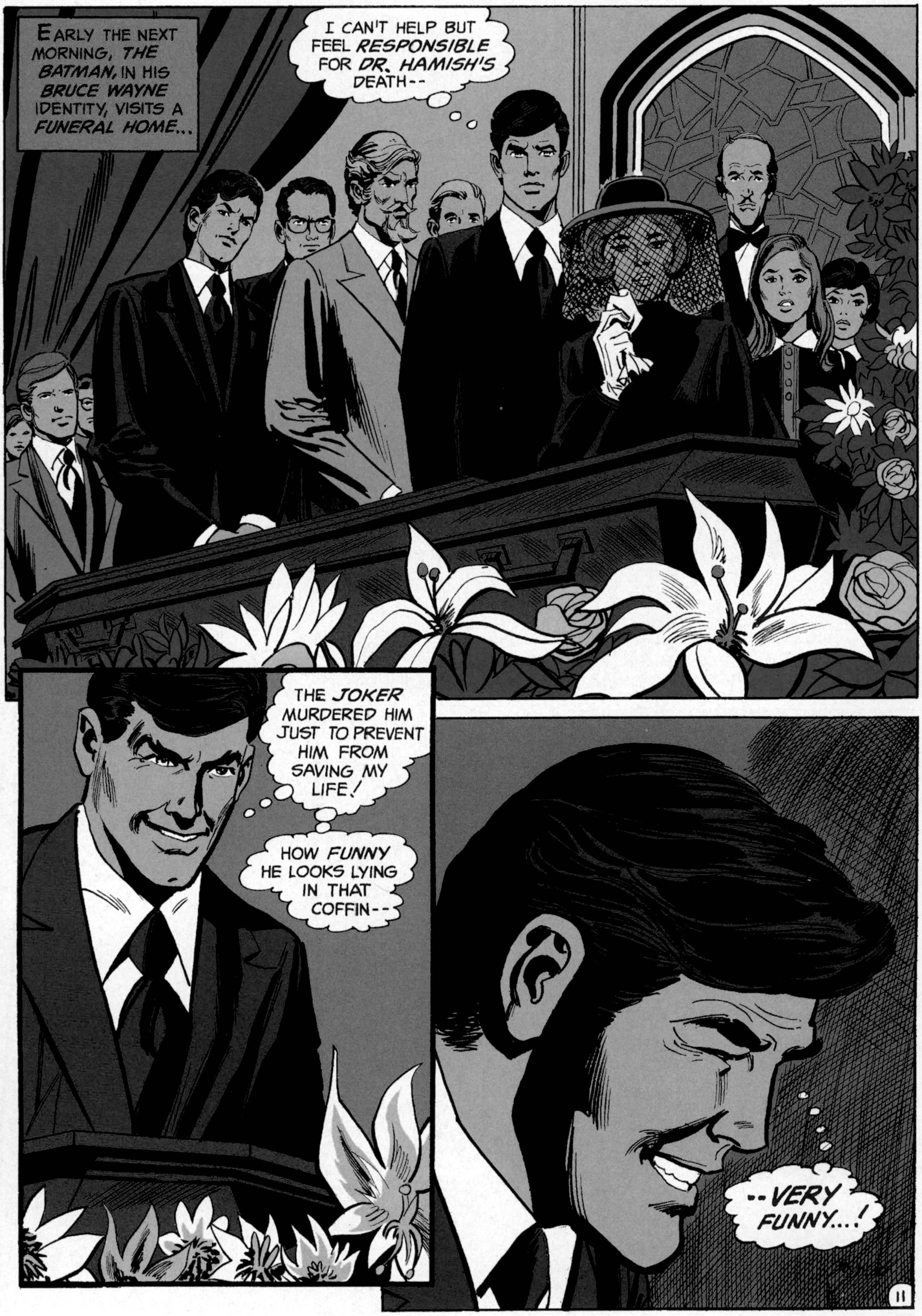
EARLY THE NEXT MORNING, THE BATMAN, IN HIS BRUCE WAYNE IDENTITY, VISITS A FUNERAL HOME...
I CAN'T HELP BUT FEEL RESPONSIBLE FOR DR. HAMISH'S DEATH--
THE JOKER MURDERED HIM JUST TO PREVENT HIM FROM SAVING MY LIFE!
HOW FUNNY HE LOOKS LYING IN THAT COFFIN--
--VERY FUNNY...!
11

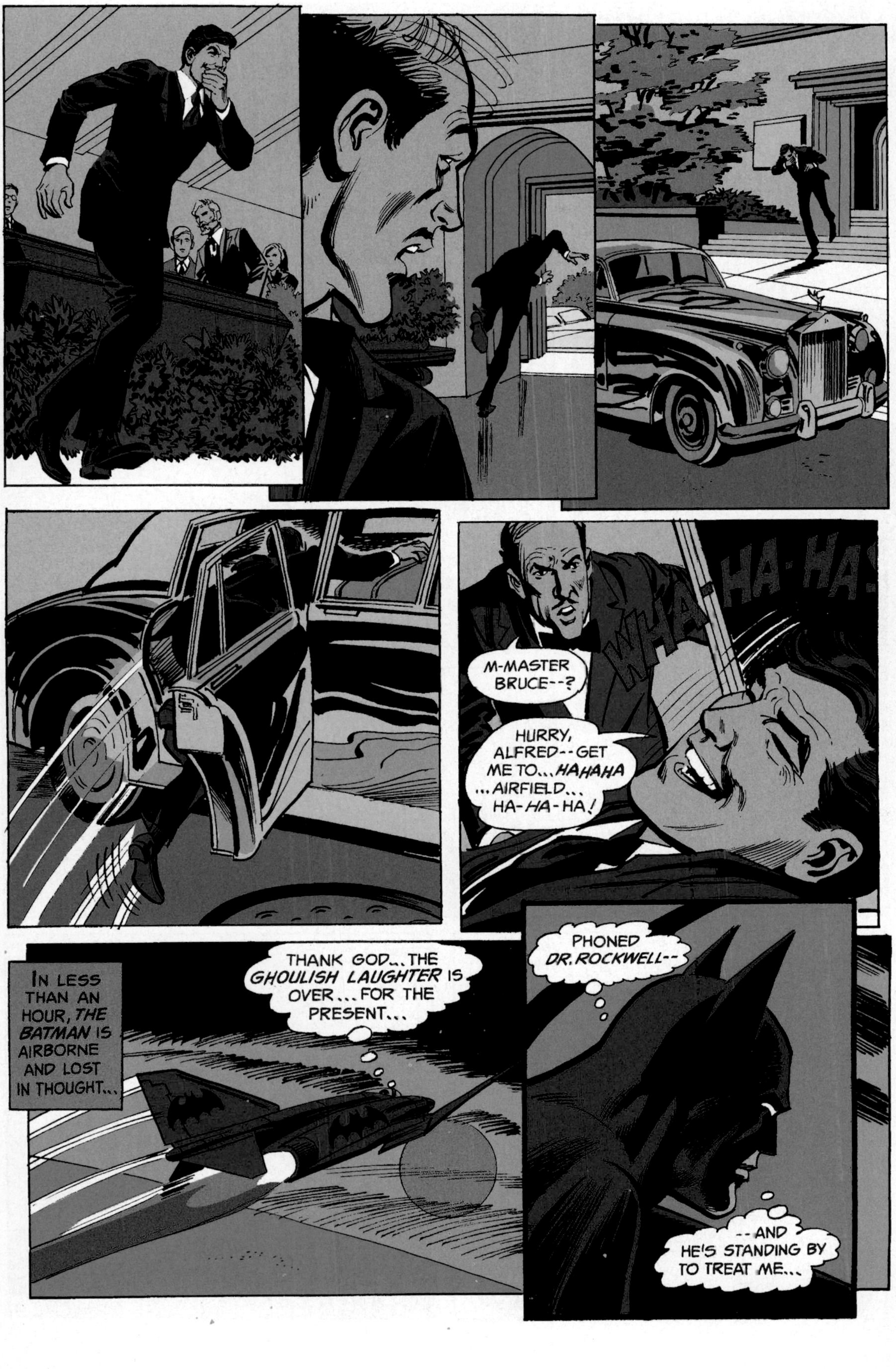
M-MASTER BRUCE--?
HURRY, ALFRED--GET ME TO...HAHAHA ...AIRFIELD... HA-HA-HA!
WHA
HA-HA
IN LESS THAN AN HOUR, THE BATMAN IS AIRBORNE AND LOST IN THOUGHT...
THANK GOD...THE GHOULISH LAUGHTER IS OVER...FOR THE PRESENT...
PHONED DR. ROCKWELL--
--AND HE'S STANDING BY TO TREAT ME...

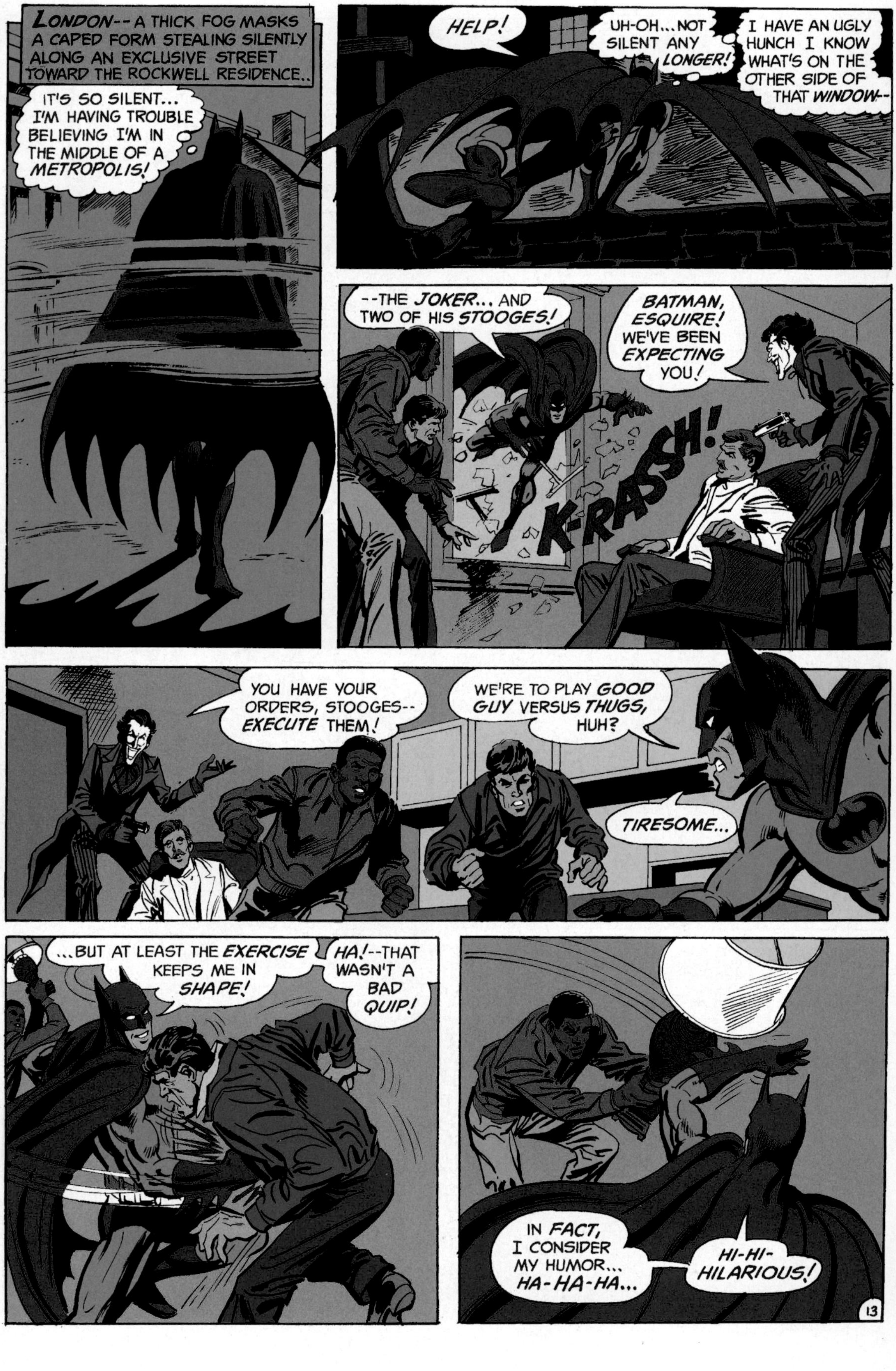
LONDON-- A THICK FOG MASKS A CAPED FORM STEALING SILENTLY ALONG AN EXCLUSIVE STREET TOWARD THE ROCKWELL RESIDENCE..
IT'S SO SILENT... I'M HAVING TROUBLE BELIEVING I'M IN THE MIDDLE OF A METROPOLIS!
HELP!
UH-OH... NOT SILENT ANY LONGER!
I HAVE AN UGLY HUNCH I KNOW WHAT'S ON THE OTHER SIDE OF THAT WINDOW--
--THE JOKER... AND TWO OF HIS STOOGES!
BATMAN, ESQUIRE! WE'VE BEEN EXPECTING YOU!
K-RASSH!
YOU HAVE YOUR ORDERS, STOOGES-- EXECUTE THEM!
WE'RE TO PLAY GOOD GUY VERSUS THUGS, HUH?
TIRESOME...
...BUT AT LEAST THE EXERCISE KEEPS ME IN SHAPE!
HA!--THAT WASN'T A BAD QUIP!
IN FACT, I CONSIDER MY HUMOR... HA-HA-HA...
HI-HI-HILARIOUS!
13

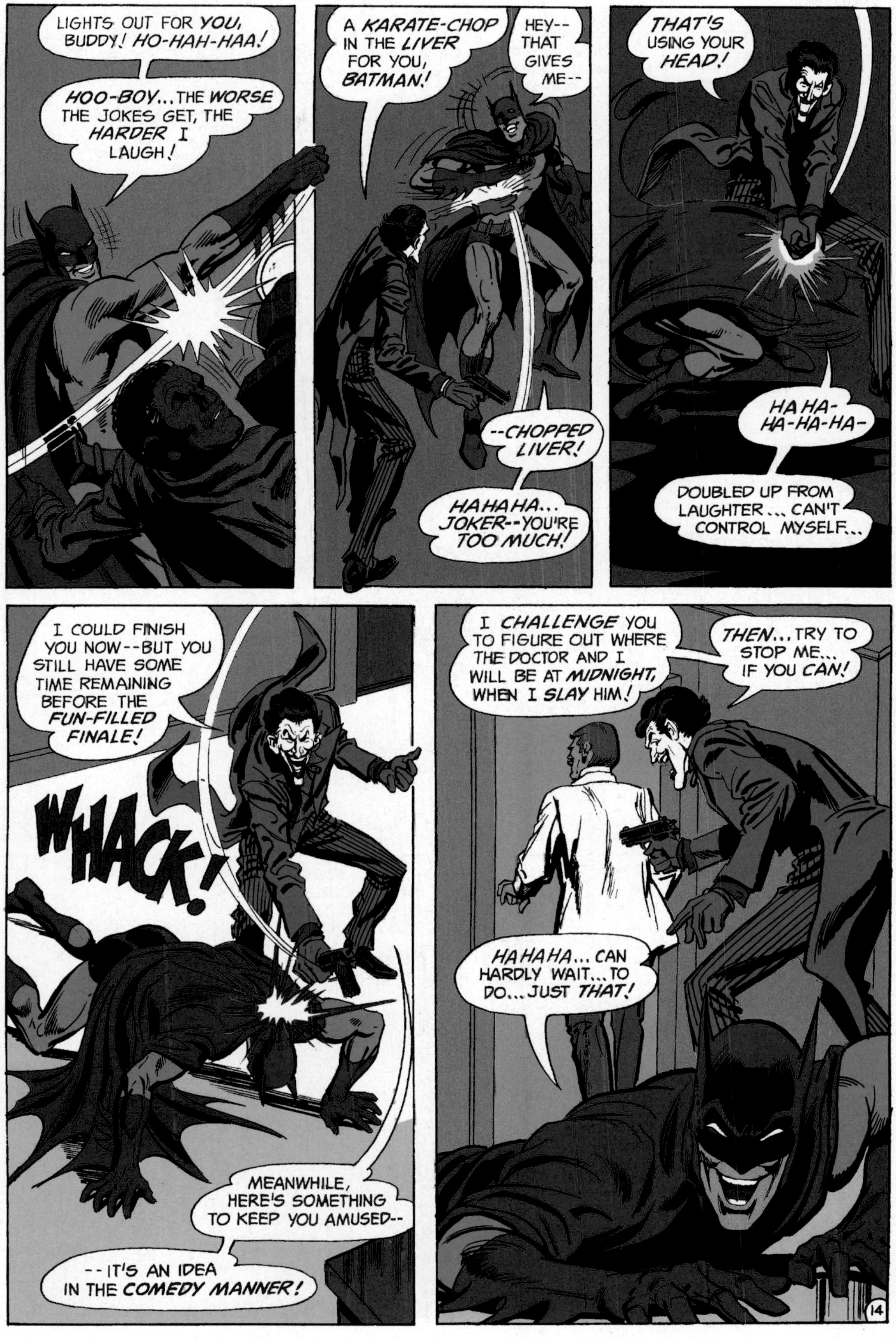
LIGHTS OUT FOR YOU, BUDDY! HO-HAH-HAA!
HOO-BOY... THE WORSE THE JOKES GET, THE HARDER I LAUGH!
A KARATE-CHOP IN THE LIVER FOR YOU, BATMAN!
HEY-- THAT GIVES ME--
--CHOPPED LIVER!
HAHAHA... JOKER--YOU'RE TOO MUCH!
THAT'S USING YOUR HEAD!
HA HA-HA-HA-HA-
DOUBLED UP FROM LAUGHTER... CAN'T CONTROL MYSELF...
I COULD FINISH YOU NOW--BUT YOU STILL HAVE SOME TIME REMAINING BEFORE THE FUN-FILLED FINALE!
WHACK!
MEANWHILE, HERE'S SOMETHING TO KEEP YOU AMUSED--
--IT'S AN IDEA IN THE COMEDY MANNER!
I CHALLENGE YOU TO FIGURE OUT WHERE THE DOCTOR AND I WILL BE AT MIDNIGHT, WHEN I SLAY HIM!
THEN... TRY TO STOP ME... IF YOU CAN!
HAHAHA... CAN HARDLY WAIT... TO DO... JUST THAT!
14

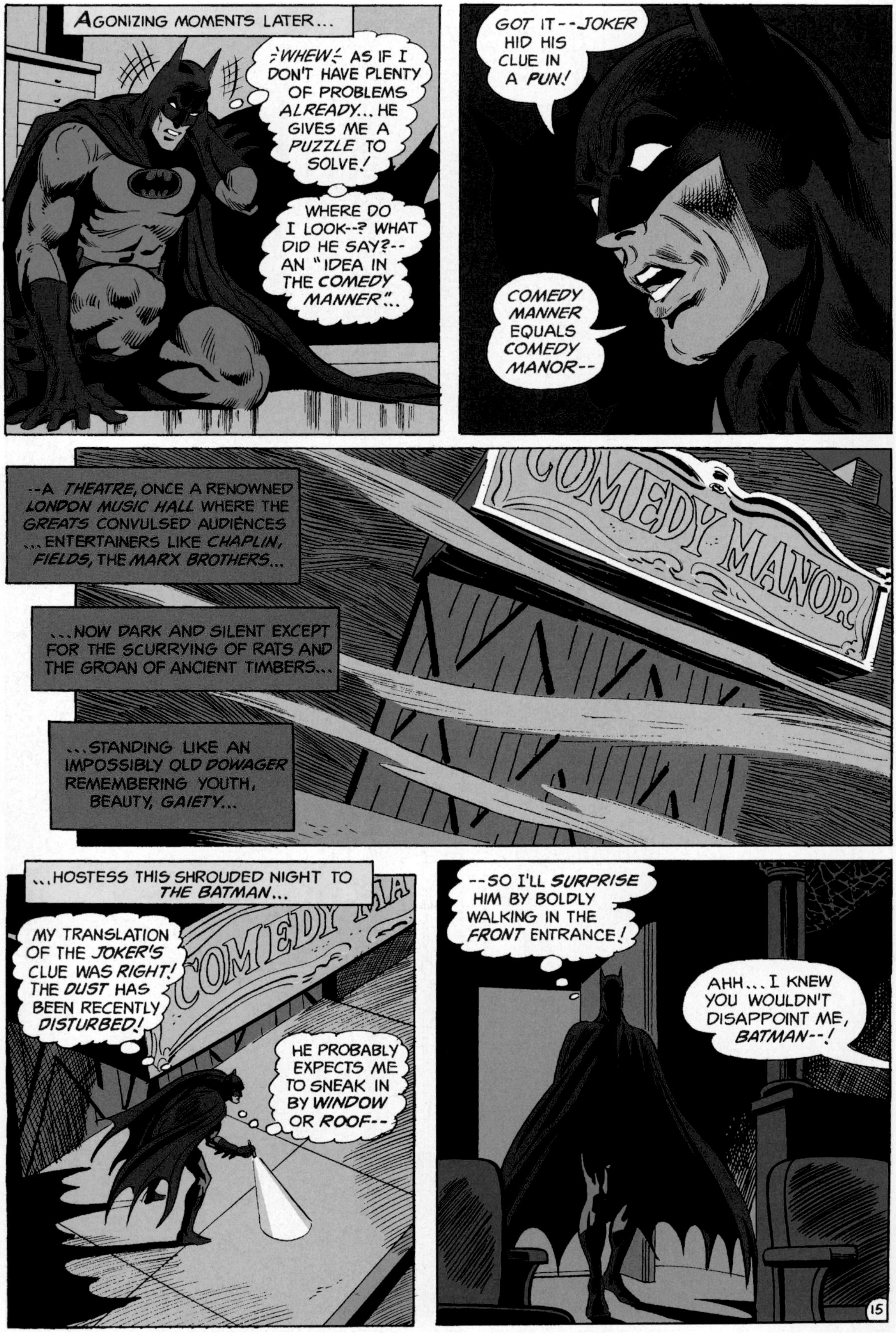
AGONIZING MOMENTS LATER...
WHEW! AS IF I DON'T HAVE PLENTY OF PROBLEMS ALREADY... HE GIVES ME A PUZZLE TO SOLVE!
WHERE DO I LOOK--? WHAT DID HE SAY?-- AN "IDEA IN THE COMEDY MANNER"...
GOT IT--JOKER HID HIS CLUE IN A PUN!
COMEDY MANNER EQUALS COMEDY MANOR--
--A THEATRE, ONCE A RENOWNED LONDON MUSIC HALL WHERE THE GREATS CONVULSED AUDIENCES ...ENTERTAINERS LIKE CHAPLIN, FIELDS, THE MARX BROTHERS...
COMEDY MANOR
...NOW DARK AND SILENT EXCEPT FOR THE SCURRYING OF RATS AND THE GROAN OF ANCIENT TIMBERS...
...STANDING LIKE AN IMPOSSIBLY OLD DOWAGER REMEMBERING YOUTH, BEAUTY, GAIETY...
...HOSTESS THIS SHROUDED NIGHT TO THE BATMAN...
MY TRANSLATION OF THE JOKER'S CLUE WAS RIGHT! THE DUST HAS BEEN RECENTLY DISTURBED!
HE PROBABLY EXPECTS ME TO SNEAK IN BY WINDOW OR ROOF--
--SO I'LL SURPRISE HIM BY BOLDLY WALKING IN THE FRONT ENTRANCE!
AHH... I KNEW YOU WOULDN'T DISAPPOINT ME, BATMAN--!
15

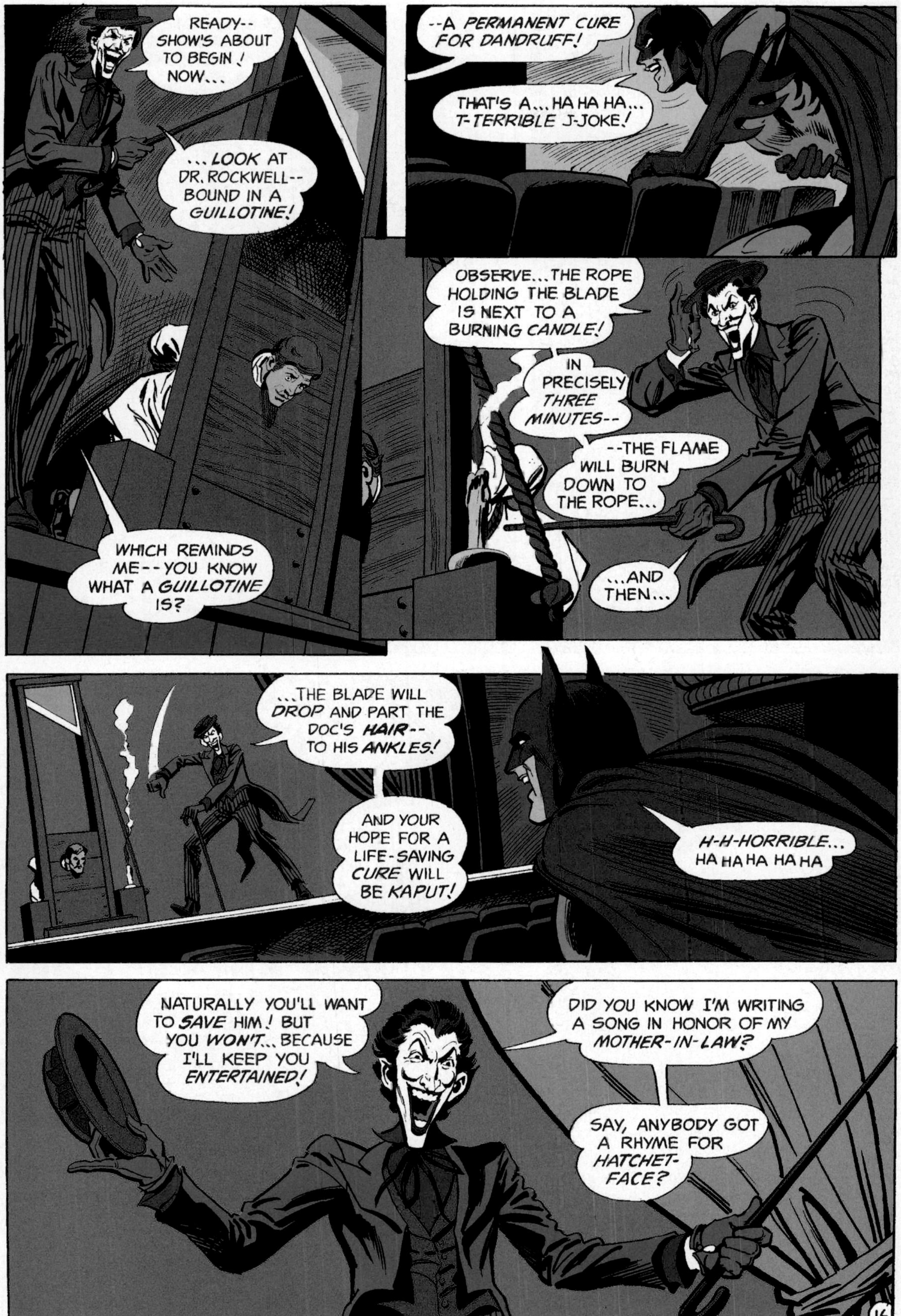

READY-- SHOW'S ABOUT TO BEGIN! NOW...
...LOOK AT DR. ROCKWELL-- BOUND IN A GUILLOTINE!
WHICH REMINDS ME--YOU KNOW WHAT A GUILLOTINE IS?
--A PERMANENT CURE FOR DANDRUFF!
THAT'S A...HA HA HA... T-TERRIBLE J-JOKE!
OBSERVE...THE ROPE HOLDING THE BLADE IS NEXT TO A BURNING CANDLE!
IN PRECISELY THREE MINUTES--
--THE FLAME WILL BURN DOWN TO THE ROPE...
...AND THEN...
...THE BLADE WILL DROP AND PART THE DOC'S HAIR-- TO HIS ANKLES!
AND YOUR HOPE FOR A LIFE-SAVING CURE WILL BE KAPUT!
H-H-HORRIBLE... HA HA HA HA HA
NATURALLY YOU'LL WANT TO SAVE HIM! BUT YOU WON'T... BECAUSE I'LL KEEP YOU ENTERTAINED!
DID YOU KNOW I'M WRITING A SONG IN HONOR OF MY MOTHER-IN-LAW?
SAY, ANYBODY GOT A RHYME FOR HATCHET-FACE?
16

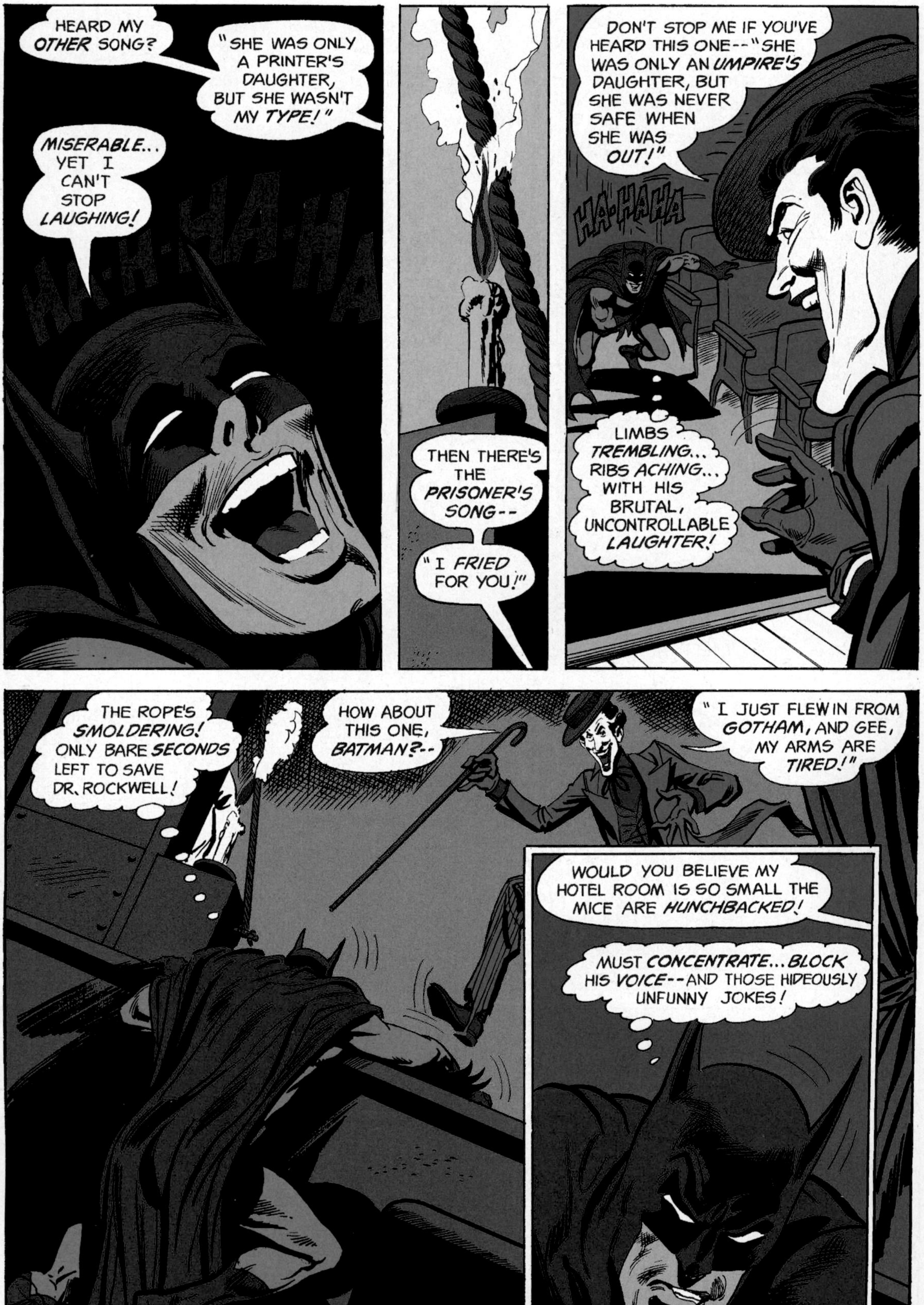
HEARD MY OTHER SONG?
"SHE WAS ONLY A PRINTER'S DAUGHTER, BUT SHE WASN'T MY TYPE!"
MISERABLE... YET I CAN'T STOP LAUGHING!
HA-HA-HA-HA
THEN THERE'S THE PRISONER'S SONG--
"I FRIED FOR YOU!"
DON'T STOP ME IF YOU'VE HEARD THIS ONE--"SHE WAS ONLY AN UMPIRE'S DAUGHTER, BUT SHE WAS NEVER SAFE WHEN SHE WAS OUT!"
HA-HAHA
LIMBS TREMBLING... RIBS ACHING... WITH HIS BRUTAL, UNCONTROLLABLE LAUGHTER!
THE ROPE'S SMOLDERING! ONLY BARE SECONDS LEFT TO SAVE DR. ROCKWELL!
HOW ABOUT THIS ONE, BATMAN?--
"I JUST FLEW IN FROM GOTHAM, AND GEE, MY ARMS ARE TIRED!"
WOULD YOU BELIEVE MY HOTEL ROOM IS SO SMALL THE MICE ARE HUNCHBACKED!
MUST CONCENTRATE... BLOCK HIS VOICE--AND THOSE HIDEOUSLY UNFUNNY JOKES!
17

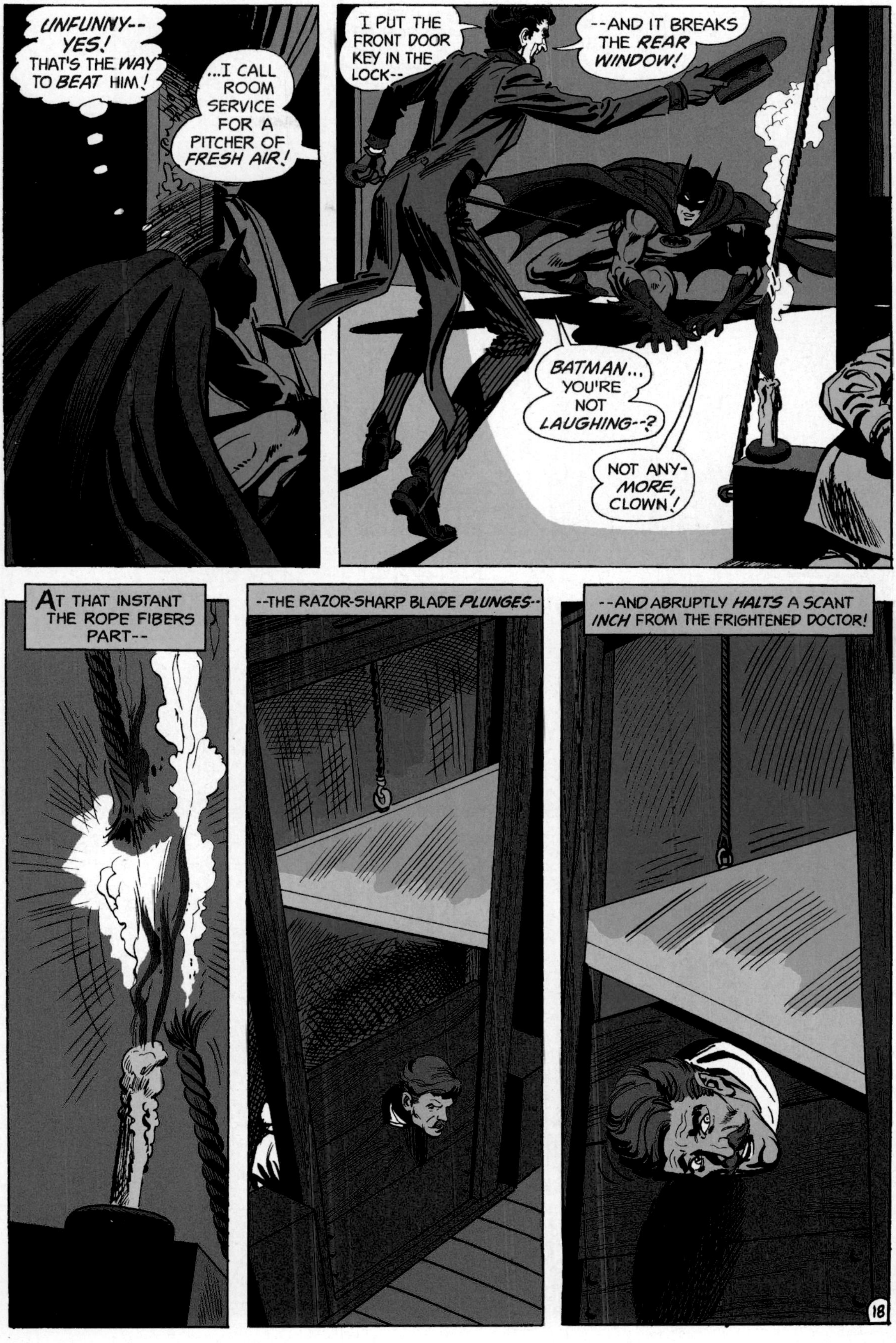
UNFUNNY-- YES! THAT'S THE WAY TO BEAT HIM!
...I CALL ROOM SERVICE FOR A PITCHER OF FRESH AIR!
I PUT THE FRONT DOOR KEY IN THE LOCK--
--AND IT BREAKS THE REAR WINDOW!
BATMAN... YOU'RE NOT LAUGHING--?
NOT ANY-MORE, CLOWN!
AT THAT INSTANT THE ROPE FIBERS PART--
--THE RAZOR-SHARP BLADE PLUNGES--
--AND ABRUPTLY HALTS A SCANT INCH FROM THE FRIGHTENED DOCTOR!
18

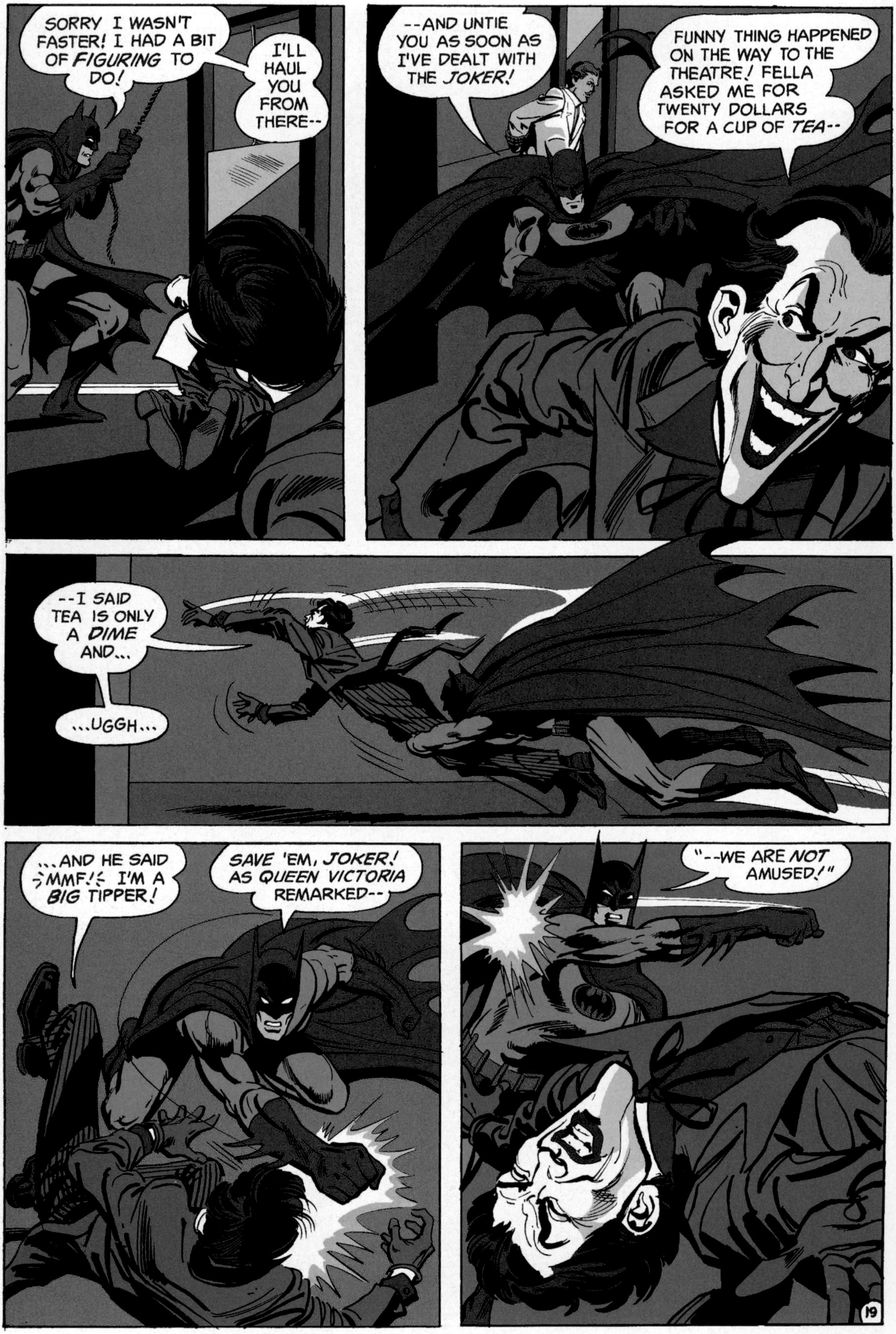

SORRY I WASN'T FASTER! I HAD A BIT OF FIGURING TO DO!
I'LL HAUL YOU FROM THERE--
--AND UNTIE YOU AS SOON AS I'VE DEALT WITH THE JOKER!
FUNNY THING HAPPENED ON THE WAY TO THE THEATRE! FELLA ASKED ME FOR TWENTY DOLLARS FOR A CUP OF TEA--
--I SAID TEA IS ONLY A DIME AND...
...UGGH...
...AND HE SAID MMF! I'M A BIG TIPPER!
SAVE 'EM, JOKER! AS QUEEN VICTORIA REMARKED--
"--WE ARE NOT AMUSED!"
19

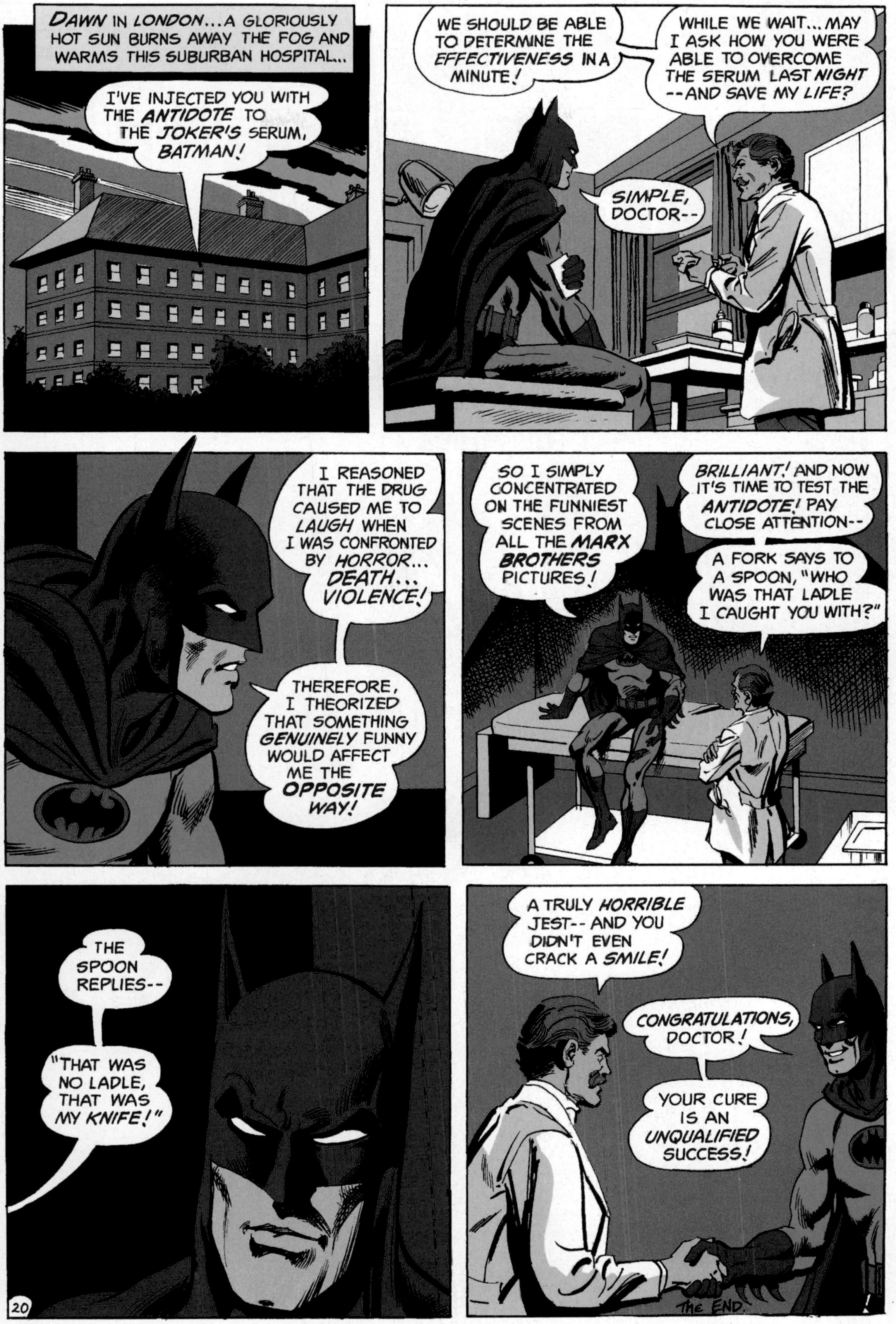
DAWN IN LONDON... A GLORIOUSLY HOT SUN BURNS AWAY THE FOG AND WARMS THIS SUBURBAN HOSPITAL...
I'VE INJECTED YOU WITH THE ANTIDOTE TO THE JOKER'S SERUM, BATMAN!
WE SHOULD BE ABLE TO DETERMINE THE EFFECTIVENESS IN A MINUTE!
WHILE WE WAIT... MAY I ASK HOW YOU WERE ABLE TO OVERCOME THE SERUM LAST NIGHT --AND SAVE MY LIFE?
SIMPLE, DOCTOR--
I REASONED THAT THE DRUG CAUSED ME TO LAUGH WHEN I WAS CONFRONTED BY HORROR... DEATH... VIOLENCE!
THEREFORE, I THEORIZED THAT SOMETHING GENUINELY FUNNY WOULD AFFECT ME THE OPPOSITE WAY!
SO I SIMPLY CONCENTRATED ON THE FUNNIEST SCENES FROM ALL THE MARX BROTHERS PICTURES!
BRILLIANT! AND NOW IT'S TIME TO TEST THE ANTIDOTE! PAY CLOSE ATTENTION--
A FORK SAYS TO A SPOON, "WHO WAS THAT LADLE I CAUGHT YOU WITH?"
THE SPOON REPLIES--
"THAT WAS NO LADLE, THAT WAS MY KNIFE!"
20
A TRULY HORRIBLE JEST-- AND YOU DIDN'T EVEN CRACK A SMILE!
CONGRATULATIONS, DOCTOR!
YOUR CURE IS AN UNQUALIFIED SUCCESS!
THE END.

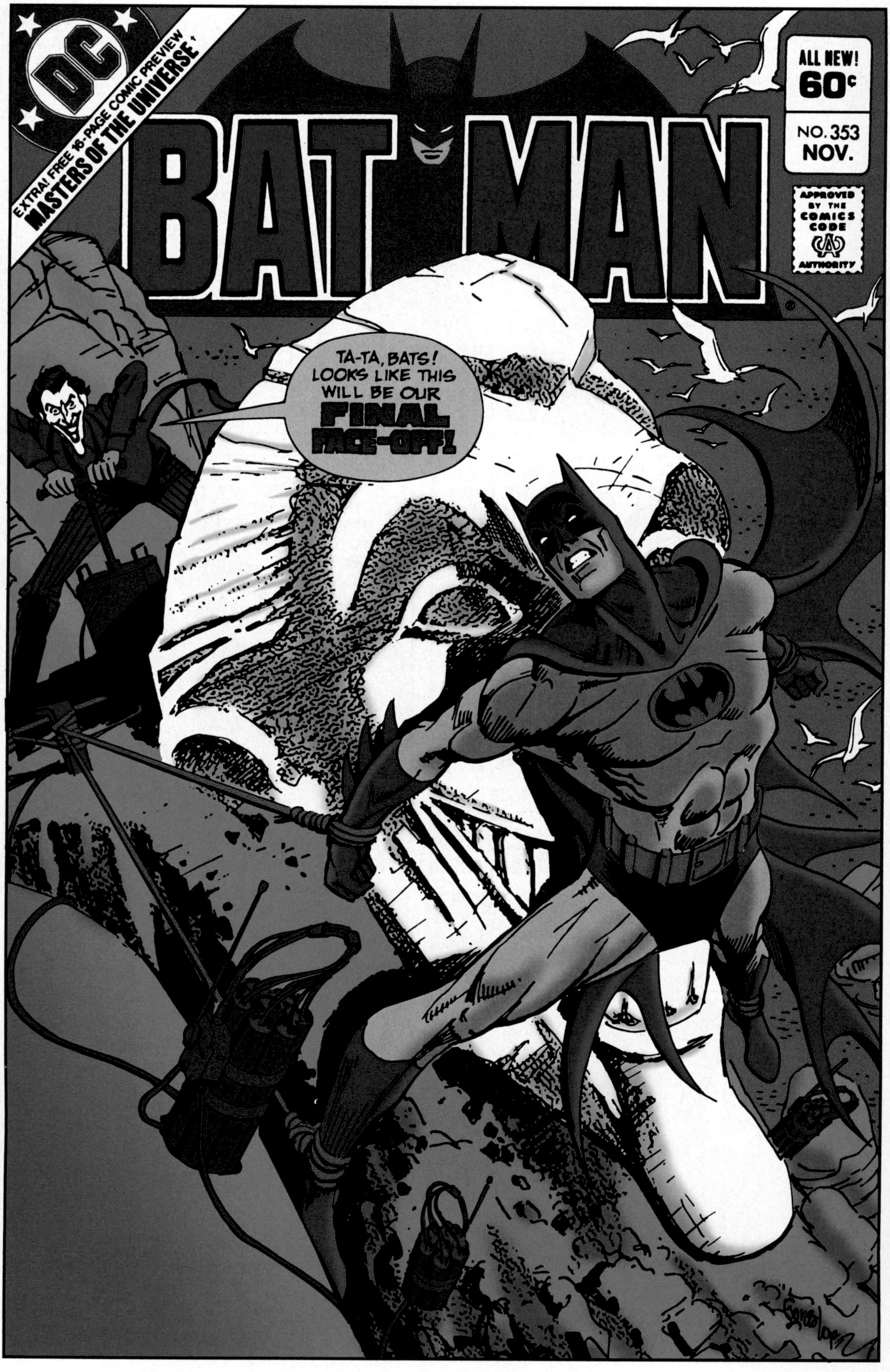
EXTRA! FREE 16-PAGE COMIC PREVIEW
MASTERS OF THE UNIVERSE
BATMAN
ALL NEW! 60¢
NO. 353 NOV.
APPROVED BY THE COMICS CODE AUTHORITY
TA-TA, BATS! LOOKS LIKE THIS WILL BE OUR FINAL FACE-OFF!

CONSIDER THIS A FRIENDLY WARNING, DETECTIVE!
INTERFERE WITH MY LATEST PROJECT, AND AS SURELY AS THERE'S A JOKER IN EVERY DECK--
BATMAN
WILL DIE!
GERRY CONWAY WRITER
JOSE GARCIA LOPEZ GUEST ARTIST
DAN ADKINS INKER
BEN ODA LETTERER
ADRIENNE ROY COLORIST
LEN WEIN EDITOR
FTWANG
FTWANG
FTWANG!

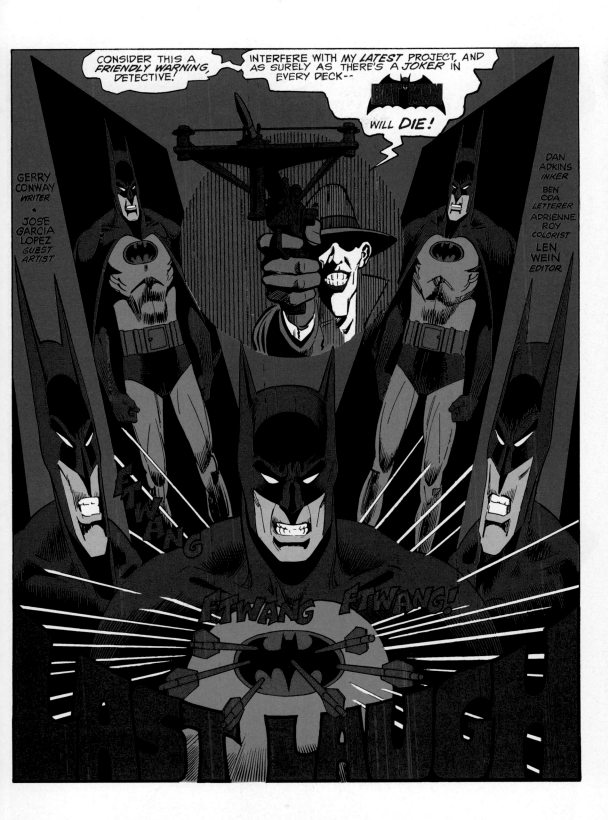

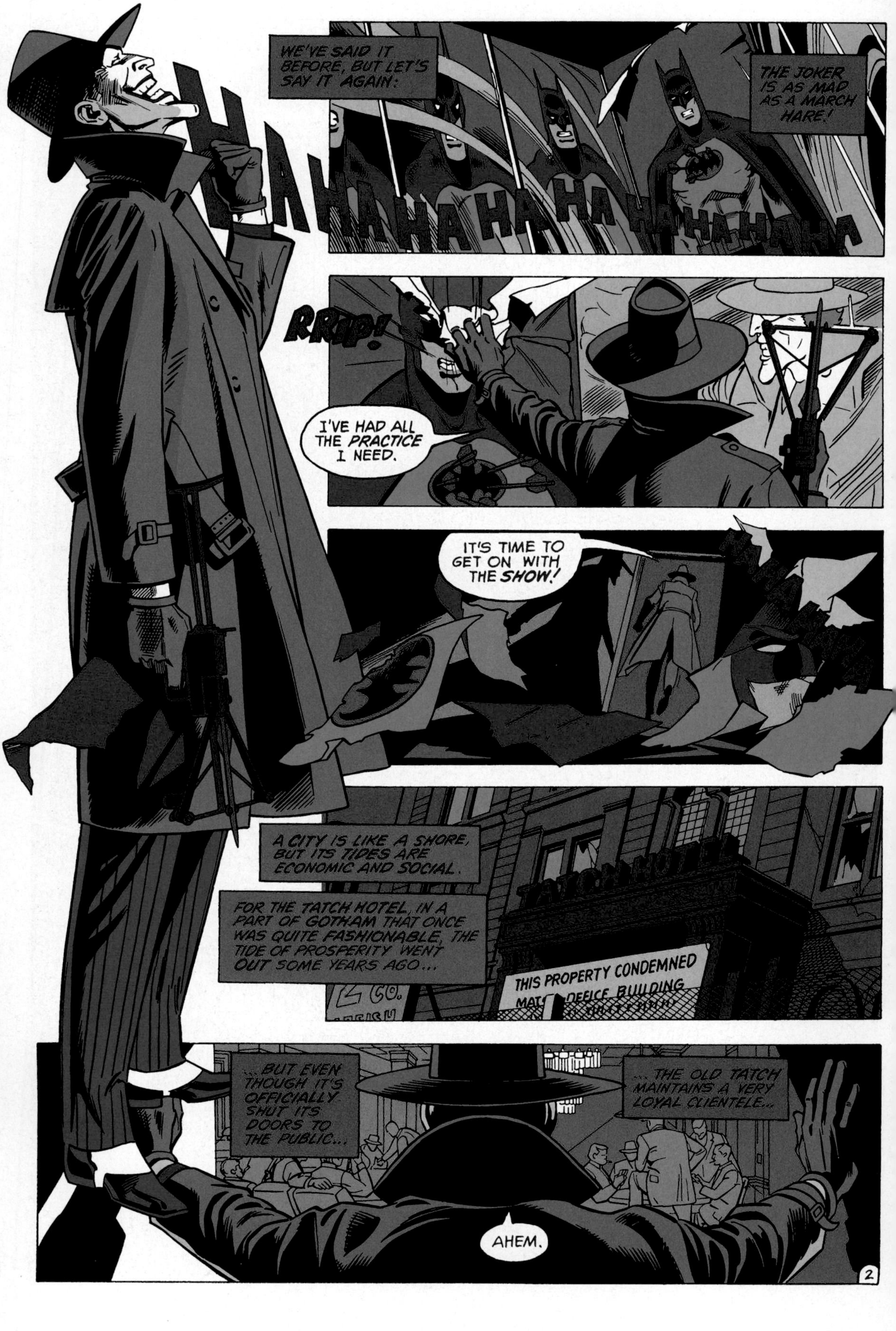

WE'VE SAID IT BEFORE, BUT LET'S SAY IT AGAIN:
THE JOKER IS AS MAD AS A MARCH HARE!
HAHAHAHAHA HA HA HAHAHAHAHA
RRIP!
I'VE HAD ALL THE PRACTICE I NEED.
IT'S TIME TO GET ON WITH THE SHOW!
A CITY IS LIKE A SHORE, BUT ITS TIDES ARE ECONOMIC AND SOCIAL.
FOR THE TATCH HOTEL, IN A PART OF GOTHAM THAT ONCE WAS QUITE FASHIONABLE, THE TIDE OF PROSPERITY WENT OUT SOME YEARS AGO...
THIS PROPERTY CONDEMNED
...BUT EVEN THOUGH IT'S OFFICIALLY SHUT ITS DOORS TO THE PUBLIC...
...THE OLD TATCH MAINTAINS A VERY LOYAL CLIENTELE...
AHEM.
2

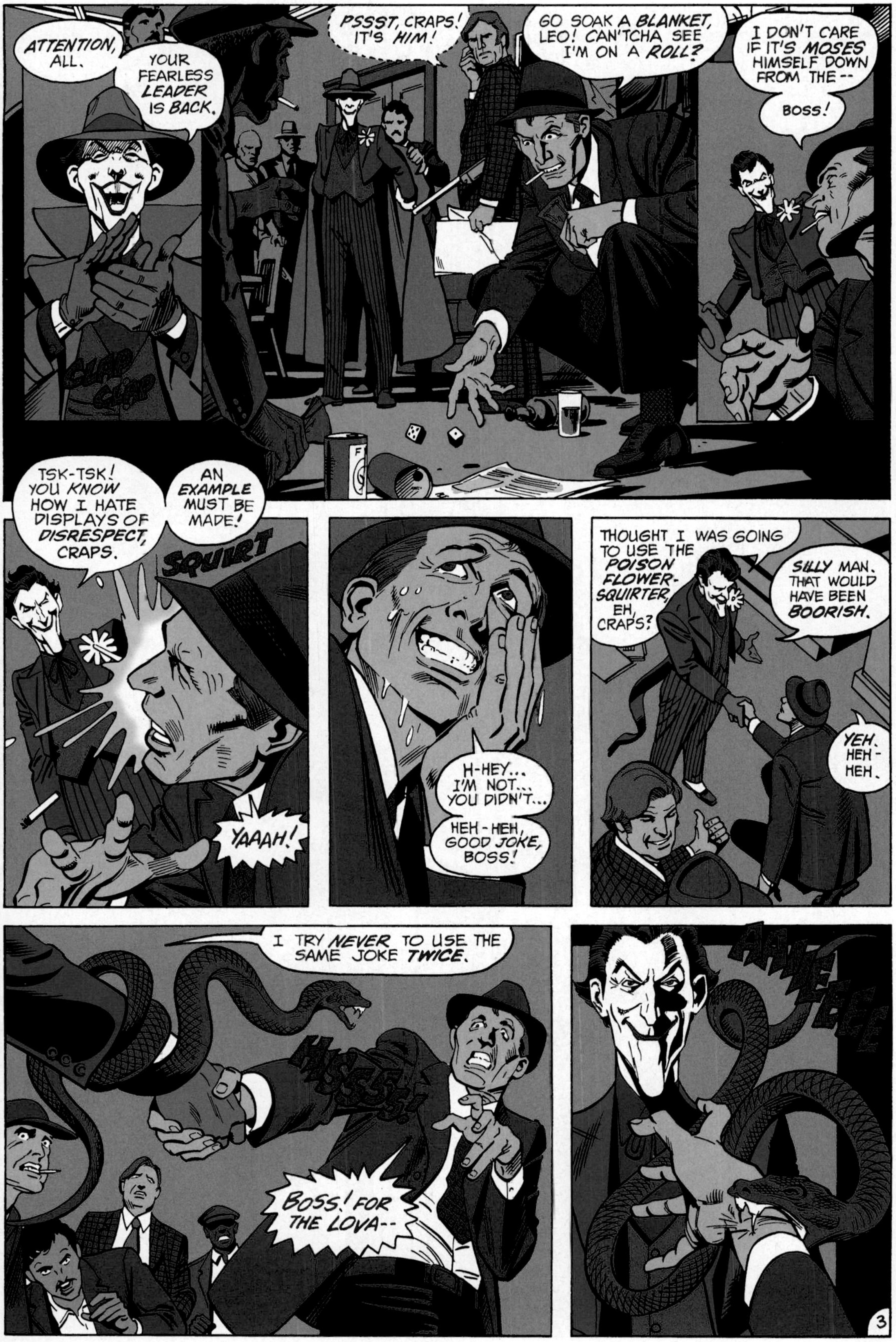
ATTENTION, ALL.
YOUR FEARLESS LEADER IS BACK.
PSSST, CRAPS! IT'S HIM!
GO SOAK A BLANKET, LEO! CAN'TCHA SEE I'M ON A ROLL?
I DON'T CARE IF IT'S MOSES HIMSELF DOWN FROM THE --
BOSS!
TSK-TSK! YOU KNOW HOW I HATE DISPLAYS OF DISRESPECT, CRAPS.
AN EXAMPLE MUST BE MADE!
SQUIRT
YAAAH!
H-HEY... I'M NOT... YOU DIDN'T...
HEH-HEH, GOOD JOKE, BOSS!
THOUGHT I WAS GOING TO USE THE POISON FLOWER-SQUIRTER, EH, CRAPS?
SILLY MAN. THAT WOULD HAVE BEEN BOORISH.
YEH. HEH-HEH.
I TRY NEVER TO USE THE SAME JOKE TWICE.
BOSS! FOR THE LOVA--
3

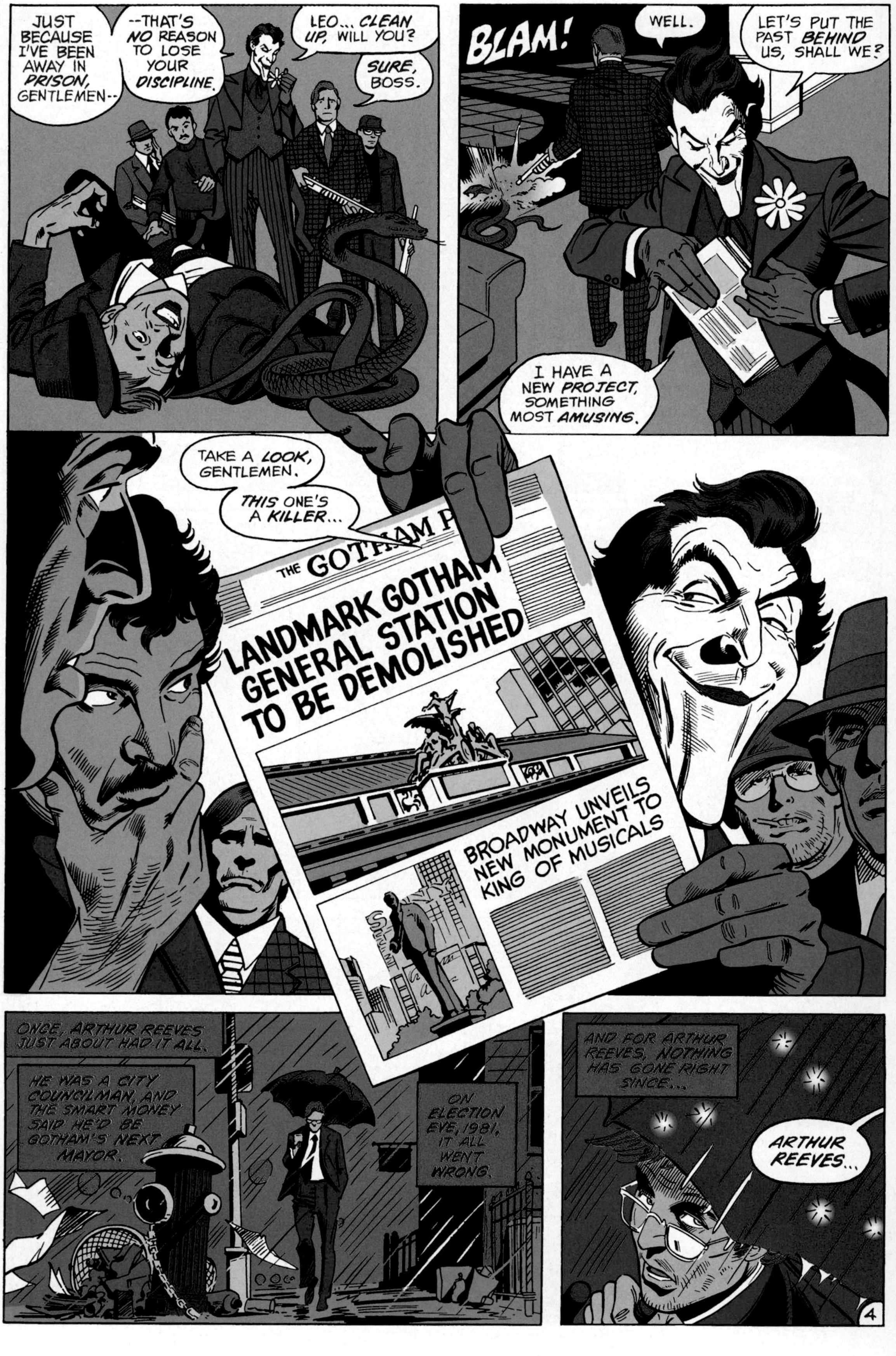
JUST BECAUSE I'VE BEEN AWAY IN PRISON, GENTLEMEN--
--THAT'S NO REASON TO LOSE YOUR DISCIPLINE.
LEO... CLEAN UP, WILL YOU?
SURE, BOSS.
BLAM!
WELL.
LET'S PUT THE PAST BEHIND US, SHALL WE?
I HAVE A NEW PROJECT, SOMETHING MOST AMUSING.
TAKE A LOOK, GENTLEMEN.
THIS ONE'S A KILLER...
THE GOTHAM P
LANDMARK GOTHAM GENERAL STATION TO BE DEMOLISHED
BROADWAY UNVEILS NEW MONUMENT TO KING OF MUSICALS
ONCE, ARTHUR REEVES JUST ABOUT HAD IT ALL.
HE WAS A CITY COUNCILMAN, AND THE SMART MONEY SAID HE'D BE GOTHAM'S NEXT MAYOR.
ON ELECTION EVE, 1981, IT ALL WENT WRONG.
AND FOR ARTHUR REEVES, NOTHING HAS GONE RIGHT SINCE...
ARTHUR REEVES...
4

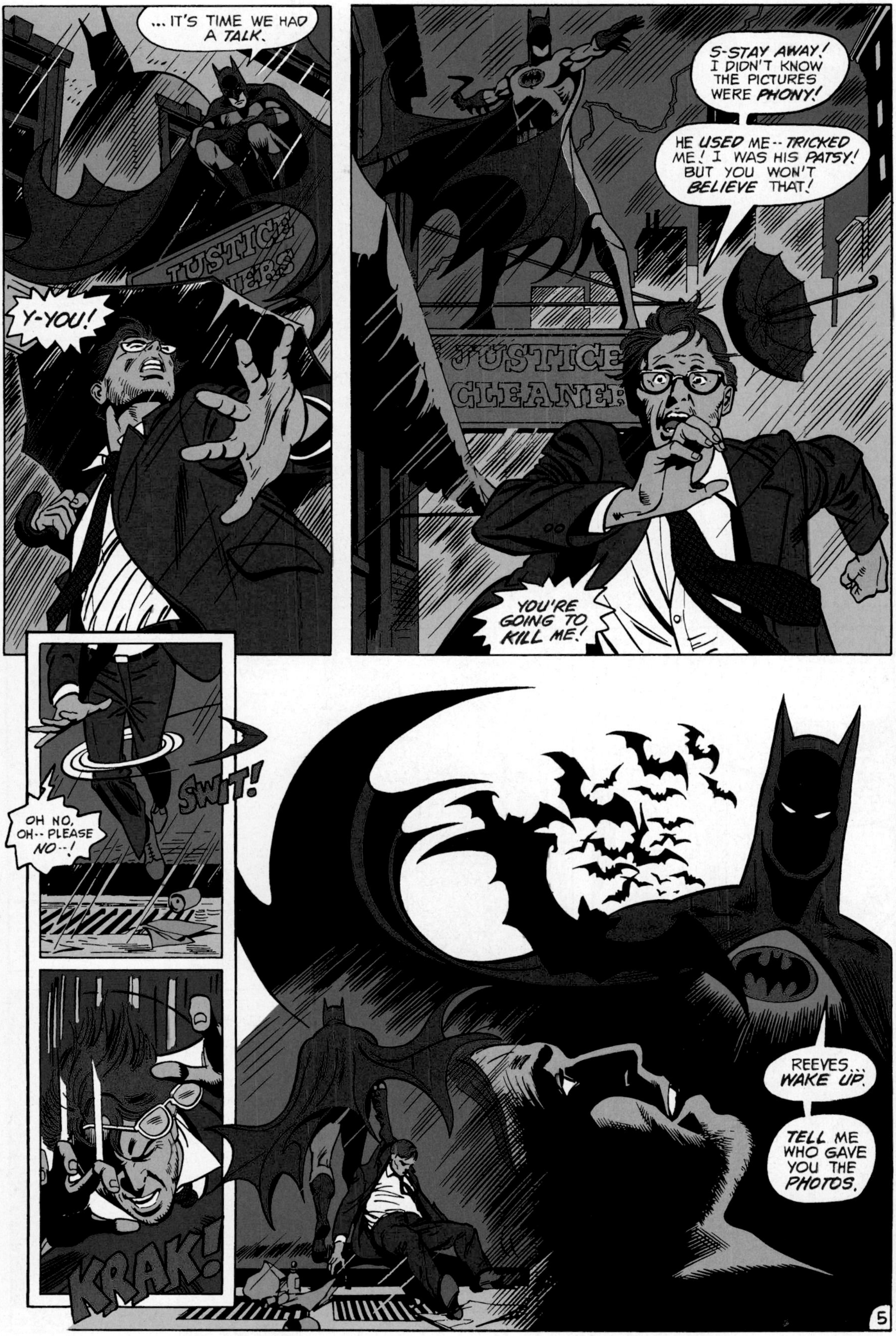
...IT'S TIME WE HAD A TALK.
Y-YOU!
S-STAY AWAY! I DIDN'T KNOW THE PICTURES WERE PHONY!
HE USED ME--TRICKED ME! I WAS HIS PATSY! BUT YOU WON'T BELIEVE THAT!
JUSTICE CLEANER
YOU'RE GOING TO KILL ME!
SWIT!
OH NO, OH--PLEASE NO--!
KRAK!
REEVES... WAKE UP.
TELL ME WHO GAVE YOU THE PHOTOS.
5

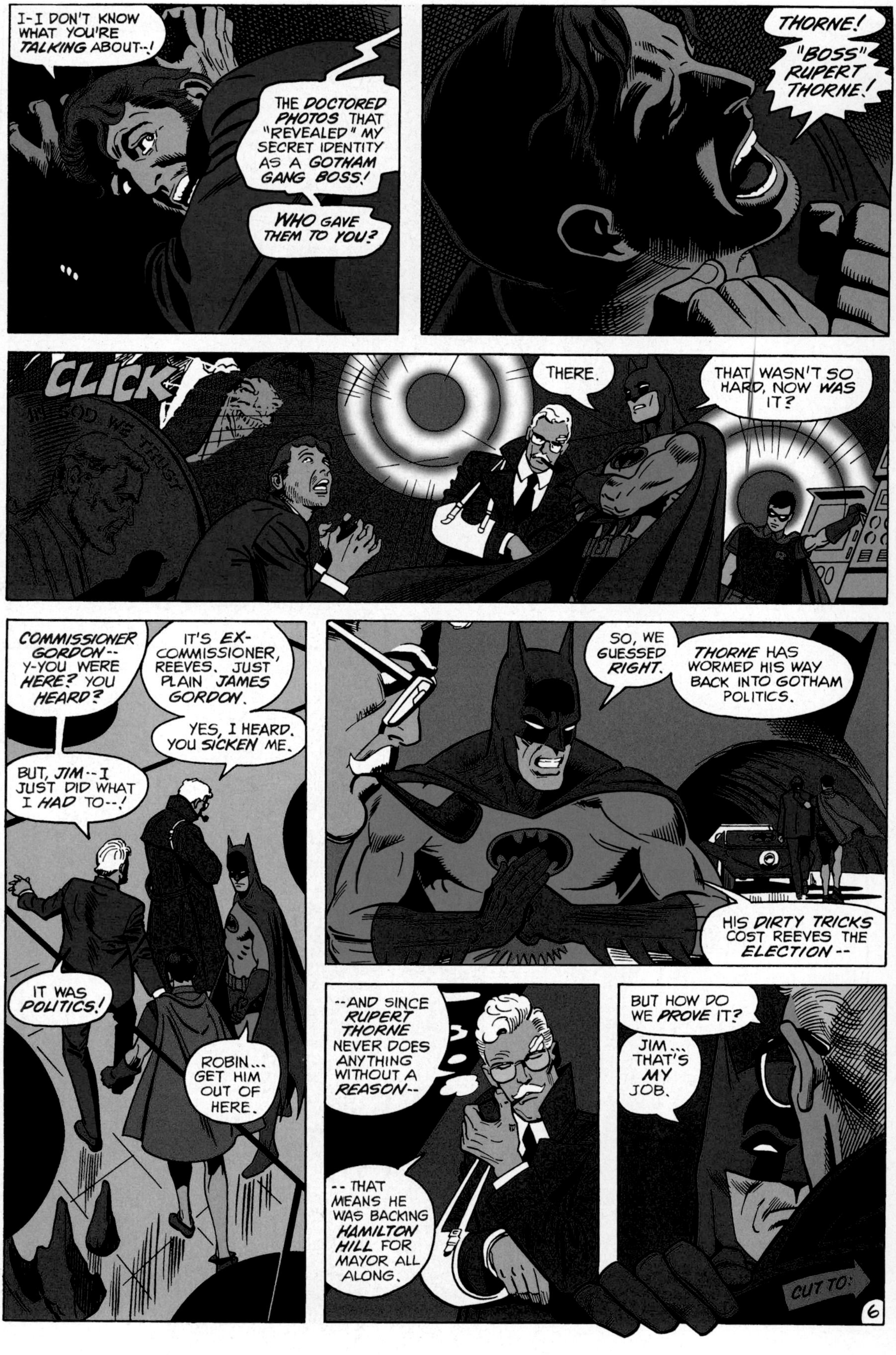
I-I DON'T KNOW WHAT YOU'RE TALKING ABOUT--!
THE DOCTORED PHOTOS THAT "REVEALED" MY SECRET IDENTITY AS A GOTHAM GANG BOSS!
WHO GAVE THEM TO YOU?
...
THORNE!
"BOSS" RUPERT THORNE!
CLICK
THERE.
THAT WASN'T SO HARD, NOW WAS IT?
COMMISSIONER GORDON-- Y-YOU WERE HERE? YOU HEARD?
IT'S EX-COMMISSIONER, REEVES. JUST PLAIN JAMES GORDON.
YES, I HEARD. YOU SICKEN ME.
BUT, JIM--I JUST DID WHAT I HAD TO--!
IT WAS POLITICS!
ROBIN... GET HIM OUT OF HERE.
SO, WE GUESSED RIGHT.
THORNE HAS WORMED HIS WAY BACK INTO GOTHAM POLITICS.
HIS DIRTY TRICKS COST REEVES THE ELECTION--
--AND SINCE RUPERT THORNE NEVER DOES ANYTHING WITHOUT A REASON--
--THAT MEANS HE WAS BACKING HAMILTON HILL FOR MAYOR ALL ALONG.
BUT HOW DO WE PROVE IT?
JIM... THAT'S MY JOB.
CUT TO:
6

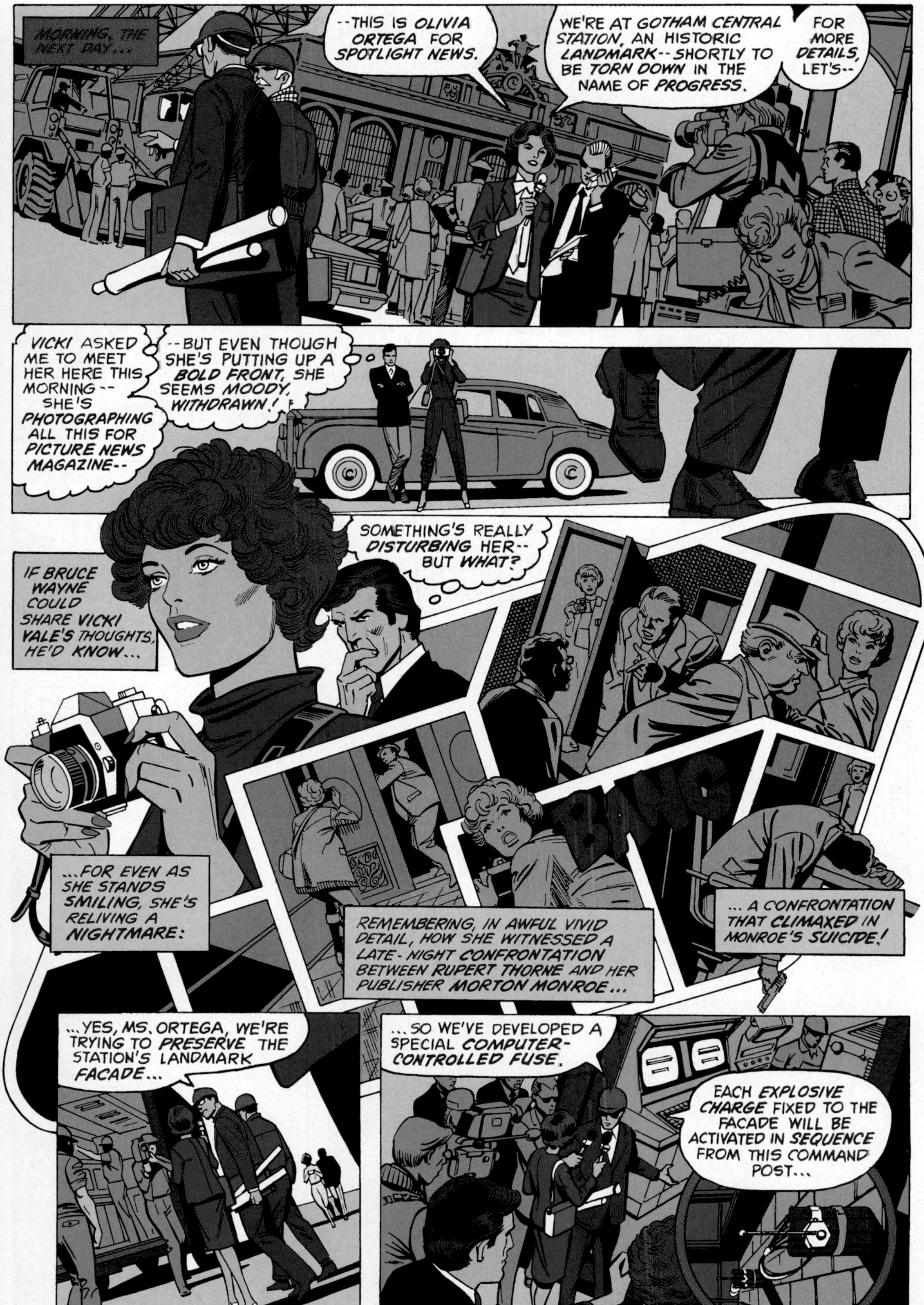

MORNING, THE NEXT DAY...
--THIS IS OLIVIA ORTEGA FOR SPOTLIGHT NEWS.
WE'RE AT GOTHAM CENTRAL STATION, AN HISTORIC LANDMARK-- SHORTLY TO BE TORN DOWN IN THE NAME OF PROGRESS.
FOR MORE DETAILS, LET'S--
VICKI ASKED ME TO MEET HER HERE THIS MORNING -- SHE'S PHOTOGRAPHING ALL THIS FOR PICTURE NEWS MAGAZINE--
--BUT EVEN THOUGH SHE'S PUTTING UP A BOLD FRONT, SHE SEEMS MOODY, WITHDRAWN!
SOMETHING'S REALLY DISTURBING HER-- BUT WHAT?
IF BRUCE WAYNE COULD SHARE VICKI VALE'S THOUGHTS, HE'D KNOW...
...FOR EVEN AS SHE STANDS SMILING, SHE'S RELIVING A NIGHTMARE:
REMEMBERING, IN AWFUL VIVID DETAIL, HOW SHE WITNESSED A LATE-NIGHT CONFRONTATION BETWEEN RUPERT THORNE AND HER PUBLISHER MORTON MONROE...
BLANG
... A CONFRONTATION THAT CLIMAXED IN MONROE'S SUICIDE!
...YES, MS. ORTEGA, WE'RE TRYING TO PRESERVE THE STATION'S LANDMARK FACADE...
...SO WE'VE DEVELOPED A SPECIAL COMPUTER-CONTROLLED FUSE.
EACH EXPLOSIVE CHARGE FIXED TO THE FACADE WILL BE ACTIVATED IN SEQUENCE FROM THIS COMMAND POST...
7

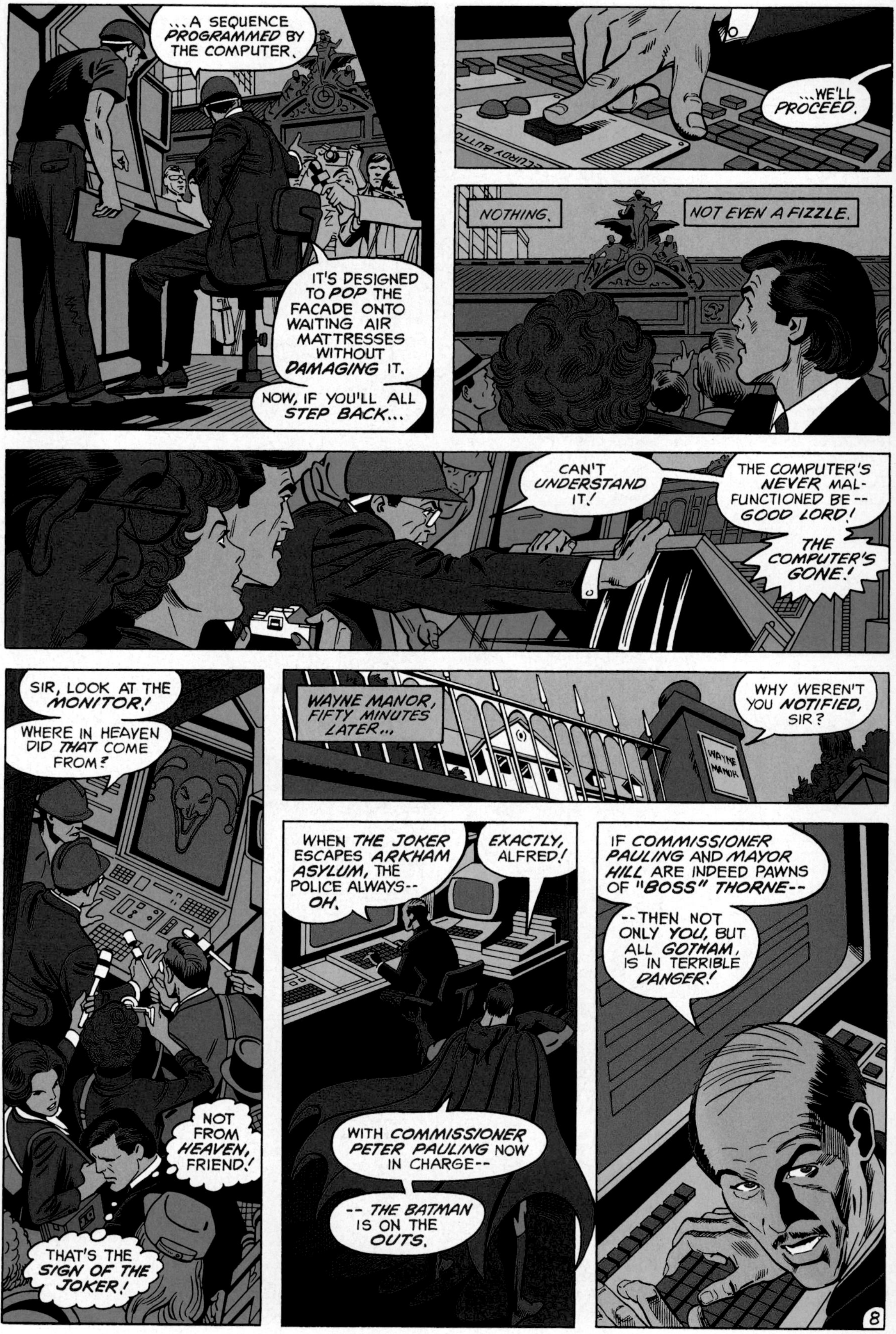
...A SEQUENCE PROGRAMMED BY THE COMPUTER.
IT'S DESIGNED TO POP THE FACADE ONTO WAITING AIR MATTRESSES WITHOUT DAMAGING IT.
NOW, IF YOU'LL ALL STEP BACK...
...WE'LL PROCEED.
NOTHING.
NOT EVEN A FIZZLE.
CAN'T UNDERSTAND IT!
THE COMPUTER'S NEVER MAL-FUNCTIONED BE-- GOOD LORD!
THE COMPUTER'S GONE!
SIR, LOOK AT THE MONITOR!
WHERE IN HEAVEN DID THAT COME FROM?
NOT FROM HEAVEN, FRIEND!
THAT'S THE SIGN OF THE JOKER!
WAYNE MANOR, FIFTY MINUTES LATER...
WHY WEREN'T YOU NOTIFIED, SIR?
WHEN THE JOKER ESCAPES ARKHAM ASYLUM, THE POLICE ALWAYS-- OH.
EXACTLY, ALFRED!
WITH COMMISSIONER PETER PAULING NOW IN CHARGE--
-- THE BATMAN IS ON THE OUTS.
IF COMMISSIONER PAULING AND MAYOR HILL ARE INDEED PAWNS OF "BOSS" THORNE--
--THEN NOT ONLY YOU, BUT ALL GOTHAM, IS IN TERRIBLE DANGER!
8

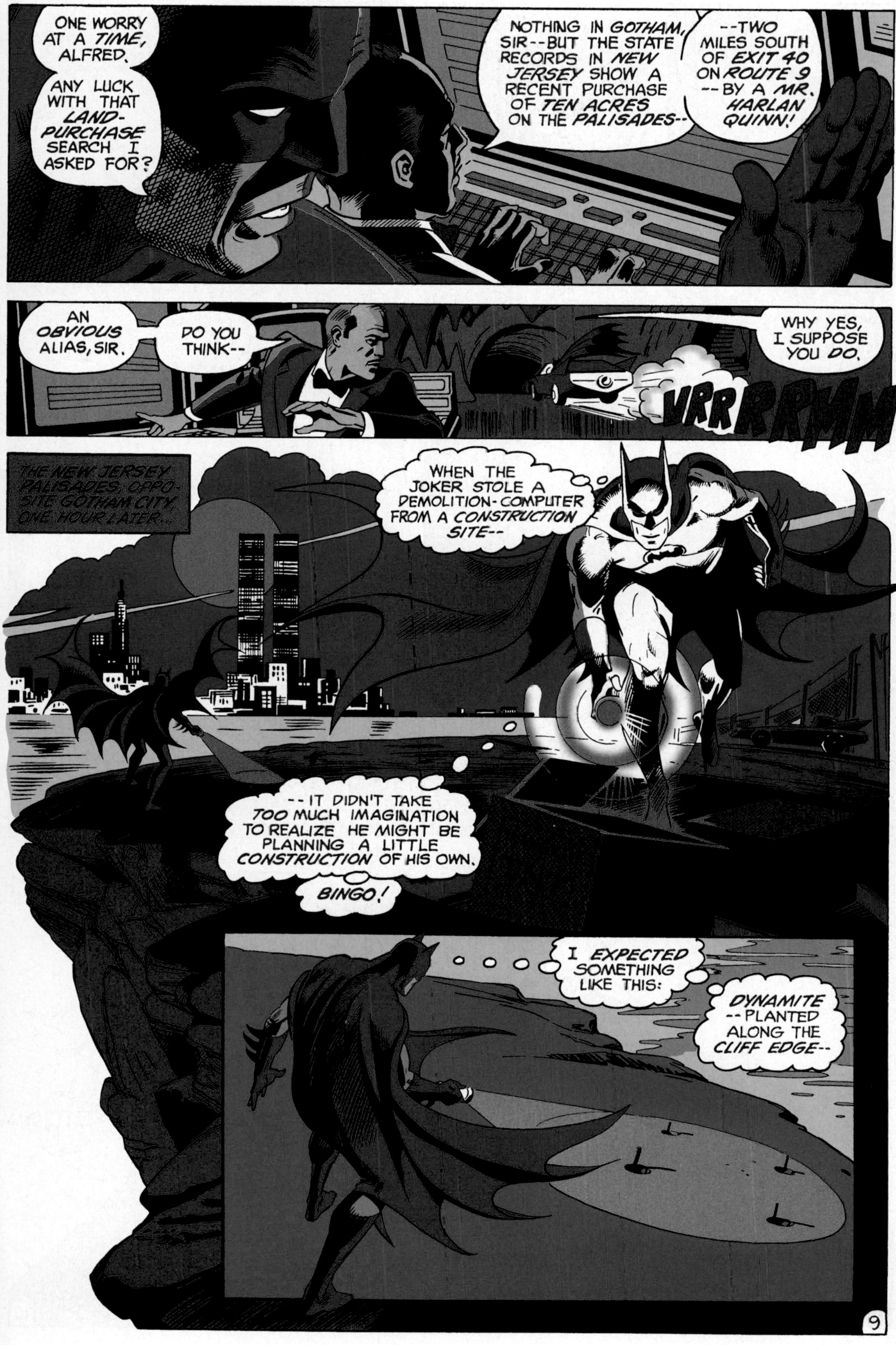
ONE WORRY AT A TIME, ALFRED.
ANY LUCK WITH THAT LAND-PURCHASE SEARCH I ASKED FOR?
NOTHING IN GOTHAM, SIR--BUT THE STATE RECORDS IN NEW JERSEY SHOW A RECENT PURCHASE OF TEN ACRES ON THE PALISADES--
--TWO MILES SOUTH OF EXIT 40 ON ROUTE 9 --BY A MR. HARLAN QUINN!
AN OBVIOUS ALIAS, SIR.
DO YOU THINK--
WHY YES, I SUPPOSE YOU DO.
VRRRRMM
THE NEW JERSEY PALISADES, OPPOSITE GOTHAM CITY, ONE HOUR LATER...
WHEN THE JOKER STOLE A DEMOLITION-COMPUTER FROM A CONSTRUCTION SITE--
--IT DIDN'T TAKE TOO MUCH IMAGINATION TO REALIZE HE MIGHT BE PLANNING A LITTLE CONSTRUCTION OF HIS OWN.
BINGO!
I EXPECTED SOMETHING LIKE THIS:
DYNAMITE --PLANTED ALONG THE CLIFF EDGE--
9

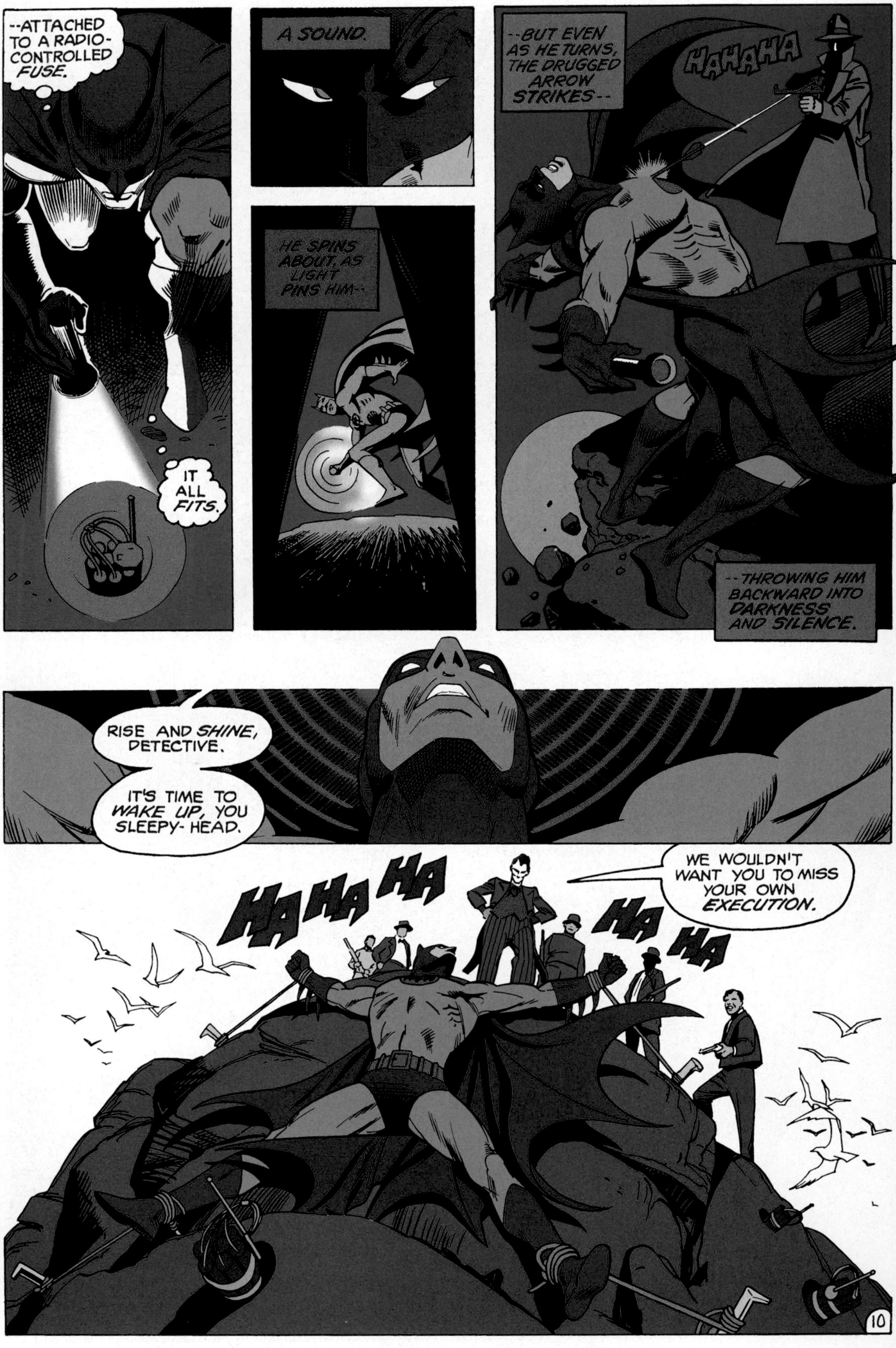
--ATTACHED TO A RADIO-CONTROLLED FUSE.
IT ALL FITS.
A SOUND.
HE SPINS ABOUT, AS LIGHT PINS HIM--
--BUT EVEN AS HE TURNS, THE DRUGGED ARROW STRIKES--
HAHAHA
--THROWING HIM BACKWARD INTO DARKNESS AND SILENCE.
RISE AND SHINE, DETECTIVE.
IT'S TIME TO WAKE UP, YOU SLEEPY- HEAD.
HA HA HA
WE WOULDN'T WANT YOU TO MISS YOUR OWN EXECUTION.
HA HA
10

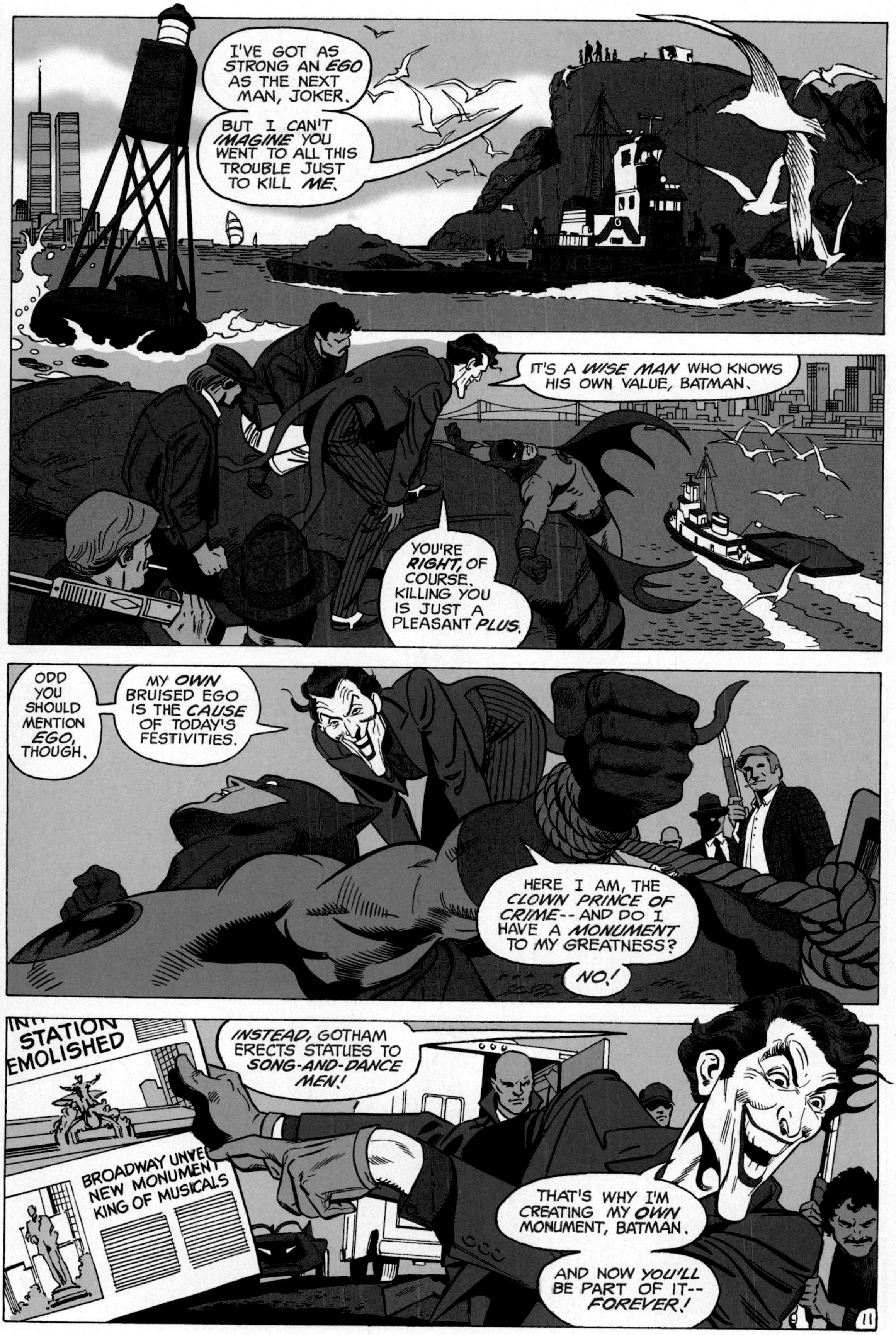

I'VE GOT AS STRONG AN EGO AS THE NEXT MAN, JOKER.
BUT I CAN'T IMAGINE YOU WENT TO ALL THIS TROUBLE JUST TO KILL ME.
IT'S A WISE MAN WHO KNOWS HIS OWN VALUE, BATMAN.
YOU'RE RIGHT, OF COURSE. KILLING YOU IS JUST A PLEASANT PLUS.
ODD YOU SHOULD MENTION EGO, THOUGH.
MY OWN BRUISED EGO IS THE CAUSE OF TODAY'S FESTIVITIES.
HERE I AM, THE CLOWN PRINCE OF CRIME-- AND DO I HAVE A MONUMENT TO MY GREATNESS?
NO!
STATION
EMOLISHED
INSTEAD, GOTHAM ERECTS STATUES TO SONG-AND-DANCE MEN!
BROADWAY UNVE
NEW MONUMENT
KING OF MUSICALS
THAT'S WHY I'M CREATING MY OWN MONUMENT, BATMAN.
AND NOW YOU'LL BE PART OF IT-- FOREVER!
11

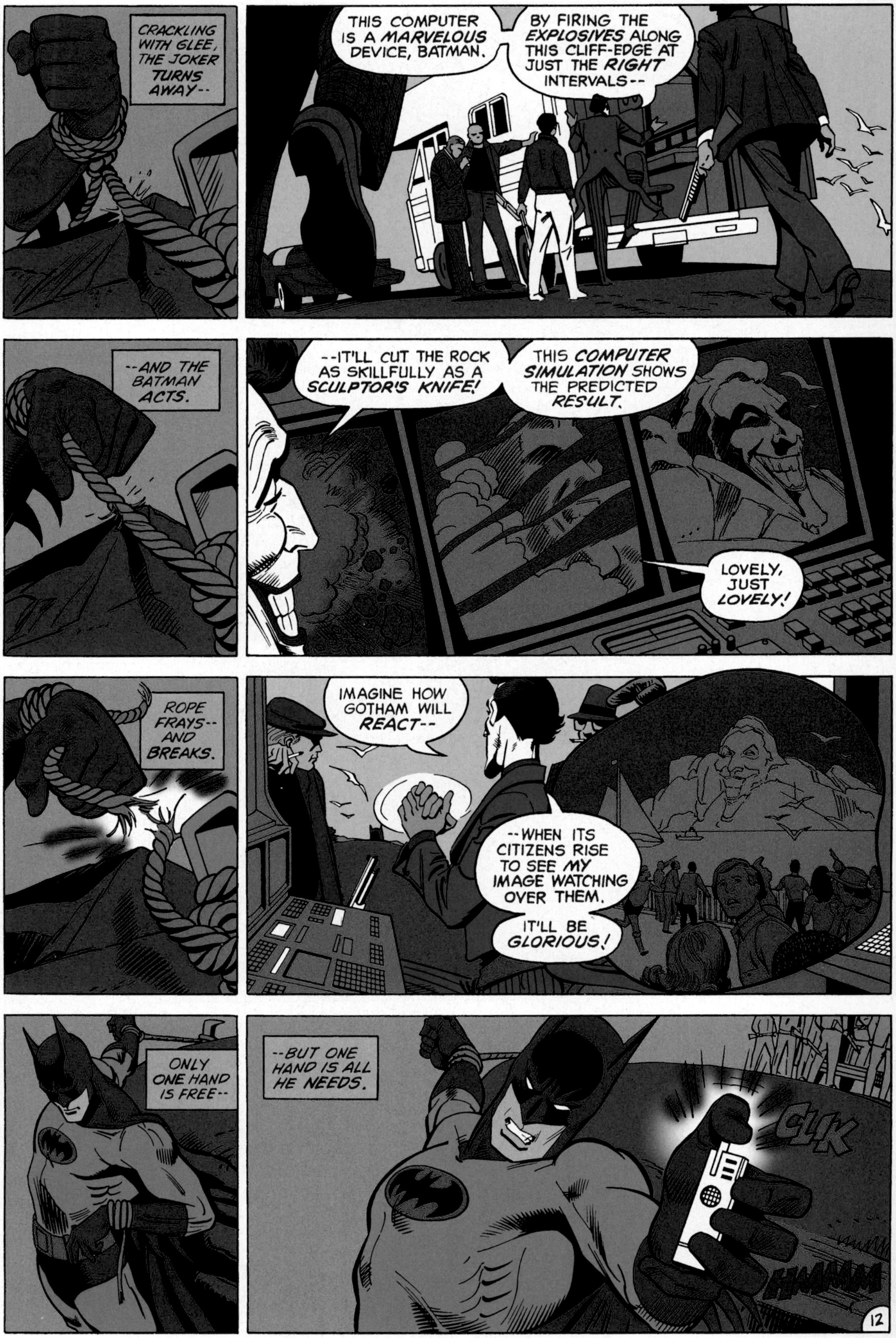
CRACKLING WITH GLEE, THE JOKER TURNS AWAY--
THIS COMPUTER IS A MARVELOUS DEVICE, BATMAN.
BY FIRING THE EXPLOSIVES ALONG THIS CLIFF-EDGE AT JUST THE RIGHT INTERVALS--
--AND THE BATMAN ACTS.
--IT'LL CUT THE ROCK AS SKILLFULLY AS A SCULPTOR'S KNIFE!
THIS COMPUTER SIMULATION SHOWS THE PREDICTED RESULT.
LOVELY, JUST LOVELY!
ROPE FRAYS-- AND BREAKS.
IMAGINE HOW GOTHAM WILL REACT--
--WHEN ITS CITIZENS RISE TO SEE MY IMAGE WATCHING OVER THEM.
IT'LL BE GLORIOUS!
ONLY ONE HAND IS FREE--
--BUT ONE HAND IS ALL HE NEEDS.
CLIK
HMMMM
12

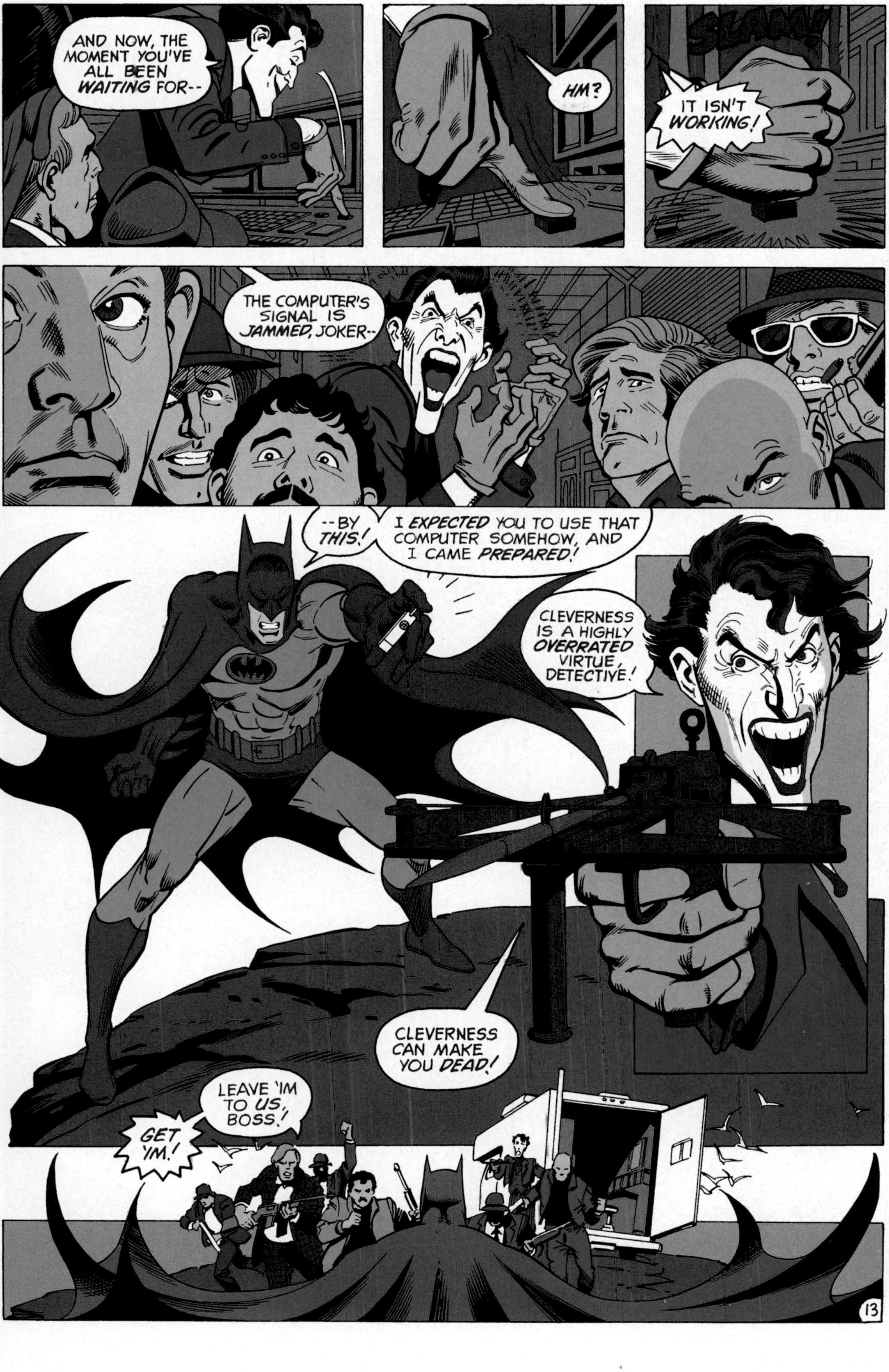
AND NOW, THE MOMENT YOU'VE ALL BEEN WAITING FOR--
HM?
SLAM!!
IT ISN'T WORKING!
THE COMPUTER'S SIGNAL IS JAMMED, JOKER--
--BY THIS!
I EXPECTED YOU TO USE THAT COMPUTER SOMEHOW, AND I CAME PREPARED!
CLEVERNESS IS A HIGHLY OVERRATED VIRTUE, DETECTIVE!
CLEVERNESS CAN MAKE YOU DEAD!
LEAVE 'IM TO US, BOSS!
GET 'IM!
13

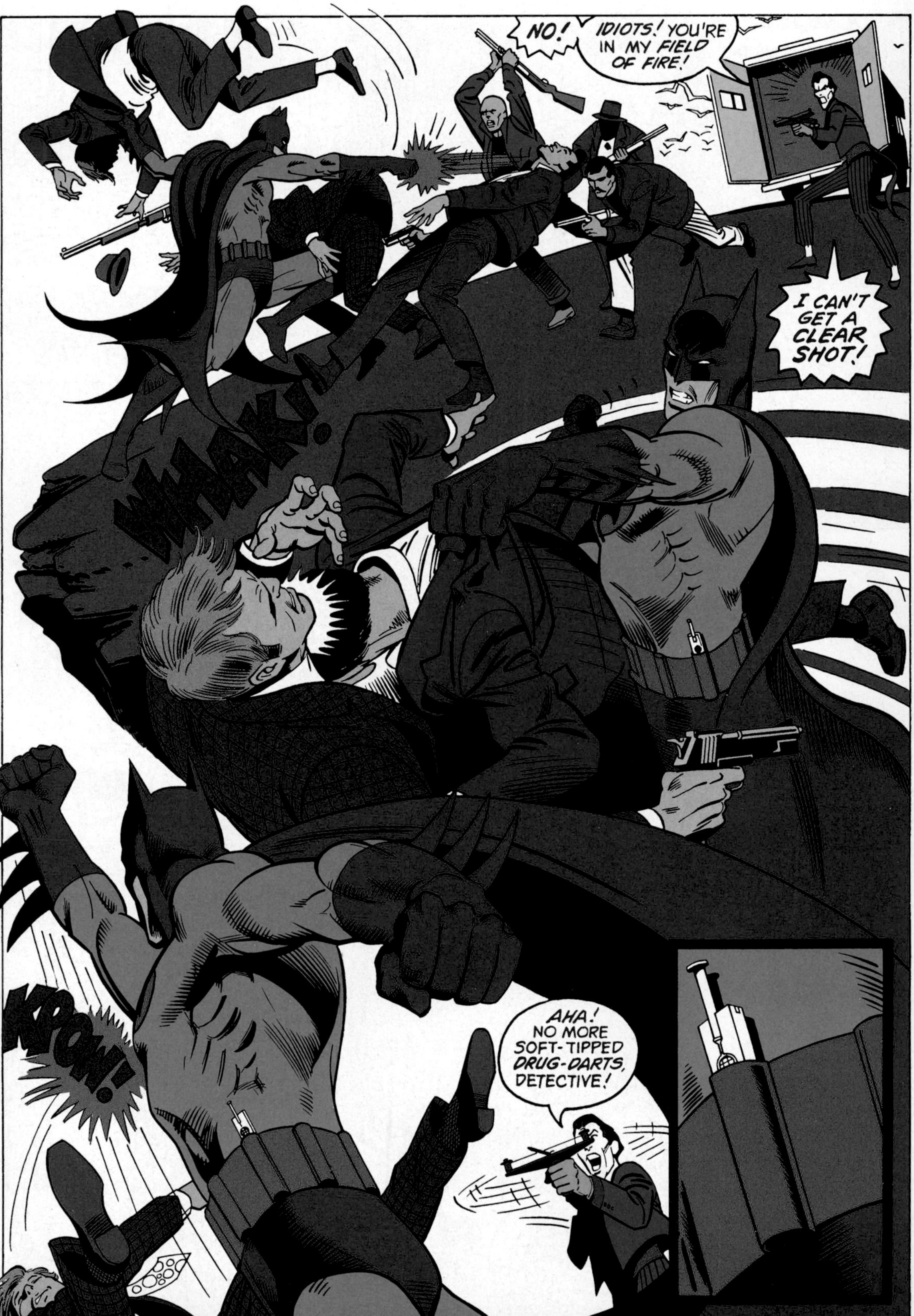
NO!
IDIOTS! YOU'RE IN MY FIELD OF FIRE!
I CAN'T GET A CLEAR SHOT!
WHAK!
KPOW!
AHA! NO MORE SOFT-TIPPED DRUG-DARTS, DETECTIVE!
14

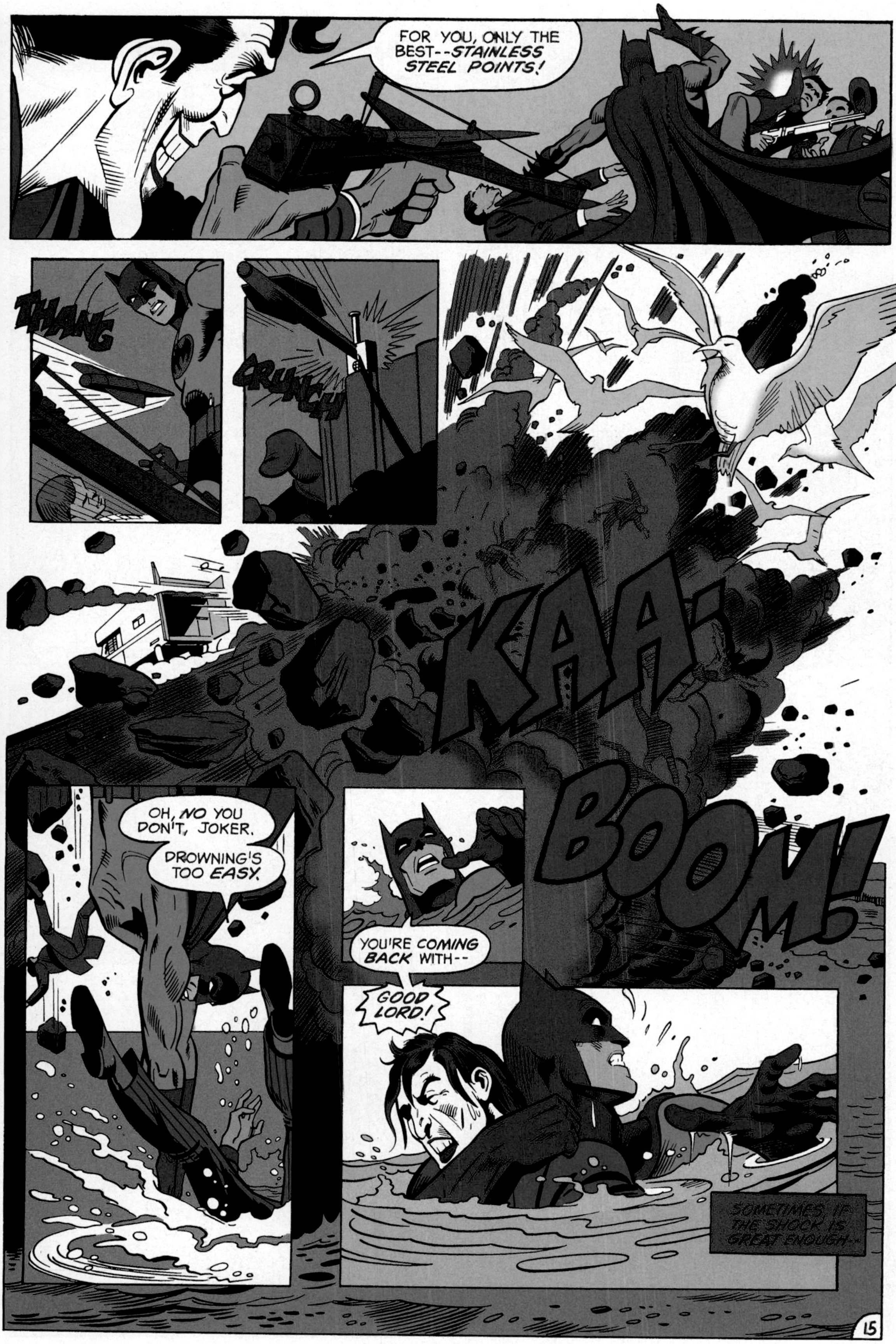
FOR YOU, ONLY THE BEST--STAINLESS STEEL POINTS!
THANG
CRUNCH
KAA-BOOM!
OH, NO YOU DON'T, JOKER.
DROWNING'S TOO EASY.
YOU'RE COMING BACK WITH--
GOOD LORD!
SOMETIMES, IF THE SHOCK IS GREAT ENOUGH--
15

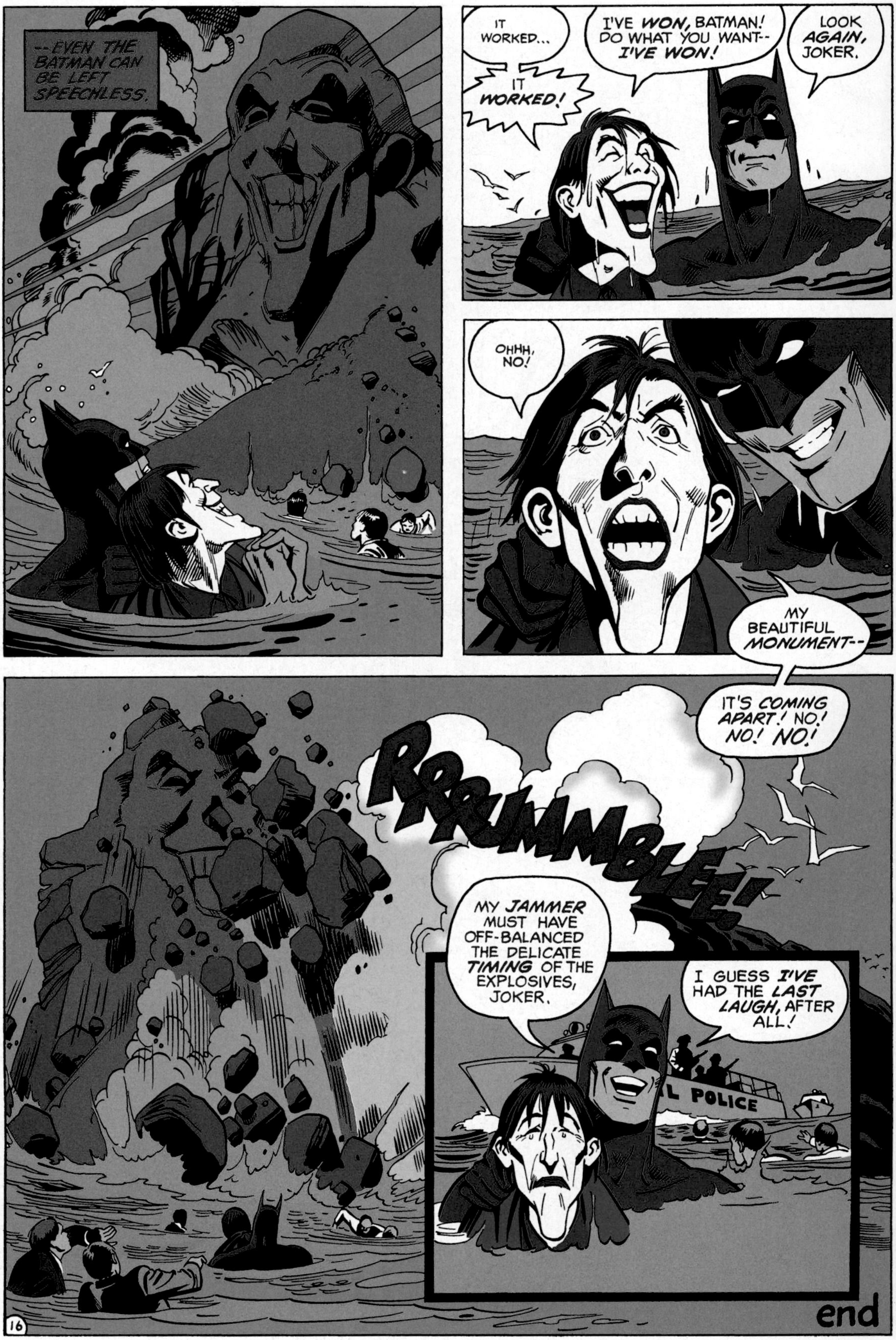
--EVEN THE BATMAN CAN BE LEFT SPEECHLESS.
IT WORKED...
IT WORKED!
I'VE WON, BATMAN! DO WHAT YOU WANT-- I'VE WON!
LOOK AGAIN, JOKER.
OHHH, NO!
MY BEAUTIFUL MONUMENT--
IT'S COMING APART! NO! NO! NO!
RRRRUMMBLEE!
MY JAMMER MUST HAVE OFF-BALANCED THE DELICATE TIMING OF THE EXPLOSIVES, JOKER.
I GUESS I'VE HAD THE LAST LAUGH, AFTER ALL!
POLICE
16
end

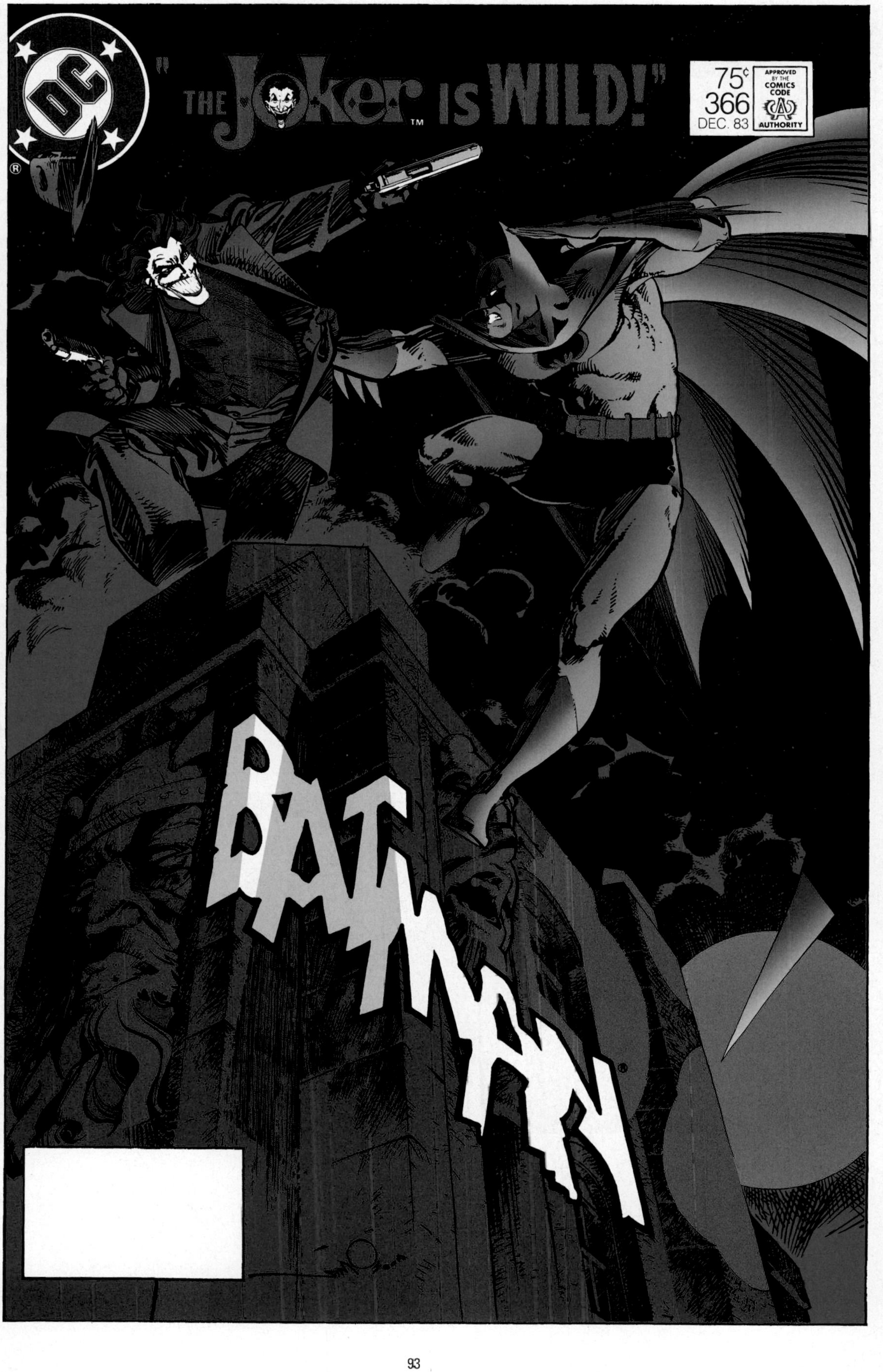
"THE JOKER IS WILD!"
75¢
366
DEC. 83
APPROVED BY THE COMICS CODE AUTHORITY
BATMAN

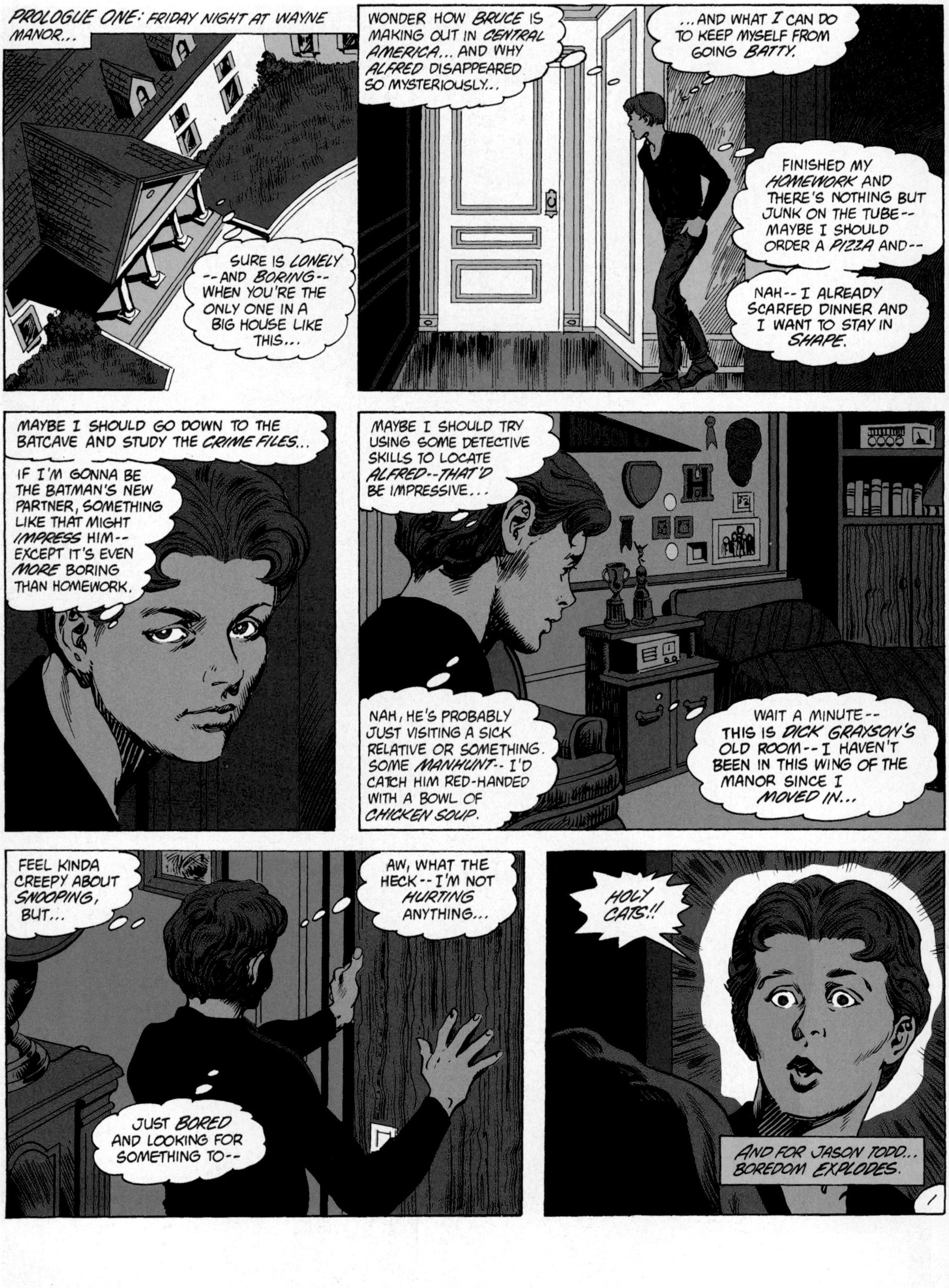
PROLOGUE ONE: FRIDAY NIGHT AT WAYNE MANOR...
SURE IS LONELY --AND BORING-- WHEN YOU'RE THE ONLY ONE IN A BIG HOUSE LIKE THIS...
WONDER HOW BRUCE IS MAKING OUT IN CENTRAL AMERICA... AND WHY ALFRED DISAPPEARED SO MYSTERIOUSLY...
...AND WHAT I CAN DO TO KEEP MYSELF FROM GOING BATTY.
FINISHED MY HOMEWORK AND THERE'S NOTHING BUT JUNK ON THE TUBE-- MAYBE I SHOULD ORDER A PIZZA AND--
NAH-- I ALREADY SCARFED DINNER AND I WANT TO STAY IN SHAPE.
MAYBE I SHOULD GO DOWN TO THE BATCAVE AND STUDY THE CRIME FILES...
IF I'M GONNA BE THE BATMAN'S NEW PARTNER, SOMETHING LIKE THAT MIGHT IMPRESS HIM-- EXCEPT IT'S EVEN MORE BORING THAN HOMEWORK.
MAYBE I SHOULD TRY USING SOME DETECTIVE SKILLS TO LOCATE ALFRED--THAT'D BE IMPRESSIVE...
NAH, HE'S PROBABLY JUST VISITING A SICK RELATIVE OR SOMETHING. SOME MANHUNT-- I'D CATCH HIM RED-HANDED WITH A BOWL OF CHICKEN SOUP.
WAIT A MINUTE-- THIS IS DICK GRAYSON'S OLD ROOM-- I HAVEN'T BEEN IN THIS WING OF THE MANOR SINCE I MOVED IN...
FEEL KINDA CREEPY ABOUT SNOOPING, BUT...
AW, WHAT THE HECK-- I'M NOT HURTING ANYTHING...
JUST BORED AND LOOKING FOR SOMETHING TO--
HOLY CATS!!
AND FOR JASON TODD... BOREDOM EXPLODES.
1

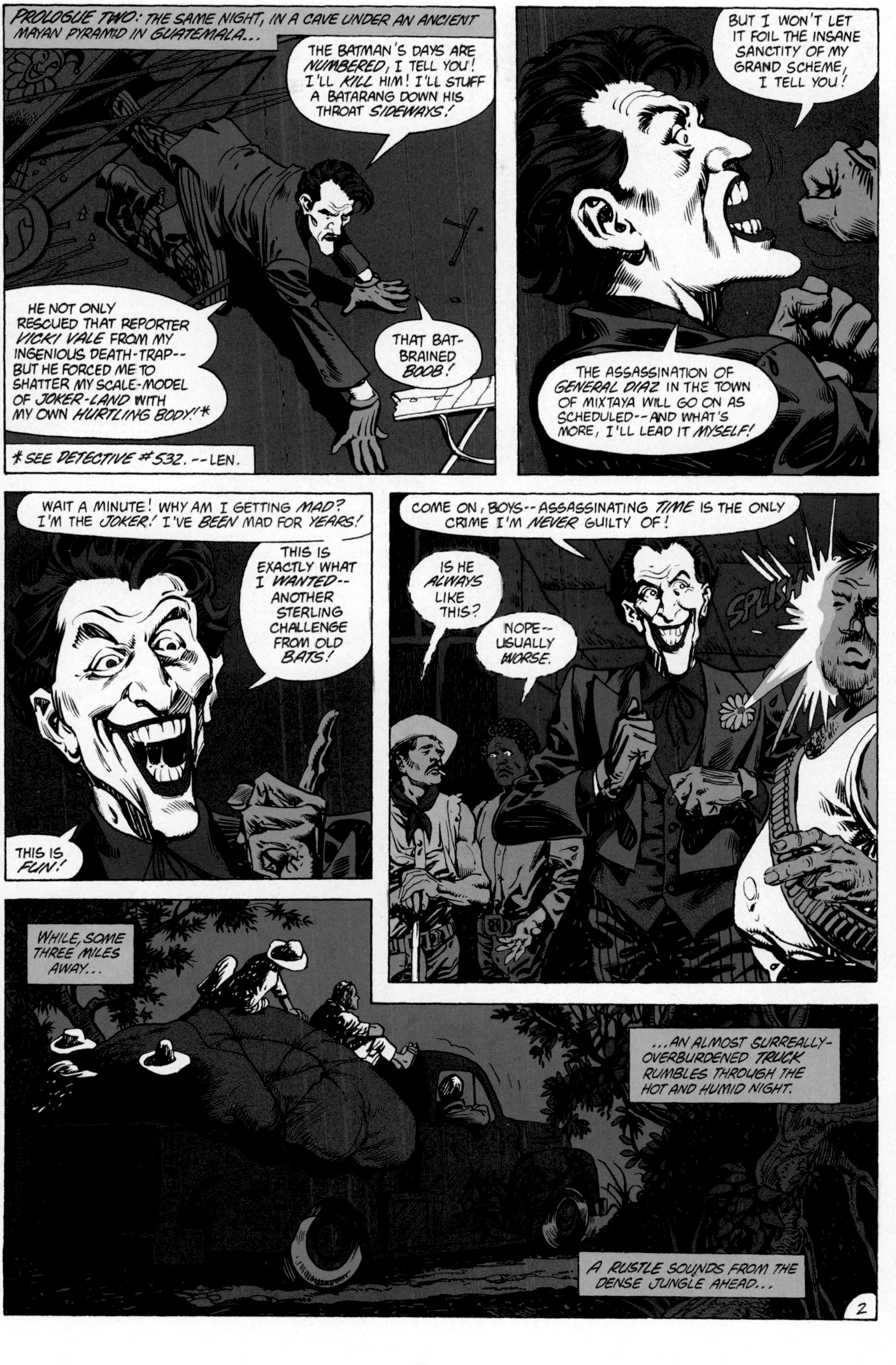
PROLOGUE TWO: THE SAME NIGHT, IN A CAVE UNDER AN ANCIENT MAYAN PYRAMID IN GUATEMALA...
THE BATMAN'S DAYS ARE NUMBERED, I TELL YOU! I'LL KILL HIM! I'LL STUFF A BATARANG DOWN HIS THROAT SIDEWAYS!
HE NOT ONLY RESCUED THAT REPORTER VICKI VALE FROM MY INGENIOUS DEATH-TRAP-- BUT HE FORCED ME TO SHATTER MY SCALE-MODEL OF JOKER-LAND WITH MY OWN HURTLING BODY!*
THAT BAT-BRAINED BOOB!
*SEE DETECTIVE #532. --LEN.
BUT I WON'T LET IT FOIL THE INSANE SANCTITY OF MY GRAND SCHEME, I TELL YOU!
THE ASSASSINATION OF GENERAL DIAZ IN THE TOWN OF MIXTAYA WILL GO ON AS SCHEDULED--AND WHAT'S MORE, I'LL LEAD IT MYSELF!
WAIT A MINUTE! WHY AM I GETTING MAD? I'M THE JOKER! I'VE BEEN MAD FOR YEARS!
THIS IS EXACTLY WHAT I WANTED-- ANOTHER STERLING CHALLENGE FROM OLD BATS!
THIS IS FUN!
COME ON, BOYS--ASSASSINATING TIME IS THE ONLY CRIME I'M NEVER GUILTY OF!
IS HE ALWAYS LIKE THIS?
NOPE-- USUALLY WORSE.
SPLISH
WHILE, SOME THREE MILES AWAY...
...AN ALMOST SURREALLY-OVERBURDENED TRUCK RUMBLES THROUGH THE HOT AND HUMID NIGHT.
A RUSTLE SOUNDS FROM THE DENSE JUNGLE AHEAD...
2

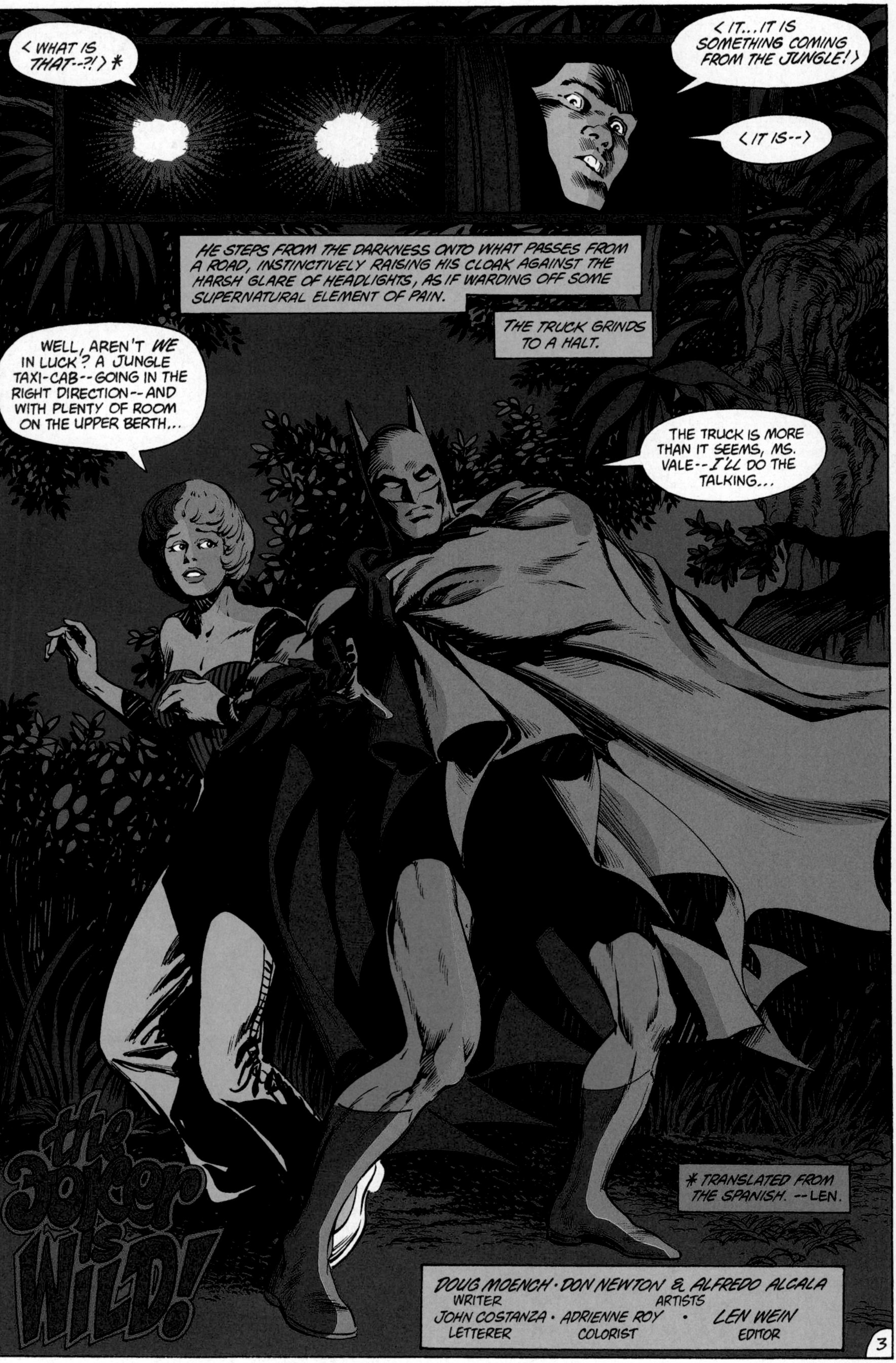

< WHAT IS THAT--?! > *
< IT...IT IS SOMETHING COMING FROM THE JUNGLE! >
< IT IS-- >
HE STEPS FROM THE DARKNESS ONTO WHAT PASSES FROM A ROAD, INSTINCTIVELY RAISING HIS CLOAK AGAINST THE HARSH GLARE OF HEADLIGHTS, AS IF WARDING OFF SOME SUPERNATURAL ELEMENT OF PAIN.
THE TRUCK GRINDS TO A HALT.
WELL, AREN'T WE IN LUCK? A JUNGLE TAXI-CAB--GOING IN THE RIGHT DIRECTION--AND WITH PLENTY OF ROOM ON THE UPPER BERTH...
THE TRUCK IS MORE THAN IT SEEMS, MS. VALE--I'LL DO THE TALKING...
the Joker is WILD!
* TRANSLATED FROM THE SPANISH. --LEN.
DOUG MOENCH · DON NEWTON & ALFREDO ALCALA
WRITER ARTISTS
JOHN COSTANZA · ADRIENNE ROY · LEN WEIN
LETTERER COLORIST EDITOR
3

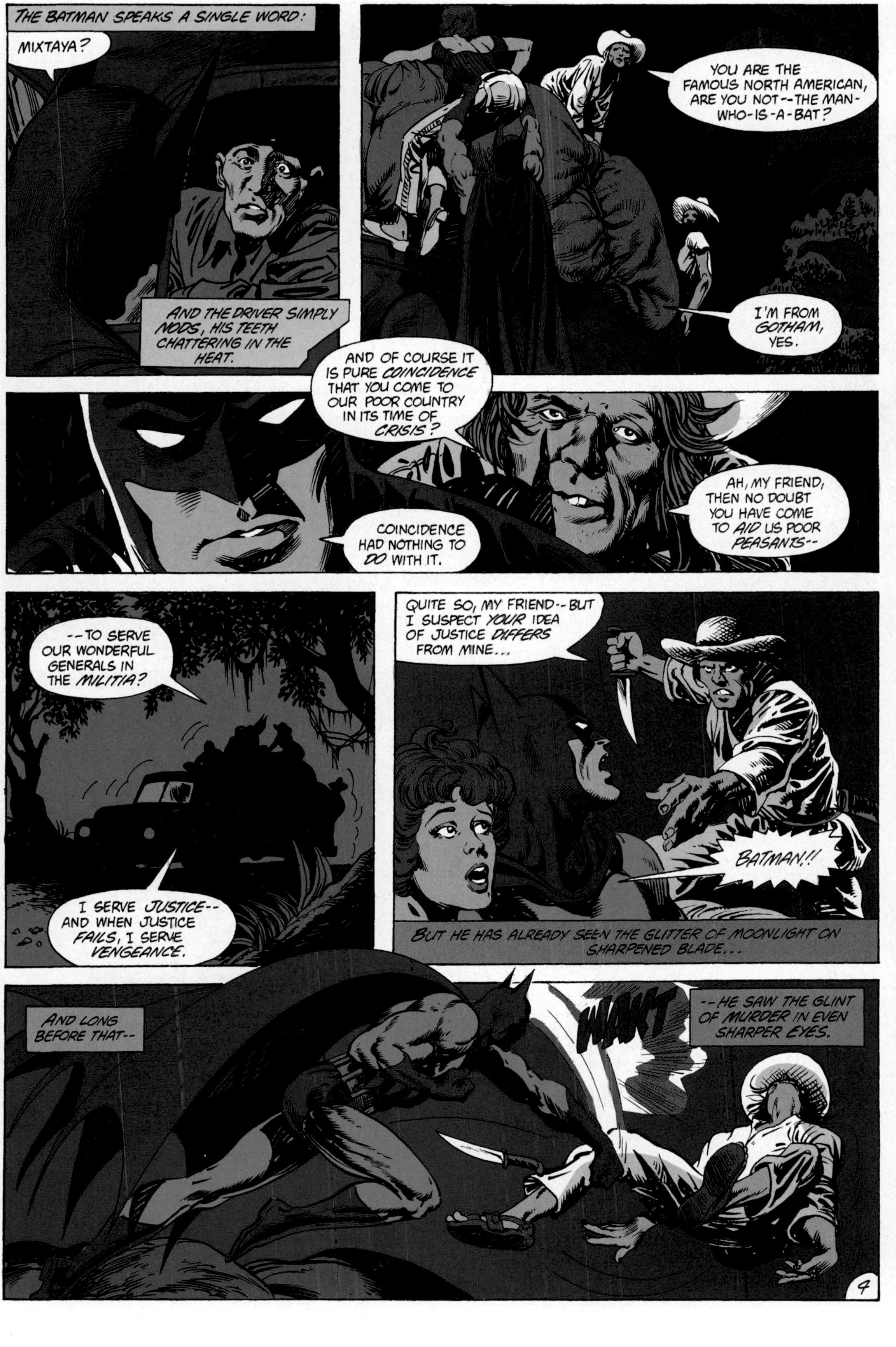

THE BATMAN SPEAKS A SINGLE WORD:
MIXTAYA?
AND THE DRIVER SIMPLY NODS, HIS TEETH CHATTERING IN THE HEAT.
YOU ARE THE FAMOUS NORTH AMERICAN, ARE YOU NOT--THE MAN-WHO-IS-A-BAT?
I'M FROM GOTHAM, YES.
AND OF COURSE IT IS PURE COINCIDENCE THAT YOU COME TO OUR POOR COUNTRY IN ITS TIME OF CRISIS?
COINCIDENCE HAD NOTHING TO DO WITH IT.
AH, MY FRIEND, THEN NO DOUBT YOU HAVE COME TO AID US POOR PEASANTS--
--TO SERVE OUR WONDERFUL GENERALS IN THE MILITIA?
I SERVE JUSTICE--AND WHEN JUSTICE FAILS, I SERVE VENGEANCE.
QUITE SO, MY FRIEND--BUT I SUSPECT YOUR IDEA OF JUSTICE DIFFERS FROM MINE...
BATMAN!!
BUT HE HAS ALREADY SEEN THE GLITTER OF MOONLIGHT ON SHARPENED BLADE...
AND LONG BEFORE THAT--
WHAM
--HE SAW THE GLINT OF MURDER IN EVEN SHARPER EYES.
4

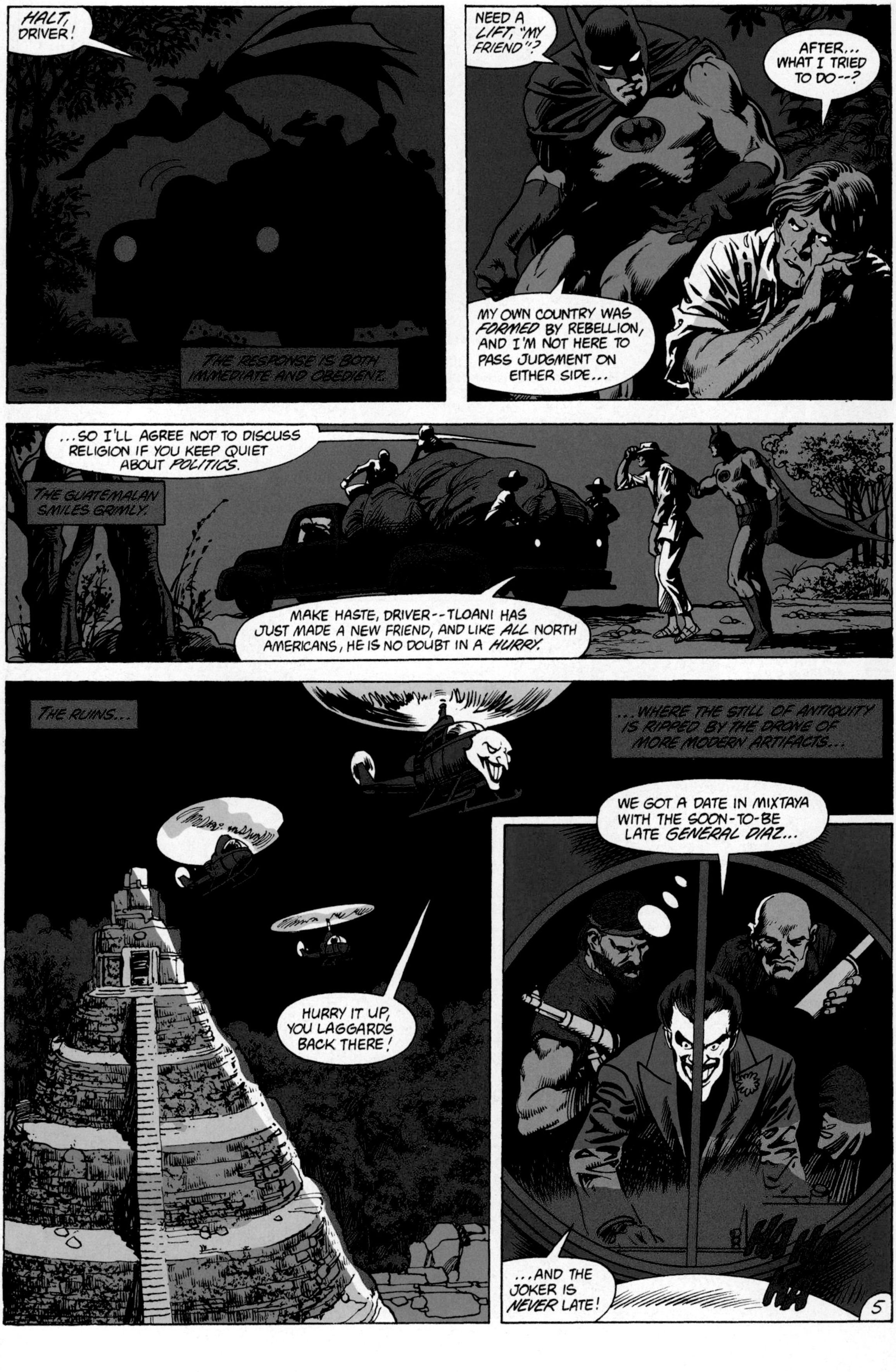

HALT, DRIVER!
THE RESPONSE IS BOTH IMMEDIATE AND OBEDIENT.
NEED A LIFT, "MY FRIEND"?
AFTER... WHAT I TRIED TO DO--?
MY OWN COUNTRY WAS FORMED BY REBELLION, AND I'M NOT HERE TO PASS JUDGMENT ON EITHER SIDE...
...SO I'LL AGREE NOT TO DISCUSS RELIGION IF YOU KEEP QUIET ABOUT POLITICS.
THE GUATEMALAN SMILES GRIMLY.
MAKE HASTE, DRIVER--TLOANI HAS JUST MADE A NEW FRIEND, AND LIKE ALL NORTH AMERICANS, HE IS NO DOUBT IN A HURRY.
THE RUINS...
...WHERE THE STILL OF ANTIQUITY IS RIPPED BY THE DRONE OF MORE MODERN ARTIFACTS...
HURRY IT UP, YOU LAGGARDS BACK THERE!
WE GOT A DATE IN MIXTAYA WITH THE SOON-TO-BE LATE GENERAL DIAZ...
...AND THE JOKER IS NEVER LATE!
5

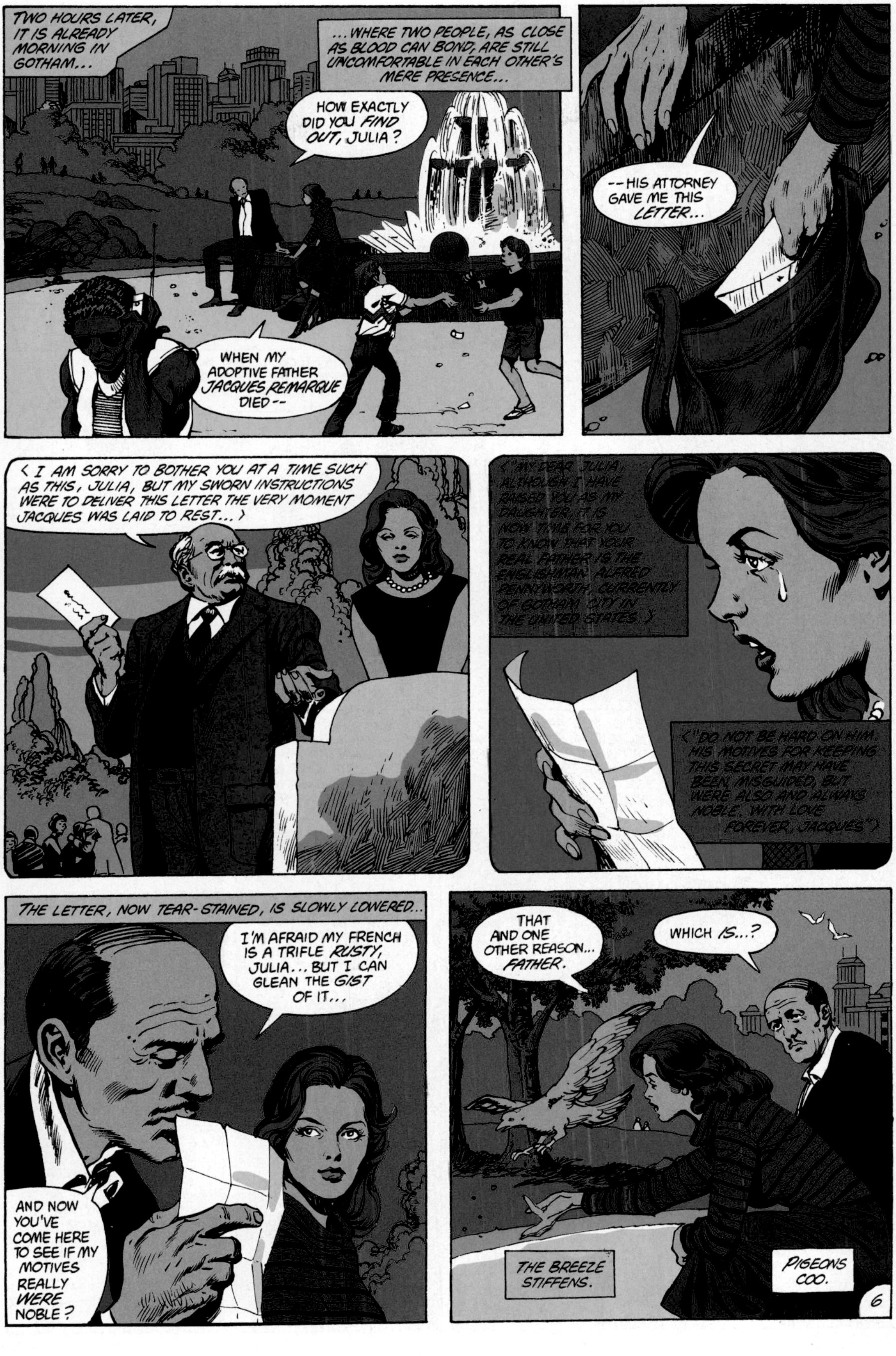
TWO HOURS LATER, IT IS ALREADY MORNING IN GOTHAM...
...WHERE TWO PEOPLE, AS CLOSE AS BLOOD CAN BOND, ARE STILL UNCOMFORTABLE IN EACH OTHER'S MERE PRESENCE...
HOW EXACTLY DID YOU FIND OUT, JULIA?
WHEN MY ADOPTIVE FATHER JACQUES REMARQUE DIED--
--HIS ATTORNEY GAVE ME THIS LETTER...
< I AM SORRY TO BOTHER YOU AT A TIME SUCH AS THIS, JULIA, BUT MY SWORN INSTRUCTIONS WERE TO DELIVER THIS LETTER THE VERY MOMENT JACQUES WAS LAID TO REST... >
< "MY DEAR JULIA, ALTHOUGH I HAVE RAISED YOU AS MY DAUGHTER, IT IS NOW TIME FOR YOU TO KNOW THAT YOUR REAL FATHER IS THE ENGLISHMAN ALFRED PENNYWORTH, CURRENTLY OF GOTHAM CITY IN THE UNITED STATES. >
< "DO NOT BE HARD ON HIM. HIS MOTIVES FOR KEEPING THIS SECRET MAY HAVE BEEN MISGUIDED, BUT WERE ALSO AND ALWAYS NOBLE. WITH LOVE FOREVER, JACQUES" >
THE LETTER, NOW TEAR-STAINED, IS SLOWLY LOWERED...
I'M AFRAID MY FRENCH IS A TRIFLE RUSTY, JULIA... BUT I CAN GLEAN THE GIST OF IT...
AND NOW YOU'VE COME HERE TO SEE IF MY MOTIVES REALLY WERE NOBLE?
THAT AND ONE OTHER REASON... FATHER.
WHICH IS...?
THE BREEZE STIFFENS.
PIGEONS COO.
6

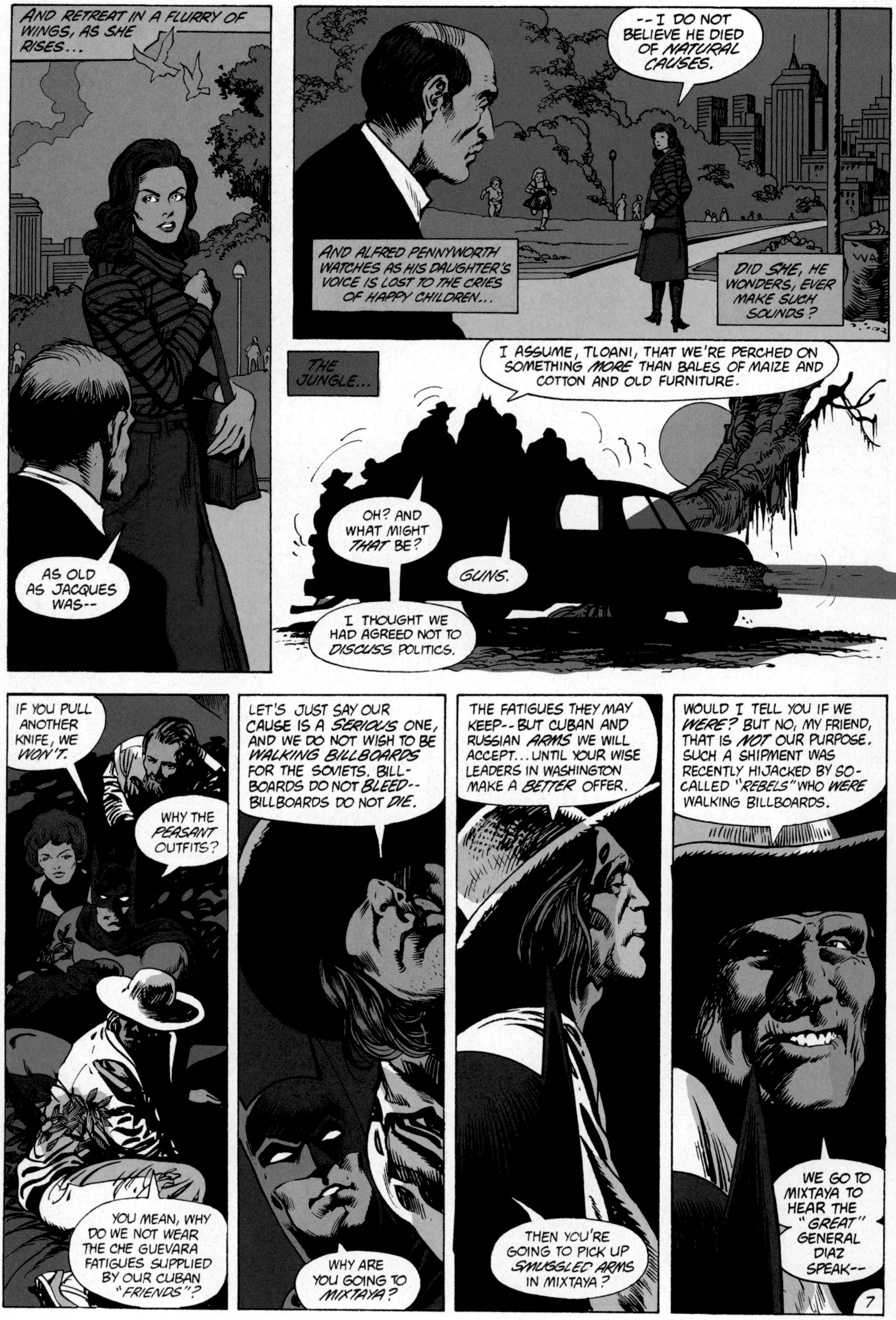
AND RETREAT IN A FLURRY OF WINGS, AS SHE RISES...
AS OLD AS JACQUES WAS--
--I DO NOT BELIEVE HE DIED OF NATURAL CAUSES.
AND ALFRED PENNYWORTH WATCHES AS HIS DAUGHTER'S VOICE IS LOST TO THE CRIES OF HAPPY CHILDREN...
DID SHE, HE WONDERS, EVER MAKE SUCH SOUNDS?
THE JUNGLE...
I ASSUME, TLOANI, THAT WE'RE PERCHED ON SOMETHING MORE THAN BALES OF MAIZE AND COTTON AND OLD FURNITURE.
OH? AND WHAT MIGHT THAT BE?
GUNS.
I THOUGHT WE HAD AGREED NOT TO DISCUSS POLITICS.
IF YOU PULL ANOTHER KNIFE, WE WON'T.
WHY THE PEASANT OUTFITS?
YOU MEAN, WHY DO WE NOT WEAR THE CHE GUEVARA FATIGUES SUPPLIED BY OUR CUBAN "FRIENDS"?
LET'S JUST SAY OUR CAUSE IS A SERIOUS ONE, AND WE DO NOT WISH TO BE WALKING BILLBOARDS FOR THE SOVIETS. BILLBOARDS DO NOT BLEED--BILLBOARDS DO NOT DIE.
WHY ARE YOU GOING TO MIXTAYA?
THE FATIGUES THEY MAY KEEP--BUT CUBAN AND RUSSIAN ARMS WE WILL ACCEPT... UNTIL YOUR WISE LEADERS IN WASHINGTON MAKE A BETTER OFFER.
THEN YOU'RE GOING TO PICK UP SMUGGLED ARMS IN MIXTAYA?
WOULD I TELL YOU IF WE WERE? BUT NO, MY FRIEND, THAT IS NOT OUR PURPOSE. SUCH A SHIPMENT WAS RECENTLY HIJACKED BY SO-CALLED "REBELS" WHO WERE WALKING BILLBOARDS.
WE GO TO MIXTAYA TO HEAR THE "GREAT" GENERAL DIAZ SPEAK--
7

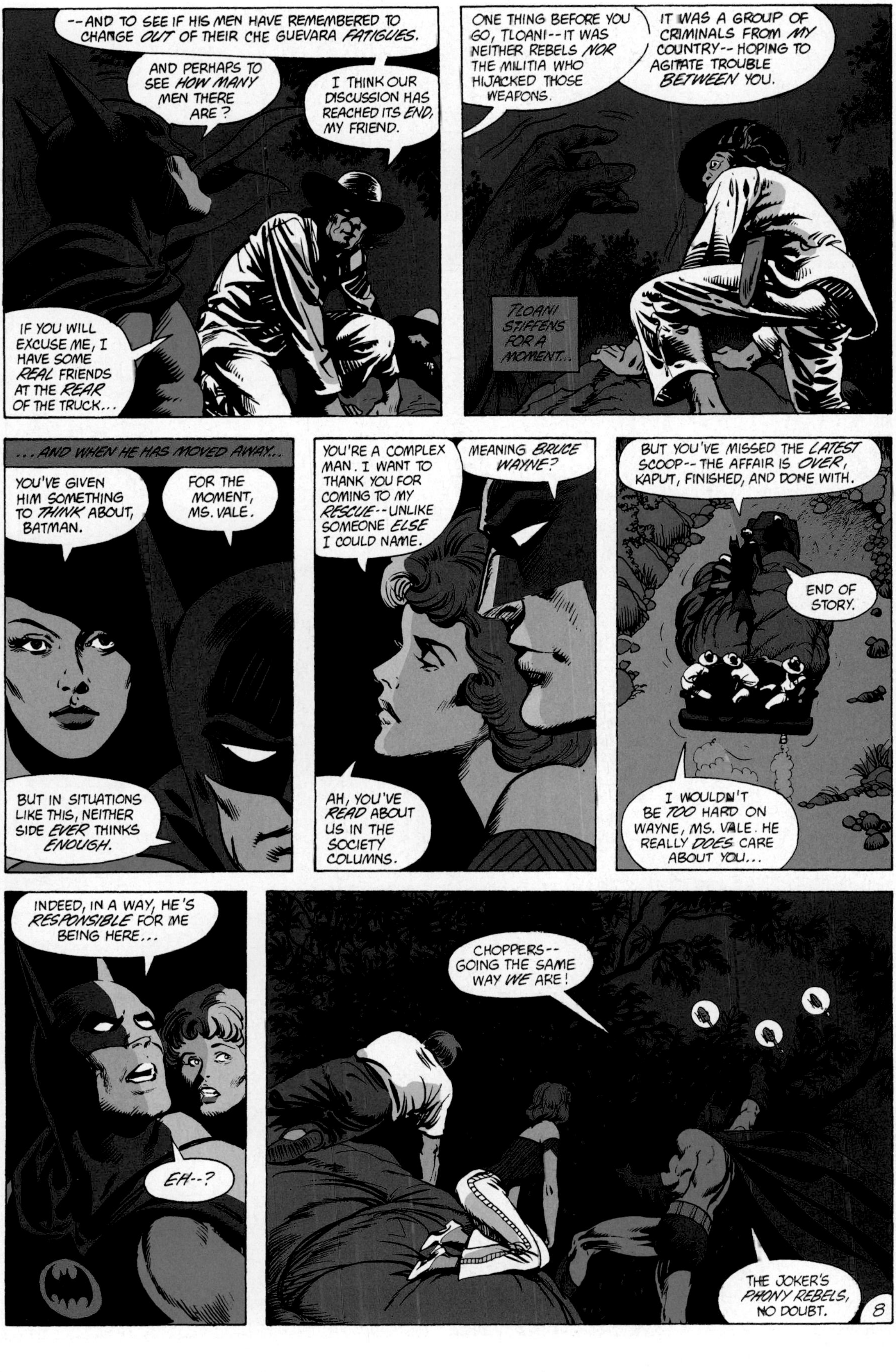
--AND TO SEE IF HIS MEN HAVE REMEMBERED TO CHANGE OUT OF THEIR CHE GUEVARA FATIGUES.
AND PERHAPS TO SEE HOW MANY MEN THERE ARE?
I THINK OUR DISCUSSION HAS REACHED ITS END, MY FRIEND.
IF YOU WILL EXCUSE ME, I HAVE SOME REAL FRIENDS AT THE REAR OF THE TRUCK...
ONE THING BEFORE YOU GO, TLOANI--IT WAS NEITHER REBELS NOR THE MILITIA WHO HIJACKED THOSE WEAPONS.
IT WAS A GROUP OF CRIMINALS FROM MY COUNTRY--HOPING TO AGITATE TROUBLE BETWEEN YOU.
TLOANI STIFFENS FOR A MOMENT...
...AND WHEN HE HAS MOVED AWAY...
YOU'VE GIVEN HIM SOMETHING TO THINK ABOUT, BATMAN.
FOR THE MOMENT, MS. VALE.
BUT IN SITUATIONS LIKE THIS, NEITHER SIDE EVER THINKS ENOUGH.
YOU'RE A COMPLEX MAN. I WANT TO THANK YOU FOR COMING TO MY RESCUE--UNLIKE SOMEONE ELSE I COULD NAME.
MEANING BRUCE WAYNE?
AH, YOU'VE READ ABOUT US IN THE SOCIETY COLUMNS.
BUT YOU'VE MISSED THE LATEST SCOOP--THE AFFAIR IS OVER, KAPUT, FINISHED, AND DONE WITH.
END OF STORY.
I WOULDN'T BE TOO HARD ON WAYNE, MS. VALE. HE REALLY DOES CARE ABOUT YOU...
INDEED, IN A WAY, HE'S RESPONSIBLE FOR ME BEING HERE...
EH--?
CHOPPERS--GOING THE SAME WAY WE ARE!
THE JOKER'S PHONY REBELS, NO DOUBT.
8

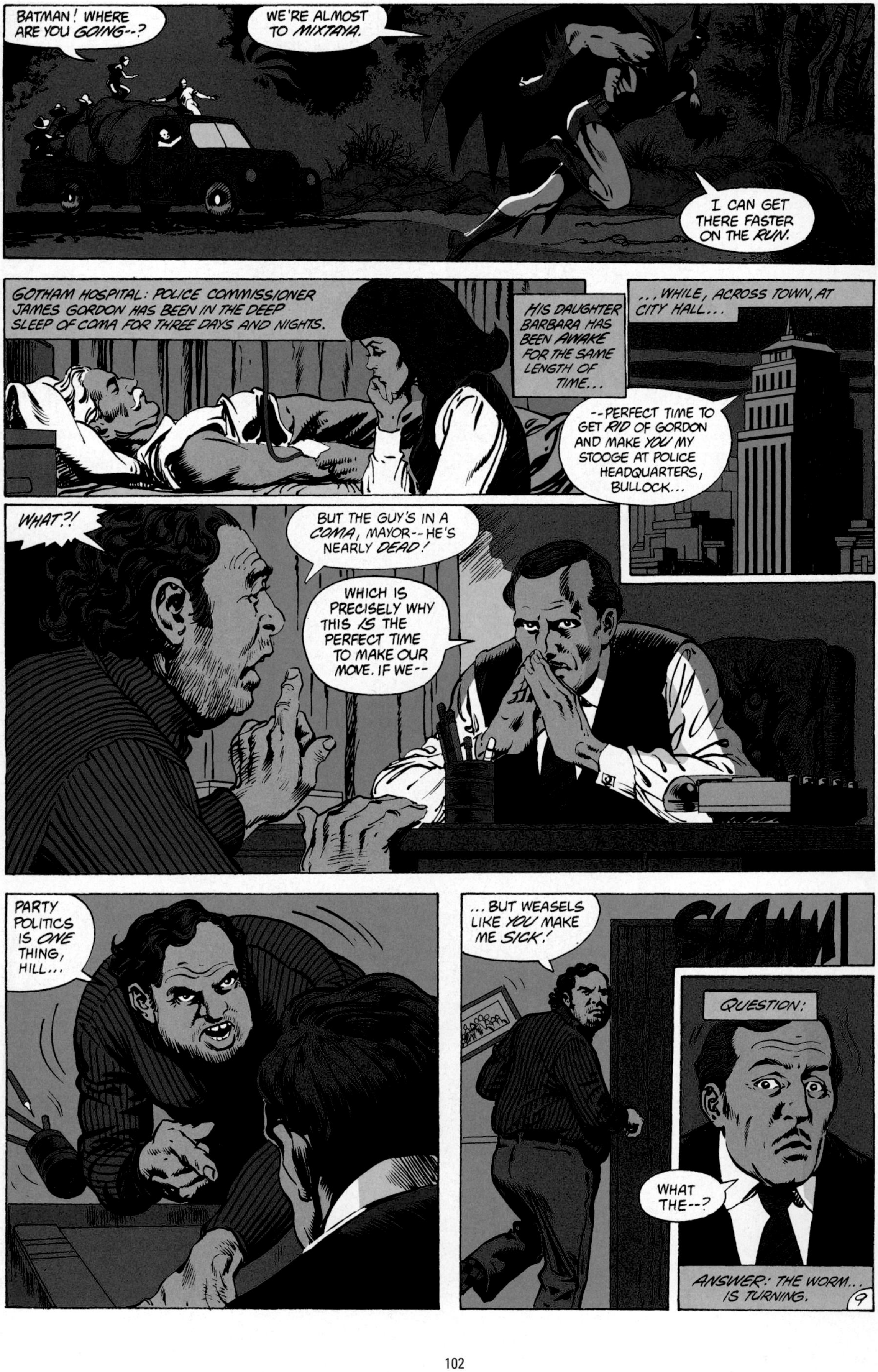
BATMAN! WHERE ARE YOU GOING--?
WE'RE ALMOST TO MIXTAYA.
I CAN GET THERE FASTER ON THE RUN.
GOTHAM HOSPITAL: POLICE COMMISSIONER JAMES GORDON HAS BEEN IN THE DEEP SLEEP OF COMA FOR THREE DAYS AND NIGHTS.
HIS DAUGHTER BARBARA HAS BEEN AWAKE FOR THE SAME LENGTH OF TIME...
...WHILE, ACROSS TOWN, AT CITY HALL...
--PERFECT TIME TO GET RID OF GORDON AND MAKE YOU MY STOOGE AT POLICE HEADQUARTERS, BULLOCK...
WHAT?!
BUT THE GUY'S IN A COMA, MAYOR--HE'S NEARLY DEAD!
WHICH IS PRECISELY WHY THIS IS THE PERFECT TIME TO MAKE OUR MOVE. IF WE--
PARTY POLITICS IS ONE THING, HILL...
...BUT WEASELS LIKE YOU MAKE ME SICK!
SLAM
QUESTION:
WHAT THE--?
ANSWER: THE WORM... IS TURNING.
9

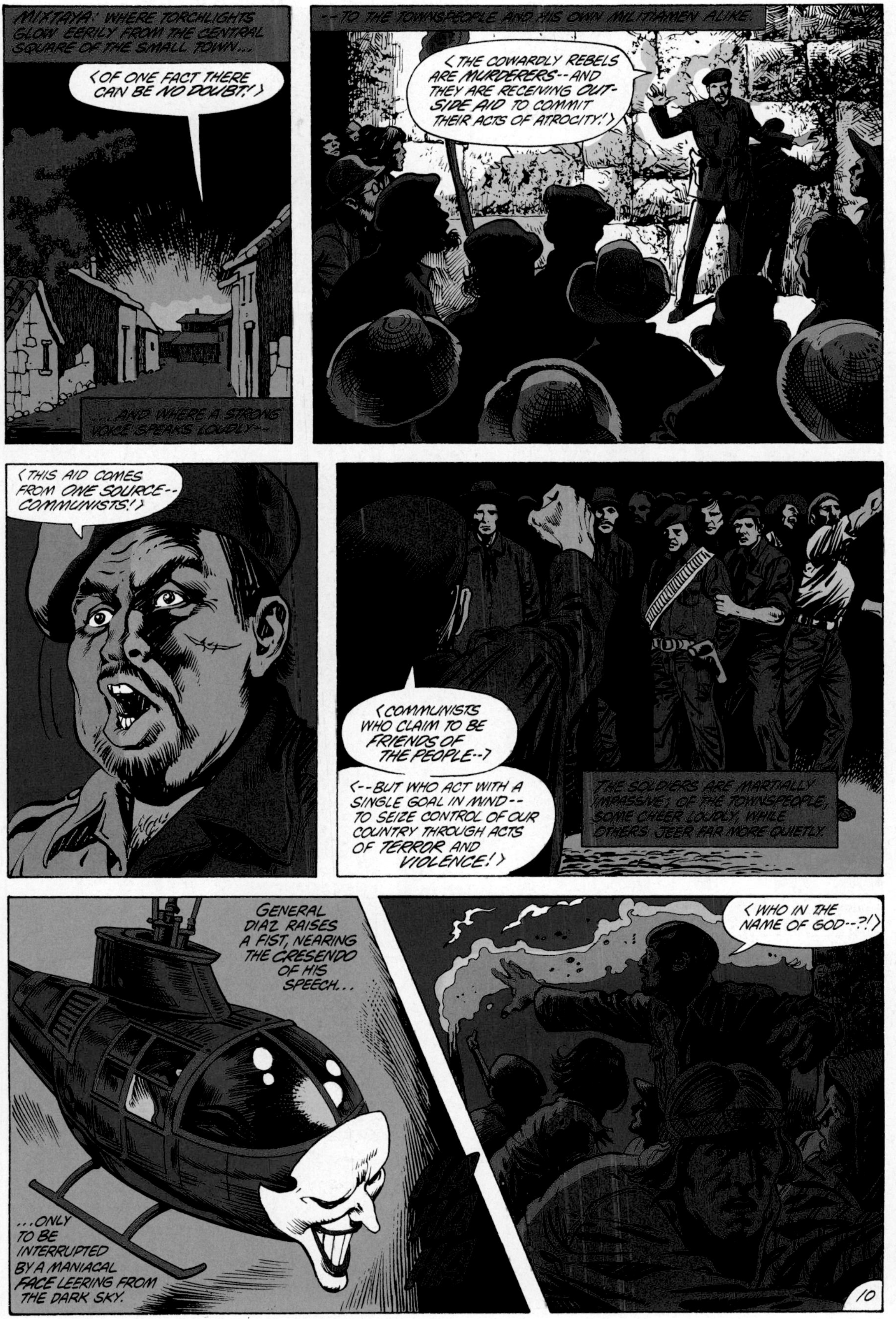
MIXTAYA: WHERE TORCHLIGHTS GLOW EERILY FROM THE CENTRAL SQUARE OF THE SMALL TOWN...
<OF ONE FACT THERE CAN BE NO DOUBT!>
...AND WHERE A STRONG VOICE SPEAKS LOUDLY--
--TO THE TOWNSPEOPLE AND HIS OWN MILITIAMEN ALIKE.
<THE COWARDLY REBELS ARE MURDERERS--AND THEY ARE RECEIVING OUTSIDE AID TO COMMIT THEIR ACTS OF ATROCITY!>
<THIS AID COMES FROM ONE SOURCE--COMMUNISTS!>
<COMMUNISTS WHO CLAIM TO BE FRIENDS OF THE PEOPLE-->
<--BUT WHO ACT WITH A SINGLE GOAL IN MIND--TO SEIZE CONTROL OF OUR COUNTRY THROUGH ACTS OF TERROR AND VIOLENCE!>
THE SOLDIERS ARE MARTIALLY IMPASSIVE; OF THE TOWNSPEOPLE, SOME CHEER LOUDLY, WHILE OTHERS JEER FAR MORE QUIETLY.
GENERAL DIAZ RAISES A FIST, NEARING THE CRESENDO OF HIS SPEECH...
...ONLY TO BE INTERRUPTED BY A MANIACAL FACE LEERING FROM THE DARK SKY.
<WHO IN THE NAME OF GOD--?!>
10

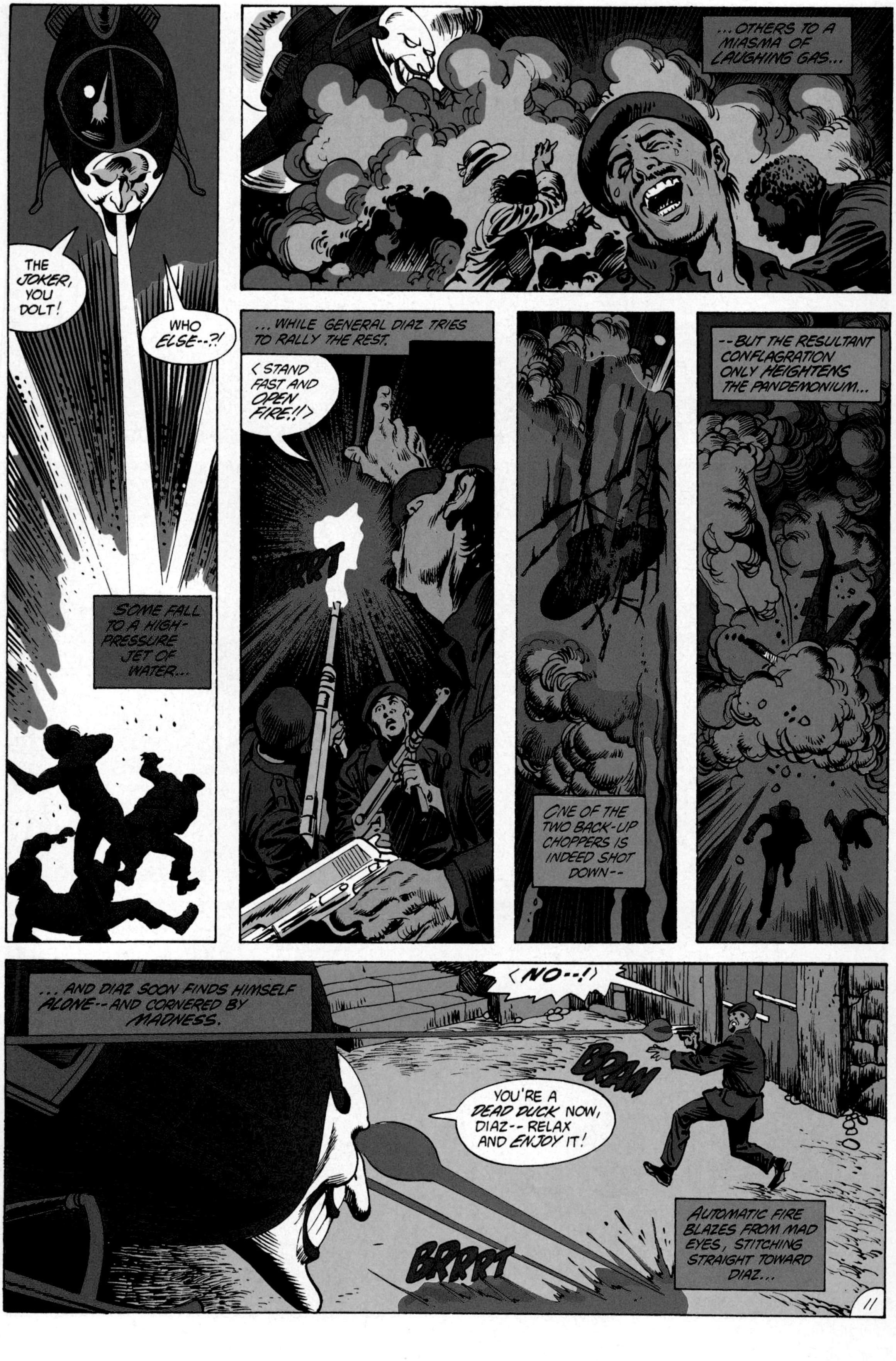
THE JOKER, YOU DOLT!
WHO ELSE--?!
SOME FALL TO A HIGH-PRESSURE JET OF WATER...
...OTHERS TO A MIASMA OF LAUGHING GAS...
...WHILE GENERAL DIAZ TRIES TO RALLY THE REST.
< STAND FAST AND OPEN FIRE!! >
BRRRT
ONE OF THE TWO BACK-UP CHOPPERS IS INDEED SHOT DOWN--
--BUT THE RESULTANT CONFLAGRATION ONLY HEIGHTENS THE PANDEMONIUM...
...AND DIAZ SOON FINDS HIMSELF ALONE--AND CORNERED BY MADNESS.
< NO--! >
BRAM
YOU'RE A DEAD DUCK NOW, DIAZ-- RELAX AND ENJOY IT!
AUTOMATIC FIRE BLAZES FROM MAD EYES, STITCHING STRAIGHT TOWARD DIAZ...
BRRRT
11

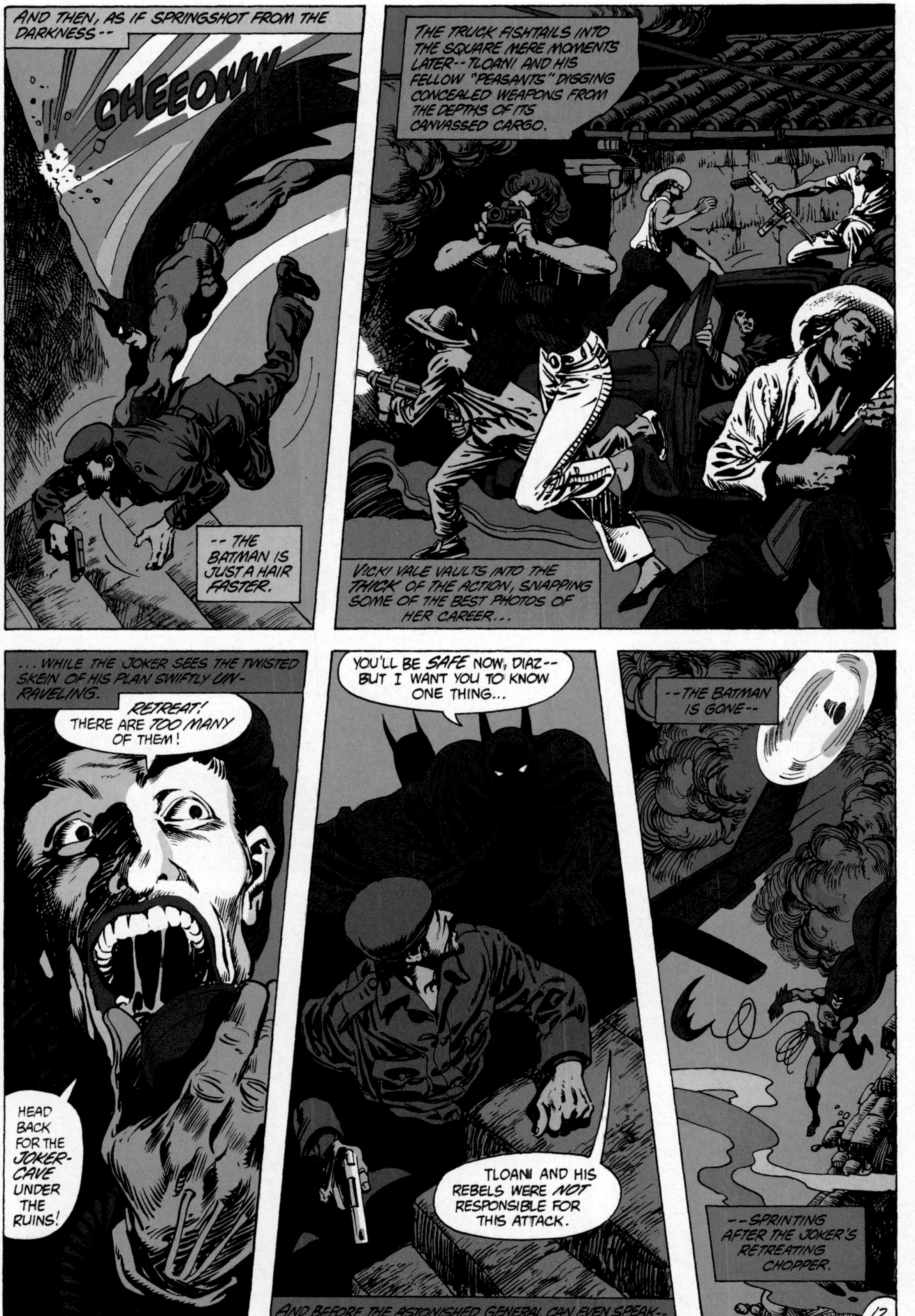
AND THEN, AS IF SPRINGSHOT FROM THE DARKNESS--
CHEEOWW
--THE BATMAN IS JUST A HAIR FASTER.
THE TRUCK FISHTAILS INTO THE SQUARE MERE MOMENTS LATER--TLOANI AND HIS FELLOW "PEASANTS" DIGGING CONCEALED WEAPONS FROM THE DEPTHS OF ITS CANVASSED CARGO.
VICKI VALE VAULTS INTO THE THICK OF THE ACTION, SNAPPING SOME OF THE BEST PHOTOS OF HER CAREER...
...WHILE THE JOKER SEES THE TWISTED SKEIN OF HIS PLAN SWIFTLY UNRAVELING.
RETREAT! THERE ARE TOO MANY OF THEM!
HEAD BACK FOR THE JOKER-CAVE UNDER THE RUINS!
YOU'LL BE SAFE NOW, DIAZ--BUT I WANT YOU TO KNOW ONE THING...
TLOANI AND HIS REBELS WERE NOT RESPONSIBLE FOR THIS ATTACK.
AND BEFORE THE ASTONISHED GENERAL CAN EVEN SPEAK--
--THE BATMAN IS GONE--
--SPRINTING AFTER THE JOKER'S RETREATING CHOPPER.
12

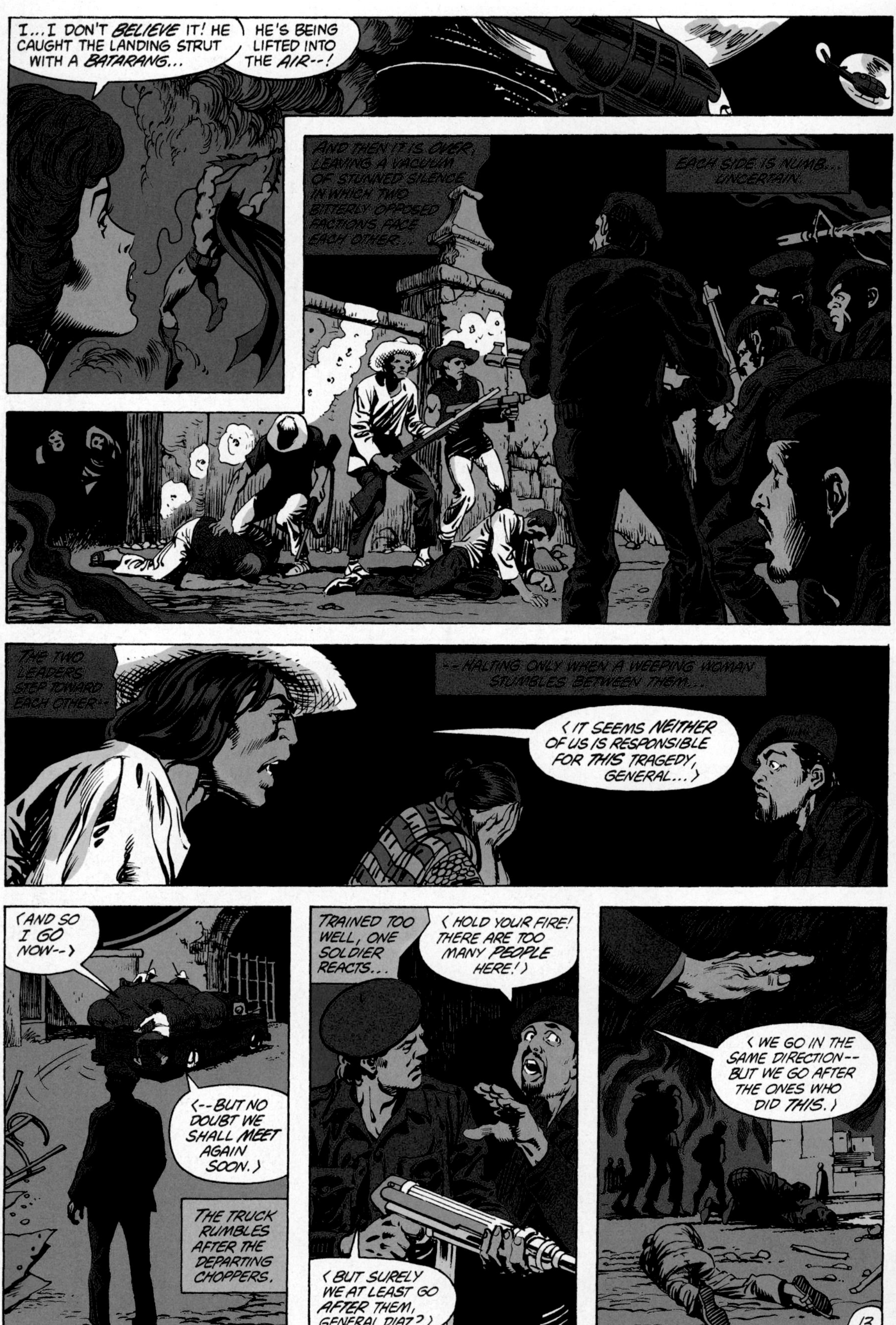
I...I DON'T BELIEVE IT! HE CAUGHT THE LANDING STRUT WITH A BATARANG...
HE'S BEING LIFTED INTO THE AIR--!
AND THEN IT IS OVER, LEAVING A VACUUM OF STUNNED SILENCE IN WHICH TWO BITTERLY OPPOSED FACTIONS FACE EACH OTHER...
EACH SIDE IS NUMB... UNCERTAIN.
THE TWO LEADERS STEP TOWARD EACH OTHER--
--HALTING ONLY WHEN A WEEPING WOMAN STUMBLES BETWEEN THEM...
< IT SEEMS NEITHER OF US IS RESPONSIBLE FOR THIS TRAGEDY, GENERAL... >
< AND SO I GO NOW-- >
< --BUT NO DOUBT WE SHALL MEET AGAIN SOON. >
THE TRUCK RUMBLES AFTER THE DEPARTING CHOPPERS.
TRAINED TOO WELL, ONE SOLDIER REACTS...
< HOLD YOUR FIRE! THERE ARE TOO MANY PEOPLE HERE! >
< BUT SURELY WE AT LEAST GO AFTER THEM, GENERAL DIAZ? >
< WE GO IN THE SAME DIRECTION-- BUT WE GO AFTER THE ONES WHO DID THIS. >
13

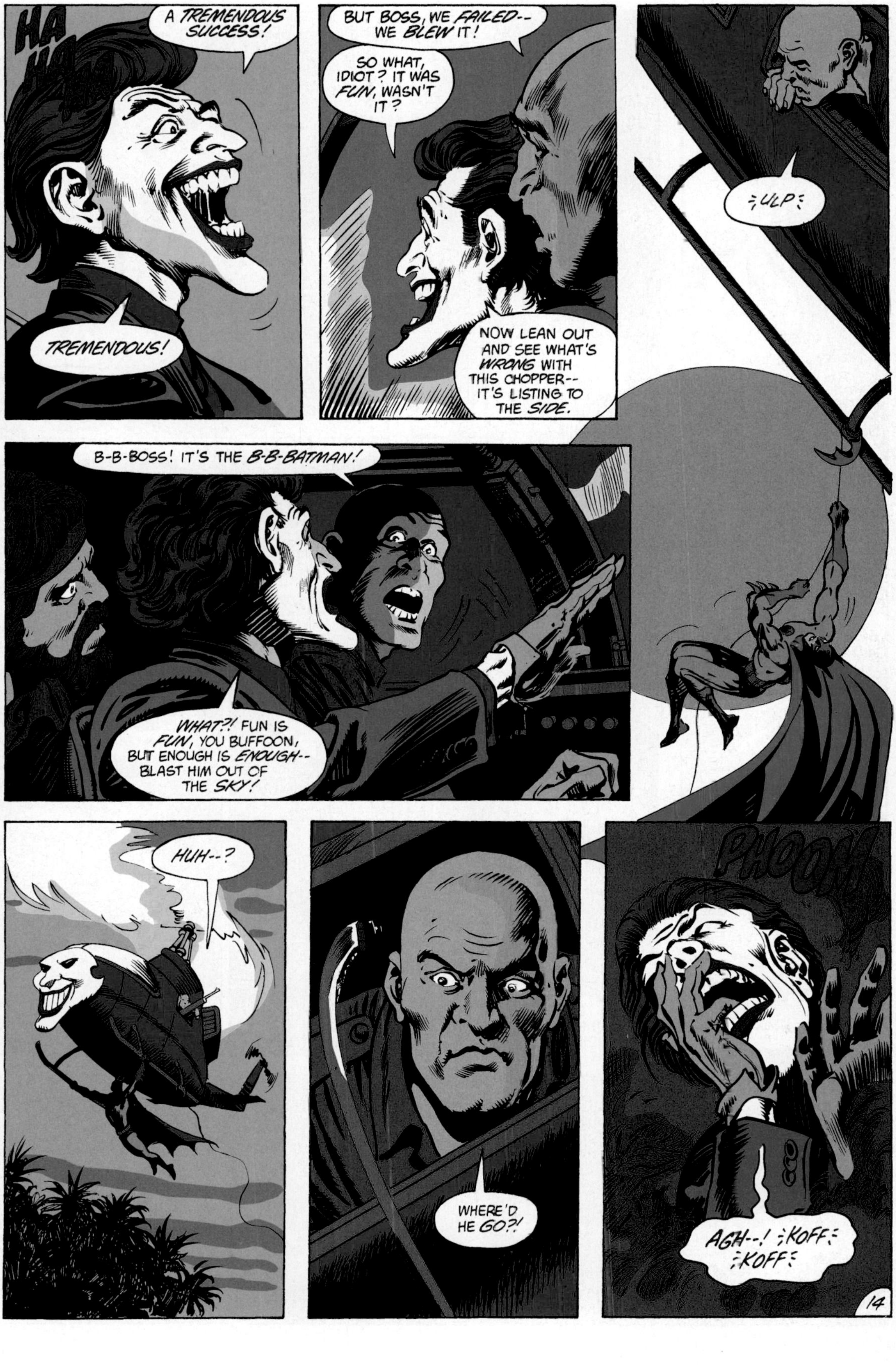
HA HA HA
A TREMENDOUS SUCCESS!
TREMENDOUS!
BUT BOSS, WE FAILED-- WE BLEW IT!
SO WHAT, IDIOT? IT WAS FUN, WASN'T IT?
NOW LEAN OUT AND SEE WHAT'S WRONG WITH THIS CHOPPER-- IT'S LISTING TO THE SIDE.
:ULP:
B-B-BOSS! IT'S THE B-B-BATMAN!
WHAT?! FUN IS FUN, YOU BUFFOON, BUT ENOUGH IS ENOUGH-- BLAST HIM OUT OF THE SKY!
HUH--?
WHERE'D HE GO?!
PHOOM
AGH--! :KOFF: :KOFF:
14

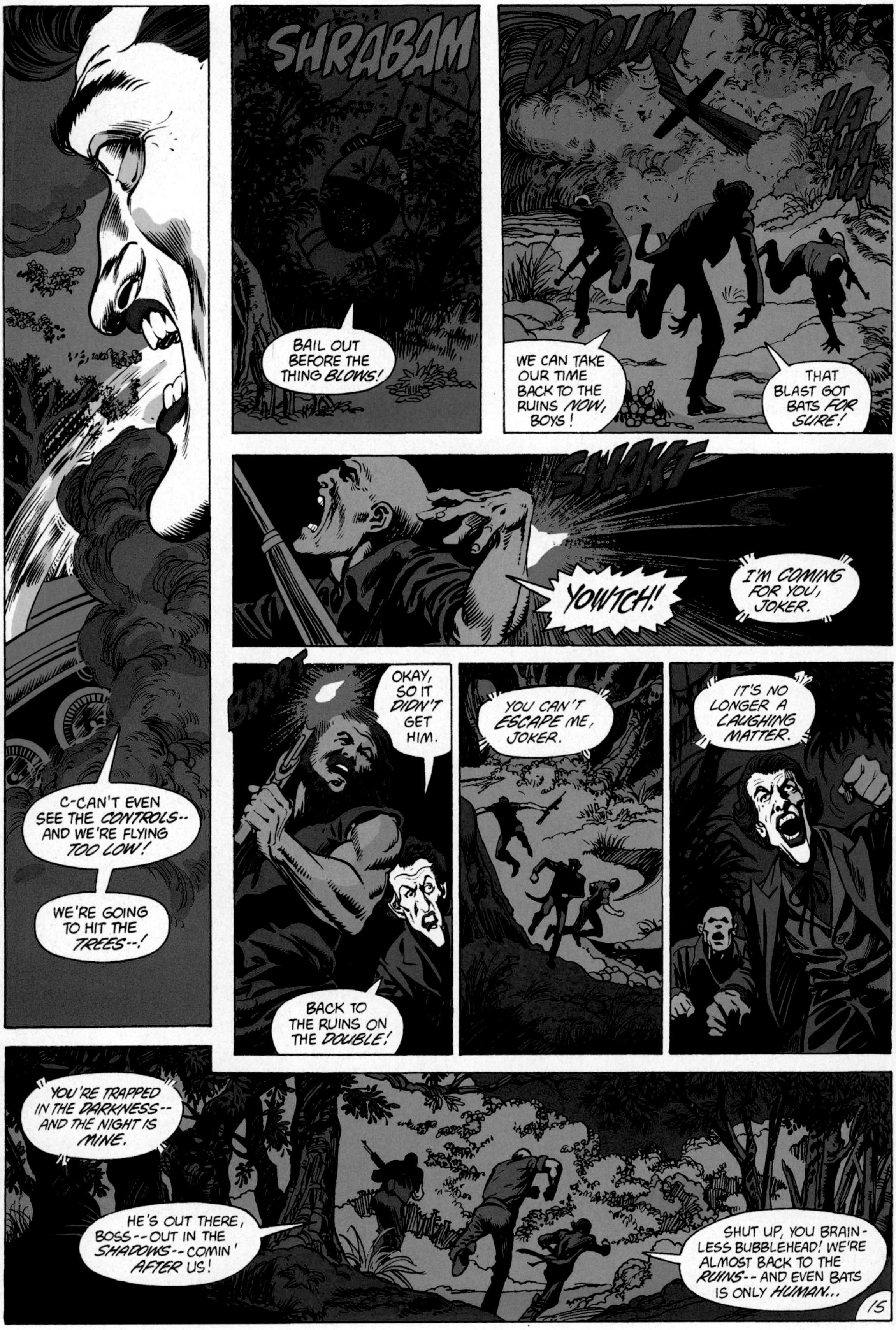
C-CAN'T EVEN SEE THE CONTROLS-- AND WE'RE FLYING TOO LOW!
WE'RE GOING TO HIT THE TREES--!
SHRABAM
BAIL OUT BEFORE THE THING BLOWS!
BADUM
HA HA HA HA
WE CAN TAKE OUR TIME BACK TO THE RUINS NOW, BOYS!
THAT BLAST GOT BATS FOR SURE!
YOWTCH!
I'M COMING FOR YOU, JOKER.
OKAY, SO IT DIDN'T GET HIM.
BACK TO THE RUINS ON THE DOUBLE!
YOU CAN'T ESCAPE ME, JOKER.
IT'S NO LONGER A LAUGHING MATTER.
YOU'RE TRAPPED IN THE DARKNESS-- AND THE NIGHT IS MINE.
HE'S OUT THERE, BOSS--OUT IN THE SHADOWS--COMIN' AFTER US!
SHUT UP, YOU BRAIN-LESS BUBBLEHEAD! WE'RE ALMOST BACK TO THE RUINS-- AND EVEN BATS IS ONLY HUMAN...
15

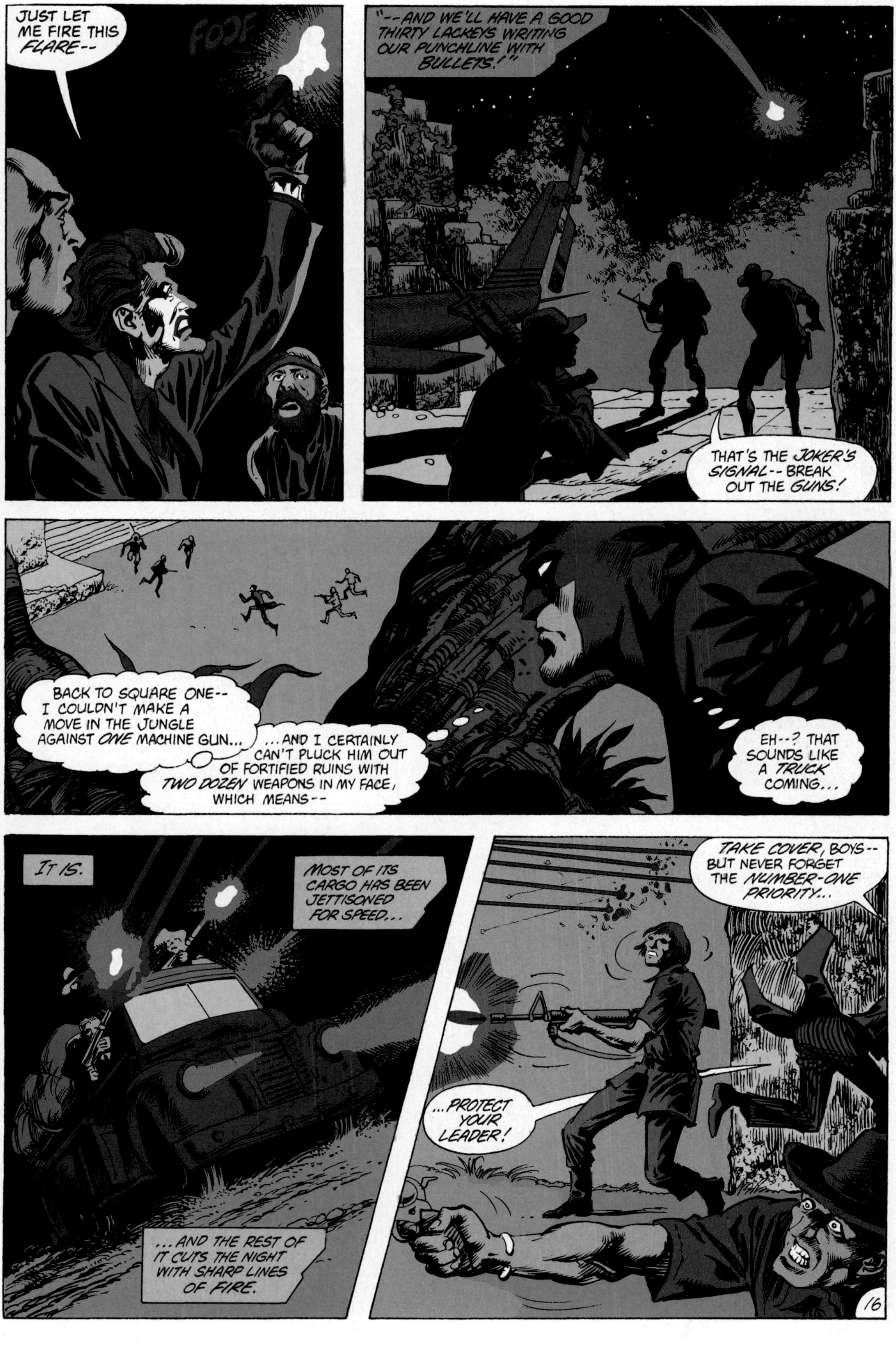
JUST LET ME FIRE THIS FLARE--
FOOF
"--AND WE'LL HAVE A GOOD THIRTY LACKEYS WRITING OUR PUNCHLINE WITH BULLETS!"
THAT'S THE JOKER'S SIGNAL--BREAK OUT THE GUNS!
BACK TO SQUARE ONE-- I COULDN'T MAKE A MOVE IN THE JUNGLE AGAINST ONE MACHINE GUN...
...AND I CERTAINLY CAN'T PLUCK HIM OUT OF FORTIFIED RUINS WITH TWO DOZEN WEAPONS IN MY FACE, WHICH MEANS--
EH--? THAT SOUNDS LIKE A TRUCK COMING...
IT IS.
MOST OF ITS CARGO HAS BEEN JETTISONED FOR SPEED...
...AND THE REST OF IT CUTS THE NIGHT WITH SHARP LINES OF FIRE.
TAKE COVER, BOYS-- BUT NEVER FORGET THE NUMBER-ONE PRIORITY...
...PROTECT YOUR LEADER!
16

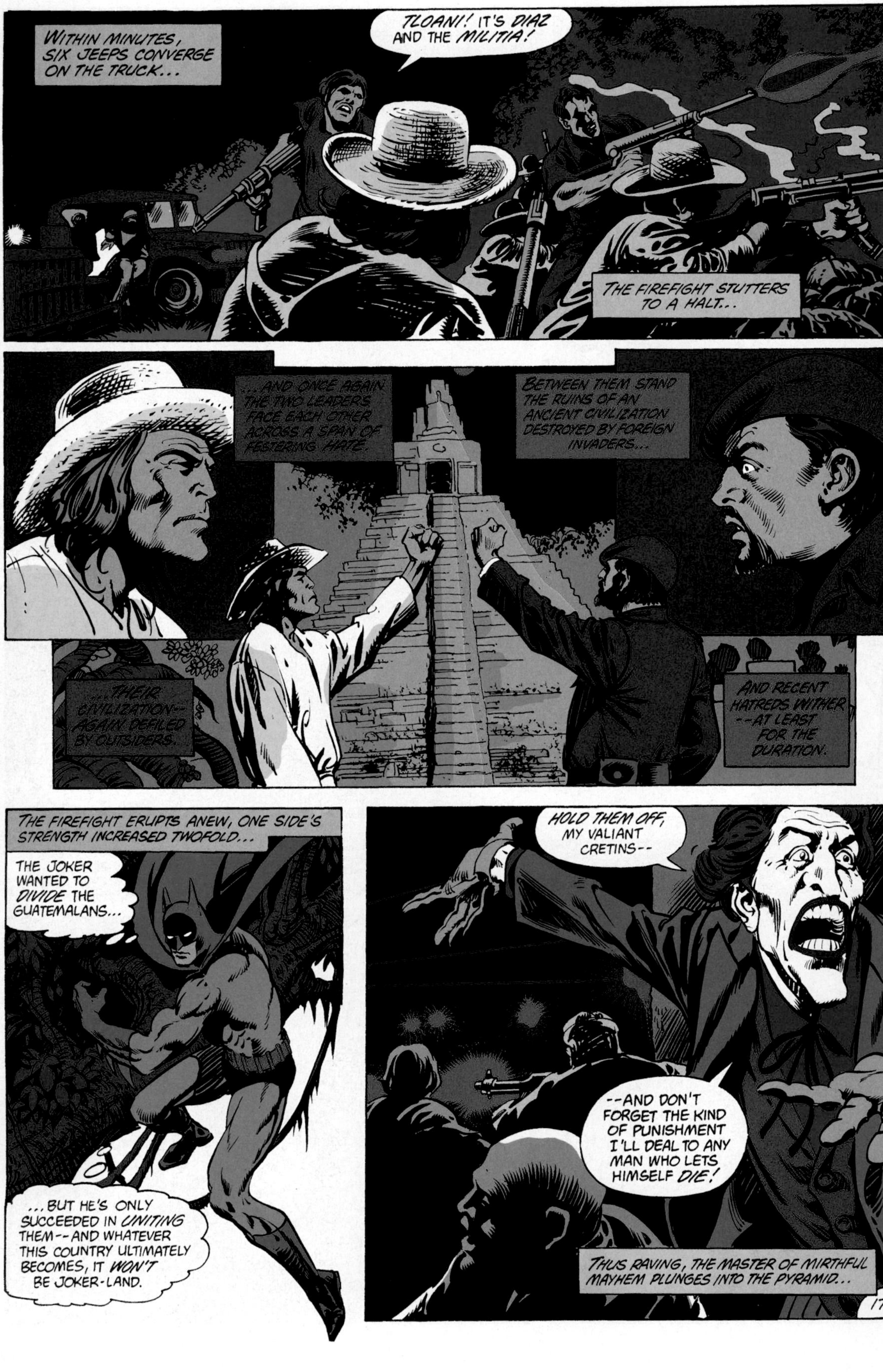
WITHIN MINUTES, SIX JEEPS CONVERGE ON THE TRUCK...
TLOANI! IT'S DIAZ AND THE MILITIA!
THE FIREFIGHT STUTTERS TO A HALT...
...AND ONCE AGAIN THE TWO LEADERS FACE EACH OTHER ACROSS A SPAN OF FESTERING HATE.
BETWEEN THEM STAND THE RUINS OF AN ANCIENT CIVILIZATION DESTROYED BY FOREIGN INVADERS...
...THEIR CIVILIZATION--AGAIN DEFILED BY OUTSIDERS.
AND RECENT HATREDS WITHER--AT LEAST FOR THE DURATION.
THE FIREFIGHT ERUPTS ANEW, ONE SIDE'S STRENGTH INCREASED TWOFOLD...
THE JOKER WANTED TO DIVIDE THE GUATEMALANS...
...BUT HE'S ONLY SUCCEEDED IN UNITING THEM--AND WHATEVER THIS COUNTRY ULTIMATELY BECOMES, IT WON'T BE JOKER-LAND.
HOLD THEM OFF, MY VALIANT CRETINS--
--AND DON'T FORGET THE KIND OF PUNISHMENT I'LL DEAL TO ANY MAN WHO LETS HIMSELF DIE!
THUS RAVING, THE MASTER OF MIRTHFUL MAYHEM PLUNGES INTO THE PYRAMID...
17

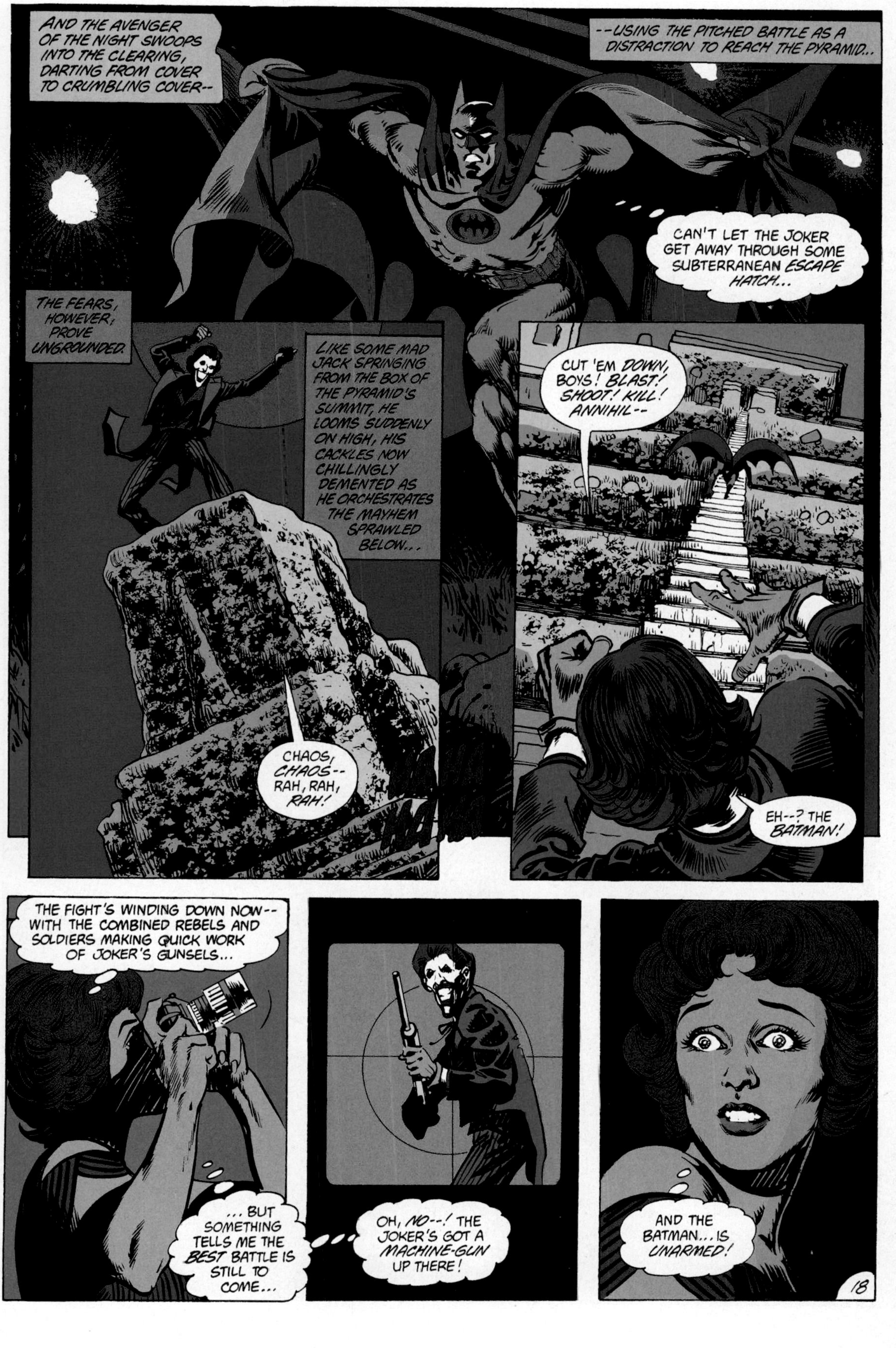

AND THE AVENGER OF THE NIGHT SWOOPS INTO THE CLEARING, DARTING FROM COVER TO CRUMBLING COVER--
--USING THE PITCHED BATTLE AS A DISTRACTION TO REACH THE PYRAMID...
CAN'T LET THE JOKER GET AWAY THROUGH SOME SUBTERRANEAN ESCAPE HATCH...
THE FEARS, HOWEVER, PROVE UNGROUNDED.
LIKE SOME MAD JACK SPRINGING FROM THE BOX OF THE PYRAMID'S SUMMIT, HE LOOMS SUDDENLY ON HIGH, HIS CACKLES NOW CHILLINGLY DEMENTED AS HE ORCHESTRATES THE MAYHEM SPRAWLED BELOW...
CHAOS, CHAOS-- RAH, RAH, RAH!
CUT 'EM DOWN, BOYS! BLAST! SHOOT! KILL! ANNIHIL--
EH--? THE BATMAN!
THE FIGHT'S WINDING DOWN NOW-- WITH THE COMBINED REBELS AND SOLDIERS MAKING QUICK WORK OF JOKER'S GUNSELS...
... BUT SOMETHING TELLS ME THE BEST BATTLE IS STILL TO COME...
OH, NO--! THE JOKER'S GOT A MACHINE-GUN UP THERE!
AND THE BATMAN... IS UNARMED!
18

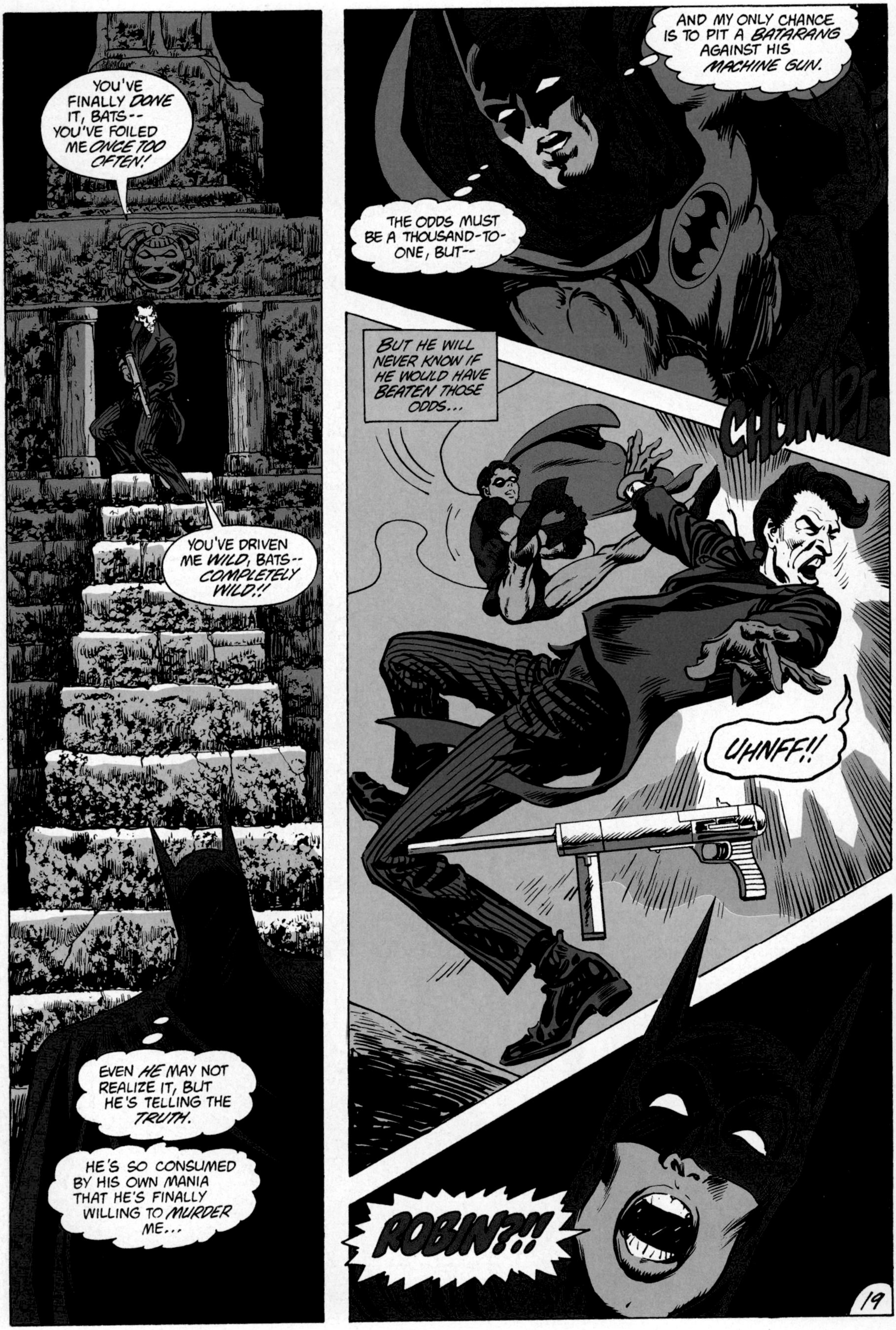
YOU'VE FINALLY DONE IT, BATS-- YOU'VE FOILED ME ONCE TOO OFTEN!
YOU'VE DRIVEN ME WILD, BATS-- COMPLETELY WILD!!
EVEN HE MAY NOT REALIZE IT, BUT HE'S TELLING THE TRUTH.
HE'S SO CONSUMED BY HIS OWN MANIA THAT HE'S FINALLY WILLING TO MURDER ME...
AND MY ONLY CHANCE IS TO PIT A BATARANG AGAINST HIS MACHINE GUN.
THE ODDS MUST BE A THOUSAND-TO-ONE, BUT--
BUT HE WILL NEVER KNOW IF HE WOULD HAVE BEATEN THOSE ODDS...
CHUMPT
UHNFF!!
ROBIN?!!
19

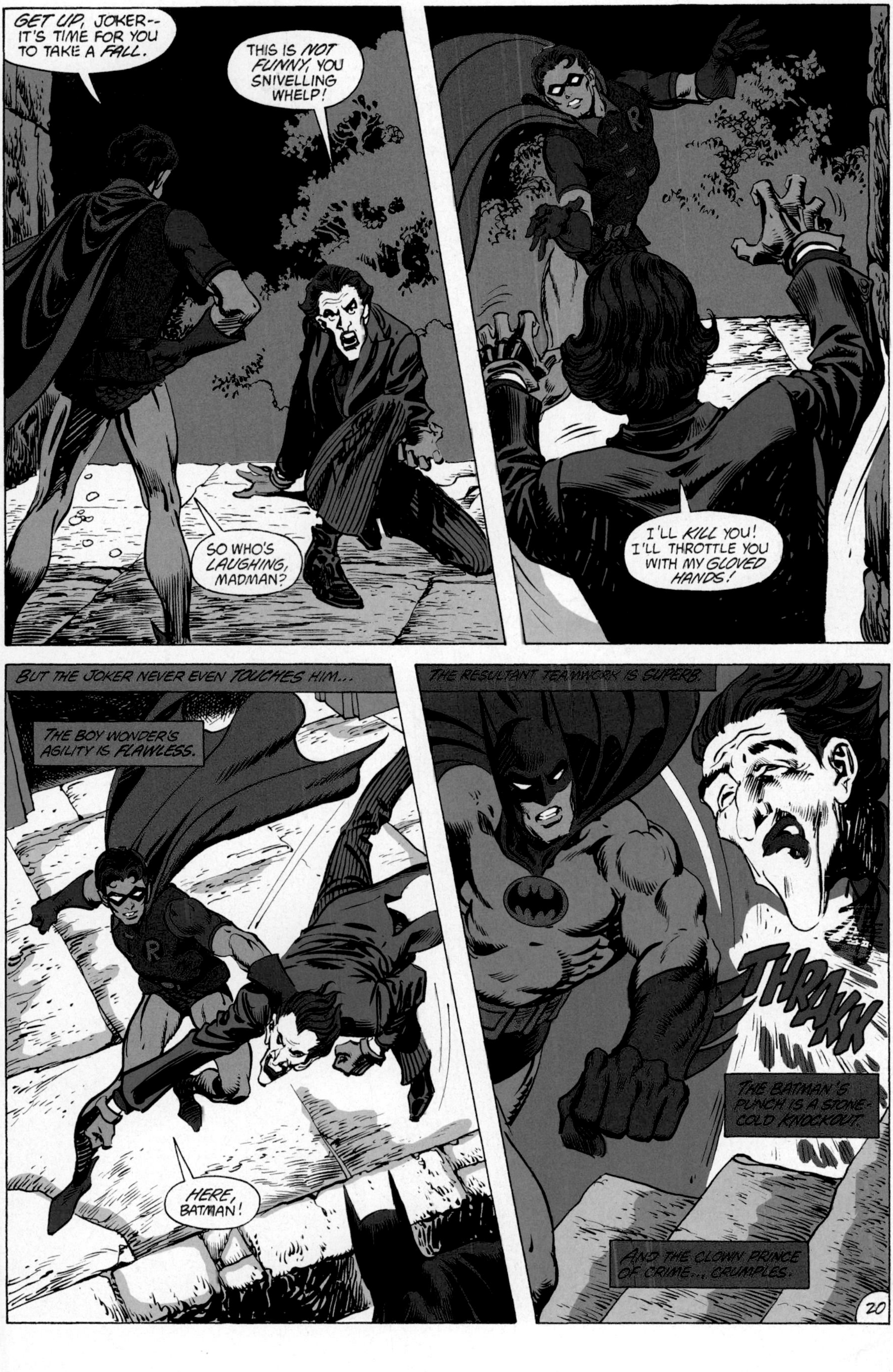
GET UP, JOKER-- IT'S TIME FOR YOU TO TAKE A FALL.
THIS IS NOT FUNNY, YOU SNIVELLING WHELP!
SO WHO'S LAUGHING, MADMAN?
I'LL KILL YOU! I'LL THROTTLE YOU WITH MY GLOVED HANDS!
BUT THE JOKER NEVER EVEN TOUCHES HIM...
THE BOY WONDER'S AGILITY IS FLAWLESS.
HERE, BATMAN!
THE RESULTANT TEAMWORK IS SUPERB.
THRAKK
THE BATMAN'S PUNCH IS A STONE-COLD KNOCKOUT.
AND THE CLOWN PRINCE OF CRIME... CRUMPLES.
20

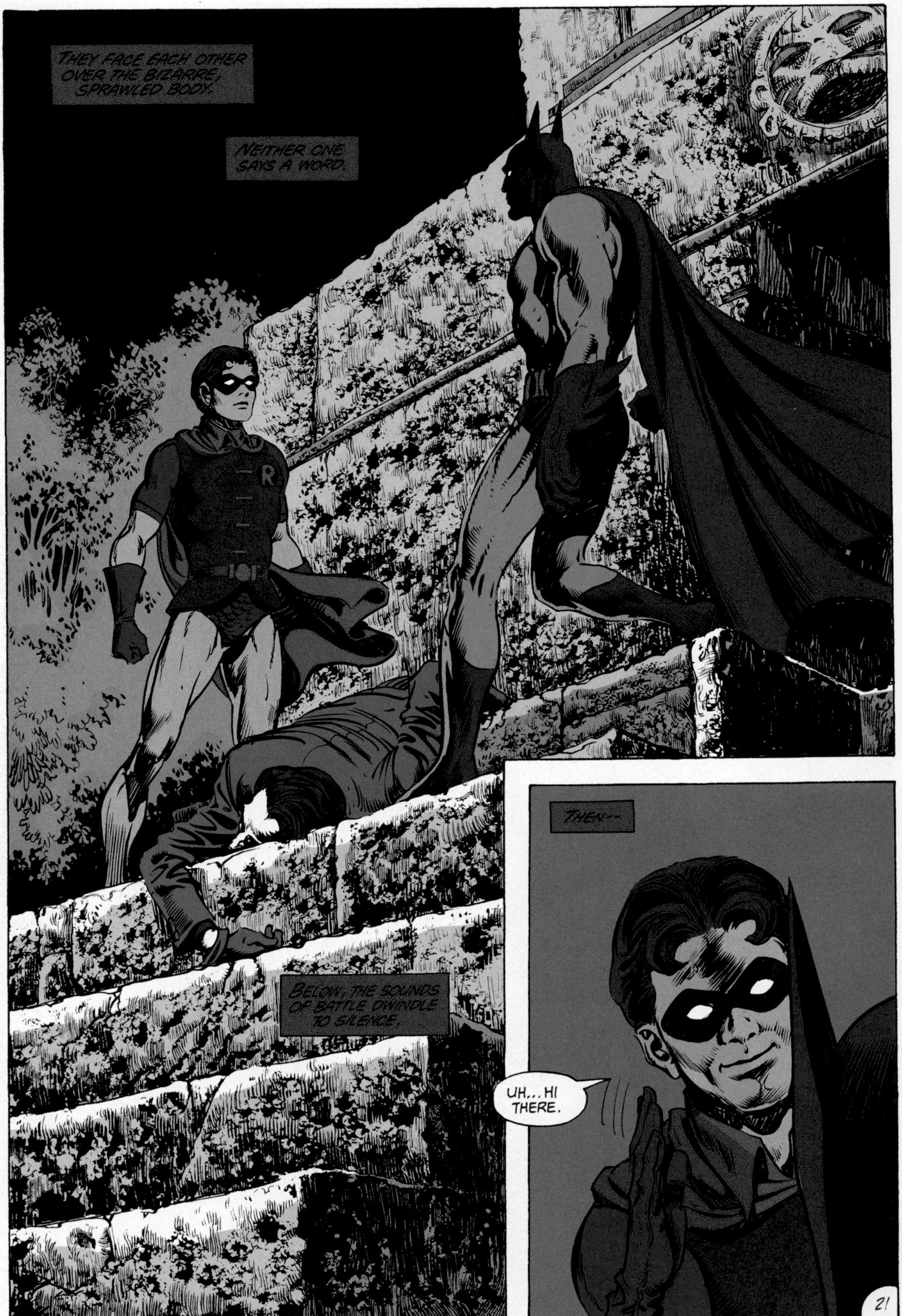
THEY FACE EACH OTHER OVER THE BIZARRE, SPRAWLED BODY.
NEITHER ONE SAYS A WORD.
BELOW, THE SOUNDS OF BATTLE DWINDLE TO SILENCE.
THEN--
UH... HI THERE.
21

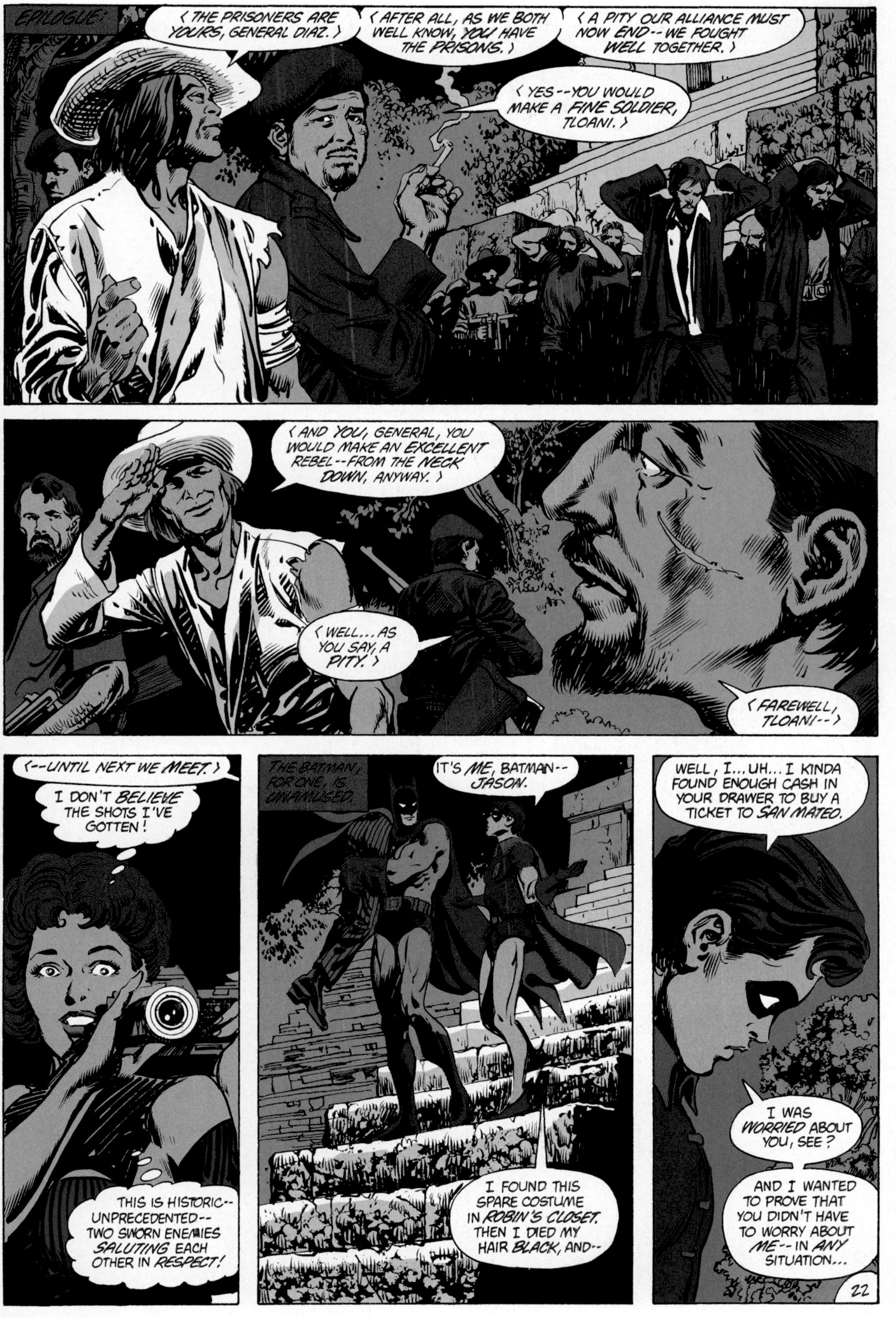
EPILOGUE:
< THE PRISONERS ARE YOURS, GENERAL DIAZ. >
< AFTER ALL, AS WE BOTH WELL KNOW, YOU HAVE THE PRISONS. >
< A PITY OUR ALLIANCE MUST NOW END-- WE FOUGHT WELL TOGETHER. >
< YES--YOU WOULD MAKE A FINE SOLDIER, TLOANI. >
< AND YOU, GENERAL, YOU WOULD MAKE AN EXCELLENT REBEL--FROM THE NECK DOWN, ANYWAY. >
< WELL... AS YOU SAY, A PITY. >
< FAREWELL, TLOANI-- >
< --UNTIL NEXT WE MEET. >
I DON'T BELIEVE THE SHOTS I'VE GOTTEN!
THIS IS HISTORIC-- UNPRECEDENTED-- TWO SWORN ENEMIES SALUTING EACH OTHER IN RESPECT!
THE BATMAN, FOR ONE, IS UNAMUSED.
IT'S ME, BATMAN-- JASON.
I FOUND THIS SPARE COSTUME IN ROBIN'S CLOSET. THEN I DIED MY HAIR BLACK, AND--
WELL, I... UH... I KINDA FOUND ENOUGH CASH IN YOUR DRAWER TO BUY A TICKET TO SAN MATEO.
I WAS WORRIED ABOUT YOU, SEE?
AND I WANTED TO PROVE THAT YOU DIDN'T HAVE TO WORRY ABOUT ME-- IN ANY SITUATION...
22

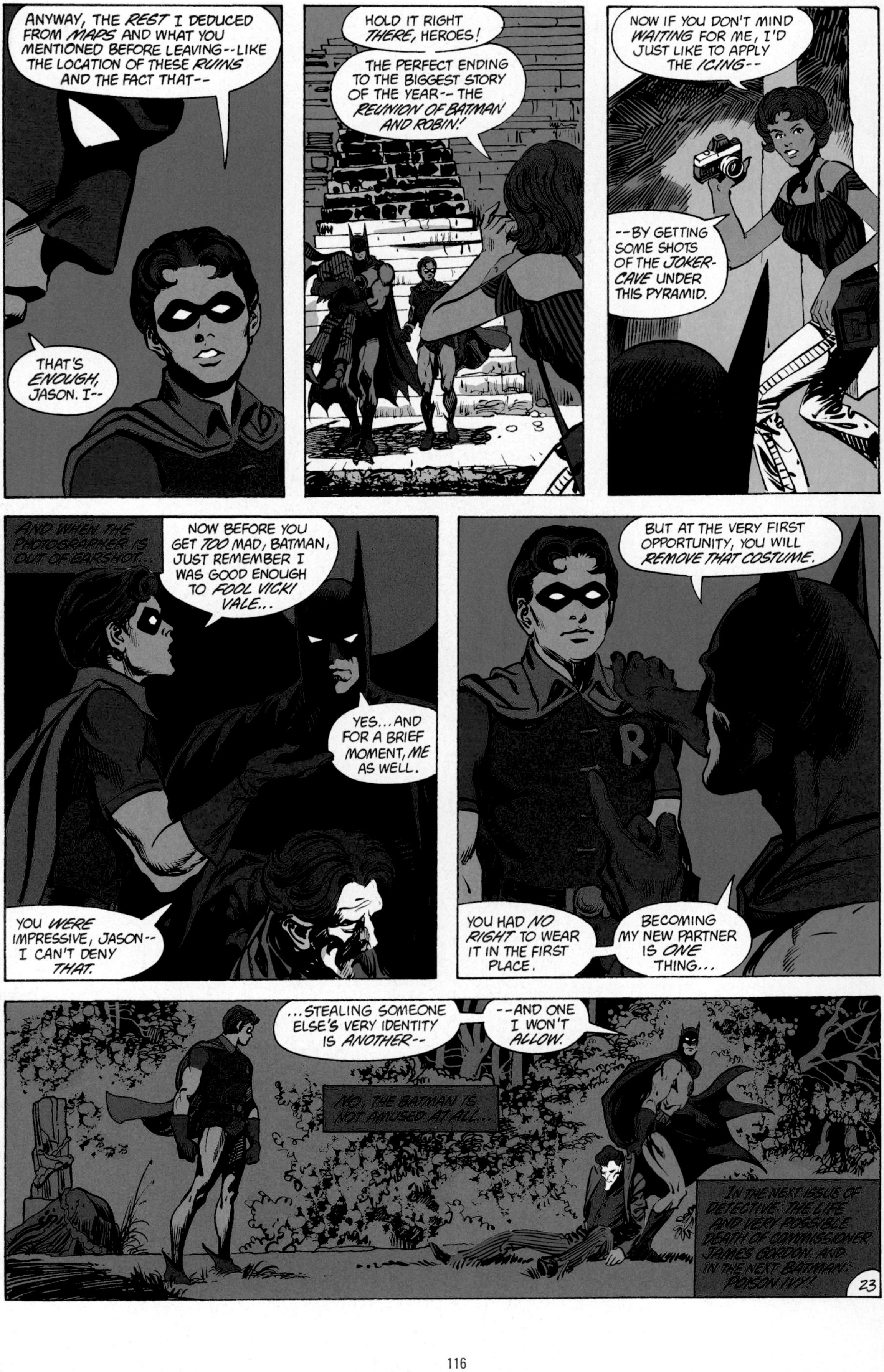
ANYWAY, THE REST I DEDUCED FROM MAPS AND WHAT YOU MENTIONED BEFORE LEAVING--LIKE THE LOCATION OF THESE RUINS AND THE FACT THAT--
THAT'S ENOUGH, JASON. I--
HOLD IT RIGHT THERE, HEROES!
THE PERFECT ENDING TO THE BIGGEST STORY OF THE YEAR--THE REUNION OF BATMAN AND ROBIN!
NOW IF YOU DON'T MIND WAITING FOR ME, I'D JUST LIKE TO APPLY THE ICING--
--BY GETTING SOME SHOTS OF THE JOKER-CAVE UNDER THIS PYRAMID.
AND WHEN THE PHOTOGRAPHER IS OUT OF EARSHOT...
NOW BEFORE YOU GET TOO MAD, BATMAN, JUST REMEMBER I WAS GOOD ENOUGH TO FOOL VICKI VALE...
YES...AND FOR A BRIEF MOMENT, ME AS WELL.
YOU WERE IMPRESSIVE, JASON--I CAN'T DENY THAT.
BUT AT THE VERY FIRST OPPORTUNITY, YOU WILL REMOVE THAT COSTUME.
YOU HAD NO RIGHT TO WEAR IT IN THE FIRST PLACE.
BECOMING MY NEW PARTNER IS ONE THING...
...STEALING SOMEONE ELSE'S VERY IDENTITY IS ANOTHER--
--AND ONE I WON'T ALLOW.
NO, THE BATMAN IS NOT AMUSED AT ALL...
IN THE NEXT ISSUE OF DETECTIVE: THE LIFE AND VERY POSSIBLE DEATH OF COMMISSIONER JAMES GORDON. AND IN THE NEXT BATMAN: POISON IVY!
23

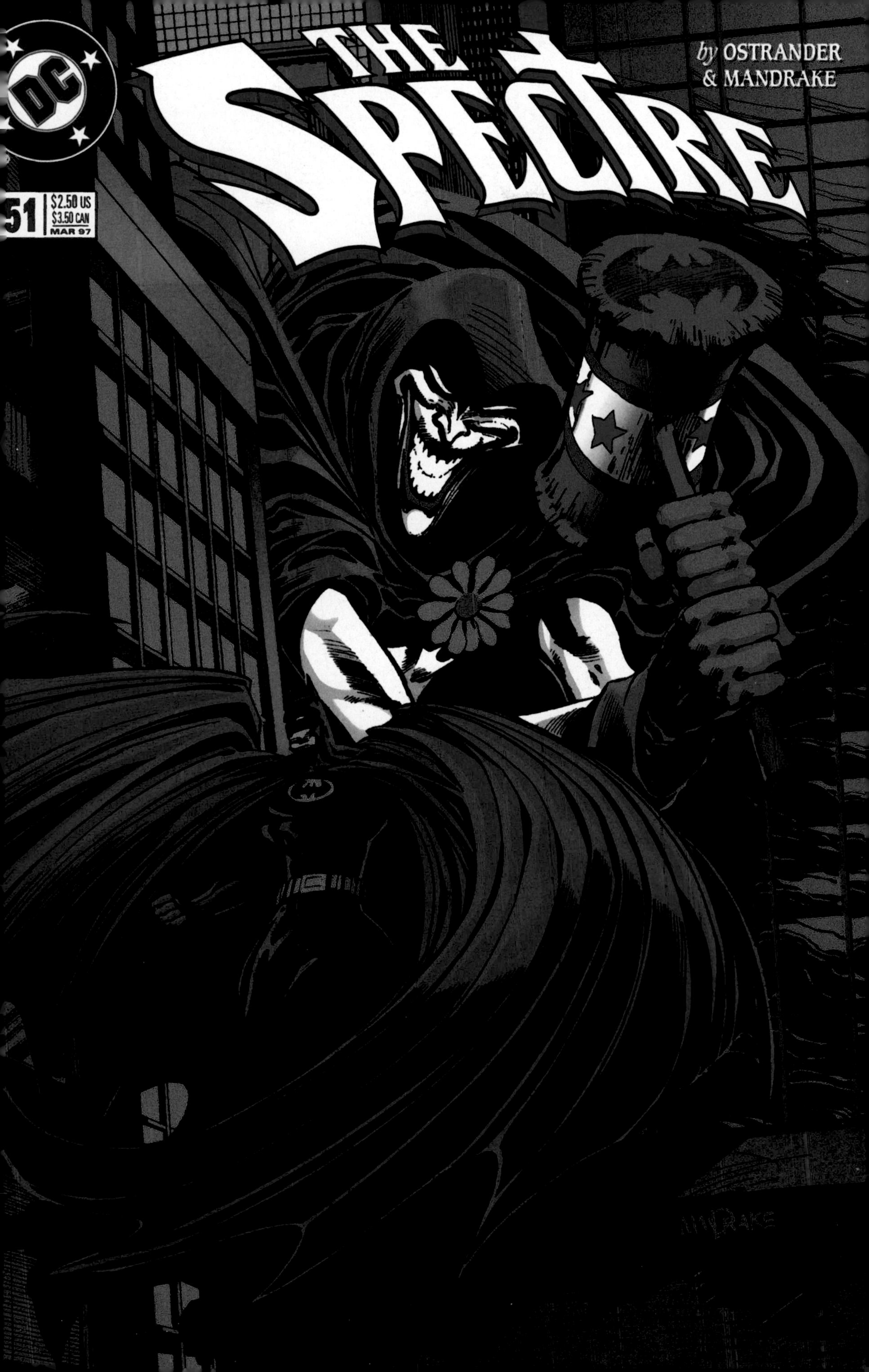
DC
THE SPECTRE
by OSTRANDER
& MANDRAKE
51
$2.50 US
$3.50 CAN
MAR 97

A SAVAGE INNOCENCE

Turning and turning in the widening gyre
The falcon cannot hear the falconer;
Things fall apart; the center cannot hold;
Mere anarchy is loosed upon the world,
The blood-dimmed tide is loosed, and everywhere
The ceremony of innocence is drowned;
The best lack all conviction, while the worst
Are full of passionate intensity.
— William Butler Yeats, *Michael Robartes and
the Dancer*, "The Second Coming" (1920)

NEW YORK CITY:

...AND THIS HUGE FREAKIN' *BAT* COMES SWOOPIN' DOWN AND BEATS THE *BEJEEZUS* OUT OF THEM THREE PUNKS WHAT WERE TRYING TO ROB US!

THE PUNKS -- OKAY, THAT'S NOO YAWK CITY! YOU ACCEPT THAT! BUT THAT FREAKIN' *BAT* AIN'T NOO YAWK! THAT'S *GOTHAM*!

I TELL YA -- I GOT A BAD *HEART*! HE ALMOST SCARES THE *LIFE* OUTTA ME! SOMETHIN' SHOULD BE *DONE*, I TELL YA!

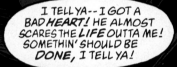

BATMAN CREATED BY *BOB KANE*

JOHN **OSTRANDER** WRITER

TOM **MANDRAKE** ARTIST

TODD **KLEIN** LETTERER

CARLA **FEENY** COLORIST

DIGITAL **CHAMELEON** COLOR SEPS.

PETER **TOMASI** ASSOC. ED.

DAN **RASPLER** EDITOR

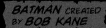

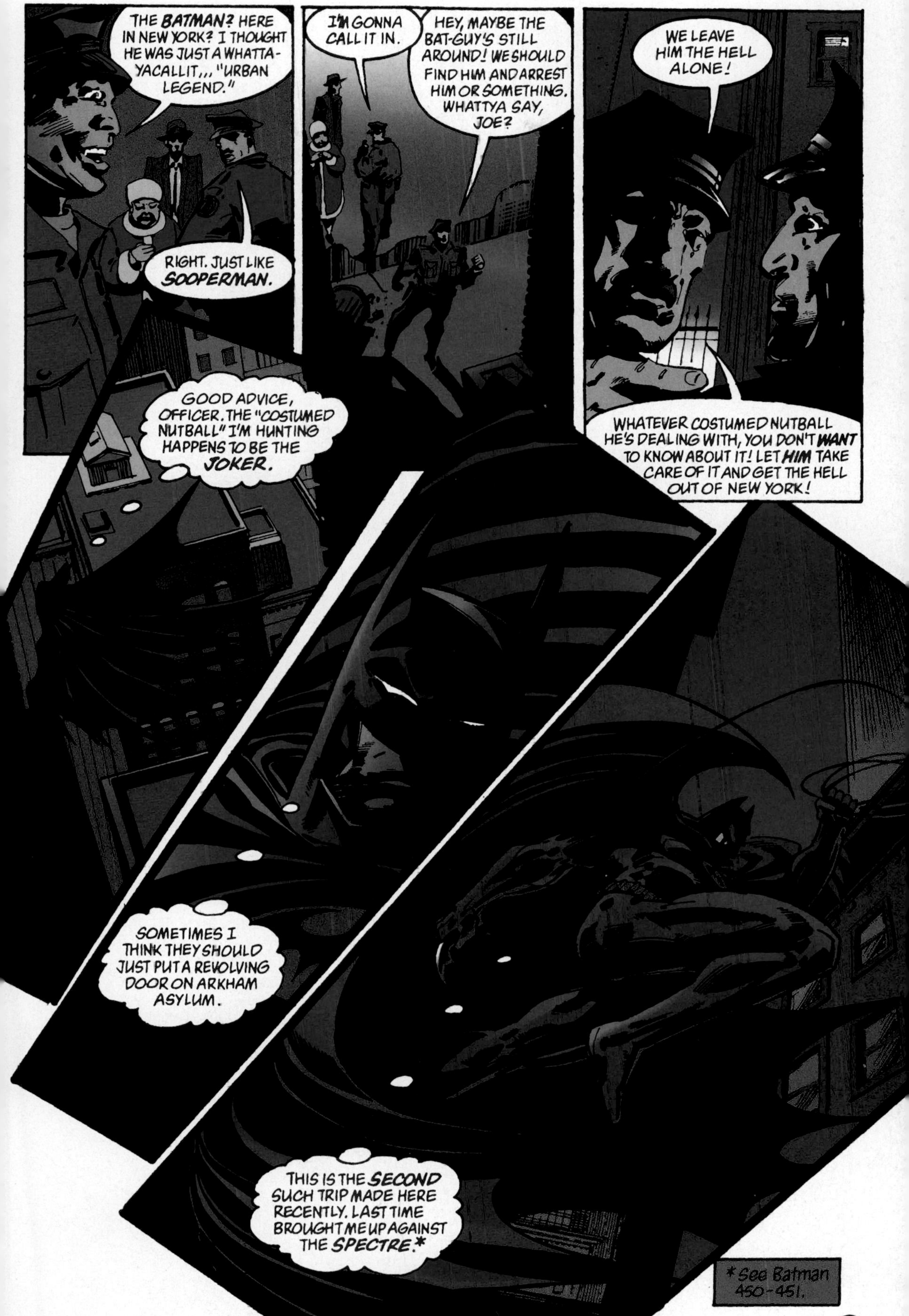
THE BATMAN? HERE IN NEW YORK? I THOUGHT HE WAS JUST A WHATTA-YACALLIT... "URBAN LEGEND."
RIGHT. JUST LIKE SOOPERMAN.
I'M GONNA CALL IT IN.
HEY, MAYBE THE BAT-GUY'S STILL AROUND! WE SHOULD FIND HIM AND ARREST HIM OR SOMETHING. WHATTYA SAY, JOE?
WE LEAVE HIM THE HELL ALONE!
WHATEVER COSTUMED NUTBALL HE'S DEALING WITH, YOU DON'T WANT TO KNOW ABOUT IT! LET HIM TAKE CARE OF IT AND GET THE HELL OUT OF NEW YORK!
GOOD ADVICE, OFFICER. THE "COSTUMED NUTBALL" I'M HUNTING HAPPENS TO BE THE JOKER.
SOMETIMES I THINK THEY SHOULD JUST PUT A REVOLVING DOOR ON ARKHAM ASYLUM.
THIS IS THE SECOND SUCH TRIP MADE HERE RECENTLY. LAST TIME BROUGHT ME UP AGAINST THE SPECTRE.*
*See Batman 450-451.
2

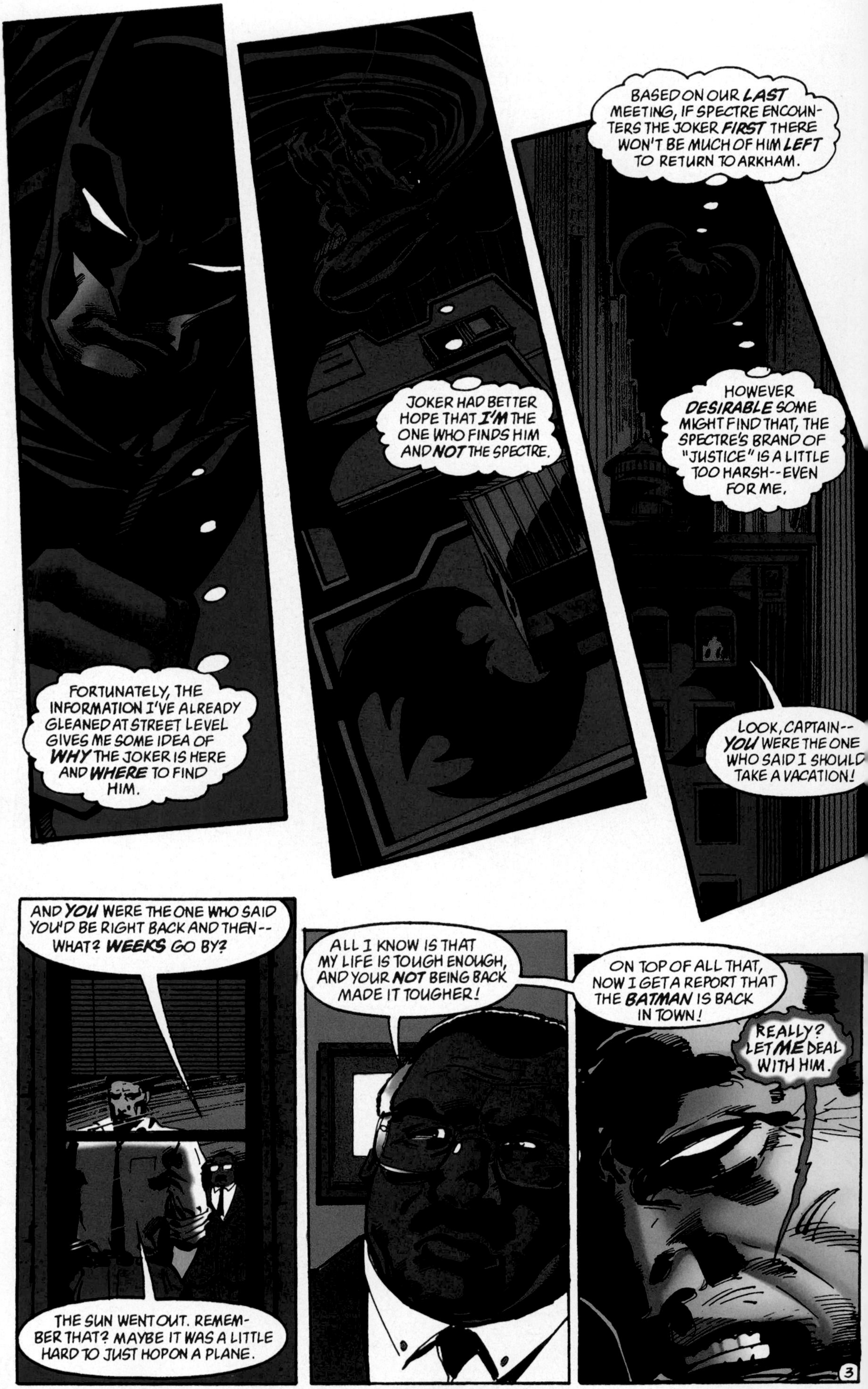
FORTUNATELY, THE INFORMATION I'VE ALREADY GLEANED AT STREET LEVEL GIVES ME SOME IDEA OF WHY THE JOKER IS HERE AND WHERE TO FIND HIM.
JOKER HAD BETTER HOPE THAT I'M THE ONE WHO FINDS HIM AND NOT THE SPECTRE.
BASED ON OUR LAST MEETING, IF SPECTRE ENCOUNTERS THE JOKER FIRST THERE WON'T BE MUCH OF HIM LEFT TO RETURN TO ARKHAM.
HOWEVER DESIRABLE SOME MIGHT FIND THAT, THE SPECTRE'S BRAND OF "JUSTICE" IS A LITTLE TOO HARSH--EVEN FOR ME.
LOOK, CAPTAIN--YOU WERE THE ONE WHO SAID I SHOULD TAKE A VACATION!
AND YOU WERE THE ONE WHO SAID YOU'D BE RIGHT BACK AND THEN--WHAT? WEEKS GO BY?
THE SUN WENT OUT. REMEMBER THAT? MAYBE IT WAS A LITTLE HARD TO JUST HOP ON A PLANE.
ALL I KNOW IS THAT MY LIFE IS TOUGH ENOUGH, AND YOUR NOT BEING BACK MADE IT TOUGHER!
ON TOP OF ALL THAT, NOW I GET A REPORT THAT THE BATMAN IS BACK IN TOWN!
REALLY? LET ME DEAL WITH HIM.

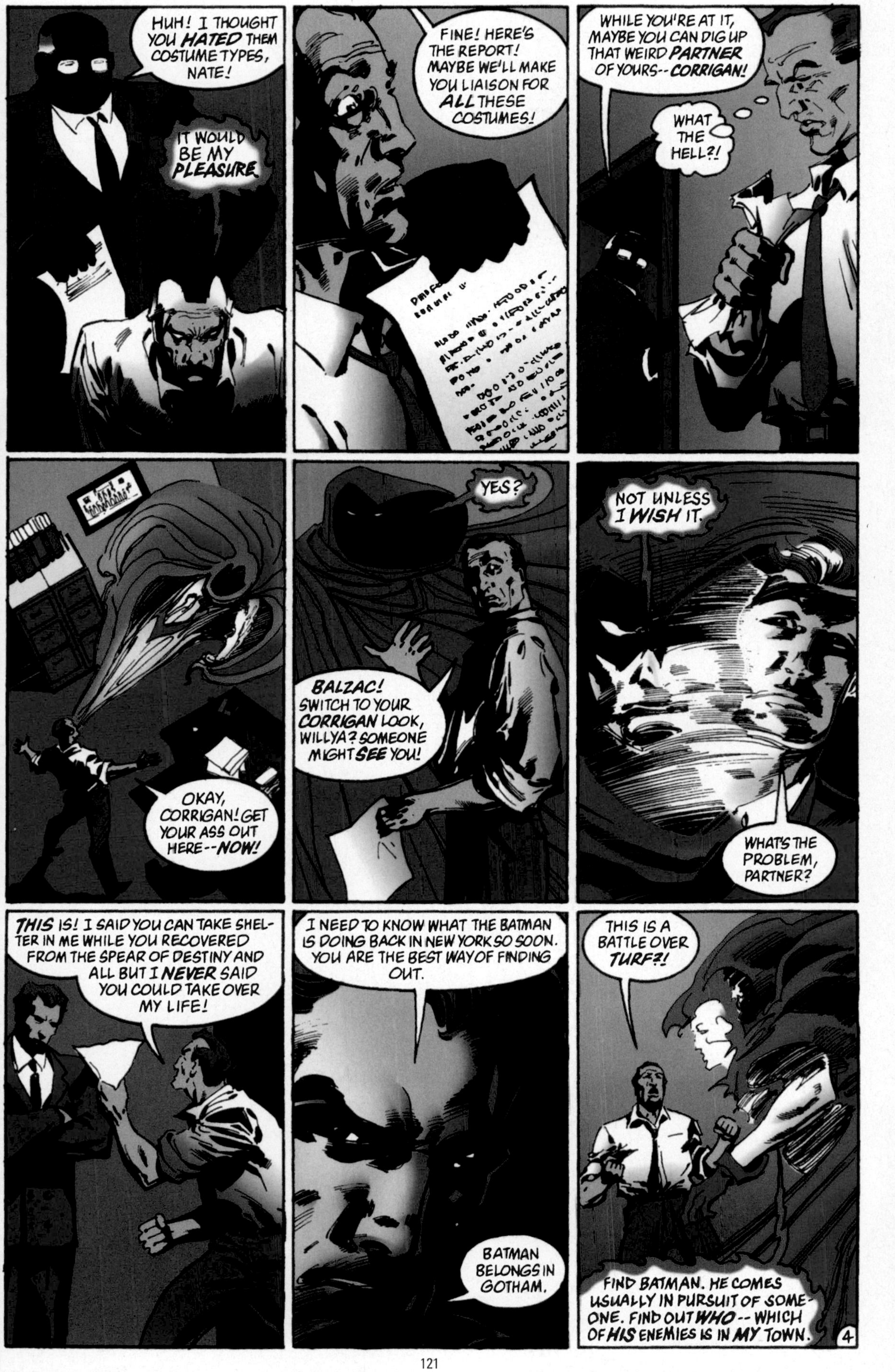
HUH! I THOUGHT YOU HATED THEM COSTUME TYPES, NATE!
IT WOULD BE MY PLEASURE
FINE! HERE'S THE REPORT! MAYBE WE'LL MAKE YOU LIAISON FOR ALL THESE COSTUMES!
WHILE YOU'RE AT IT, MAYBE YOU CAN DIG UP THAT WEIRD PARTNER OF YOURS--CORRIGAN!
WHAT THE HELL?!
OKAY, CORRIGAN! GET YOUR ASS OUT HERE--NOW!
YES?
BALZAC! SWITCH TO YOUR CORRIGAN LOOK, WILLYA? SOMEONE MIGHT SEE YOU!
NOT UNLESS I WISH IT.
WHAT'S THE PROBLEM, PARTNER?
THIS IS! I SAID YOU CAN TAKE SHELTER IN ME WHILE YOU RECOVERED FROM THE SPEAR OF DESTINY AND ALL BUT I NEVER SAID YOU COULD TAKE OVER MY LIFE!
I NEED TO KNOW WHAT THE BATMAN IS DOING BACK IN NEW YORK SO SOON. YOU ARE THE BEST WAY OF FINDING OUT.
BATMAN BELONGS IN GOTHAM.
THIS IS A BATTLE OVER TURF?!
FIND BATMAN. HE COMES USUALLY IN PURSUIT OF SOMEONE. FIND OUT WHO--WHICH OF HIS ENEMIES IS IN MY TOWN.
4

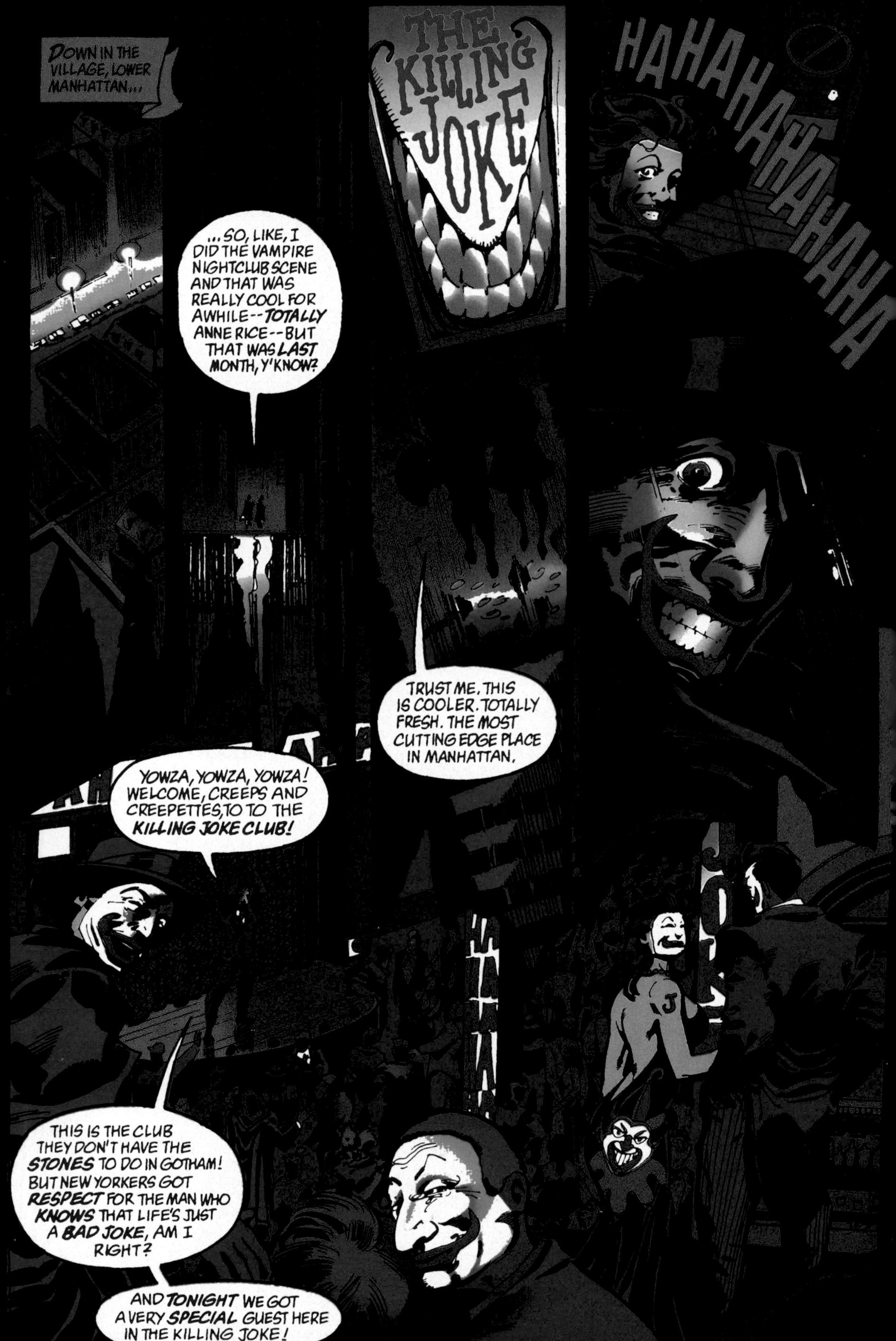
THE KILLING JOKE
HAHAHAHAHAHAHAHAHAHA
DOWN IN THE VILLAGE, LOWER MANHATTAN...
...SO, LIKE, I DID THE VAMPIRE NIGHTCLUB SCENE AND THAT WAS REALLY COOL FOR AWHILE--TOTALLY ANNE RICE--BUT THAT WAS LAST MONTH, Y'KNOW?
TRUST ME. THIS IS COOLER. TOTALLY FRESH. THE MOST CUTTING EDGE PLACE IN MANHATTAN.
YOWZA, YOWZA, YOWZA! WELCOME, CREEPS AND CREEPETTES, TO TO THE KILLING JOKE CLUB!
THIS IS THE CLUB THEY DON'T HAVE THE STONES TO DO IN GOTHAM! BUT NEW YORKERS GOT RESPECT FOR THE MAN WHO KNOWS THAT LIFE'S JUST A BAD JOKE, AM I RIGHT?
AND TONIGHT WE GOT A VERY SPECIAL GUEST HERE IN THE KILLING JOKE!

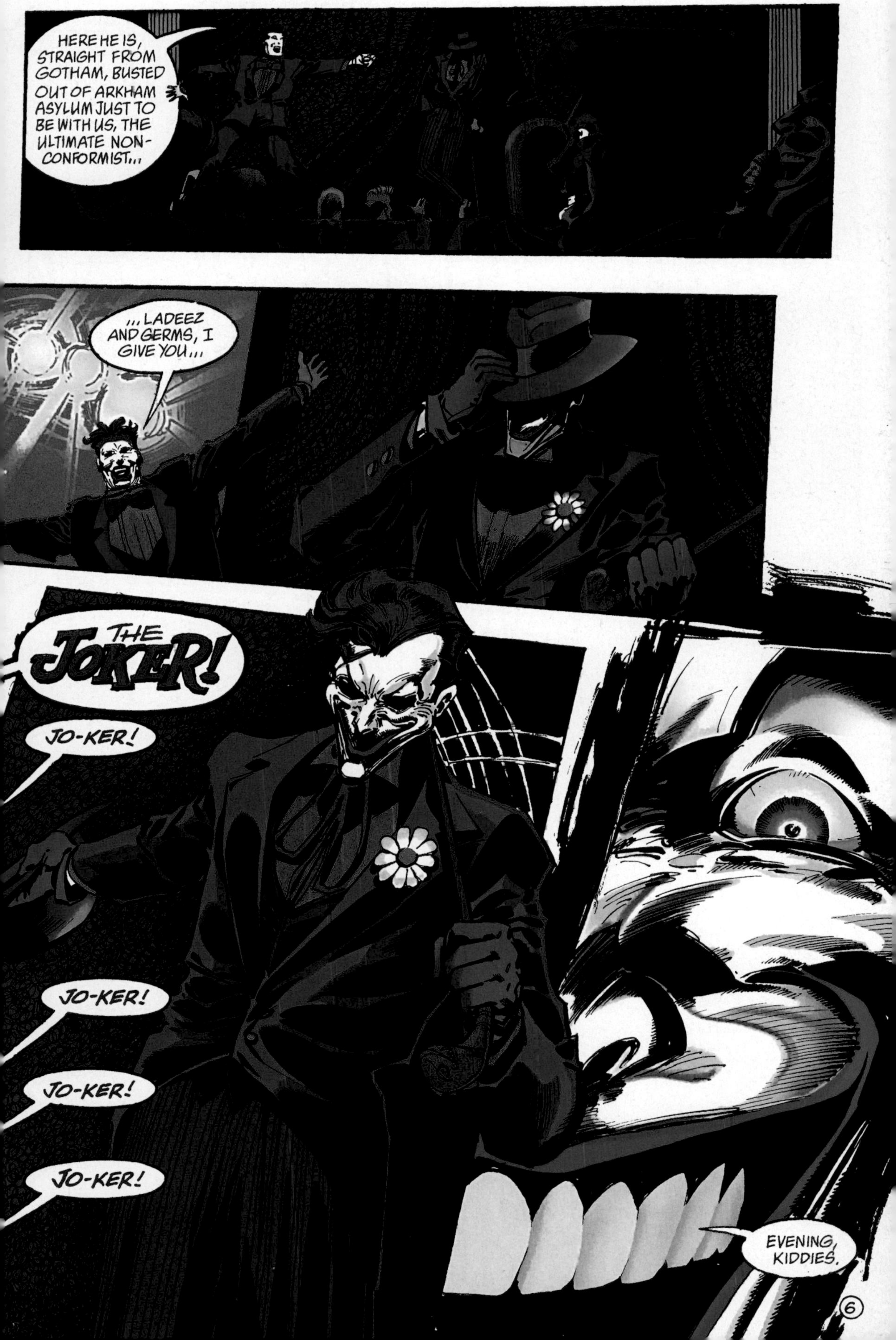
HERE HE IS, STRAIGHT FROM GOTHAM, BUSTED OUT OF ARKHAM ASYLUM JUST TO BE WITH US, THE ULTIMATE NON-CONFORMIST...
...LADEEZ AND GERMS, I GIVE YOU...
THE JOKER!
JO-KER!
JO-KER!
JO-KER!
JO-KER!
EVENING, KIDDIES.
6

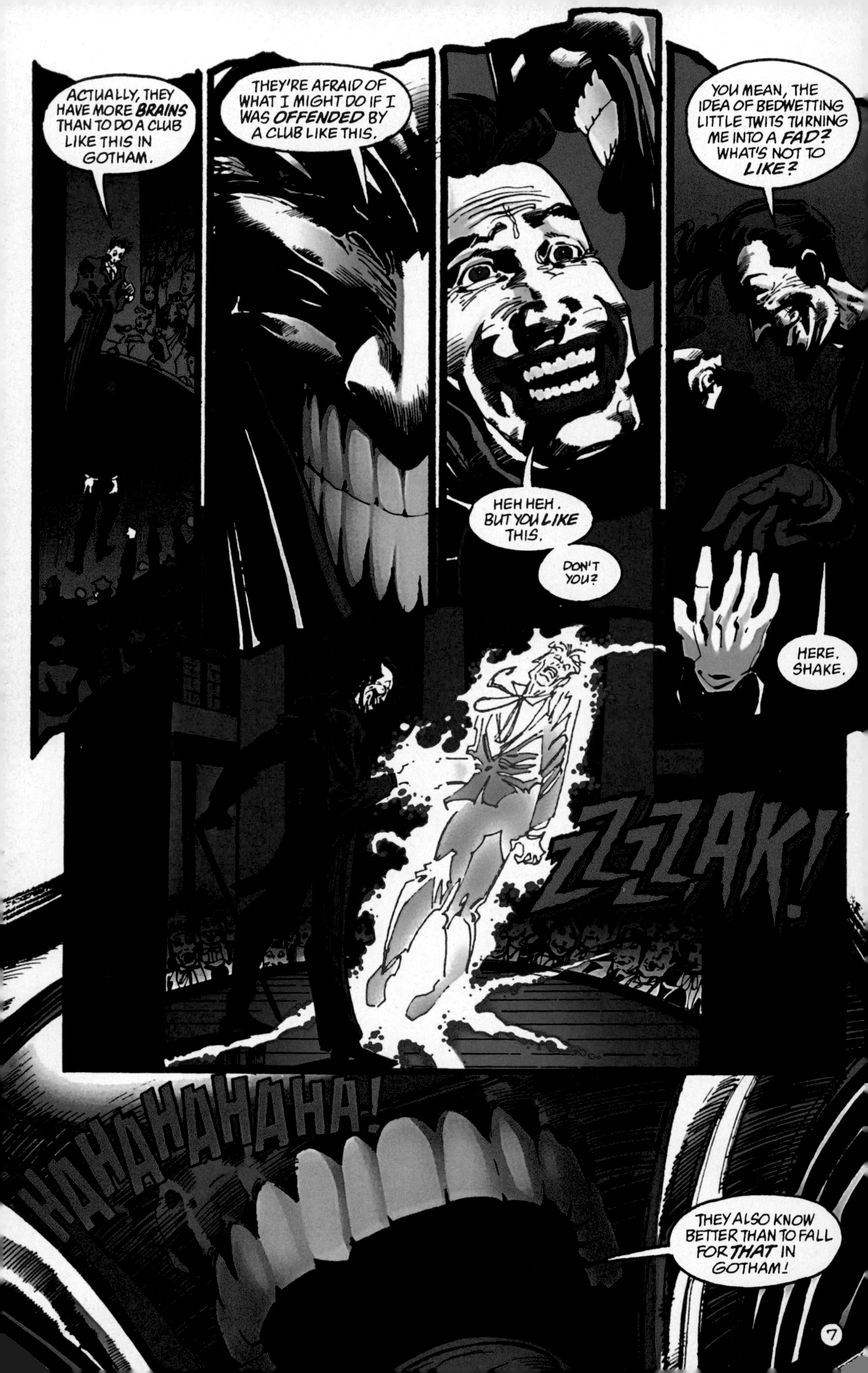
ACTUALLY, THEY HAVE MORE BRAINS THAN TO DO A CLUB LIKE THIS IN GOTHAM.
THEY'RE AFRAID OF WHAT I MIGHT DO IF I WAS OFFENDED BY A CLUB LIKE THIS.
HEH HEH. BUT YOU LIKE THIS.
DON'T YOU?
YOU MEAN, THE IDEA OF BEDWETTING LITTLE TWITS TURNING ME INTO A FAD? WHAT'S NOT TO LIKE?
HERE. SHAKE.
ZZZZAK!
HAHAHAHAHAHA!
THEY ALSO KNOW BETTER THAN TO FALL FOR THAT IN GOTHAM!

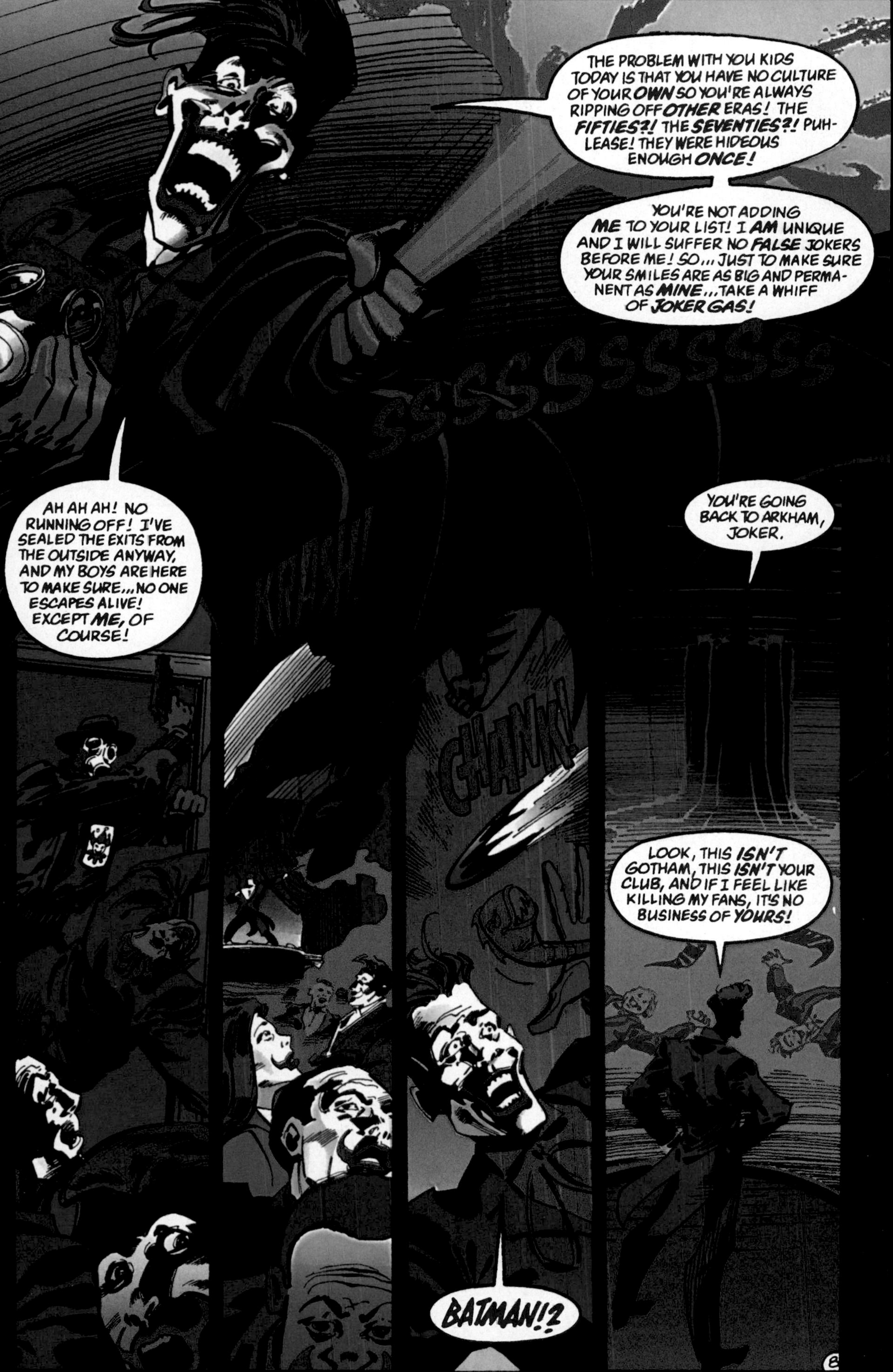
THE PROBLEM WITH YOU KIDS TODAY IS THAT YOU HAVE NO CULTURE OF YOUR OWN SO YOU'RE ALWAYS RIPPING OFF OTHER ERAS! THE FIFTIES?! THE SEVENTIES?! PUH-LEASE! THEY WERE HIDEOUS ENOUGH ONCE!
YOU'RE NOT ADDING ME TO YOUR LIST! I AM UNIQUE AND I WILL SUFFER NO FALSE JOKERS BEFORE ME! SO... JUST TO MAKE SURE YOUR SMILES ARE AS BIG AND PERMANENT AS MINE... TAKE A WHIFF OF JOKER GAS!
AH AH AH! NO RUNNING OFF! I'VE SEALED THE EXITS FROM THE OUTSIDE ANYWAY, AND MY BOYS ARE HERE TO MAKE SURE... NO ONE ESCAPES ALIVE! EXCEPT ME, OF COURSE!
CHANK!
BATMAN!?
YOU'RE GOING BACK TO ARKHAM, JOKER.
LOOK, THIS ISN'T GOTHAM, THIS ISN'T YOUR CLUB, AND IF I FEEL LIKE KILLING MY FANS, IT'S NO BUSINESS OF YOURS!

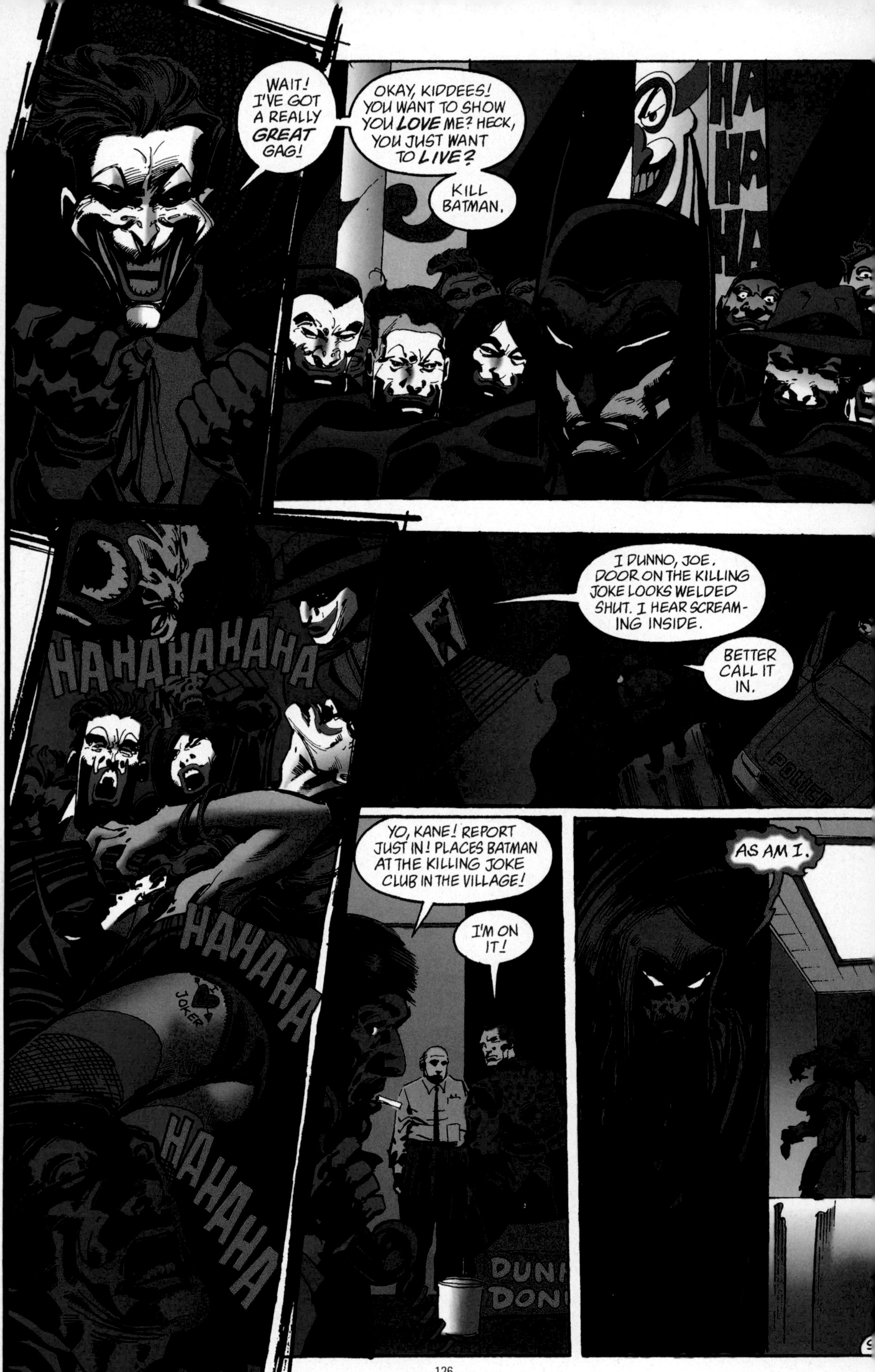
WAIT! I'VE GOT A REALLY GREAT GAG!
OKAY, KIDDEES! YOU WANT TO SHOW YOU LOVE ME? HECK, YOU JUST WANT TO LIVE?
KILL BATMAN.
HA HA HA
HAHAHAHAHA
JOKER
HAHAHA
HAHAHA
I DUNNO, JOE. DOOR ON THE KILLING JOKE LOOKS WELDED SHUT. I HEAR SCREAMING INSIDE.
BETTER CALL IT IN.
YO, KANE! REPORT JUST IN! PLACES BATMAN AT THE KILLING JOKE CLUB IN THE VILLAGE!
I'M ON IT!
AS AM I.

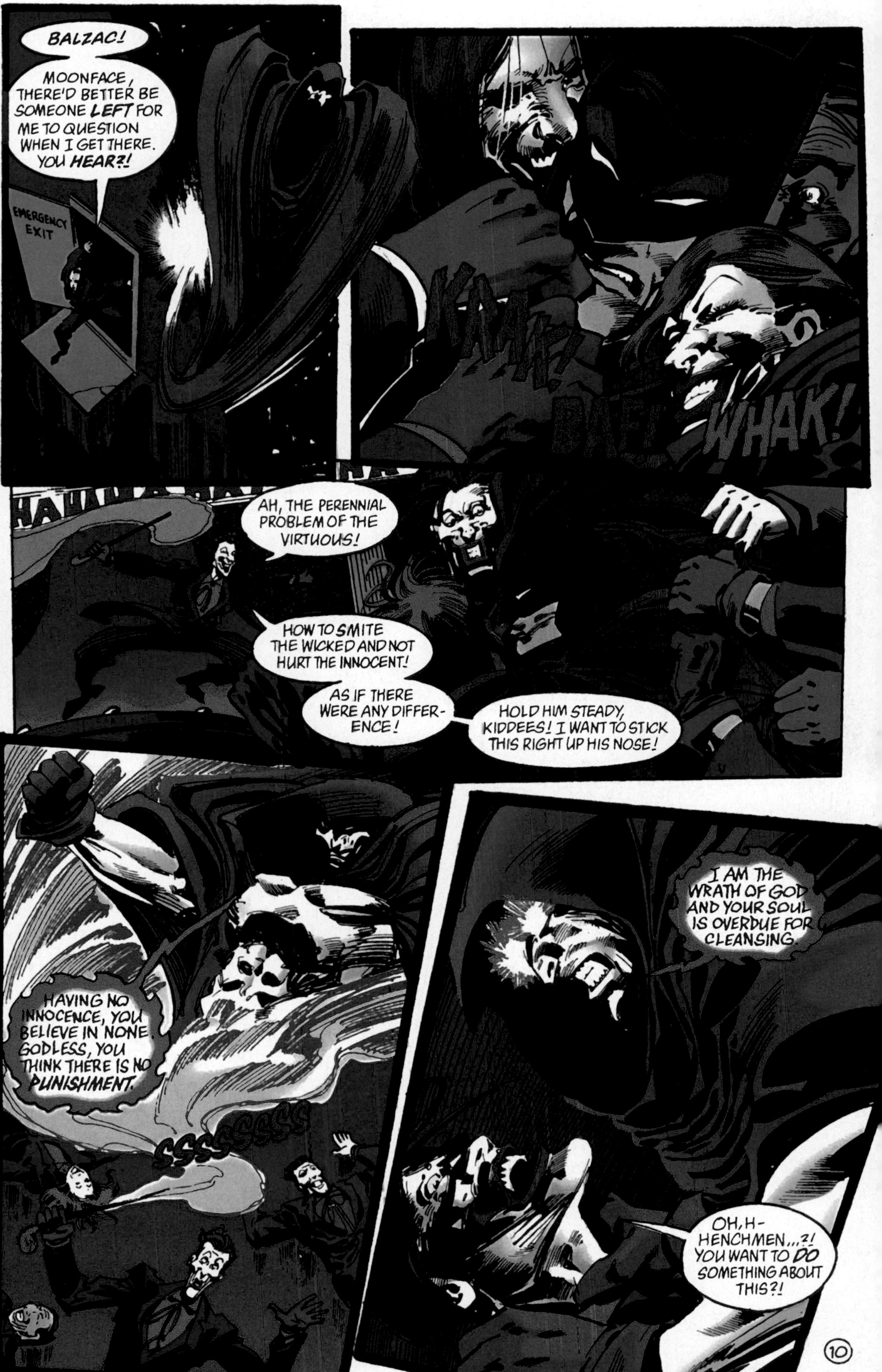
BALZAC!
MOONFACE, THERE'D BETTER BE SOMEONE LEFT FOR ME TO QUESTION WHEN I GET THERE. YOU HEAR?!
EMERGENCY EXIT
WHAK!
AH, THE PERENNIAL PROBLEM OF THE VIRTUOUS!
HOW TO SMITE THE WICKED AND NOT HURT THE INNOCENT!
AS IF THERE WERE ANY DIFFERENCE!
HOLD HIM STEADY, KIDDEES! I WANT TO STICK THIS RIGHT UP HIS NOSE!
HAVING NO INNOCENCE, YOU BELIEVE IN NONE. GODLESS, YOU THINK THERE IS NO PUNISHMENT.
SSSSSSSSS
I AM THE WRATH OF GOD AND YOUR SOUL IS OVERDUE FOR CLEANSING.
OH, H-HENCHMEN...?! YOU WANT TO DO SOMETHING ABOUT THIS?!

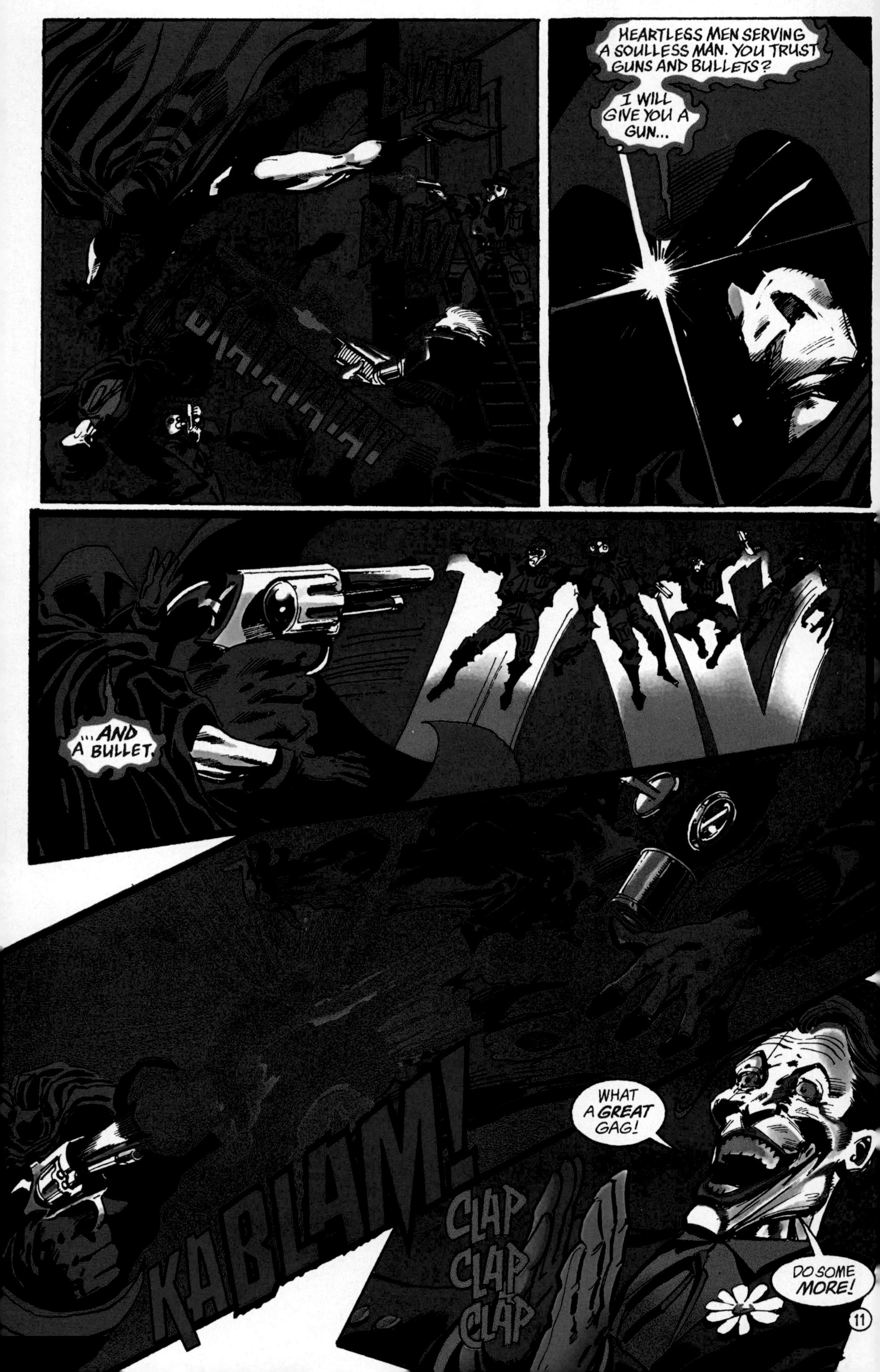
BLAM
BLAM
HEARTLESS MEN SERVING A SOULLESS MAN. YOU TRUST GUNS AND BULLETS?
I WILL GIVE YOU A GUN...
...AND A BULLET.
KABLAM!
WHAT A GREAT GAG!
CLAP CLAP CLAP
DO SOME MORE!

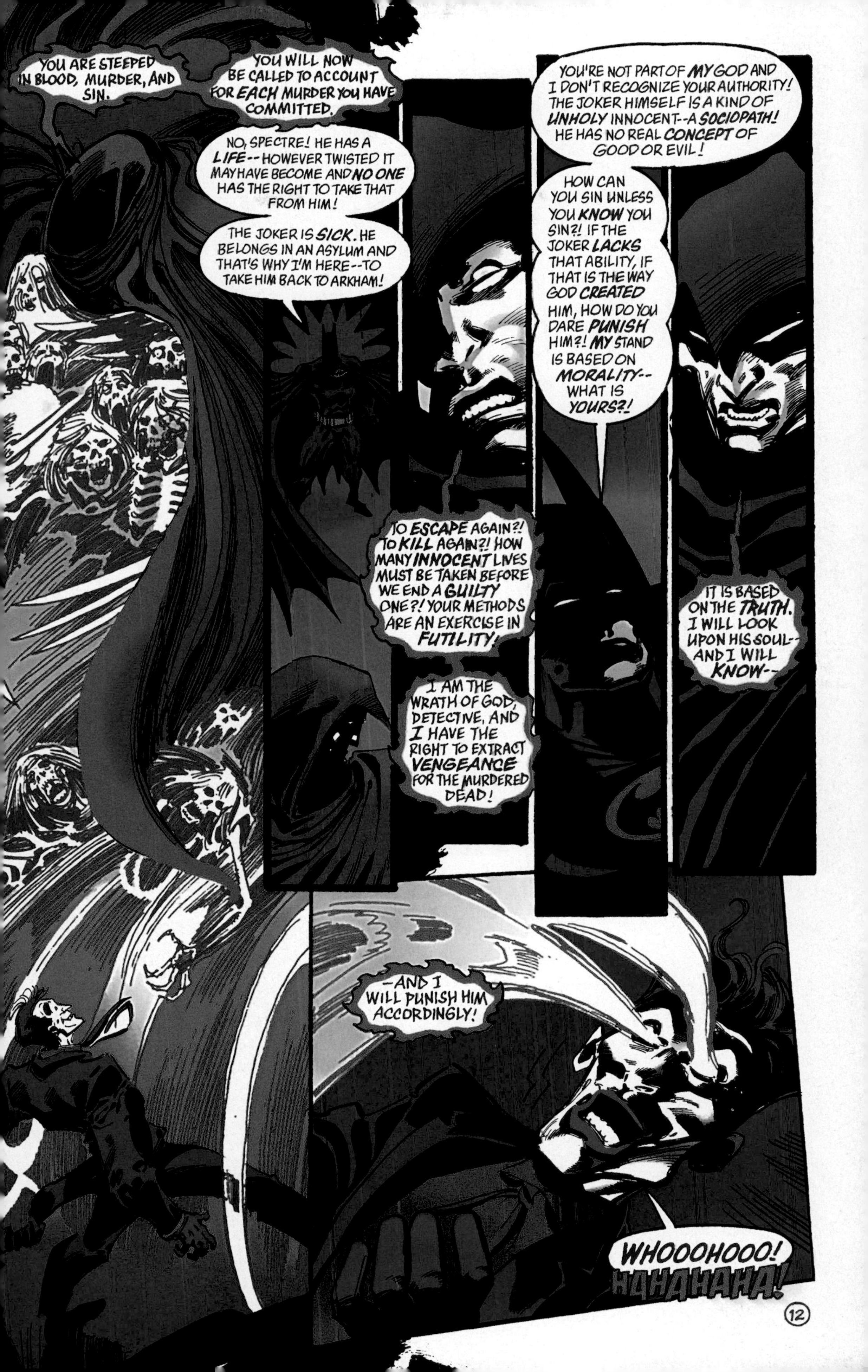
YOU ARE STEEPED IN BLOOD, MURDER, AND SIN.
YOU WILL NOW BE CALLED TO ACCOUNT FOR EACH MURDER YOU HAVE COMMITTED.
NO, SPECTRE! HE HAS A LIFE-- HOWEVER TWISTED IT MAY HAVE BECOME AND NO ONE HAS THE RIGHT TO TAKE THAT FROM HIM!
THE JOKER IS SICK. HE BELONGS IN AN ASYLUM AND THAT'S WHY I'M HERE--TO TAKE HIM BACK TO ARKHAM!
TO ESCAPE AGAIN?! TO KILL AGAIN?! HOW MANY INNOCENT LIVES MUST BE TAKEN BEFORE WE END A GUILTY ONE?! YOUR METHODS ARE AN EXERCISE IN FUTILITY!
I AM THE WRATH OF GOD, DETECTIVE, AND I HAVE THE RIGHT TO EXTRACT VENGEANCE FOR THE MURDERED DEAD!
YOU'RE NOT PART OF MY GOD AND I DON'T RECOGNIZE YOUR AUTHORITY! THE JOKER HIMSELF IS A KIND OF UNHOLY INNOCENT--A SOCIOPATH! HE HAS NO REAL CONCEPT OF GOOD OR EVIL!
HOW CAN YOU SIN UNLESS YOU KNOW YOU SIN?! IF THE JOKER LACKS THAT ABILITY, IF THAT IS THE WAY GOD CREATED HIM, HOW DO YOU DARE PUNISH HIM?! MY STAND IS BASED ON MORALITY-- WHAT IS YOURS?!
IT IS BASED ON THE TRUTH. I WILL LOOK UPON HIS SOUL-- AND I WILL KNOW--
--AND I WILL PUNISH HIM ACCORDINGLY!
WHOOOHOOO! HAHAHAHA!
12

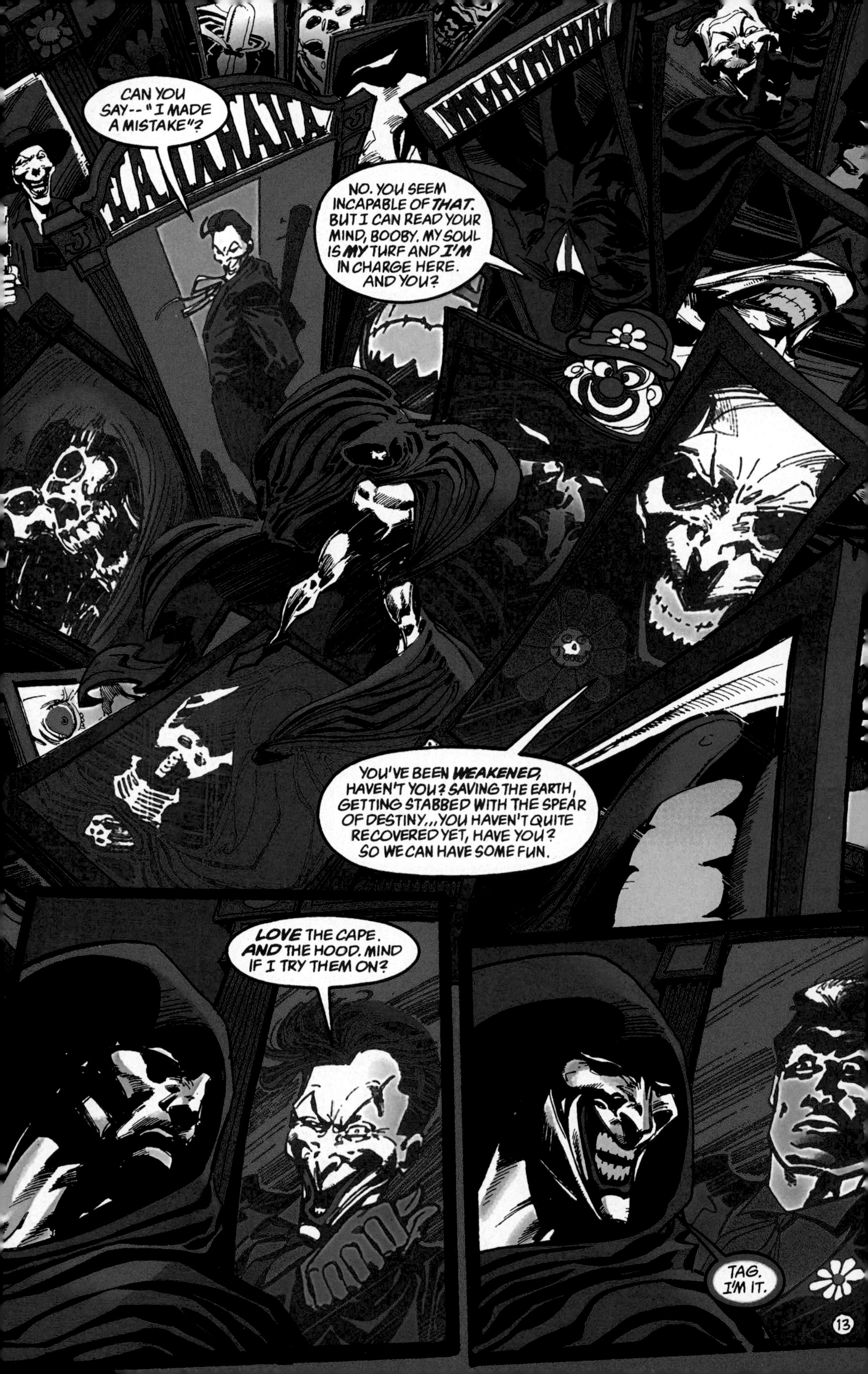
CAN YOU SAY-- "I MADE A MISTAKE"?
HAHAHAHA
HAHAHAHA
NO. YOU SEEM INCAPABLE OF THAT. BUT I CAN READ YOUR MIND, BOOBY. MY SOUL IS MY TURF AND I'M IN CHARGE HERE. AND YOU?
YOU'VE BEEN WEAKENED, HAVEN'T YOU? SAVING THE EARTH, GETTING STABBED WITH THE SPEAR OF DESTINY... YOU HAVEN'T QUITE RECOVERED YET, HAVE YOU? SO WE CAN HAVE SOME FUN.
LOVE THE CAPE. AND THE HOOD. MIND IF I TRY THEM ON?
TAG. I'M IT.

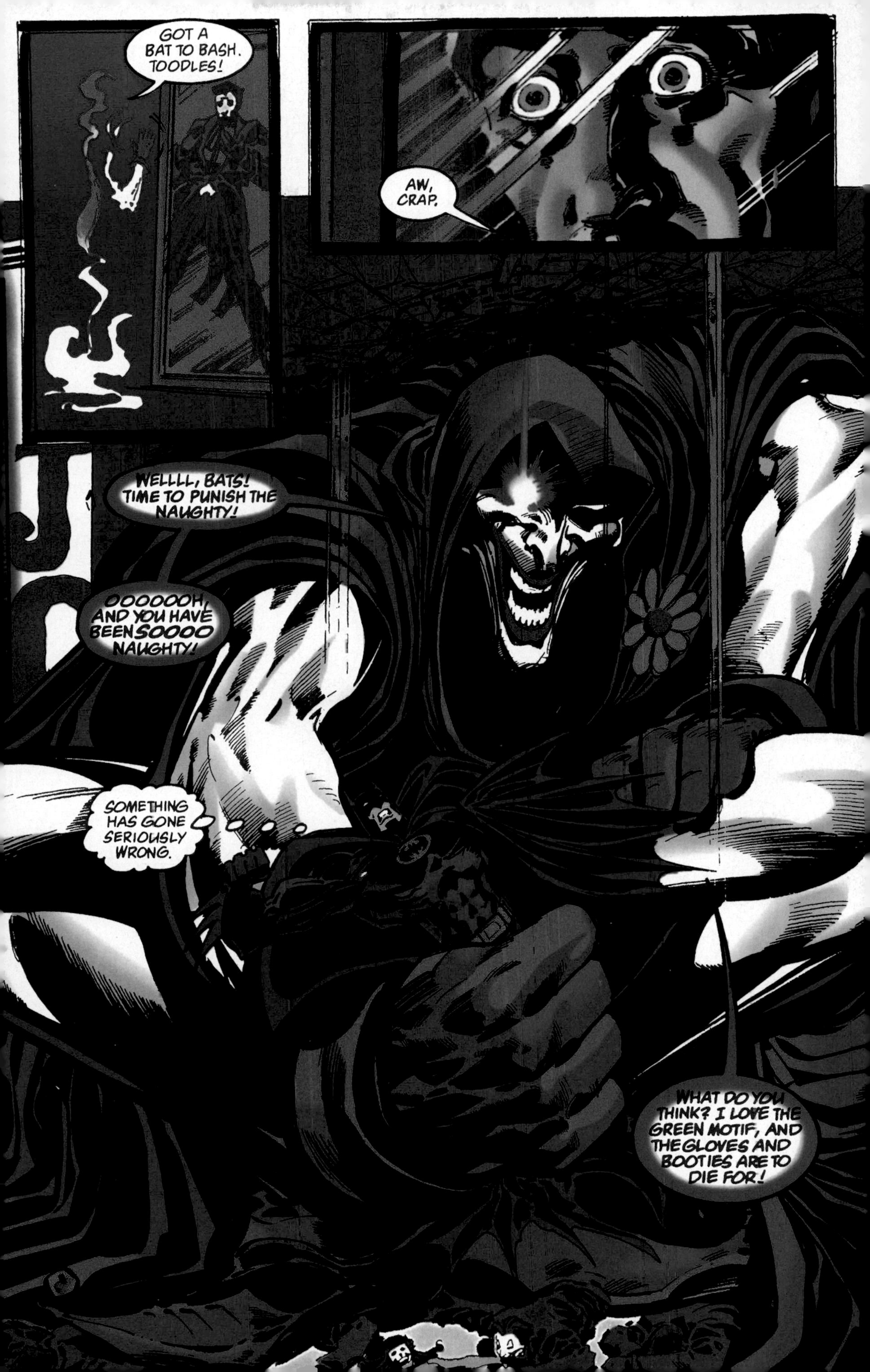
GOT A BAT TO BASH. TOODLES!
AW, CRAP.
WELLLL, BATS! TIME TO PUNISH THE NAUGHTY!
OOOOOOOH, AND YOU HAVE BEEN SOOOO NAUGHTY!
SOMETHING HAS GONE SERIOUSLY WRONG.
WHAT DO YOU THINK? I LOVE THE GREEN MOTIF, AND THE GLOVES AND BOOTIES ARE TO DIE FOR!

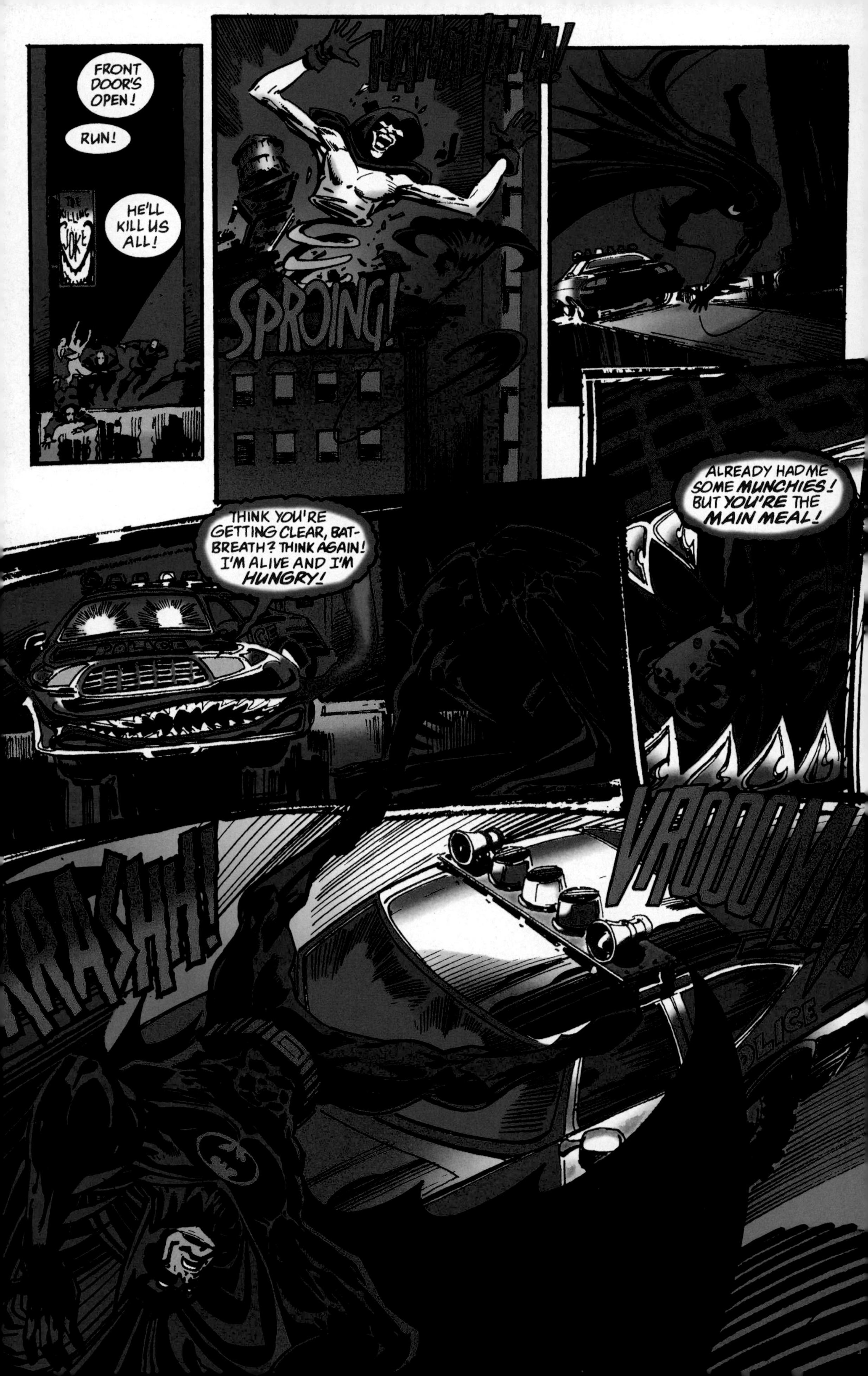

FRONT DOOR'S OPEN!
RUN!
HE'LL KILL US ALL!
SPROING!
THINK YOU'RE GETTING CLEAR, BAT-BREATH? THINK AGAIN! I'M ALIVE AND I'M HUNGRY!
ALREADY HAD ME SOME MUNCHIES! BUT YOU'RE THE MAIN MEAL!
KRASHH!
POLICE

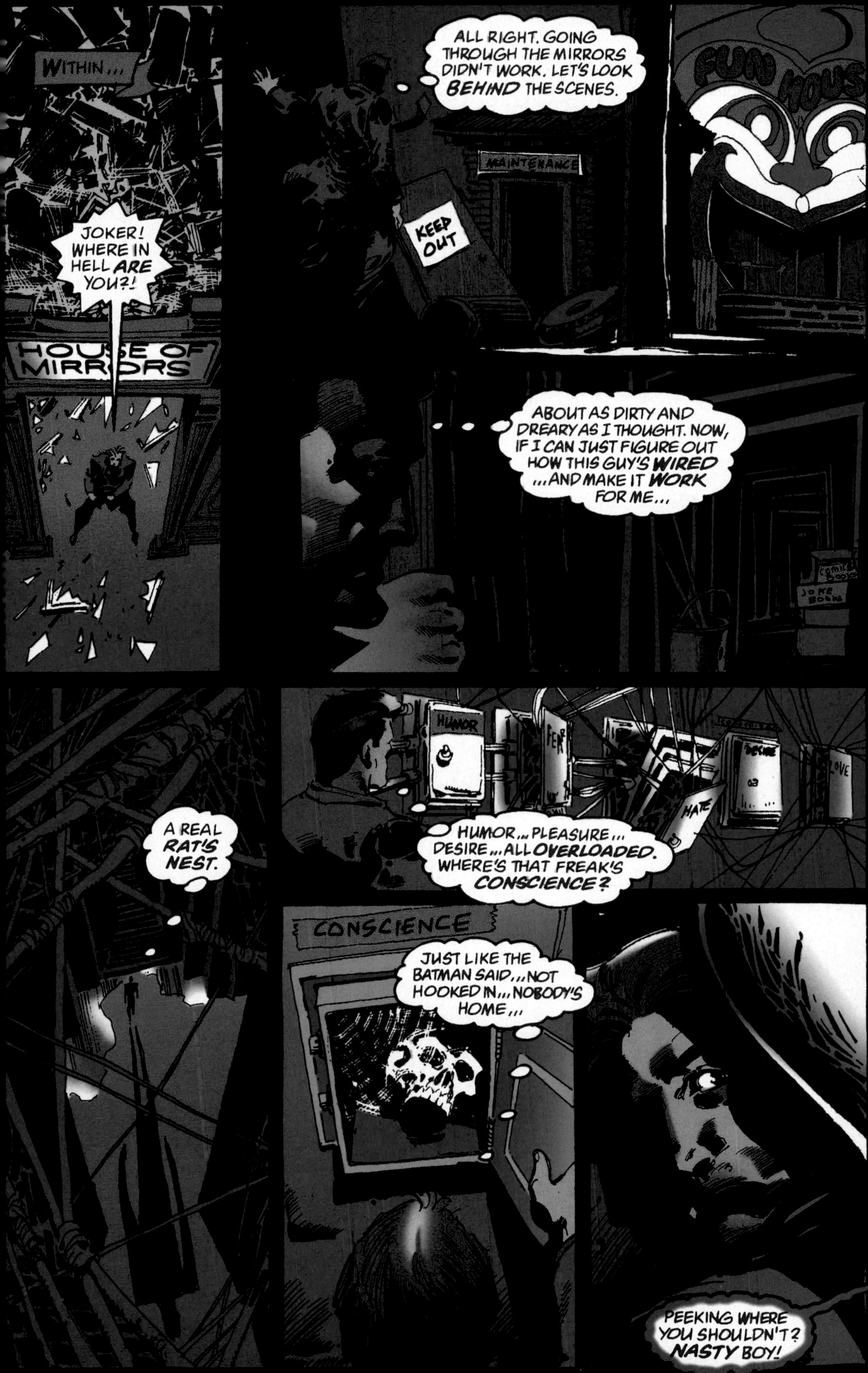

WITHIN...
JOKER! WHERE IN HELL ARE YOU?!
HOUSE OF MIRRORS
ALL RIGHT. GOING THROUGH THE MIRRORS DIDN'T WORK. LET'S LOOK BEHIND THE SCENES.
MAINTENANCE
KEEP OUT
FUN HOUSE
ABOUT AS DIRTY AND DREARY AS I THOUGHT. NOW, IF I CAN JUST FIGURE OUT HOW THIS GUY'S WIRED ...AND MAKE IT WORK FOR ME...
JOKE BOOKS
A REAL RAT'S NEST.
HUMOR
FEAR
DESIRE
LOVE
HATE
HUMOR... PLEASURE... DESIRE... ALL OVERLOADED. WHERE'S THAT FREAK'S CONSCIENCE?
CONSCIENCE
JUST LIKE THE BATMAN SAID... NOT HOOKED IN... NOBODY'S HOME...
PEEKING WHERE YOU SHOULDN'T? NASTY BOY!

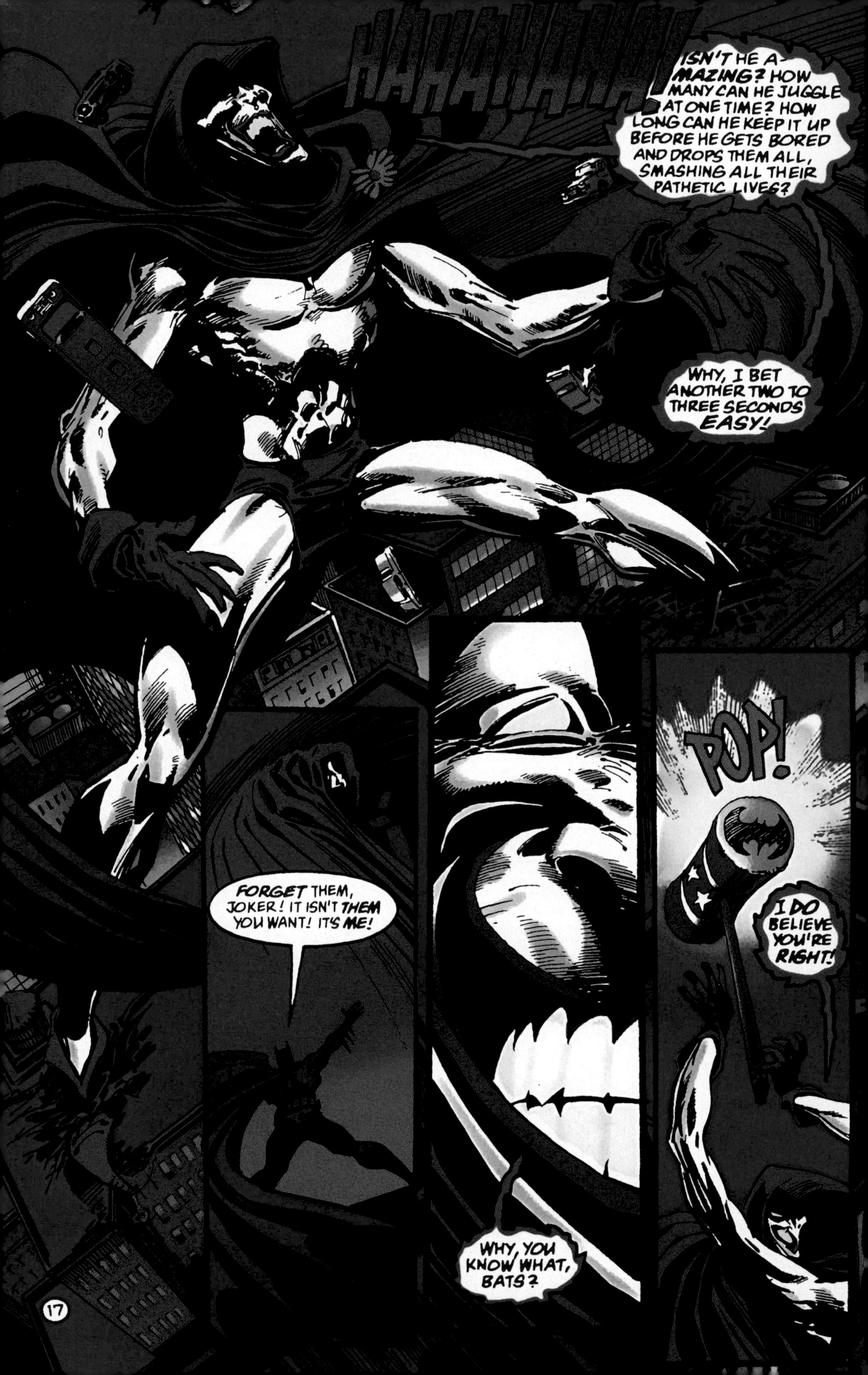
HAHAHAHAHA!
ISN'T HE A-MAZING? HOW MANY CAN HE JUGGLE AT ONE TIME? HOW LONG CAN HE KEEP IT UP BEFORE HE GETS BORED AND DROPS THEM ALL, SMASHING ALL THEIR PATHETIC LIVES?
WHY, I BET ANOTHER TWO TO THREE SECONDS EASY!
FORGET THEM, JOKER! IT ISN'T THEM YOU WANT! IT'S ME!
WHY, YOU KNOW WHAT, BATS?
POP!
I DO BELIEVE YOU'RE RIGHT!

KAWHRAM!

TOO CLOSE -- BUT I HAVE TO KEEP HIM FOCUSED ON *ME*, GIVE CORRIGAN TIME TO REASSERT HIMSELF, GRAB THE POWER BACK!

IF HE CAN...!

SO, YOU SEEK TO STRIP MY MYSTERY FROM ME, AS THE *BARD* ONCE SAID. OR SHOULD HAVE.

YOU'RE A PETTY LITTLE *BUG.* YOU'RE GETTING ON MY *NERVES,* LITTLE BUG! SLOWING ME DOWN!

GUESS THE ONLY INTELLIGENT THING TO DO IS *KILL* YOU.

BATMAN WAS *RIGHT* ABOUT YOU. YOUR BIG PROBLEM IS THAT YOU DON'T HAVE A *CONSCIENCE,* JOKER.

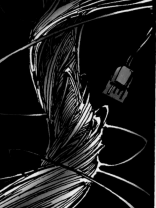

ME? I GOT THAT IN *SPADES.*

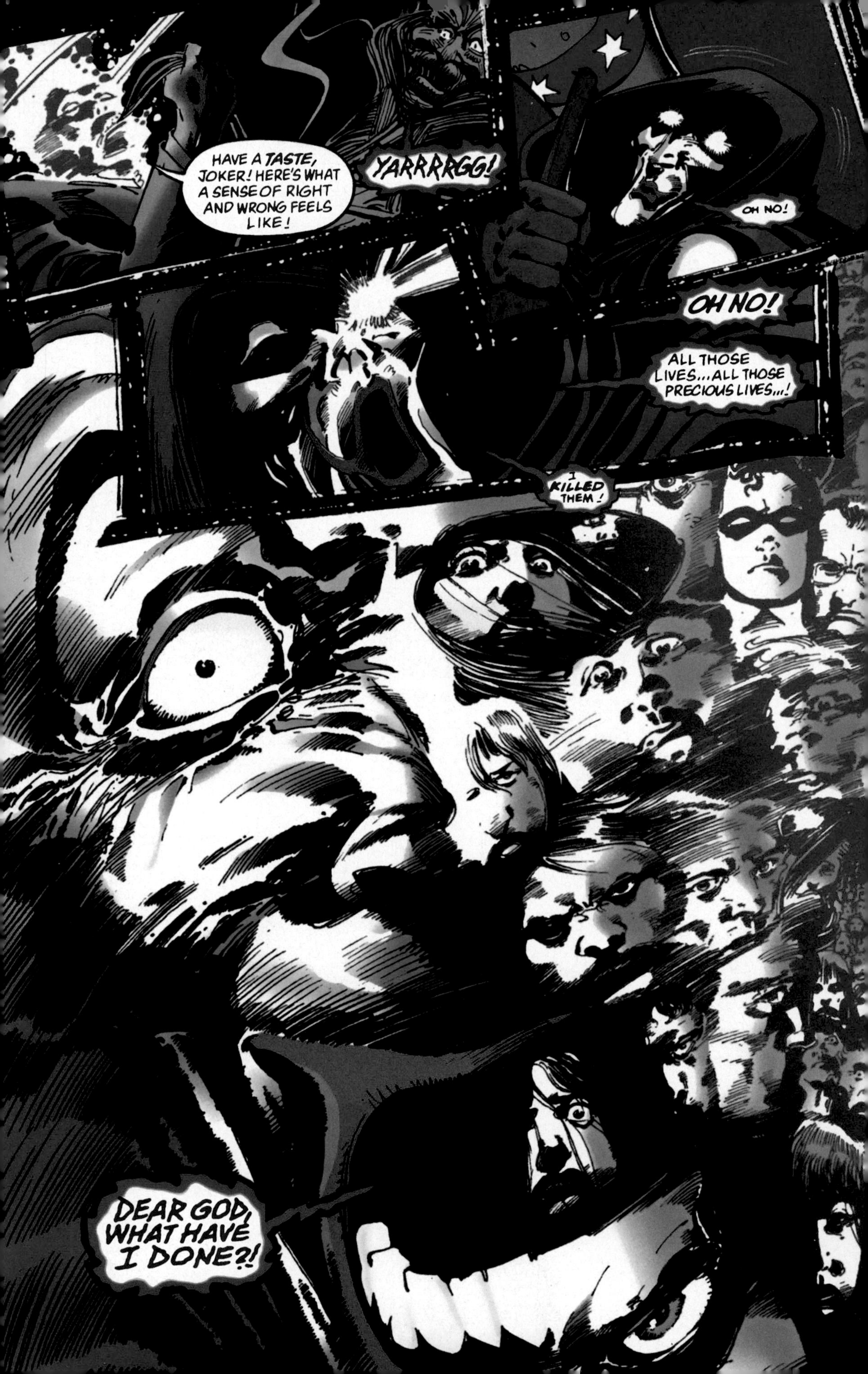
HAVE A TASTE, JOKER! HERE'S WHAT A SENSE OF RIGHT AND WRONG FEELS LIKE!
YARRRRGG!
OH NO!
OH NO!
ALL THOSE LIVES... ALL THOSE PRECIOUS LIVES...!
I KILLED THEM!
DEAR GOD, WHAT HAVE I DONE?!

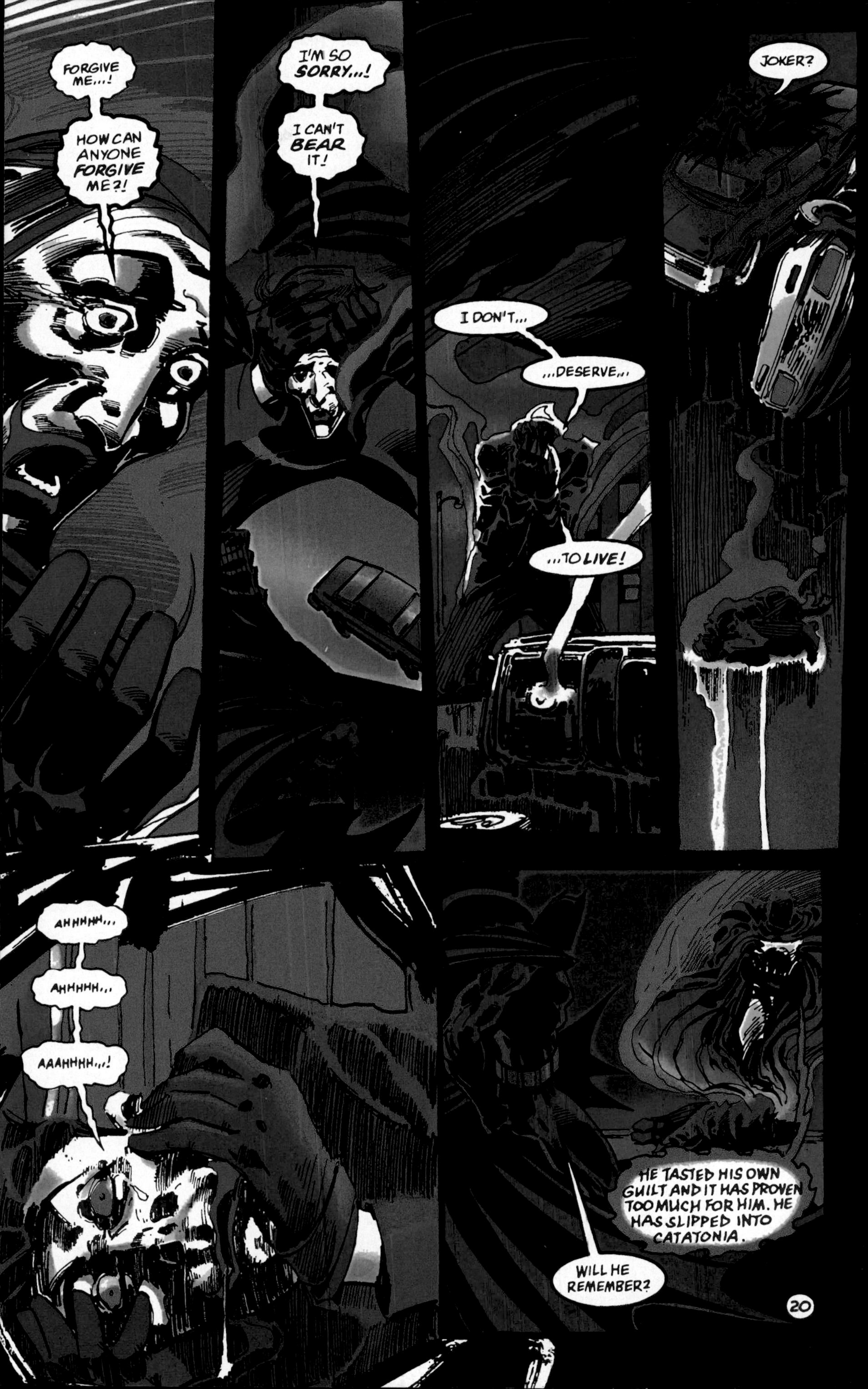
FORGIVE ME...!
HOW CAN ANYONE FORGIVE ME?!
I'M SO SORRY...!
I CAN'T BEAR IT!
I DON'T...
...DESERVE...
...TO LIVE!
JOKER?
AHHHHH...
AHHHHH...
AAAHHHH...!
HE TASTED HIS OWN GUILT AND IT HAS PROVEN TOO MUCH FOR HIM. HE HAS SLIPPED INTO CATATONIA.
WILL HE REMEMBER?

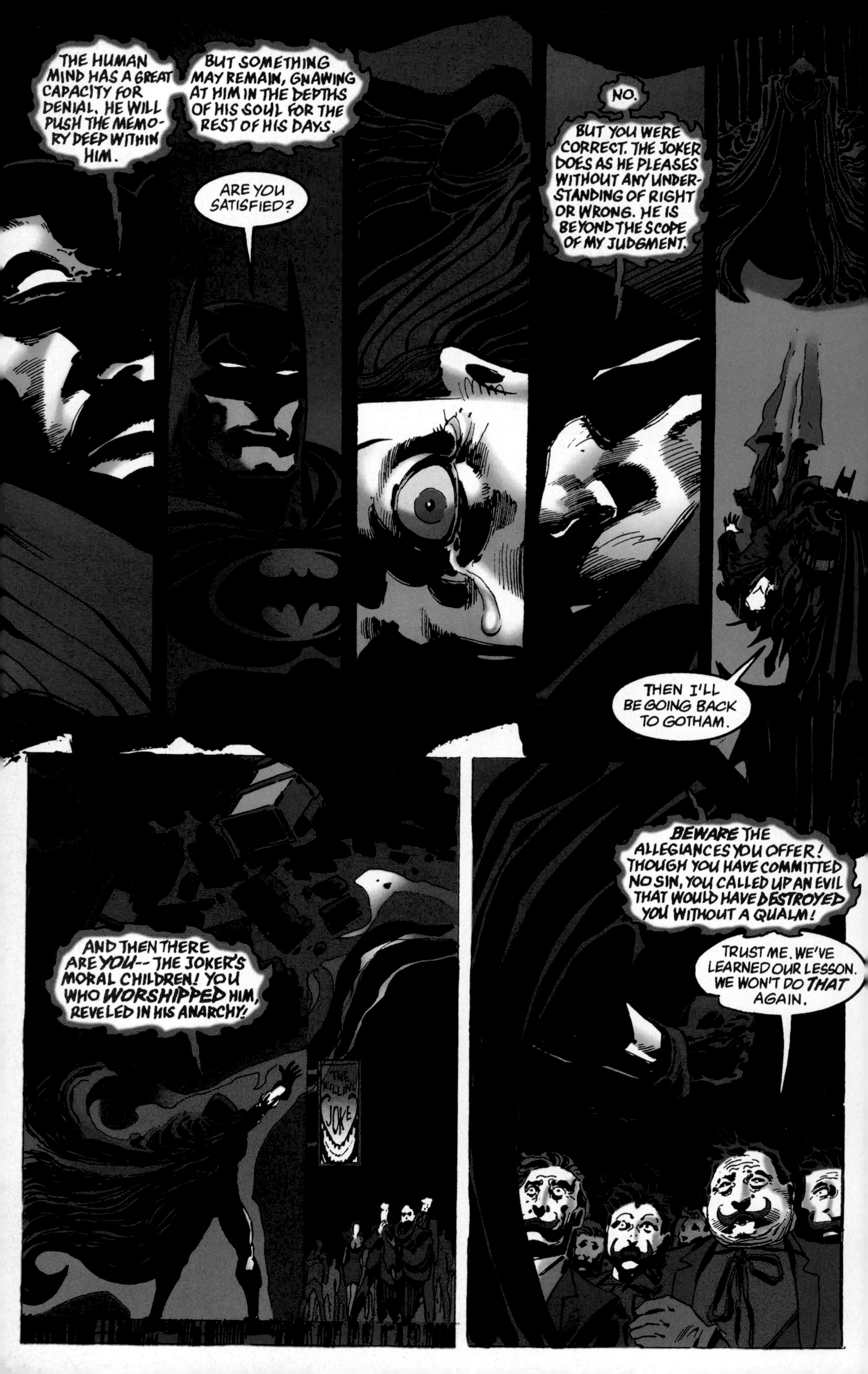
THE HUMAN MIND HAS A GREAT CAPACITY FOR DENIAL. HE WILL PUSH THE MEMORY DEEP WITHIN HIM.
BUT SOMETHING MAY REMAIN, GNAWING AT HIM IN THE DEPTHS OF HIS SOUL FOR THE REST OF HIS DAYS.
ARE YOU SATISFIED?
NO.
BUT YOU WERE CORRECT. THE JOKER DOES AS HE PLEASES WITHOUT ANY UNDERSTANDING OF RIGHT OR WRONG. HE IS BEYOND THE SCOPE OF MY JUDGMENT.
THEN I'LL BE GOING BACK TO GOTHAM.
AND THEN THERE ARE YOU-- THE JOKER'S MORAL CHILDREN! YOU WHO WORSHIPPED HIM, REVELED IN HIS ANARCHY!
BEWARE THE ALLEGIANCES YOU OFFER! THOUGH YOU HAVE COMMITTED NO SIN, YOU CALLED UP AN EVIL THAT WOULD HAVE DESTROYED YOU WITHOUT A QUALM!
TRUST ME. WE'VE LEARNED OUR LESSON. WE WON'T DO THAT AGAIN.

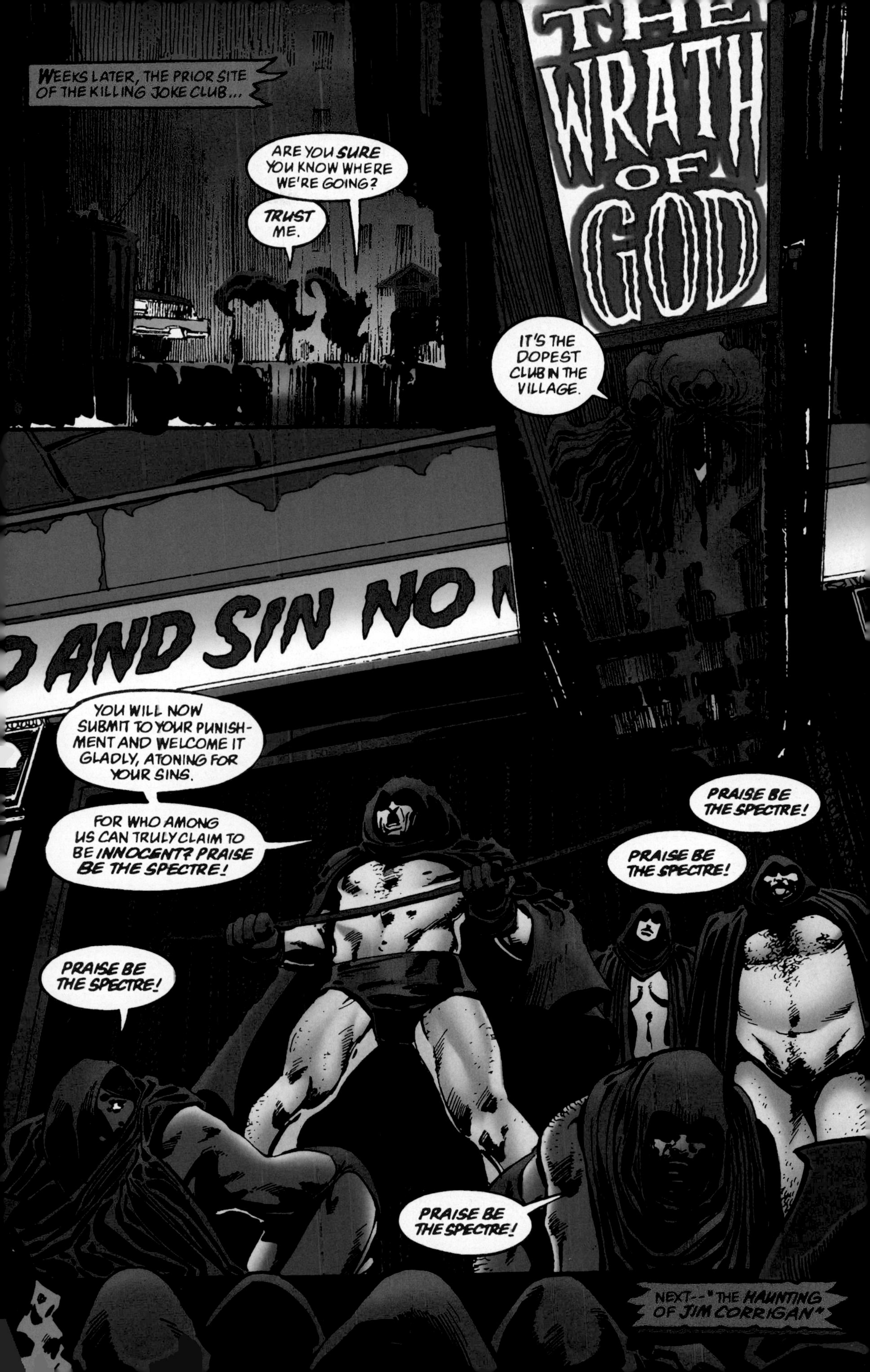
WEEKS LATER, THE PRIOR SITE OF THE KILLING JOKE CLUB...
THE WRATH OF GOD
ARE YOU SURE YOU KNOW WHERE WE'RE GOING?
TRUST ME.
IT'S THE DOPEST CLUB IN THE VILLAGE.
AND SIN NO
YOU WILL NOW SUBMIT TO YOUR PUNISHMENT AND WELCOME IT GLADLY, ATONING FOR YOUR SINS.
FOR WHO AMONG US CAN TRULY CLAIM TO BE INNOCENT? PRAISE BE THE SPECTRE!
PRAISE BE THE SPECTRE!
PRAISE BE THE SPECTRE!
PRAISE BE THE SPECTRE!
PRAISE BE THE SPECTRE!
NEXT-- "THE HAUNTING OF JIM CORRIGAN"

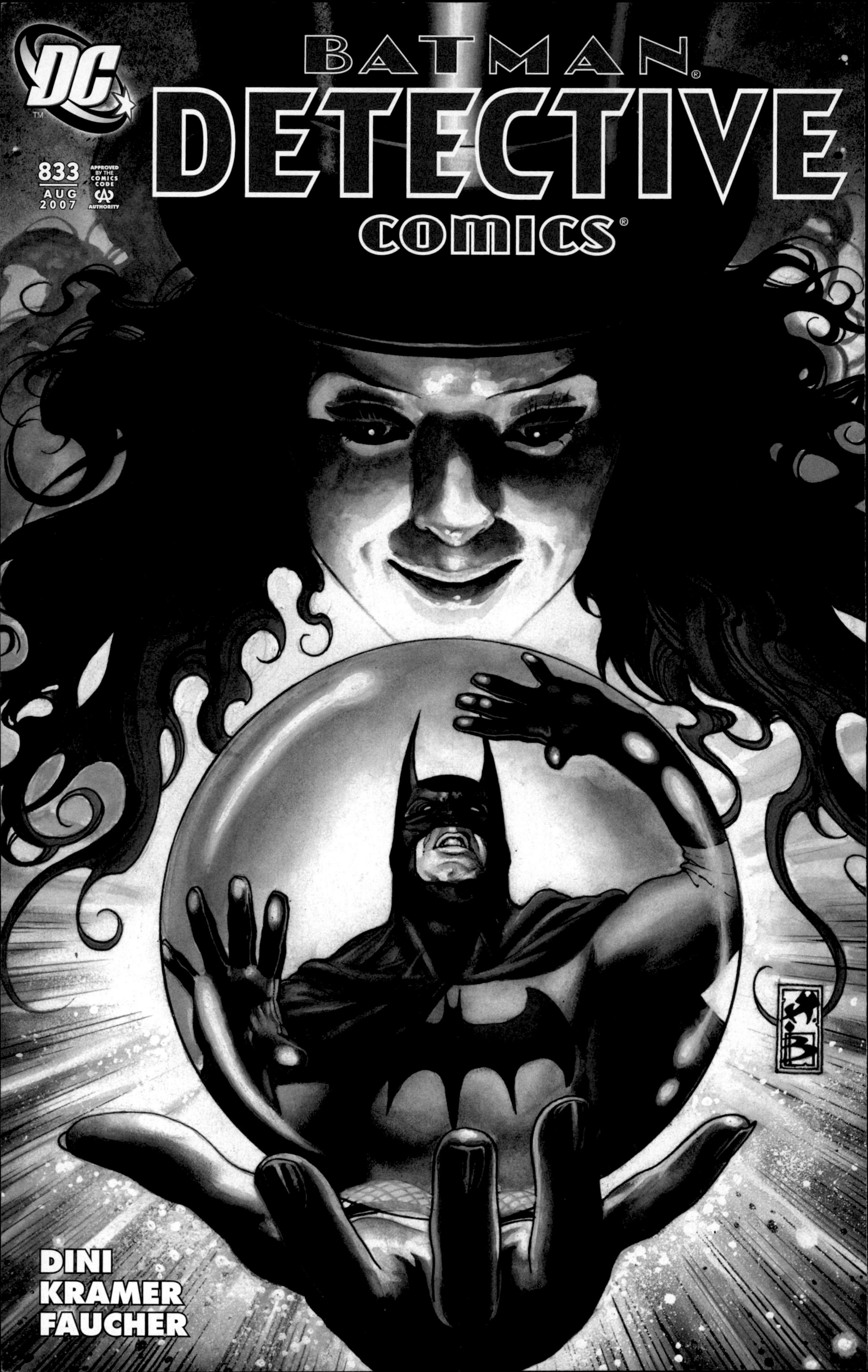
DC
BATMAN
DETECTIVE
COMICS
833
AUG
2007
APPROVED BY THE COMICS CODE AUTHORITY
DINI
KRAMER
FAUCHER

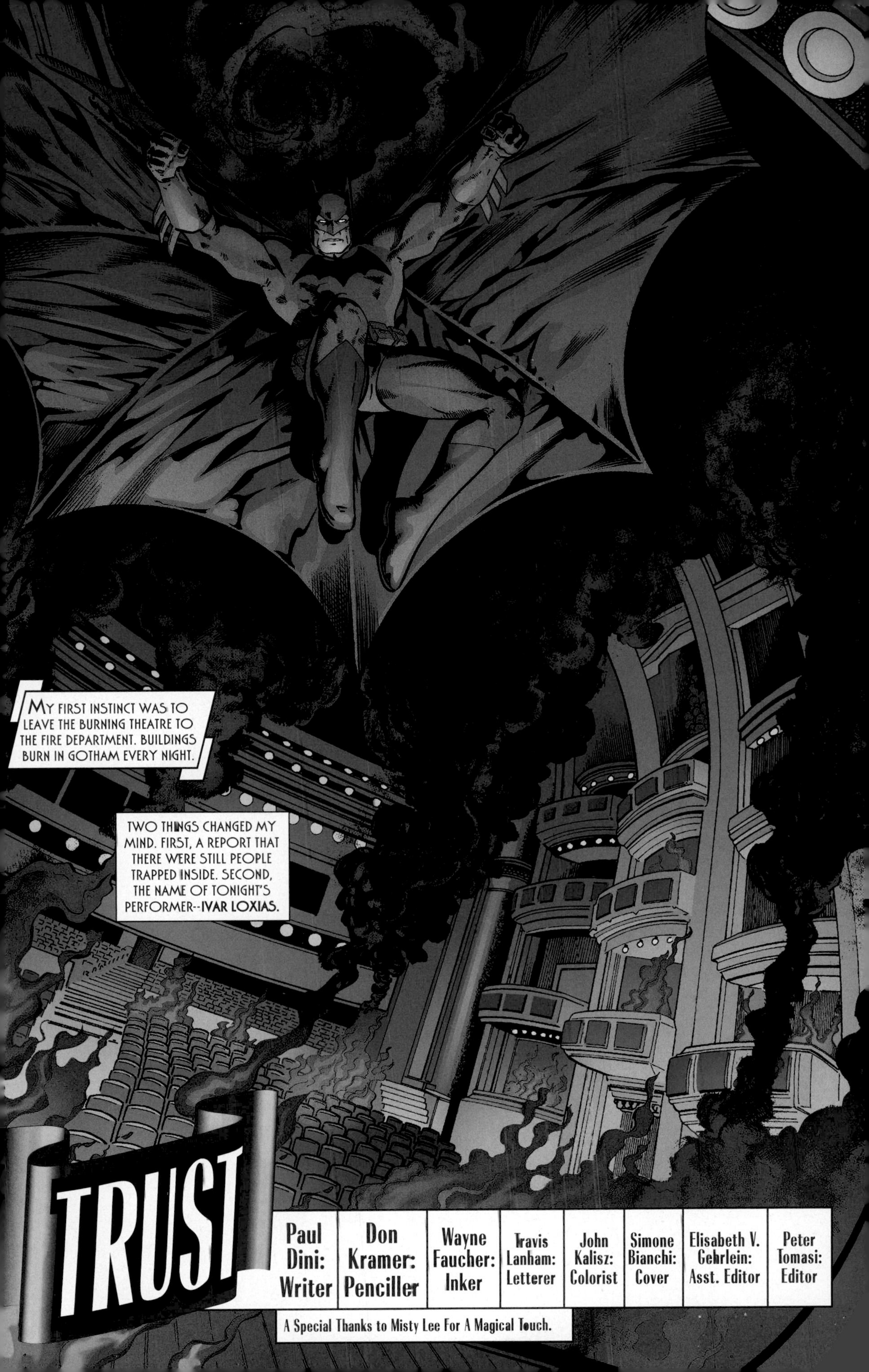
MY FIRST INSTINCT WAS TO LEAVE THE BURNING THEATRE TO THE FIRE DEPARTMENT. BUILDINGS BURN IN GOTHAM EVERY NIGHT.
TWO THINGS CHANGED MY MIND. FIRST, A REPORT THAT THERE WERE STILL PEOPLE TRAPPED INSIDE. SECOND, THE NAME OF TONIGHT'S PERFORMER--IVAR LOXIAS.
TRUST
Paul Dini: Writer
Don Kramer: Penciller
Wayne Faucher: Inker
Travis Lanham: Letterer
John Kalisz: Colorist
Simone Bianchi: Cover
Elisabeth V. Gehrlein: Asst. Editor
Peter Tomasi: Editor
A Special Thanks to Misty Lee For A Magical Touch.

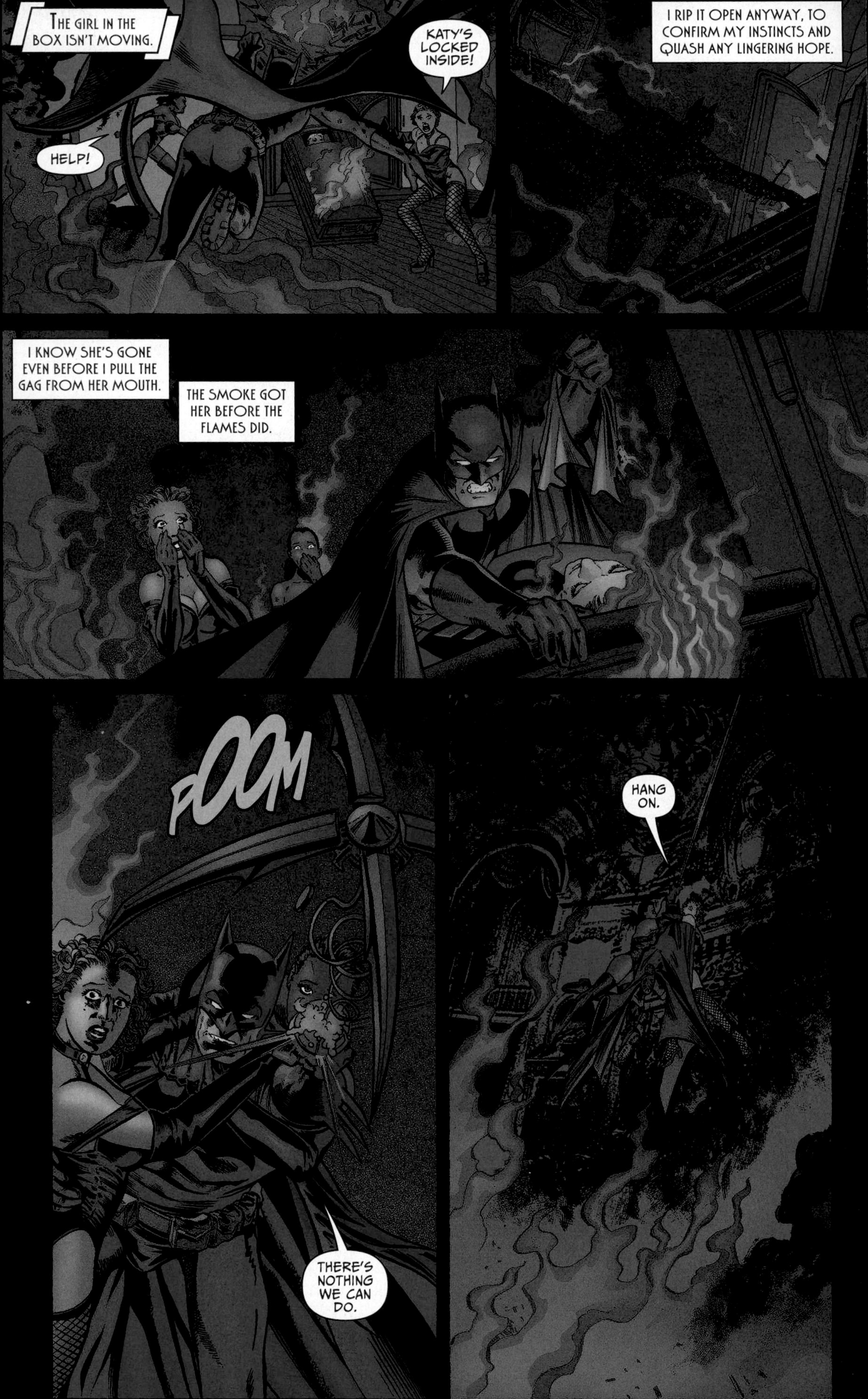
THE GIRL IN THE BOX ISN'T MOVING.
HELP!
KATY'S LOCKED INSIDE!
I RIP IT OPEN ANYWAY, TO CONFIRM MY INSTINCTS AND QUASH ANY LINGERING HOPE.
I KNOW SHE'S GONE EVEN BEFORE I PULL THE GAG FROM HER MOUTH.
THE SMOKE GOT HER BEFORE THE FLAMES DID.
POOM
THERE'S NOTHING WE CAN DO.
HANG ON.

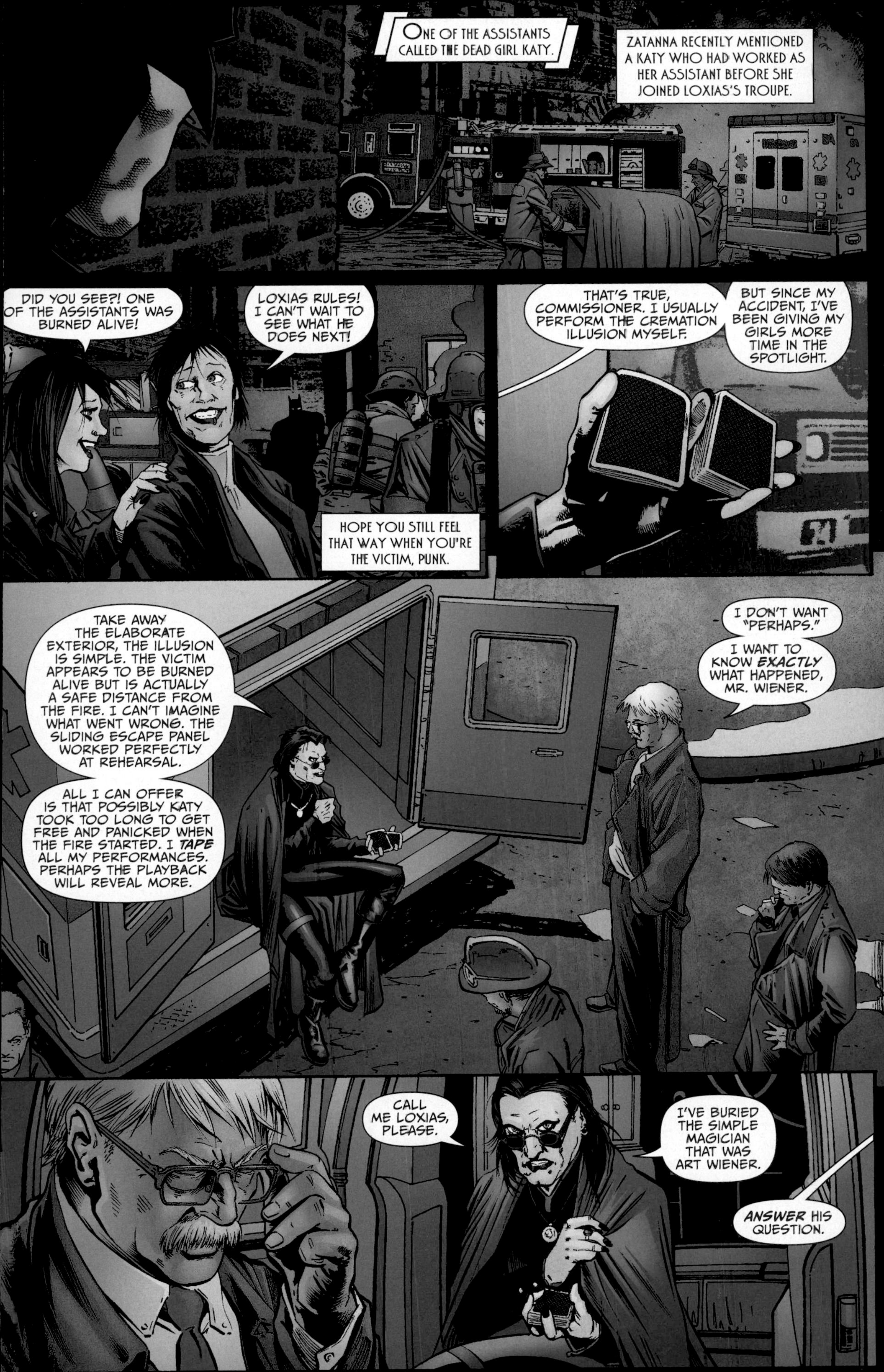

ONE OF THE ASSISTANTS CALLED THE DEAD GIRL KATY.
ZATANNA RECENTLY MENTIONED A KATY WHO HAD WORKED AS HER ASSISTANT BEFORE SHE JOINED LOXIAS'S TROUPE.
DID YOU SEE?! ONE OF THE ASSISTANTS WAS BURNED ALIVE!
LOXIAS RULES! I CAN'T WAIT TO SEE WHAT HE DOES NEXT!
HOPE YOU STILL FEEL THAT WAY WHEN YOU'RE THE VICTIM, PUNK.
THAT'S TRUE, COMMISSIONER. I USUALLY PERFORM THE CREMATION ILLUSION MYSELF.
BUT SINCE MY ACCIDENT, I'VE BEEN GIVING MY GIRLS MORE TIME IN THE SPOTLIGHT.
TAKE AWAY THE ELABORATE EXTERIOR, THE ILLUSION IS SIMPLE. THE VICTIM APPEARS TO BE BURNED ALIVE BUT IS ACTUALLY A SAFE DISTANCE FROM THE FIRE. I CAN'T IMAGINE WHAT WENT WRONG. THE SLIDING ESCAPE PANEL WORKED PERFECTLY AT REHEARSAL.
ALL I CAN OFFER IS THAT POSSIBLY KATY TOOK TOO LONG TO GET FREE AND PANICKED WHEN THE FIRE STARTED. I *TAPE* ALL MY PERFORMANCES. PERHAPS THE PLAYBACK WILL REVEAL MORE.
I DON'T WANT "PERHAPS."
I WANT TO KNOW *EXACTLY* WHAT HAPPENED, MR. WIENER.
CALL ME LOXIAS, PLEASE.
I'VE BURIED THE SIMPLE MAGICIAN THAT WAS ART WIENER.
ANSWER HIS QUESTION.

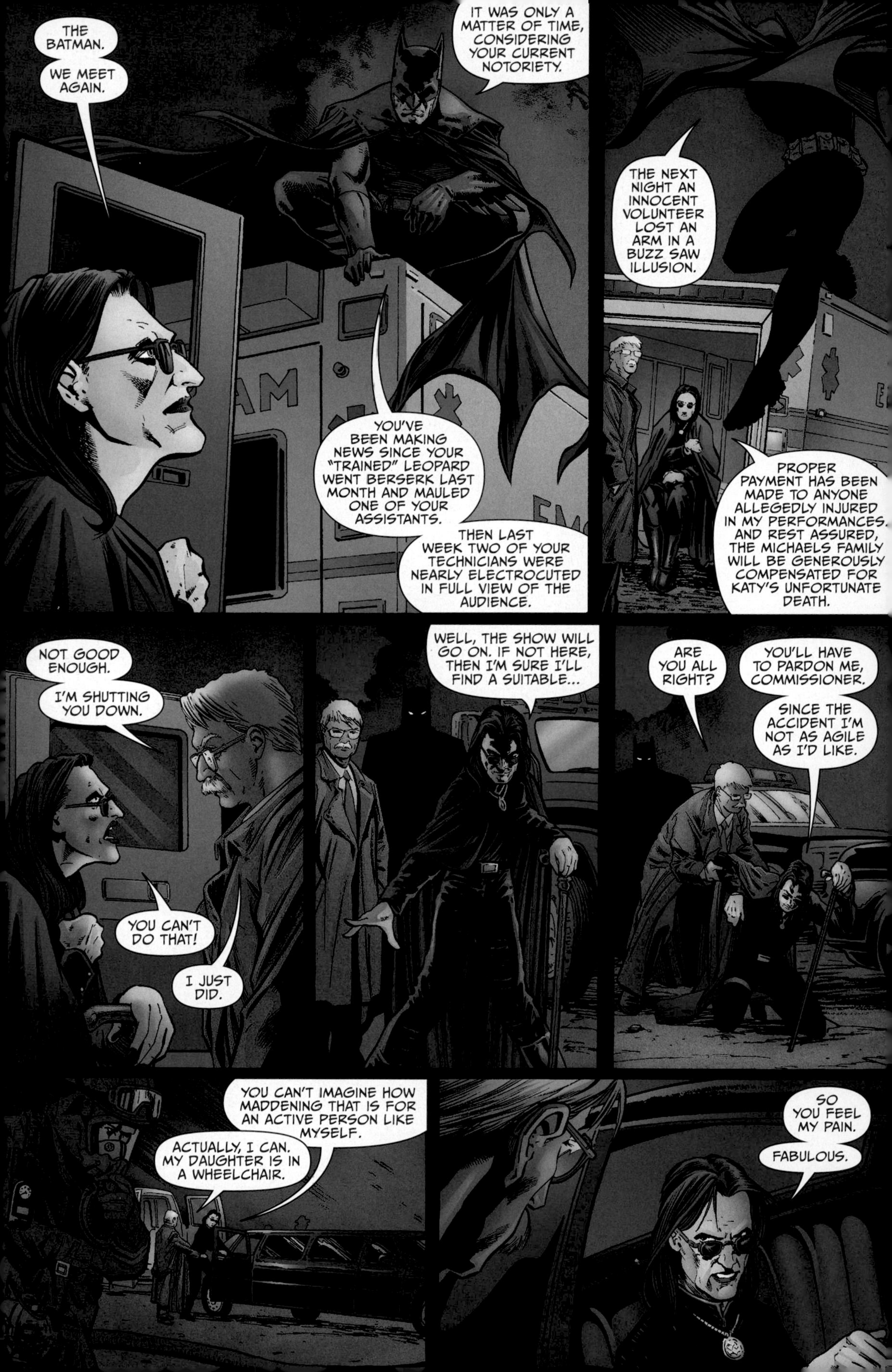
THE BATMAN.
WE MEET AGAIN.
IT WAS ONLY A MATTER OF TIME, CONSIDERING YOUR CURRENT NOTORIETY.
YOU'VE BEEN MAKING NEWS SINCE YOUR "TRAINED" LEOPARD WENT BERSERK LAST MONTH AND MAULED ONE OF YOUR ASSISTANTS.
THEN LAST WEEK TWO OF YOUR TECHNICIANS WERE NEARLY ELECTROCUTED IN FULL VIEW OF THE AUDIENCE.
THE NEXT NIGHT AN INNOCENT VOLUNTEER LOST AN ARM IN A BUZZ SAW ILLUSION.
PROPER PAYMENT HAS BEEN MADE TO ANYONE ALLEGEDLY INJURED IN MY PERFORMANCES. AND REST ASSURED, THE MICHAELS FAMILY WILL BE GENEROUSLY COMPENSATED FOR KATY'S UNFORTUNATE DEATH.
NOT GOOD ENOUGH.
I'M SHUTTING YOU DOWN.
YOU CAN'T DO THAT!
I JUST DID.
WELL, THE SHOW WILL GO ON. IF NOT HERE, THEN I'M SURE I'LL FIND A SUITABLE...
ARE YOU ALL RIGHT?
YOU'LL HAVE TO PARDON ME, COMMISSIONER.
SINCE THE ACCIDENT I'M NOT AS AGILE AS I'D LIKE.
YOU CAN'T IMAGINE HOW MADDENING THAT IS FOR AN ACTIVE PERSON LIKE MYSELF.
ACTUALLY, I CAN. MY DAUGHTER IS IN A WHEELCHAIR.
SO YOU FEEL MY PAIN.
FABULOUS.

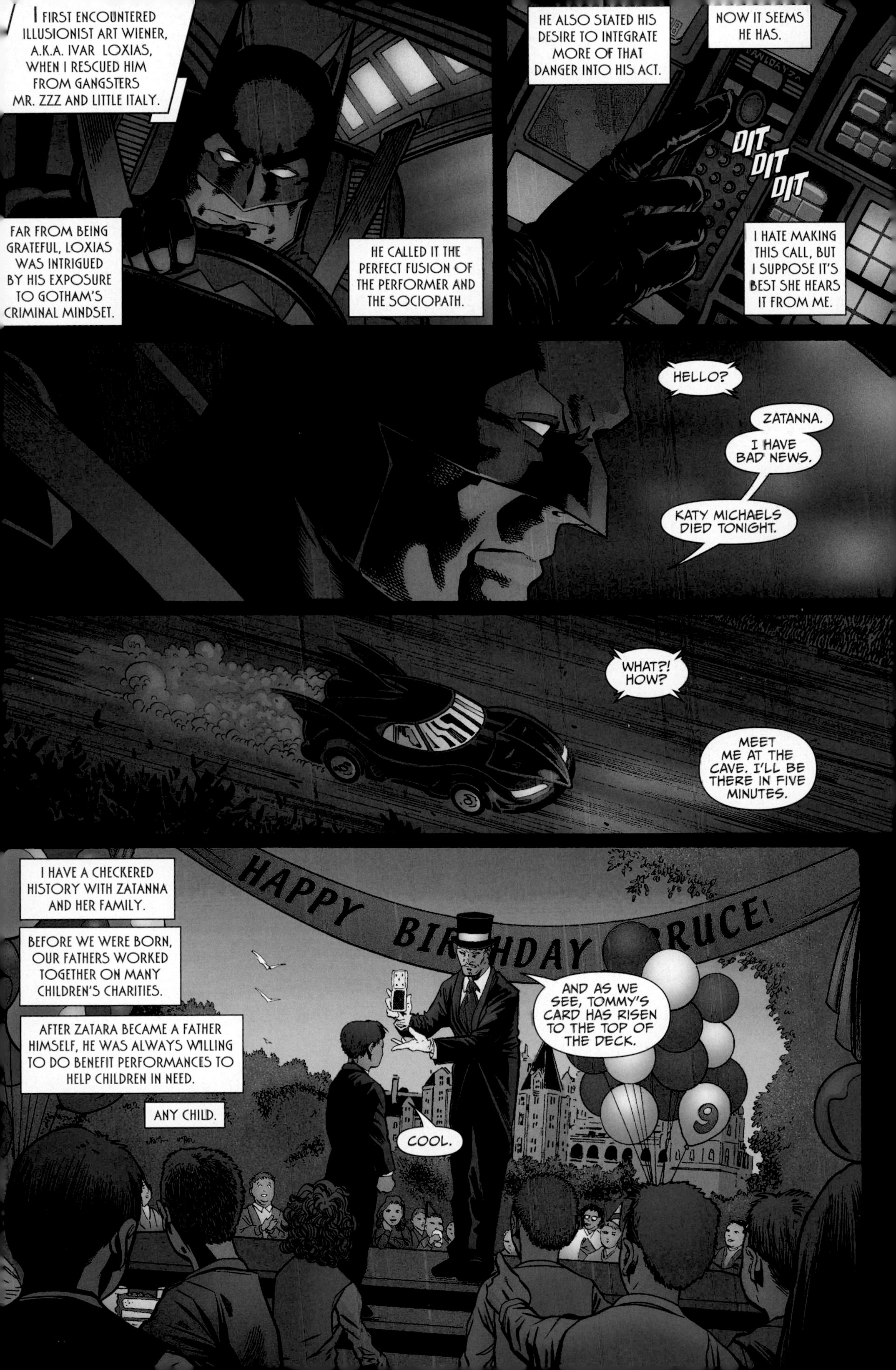
I FIRST ENCOUNTERED ILLUSIONIST ART WIENER, A.K.A. IVAR LOXIAS, WHEN I RESCUED HIM FROM GANGSTERS MR. ZZZ AND LITTLE ITALY.
FAR FROM BEING GRATEFUL, LOXIAS WAS INTRIGUED BY HIS EXPOSURE TO GOTHAM'S CRIMINAL MINDSET.
HE CALLED IT THE PERFECT FUSION OF THE PERFORMER AND THE SOCIOPATH.
HE ALSO STATED HIS DESIRE TO INTEGRATE MORE OF THAT DANGER INTO HIS ACT.
NOW IT SEEMS HE HAS.
DIT DIT DIT
I HATE MAKING THIS CALL, BUT I SUPPOSE IT'S BEST SHE HEARS IT FROM ME.
HELLO?
ZATANNA.
I HAVE BAD NEWS.
KATY MICHAELS DIED TONIGHT.
WHAT?! HOW?
MEET ME AT THE CAVE. I'LL BE THERE IN FIVE MINUTES.
HAPPY BIRTHDAY BRUCE!
I HAVE A CHECKERED HISTORY WITH ZATANNA AND HER FAMILY.
BEFORE WE WERE BORN, OUR FATHERS WORKED TOGETHER ON MANY CHILDREN'S CHARITIES.
AFTER ZATARA BECAME A FATHER HIMSELF, HE WAS ALWAYS WILLING TO DO BENEFIT PERFORMANCES TO HELP CHILDREN IN NEED.
ANY CHILD.
AND AS WE SEE, TOMMY'S CARD HAS RISEN TO THE TOP OF THE DECK.
COOL.
9

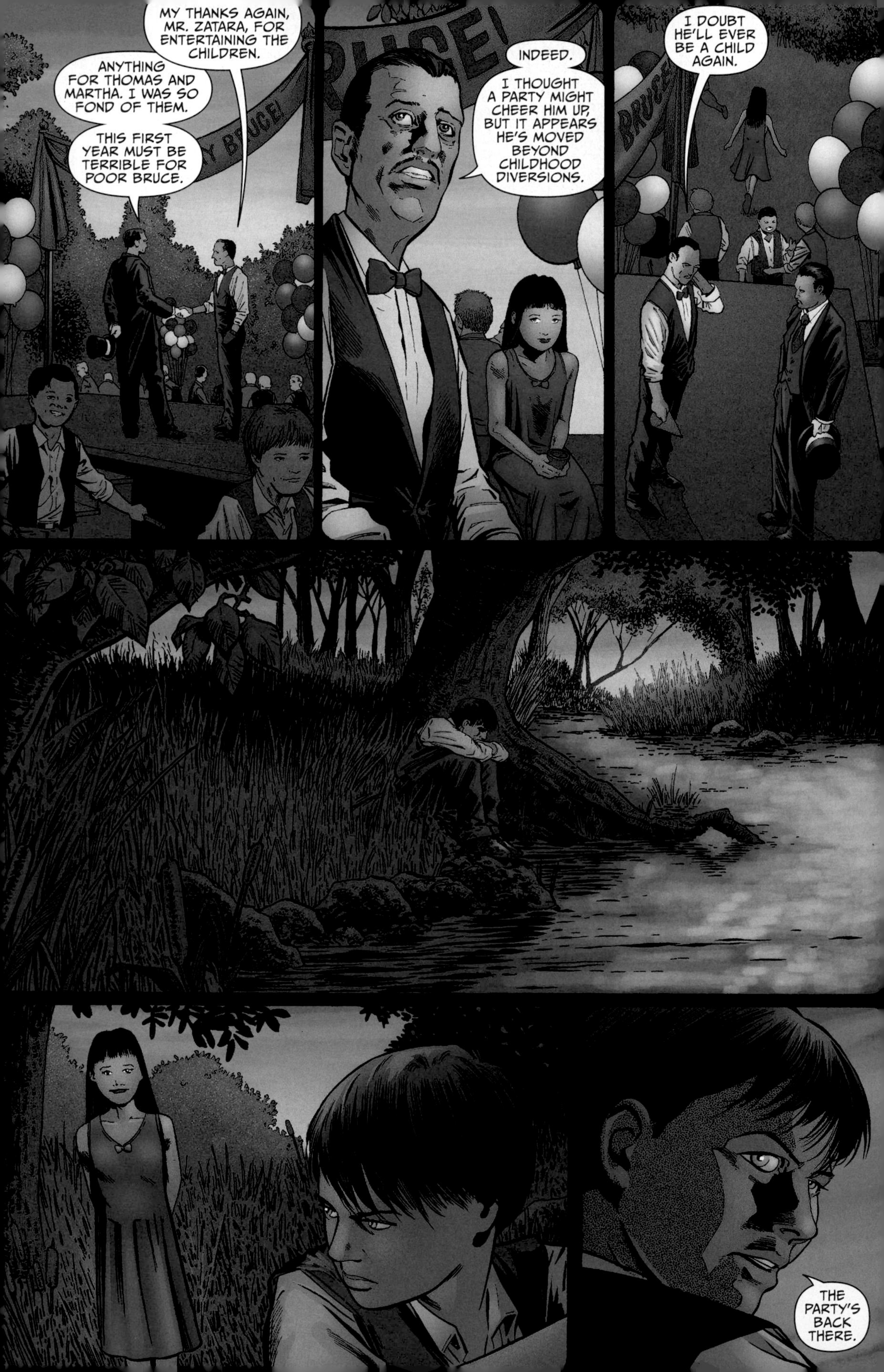
MY THANKS AGAIN, MR. ZATARA, FOR ENTERTAINING THE CHILDREN.
ANYTHING FOR THOMAS AND MARTHA. I WAS SO FOND OF THEM.
THIS FIRST YEAR MUST BE TERRIBLE FOR POOR BRUCE.
INDEED.
I THOUGHT A PARTY MIGHT CHEER HIM UP, BUT IT APPEARS HE'S MOVED BEYOND CHILDHOOD DIVERSIONS.
I DOUBT HE'LL EVER BE A CHILD AGAIN.
THE PARTY'S BACK THERE.

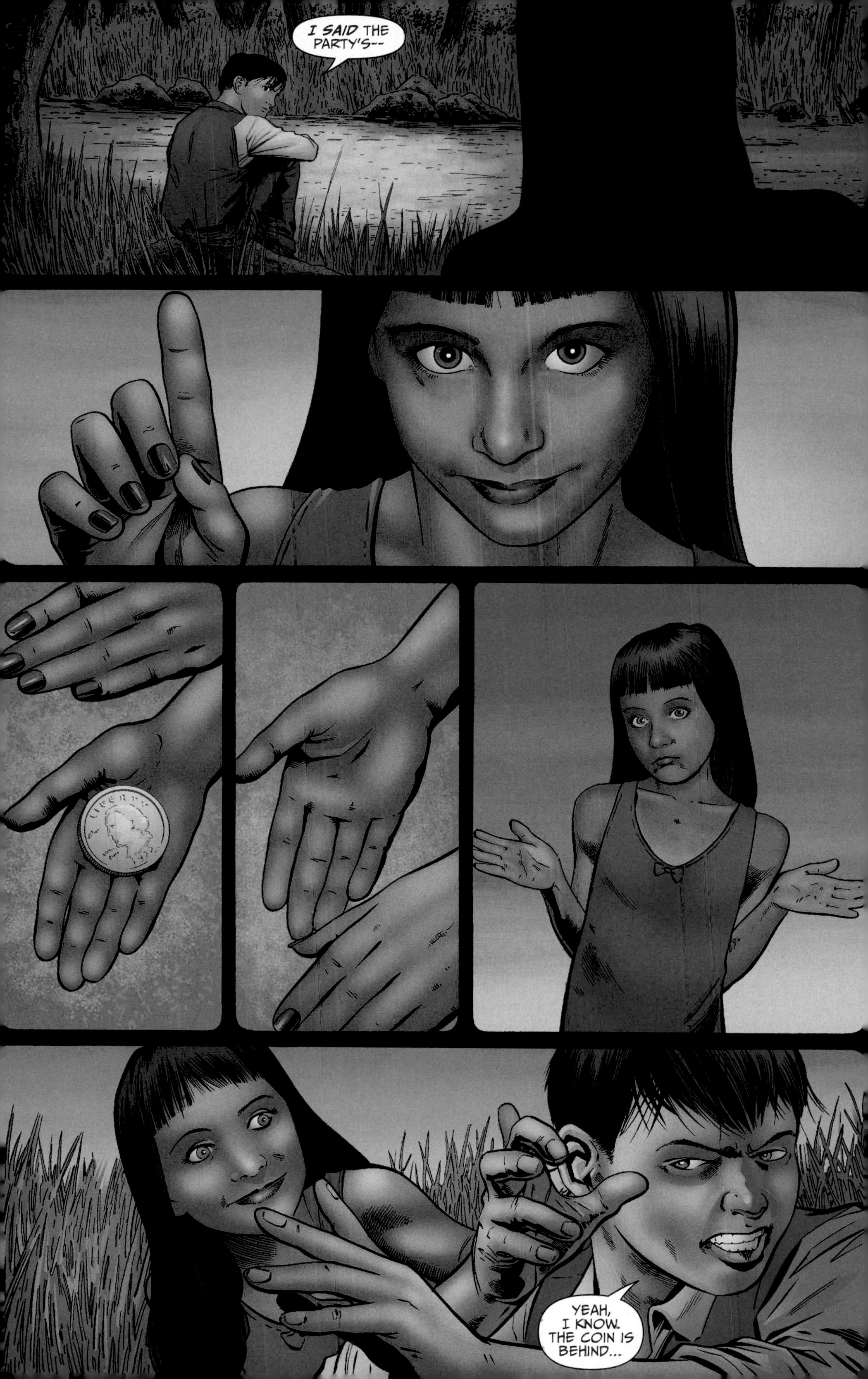
I SAID THE PARTY'S--
YEAH, I KNOW. THE COIN IS BEHIND...

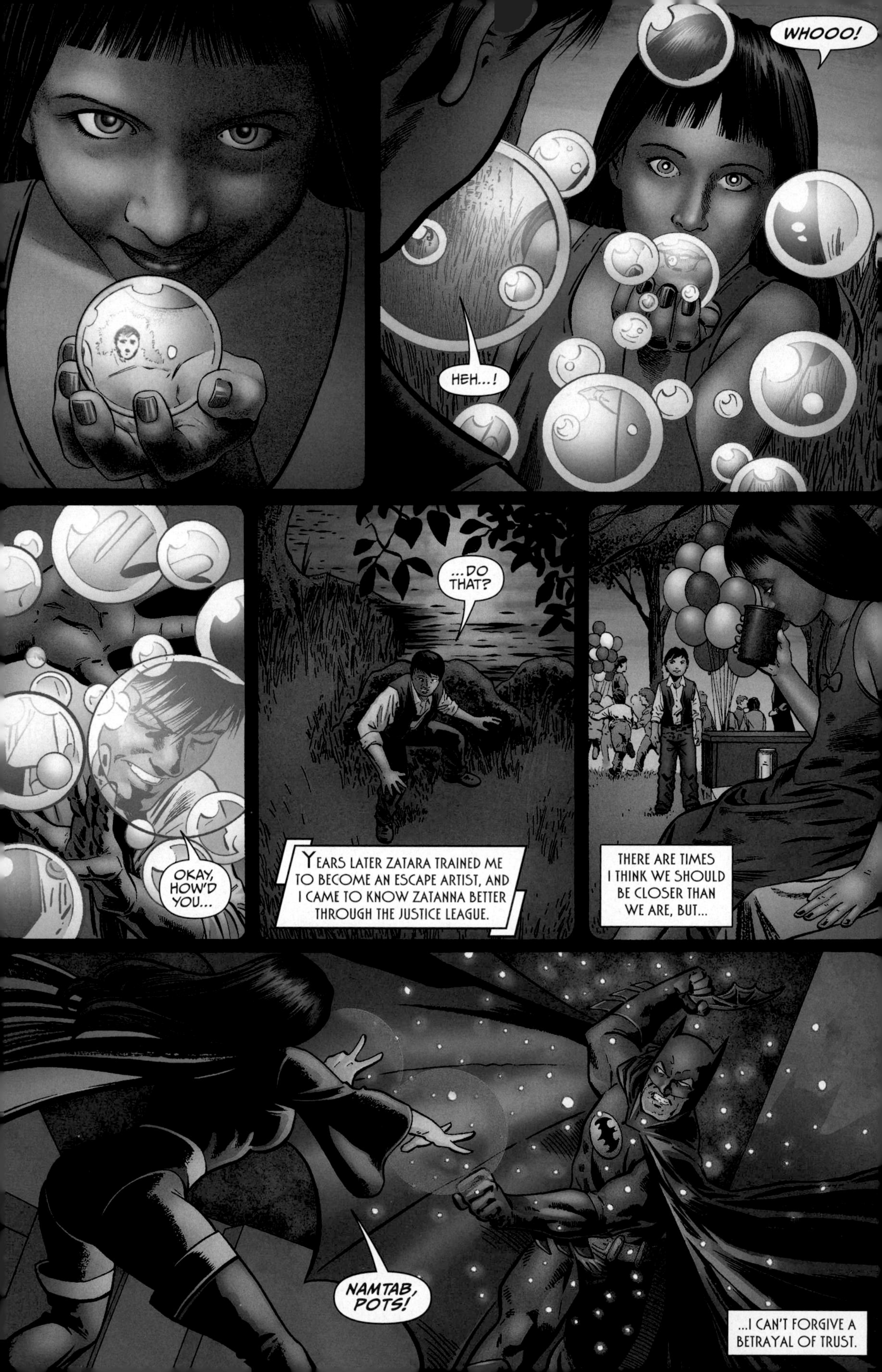
WHOOO!
HEH...!
OKAY, HOW'D YOU...
...DO THAT?
YEARS LATER ZATARA TRAINED ME TO BECOME AN ESCAPE ARTIST, AND I CAME TO KNOW ZATANNA BETTER THROUGH THE JUSTICE LEAGUE.
THERE ARE TIMES I THINK WE SHOULD BE CLOSER THAN WE ARE, BUT...
NAMTAB, POTS!
...I CAN'T FORGIVE A BETRAYAL OF TRUST.

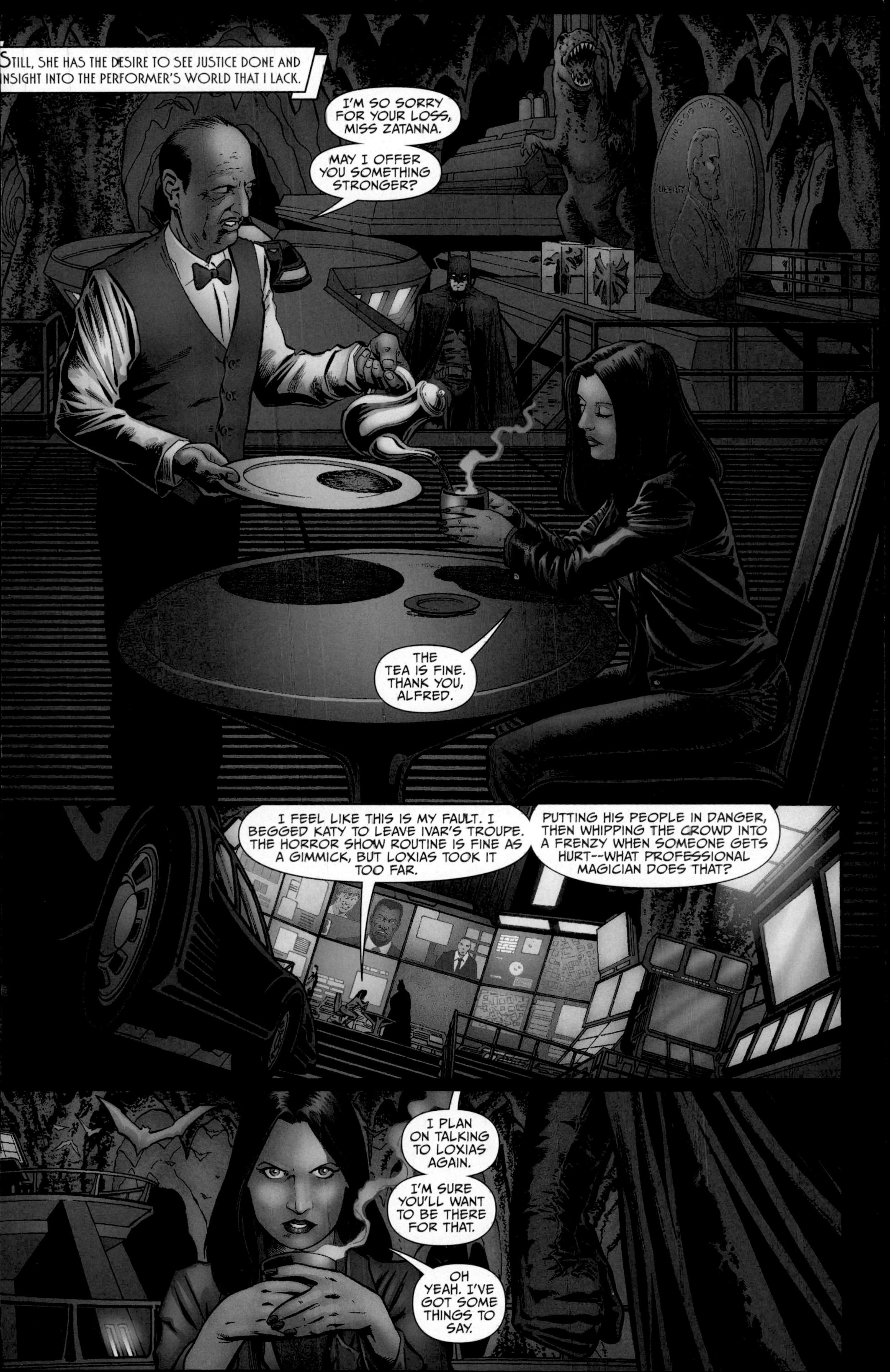
STILL, SHE HAS THE DESIRE TO SEE JUSTICE DONE AND INSIGHT INTO THE PERFORMER'S WORLD THAT I LACK.
I'M SO SORRY FOR YOUR LOSS, MISS ZATANNA.
MAY I OFFER YOU SOMETHING STRONGER?
THE TEA IS FINE. THANK YOU, ALFRED.
I FEEL LIKE THIS IS MY FAULT. I BEGGED KATY TO LEAVE IVAR'S TROUPE. THE HORROR SHOW ROUTINE IS FINE AS A GIMMICK, BUT LOXIAS TOOK IT TOO FAR.
PUTTING HIS PEOPLE IN DANGER, THEN WHIPPING THE CROWD INTO A FRENZY WHEN SOMEONE GETS HURT--WHAT PROFESSIONAL MAGICIAN DOES THAT?
I PLAN ON TALKING TO LOXIAS AGAIN.
I'M SURE YOU'LL WANT TO BE THERE FOR THAT.
OH YEAH. I'VE GOT SOME THINGS TO SAY.

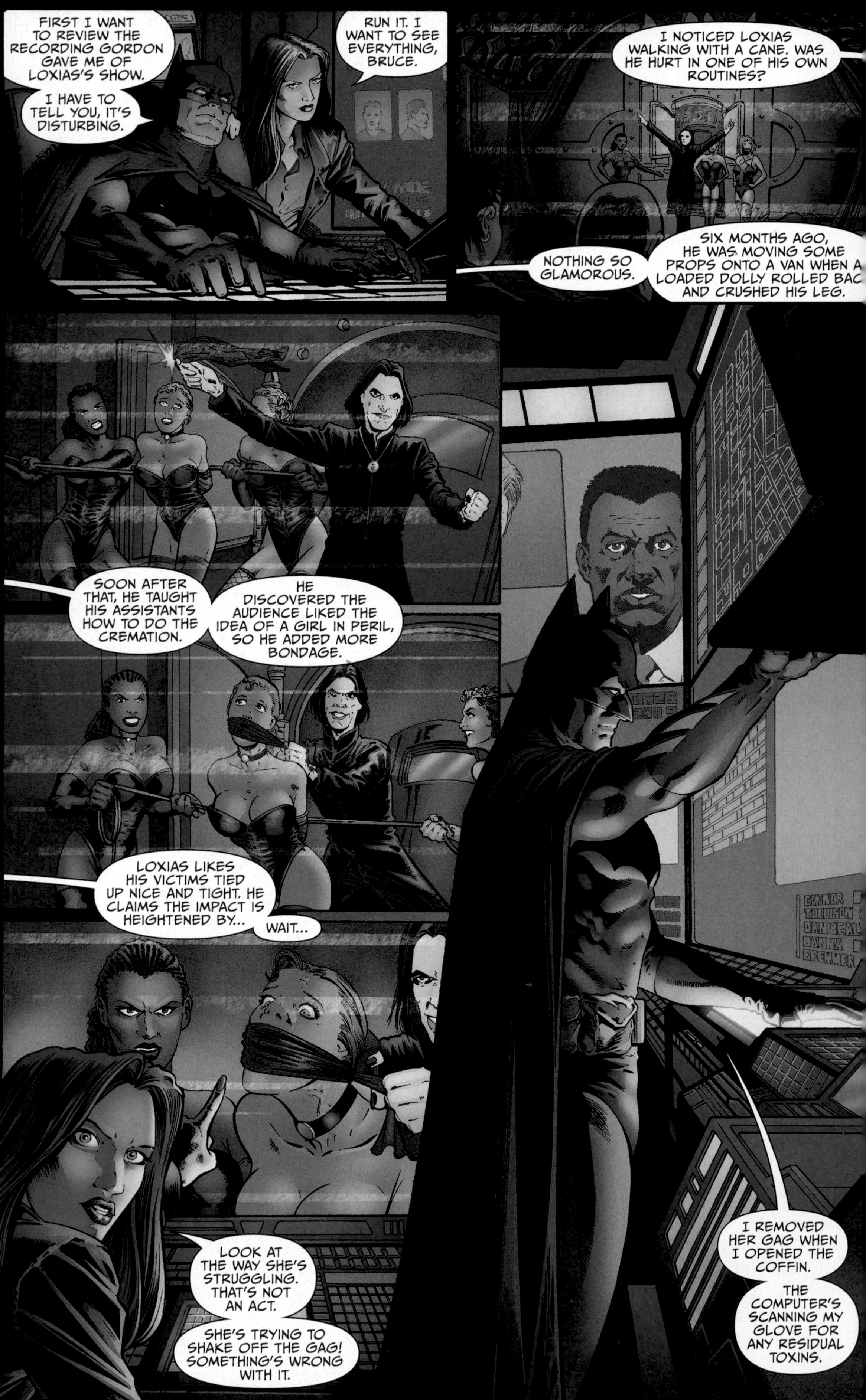
FIRST I WANT TO REVIEW THE RECORDING GORDON GAVE ME OF LOXIAS'S SHOW.
I HAVE TO TELL YOU, IT'S DISTURBING.
RUN IT. I WANT TO SEE EVERYTHING, BRUCE.
I NOTICED LOXIAS WALKING WITH A CANE. WAS HE HURT IN ONE OF HIS OWN ROUTINES?
NOTHING SO GLAMOROUS.
SIX MONTHS AGO, HE WAS MOVING SOME PROPS ONTO A VAN WHEN A LOADED DOLLY ROLLED BAC AND CRUSHED HIS LEG.
SOON AFTER THAT, HE TAUGHT HIS ASSISTANTS HOW TO DO THE CREMATION.
HE DISCOVERED THE AUDIENCE LIKED THE IDEA OF A GIRL IN PERIL, SO HE ADDED MORE BONDAGE.
LOXIAS LIKES HIS VICTIMS TIED UP NICE AND TIGHT. HE CLAIMS THE IMPACT IS HEIGHTENED BY...
WAIT...
LOOK AT THE WAY SHE'S STRUGGLING. THAT'S NOT AN ACT.
SHE'S TRYING TO SHAKE OFF THE GAG! SOMETHING'S WRONG WITH IT.
I REMOVED HER GAG WHEN I OPENED THE COFFIN.
THE COMPUTER'S SCANNING MY GLOVE FOR ANY RESIDUAL TOXINS.

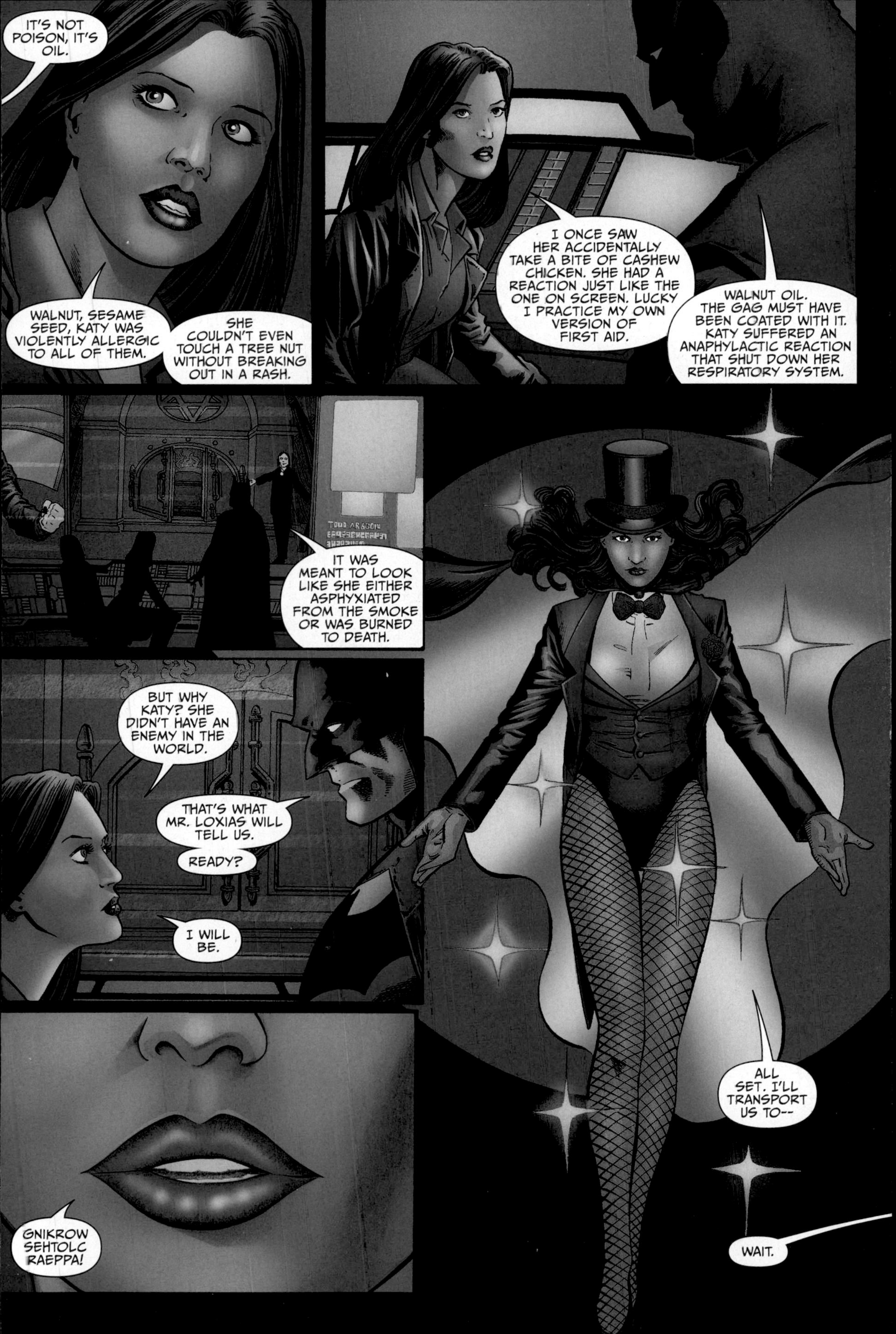
IT'S NOT POISON, IT'S OIL.
WALNUT, SESAME SEED, KATY WAS VIOLENTLY ALLERGIC TO ALL OF THEM.
SHE COULDN'T EVEN TOUCH A TREE NUT WITHOUT BREAKING OUT IN A RASH.
I ONCE SAW HER ACCIDENTALLY TAKE A BITE OF CASHEW CHICKEN. SHE HAD A REACTION JUST LIKE THE ONE ON SCREEN. LUCKY I PRACTICE MY OWN VERSION OF FIRST AID.
WALNUT OIL. THE GAG MUST HAVE BEEN COATED WITH IT. KATY SUFFERED AN ANAPHYLACTIC REACTION THAT SHUT DOWN HER RESPIRATORY SYSTEM.
TODD ARAGON
IT WAS MEANT TO LOOK LIKE SHE EITHER ASPHYXIATED FROM THE SMOKE OR WAS BURNED TO DEATH.
BUT WHY KATY? SHE DIDN'T HAVE AN ENEMY IN THE WORLD.
THAT'S WHAT MR. LOXIAS WILL TELL US.
READY?
I WILL BE.
GNIKROW SEHTOLC RAEPPA!
ALL SET. I'LL TRANSPORT US TO--
WAIT.

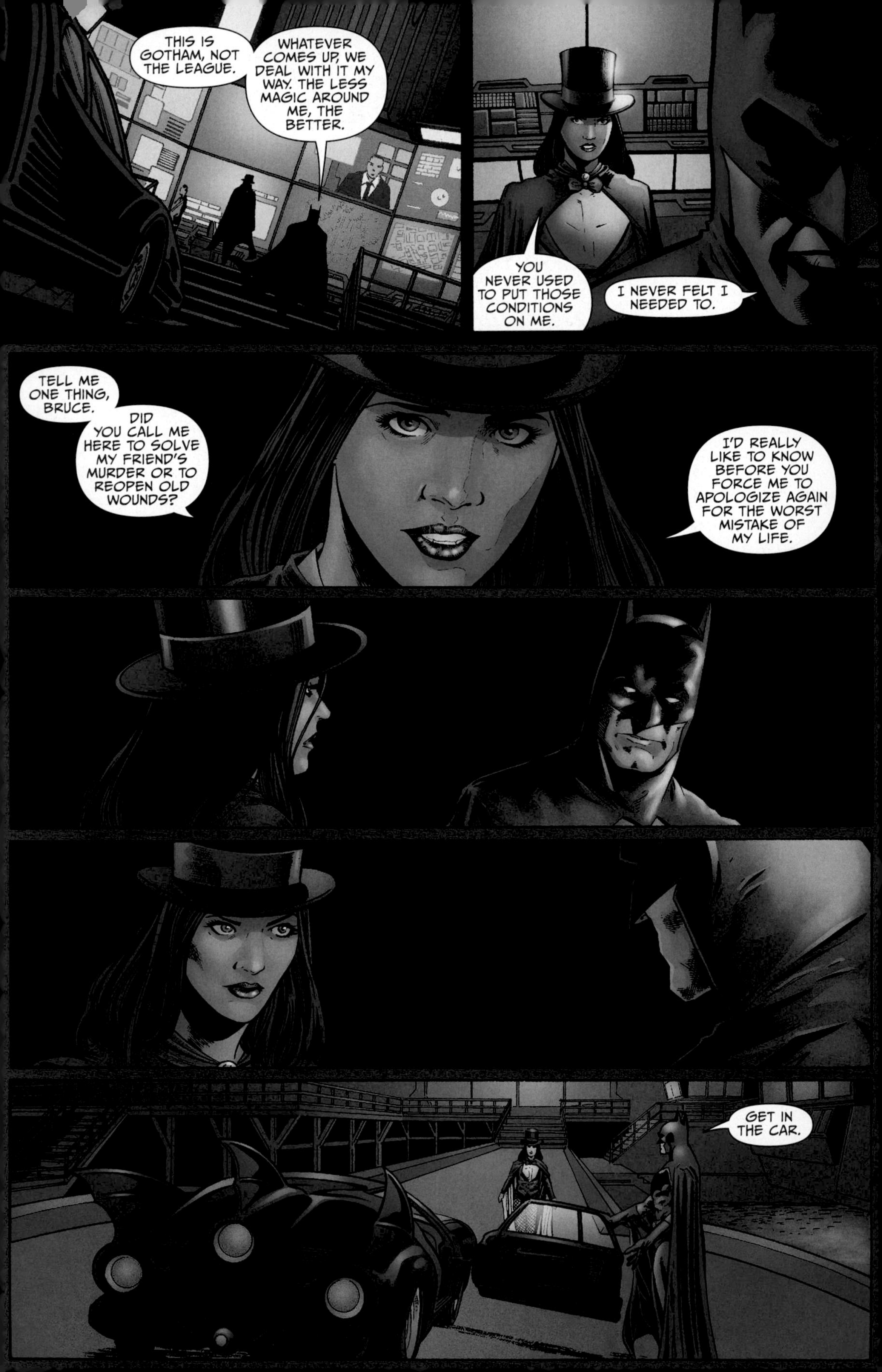
THIS IS GOTHAM, NOT THE LEAGUE.
WHATEVER COMES UP, WE DEAL WITH IT MY WAY. THE LESS MAGIC AROUND ME, THE BETTER.
YOU NEVER USED TO PUT THOSE CONDITIONS ON ME.
I NEVER FELT I NEEDED TO.
TELL ME ONE THING, BRUCE.
DID YOU CALL ME HERE TO SOLVE MY FRIEND'S MURDER OR TO REOPEN OLD WOUNDS?
I'D REALLY LIKE TO KNOW BEFORE YOU FORCE ME TO APOLOGIZE AGAIN FOR THE WORST MISTAKE OF MY LIFE.
GET IN THE CAR.

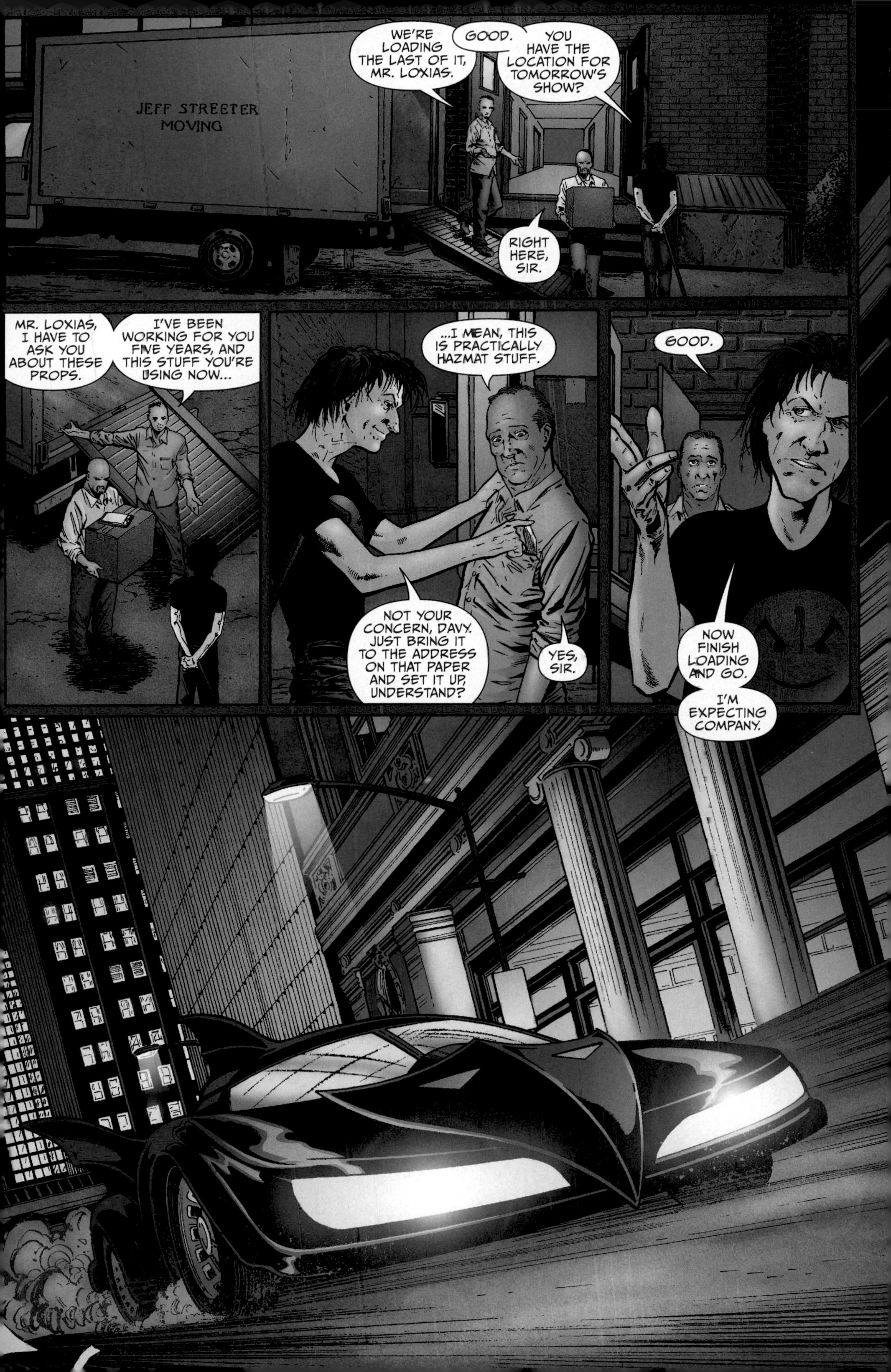
JEFF STREETER
MOVING
WE'RE LOADING THE LAST OF IT, MR. LOXIAS.
GOOD.
YOU HAVE THE LOCATION FOR TOMORROW'S SHOW?
RIGHT HERE, SIR.
MR. LOXIAS, I HAVE TO ASK YOU ABOUT THESE PROPS.
I'VE BEEN WORKING FOR YOU FIVE YEARS, AND THIS STUFF YOU'RE USING NOW...
...I MEAN, THIS IS PRACTICALLY HAZMAT STUFF.
NOT YOUR CONCERN, DAVY. JUST BRING IT TO THE ADDRESS ON THAT PAPER AND SET IT UP, UNDERSTAND?
YES, SIR.
GOOD.
NOW FINISH LOADING AND GO.
I'M EXPECTING COMPANY.

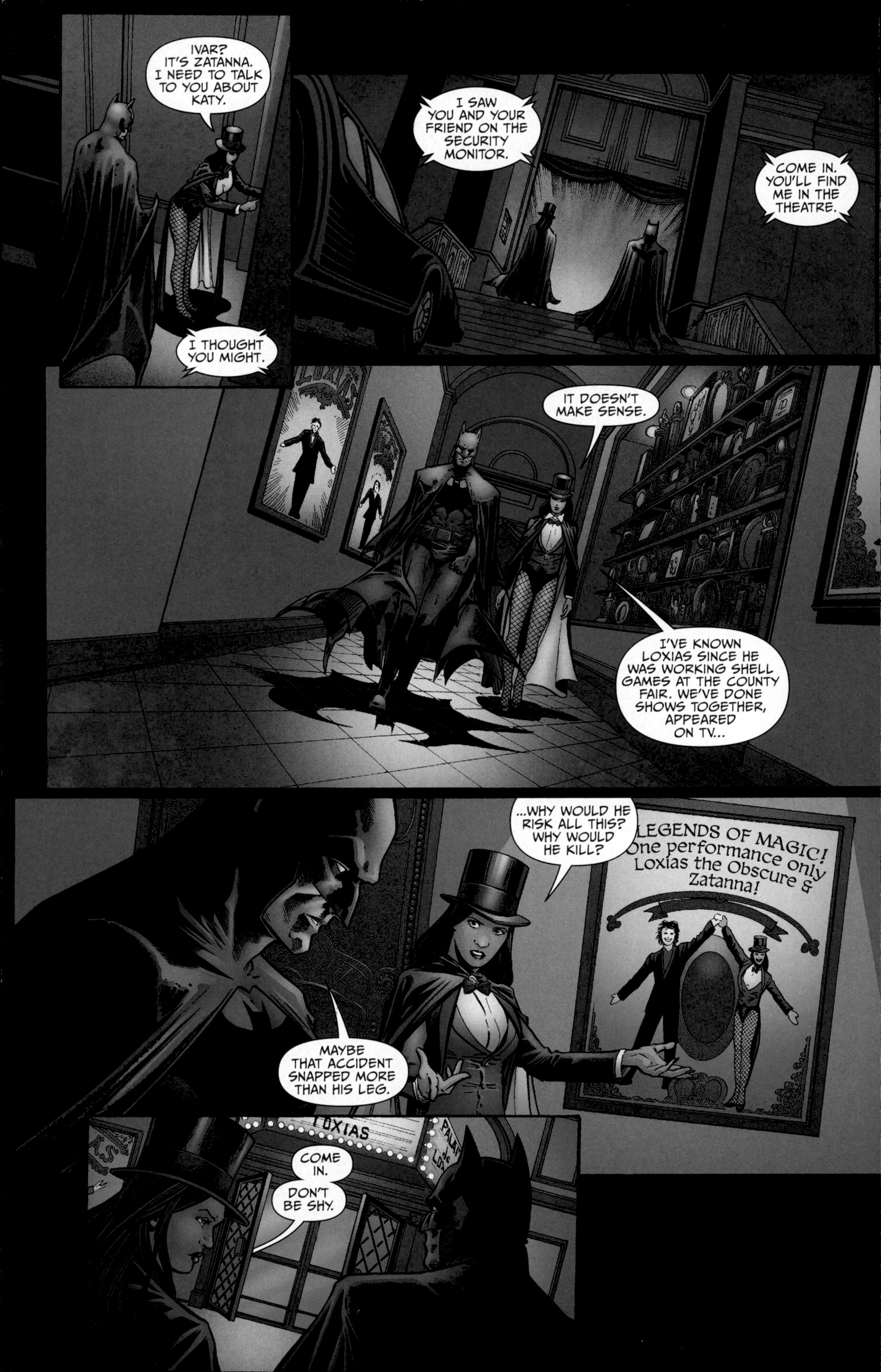
IVAR? IT'S ZATANNA. I NEED TO TALK TO YOU ABOUT KATY.
I THOUGHT YOU MIGHT.
I SAW YOU AND YOUR FRIEND ON THE SECURITY MONITOR.
COME IN. YOU'LL FIND ME IN THE THEATRE.
LOXIAS
IT DOESN'T MAKE SENSE.
I'VE KNOWN LOXIAS SINCE HE WAS WORKING SHELL GAMES AT THE COUNTY FAIR. WE'VE DONE SHOWS TOGETHER, APPEARED ON TV...
...WHY WOULD HE RISK ALL THIS? WHY WOULD HE KILL?
LEGENDS OF MAGIC! One performance only Loxias the Obscure & Zatanna!
MAYBE THAT ACCIDENT SNAPPED MORE THAN HIS LEG.
LOXIAS
COME IN.
DON'T BE SHY.

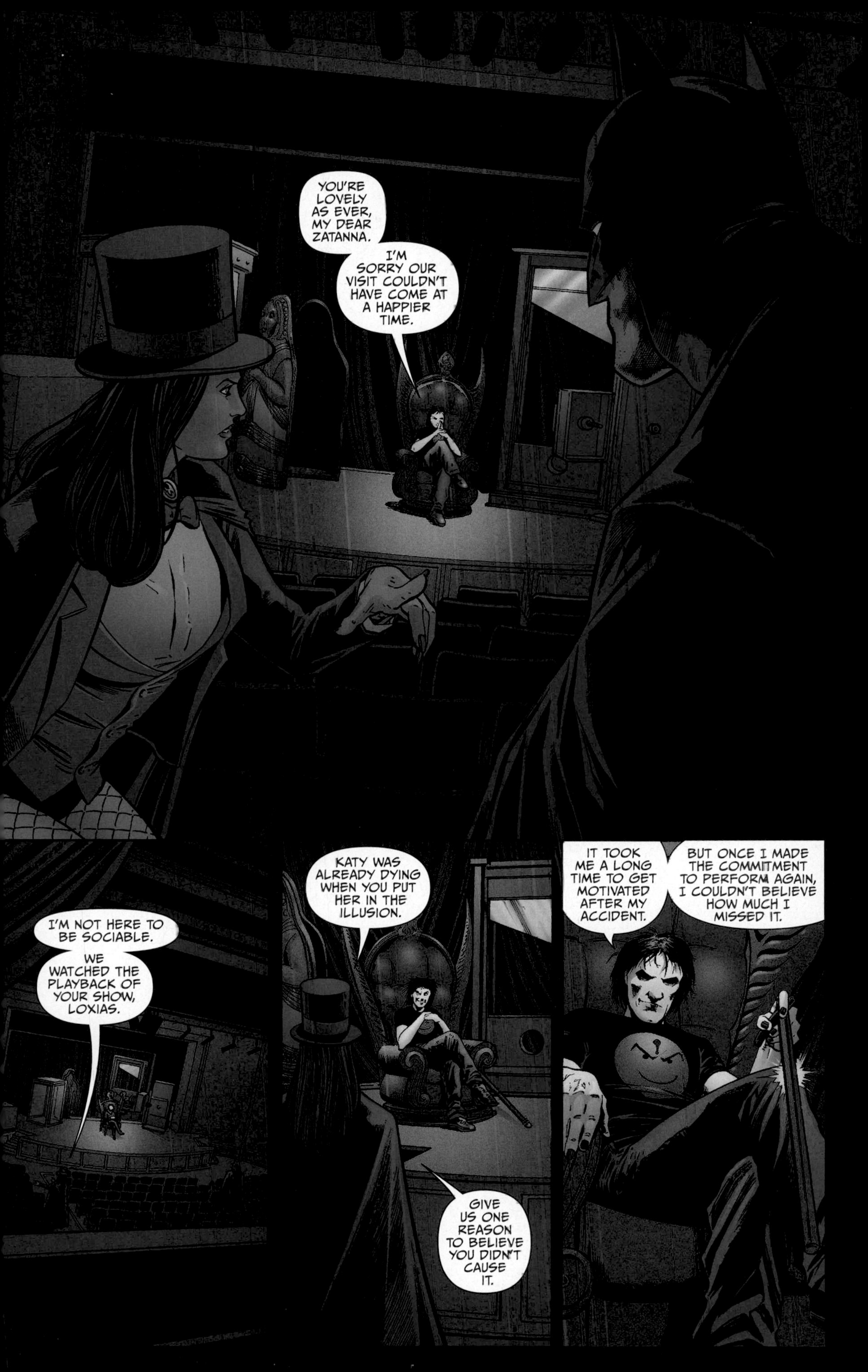
YOU'RE LOVELY AS EVER, MY DEAR ZATANNA.
I'M SORRY OUR VISIT COULDN'T HAVE COME AT A HAPPIER TIME.
I'M NOT HERE TO BE SOCIABLE.
WE WATCHED THE PLAYBACK OF YOUR SHOW, LOXIAS.
KATY WAS ALREADY DYING WHEN YOU PUT HER IN THE ILLUSION.
GIVE US ONE REASON TO BELIEVE YOU DIDN'T CAUSE IT.
IT TOOK ME A LONG TIME TO GET MOTIVATED AFTER MY ACCIDENT.
BUT ONCE I MADE THE COMMITMENT TO PERFORM AGAIN, I COULDN'T BELIEVE HOW MUCH I MISSED IT.

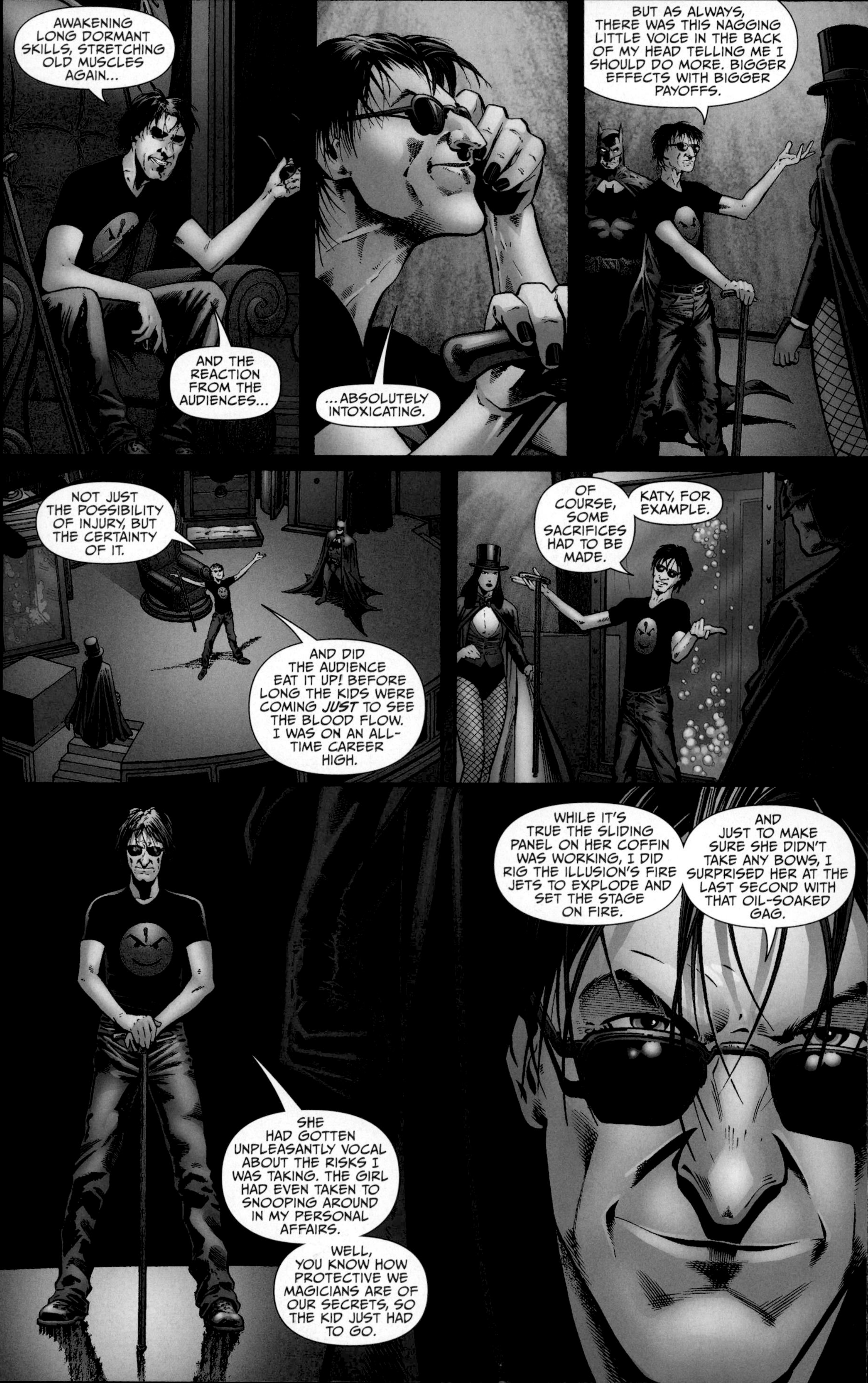
AWAKENING LONG DORMANT SKILLS, STRETCHING OLD MUSCLES AGAIN...
AND THE REACTION FROM THE AUDIENCES...
...ABSOLUTELY INTOXICATING.
BUT AS ALWAYS, THERE WAS THIS NAGGING LITTLE VOICE IN THE BACK OF MY HEAD TELLING ME I SHOULD DO MORE. BIGGER EFFECTS WITH BIGGER PAYOFFS.
NOT JUST THE POSSIBILITY OF INJURY, BUT THE CERTAINTY OF IT.
AND DID THE AUDIENCE EAT IT UP! BEFORE LONG THE KIDS WERE COMING JUST TO SEE THE BLOOD FLOW. I WAS ON AN ALL-TIME CAREER HIGH.
OF COURSE, SOME SACRIFICES HAD TO BE MADE.
KATY, FOR EXAMPLE.
SHE HAD GOTTEN UNPLEASANTLY VOCAL ABOUT THE RISKS I WAS TAKING. THE GIRL HAD EVEN TAKEN TO SNOOPING AROUND IN MY PERSONAL AFFAIRS.
WELL, YOU KNOW HOW PROTECTIVE WE MAGICIANS ARE OF OUR SECRETS, SO THE KID JUST HAD TO GO.
WHILE IT'S TRUE THE SLIDING PANEL ON HER COFFIN WAS WORKING, I DID RIG THE ILLUSION'S FIRE JETS TO EXPLODE AND SET THE STAGE ON FIRE.
AND JUST TO MAKE SURE SHE DIDN'T TAKE ANY BOWS, I SURPRISED HER AT THE LAST SECOND WITH THAT OIL-SOAKED GAG.

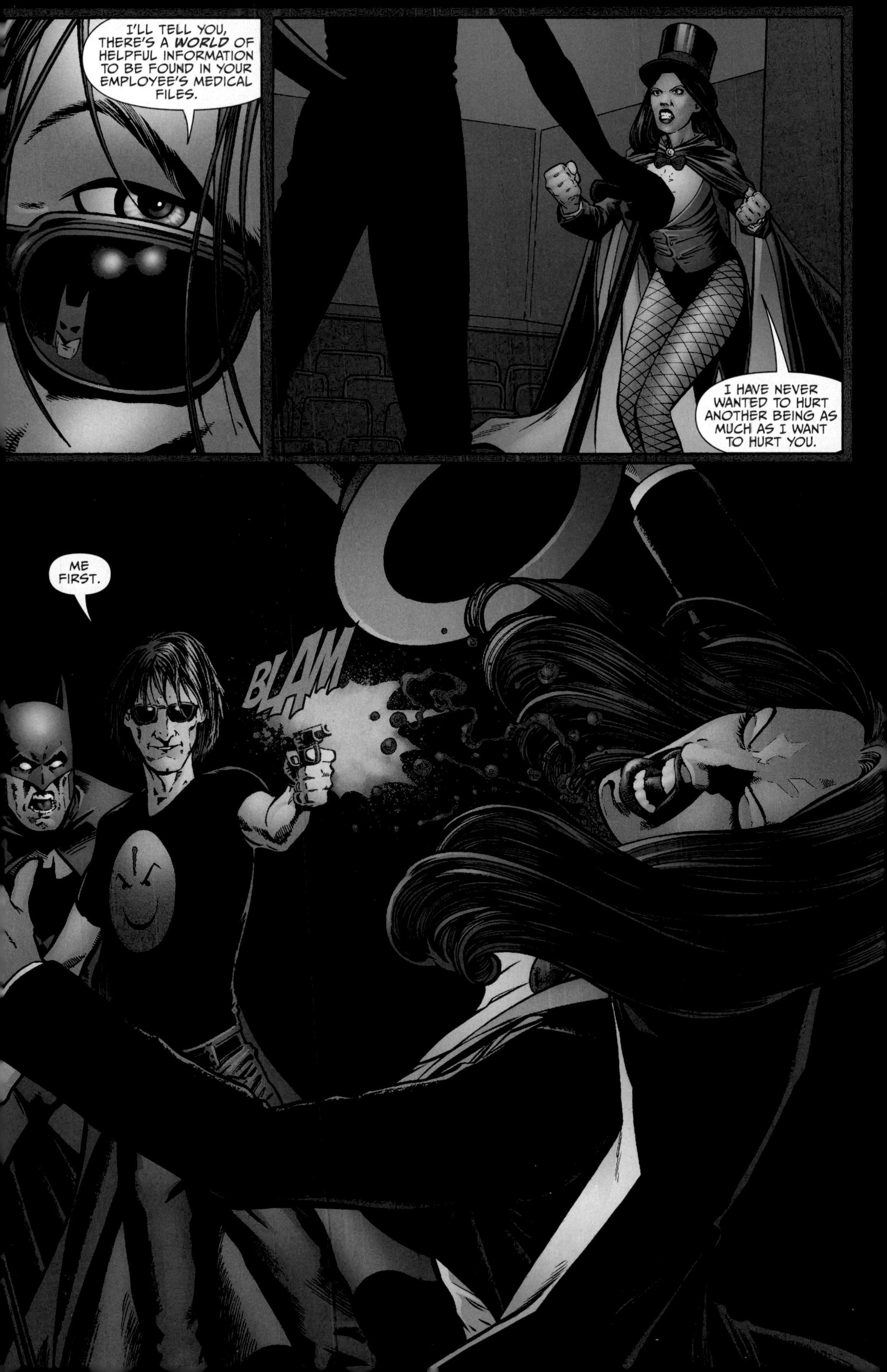
I'LL TELL YOU, THERE'S A WORLD OF HELPFUL INFORMATION TO BE FOUND IN YOUR EMPLOYEE'S MEDICAL FILES.
I HAVE NEVER WANTED TO HURT ANOTHER BEING AS MUCH AS I WANT TO HURT YOU.
ME FIRST.
BLAM

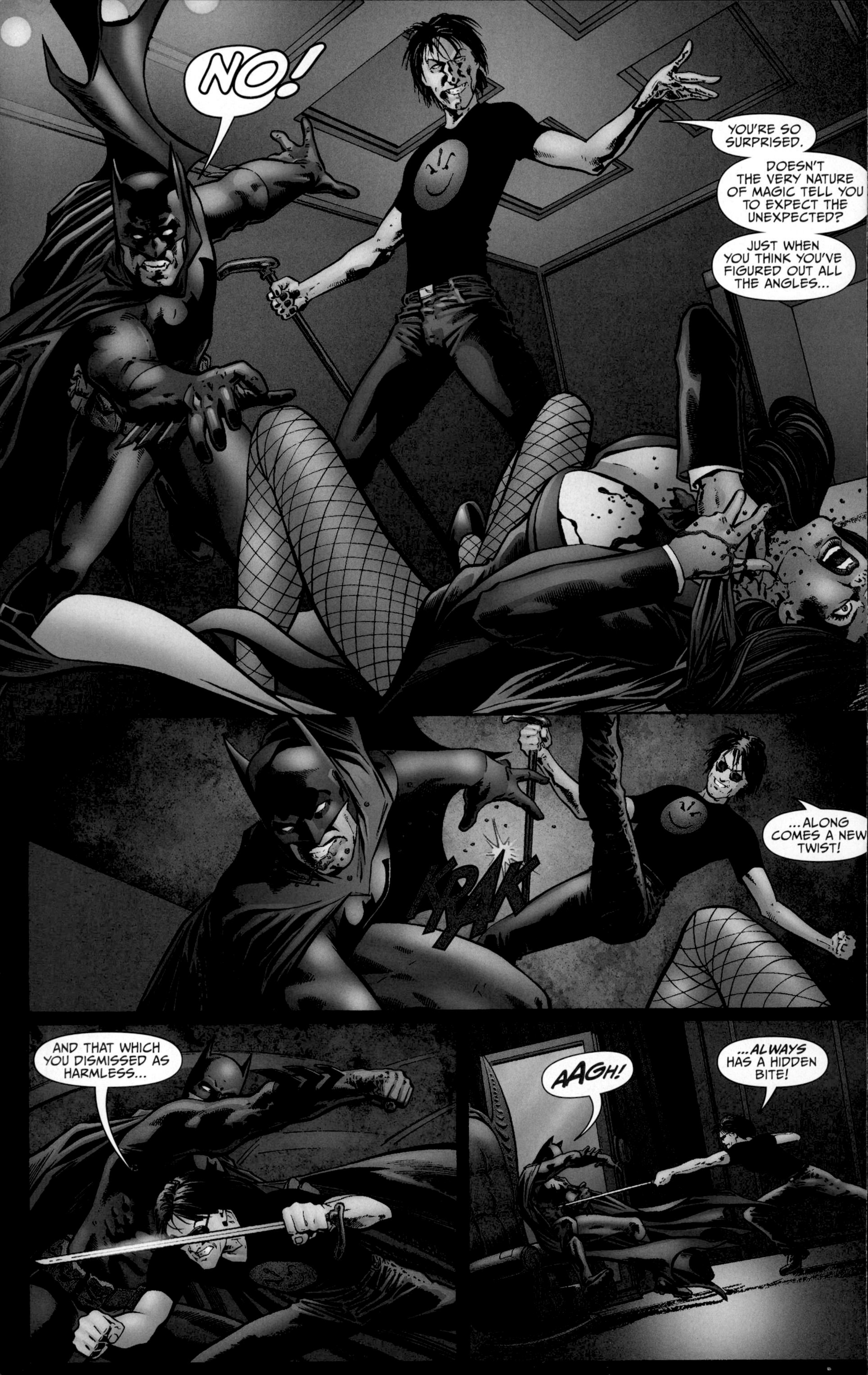
NO!
YOU'RE SO SURPRISED.
DOESN'T THE VERY NATURE OF MAGIC TELL YOU TO EXPECT THE UNEXPECTED?
JUST WHEN YOU THINK YOU'VE FIGURED OUT ALL THE ANGLES...
...ALONG COMES A NEW TWIST!
KRAK
AND THAT WHICH YOU DISMISSED AS HARMLESS...
AAGH!
...ALWAYS HAS A HIDDEN BITE!

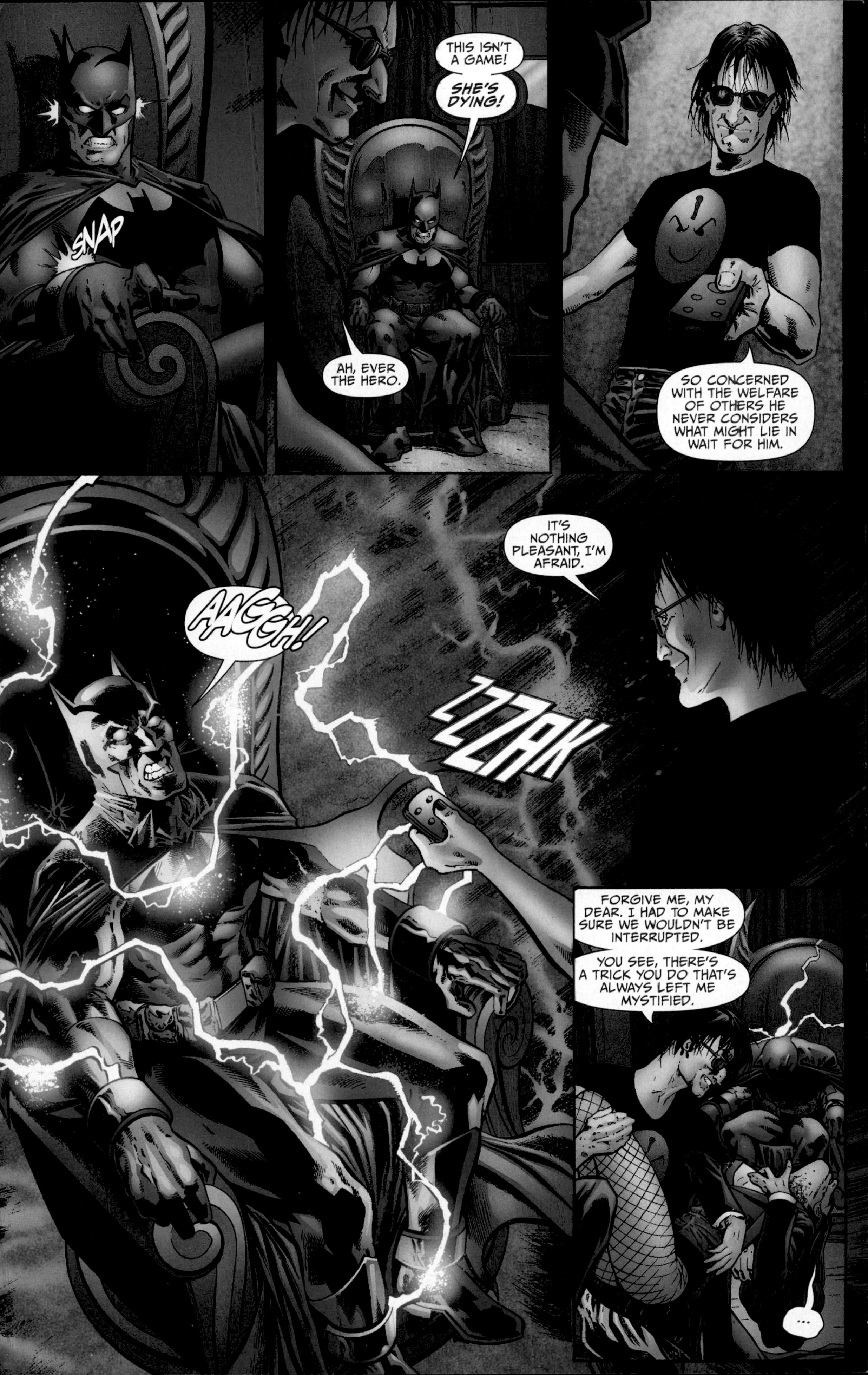
SNAP
THIS ISN'T A GAME!
SHE'S DYING!
AH, EVER THE HERO.
SO CONCERNED WITH THE WELFARE OF OTHERS HE NEVER CONSIDERS WHAT MIGHT LIE IN WAIT FOR HIM.
IT'S NOTHING PLEASANT, I'M AFRAID.
AAGGGH!
ZZZAK
FORGIVE ME, MY DEAR. I HAD TO MAKE SURE WE WOULDN'T BE INTERRUPTED.
YOU SEE, THERE'S A TRICK YOU DO THAT'S ALWAYS LEFT ME MYSTIFIED.
...

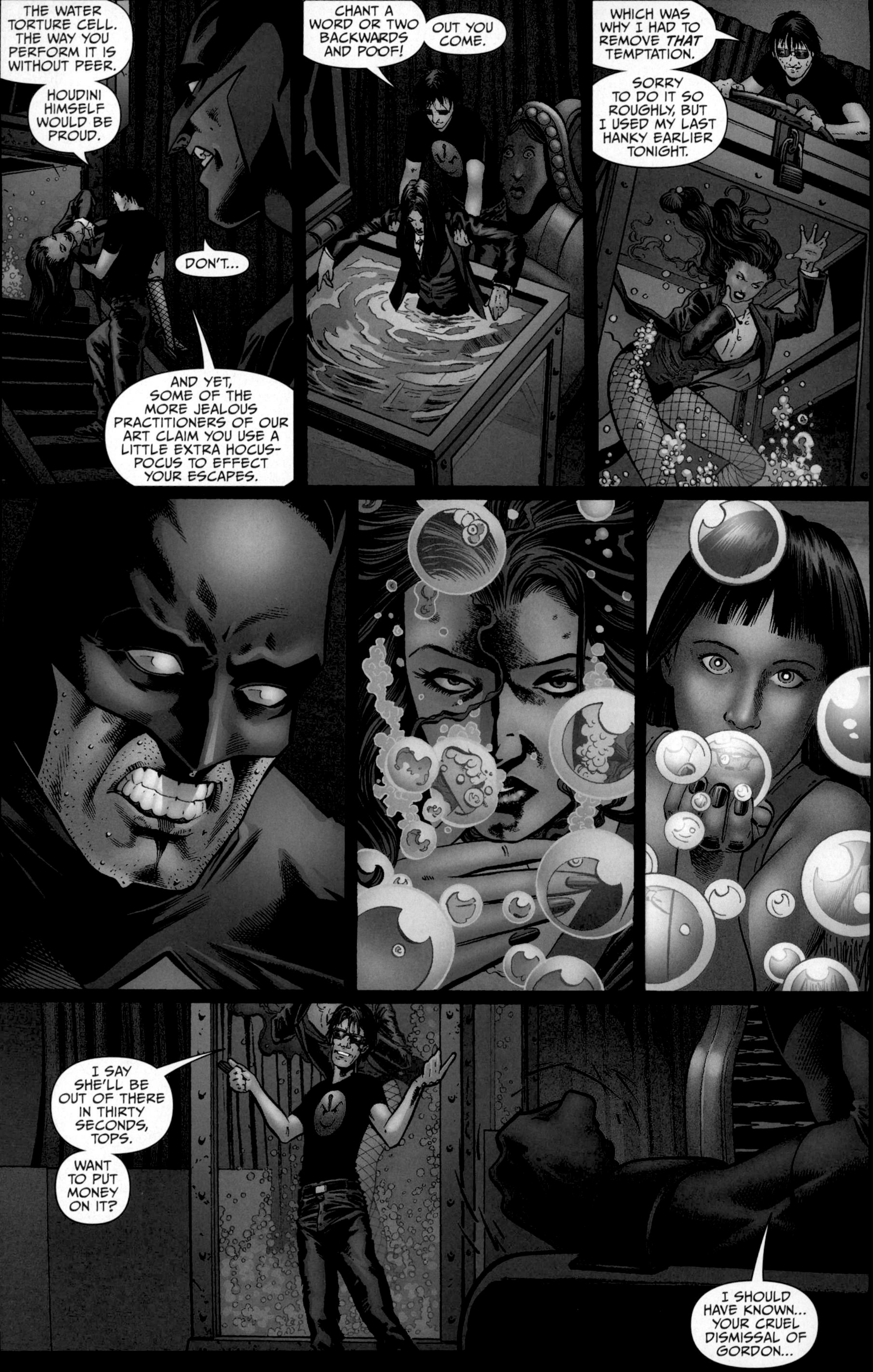

THE WATER TORTURE CELL. THE WAY YOU PERFORM IT IS WITHOUT PEER.
HOUDINI HIMSELF WOULD BE PROUD.
DON'T...
AND YET, SOME OF THE MORE JEALOUS PRACTITIONERS OF OUR ART CLAIM YOU USE A LITTLE EXTRA HOCUS-POCUS TO EFFECT YOUR ESCAPES.
CHANT A WORD OR TWO BACKWARDS AND POOF!
OUT YOU COME.
WHICH WAS WHY I HAD TO REMOVE *THAT* TEMPTATION.
SORRY TO DO IT SO ROUGHLY, BUT I USED MY LAST HANKY EARLIER TONIGHT.
I SAY SHE'LL BE OUT OF THERE IN THIRTY SECONDS, TOPS.
WANT TO PUT MONEY ON IT?
I SHOULD HAVE KNOWN... YOUR CRUEL DISMISSAL OF GORDON...

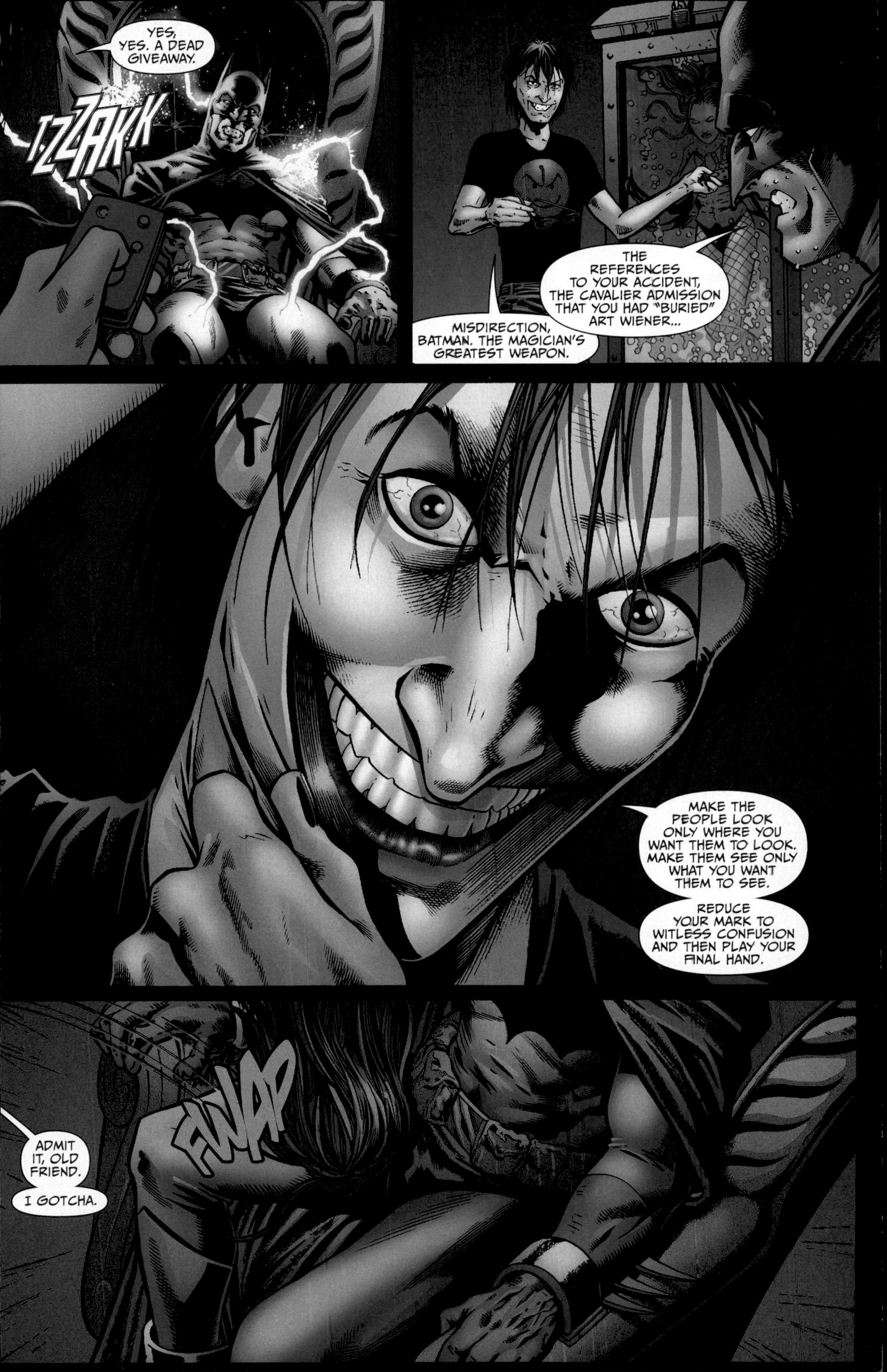
YES, YES. A DEAD GIVEAWAY.
TZZZAKK
THE REFERENCES TO YOUR ACCIDENT, THE CAVALIER ADMISSION THAT YOU HAD "BURIED" ART WIENER...
MISDIRECTION, BATMAN. THE MAGICIAN'S GREATEST WEAPON.
MAKE THE PEOPLE LOOK ONLY WHERE YOU WANT THEM TO LOOK. MAKE THEM SEE ONLY WHAT YOU WANT THEM TO SEE.
REDUCE YOUR MARK TO WITLESS CONFUSION AND THEN PLAY YOUR FINAL HAND.
FWAP
ADMIT IT, OLD FRIEND.
I GOTCHA.

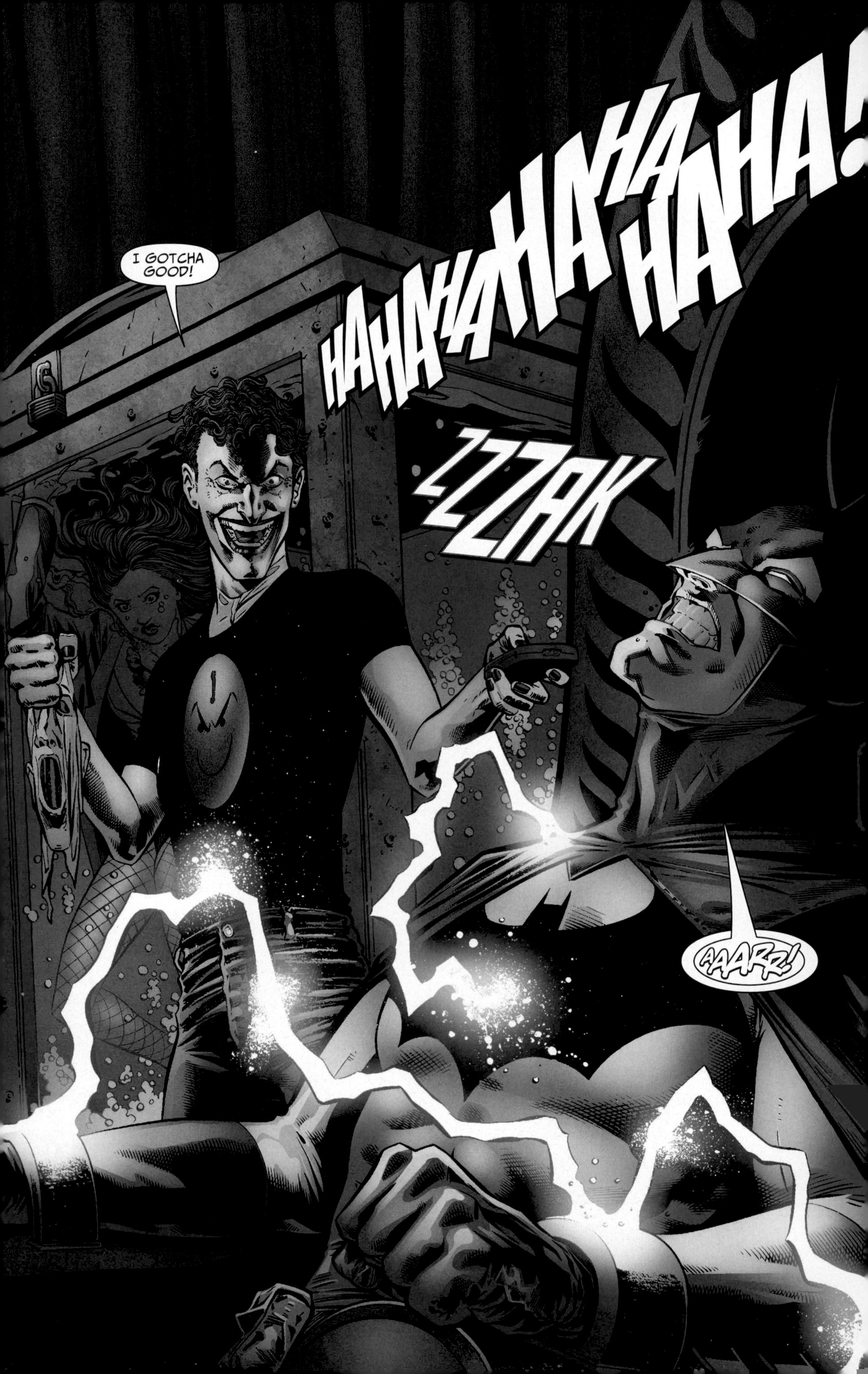
I GOTCHA GOOD!
HAHAHAHAHAHAHAHAHA!
ZZZAK
AAARR!

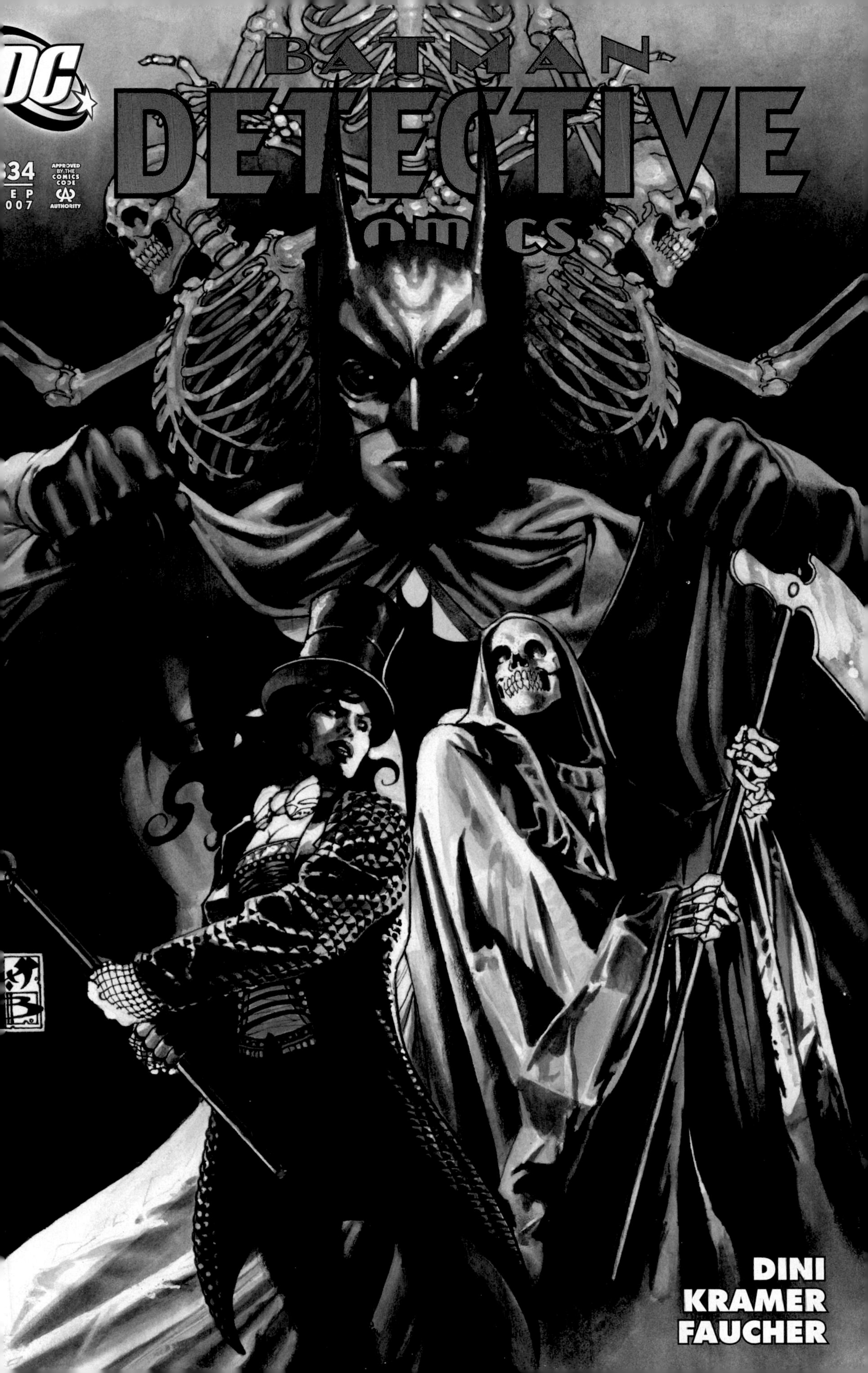

BATMAN
DETECTIVE
COMICS
APPROVED BY THE COMICS CODE AUTHORITY
DINI
KRAMER
FAUCHER

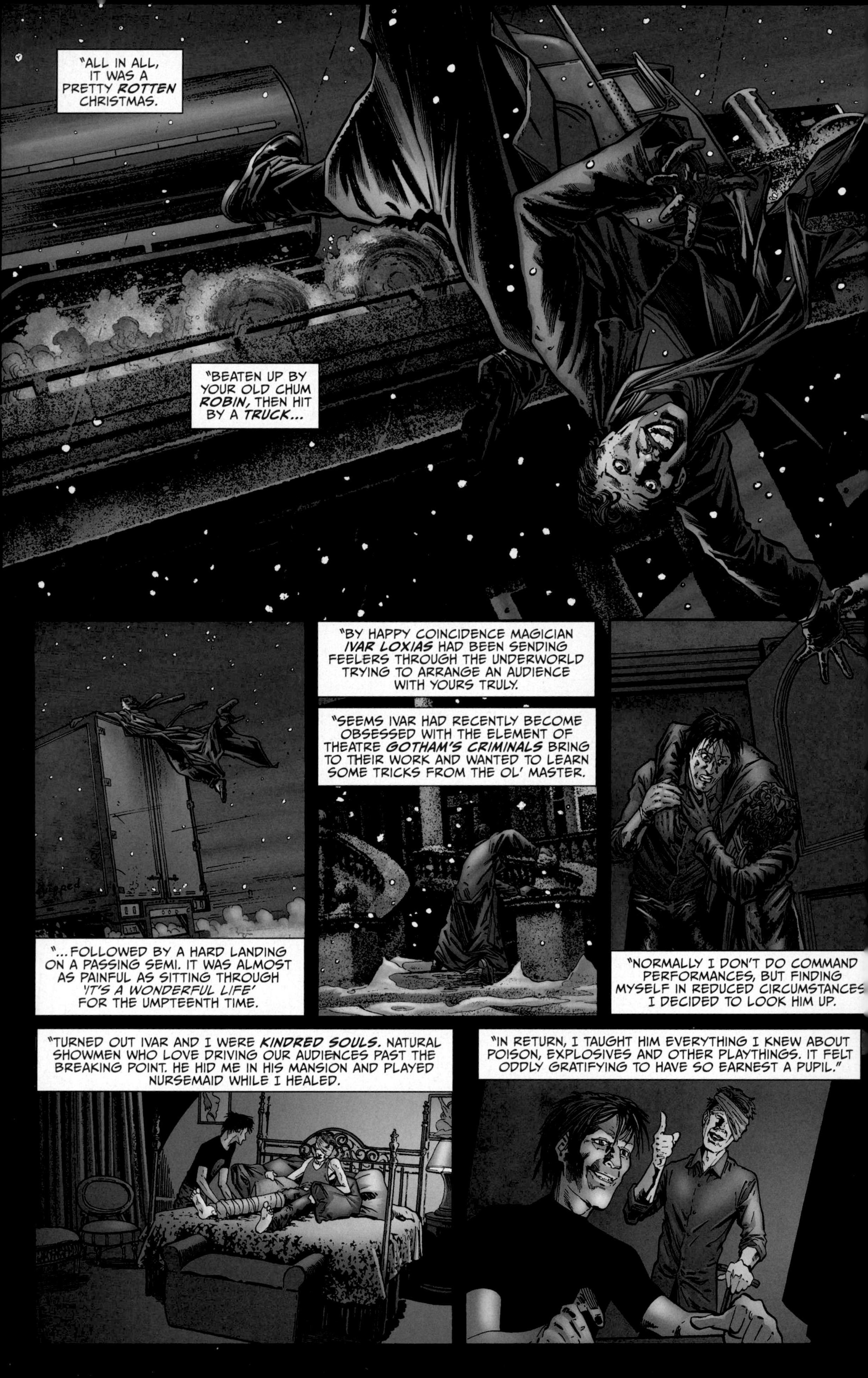
"ALL IN ALL, IT WAS A PRETTY *ROTTEN* CHRISTMAS.
"BEATEN UP BY YOUR OLD CHUM *ROBIN,* THEN HIT BY A *TRUCK...*
"...FOLLOWED BY A HARD LANDING ON A PASSING SEMI. IT WAS ALMOST AS PAINFUL AS SITTING THROUGH *'IT'S A WONDERFUL LIFE'* FOR THE UMPTEENTH TIME.
"BY HAPPY COINCIDENCE MAGICIAN *IVAR LOXIAS* HAD BEEN SENDING FEELERS THROUGH THE UNDERWORLD TRYING TO ARRANGE AN AUDIENCE WITH YOURS TRULY.
"SEEMS IVAR HAD RECENTLY BECOME OBSESSED WITH THE ELEMENT OF THEATRE *GOTHAM'S CRIMINALS* BRING TO THEIR WORK AND WANTED TO LEARN SOME TRICKS FROM THE OL' MASTER.
"NORMALLY I DON'T DO COMMAND PERFORMANCES, BUT FINDING MYSELF IN REDUCED CIRCUMSTANCES I DECIDED TO LOOK HIM UP.
"TURNED OUT IVAR AND I WERE *KINDRED SOULS.* NATURAL SHOWMEN WHO LOVE DRIVING OUR AUDIENCES PAST THE BREAKING POINT. HE HID ME IN HIS MANSION AND PLAYED NURSEMAID WHILE I HEALED.
"IN RETURN, I TAUGHT HIM EVERYTHING I KNEW ABOUT POISON, EXPLOSIVES AND OTHER PLAYTHINGS. IT FELT ODDLY GRATIFYING TO HAVE SO EARNEST A PUPIL."

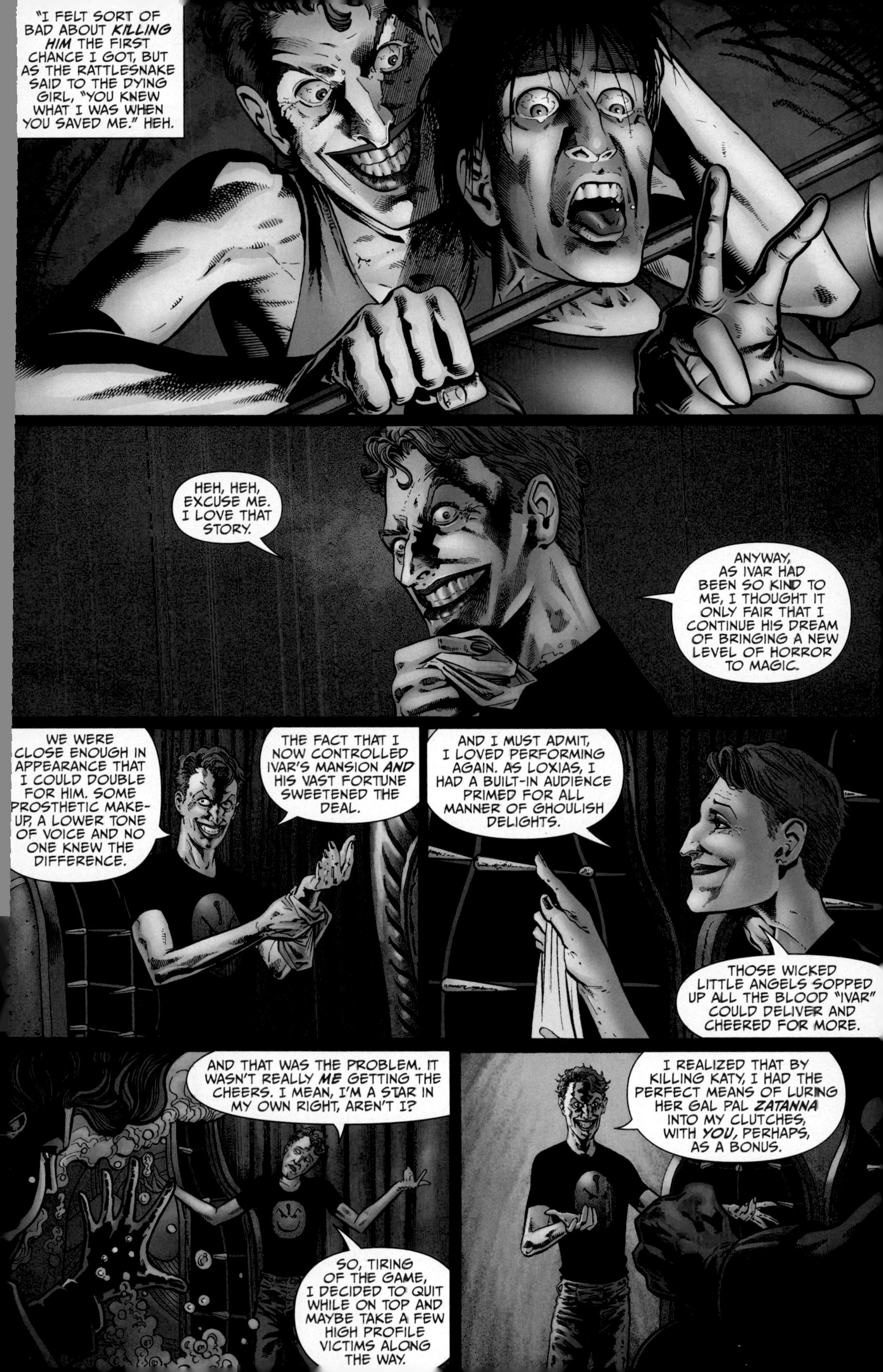
"I FELT SORT OF BAD ABOUT KILLING HIM THE FIRST CHANCE I GOT, BUT AS THE RATTLESNAKE SAID TO THE DYING GIRL, "YOU KNEW WHAT I WAS WHEN YOU SAVED ME." HEH.
HEH, HEH, EXCUSE ME. I LOVE THAT STORY.
ANYWAY, AS IVAR HAD BEEN SO KIND TO ME, I THOUGHT IT ONLY FAIR THAT I CONTINUE HIS DREAM OF BRINGING A NEW LEVEL OF HORROR TO MAGIC.
WE WERE CLOSE ENOUGH IN APPEARANCE THAT I COULD DOUBLE FOR HIM. SOME PROSTHETIC MAKE-UP, A LOWER TONE OF VOICE AND NO ONE KNEW THE DIFFERENCE.
THE FACT THAT I NOW CONTROLLED IVAR'S MANSION AND HIS VAST FORTUNE SWEETENED THE DEAL.
AND I MUST ADMIT, I LOVED PERFORMING AGAIN. AS LOXIAS, I HAD A BUILT-IN AUDIENCE PRIMED FOR ALL MANNER OF GHOULISH DELIGHTS.
THOSE WICKED LITTLE ANGELS SOPPED UP ALL THE BLOOD "IVAR" COULD DELIVER AND CHEERED FOR MORE.
AND THAT WAS THE PROBLEM. IT WASN'T REALLY ME GETTING THE CHEERS. I MEAN, I'M A STAR IN MY OWN RIGHT, AREN'T I?
SO, TIRING OF THE GAME, I DECIDED TO QUIT WHILE ON TOP AND MAYBE TAKE A FEW HIGH PROFILE VICTIMS ALONG THE WAY.
I REALIZED THAT BY KILLING KATY, I HAD THE PERFECT MEANS OF LURING HER GAL PAL ZATANNA INTO MY CLUTCHES, WITH YOU, PERHAPS, AS A BONUS.

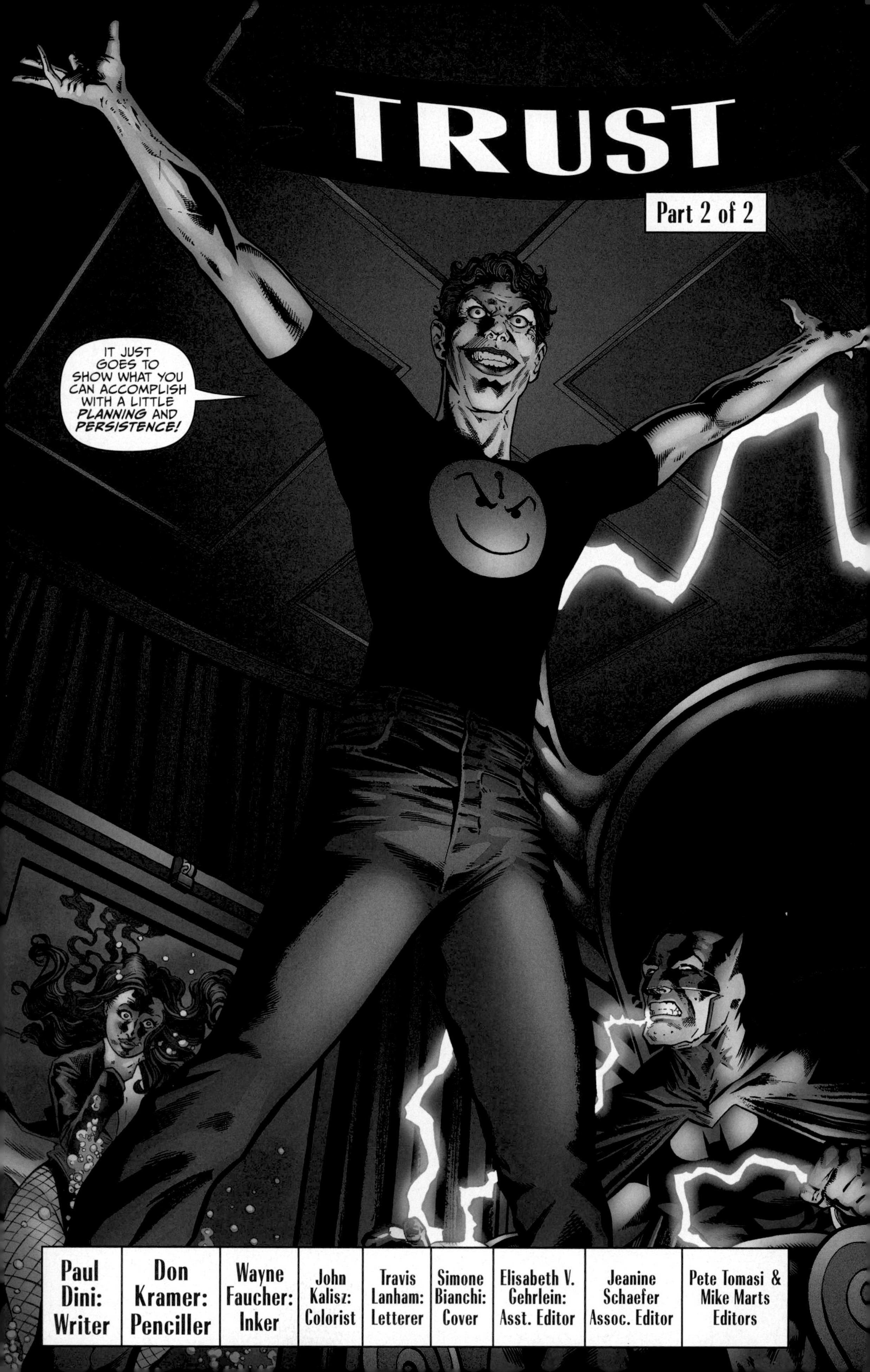
TRUST
Part 2 of 2
IT JUST GOES TO SHOW WHAT YOU CAN ACCOMPLISH WITH A LITTLE PLANNING AND PERSISTENCE!
Paul Dini: Writer
Don Kramer: Penciller
Wayne Faucher: Inker
John Kalisz: Colorist
Travis Lanham: Letterer
Simone Bianchi: Cover
Elisabeth V. Gehrlein: Asst. Editor
Jeanine Schaefer Assoc. Editor
Pete Tomasi & Mike Marts Editors

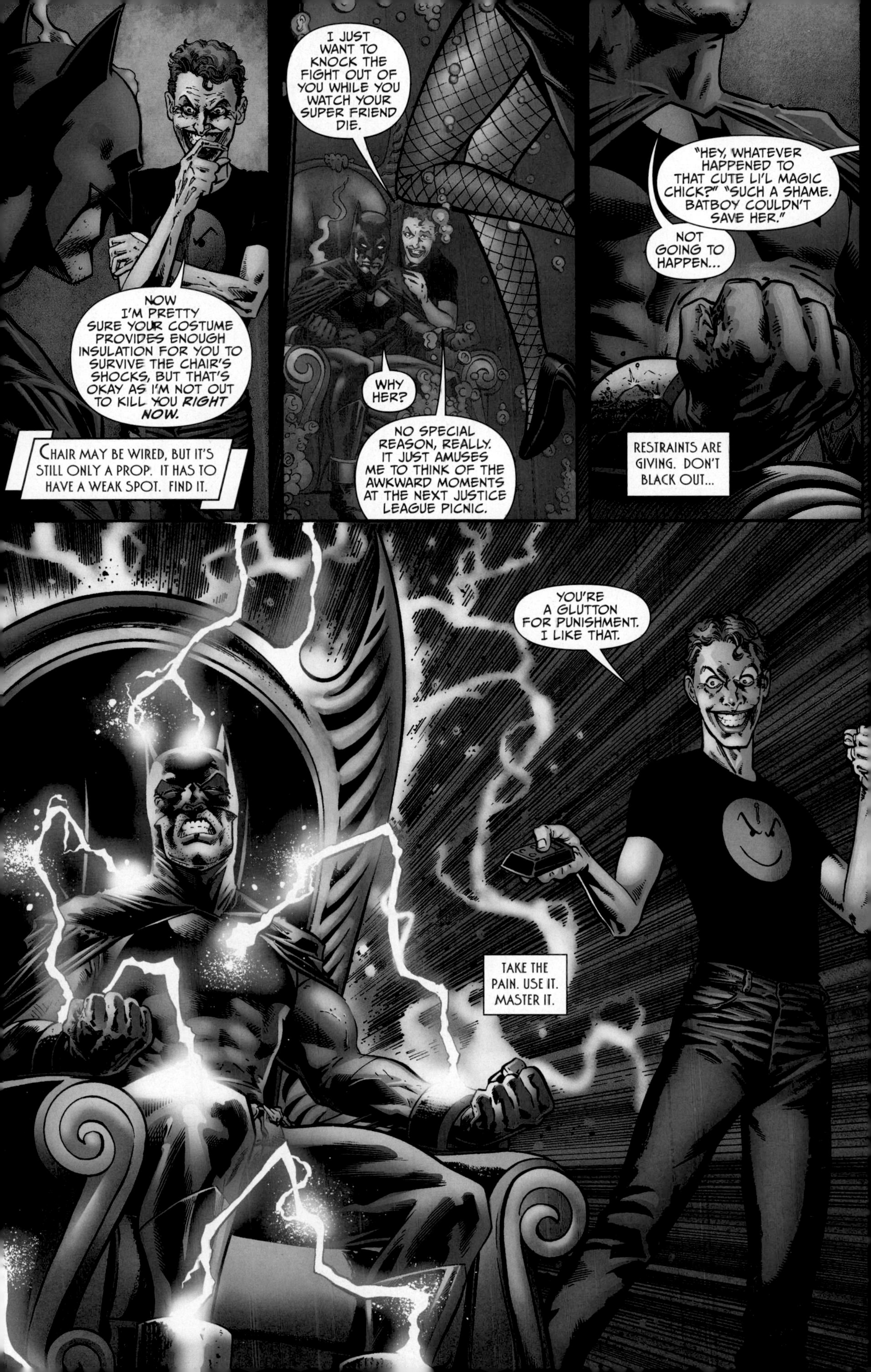
NOW I'M PRETTY SURE YOUR COSTUME PROVIDES ENOUGH INSULATION FOR YOU TO SURVIVE THE CHAIR'S SHOCKS, BUT THAT'S OKAY AS I'M NOT OUT TO KILL YOU *RIGHT NOW.*
CHAIR MAY BE WIRED, BUT IT'S STILL ONLY A PROP. IT HAS TO HAVE A WEAK SPOT. FIND IT.
I JUST WANT TO KNOCK THE FIGHT OUT OF YOU WHILE YOU WATCH YOUR SUPER FRIEND DIE.
WHY HER?
NO SPECIAL REASON, REALLY. IT JUST AMUSES ME TO THINK OF THE AWKWARD MOMENTS AT THE NEXT JUSTICE LEAGUE PICNIC.
"HEY, WHATEVER HAPPENED TO THAT CUTE LI'L MAGIC CHICK?" "SUCH A SHAME. BATBOY COULDN'T SAVE HER."
NOT GOING TO HAPPEN...
RESTRAINTS ARE GIVING. DON'T BLACK OUT...
YOU'RE A GLUTTON FOR PUNISHMENT. I LIKE THAT.
TAKE THE PAIN. USE IT. MASTER IT.

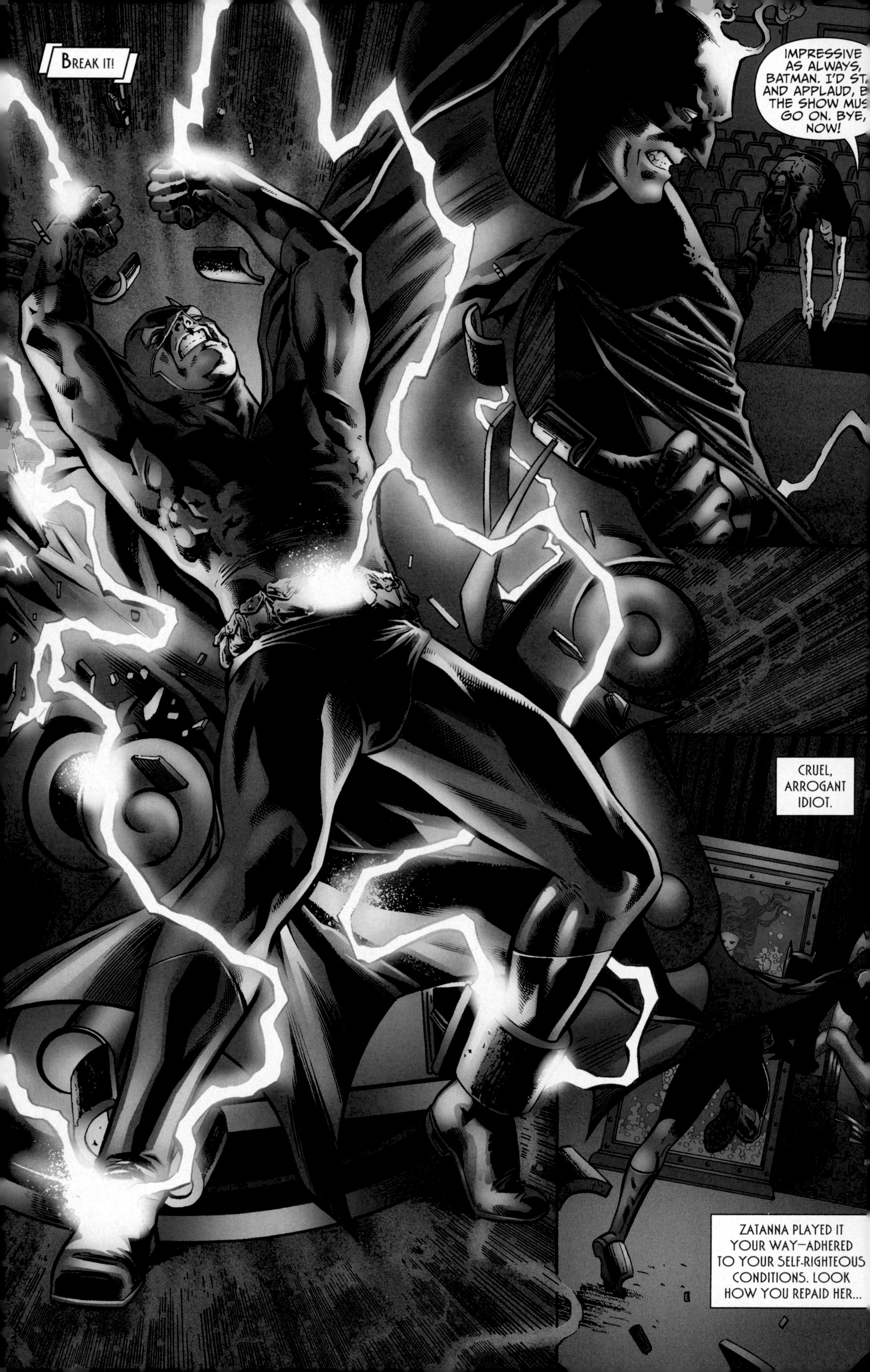
BREAK IT!
IMPRESSIVE AS ALWAYS, BATMAN. I'D ST AND APPLAUD, B THE SHOW MUS GO ON. BYE, NOW!
CRUEL, ARROGANT IDIOT.
ZATANNA PLAYED IT YOUR WAY—ADHERED TO YOUR SELF-RIGHTEOUS CONDITIONS. LOOK HOW YOU REPAID HER...

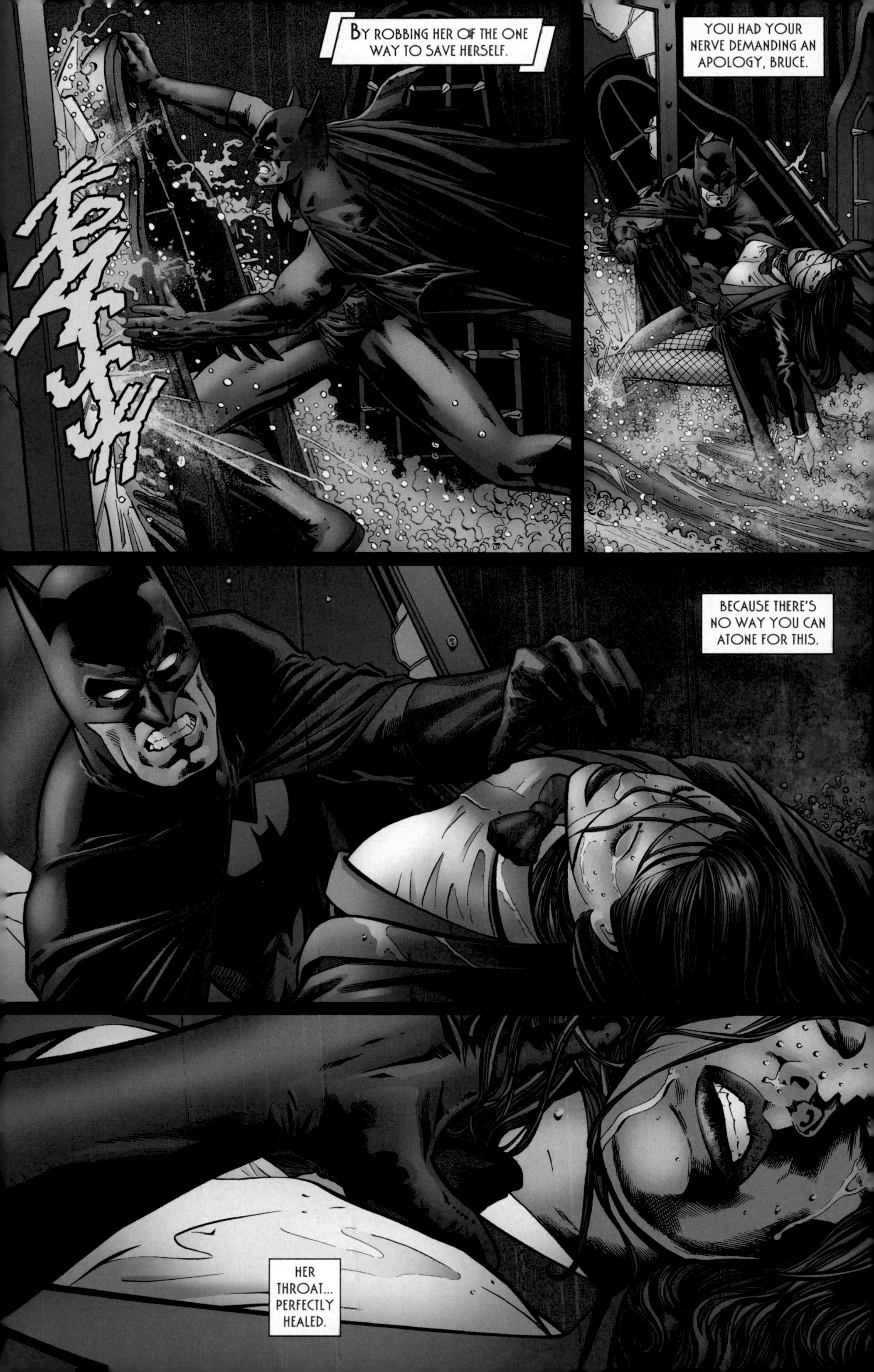
BY ROBBING HER OF THE ONE WAY TO SAVE HERSELF.
YOU HAD YOUR NERVE DEMANDING AN APOLOGY, BRUCE.
BECAUSE THERE'S NO WAY YOU CAN ATONE FOR THIS.
HER THROAT... PERFECTLY HEALED.

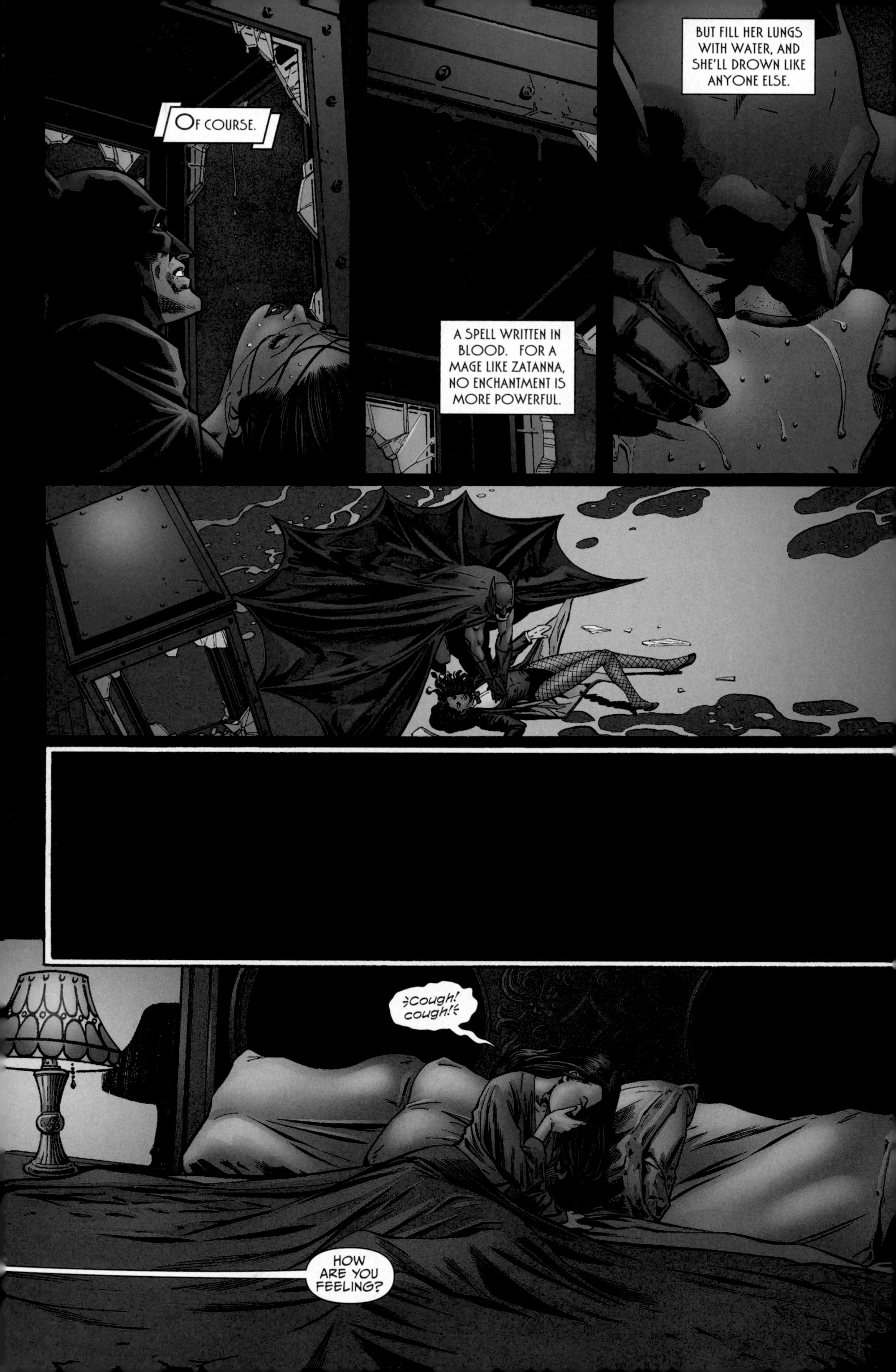

OF COURSE.
A SPELL WRITTEN IN BLOOD. FOR A MAGE LIKE ZATANNA, NO ENCHANTMENT IS MORE POWERFUL.
BUT FILL HER LUNGS WITH WATER, AND SHE'LL DROWN LIKE ANYONE ELSE.
COUGH! COUGH!
HOW ARE YOU FEELING?

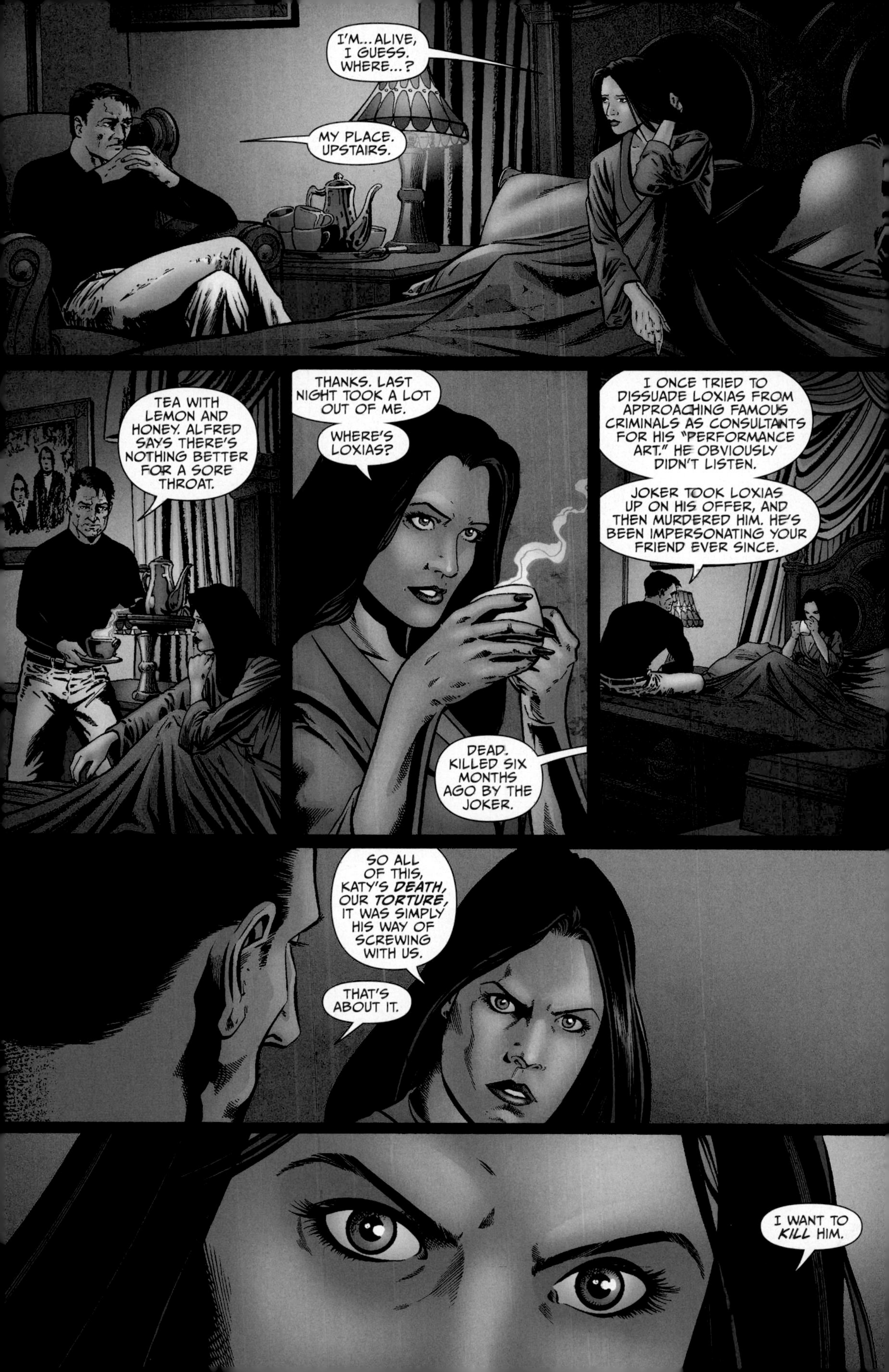
I'M... ALIVE, I GUESS. WHERE...?
MY PLACE. UPSTAIRS.
TEA WITH LEMON AND HONEY. ALFRED SAYS THERE'S NOTHING BETTER FOR A SORE THROAT.
THANKS. LAST NIGHT TOOK A LOT OUT OF ME.
WHERE'S LOXIAS?
DEAD. KILLED SIX MONTHS AGO BY THE JOKER.
I ONCE TRIED TO DISSUADE LOXIAS FROM APPROACHING FAMOUS CRIMINALS AS CONSULTANTS FOR HIS "PERFORMANCE ART." HE OBVIOUSLY DIDN'T LISTEN.
JOKER TOOK LOXIAS UP ON HIS OFFER, AND THEN MURDERED HIM. HE'S BEEN IMPERSONATING YOUR FRIEND EVER SINCE.
SO ALL OF THIS, KATY'S ***DEATH,*** OUR ***TORTURE,*** IT WAS SIMPLY HIS WAY OF SCREWING WITH US.
THAT'S ABOUT IT.
I WANT TO ***KILL*** HIM.

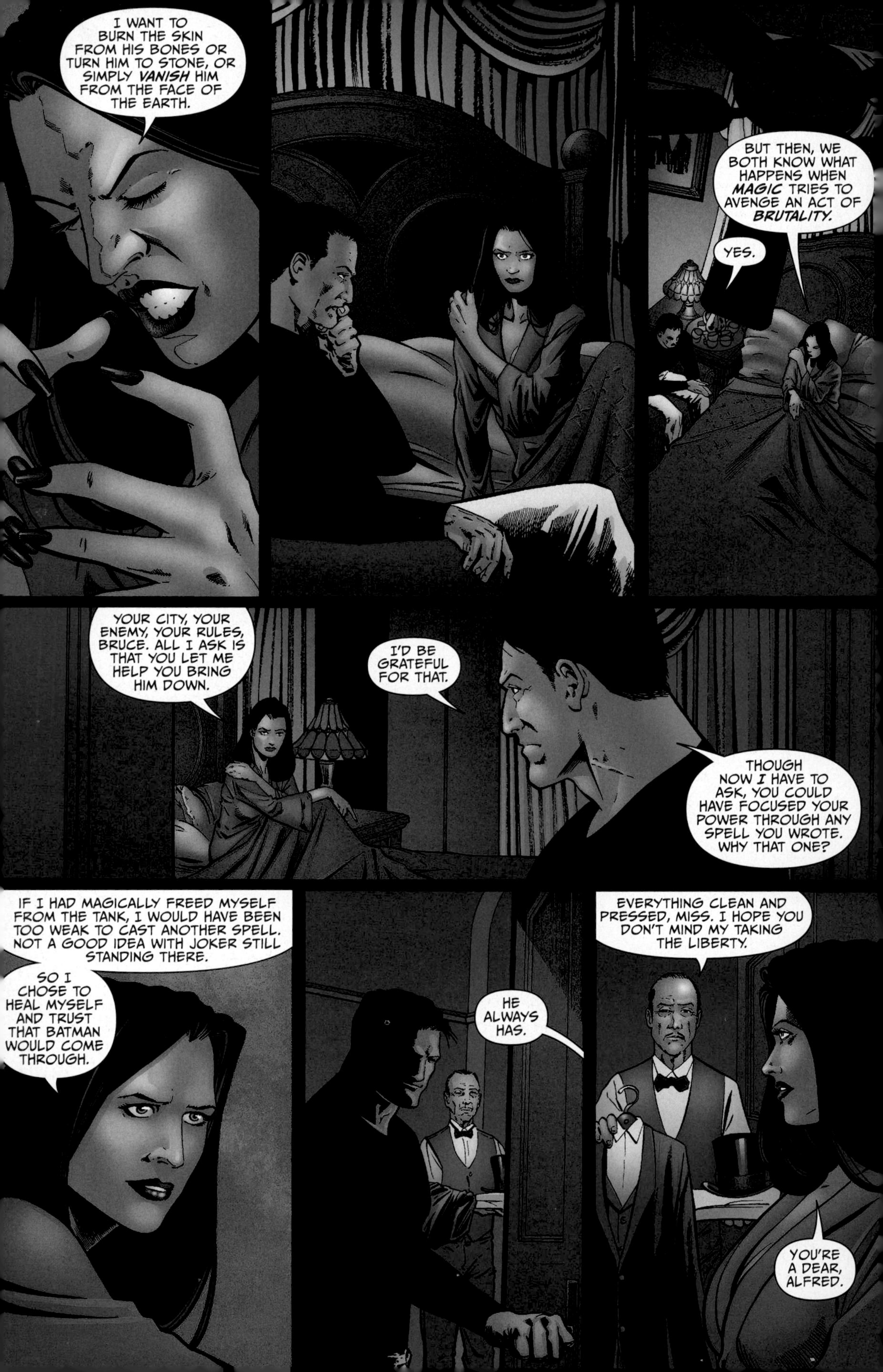
I WANT TO BURN THE SKIN FROM HIS BONES OR TURN HIM TO STONE, OR SIMPLY VANISH HIM FROM THE FACE OF THE EARTH.
BUT THEN, WE BOTH KNOW WHAT HAPPENS WHEN MAGIC TRIES TO AVENGE AN ACT OF BRUTALITY.
YES.
YOUR CITY, YOUR ENEMY, YOUR RULES, BRUCE. ALL I ASK IS THAT YOU LET ME HELP YOU BRING HIM DOWN.
I'D BE GRATEFUL FOR THAT.
THOUGH NOW I HAVE TO ASK, YOU COULD HAVE FOCUSED YOUR POWER THROUGH ANY SPELL YOU WROTE. WHY THAT ONE?
IF I HAD MAGICALLY FREED MYSELF FROM THE TANK, I WOULD HAVE BEEN TOO WEAK TO CAST ANOTHER SPELL. NOT A GOOD IDEA WITH JOKER STILL STANDING THERE.
SO I CHOSE TO HEAL MYSELF AND TRUST THAT BATMAN WOULD COME THROUGH.
HE ALWAYS HAS.
EVERYTHING CLEAN AND PRESSED, MISS. I HOPE YOU DON'T MIND MY TAKING THE LIBERTY.
YOU'RE A DEAR, ALFRED.

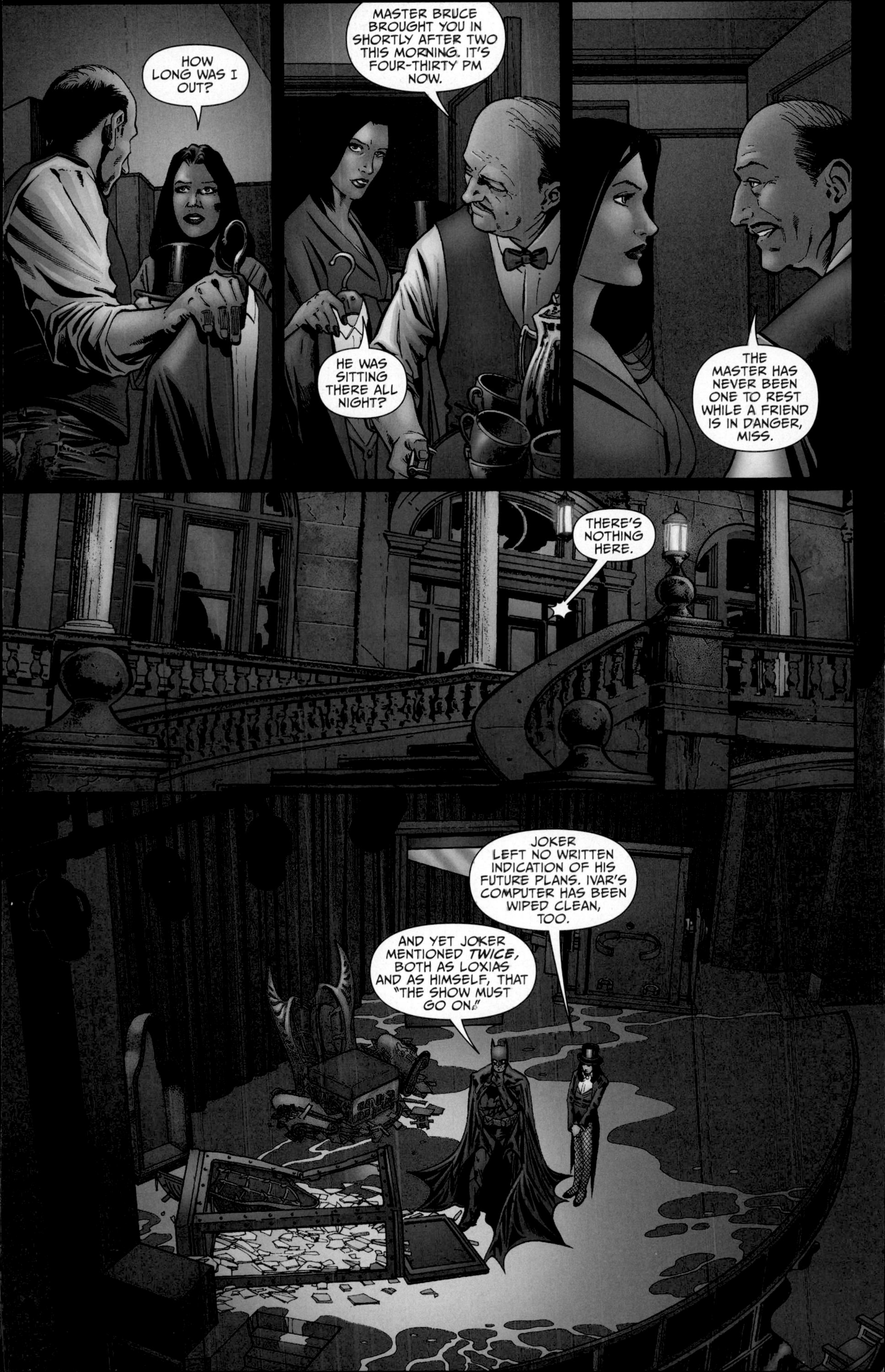
HOW LONG WAS I OUT?
MASTER BRUCE BROUGHT YOU IN SHORTLY AFTER TWO THIS MORNING. IT'S FOUR-THIRTY PM NOW.
HE WAS SITTING THERE ALL NIGHT?
THE MASTER HAS NEVER BEEN ONE TO REST WHILE A FRIEND IS IN DANGER, MISS.
THERE'S NOTHING HERE.
JOKER LEFT NO WRITTEN INDICATION OF HIS FUTURE PLANS. IVAR'S COMPUTER HAS BEEN WIPED CLEAN, TOO.
AND YET JOKER MENTIONED TWICE, BOTH AS LOXIAS AND AS HIMSELF, THAT "THE SHOW MUST GO ON."

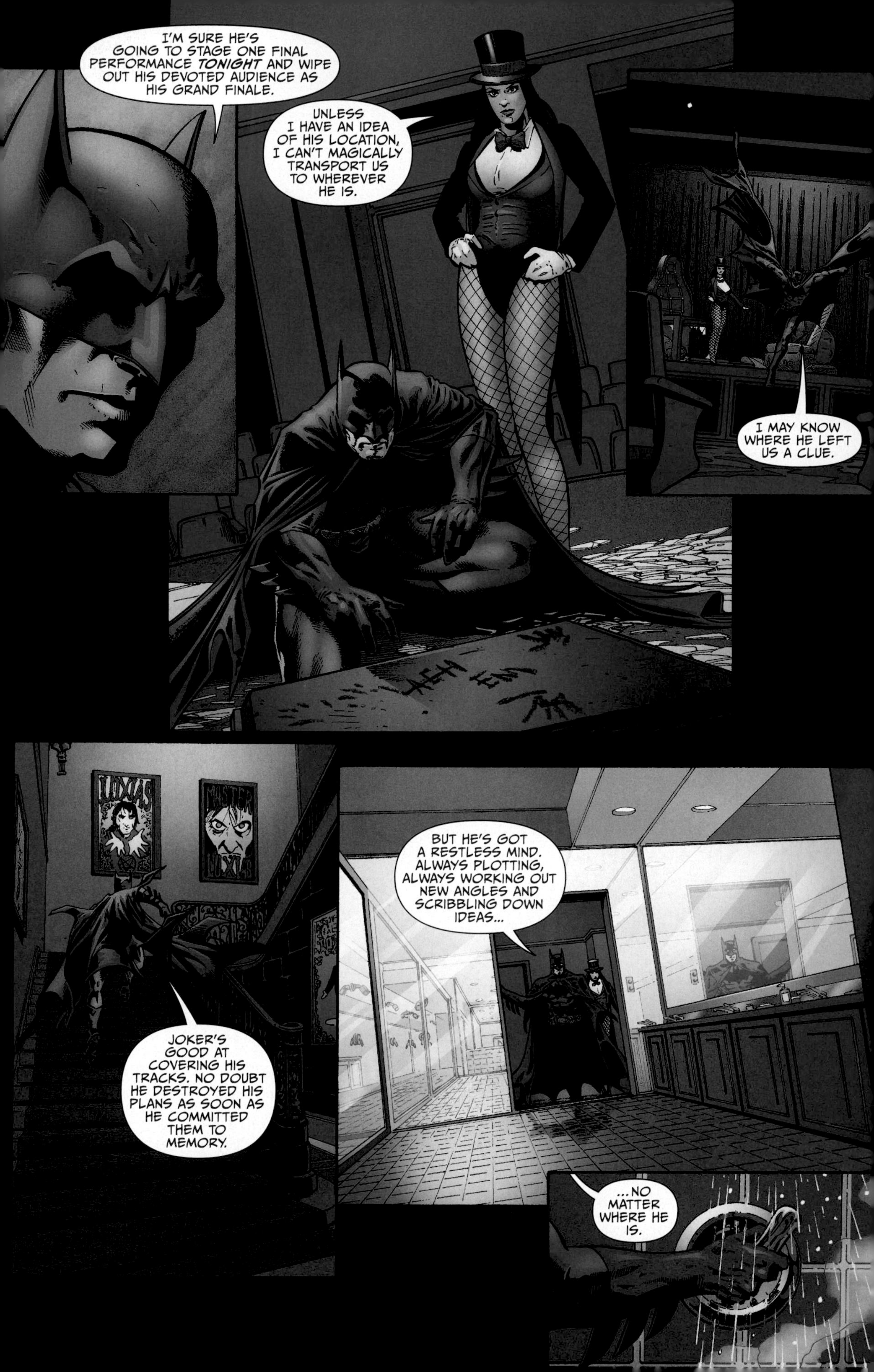
I'M SURE HE'S GOING TO STAGE ONE FINAL PERFORMANCE *TONIGHT* AND WIPE OUT HIS DEVOTED AUDIENCE AS HIS GRAND FINALE.
UNLESS I HAVE AN IDEA OF HIS LOCATION, I CAN'T MAGICALLY TRANSPORT US TO WHEREVER HE IS.
I MAY KNOW WHERE HE LEFT US A CLUE.
JOKER'S GOOD AT COVERING HIS TRACKS. NO DOUBT HE DESTROYED HIS PLANS AS SOON AS HE COMMITTED THEM TO MEMORY.
BUT HE'S GOT A RESTLESS MIND. ALWAYS PLOTTING, ALWAYS WORKING OUT NEW ANGLES AND SCRIBBLING DOWN IDEAS...
...NO MATTER WHERE HE IS.

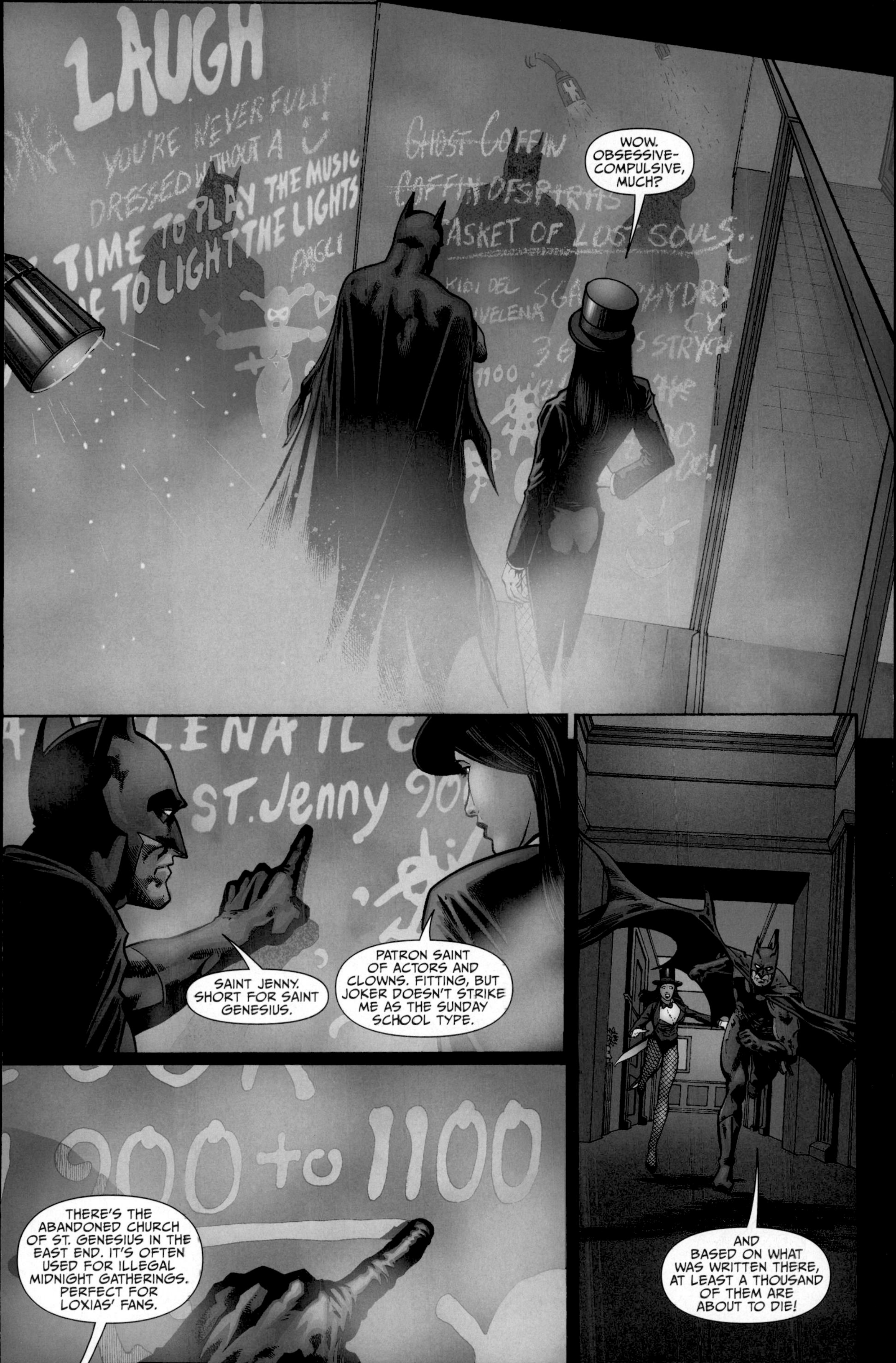

LAUGH
YOU'RE NEVER FULLY DRESSED WITHOUT A
TIME TO PLAY THE MUSIC
TO LIGHT THE LIGHTS
Ghost Coffin
CASKET OF LOST SOULS
WOW. OBSESSIVE-COMPULSIVE, MUCH?
ST. Jenny
SAINT JENNY. SHORT FOR SAINT GENESIUS.
PATRON SAINT OF ACTORS AND CLOWNS. FITTING, BUT JOKER DOESN'T STRIKE ME AS THE SUNDAY SCHOOL TYPE.
900 to 1100
THERE'S THE ABANDONED CHURCH OF ST. GENESIUS IN THE EAST END. IT'S OFTEN USED FOR ILLEGAL MIDNIGHT GATHERINGS. PERFECT FOR LOXIAS' FANS.
AND BASED ON WHAT WAS WRITTEN THERE, AT LEAST A THOUSAND OF THEM ARE ABOUT TO DIE!

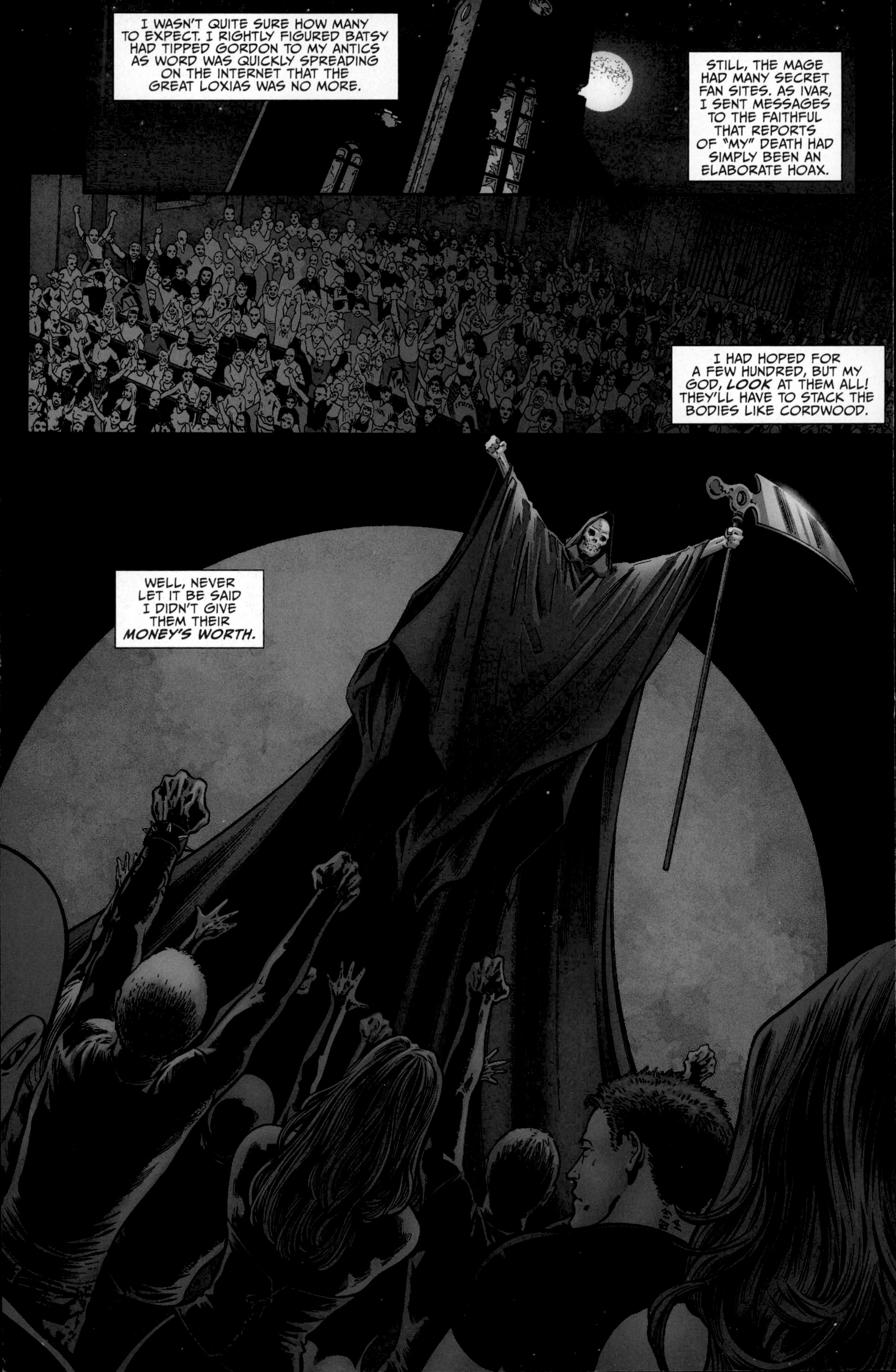
I WASN'T QUITE SURE HOW MANY TO EXPECT. I RIGHTLY FIGURED BATSY HAD TIPPED GORDON TO MY ANTICS AS WORD WAS QUICKLY SPREADING ON THE INTERNET THAT THE GREAT LOXIAS WAS NO MORE.
STILL, THE MAGE HAD MANY SECRET FAN SITES. AS IVAR, I SENT MESSAGES TO THE FAITHFUL THAT REPORTS OF "MY" DEATH HAD SIMPLY BEEN AN ELABORATE HOAX.
I HAD HOPED FOR A FEW HUNDRED, BUT MY GOD, *LOOK* AT THEM ALL! THEY'LL HAVE TO STACK THE BODIES LIKE CORDWOOD.
WELL, NEVER LET IT BE SAID I DIDN'T GIVE THEM THEIR *MONEY'S WORTH.*

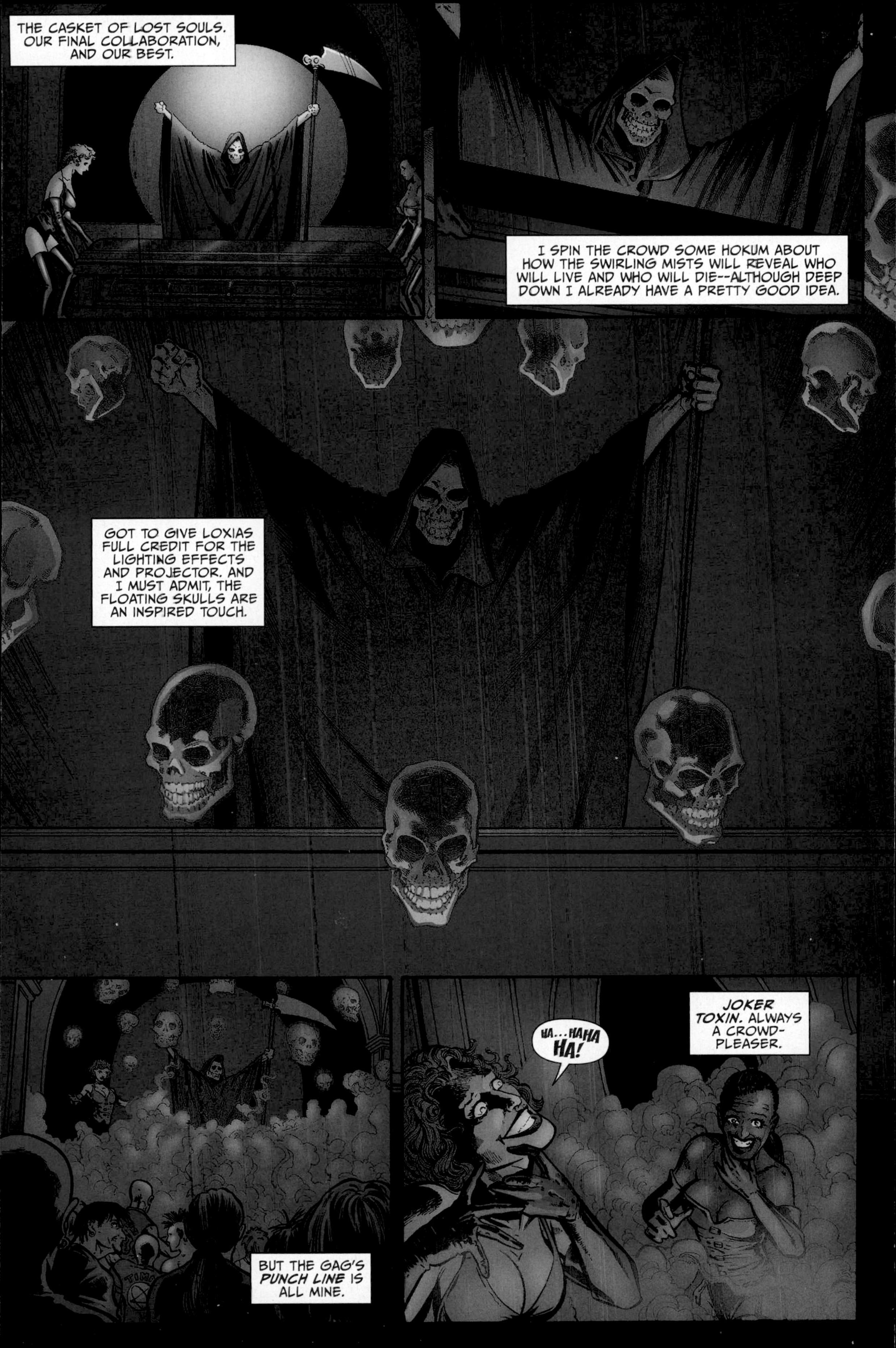
THE CASKET OF LOST SOULS. OUR FINAL COLLABORATION, AND OUR BEST.
I SPIN THE CROWD SOME HOKUM ABOUT HOW THE SWIRLING MISTS WILL REVEAL WHO WILL LIVE AND WHO WILL DIE--ALTHOUGH DEEP DOWN I ALREADY HAVE A PRETTY GOOD IDEA.
GOT TO GIVE LOXIAS FULL CREDIT FOR THE LIGHTING EFFECTS AND PROJECTOR. AND I MUST ADMIT, THE FLOATING SKULLS ARE AN INSPIRED TOUCH.
BUT THE GAG'S *PUNCH LINE* IS ALL MINE.
HA...HAHA HA!
JOKER TOXIN. ALWAYS A CROWD-PLEASER.

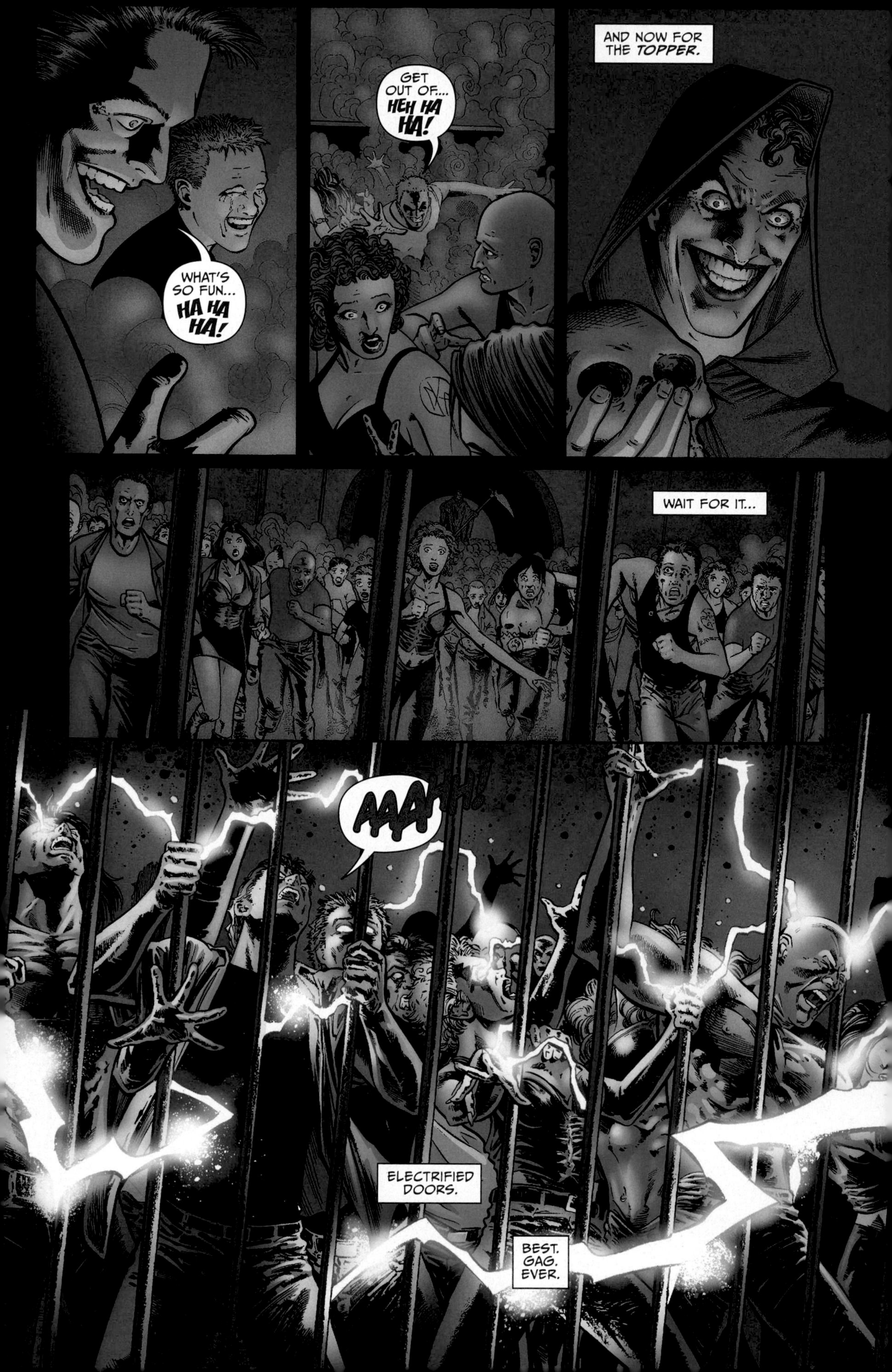
WHAT'S SO FUN... HA HA HA!
GET OUT OF... HEH HA HA!
AND NOW FOR THE TOPPER.
WAIT FOR IT...
AAAHHH!
ELECTRIFIED DOORS.
BEST. GAG. EVER.

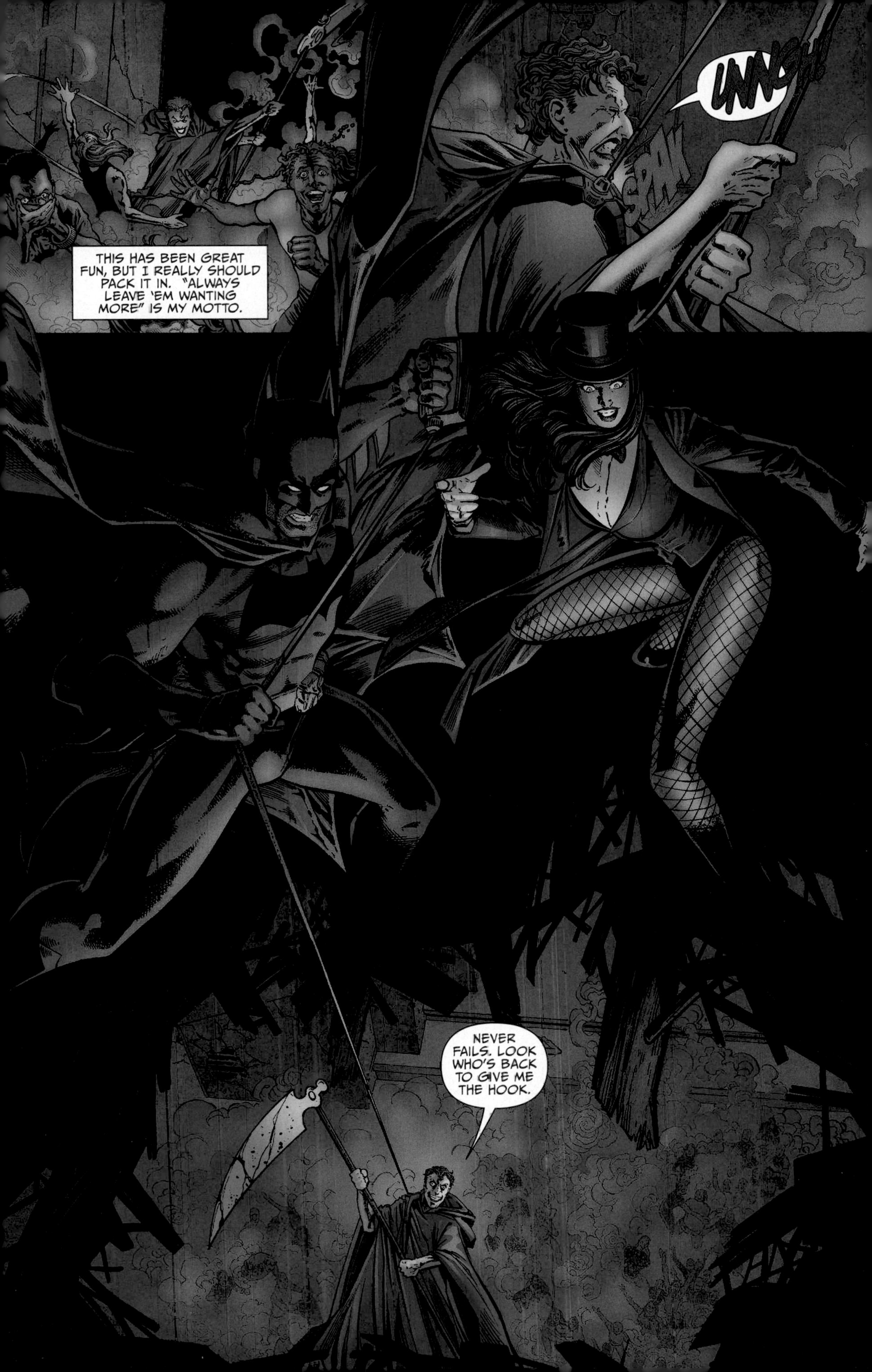
UNNGH!
SPAK
THIS HAS BEEN GREAT FUN, BUT I REALLY SHOULD PACK IT IN. "ALWAYS LEAVE 'EM WANTING MORE" IS MY MOTTO.
NEVER FAILS. LOOK WHO'S BACK TO GIVE ME THE HOOK.

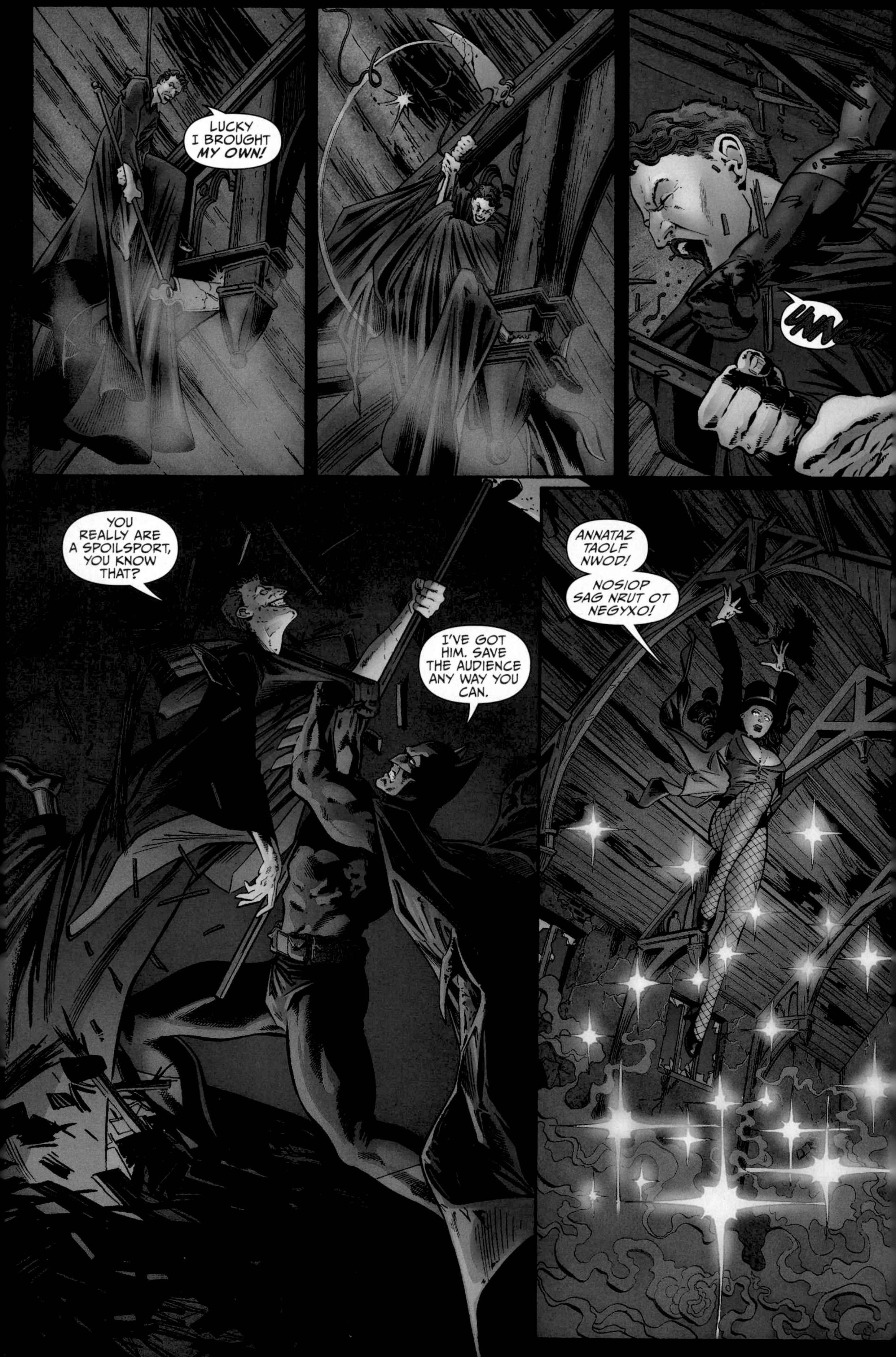
LUCKY I BROUGHT MY OWN!
UNNGH!
YOU REALLY ARE A SPOILSPORT, YOU KNOW THAT?
I'VE GOT HIM. SAVE THE AUDIENCE ANY WAY YOU CAN.
ANNATAZ TAOLF NWOD!
NOSIOP SAG NRUT OT NEGYXO!

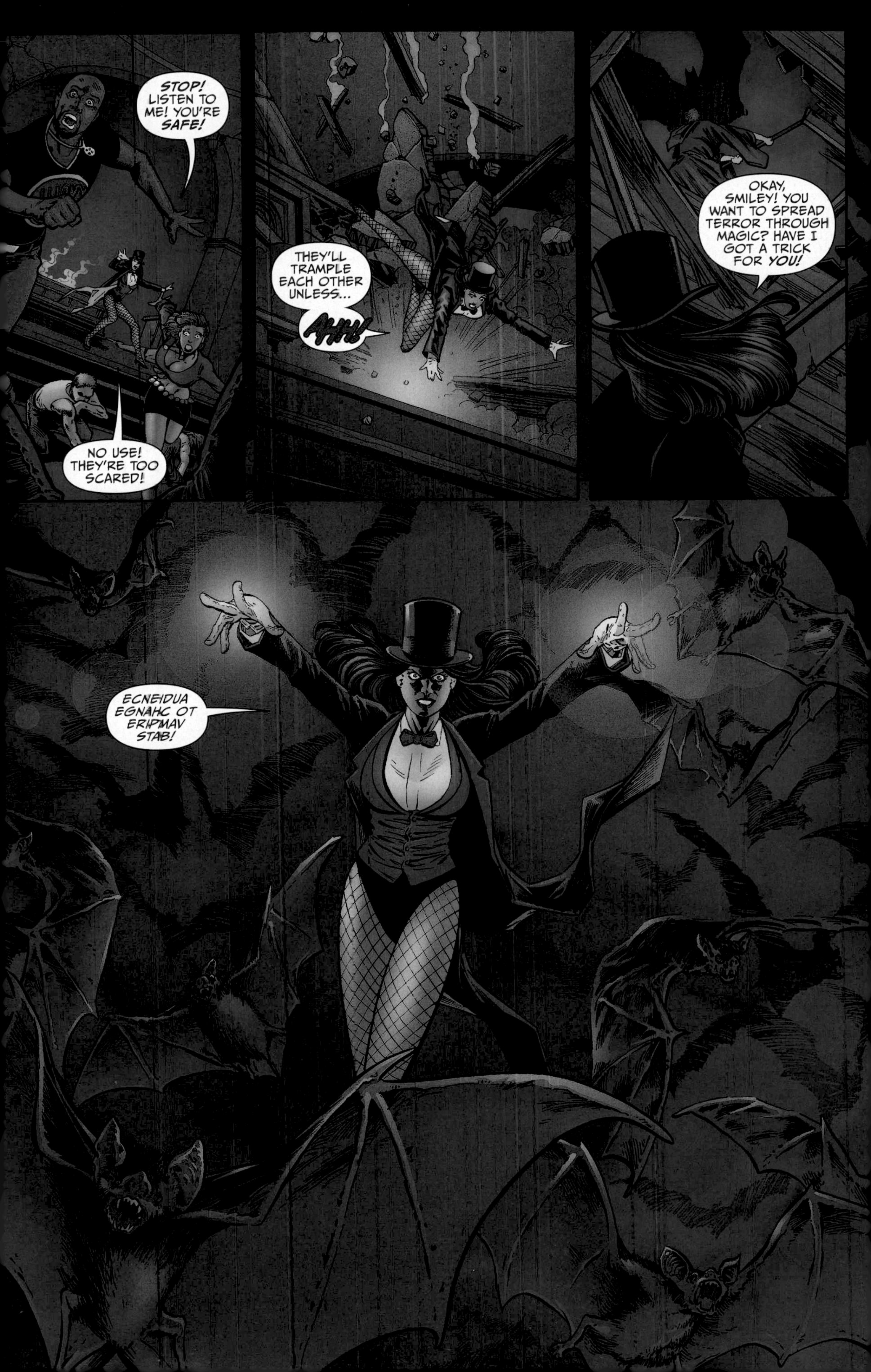

STOP! LISTEN TO ME! YOU'RE SAFE!
NO USE! THEY'RE TOO SCARED!
THEY'LL TRAMPLE EACH OTHER UNLESS...
AHH!
OKAY, SMILEY! YOU WANT TO SPREAD TERROR THROUGH MAGIC? HAVE I GOT A TRICK FOR YOU!
ECNEIDUA EGNAHC OT ERIPMAV STAB!

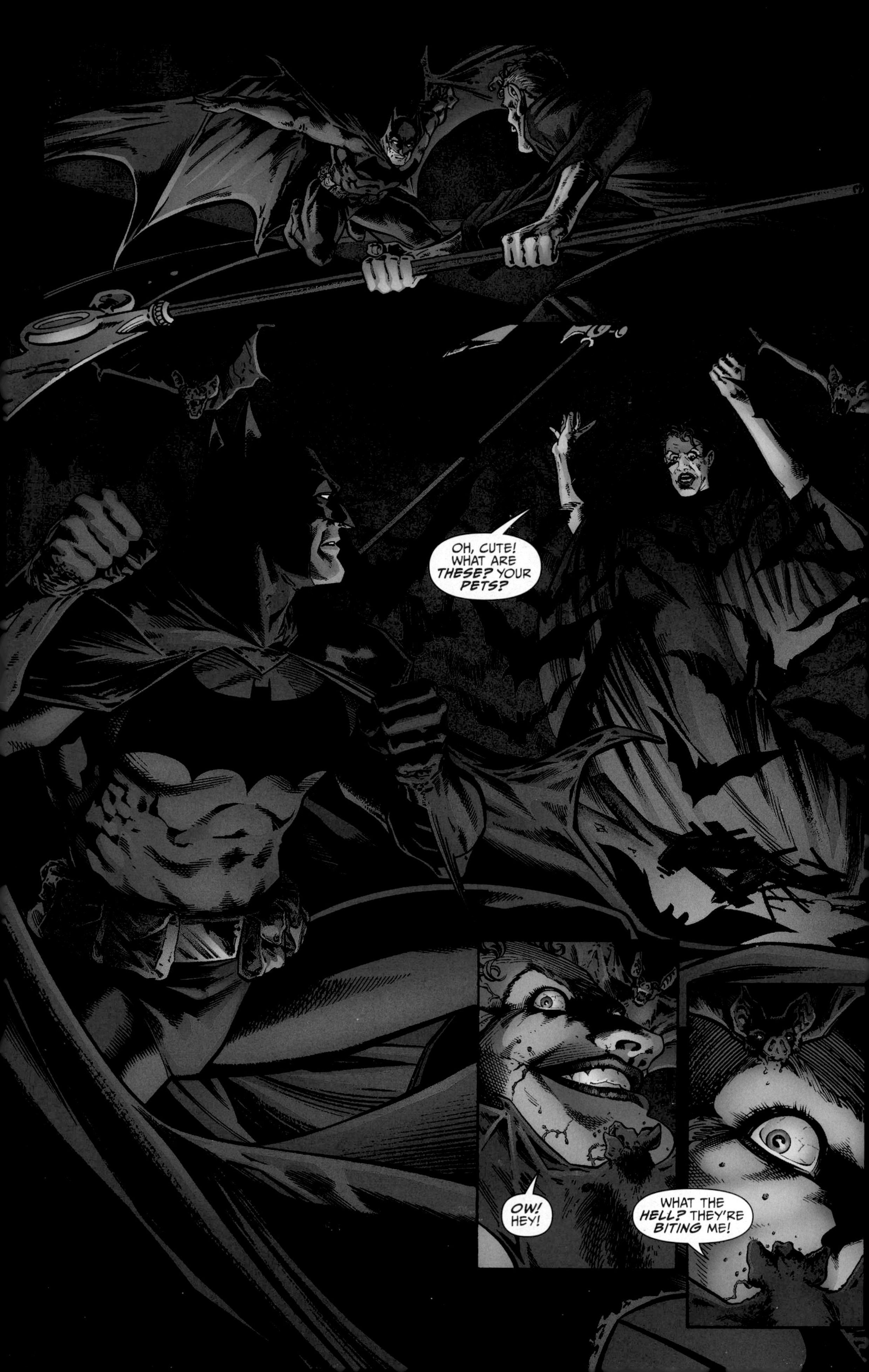
OH, CUTE! WHAT ARE THESE? YOUR PETS?
OW! HEY!
WHAT THE HELL? THEY'RE BITING ME!

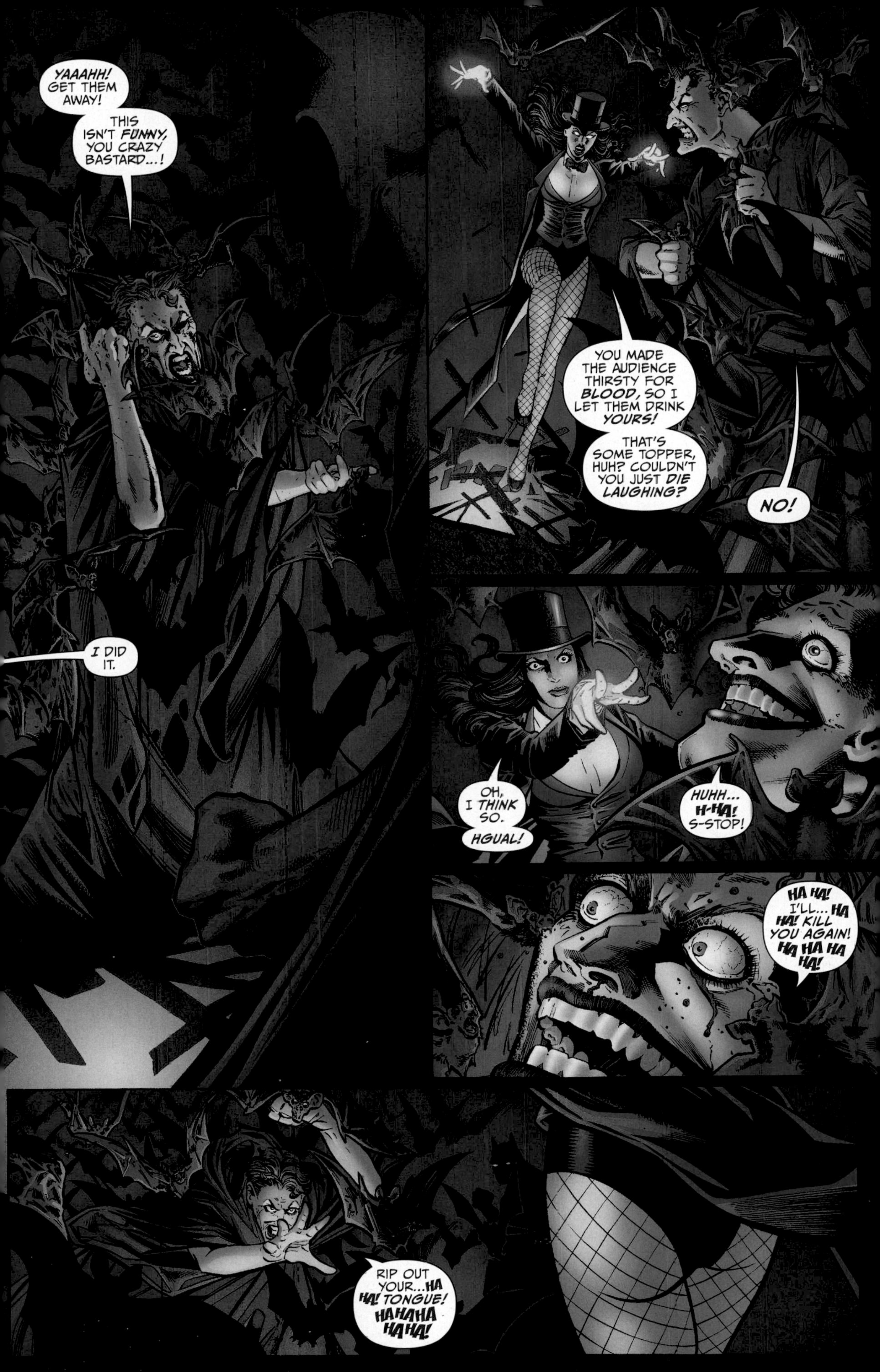
YAAAHH! GET THEM AWAY!
THIS ISN'T FUNNY, YOU CRAZY BASTARD...!
YOU MADE THE AUDIENCE THIRSTY FOR BLOOD, SO I LET THEM DRINK YOURS!
THAT'S SOME TOPPER, HUH? COULDN'T YOU JUST DIE LAUGHING?
NO!
I DID IT.
OH, I THINK SO. HGUAL!
HUHH... H-HA! S-STOP!
HA HA! I'LL... HA HA! KILL YOU AGAIN! HA HA HA HA!
RIP OUT YOUR... HA HA! TONGUE! HAHAHA HAHA!

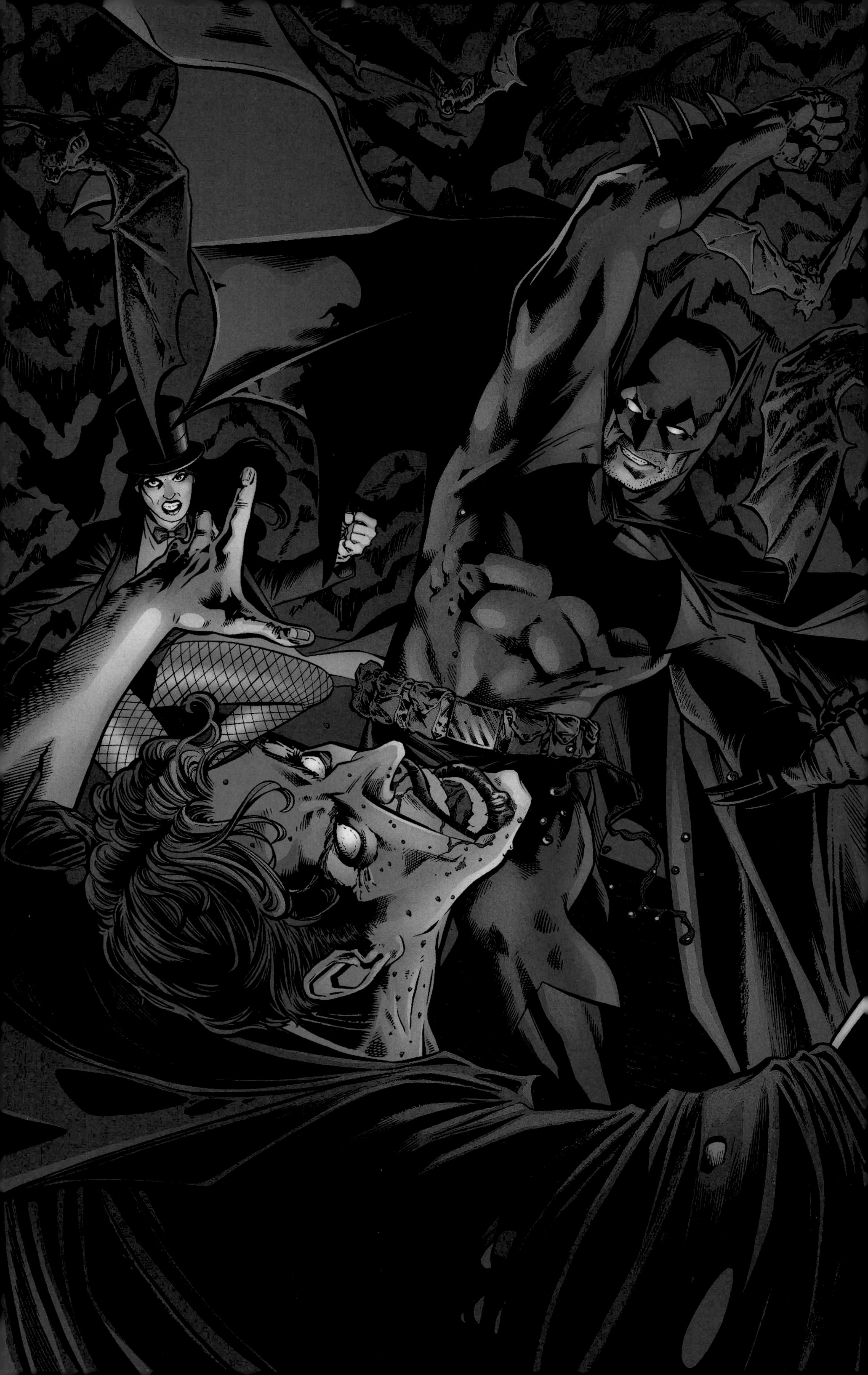

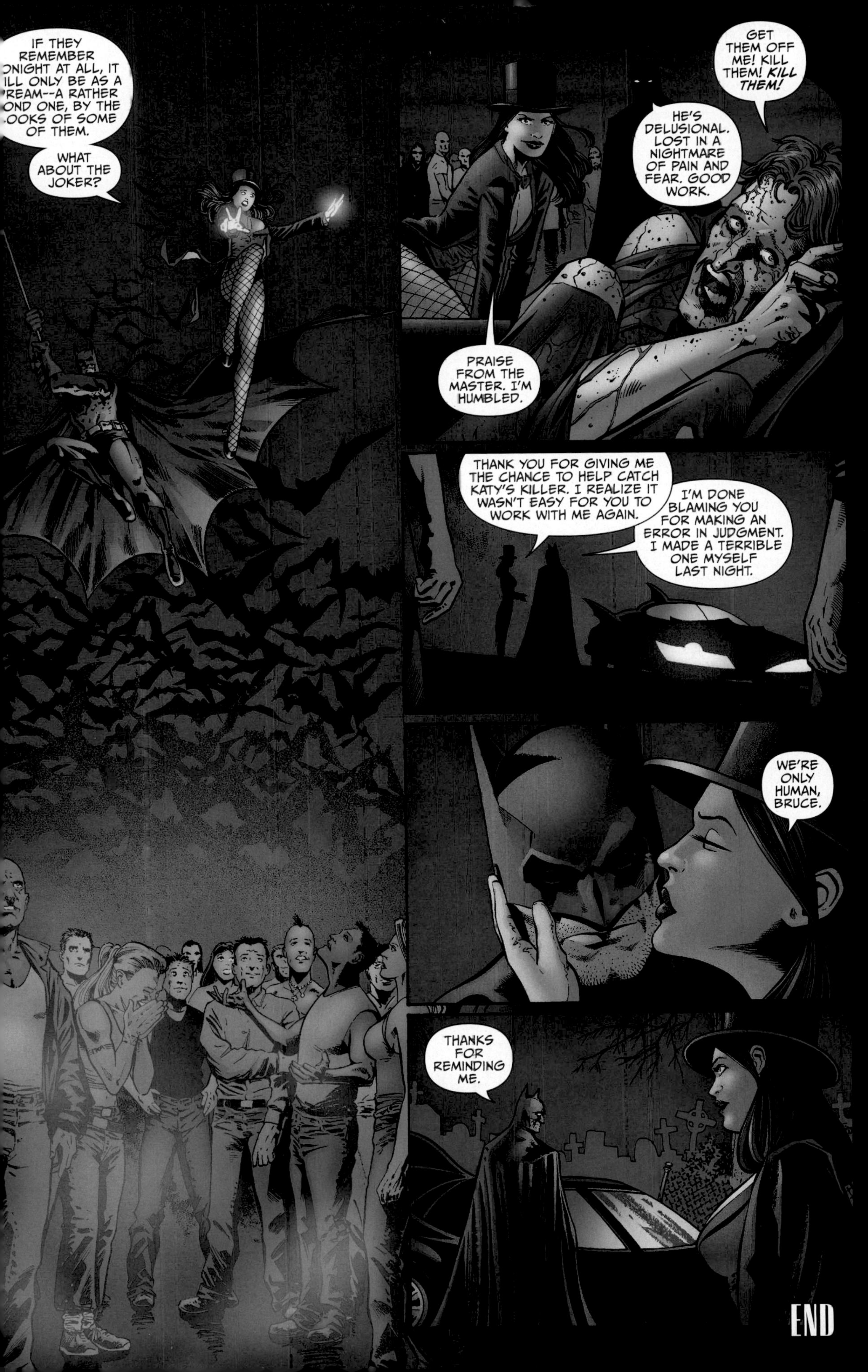
IF THEY REMEMBER ONIGHT AT ALL, IT ILL ONLY BE AS A REAM--A RATHER OND ONE, BY THE OOKS OF SOME OF THEM.
WHAT ABOUT THE JOKER?
GET THEM OFF ME! KILL THEM! *KILL THEM!*
HE'S DELUSIONAL. LOST IN A NIGHTMARE OF PAIN AND FEAR. GOOD WORK.
PRAISE FROM THE MASTER. I'M HUMBLED.
THANK YOU FOR GIVING ME THE CHANCE TO HELP CATCH KATY'S KILLER. I REALIZE IT WASN'T EASY FOR YOU TO WORK WITH ME AGAIN.
I'M DONE BLAMING YOU FOR MAKING AN ERROR IN JUDGMENT. I MADE A TERRIBLE ONE MYSELF LAST NIGHT.
WE'RE ONLY HUMAN, BRUCE.
THANKS FOR REMINDING ME.
END

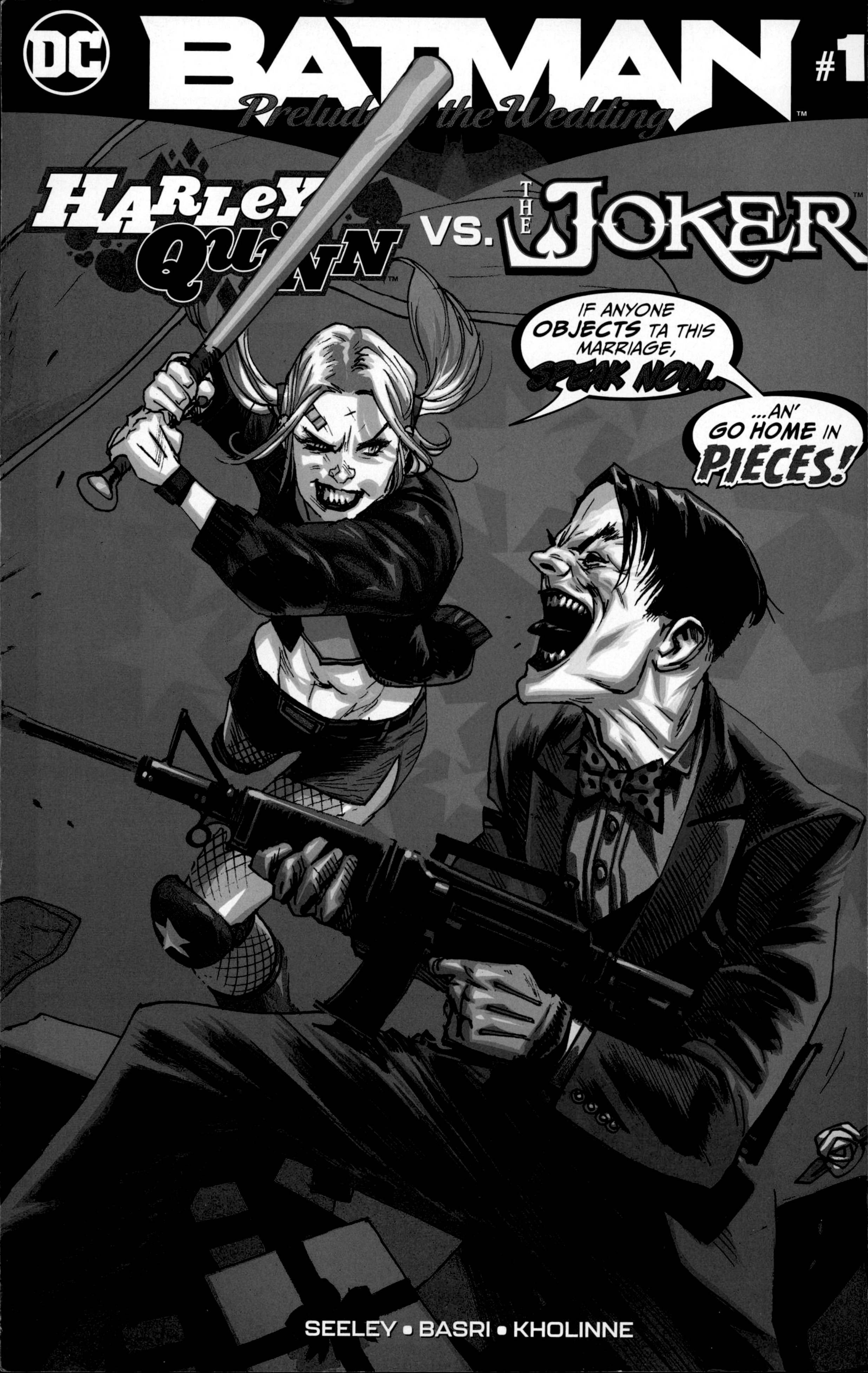

DC
BATMAN
#1
Prelude to the Wedding
HARLEY QUINN
VS.
THE JOKER
IF ANYONE OBJECTS TA THIS MARRIAGE, SPEAK NOW...
...AN' GO HOME IN PIECES!
SEELEY • BASRI • KHOLINNE

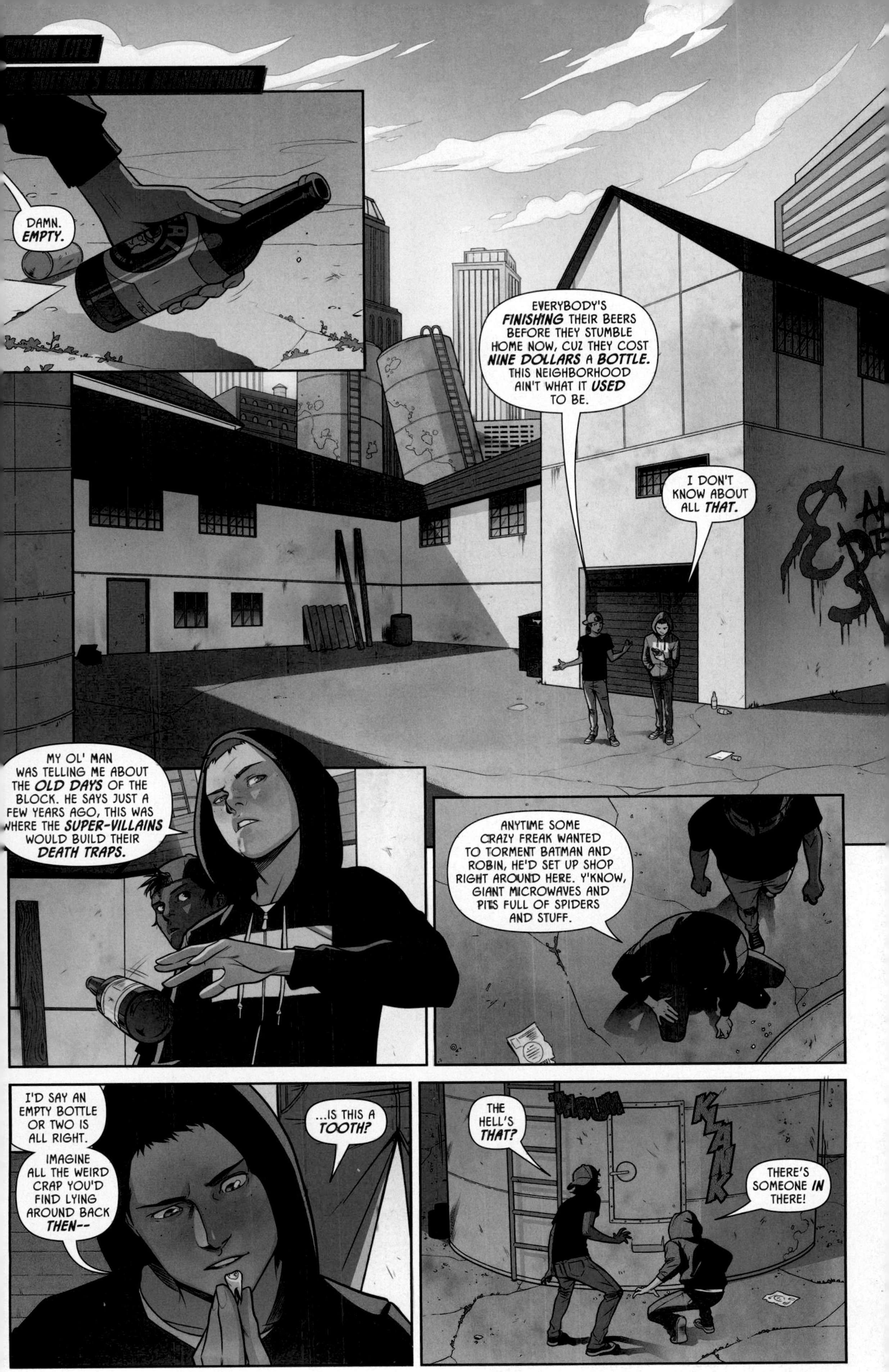
GOTHAM CITY.
THE BUTCHER'S BLOCK NEIGHBORHOOD.
DAMN. EMPTY.
EVERYBODY'S FINISHING THEIR BEERS BEFORE THEY STUMBLE HOME NOW, CUZ THEY COST NINE DOLLARS A BOTTLE. THIS NEIGHBORHOOD AIN'T WHAT IT USED TO BE.
I DON'T KNOW ABOUT ALL THAT.
MY OL' MAN WAS TELLING ME ABOUT THE OLD DAYS OF THE BLOCK. HE SAYS JUST A FEW YEARS AGO, THIS WAS WHERE THE SUPER-VILLAINS WOULD BUILD THEIR DEATH TRAPS.
ANYTIME SOME CRAZY FREAK WANTED TO TORMENT BATMAN AND ROBIN, HE'D SET UP SHOP RIGHT AROUND HERE. Y'KNOW, GIANT MICROWAVES AND PITS FULL OF SPIDERS AND STUFF.
I'D SAY AN EMPTY BOTTLE OR TWO IS ALL RIGHT.
IMAGINE ALL THE WEIRD CRAP YOU'D FIND LYING AROUND BACK THEN--
...IS THIS A TOOTH?
THE HELL'S THAT?
THRUM
KLANK
THERE'S SOMEONE IN THERE!

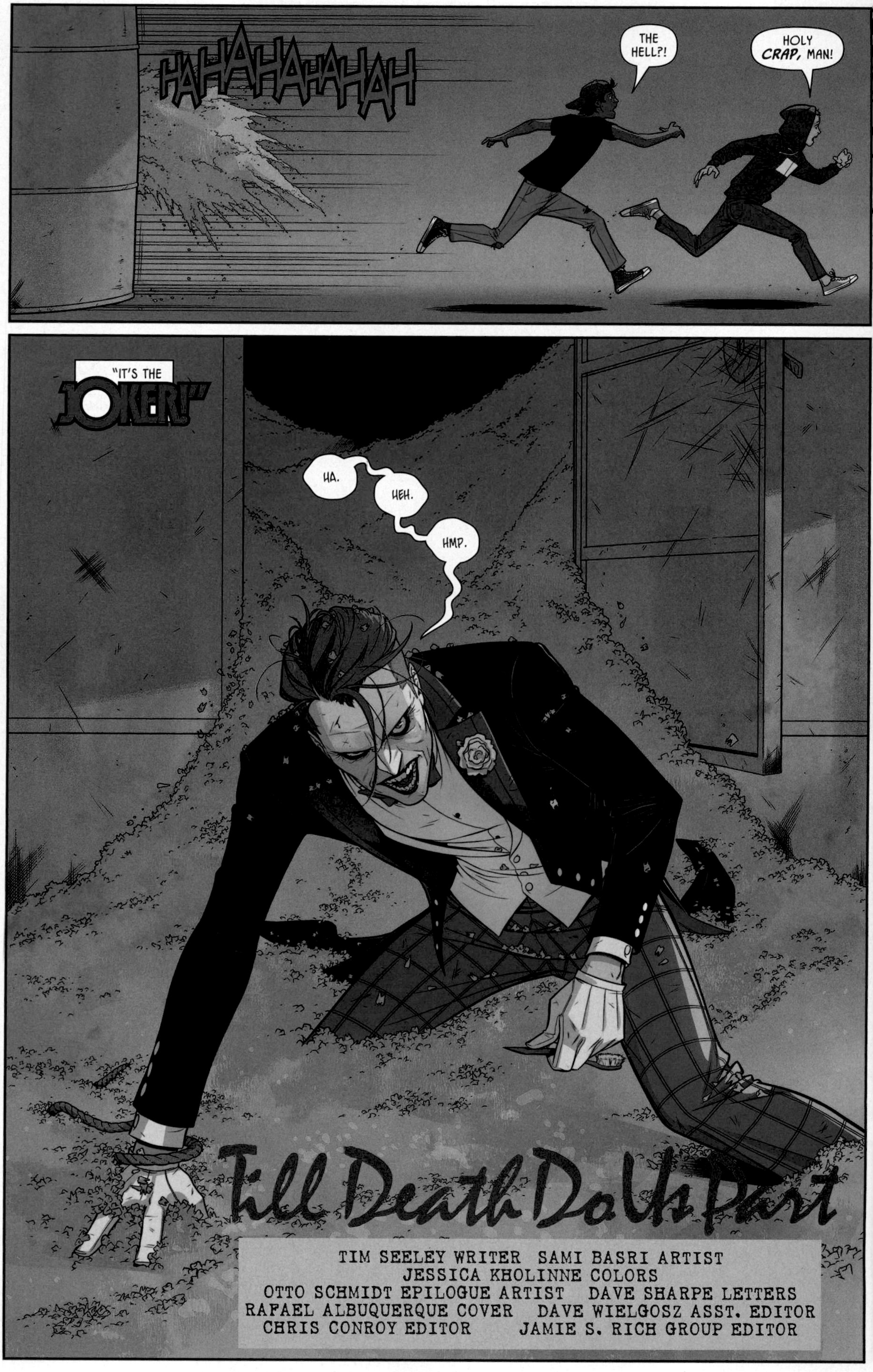
HAHAHAHAHAH
THE HELL?!
HOLY CRAP, MAN!
"IT'S THE JOKER!"
HA.
HEH.
HMP.
Till Death Do Us Part
TIM SEELEY WRITER SAMI BASRI ARTIST
JESSICA KHOLINNE COLORS
OTTO SCHMIDT EPILOGUE ARTIST DAVE SHARPE LETTERS
RAFAEL ALBUQUERQUE COVER DAVE WIELGOSZ ASST. EDITOR
CHRIS CONROY EDITOR JAMIE S. RICH GROUP EDITOR

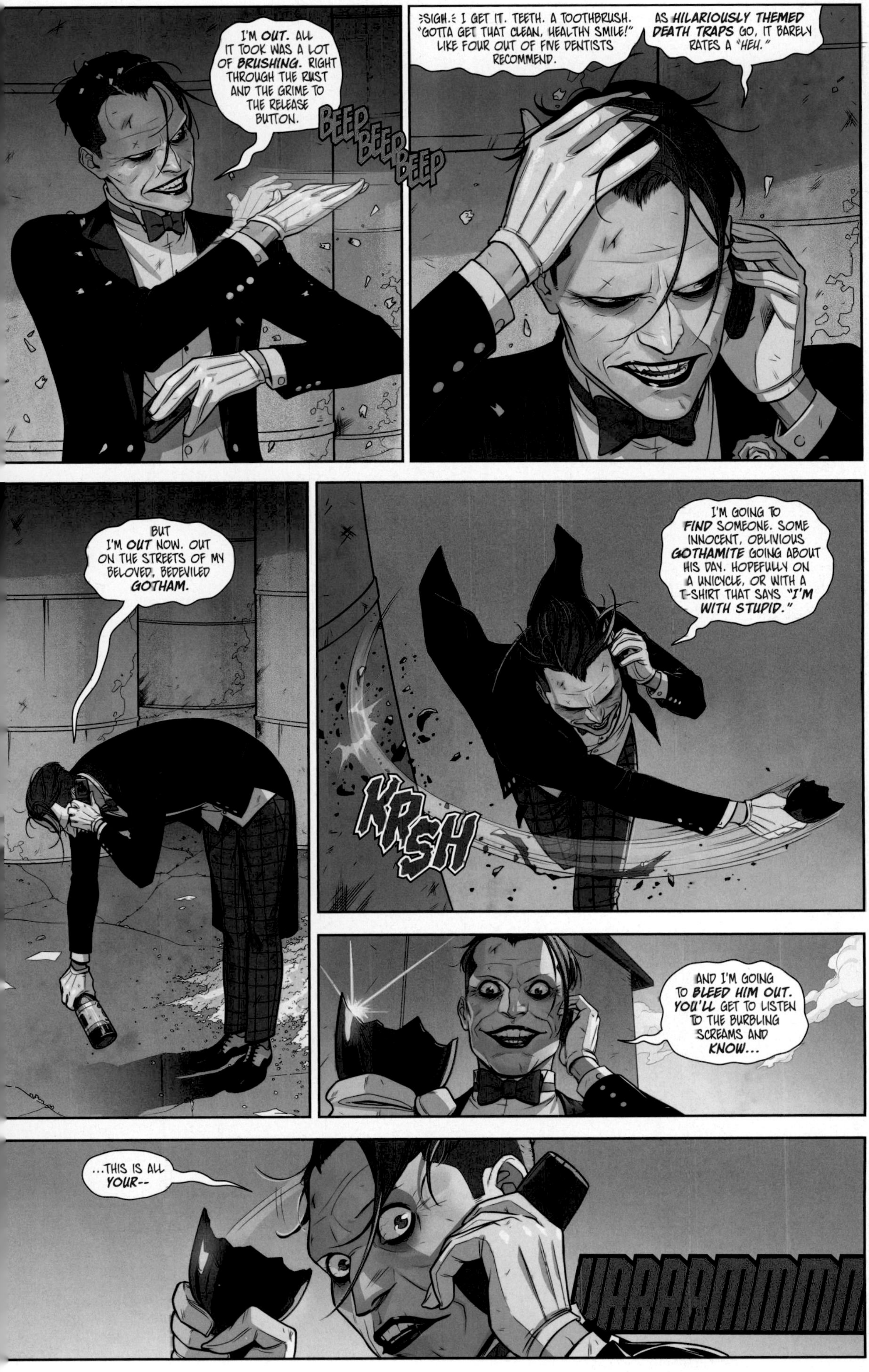
I'M OUT. ALL IT TOOK WAS A LOT OF BRUSHING. RIGHT THROUGH THE RUST AND THE GRIME TO THE RELEASE BUTTON.
BEEP BEEP BEEP
SIGH. I GET IT. TEETH. A TOOTHBRUSH. "GOTTA GET THAT CLEAN, HEALTHY SMILE!" LIKE FOUR OUT OF FIVE DENTISTS RECOMMEND.
AS HILARIOUSLY THEMED DEATH TRAPS GO, IT BARELY RATES A "HEH."
BUT I'M OUT NOW. OUT ON THE STREETS OF MY BELOVED, BEDEVILED GOTHAM.
I'M GOING TO FIND SOMEONE. SOME INNOCENT, OBLIVIOUS GOTHAMITE GOING ABOUT HIS DAY. HOPEFULLY ON A UNICYCLE, OR WITH A T-SHIRT THAT SAYS "I'M WITH STUPID."
KRSH
AND I'M GOING TO BLEED HIM OUT. YOU'LL GET TO LISTEN TO THE BURBLING SCREAMS AND KNOW...
...THIS IS ALL YOUR--
VRRRRMMMM

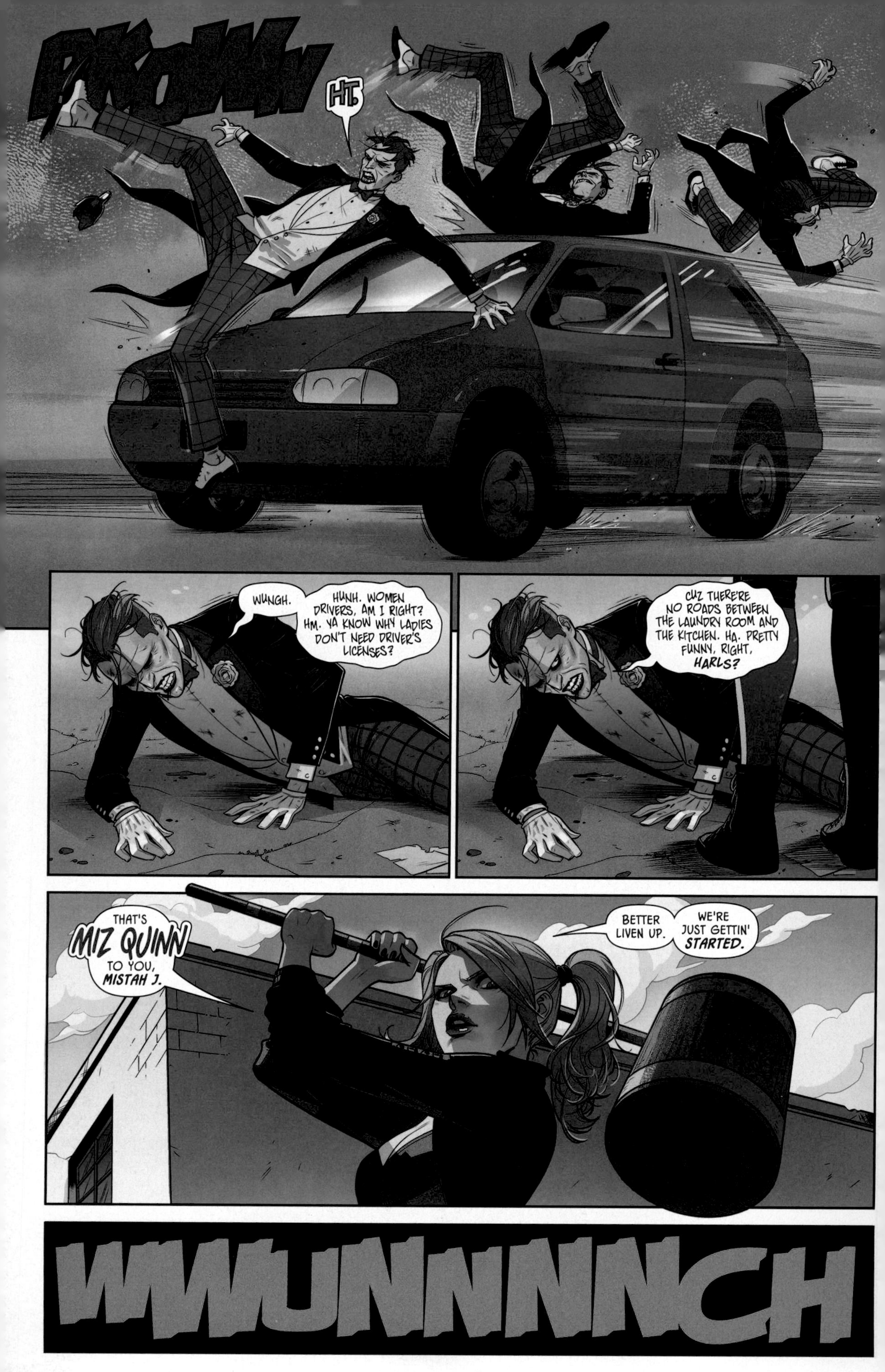
PKOWW
HT.
WUNGH.
HUNH. WOMEN DRIVERS, AM I RIGHT? HM. YA KNOW WHY LADIES DON'T NEED DRIVER'S LICENSES?
CUZ THERE'RE NO ROADS BETWEEN THE LAUNDRY ROOM AND THE KITCHEN. HA. PRETTY FUNNY, RIGHT, HARLS?
THAT'S MIZ QUINN TO YOU, MISTAH J.
BETTER LIVEN UP.
WE'RE JUST GETTIN' STARTED.
WWUNNNNCH

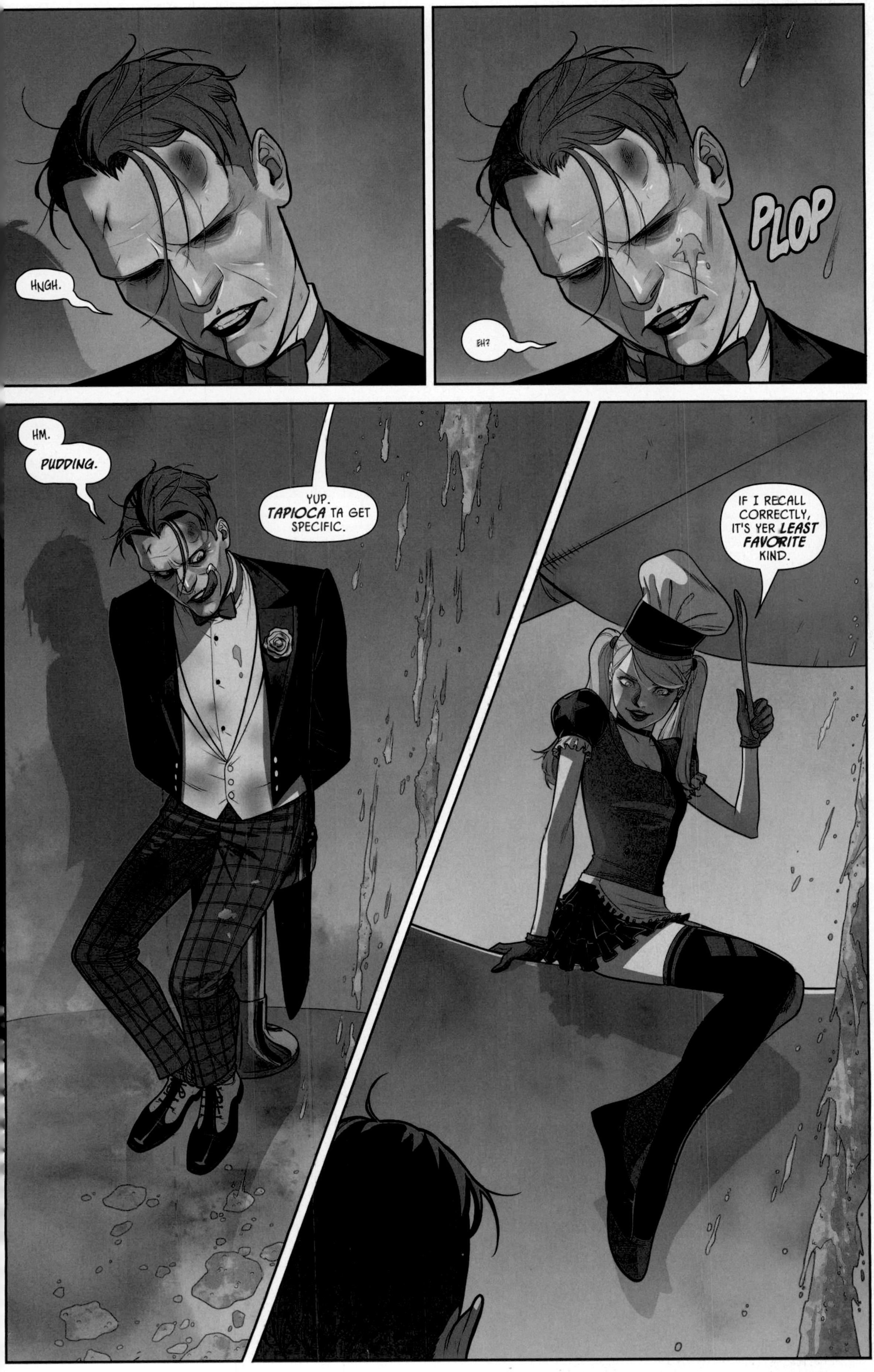
HNGH.
PLOP
EH?
HM.
PUDDING.
YUP. TAPIOCA TA GET SPECIFIC.
IF I RECALL CORRECTLY, IT'S YER LEAST FAVORITE KIND.

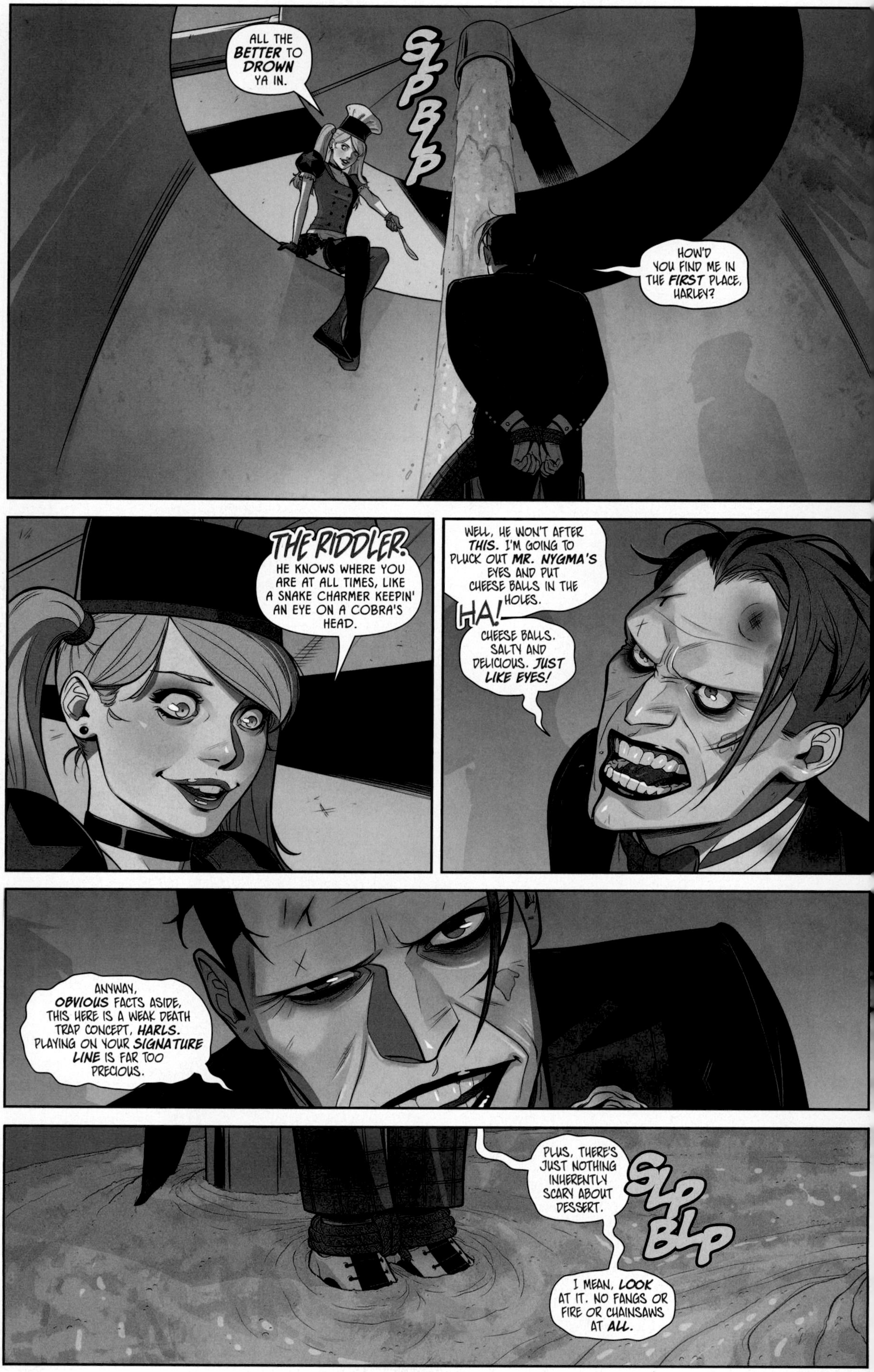
ALL THE BETTER TO DROWN YA IN.
SLP BLP
HOW'D YOU FIND ME IN THE FIRST PLACE, HARLEY?
THE RIDDLER.
HE KNOWS WHERE YOU ARE AT ALL TIMES, LIKE A SNAKE CHARMER KEEPIN' AN EYE ON A COBRA'S HEAD.
WELL, HE WON'T AFTER THIS. I'M GOING TO PLUCK OUT MR. NYGMA'S EYES AND PUT CHEESE BALLS IN THE HOLES.
HA!
CHEESE BALLS. SALTY AND DELICIOUS. JUST LIKE EYES!
ANYWAY, OBVIOUS FACTS ASIDE, THIS HERE IS A WEAK DEATH TRAP CONCEPT, HARLS. PLAYING ON YOUR SIGNATURE LINE IS FAR TOO PRECIOUS.
PLUS, THERE'S JUST NOTHING INHERENTLY SCARY ABOUT DESSERT.
SLP BLP
I MEAN, LOOK AT IT. NO FANGS OR FIRE OR CHAINSAWS AT ALL.

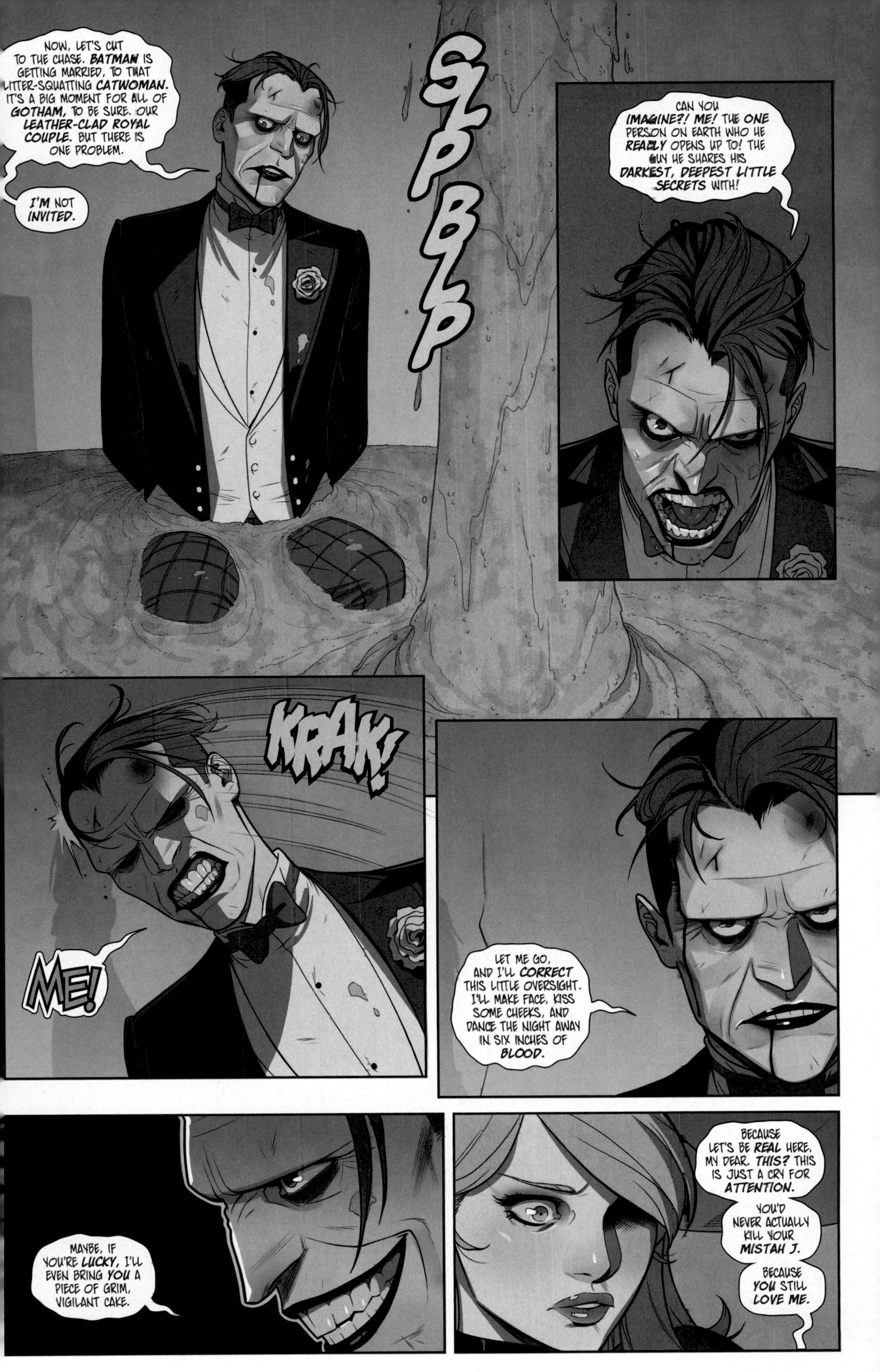
NOW, LET'S CUT TO THE CHASE. BATMAN IS GETTING MARRIED, TO THAT LITTER-SQUATTING CATWOMAN. IT'S A BIG MOMENT FOR ALL OF GOTHAM, TO BE SURE. OUR LEATHER-CLAD ROYAL COUPLE. BUT THERE IS ONE PROBLEM.
I'M NOT INVITED.
SLPBLP
CAN YOU IMAGINE?! ME! THE ONE PERSON ON EARTH WHO HE REALLY OPENS UP TO! THE GUY HE SHARES HIS DARKEST, DEEPEST LITTLE SECRETS WITH!
KRAK!
ME!
LET ME GO, AND I'LL CORRECT THIS LITTLE OVERSIGHT. I'LL MAKE FACE, KISS SOME CHEEKS, AND DANCE THE NIGHT AWAY IN SIX INCHES OF BLOOD.
MAYBE, IF YOU'RE LUCKY, I'LL EVEN BRING YOU A PIECE OF GRIM, VIGILANT CAKE.
BECAUSE LET'S BE REAL HERE, MY DEAR. THIS? THIS IS JUST A CRY FOR ATTENTION.
YOU'D NEVER ACTUALLY KILL YOUR MISTAH J.
BECAUSE YOU STILL LOVE ME.

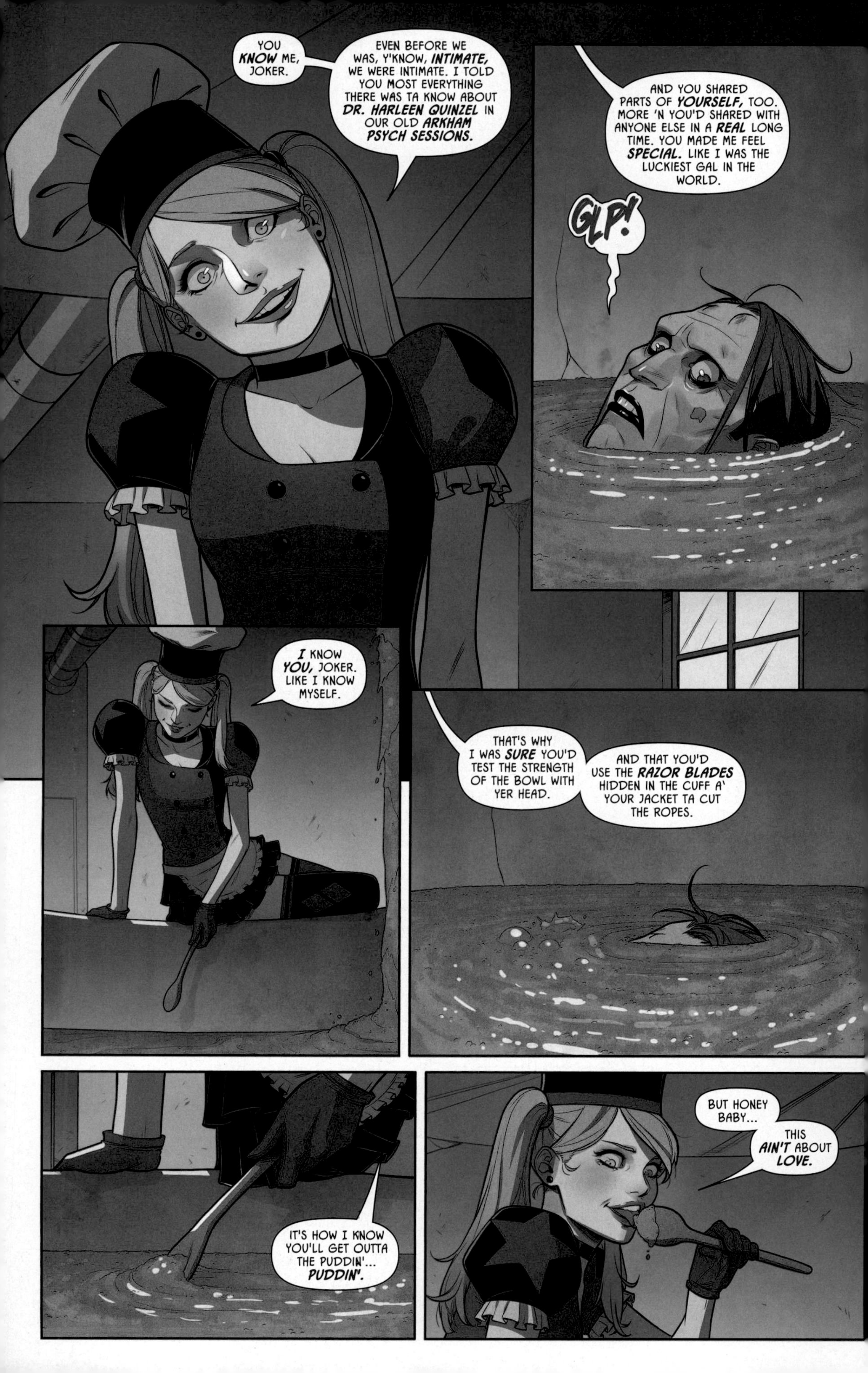
YOU KNOW ME, JOKER.
EVEN BEFORE WE WAS, Y'KNOW, INTIMATE, WE WERE INTIMATE. I TOLD YOU MOST EVERYTHING THERE WAS TA KNOW ABOUT DR. HARLEEN QUINZEL IN OUR OLD ARKHAM PSYCH SESSIONS.
AND YOU SHARED PARTS OF YOURSELF, TOO. MORE 'N YOU'D SHARED WITH ANYONE ELSE IN A REAL LONG TIME. YOU MADE ME FEEL SPECIAL. LIKE I WAS THE LUCKIEST GAL IN THE WORLD.
GLP!
I KNOW YOU, JOKER. LIKE I KNOW MYSELF.
THAT'S WHY I WAS SURE YOU'D TEST THE STRENGTH OF THE BOWL WITH YER HEAD.
AND THAT YOU'D USE THE RAZOR BLADES HIDDEN IN THE CUFF A' YOUR JACKET TA CUT THE ROPES.
IT'S HOW I KNOW YOU'LL GET OUTTA THE PUDDIN'... PUDDIN'.
BUT HONEY BABY...
THIS AIN'T ABOUT LOVE.

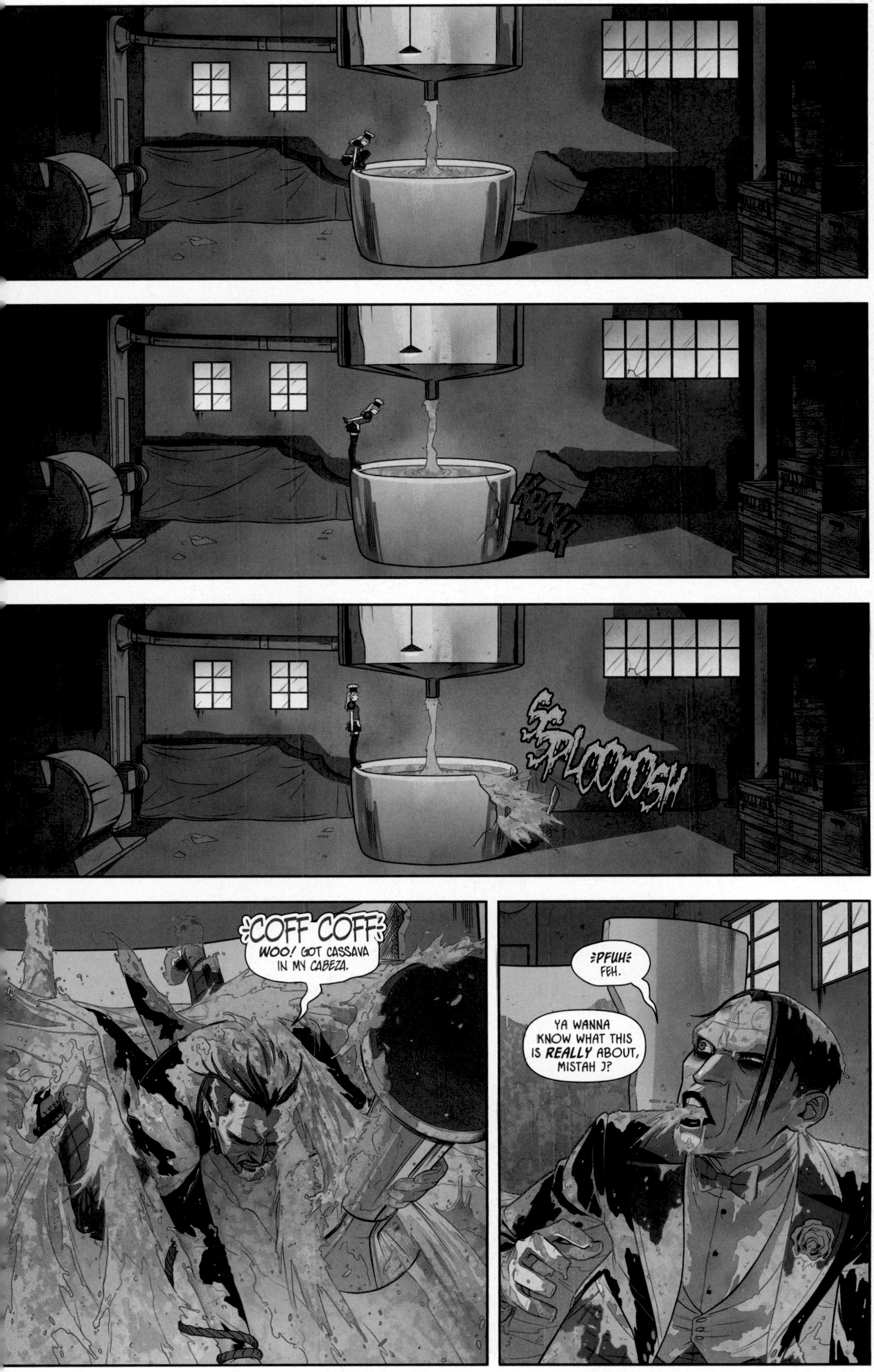
KRAAK
SPLOOOOSH
COFF COFF
WOO! GOT CASSAVA IN MY CABEZA.
PFUH
FEH.
YA WANNA KNOW WHAT THIS IS REALLY ABOUT, MISTAH J?

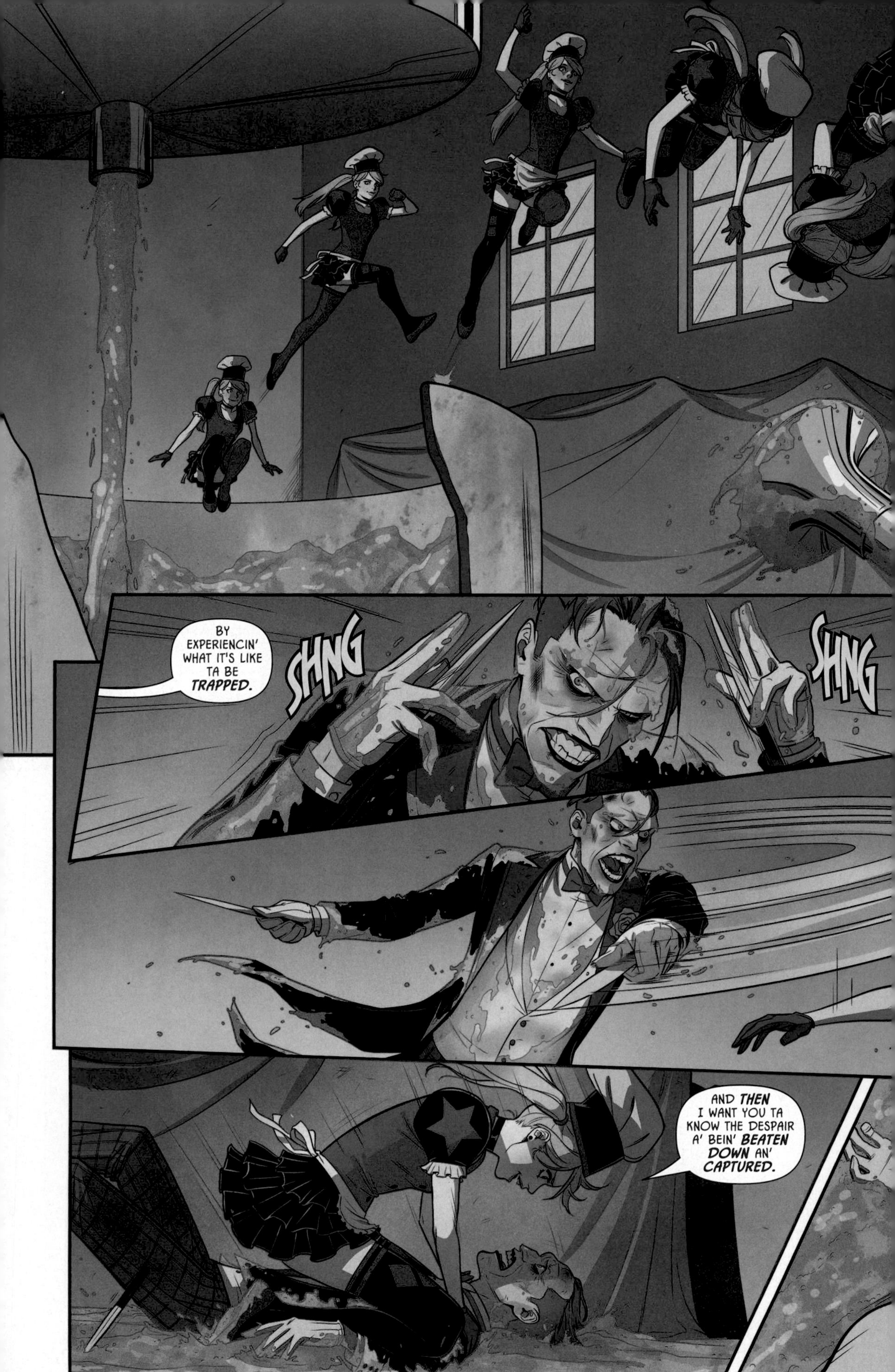
BY EXPERIENCIN' WHAT IT'S LIKE TA BE **TRAPPED**.
SHNG
SHNG
AND **THEN** I WANT YOU TA KNOW THE DESPAIR A' BEIN' **BEATEN DOWN** AN' **CAPTURED**.

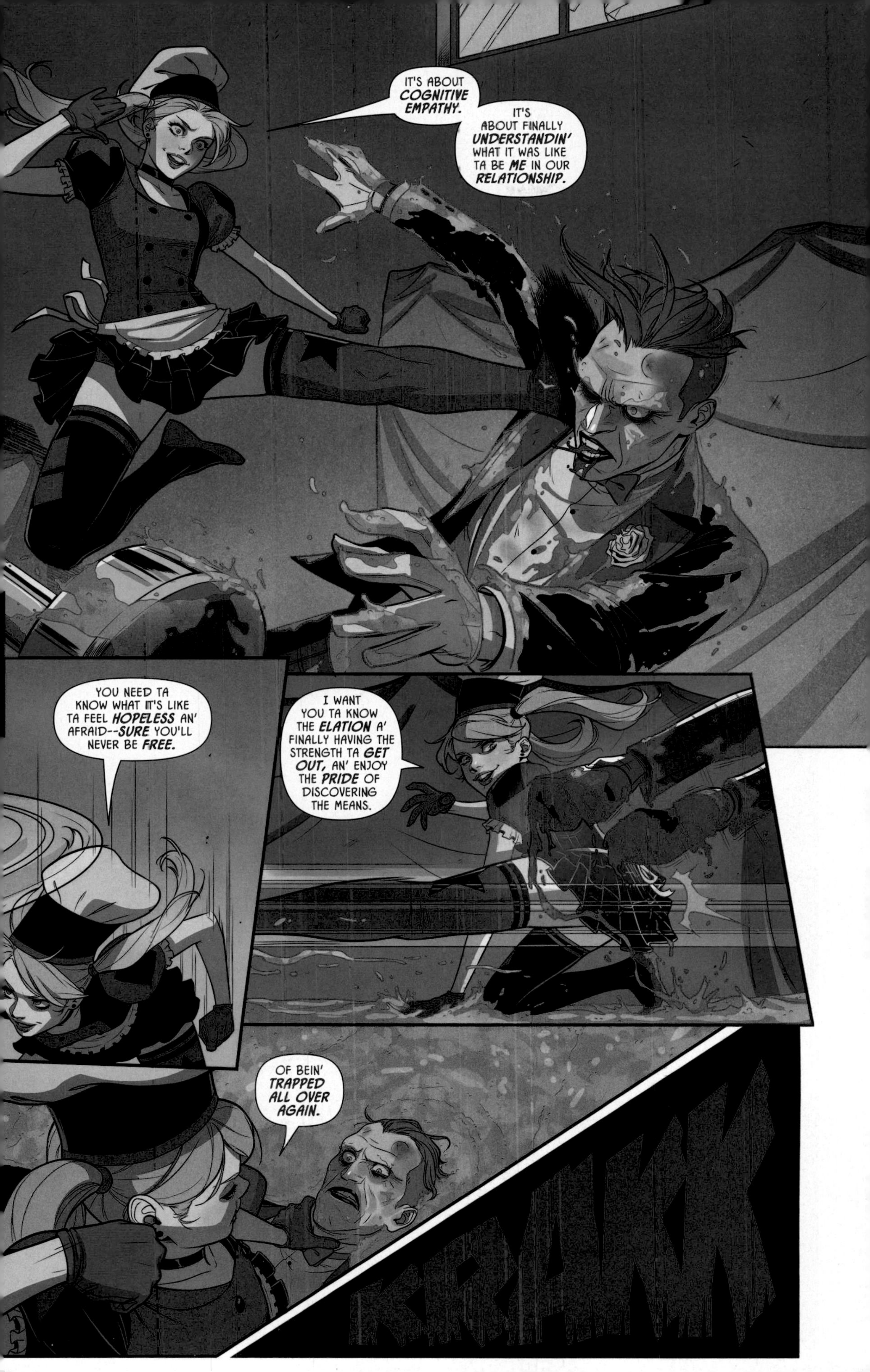
IT'S ABOUT *COGNITIVE EMPATHY.*
IT'S ABOUT FINALLY *UNDERSTANDIN'* WHAT IT WAS LIKE TA BE *ME* IN OUR *RELATIONSHIP.*
YOU NEED TA KNOW WHAT IT'S LIKE TA FEEL *HOPELESS* AN' AFRAID--*SURE* YOU'LL NEVER BE *FREE.*
I WANT YOU TA KNOW THE *ELATION* A' FINALLY HAVING THE STRENGTH TA *GET OUT,* AN' ENJOY THE *PRIDE* OF DISCOVERING THE MEANS.
OF BEIN' *TRAPPED ALL OVER AGAIN.*
KRAKKK

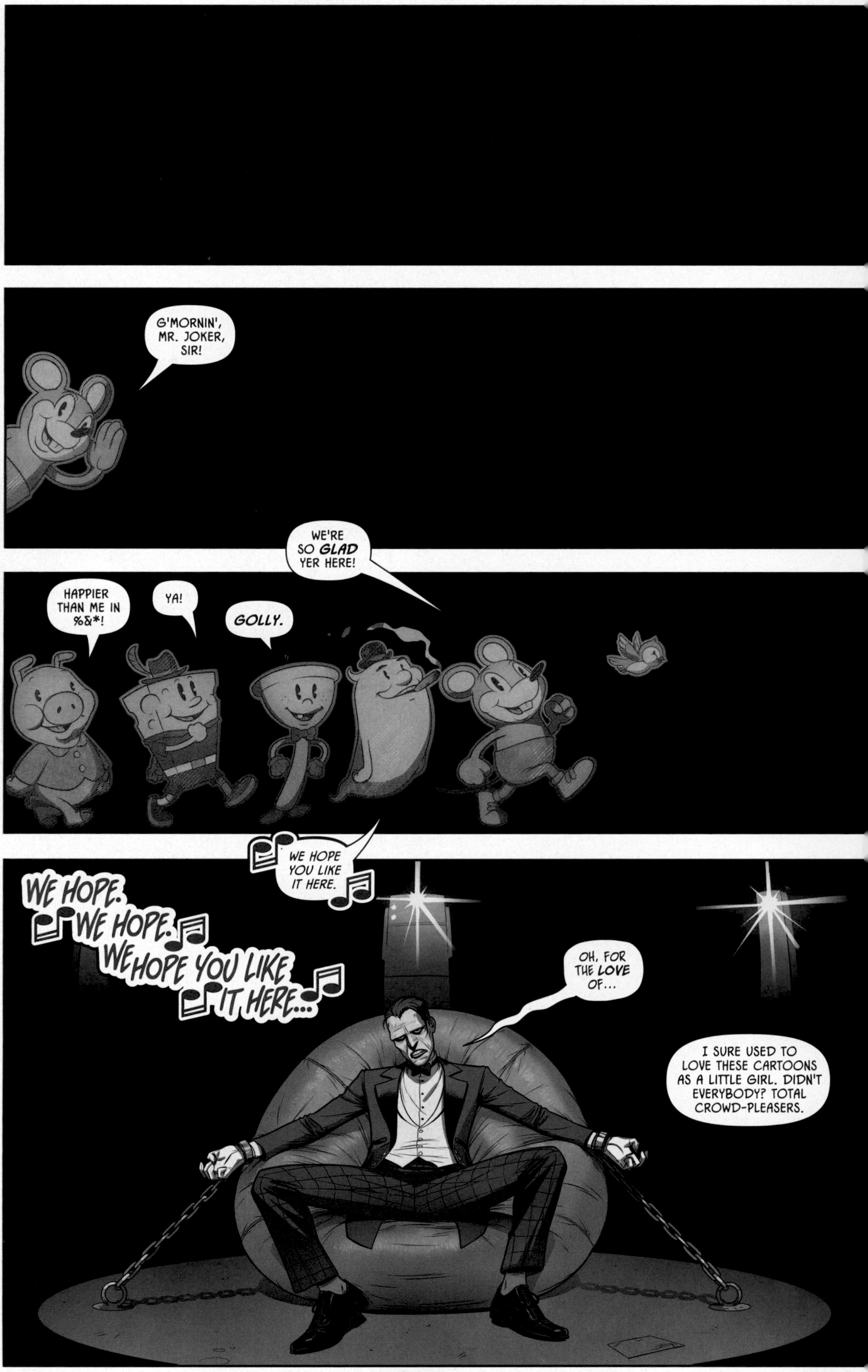
G'MORNIN', MR. JOKER, SIR!
HAPPIER THAN ME IN %&*!
YA!
GOLLY.
WE'RE SO GLAD YER HERE!
WE HOPE YOU LIKE IT HERE.
WE HOPE. WE HOPE. WE HOPE YOU LIKE IT HERE...
OH, FOR THE LOVE OF...
I SURE USED TO LOVE THESE CARTOONS AS A LITTLE GIRL. DIDN'T EVERYBODY? TOTAL CROWD-PLEASERS.

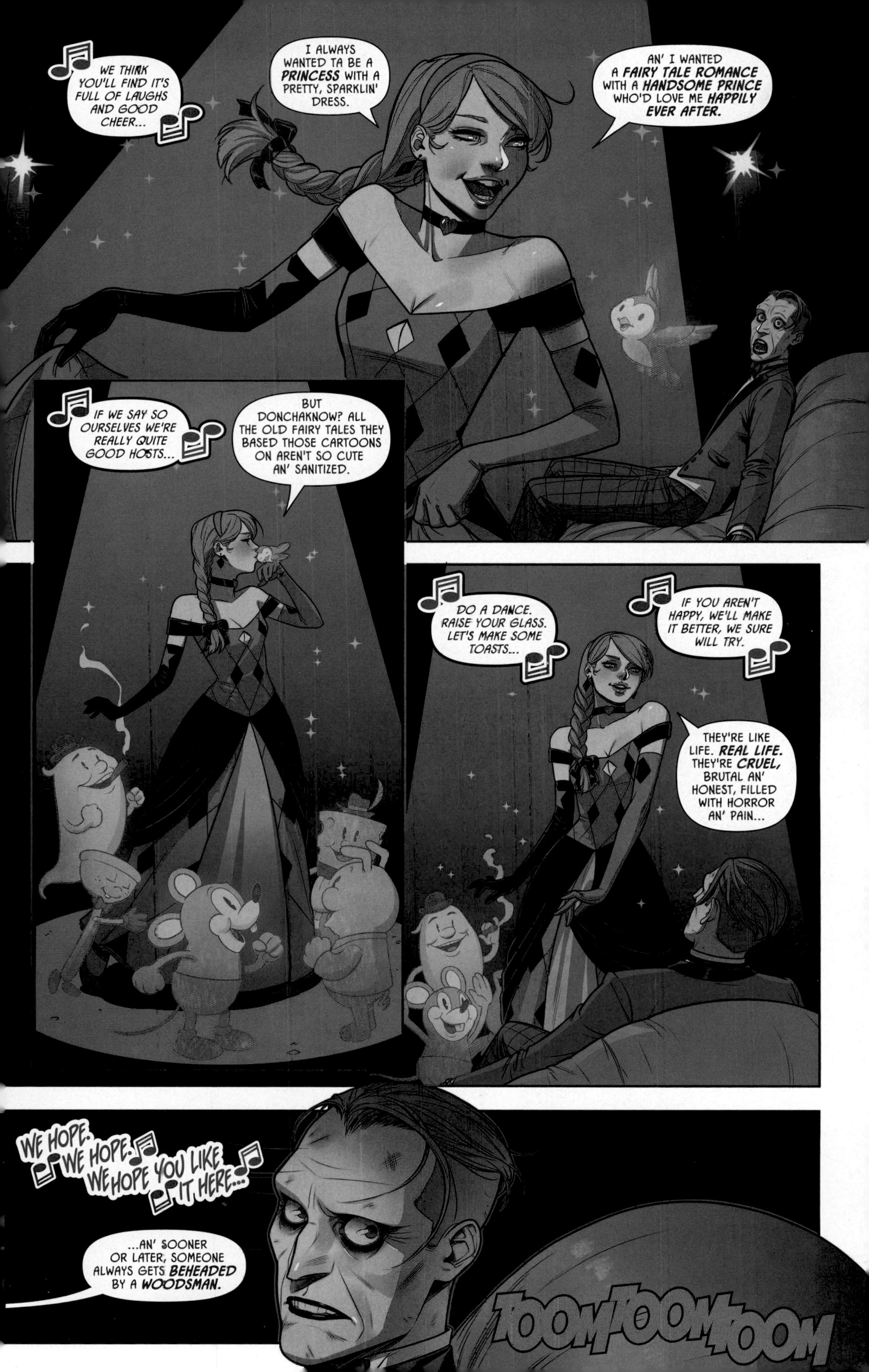
WE THINK YOU'LL FIND IT'S FULL OF LAUGHS AND GOOD CHEER...
I ALWAYS WANTED TA BE A PRINCESS WITH A PRETTY, SPARKLIN' DRESS.
AN' I WANTED A FAIRY TALE ROMANCE WITH A HANDSOME PRINCE WHO'D LOVE ME HAPPILY EVER AFTER.
IF WE SAY SO OURSELVES WE'RE REALLY QUITE GOOD HOSTS...
BUT DONCHAKNOW? ALL THE OLD FAIRY TALES THEY BASED THOSE CARTOONS ON AREN'T SO CUTE AN' SANITIZED.
DO A DANCE. RAISE YOUR GLASS. LET'S MAKE SOME TOASTS...
IF YOU AREN'T HAPPY, WE'LL MAKE IT BETTER, WE SURE WILL TRY.
THEY'RE LIKE LIFE. REAL LIFE. THEY'RE CRUEL, BRUTAL AN' HONEST, FILLED WITH HORROR AN' PAIN...
WE HOPE. WE HOPE. WE HOPE YOU LIKE IT HERE...
...AN' SOONER OR LATER, SOMEONE ALWAYS GETS BEHEADED BY A WOODSMAN.
TOOM TOOM TOOM

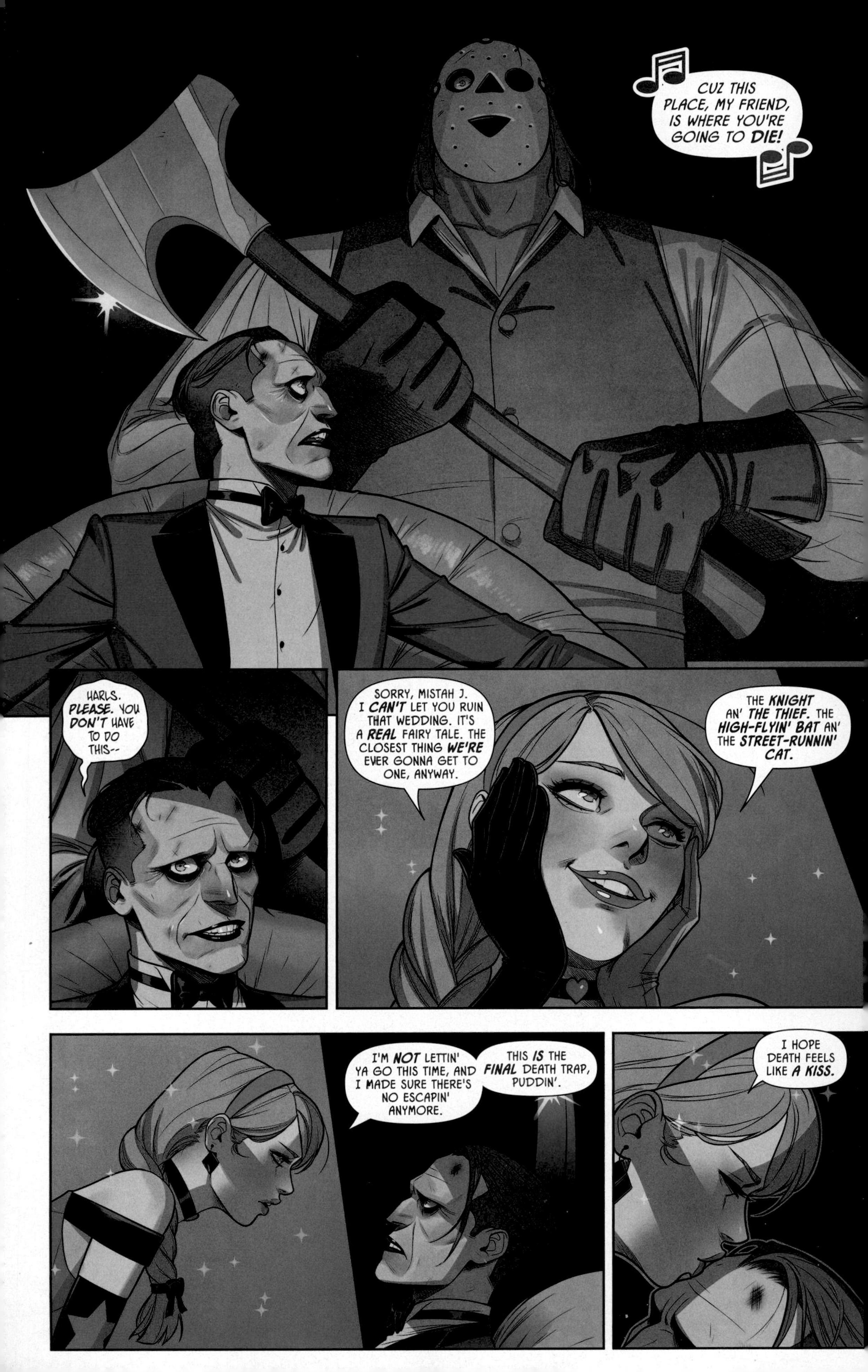

CUZ THIS PLACE, MY FRIEND, IS WHERE YOU'RE GOING TO DIE!
HARLS. PLEASE. YOU DON'T HAVE TO DO THIS--
SORRY, MISTAH J. I CAN'T LET YOU RUIN THAT WEDDING. IT'S A REAL FAIRY TALE. THE CLOSEST THING WE'RE EVER GONNA GET TO ONE, ANYWAY.
THE KNIGHT AN' THE THIEF. THE HIGH-FLYIN' BAT AN' THE STREET-RUNNIN' CAT.
I'M NOT LETTIN' YA GO THIS TIME, AND I MADE SURE THERE'S NO ESCAPIN' ANYMORE.
THIS IS THE FINAL DEATH TRAP, PUDDIN'.
I HOPE DEATH FEELS LIKE A KISS.

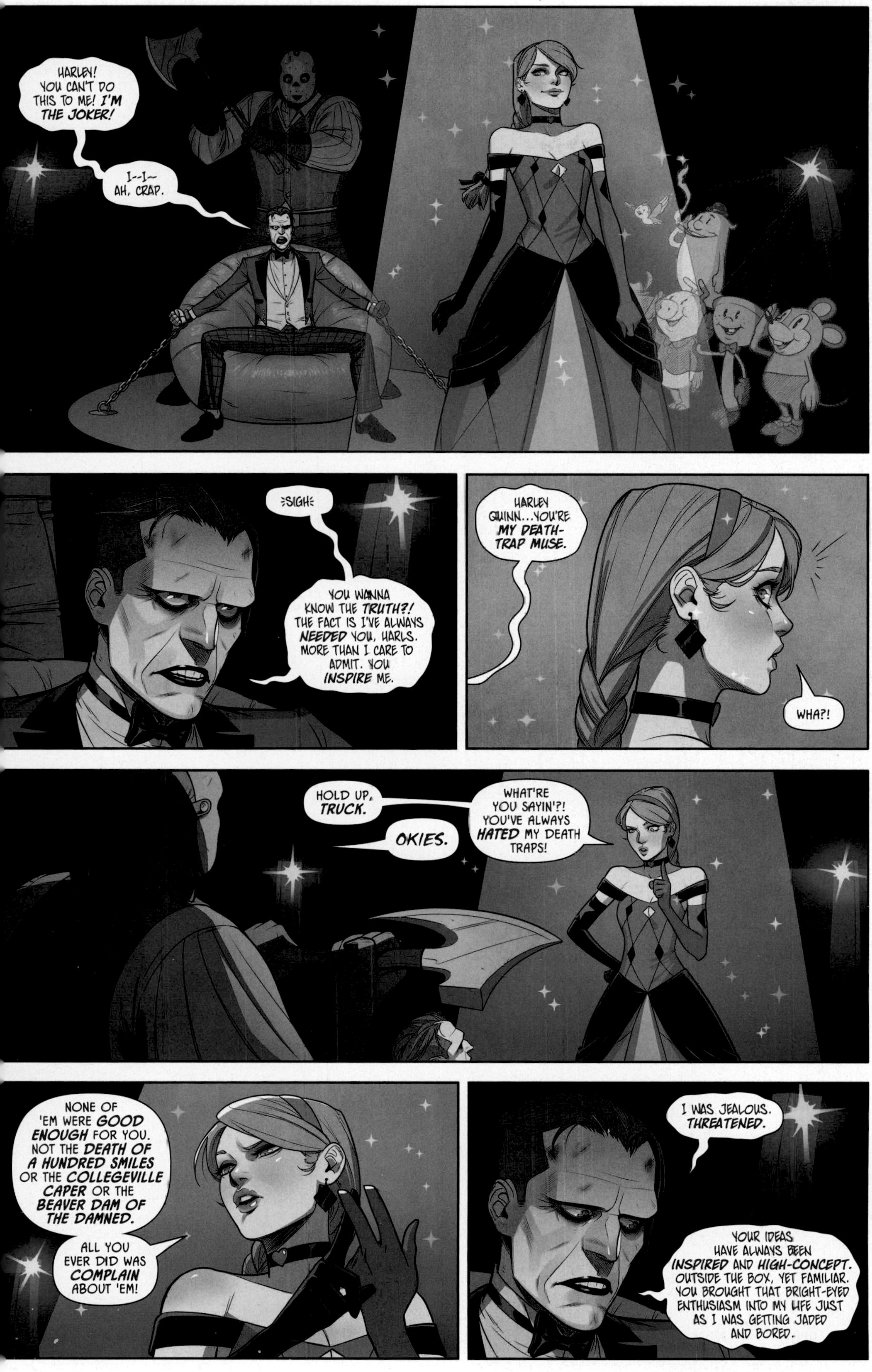
HARLEY! YOU CAN'T DO THIS TO ME! I'M THE JOKER!
I--I-- AH, CRAP.
SIGH
YOU WANNA KNOW THE TRUTH?! THE FACT IS I'VE ALWAYS NEEDED YOU, HARLS. MORE THAN I CARE TO ADMIT. YOU INSPIRE ME.
HARLEY QUINN...YOU'RE MY DEATH-TRAP MUSE.
WHA?!
HOLD UP, TRUCK.
OKIES.
WHAT'RE YOU SAYIN'?! YOU'VE ALWAYS HATED MY DEATH TRAPS!
NONE OF 'EM WERE GOOD ENOUGH FOR YOU. NOT THE DEATH OF A HUNDRED SMILES OR THE COLLEGEVILLE CAPER OR THE BEAVER DAM OF THE DAMNED.
ALL YOU EVER DID WAS COMPLAIN ABOUT 'EM!
I WAS JEALOUS. THREATENED.
YOUR IDEAS HAVE ALWAYS BEEN INSPIRED AND HIGH-CONCEPT. OUTSIDE THE BOX, YET FAMILIAR. YOU BROUGHT THAT BRIGHT-EYED ENTHUSIASM INTO MY LIFE JUST AS I WAS GETTING JADED AND BORED.

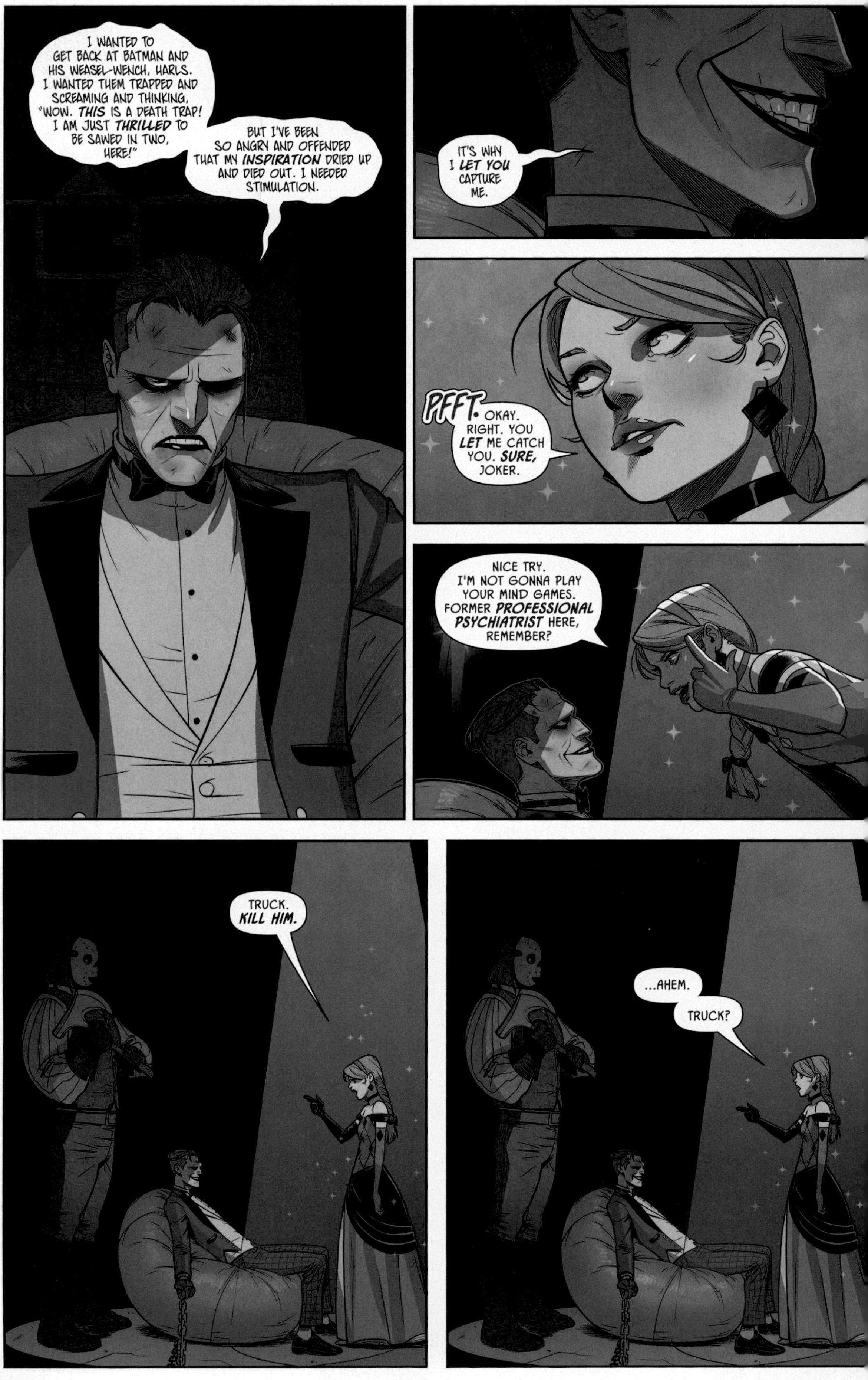
I WANTED TO GET BACK AT BATMAN AND HIS WEASEL-WENCH, HARLS. I WANTED THEM TRAPPED AND SCREAMING AND THINKING, "WOW. THIS IS A DEATH TRAP! I AM JUST THRILLED TO BE SAWED IN TWO, HERE!"
BUT I'VE BEEN SO ANGRY AND OFFENDED THAT MY INSPIRATION DRIED UP AND DIED OUT. I NEEDED STIMULATION.
IT'S WHY I LET YOU CAPTURE ME.
PFFT.
OKAY. RIGHT. YOU LET ME CATCH YOU. SURE, JOKER.
NICE TRY. I'M NOT GONNA PLAY YOUR MIND GAMES. FORMER PROFESSIONAL PSYCHIATRIST HERE, REMEMBER?
TRUCK. KILL HIM.
...AHEM.
TRUCK?

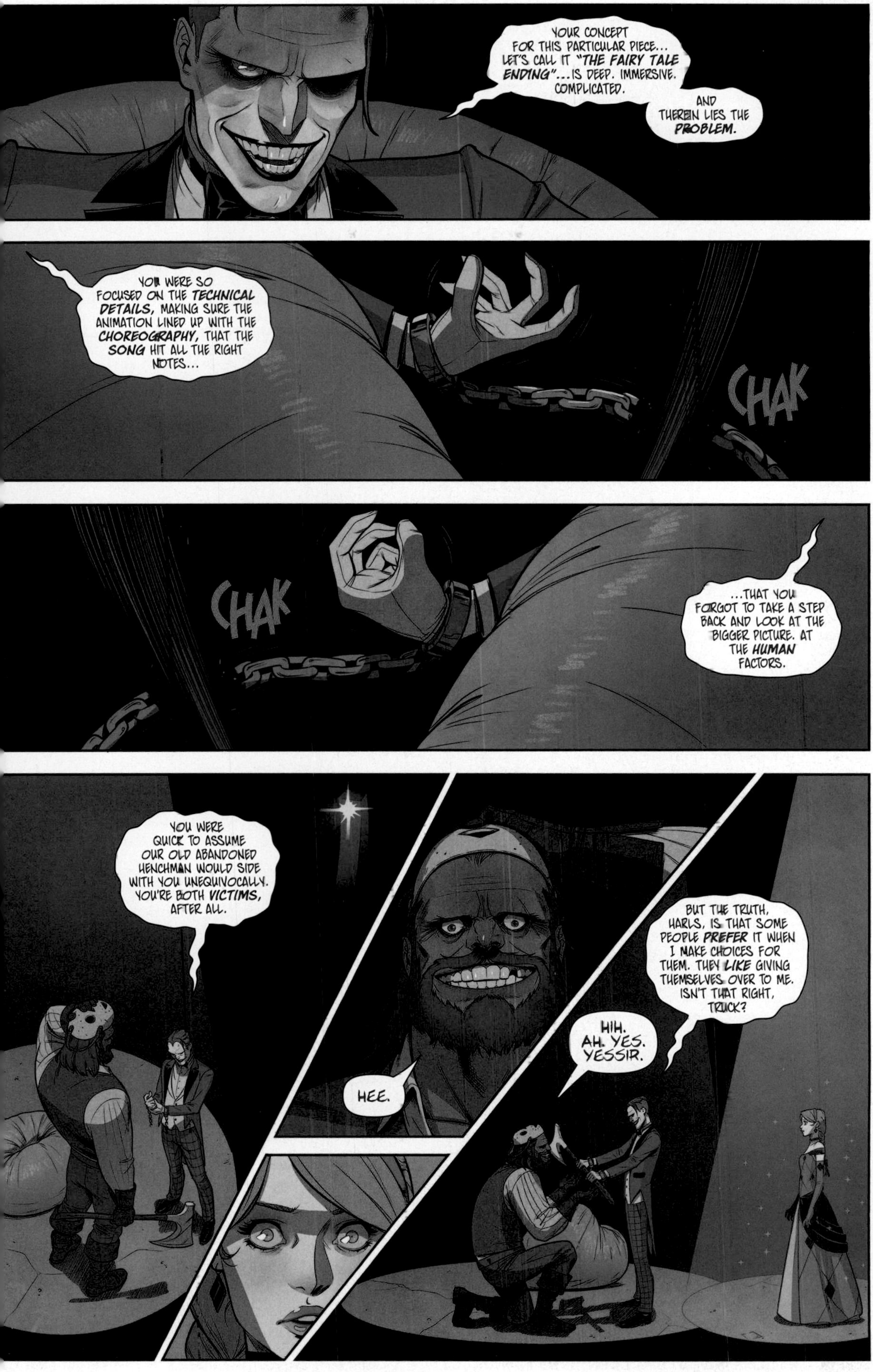

YOUR CONCEPT FOR THIS PARTICULAR PIECE... LET'S CALL IT "THE FAIRY TALE ENDING"... IS DEEP. IMMERSIVE. COMPLICATED.
AND THEREIN LIES THE PROBLEM.
YOU WERE SO FOCUSED ON THE TECHNICAL DETAILS, MAKING SURE THE ANIMATION LINED UP WITH THE CHOREOGRAPHY, THAT THE SONG HIT ALL THE RIGHT NOTES...
CHAK
CHAK
...THAT YOU FORGOT TO TAKE A STEP BACK AND LOOK AT THE BIGGER PICTURE. AT THE HUMAN FACTORS.
YOU WERE QUICK TO ASSUME OUR OLD ABANDONED HENCHMAN WOULD SIDE WITH YOU UNEQUIVOCALLY. YOU'RE BOTH VICTIMS, AFTER ALL.
HEE.
BUT THE TRUTH, HARLS, IS THAT SOME PEOPLE PREFER IT WHEN I MAKE CHOICES FOR THEM. THEY LIKE GIVING THEMSELVES OVER TO ME. ISN'T THAT RIGHT, TRUCK?
HIH. AH. YES. YESSIR.

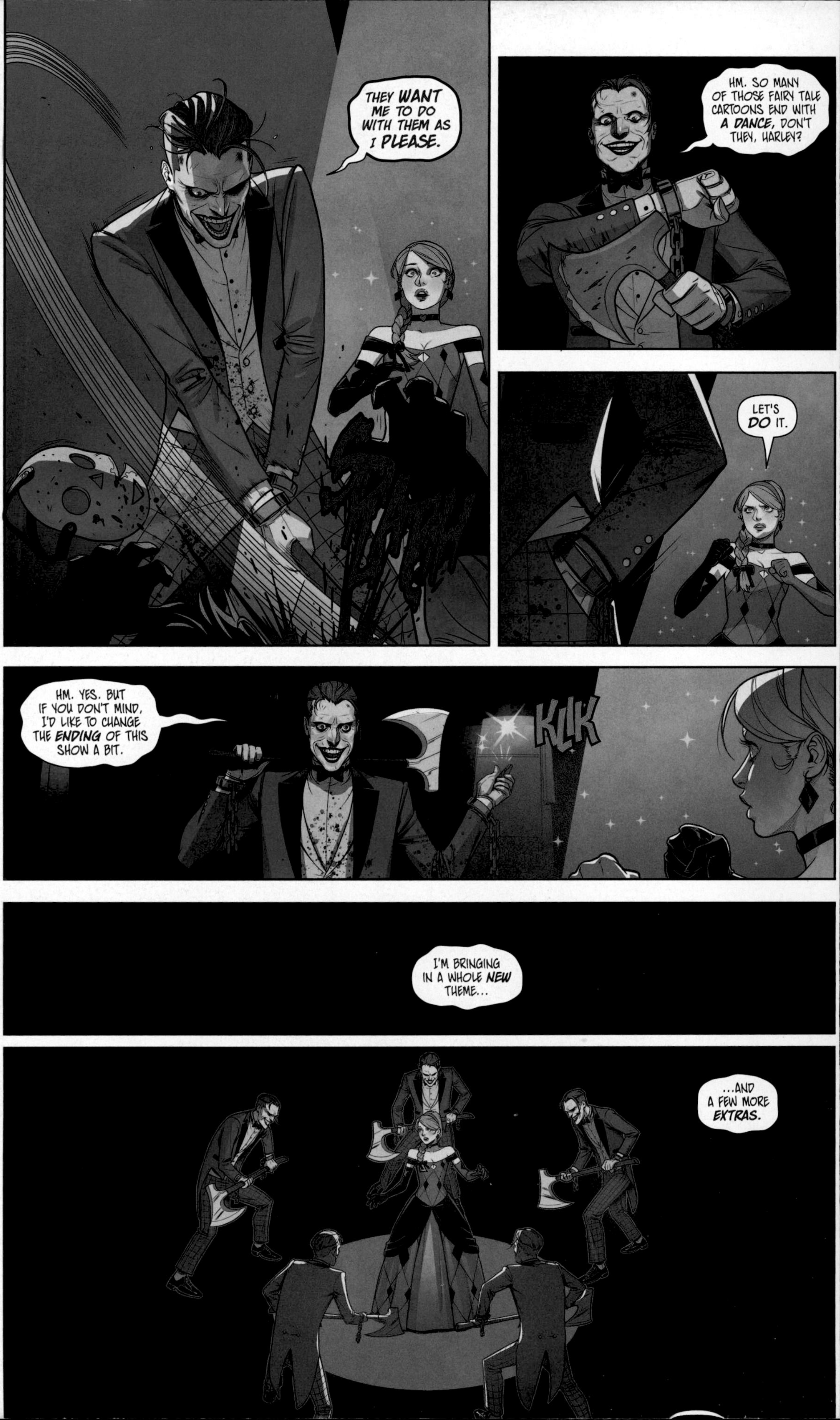

THEY WANT ME TO DO WITH THEM AS I PLEASE.
HM. SO MANY OF THOSE FAIRY TALE CARTOONS END WITH A DANCE, DON'T THEY, HARLEY?
LET'S DO IT.
HM. YES. BUT IF YOU DON'T MIND, I'D LIKE TO CHANGE THE ENDING OF THIS SHOW A BIT.
KLIK
I'M BRINGING IN A WHOLE NEW THEME...
...AND A FEW MORE EXTRAS.

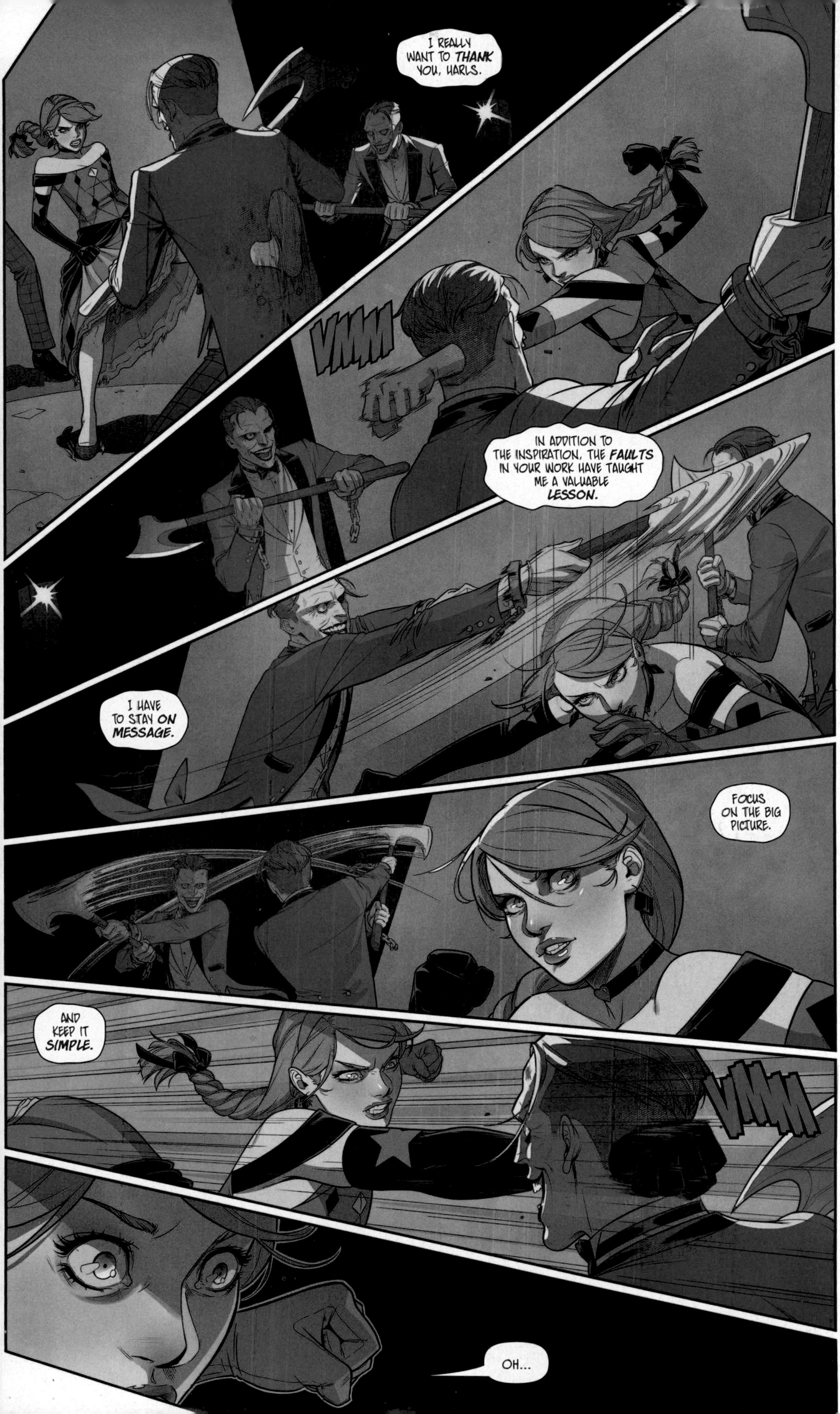
I REALLY WANT TO THANK YOU, HARLS.
VMM
IN ADDITION TO THE INSPIRATION, THE FAULTS IN YOUR WORK HAVE TAUGHT ME A VALUABLE LESSON.
I HAVE TO STAY ON MESSAGE.
FOCUS ON THE BIG PICTURE.
AND KEEP IT SIMPLE.
VMM
OH...

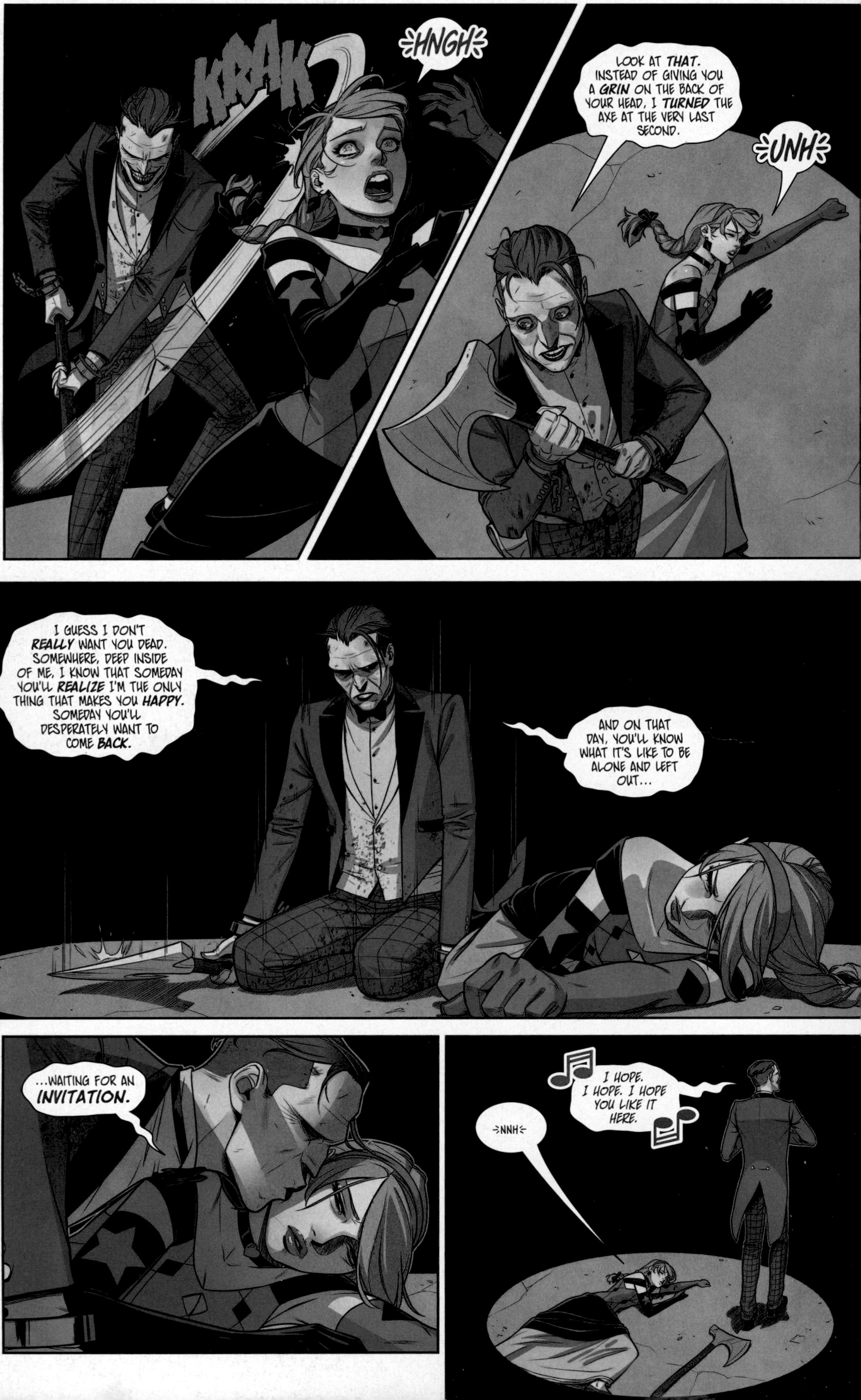
KRAK
HNGH
LOOK AT THAT. INSTEAD OF GIVING YOU A GRIN ON THE BACK OF YOUR HEAD, I TURNED THE AXE AT THE VERY LAST SECOND.
UNH
I GUESS I DON'T REALLY WANT YOU DEAD. SOMEWHERE, DEEP INSIDE OF ME, I KNOW THAT SOMEDAY YOU'LL REALIZE I'M THE ONLY THING THAT MAKES YOU HAPPY. SOMEDAY YOU'LL DESPERATELY WANT TO COME BACK.
AND ON THAT DAY, YOU'LL KNOW WHAT IT'S LIKE TO BE ALONE AND LEFT OUT...
...WAITING FOR AN INVITATION.
I HOPE. I HOPE. I HOPE YOU LIKE IT HERE.
NNH

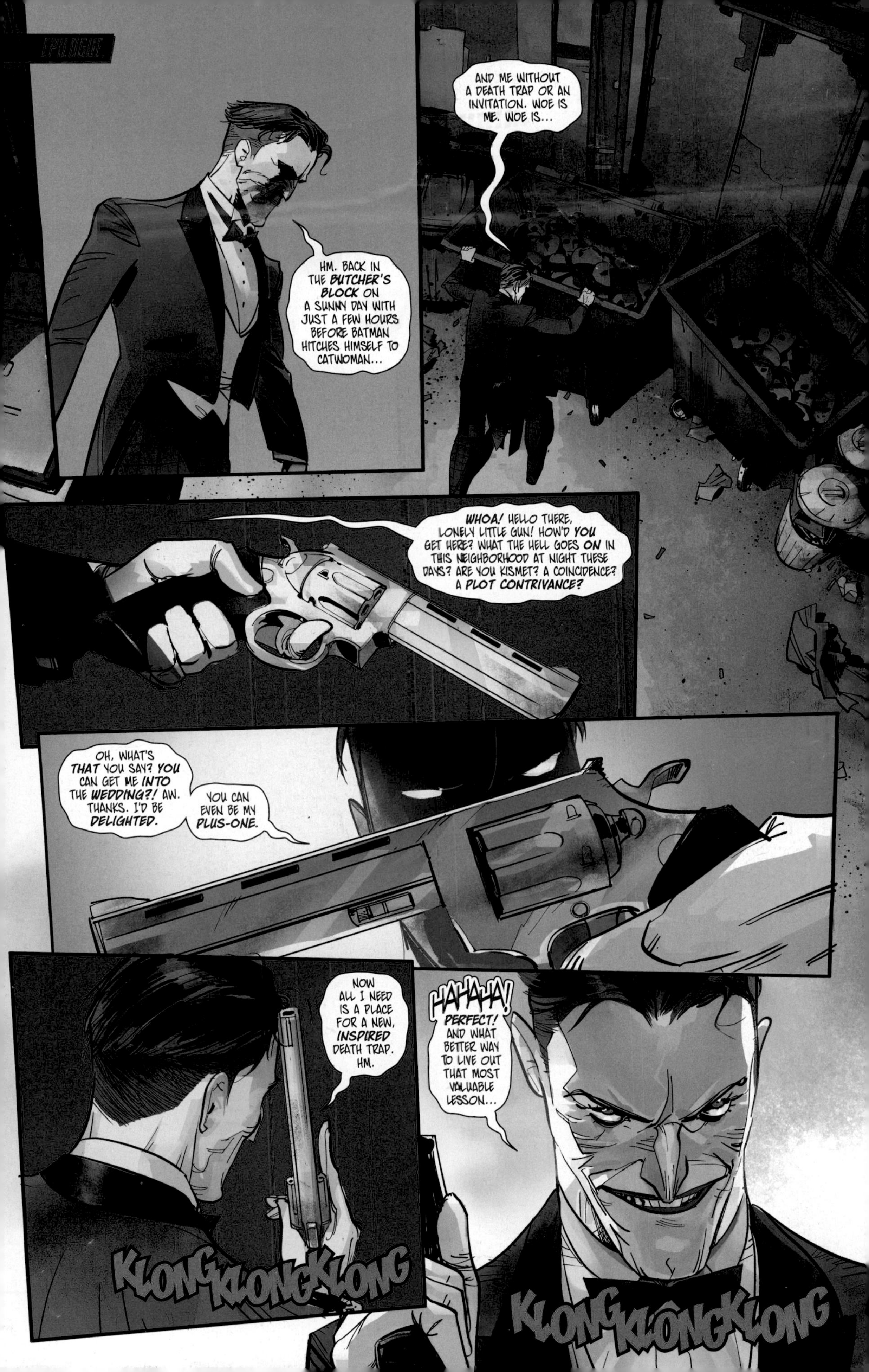
EPILOGUE
HM. BACK IN THE BUTCHER'S BLOCK ON A SUNNY DAY WITH JUST A FEW HOURS BEFORE BATMAN HITCHES HIMSELF TO CATWOMAN...
AND ME WITHOUT A DEATH TRAP OR AN INVITATION. WOE IS ME. WOE IS...
WHOA! HELLO THERE, LONELY LITTLE GUN! HOW'D YOU GET HERE? WHAT THE HELL GOES ON IN THIS NEIGHBORHOOD AT NIGHT THESE DAYS? ARE YOU KISMET? A COINCIDENCE? A PLOT CONTRIVANCE?
OH, WHAT'S THAT YOU SAY? YOU CAN GET ME INTO THE WEDDING?! AW. THANKS. I'D BE DELIGHTED.
YOU CAN EVEN BE MY PLUS-ONE.
NOW ALL I NEED IS A PLACE FOR A NEW, INSPIRED DEATH TRAP. HM.
KLONG KLONG KLONG
HAHAHA! PERFECT! AND WHAT BETTER WAY TO LIVE OUT THAT MOST VALUABLE LESSON...
KLONG KLONG KLONG

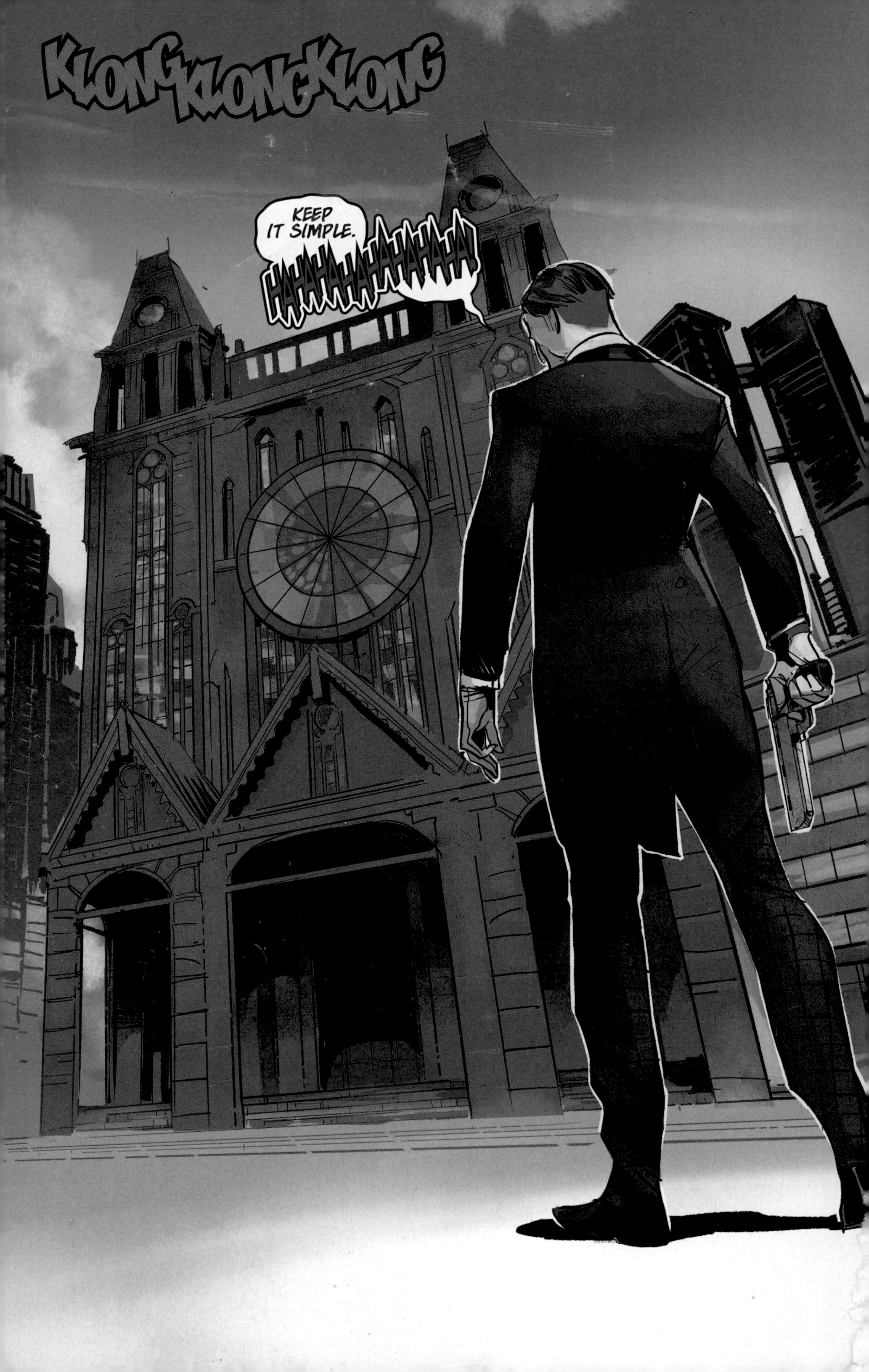
KLONG KLONG KLONG
KEEP IT SIMPLE.
HAHAHAHAHAHAHAHA!